Alternatives t<

Routledge Studies in Development and Society

Alternatives to Privatization

Public Options for Essential
Services in the Global South

**Edited by David A. McDonald
and Greg Ruiters**

Routledge
Taylor & Francis Group

NEW YORK   LONDON

First published 2012
by Routledge
711 Third Avenue, New York, NY 10017

Simultaneously published in the UK
by Routledge
2 Park Square, Milton Park, Abingdon, Oxon OX14 4RN

*Routledge is an imprint of the Taylor & Francis Group,
an informa business*

Typeset in Sabon by IBT Global.
Printed and bound in the United States of America on acid-free paper by
IBT Global.

Library of Congress Cataloging-in-Publication Data
    Alternatives to privatization : public options for essential services in the
Global South / edited by David A. McDonald, Greg Ruiters.
        p. cm. — (Routledge studies in development and society ; 29)
    Includes bibliographical references and index.
    1.   Privatization—Developing countries. 2.   Public utilities—
Developing countries. I. McDonald, David A. (David Alexander)
    II. Ruiters, Greg, 1959-
    HD3850.A486 2011
    363.609172'4—dc23
    2011025816

ISBN: 978-0-415-88668-0 (hbk)
ISBN: 978-0-203-14706-1 (ebk)

Contents

PART III
Looking Ahead

Tables

Figures

Acknowledgements

We would like to thank Amanda Wilson and Julie Borland for their invaluable assistance with the coordination of this research and publishing project and the anonymous peer reviewers of the original manuscript for their insightful suggestions for revisions. Special thanks as well to Madeleine Bélanger Dumontier for her meticulous copy editing on the final versions of the manuscript; a substantial undertaking with such a diverse range of topics and contributors. We would also like to thank our primary funders, the International Development Research Centre of Canada (IDRC) and in particular the Governance, Equity and Health Group, for their ongoing support and encouragement.

Special thanks go to the authors of this book for their willingness to work through a collective research agenda, as well as to the dozens of other activists, unionists, policy makers, and academics who gave of their time to assist with the data gathering and analysis.

1 Introduction
In Search of Alternatives to Privatization

David A. McDonald and Greg Ruiters

In the ongoing debates about privatization, it is often argued that those who oppose private sector involvement in service delivery do not present concrete alternatives. There is some truth to this claim, springing in part from the deep impoverishment of debate since the onset of neoliberalism, which pronounced that "there is no alternative" to privatization. This also needs to be seen in contrast to the 1930s, and the post-World War II period when there was a strong sense of the limits and dangers of excessive domination of society by unfettered markets and private sector service provision and much greater scope for understanding the limits of capitalism and the use of state powers to ensure social integration and secure basic needs and wants.

Yet in the recent past, with the limits to privatization and financialization becoming more apparent, a burgeoning field of enquiry around alternatives has emerged, albeit in a fragmented and inconsistent way. Social movements have developed powerful rhetoric—such as "another world is possible" and "there must be alternatives"—but with little detail on how alternatives are constructed, to what extent they are reproducible, and what normative values might guide them (if any). The literature and practices that do speak directly to "alternatives to privatization" tend to be highly localized and sector-specific and lacking in conceptual and methodological consistency, leading to interesting but somewhat variegated case studies.

This book is an attempt to help fill this analytical and empirical gap by synthesizing existing work and generating new conceptual frameworks, which directly address questions of what constitutes alternatives, what makes them successful (or not), what improvements have been achieved, and what lessons are to be learned for future service delivery debates. The analysis is backed up by a comprehensive examination of initiatives in over 50 countries in Africa, Asia, and Latin America. It covers three sectors—health care, water/sanitation, and electricity—and is the first global survey of its kind, providing a more rigorous and robust platform for evaluating alternatives than has existed to date and allowing for better (though still challenging) comparisons across regions and sectors.

Although our research focuses on particular sectors in particular regions, the findings are relevant to other services and to other parts of the world, at least in broad conceptual terms. Information of this type is urgently required by practitioners, unionists, social movements, and analysts alike, all of whom are seeking reliable knowledge on what kinds of public models work and their main strengths and weaknesses.

To this end, the book is intended as a first step in a multipronged research process. The findings presented here offer a preliminary review of the scope and character of "successful" alternatives in the different regions and sectors investigated, while at the same time providing a testing ground for conceptual frameworks and research methods. Subsequent research will provide more fine-tuned case studies in sectors and regions identified from this research to be of particular interest, with a focus on key themes that have emerged from the studies (such as the trend towards remunicipalizing water services and the tensions inherent in corporatized service delivery models). The book is therefore a starting point, not an endpoint, and is intended to act as a guide for our own future research as well as a catalyst for others.

The orientation of the research is academic but has involved activists, unionists, social movements, and non-governmental organizations (NGOs) from the outset. As with previous research by the Municipal Services Project,[1] the involvement of frontline workers, service users, policy makers, and others has been an essential part of the design and implementation of research, as well as of outputs and outreach. The perspectives and practices brought to the table by these various groups, based in various regions and sectors, complicate the traditional academic process, but the outcome is much richer for it. The book has thus been written to be academically rigorous but also to be accessible to policy makers, analysts, unionists, activists, and others familiar with the debates on privatization and its alternatives. Not all chapters will resonate with all readers, but the intention is that the book will help advance our understanding of alternatives to privatization in general and stimulate further research in this critically important area.

The book has been divided into three sections. The first looks at conceptual questions around the nature of the state in service provision, the role of labour and social movements, gendered outcomes of different service mechanisms, and the ways in which neoliberal practices and ideologies construct and constrict the push for alternative delivery systems. The second section is an empirical review of alternative models of service delivery broken down by region (Asia, Africa, and Latin America) and sector (health care, water/sanitation, and electricity). In this latter section, regionally based research teams were asked to identify as many "successful" alternatives as they could find in a given region and sector, categorize them according to predefined typologies, and evaluate their achievements based on a set of normative criteria. The book concludes with a chapter that summarizes the findings of the research and points to future directions for study, policy, and activism.

WHAT IS AN "ALTERNATIVE TO PRIVATIZATION"?

An extended discussion of the methods and typologies developed for the collaborative research in this book is provided in Chapter 2, but it is useful to first explain what we mean by an "alternative to privatization". We have defined alternatives in this book as (i) "public" entities that are entirely state-owned and operated (such as a municipal water utility or a provincial electricity generator) and (ii) "non-state" organizations that operate independently of the state on a not-for-profit basis and are oriented to principles of equality and social citizenship (such as certain types of NGOs or community groups). These two broadly defined groups might operate independently from each other or in some form of partnership (with "partnerships" forming a third category of sorts).

Notably, this definition includes non-state actors in notions of "public", helping to get beyond the "stale positions staked out in the public-versus-private debate", which has often limited the discussion to states versus the private sector (Bakker 2010, 218). More controversially, however, our definition excludes all forms of private, for-profit actors, be they large corporations or for-profit NGOs. In this regard our definition of privatization covers all forms of "private" ownership and/or management, including governmental, non-governmental, or community-based organizations operating on a for-profit basis.

There are fuzzy margins here, of course, many of which complicated our data collection and analysis. After all, the majority of public services operates within capitalist environments and procure goods and services from private firms and rely on certain private distribution and collection networks. There are also many highly regarded public services that have outsourced small aspects of their operations (e.g. meter reading) but otherwise operate on a non-commercial basis. Being "purist" in this regard was not logistically practical and might have unnecessarily eliminated some interesting examples of "alternatives" from our study. There are also NGOs that offer interesting alternative service delivery schemes on a not-for-profit basis in one location but have ties to profit-making ventures in other areas. To rule out these forms of service delivery could also have meant the loss of interesting case studies. Similar parameters apply to "community" service providers, many of which can be "private" (to the extent that they are not always accountable to political authorities or to the communities within which they operate) but could not necessarily be ruled out as "public" actors, particularly if they operated in non-marketized ways.

But the most vexing question of all was (and remains) what to make of "corporatized" services—i.e. state-owned and state-operated services run (to varying degrees) on commercial principles. Corporatized entities have become extremely popular over the past 20–30 years, and some have become more private than public in their orientation. They may not operate on a for-profit basis, but they function using market doctrines, valorizing the exchange rate of a service over its use value, prioritizing financial cost-benefit analysis in decision making, and employing private sector management techniques such as performance-based salaries. These corporatized entities often see their service delivery mandates framed in market terms of maximizing efficiency, promoting free enterprise, and serving individual consumer sovereignty (Shirley 1999, Bollier 2003, Preker and Harding 2003, Whincop 2003).

It is here that we found the biggest divisions amongst ourselves over the publicness of these corporatized entities and whether they should be considered "alternatives to privatization". In the end it was decided that being purist on this point would not have been helpful either, knowing that some corporatized public entities have performed well when relying on (some) private sector operating principles and that democratic political processes can be used to buffer against overly marketized processes and outcomes (on the latter point, see Warner and Hefetz 2008). Individual research groups were therefore asked to determine whether they thought a particular corporatized entity was sufficiently "non-private" in its operational practice and ideologies to be included in the study. The outcome was that some corporatized service providers were included as positive examples of "alternatives to privatization", and some were not. Uruguay's corporatized water entity, *Obras Sanitarias del Estado* (OSE), is an example of the former, having been instrumental in the transformation of water services in that country into fairer and more transparent service provision (see Chapter 15, this volume). Many others were left out, such as South Africa's parastatal electricity producer, Eskom, which initially extended subsidized electricity to millions after the end of apartheid but now acts much like a private company, cutting off low-income households for non-payment of services and aggressively pursuing privatized contracts in other parts of Africa (Greenberg 2009). This diffusion is a reflection of the conceptual differences of opinion within our research group, as well as a product of different interpretations and measurements of the more objective empirical evaluations of service performance captured in our "criteria for success", such as accountability, equity, and quality of services (on which more will be said in Chapter 2, this volume).

In other words, there are no hard and fast boundaries between a "privatized" service and an "alternative to privatization". Rather than lying along a linear trajectory of state ownership at one extreme and private ownership at the other, there are multiple criteria across different forms of provision that are fractured in relation to one another and in terms of more or less progressive outcomes; state (i.e. public) ownership can serve elite and corporate needs and marginalize the poor, for example. The degree of state or non-state ownership and control is neither a singular nor exclusive marker of "alternatives". It is a matter of who is served and how, with substantial contextual content. And while we can argue for a definition of alternatives that is as free of private sector influence as possible—and we certainly need a stricter definition than the rather flaccid and overly compromised notions of "public" services being promoted by many United Nations (UN) agencies and international financial institutions, which can even include multinational corporations (UN-Habitat 2007, World Bank 2009)—we felt it was conceptually and politically mistaken to impose too tight a definition at this early stage of our research agenda.

We have therefore used this initial "mapping exercise" as an opportunity for constructive debate within and across the different sectors and regions we are studying to understand better how "public" service provision can be progressively sustained, rather than establishing firm guidelines for how boundaries for "alternatives" should be drawn or where these boundary lines should lie. Both the nature *and* dynamic of alternative provision are of significance. It is important to advance and defend definitions and not simply to try and stay the right side of the border, as it were. The material presented in this book reflects some of these unresolved debates and will serve as the subject of further empirical and conceptual study.

Having said that, the overwhelming majority of "successful" alternatives to privatization identified in this book are those run on a non-commercial basis by the state and/or by non-governmental or civic associations. The details of these services differ from place to place and are often as dissimilar to the "old style" state-run services that preceded them as they are from their more contemporary privatized counterparts. These differences are due in part to the dramatic changes that have been imposed by decentralization and supranationalization (with everything from local authorities to international governing bodies now taking part in service delivery), as well as the direct involvement that NGOs, social movements, and community-based groups have earned at various levels of decision making and service delivery. As a result, the divisions between governmental and non-governmental have also blurred, and this is particularly pronounced in the realm of alternatives.

Despite this fuzziness we have attempted to typologize state and non-state service delivery systems in ways that give sharper definition to alternatives than simply the term "public" (or "public-public" in cases in which there is more than one entity working together). We do so by more clearly distinguishing between governmental and non-governmental actors than has been done in the past and by differentiating between single and multiple actors (see Chapter 2 for more details, this volume). Though rather inelegant in the names and acronyms this produces—e.g. SiNP (single non-profit sector), NPNPP (non-profit/non-profit partnership)—there is a need for more clarity around the institutional composition of alternatives if we are to comprehend better the nature and shifting differentiation of public sector alternatives.

IDENTIFYING ALTERNATIVES BY THEIR "OBJECTIVES"

We have also attempted to identify alternatives by their intended objectives and have broken them into five categories, based on how they emerged from the research. The first category refers to alternatives whose primary objective is *"defending the status quo"*. In the fight against privatization, we often forget that the vast majority of services that exist are still provided by the public sector (an estimated 90%–95% of the world's water services, for example). There is much that can be improved (even rejected) about these public sector service delivery models, but some of it is done exceptionally well, and we should not fall victim to the negative rhetoric of public sector service bashing that has become part and parcel of today's neoliberal political objective.

Our primary interest, however, lies with identifying and evaluating positive examples of alternatives to privatization that are aimed at *"revising the status quo"*. We acknowledge that many existing public services are poorly run—or non-existent—and do not meet many of our "criteria for success". Defending these services is not an acceptable route to developing alternatives. It is important therefore to explore efforts that have gone into making public services more democratic, more participatory, more equitable, more transparent, more environmentally sound, more secure, and so on, and it is essential that we understand the scope and character of these reforms. Examples range from the well-known participatory budgeting models of Latin America to lesser known initiatives in cities, towns, and villages in Asia and Africa. In some cases the reforms leave institutional structures intact, while in others they dismantle old forms of the state with a much broader set of actors and innovative forms of governance, opening up new *vistas* for thinking about how the "public" can operate.

Our third category is that of *"reclaiming public services"*. After the privatization euphoria of the 1980s and 1990s, many national and municipal governments are finding themselves once again in control of essential services, either as a result of a political struggle to remove a private firm (such as the "Water War" of Cochabamba, Bolivia) or because the private sector service provider fled what they perceived to be an unprofitable situation, leaving the state/community to pick up the pieces (as with water services in Buenos Aires in the early 2000s). Whatever the cause (an understanding of which is essential to assessing the outcomes), there is a large and growing swathe of previously privatized services that are now back in public hands. We have attempted to identify as many positive examples of this as possible and discuss the lessons learned (we have also completed separate, in-depth research comparing water remunicipalization in five countries, in a forthcoming publication).

Fourth, we are interested in what we call *"utopian"* models of service delivery. These are proposed/theorized systems that do not yet exist but which animate academic and popular debate. There is value in utopian thinking for several reasons. First, much policy scholarship originates from narrow-minded thinking based on what advocates believe will be acceptable to powerful interest groups and state bureaucrats. The horizons of thought are predetermined by the deadweight of the present. Utopian thinking, by contrast, allows us to start with probing questions about the ethical principles and necessity of change, rather than its feasibility as shaped by existing power relations and balance of forces (Friedmann 2000, Harvey 2000, Tormey 2005). Against having a blueprint for the future, the kind of utopian thinking we suggest allows for a discussion of processes that produce things in the present. Utopian thinking might also allow us to ask fundamental questions about the social creation of needs in contemporary society and what kind of ecological footprint we might want to leave, focusing our minds on alternative social forms, alliances, politics of scale, and processes of how we might get there.

Our final category is *"historical models"* of non-private service delivery, which we hope can shed light on what has worked and not worked in places such as the Soviet bloc, early communist China, 19th century municipal socialisms, "African socialisms", and so on. Most of this historical research is being conducted separate from this book (such as a review of "municipal socialism" from the late-1800s to the 1940s), but some historical models find their way into the current chapters, either because they continue to operate (such as Cuba's much-vaunted medical system) or because they provide useful comparators for what is happening today (e.g. the now-defunct "Semashko" health model developed by the Soviets).

Looking at historical models is also a useful way to remind ourselves that this is not the first time there has been a debate about "alternatives to privatization". Much of what we call "public" services today started out as private entities and were nationalized or municipalized as far back as the mid-1800s, often because privatization was deemed to be too inefficient and unpredictable by the private sector itself (see Chapter 7 for an extended discussion, this volume). Some services have experienced several public-private swings, offering temporal insights into the rationale for, and debates over, public versus private service delivery today. Contemporary struggles have different social, technological, and ecological overtones, but many of the issues remain the same, and it is important that we locate current efforts to build alternatives in historical context.

STRUCTURE OF THE BOOK

Our objective with this book is to be "critically positive" about the nature of alternatives. While it is important to celebrate notions of "publicness" that have been so demeaned over the years, there is little value in uncritically promoting service options that have proven to be problematic or that have been inadequately researched. As such, our evaluations may appear overly negative at times, airing on the side of caution when we are unsure of the full scope of particular changes or when we see real or potential problems lurking behind the scenes (as with some forms of corporatization). We therefore recognize public sector failures and highlight the challenges ahead.

Having said that, we also recognize the David and Goliath nature of the battle over privatization and want to speak loudly in favour of efforts to find, initiate, and promote positive alternatives. The dominance of institutions that back the privatization and marketization of essential services remains strong, as does the volume of pro-privatization/commercialization research by international funding agencies, NGOs, think tanks, and governments. This book has been written in direct response to this political and financial hegemony, and in doing so, joins a growing counter-narrative that has become increasingly networked and effective in its knowledge base and tactics. There may be relatively little in the way of direct funding for research and development on alternatives when compared to the billions of dollars that flow into privatization and commercialization initiatives each year, but unions (e.g. Unison, Canadian Union of Public Employees, South African Municipal Workers Union, Public Services International), NGOs (e.g. Food and Water Watch, Transnational Institute, Corporate Europe Observatory, Focus on the Global South, World Development Movement), social movements (e.g. Red Vida, Africa Water Network, People's Health Movement), and others have become increasingly focused on moving beyond critiques of privatization and proposing new ways forward. There are even small pockets of resources being made available for these purposes by aid agencies and international governance institutions such as the UN. The creation of the Global Water Operators' Partnerships Alliance (GWOPA) by UN-Habitat to explore "public-public partnerships" is one example, as is recognition by the European Parliament that "financing and technical support available from a variety of donors for PPPs" needs to be balanced by "dedicated funds made available for PuPs [public-public partnerships] . . . to ensure that PuPs are an accessible option for governments seeking to enter into partnerships, and to enable PuPs to develop so that their potential can be better understood" (Tucker et al, 2010). But the fact that the first example is compromised by the presence of multinational corporations (Miranda 2007), and the latter is but a drop in the proverbial funding bucket, illustrates just how unbalanced this debate remains. Nevertheless, there are indications of a growing awareness from mainstream actors of the need to put resources into a more systematic exploration of alternatives to privatization—if for no other reason than the private sector continues to shun the risk of service delivery in many parts of the global South.

This book hopes to address this imbalance by bringing together academics, activists, unionists, social movements, and non-governmental organizations involved in the debates over alternatives to privatization, all of whom are seeking better conceptual models and methodologies for more rigorous, comparative research on public service provision. Chapter 2 lays out our collective thinking on definitions of "successful" alternatives and how we went about identifying and studying them. This is followed by a series of chapters in Part I that provide insights on actors, issues and ideologies associated with alternative service delivery models, with a combination of theory and empirical evidence that covers some of the overarching themes of the book, such as the role of social movements, organized labour, community-based groups, contested notions of the state, and the challenges of incorporating gender into our understandings of what makes for a successful alternative system. We also include an overview of contemporary neoliberalism and how this phenomenon both constrains and energizes alternatives to privatization. Although the aim of the book is to get beyond a critique of privatization, it is important to situate ourselves within a particular understanding of the contemporary neoliberal world order and how this shapes thinking and practice on what kinds of alternatives are possible.

Part II of the book is a series of regional and sectoral studies looking at the evolution of alternative services in health care, water/sanitation, and electricity in Asia, Africa, and Latin America—a total of nine chapters. We have opted to organize these discussions by region due to the strong geographic similarities we found across sectors and have provided short regional overviews that offer basic historical and political-economic context for readers less familiar with these regions and minimize repetition in the chapters.

Finally, we conclude in Part III with a discussion of ways forward. As noted earlier, we see this book as a starting point for a more coherent and coordinated set of research activities on alternatives, and we use this final chapter to point to potential future research activities for ourselves and to encourage others to develop related research programmes, conceptual models, and methodologies.

MAIN RESEARCH FINDINGS

There are no simple or singular lessons to be taken from this book. It is important to read each chapter for what is has to offer. This is due in part to the enormous variations across regions, sectors, and actors. It is also a product of new conceptual and methodological frameworks that allow for competing interpretations of what constitutes "public" and how one defines a "successful" alternative to privatization. Some contributors, for example, are more supportive of NGO involvement in services than others. Some contributors are insistent on strong state roles while others are more skeptical. Some are accepting/supportive of corporatization. We take this as a healthy sign of a diverse and complex research topic and of the need to see alternatives in context. Nevertheless, there are a few broad generalizations that we can make about the research findings.

Vibrant debates

The first, and most important, finding to highlight is that there is considerable vibrancy in the world of alternatives to privatization. Despite what the mainstream press would have us believe, debate and practice in this area is robust, and there are a myriad of positive examples of "public" service delivery across all sectors and regions.

Water appears to be the most dynamic. This is likely due to the fact that it has been one of the services most affected and politicized by privatization, but also because it is the only truly "non-substitutable" service of the three sectors under study and because it is also relatively simple, technologically speaking, and the easiest to imagine having more community/public control over. There is also an effective and well-coordinated cluster of regional and international groups that have opposed water privatization and which are now proposing alternatives.

Electricity is by far the *least* organized of the sectors, mainly in terms of the development and conceptualization of alternatives, largely for the opposite reasons as those given for water—i.e. alternative forms of energy exist, it is highly technical and capital intensive (though it need not be), and there has been relatively little understanding of the complex nature of unbundling that has taken place in the sector. As a result, few regional—and no international—fora exist that are working on alternatives to privatization in electricity. Positive examples of alternatives exist, but they are fewer in number and more isolated in their activities.

The health sector, for its part, also has many positive "alternatives" to point to, but it is more fragmented than the other two sectors in its capacity to recognize and promote these models. This is due in part to the existence of primary, secondary, and tertiary systems that often do not interact with one another, making health less vertically integrated than the other two sectors in its structures and governance (though they need not be). There are also highly personal aspects to the user-provider relationship that make the experience with health care less predictable or homogenous than that with water or electricity. Nevertheless, experiences with privatized systems have served to bring together otherwise disparate groups, and renewed interest in alternative forms of health care have further contributed to thinking about alternative delivery mechanisms.

In short, all three sectors are experiencing debates about alternatives to privatization, but there is as much that differentiates these discussions as binds them together. The intersectoral approach we have taken in this book is therefore both its strength and its challenge, attempting to find common ground and promote intersectoral dialogue and practice, while at the same time recognizing and respecting the unique realities of each.

In the end, we are advancing a notion of *health systems*, which, drawing on the World Health Organization's definition, involves "all actions whose primary purpose is to promote, restore, or maintain health" (WHO 2000). In other words, health includes "upstream" social determinants (in this case, water/sanitation and electricity), as well as the potential for the health sector itself to act as social determinant by shaping "downstream" access to health care services by the disadvantaged, reaching back upwards to shape the socio-political environment (Gilson et al, 2007, viii). Taken this way, health systems are a totality of interactions, with different sectors having reciprocating effects on one another and reshaping the health system as a whole.

From a geographic point of view, the largest number of interesting alternatives are to be found in Latin America. This will come as no surprise to readers familiar with the region's larger set of experiments with socialism, and alternatives to neoliberalism more generally, as well as its long history of anti-corporate struggle. Africa, by contrast, is the weakest region in terms of "successful" alternatives, constrained in large part by the ongoing stranglehold of international financial institutions such as the World Bank, the relatively conservative/neoliberal regimes in power, and limited state capacities. There is robust resistance to privatization on the continent, but this has not yet morphed into as effective a voice on alternatives to privatization as we have seen in the other two regions. Despite the differences, it is hoped that lessons learned from each region—whether positive or negative—will be of use in the others, as well as in the struggles for alternative service delivery systems in the global North.

No "ideal models"

We found many different types of alternatives to privatization, but there are no "ideal models". None excelled at *all* of the criteria we identified for "success" and few could be neatly typologized into the categories we created. This too should come as no surprise. Context, empowerment, and democracy are remarkably important. This is stating the obvious, of course, but given the one-size-fits-all approach of the proponents of privatization/commercialization (or even a mix-of-templates-fits-all), it is important to state that "alternatives to privatization" need not fit into neat little boxes and need not be replicable elsewhere. The ideological milieu, the institutional makeup, the capacity of states and civil society, the availability of capital, and environmental conditions are but some of the factors that can make or break an alternative, and a model that works in one place may prove a failure in another, for any combination of reasons. Uganda is not Uruguay is not Ulan Bator.

This does not mean we should abandon a commitment to certain universal norms and expectations—we have built our study around such normative criteria, such as equity, sustainability, and transparency—but these must be contextually meaningful and practical. Research methods must be equally elastic, with sufficiently flexible conceptual frameworks needed to take into account particularities, while at the same time allowing for meaningful comparisons across regions and sectors. There may be no single model that works for every sector in every place, but there may be certain factors that raise the likelihood of an alternative to privatization being considered successful. Chapter 2 discusses this methodological challenge at length.

Scale matters (but not too much)

We identified successful alternatives to privatization across a wide range of scales; from highly localized water provision systems in small rural areas that service several hundred people, to national health systems that service millions. The scale of a service system is not, therefore, an a priori *determinant* of success, but it is important when considering efficiency, universal standards of coverage, resource requirements, ease of regulation, and so on. Being big can be beneficial in some ways (economies of scale, national standards) but detrimental in others (public participation, cultural appropriateness). Ditto for being small, where we must be particularly watchful of the sometimes blind push for decentralization of services over the past few decades (largely from neoliberals but also from the left) and the potential to fetishize the local. Small may be beautiful at times, and large may be efficient at others, but neither should be considered ontological categories of their own, and there is nothing axiomatic about scale when it comes to alternatives to privatization.

Technological (r)evolutions

A related point is the question of technology. Whereas much of the scalar debate takes place with reference to politics (participation, democratic oversight, etc), the kinds of technologies employed can have equally important influences on the success or failure of an alternative service delivery system. That so little exists in the way of coordinated alternatives to privatization in the electricity sector is in part because most electricity systems are national/regional high-voltage grids that require coordination on an equally large political scale, with massive amounts of capital and considerable technical knowledge. Water production, on the other hand, is still artisanal in places and even where it is fully industrialized it tends to be locally managed due to transport issues. Water treatment and distribution involves relatively simple technology, as can some health care provision, with localized health systems able to use relatively simple techniques such as oral rehydration that can be provided with minimal training (very different, of course, from high-end tertiary health care, which has tended to use technology as a way of insulating itself from public accountability, a point that is taken up at length in each of the chapters on health in this book). Some service sectors therefore lend themselves better to technological innovations that are appropriate for de-scaled applications with community control and ownership. However, within sectors, technology choices are also important, and evidence exists that high-end technology is not always the most efficient and cost-effective option available.

These technologically determined scenarios need not be the case, but it is critical to see the roles that technology can play in shaping alternatives to privatization. This is highlighted most poignantly in the chapter on electricity in Africa (Chapter 13, this volume), whereby small-scale electricity production systems are seen as one way out of the highly commercialized giganticism of continental dams and grids that hand power to multinational capital and unaccountable (regional) governments.

And finally, gender

Whereas there is a growing literature on the gendered dimensions of privatization, virtually nothing has been written about gender and "alternatives to privatization". The chapter on gender included in this book is seen as both a preliminary corrective to this lacuna as well as a call for better conceptual and methodological modelling for future studies.

The methodological frameworks employed for the current research included specific references to gender (equity, participation, access, etc), and efforts were made to identify important gender gains/gaps in the alternatives that were identified, but given the desktop nature of this "mapping exercise", we have not been able to disaggregate adequately the gendered dimensions of the models we explored (nor for class, race, age, and other important socio-demographic characteristics). It is hoped that the discussion provided in the chapter on gender will help us better investigate these finer-tuned aspects of alternatives in the future, as well as contribute to ongoing struggles for more gender-equitable service provision on the ground.

CONCLUSION

In this book we proceed both empirically and theoretically to look at the question of alternatives to privatization and, more broadly, of alternatives to neoliberalism. We will not necessarily just "find" alternatives waiting to be discovered. But by combining historical, contemporary, and future (imagined) insights into alternatives, with a theoretically informed understanding of political economy and the state, we hope to provide helpful ways forward. While we seek to distill key lessons and exemplary cases from "what was and is out there", we realize there remains a deep poverty of practice and thinking around alternatives, and that many public entities have too often imbibed the neoliberal spirit. Yet the sheer variety of alternatives and achievements that do exist (from traditional welfare and socialist states to more contemporary innovations), and the multitude of large- and small-scale efforts to produce them, provides hope.

Human beings have the capacity to develop new ideas of social life and species being, but as Harvey argues,

> to propose different rights from those held sacrosanct by neoliberalism carries with it an obligation to specify alternative social processes within which such alternative rights can inhere. The profoundly antidemocratic nature of neoliberalism backed by the authoritarianism of the neoconservatives should surely be the main focus of political struggle. (2005, 204–205)

Democracy, understood as popular control of state institutions with social equality and open democratic institutions means liberating the state from the control of narrow elites and corporations and rolling back the frontiers of market power. Alternative service delivery models in water, health care, and electricity may only be a small part of this larger frontier, but they are important pieces of the puzzle.

NOTES

1. For more information on the project, see www.municipalservicesproject.org.

REFERENCES

Bakker, K. 2010. *Privatizing water: Governance failure and the word's urban water crisis*. Ithaca: Cornell University Press.
Bollier, D. 2003. *Silent theft: The private plunder of our common wealth*. London: Routledge.
Friedmann, J. 2000. The good city: In defense of utopian thinking. *International Journal of Urban and Regional Research* 24(2): 460–472.
Gilson, L., Doherty, J., Loewenson, R. and Francis, V. 2007. *Challenging inequality through health systems*. Knowledge Network on Health Systems, WHO Commission on the Social Determinants of Health. Geneva: WHO.
Greenberg, S. 2009. Market liberalisation and continental expansion: The repositioning of eskom in post-apartheid South Africa. In McDonald, D.A. (Ed), *Electric capitalism: Recolonizing Africa on the power grid*, pp. 73–108. London: Earthscan.
Harvey, D. 2000. *Spaces of hope*. Berkeley: University of California Press.
———. 2005. *A brief history of neoliberalism*. Oxford: Oxford University Press.
Miranda, A. 2007. Developing public-public partnerships: Why and how not-for-profit partnerships can improve water and sanitation services worldwide. In Warwick, H. and Cann, V. (Eds), *Going public: Southern solutions to the global water crisis*, pp. 63–70. London: World Development Movement.

Preker, A.S. and Harding, A. (Eds). 2003. *Innovations in health service delivery: The corporatization of public hospitals.* Washington, DC: World Bank.

Shirley, M.M. 1999. The roles of privatization versus corporatization in state-owned enterprise reform. *World Development* 27(1): 115–136.

Tormey, S. 2005. From utopian worlds to utopian spaces: Reflections on the contemporary radical imaginary and the social forum process. *Ephemera: Theory and Politics in Organization* 5(2): 394–408.

Tucker, J., Calow, R., Nickel, D. and Thaler, T. 2010. A comparative evaluation of public-private partnerships for urban water services in ACP countries. www.europarl.europa.eu/activities/committees/studies.do?language=EN (accessed 10 September 2010).

UN-Habitat. 2007. Framework for Global Water Operators Partnerships Alliance. Water, sanitation and infrastructure branch. www.unhabitat.org/downloads/docs/5377_74541_frame.pdf (accessed 14 March 2008).

Warner, M.E. and Hefetz, A. 2008. Managing markets for public service: The role of mixed public-private delivery of city services. *Public Administration Review* 68(1): 155–166.

Whincop, M.J. (Ed). 2003. *From bureaucracy to business enterprise: Legal and policy issues in the transformation of government services.* Aldershot, UK: Ashgate.

WHO. 2000. *World health report: Health systems improving performance.* Geneva: WHO.

World Bank. 2009. Governance and public sector reform: Accountability, transparency and corruption in decentralized governance. www.go.worldbank.org/IEQXV96ZQ0 (accessed on 15 January 2009).

2 Weighing the Options
Methodological Considerations

David A. McDonald and Greg Ruiters[1]

"There is nothing more boring than a chapter on research methodology".

Although no one has written this opening quote (to our knowledge), many a researcher, and many more an activist and policy maker, have thought it. And yet, what comes out of a research project is dependent on what goes into it, and nowhere is this more important than in a field of study with few, if any, established research criteria. Such is the case with "alternatives to privatization".

Our intention in placing this chapter at the start of the book is twofold. The first is to explain in detail the ways in which we have identified and evaluated "successful" alternatives to privatization. Our aim is to be as transparent as possible about our data gathering and conclusions and to allow readers to assess better for themselves the significance of our findings. The second reason is to provide baseline methodological frameworks that can be taken up (and altered) by others, with the aim of expanding the volume, reliability, and comparability of research in this field. We will continue to employ some modified versions of this methodology in our own future research but expect that it will morph into different shapes as we learn about its strengths and weaknesses and as we test the pros and cons of employing universal norms in a heterogeneous world of service delivery. Indeed, we have already learned much from this initial "mapping exercise" and will adjust some aspects of our work in the future. What we present here, however, are the frameworks and terms of reference given to our research teams at the outset of this project—warts and all—to contextualize the data gathering in this book as accurately as possible.

The lack of a consistent and transparent set of research methods on alternatives to privatization has been our primary motivation in this regard. Despite the best intentions of those who have done research in this area—including many of the contributors to this volume—a review of the literature on alternatives is akin to comparing apples and oranges (and several other fruits). Although interesting in its insights on how and why particular alternatives developed, the existing case study material is largely descriptive in its orientation, has no established criteria for what constitutes an "alternative", and no consistent ways of evaluating success or failure. At best, the writing provides interesting accounts of how particular alternative models developed and what they have accomplished (or not). At worst, it offers competing, even contradictory, notions of what is meant by a "public" service with no explicit definitions or evaluative criteria to allow for objective evaluation or to compare experiences across sectors or regions.

We do not expect, or want, to resolve all of these tensions in the literature. Nor do we wish to uncritically universalize notions of "public" or "success". We are not looking for blueprint solutions. A rigid research methodology that ignores uneven economic, social and political developments, and vastly different cultural formations, erases diversity and would be counterproductive in many ways. It is simply not reasonable to expect to be able to compare different service sectors in different places on a linear, item-by-item basis with a single, inelastic research model. As Hachfeld et al note with regard to water services:

> There is no exemplary model of 'good' or 'progressive' public water management. The quantity and quality of water, as well as the need for water, vary from place to place. Water is also an important cultural good, and different societies have developed historically different cultures of water. These cultures reflect existing and often uneven power relations in societies. Therefore, the public systems of water and sanitation services are historically grown and some existing cultures of water are highly problematic. It would neither be possible nor desirable to develop one model of water management to be implemented everywhere. Instead, responsible ways of handling water need to be developed around existing local structures. (2009, 4)

Finding an appropriate methodological approach to this contextual diversity is therefore a major challenge. The neoliberal approach has been to sweep away difference by arguing that all human behaviour is ultimately based on self-interest that responds to signals from the market. There may be differences in the way people produce and consume a service, but self-maximization is seen to be central to all service behaviours, with concepts of marginal utility serving as a universal indicator to explain everything from "willingness to pay" to the creation of "social capital" (Whittington et al, 1991, Harriss 2001, Merrett 2002; for a critique, see Fine 2001). Using this rationale, neoliberal researchers see individualized behaviour behind every action, allowing them to argue that marketized forms of service delivery are necessary, despite (indeed because of) a diverse cultural world.

At the other extreme, some post-modernists have rejected any notion of universality, seeing universal norms as "a mere stepchild of erroneous patterns of Enlightenment thought, incapable of adaption to a world of incommunicability and irreconcilable cultural difference" (Harvey 2000, 86). Cultural perceptions of water, historical practices of medicine, and localized forms of energy production are seen to be too different from place to place to allow for consistent forms of assessment, or reproducibility, and should not be subject to imposed globalized norms. Post-modernists (and some Marxists) have also cast aside talk of universal norms and values, especially notions of "human rights" that are seen to be captive to bourgeois institutions and prone to mere reformism—giving people the "right" to water, for example, but also imposing the "responsibility" to pay for it via wage labour (for a discussion, see Boyd 2009).

Yet human rights and social justice (even if vague slogans) remain amongst the most powerful ideas in social movements, attracting and requiring some kind of methodological middle ground. Following Harvey (2000, 83–93, 246–55), our aim has been to construct a dialectical bridge between universals and particulars, one that allows for the use of widely acknowledged objectives (such as "equity" and "accountability"), while at the same time recognizing that such generalizations are fraught with cultural and political tensions that disallow easy comparisons and may be irreconcilable at times.

The challenge is how to apply universal values and notions of justice while still accommodating difference, a task made all the more difficult by the rapidly changing political, technological, and demographic terrain of service delivery. We can reject the linear, teleological notion that advanced capitalist countries will show the way but being *opposed* to privatization (or "modernization") is not enough. It is important to have a *positive* philosophical orientation.

Our approach has been to propose a normative set of "criteria for success" against which alternative service delivery models can be evaluated. These criteria are intended as a reference point for research, not an anchor point, and are open to debate and change. The objective is to provide explicit and transparent criteria in a field with no few analytical markers.

The selection of criteria should come as little surprise to readers familiar with the debates over privatization. Much of what we have selected as "criteria for success" are the polar opposite of what has been seen to be wrong with privatization—e.g. lack of transparency, inequality, unaccountability, and so on. But once again we are not only *reacting* to privatization. The emergent literature on alternatives has begun to establish its own universal objectives (though not always explicitly or clearly), on which we have drawn. And finally, we have modified and developed some concepts that have been inadequately articulated in the literature on alternatives to date (such as "public ethos").

Asserting universal categories is the easy part. The difficulty is making them dialectical, allowing for some universal notion of what constitutes an acceptable standard while allowing for differences across sector/place. We have attempted to do this in several ways. First, we have chosen criteria (such as equity) with sufficient elasticity of meaning to allow for variations in interpretation on whether they have been adequately met. This is particularly useful for the survey-oriented nature of the research that has been conducted for this book, where data are typically highly aggregated and where fine-tuned analyses are generally not possible. Second, and notwithstanding the aggregate nature of data availability, we created subcategories within our criteria that allowed (or forced) researchers to probe specific aspects of the ways services are provided, allowing for partially disaggregated evaluations and lending some degree of objectivity to the criteria (such as the impact of tariffs on equity). And finally, by associating our research with critiques of privatization we rule out many of the neoliberal interpretations of the criteria we are using, such as the marketized notion that "efficiency" should be defined in narrow financial terms.

By providing researchers with a strong normative vision of alternative services, while still allowing for subjectivity, we feel we are advancing understandings of what constitutes an alternative to privatization and what makes it successful or not—as realized by the different interpretations of service delivery models within the pages of this book. By the same token, our methodological approach cannot and should not hold permanently, especially as an index of its own success. It will require refinement in application and more explicit ideological orientations towards the influence of larger market forces.

There is certainly a practical and political need for such an approach. As Harvey also notes with reference to the development of universal norms for human rights, "To turn our backs on such universals at this stage in our history, however fraught or even tainted, is to turn our backs on all manner of prospects for political action" (2000, 94). Such expediency is all the more relevant in the world of service delivery, given the abject failures of privatization and the immediate life-and-death realities of health, water/sanitation, and electricity affecting at least one-third of the people on the planet. Applying universal concepts across different sectors and regions, while still allowing for local interpretation, is not only justifiable academically, but is necessary politically if we are going to have a coherent global dialogue about the kinds of service delivery alternatives we want to propose and achieve in the 21st century.

PLANNING THE RESEARCH

The research for this book was part of a larger process of designing a five-year plan for the third phase of the Municipal Services Project (MSP).[2] The first two phases of the project focused on a critique of the commercialization and privatization of public services, with a focus on South(ern) Africa. After seven years of investigating models to which we were opposed, we felt it was time to design research on service delivery systems of which we were supportive. We also felt it was necessary to be more global in our scope, in part because of the dearth of "alternatives to privatization" in Southern Africa (as indicated in the section in this book that deals with that continent) and in part because of the vibrant debate that was taking place about service delivery alternatives in other parts of the world, notably Latin America and parts of Asia. We had established working relationships with many of the individuals and organizations involved with this book and asked if they would be interested in collaborating on an international initiative to explore alternatives more systematically. Having already recognized some of the limitations of the research in the field to date, there was a keen collective commitment to moving research (and advocacy) forward in a more coordinated manner.

An initial planning meeting of about a dozen academics, activists, social movement organizers, and NGO and labour representatives resulted in a plan for a three-stage research initiative. The first stage—the product of which is this book—is intended as a "mapping exercise" to gauge the scope and character of alternatives to privatization in water, health, and electricity in Asia, Africa, and Latin America. The aim has been to provide a rough indication of the types and numbers of alternatives that exist, the extent to which they can be considered successes or failures, how they compare with one another across regions and sectors, and the usefulness of the methodological tools employed to categorize and assess them. The next stage of the research involves a closer examination of key cases and thematic issues, while the third stage will examine the lessons to be learned from the global research for Southern Africa.

A mid-research workshop of some 35 researchers and other interested parties allowed for discussion of preliminary findings of the mapping exercise research, and an evaluation and recalibration of some methodological tools (such as whether or not to include "corporatized" service entities in our definition of alternatives). Regular telephonic and electronic communications allowed for further refinements, as did close collaboration of most regional researchers, contributing to dialogue across sectors.

As discussed in Chapter 1, the book is divided into three sections. The first is largely conceptual in orientation, exploring ideas and actors related to alternatives to privatization. These chapters in Part I are intended to advance our understanding of the possibilities for, and limitations of, alternatives to privatization. Hence the chapter on social movements is designed to evaluate the impact and influence of social movements on the delivery of basic services such as water/sanitation, electricity, and primary health care in countries in the South, with a focus on the role of social movements in developing, advocating for, and/or participating in the delivery of such services that have an explicitly anti-privatization focus. Because a reasonable literature on this subject already existed, the authors were able to comment on the state of the debate and draw global conclusions on the significance of social movements in this field. The chapters on the state, labour organizations, and the current status of neoliberalism had similar mandates.

The chapter on gender, by contrast, is more pioneering because there has been virtually nothing written about gender and alternatives to privatization. The authors were therefore tasked with providing a literature review summarizing the existing scholarship on the gendered power relations in public services and social reproduction, the implications of privatization and marketization of basic services for women's rights and citizenship, insights into the gendered considerations for the study of the construction of alternatives to privatization, and an assessment of the kind of empirical and theoretical research required to further our understanding of the gendered dimensions of alternatives to privatization.

The empirical studies in the second section of the book were more uniform in their research mandates, with researchers in each of the three sectors and three regions being given the same terms of reference in an effort to create as comparable a set of studies as possible, as follows:

- implement and evaluate the methodological tools for classifying and evaluating "alternatives to privatization" in your sector (water/sanitation, electricity or primary health care) and in your region (Asia, Africa or Latin America)
- advance our empirical and conceptual understanding of these alternatives in your region/sector
- advance our understanding of what constitutes "success" with the alternatives in your region/sector
- identify interesting and important case studies for the next stages of the project
- advance communication between researchers and activists working on alternatives in your region/sector and, where possible, across regions/sectors
- develop research and advocacy networks for the next stages of the project

We explain the first three aspects of this mandate in more detail below.

IDENTIFYING AND CLASSIFYING ALTERNATIVES

Researchers were asked to identify as many alternatives to privatization in their region/sector as possible, using a predefined typology. Our objective in constructing this typology was to give better definition to what constitutes an alternative to privatization and how one should determine whether or not a particular example should be included. Our starting point here was to use a "negative" definition, excluding private and for-profit operators from what we consider to be an alternative. This exclusionary method removed all forms of public-private partnerships (PPPs) from our investigation, as well as services that involved governmental, non-governmental, or community-based organizations operating on a for-profit basis—the rationale for this being that profit-seeking behaviour is at the core of the problems associated with privatization and commercialization.

This negative definition was enhanced by "positive" characteristics of defining alternatives as service entities that are composed of (i) state bodies that operate on a non-commercial basis and are subject to political control and oversight and (ii) non-state organizations operating on a non-commercial basis. A third category involves partnerships within and between these individual institutional formations.

These definitions explicitly avoid attaching social, ideological, scalar, or other subjective criteria to our categorization of an "alternative". These latter factors were left as variables to be evaluated in the assessment of how well an alternative service model performed (on which more, below). In other words, the only criteria for a service to be considered an "alternative to privatization" were that it be not directly linked to the private sector, not profit-oriented in its operations, and that it be run either by a state or non-state entity operating with the express purpose of providing services in a non-profit manner.

The end result of this typologization is provided in Table 2.1. The categories are overly simplistic—and the acronyms clunky and in need of refinement—but the result is a more clearly delineated notion of alternatives than has been used to date and certainly an improvement on the ambiguous use of the term "public" that has served as proxy for a diverse range of alternatives in the literature.

Most importantly, these typologies make a sharper and more explicit distinction between public and private than has been developed to date, without drawing a hard and fast boundary between the two. There remains considerable debate (including within our own project) about the "public" nature of corporatized services (i.e. those that are state-owned and operated but run like private corporations), and there are other fuzzy areas of public/private overlap. It was felt that the definitions we established gave sufficiently objective boundaries, while, at the same time, allowing for subjective decision making for determining whether or not to classify a particular entity as an alternative to privatization. Though not flawless, this methodology is another illustration of the creative tension that we have tried to construct in the early stages of the research as we surf between the universal and the particularist aspects of the criteria we have employed.

Table 2.1 Typology of "Alternatives to Privatization"

Institutional type	Description	Examples	Name/acronym
Public entity A single public sector agency working on its own to deliver a service	Any state body that is publicly owned, managed, and financed, and subject to political control and oversight.	Government bodies and departments (at all levels of state—local, district, provincial, national, regional); state utilities and parastatals; state development agencies (bilateral, multilateral). This category can include "corporatized" service entities run on private sector operating principles, subject to an evaluation of their "success".	SiP (single public sector)
Non-profit entity A single non-profit agency working on its own to deliver a service	Any non-state, non-commercial organization with an identifiable membership base (formal or otherwise) that operates on a non-profit basis and willingly plays a role in one or more aspects of service delivery with no significant involvement by the state.	Community-based organizations (CBOs), non-governmental organizations (NGOs), churches, foundations, social movements, trade unions, etc. There may also be hybrid cases in which the state provides some resource and management support to non-profit entities (e.g. government-organized NGOs [GONGOs]).	SiNP (single non-profit sector)
Partnership Two or more public and/or non-profit entities working together to deliver a service	A partnership refers to any substantial contractual collaboration between two or more agencies in the public and/or non-profit sector for the purpose of operating and/or financing the delivery of a service over an extended period of time.	Partnership combinations can include two or more public entities working together (within the same level of government or across levels and boundaries of government), two or more "non-profit" entities working together, or combinations thereof.	PuP (public-public partnership) NPNPP (non-profit/non-profit partnership) PuNPP (public/non-profit partnership)

"CRITERIA FOR SUCCESS"

Once identified, alternatives were then subject to an assessment of their "success". Our approach to this evaluation, as noted above, was to use a limited number of predefined norms that we considered to be positive indicators of success, with the understanding that none of these criteria can be entirely objectively assessed and that they are open to re-evaluation as part of the research exercise. Our choice of criteria was drawn from the global anti-privatization literature, the literature on alternatives to privatization, and our own (re)configuration of criteria based on our familiarity with the debates.

These criteria, and the evaluations they informed, are intended as preliminary, first-cut attempts at providing broad-based comparisons of the successes/failures of different alternatives and attempts at improvements and reforms in public sector provision. They are not intended to be comprehensive assessments. As such, researchers were asked to provide general insights on broad categories of success, with the understanding that all of the criteria were open to subjective evaluation, that no single service entity could possibly meet all of the criteria, and that there was the potential for significant tensions between categories (e.g. increased efficiency at the expense of jobs). Researchers were asked to evaluate each service they identified as a potential example of a successful alternative to privatization and to record these evaluations in "data sheets".

The remainder of this chapter discusses the normative categories we chose and the subcategories we consider to be of importance within them. Entire books can (and have) been written on the items listed here, but our review is intentionally brief, intended to give general indications of the rationale for choosing the criteria and the key questions related to them. This is in part to reflect the reality of the terms of reference given to the individual research teams and in part to indicate the preliminary, scoping nature of the research. It did not make sense to place too tight or complex a set of methodological constraints at this initial stage, particularly when the national/regional level of data gathering did not allow for detailed, disaggregated analysis, and when our approach is an explicitly iterative one.

Table 2.2 provides a summary of the normative categories developed for the research and the relevant analytical criteria that apply to each. A more detailed narrative of each category is provided below.

Equity

Inequity is arguably the single largest concern with privatization, with low-income households and other marginalized groups being left out of the service delivery equation (or being offered substandard services) because they cannot afford to pay market rates. Not surprisingly, providing more

Table 2.2   Normative "Criteria for Success" Employed in the Research

Normative category	Related analytical criteria
Equity	• Is physical availability of the service equitable for different social groups (e.g. location, time-distance, gender, age, race, class, ethnicity, etc)? • Is the quality of the service equitable (e.g. product, end-user relations, etc)? • Are quantities of the service equitable (e.g. amounts of water, amperage of electricity, levels of health care)? • Are pricing systems equitable? • Is equity formalized, legalized, or institutionalized in some way?
Participation	• Is the depth of participation adequate (e.g. meaningful participation versus mere consultation, etc)? • Is the scope of participation adequate (i.e. what is open to participation and is it sufficient—policy making, budget decisions, day-to-day service operations, etc)? • Is participation taking place at appropriate scales (i.e. local, national, regional, etc)? • What powers do constituents have to make substantive changes? • Is participation equitable (in terms of gender, race, ethnicity, ability, income, education, workers, NGOs, CBOs, etc)? • Is participation sufficiently representative (i.e. if not everyone participates, are the participants representative of "stakeholder" groups)? • Are there adequate resources for participation by a diverse range of society (transportation, time off work, etc)? • Is participation conducted in culturally appropriate ways? • Are appropriate and adequate amounts of information made available to participants? • Is participation formalized, legalized, or institutionalized in some way? • Is the model of participation robust (i.e. can it adjust to new situations, is it learning as it goes)? • Was there adequate preparation and consultation before beginning the participation process?
Efficiency	• Is the service delivered in a financially efficient manner (e.g. per unit of service delivered)? • Is the service delivered in a resource efficient manner (e.g. water and electricity losses, administration costs, environmental impacts, etc)? • Are adequate investments being made in long-term maintenance? • Do efficiency gains undermine other potentially positive outcomes (e.g. equity, affordability, environment, wages, health and safety, quality, etc)? • Do efficiency gains take into account other services and/or levels of government (e.g. downloading, ring-fencing, etc)?

(continued)

Table 2.2 (continued)

Normative category	Related analytical criteria
Quality of service	• Is the overall quality of the service acceptable in terms of end product (e.g. primary health, water quality, etc) and relations with end users? • Is quality improving?
Accountability	• Are policy makers and service providers accountable to end users? • Is accountability provided at the appropriate scales (i.e. local, national, regional, etc)? • Is the quality of accountability high (i.e. trustworthy, understandable, verifiable)? • Is accountability equitable (i.e. do all service users receive the same depth and quality of accountability)? • Are there clear chains and/or mechanisms of accountability that are formalized, legalized, or institutionalized in some way? • Are there adequate resources to ensure/enforce accountability?
Transparency	• Are operational mandates of the service readily available to the public and understandable? • Are policy decisions about the service readily available to the public and understandable? • Are capital and operating budgets of the service readily available to the public and understandable? • Are there sufficient resources to ensure/enforce transparency?
Quality of the workplace	• Are there mechanisms for workers/unions to participate in the operation, management, or policy making of the service? • Are workers paid a fair salary and benefits? • Do workers feel "empowered"? • Do workers have adequate training and education? • Are there adequate numbers of workers (to ensure quality, safety, sustainability, etc)? • Are there good relations between frontline workers, managers, and end users of the service? • Is there equity amongst workers (gender, race, ethnicity, etc)?

Sustainability
- *Financial sustainability*
  - o Is there sufficient (state) spending to ensure continuity of the service model in terms of operating and capital funds?
  - o Does the service model rely heavily on donor support?
- *Social sustainability*
  - o Can the social engagement mechanism (e.g. volunteerism) be sustained?
- *Political sustainability*
  - o Is there sufficient political support for the model at different levels?
  - o Can the alternative be sustained in a global context of neoliberalism (i.e. is it robust enough to survive serious opposition)?
- *Environmental sustainability*
  - o Are adequate resources available in a sustainable way to support the service and its growth?
  - o Are appropriate types of technologies and resources being used (e.g. coal vs. solar)?
  - o Are appropriate scales of resource use being employed?

Solidarity
- Does the service help build solidarity between workers, community, bureaucrats, politicians, NGOs, end users, etc?
- Does the service help to build solidarity with other service sectors (health, water, electricity, other)?
- Does the service help to build solidarity between other levels of service delivery (regional, international)?

Public ethos
- Does the model help to create/build a stronger "public ethos" around service delivery amongst some or all of the following groups: community, workers, government officials, and politicians?
- Does the model suggest new ways of thinking about the concept of public ownership/workers' control/community control?
- Does the service model explicitly oppose privatization and commercialization?

Transferability
- Is the model transferable to other places in the country/region/world in whole or in part?

equitable services is a central objective of most, if not all, alternative service delivery experiments (Equinet 2007, McIntyre and Mooney 2007).

But equity is not an easy concept to measure. For some countries/cases, it is about policies that ensure distribution of resources according to need and policies that *reduce* inequality by treating unequals unequally (vertical equity). For others, it might be couched as a state-provided basic minimum package of benefits for all or for "targeted groups" ensuring that nobody falls below a certain level (e.g. "free basic water" in South Africa). Differences between countries reflect different equity goals (Wagstaff et al, 1991). It is therefore critical to break the concept into a series of subcategories that probe specific areas.

Much of the case study literature highlights improvements made in accessibility, particularly in terms of class and location. Information on other indicators, such as gender and ethnicity, is not as readily available. There is also a dearth of information on the reliability of a service. Particularly for water and electricity services, many countries are faced with chronic shortages or outages in service (Nakhooda et al, 2007). Part of equity is overcoming physical, economic, and cultural barriers that people encounter in accessing services and participating in decision making. It involves recognition that "social disadvantage and powerlessness underlies the social stratification that generates (health) inequity" (Equinet 2007, 173; see also McIntyre and Mooney 2007).

There is little to draw on from existing research for suggestions on how to evaluate equity in terms of quality. It is likely that this will be a function of both equity and quality in a broad sense—meaning that if a case study ranks high in both quality and equity, it is likely it will have strong equity in terms of quality. However, it is possible that a service could have strong quality but due to poor levels of equity fail to provide a quality end product to all end users.

There are also important political debates about what constitutes sufficient amounts of water, electricity, or health care, in part because they are environmentally and socially determined and in part because it imposes definitions of needs (Ruiters 2007, Dugard 2009). There are baselines below which most "experts" agree quantities are insufficient. At the same time, there are debates about what constitutes adequate services for effective citizenship, as well as how this impacts on overall designs of systems. Health systems are largely geared to curative needs of the wealthy and large water systems are designed for middle-class users, while the poor are relegated to "basic" use. The questions of how much and whether needs and wants or only "effective" demands are met are fundamental questions of the relative power of social classes and the commodification of nature and its instrumentalization as a resource (Harvey 1996).

Another relevant equity question is whether water, electricity, and health as social rights of citizenship are to be free, universal, and paid from taxes. Where differential costs are imposed, the issue is that higher-income households may pay twice as much for a service as lower-income households, but if their household incomes are 10 times as high, then pricing is unfair. One argument says that unequals need to be treated unequally through cross-subsidies. Tariff structures (rates-based, block rates, lifelines, internal cross-subsidies, etc) are important factors in determining equity, for consumption of a service as well as for fixed connection fees. There is general agreement in the municipal services literature on the need for a progressive tariff system, including a base amount of inexpensive or free access (either on a universal or selective basis). These two elements stem from the recognition of a "right" to particular services, with those who use more or hold more financial resources paying more than those who are poor or use less. Cross-subsidies from other sectors and tiers of government are also important here. Some countries use local taxes to fund services and others use intergovernmental transfers to fund services. The degree of progressivity in tax regimes is important. So too is the question of residential versus commercial rates.

Within the literature equity is described both in terms of practice and as a formal procedure. While both are important, without formal or institutional commitments to equity, there can be questions over how it can be guaranteed or applied in a consistent manner. In the case of the public-public partnership (PuP) between Rand Water and the municipality of Harrismith in South Africa, for example, there was an informal practice of not cutting off service to households if they failed to pay. However in the absence of a formal policy or commitment guaranteeing this practice, residents cannot be sure they will all receive such treatment or for how long it may last. Moreover, in assessing alternatives, we would like to explore whether nominal equitable access is reflected in imputed benefits and outcomes and whether they can be measured. For example, what is the under-five mortality rate in areas in which alternatives are being tried?

Participation

Participation of citizens and non-governmental organizations in decision making and implementation of services has become something of a mantra in all of the services literature, be it pro- or anti-privatization, with references having sprung up in what might seem like unlikely places, such as the private sector-dominated World Water Council. For some, participation refers to clear transfers of power and decision-making abilities, while for others it is seen more as a form of consultation and education. When everyone from radical community activists to neoliberal institutions is talking about participation, it is likely that they are not talking about the same thing (Murthy and Klugman 2004; Balanyá et al, 2005, 254). It is therefore critical to be as specific as possible about the forms of participation that can be considered "successful".

The scope and depth of participation will likely be influenced by factors of scale. If participation happens only at the local level it may be difficult to affect policy decisions that take place at regional, national or international levels. Similarly, if participation occurs only at a regional or national level, the depth of local participation may be weak or insufficiently representative of the communities directly affected by the service.

There is often no special consideration given to how to incorporate and empower marginalized groups within "the community"; power dynamics often continue to exist in these spaces (Murthy and Klugman 2004, 78). Equinet, commenting on the experience of representative participation in health care systems in Zambia, argues that representative mechanisms often fail to represent communities fully, particularly vulnerable groups (2007, 185). There is also a growing feminist literature that has drawn attention to the (potentially) high costs of participation on the part of women, since many development projects—especially in the water sector—focus on women's participation while ignoring the gendered aspects of household management. Indeed, participation might just add more work with little benefit (Cleaver 1998, 2000).

Even if marginalized groups are included in participatory mechanisms the question of representativeness must be considered: Do representatives reflect the diversity of the population in terms of gender, ethnicity, class, location, and age? Are representatives of groups fairly chosen/elected? Is representativeness even an appropriate mechanism if broad-based participation is the objective?

Nakhooda et al note that the capacity of community members to participate is constrained by financial and human resources and access to technical expertise (2007, 43). It is one thing for the state to make a commitment to community participation and decision making; it is quite another to devote time and resources to ensuring that everyone is able to participate. There needs to be adequate resources allocated for communications, training, fora, and outreach.

Conducting participation in culturally appropriate ways may help lead to a meaningful experience for participants and may also help to increase the effectiveness of the process. Cultural practices pertaining to everything from discussion styles and leadership structure may need to be taken into account.

Participants must be provided with sufficient information on which to make informed decisions and interventions. This may include technical, financial, and other information. The availability of information in multiple formats is significant because community members will have different access points depending on income, location, etc. This includes having information presented in ways that allow all participants to understand technical or bureaucratic language.

Murthy and Klugman also suggest the creation of "participation contracts" (2004, 84) to detail clearly the relationship between community/civil society and the government/institutions, guaranteeing equal decision-making power in setting priorities, specific policies and monitoring implementation. Such contracts can help to outline the scope, level of participation and the inclusion of marginalized voices. Equinet echoes that sentiment, believing that in order to assure that real community participation occurs in health systems, the role of communities must be formally recognized in law and institutional practice (2007, 212).

Although models must have a certain degree of permanence if they are to be consistent, there may also be reasons for adjusting practices due to changing circumstances, recognition of mistakes, etc. Does the model in question allow for this kind of dynamism, learning, and flexibility? Hall et al note the importance of early community involvement to ensuring successful and effective participation. Not only are the "hows" of community participation important but also the "whens". These authors concluded, in their study on PuPs in the health sector, that "the most effective PuPs had the longest lead-in times and had the community as a partner" (Hall et al, 2005, 36).

Efficiency

"Public" systems are often assumed to be less efficient than their private counterparts, despite research that suggests otherwise. It is therefore critical to assess the efficiency of alternative models of service delivery by similar and different criteria as well as broaden our definitions of the concept.

Efficiency is typically described when "x" inputs produce "y" outputs, and these benchmark criteria need to be considered with alternatives as well. But it is important to contextualize the analysis and to give it longer time horizons. Health care, for example, does not produce homogeneous outputs, with "curing" and "caring" requiring very different forms of measurement. The effects of health prevention may also only be registered many years later and require new forms of evaluation.

Privatized entities often claim better efficiencies but this can be at the expense of long-term investments in equipment and personnel. Factoring in these longer term costs and benefits into efficiency measurements of alternatives is important. In the case of the remunicipalization of the water utility in Grenoble, France, Avrillier writes that maintenance, renewal and improvement of technical systems have improved threefold compared with the experience of privatization (2005, 64).

Some efficiency criteria can also be at odds with others. Financial efficiency, for example, may come at the cost of workers' health and safety and working conditions or community participation. In the example of Honduras's national water authority, SANAA, efficiency appears to have been achieved at the cost of workers, with the loss of 35% of jobs having gone unnoticed in most evaluations of the programme (Lobina and Hall 2000, 48). More broadly, there is a need to challenge the belief that the private sector is more efficient than the public, despite ambiguous empirical evidence and despite the fact that mainstream definitions fail to adequately address the social goals of service delivery such as quality of life and dignity (Spronk 2010). An accounting of "social efficiency" would be more appropriate, though difficult.

It is also important to note if efficiency gains of a particular service are occurring at the expense of another sector or another level of government (e.g. downloading or uploading). Scale is a factor in assessing efficiency since many private sector studies ignore wider impacts and focus on narrow criteria. Finally there are intangible, unmeasured outcomes that public services can provide for societies that must be taken into account (such as promoting cultural practices and providing safe environments).

Quality of service

Perceived poor quality is another justification used by neoliberal policy makers to privatize public services. Yet quality is also a problematic concept, shaped by cultural perceptions and market demands. Evaluating alternatives on this basis is therefore an important, but tricky, counter to the argument that the public sector has to keep up with private sector expectations. The false argument that private bottled water is better than public tap water is a case in point (Clarke 2005).

Accountability

While the World Bank defines accountability as "the degree to which governments have to explain or justify what they have done or failed to do" (World Bank 1999, 284), Murthy and Klugman note that there are richer understandings of the concept than simple "answerability", making distinctions between the scope of accountability (who is accountable and to whom) and whether the accountability mechanisms have any enforceability (2004, 79–80). The World Bank definition, like that for corruption, surreptitiously places the focus, and generally the blame, on the public as opposed to the private sector as a matter of definition (with the false presumption that the market makes the private sector accountable). At higher levels, accountability is something to be negotiated, not limited to immediate interests but global ones. Accountability extends both vertically and horizontally, as the community has the power to hold a service provider accountable through legal mechanisms, not just internally from one level of personnel to another.

The literature provides several examples of how this might be achieved. Montemayor's (2005) understanding of accountability emphasizes the need for a clear chain of accountability to respond to, and deal with, community concerns and comments. Nakhooda et al (2007) argue that an independent regulatory body can improve transparency, participation, and accountability. Gomez and Terhorst emphasize the need for accountability via a unit of "vigilance and social control" composed of citizens/civil society (2005, 123).

Transparency

Having access to information about the operation of a service is crucial to creating a transparent environment. In the case of water remunicipalization in Grenoble, France, Avrillier notes that citizens have access to information on water services and costs and have open debates about them, but it is not clear whether this information is easily accessible or understandable to the public (2005, 67). Having access to financial information also allows citizens and community groups to put the policy and operational information in context, giving them the tools to challenge policies if budgets do not follow stated aims.

Quality of the workplace

Frontline workers are essential to the delivery of services whether they are public or private, with many workers exposed to serious health risks. Any alternative to privatization must take into account workplace health and safety as well as systems that allow for worker participation.

While discussions of participation generally focus on community, there is also the question of workforce participation and forms of workplace organization. Depending on the model being used (cooperative, PuP, public utility) different types of worker participation/organization will exist, from full control to joint-management committees to minor input on issues directly related to the workplace. *Aguas Bonaerenses SA* in Buenos Aires, Argentina, is a public sector operator with representation from water workers and users in the regulatory body and management of the water company. This participation has led to increased coverage in water and sewage, the building of new pipelines and improved water pressure (Hall and Lobina 2006, 13). In Kampala, Uganda, the 1999 reform process brought in a new collective agreement with the union, guaranteeing them involvement in all aspects of restructuring and a new unit management committee was created, with a seat for the union. There are many cases in which workers performing important and sometimes dangerous tasks are extremely poorly paid. This can force workers to resort to bribes and extra payments to survive. In this environment it is hard for things not to be inefficient (Hall and Lobina 2006, 13).

Workers' sense of "empowerment" is important as well, but hard to quantify in any comparative sense, and can come from many different sources for different workers. Evaluating this component will require observation of, and interaction with, workers themselves. Other indicators, such as worker participation, pay and benefits, and relations between worker and management, may help to evaluate objectively the degree to which workers feel empowered in an alternative service delivery system.

A major part of investing in workers is providing proper and adequate training to perform in their jobs. In Ho Chi Minh City, Vietnam, the water utility received an Asian Development Bank loan that provided support for training on several key issues: organizational development, water supply maintenance and management, financial management and accounting, computer systems, and English language skills. In Porto Alegre, Sabesp operates a continual training and education programme for employees covering technical aspects and administrative and managerial issues. It also runs computer classes and literacy programmes for the workers (Hall and Lobina 2006, 14).

Many regions lack sufficient health care professionals to implement essential services; those that remain often feel frustrated and undervalued and are forced to work in under-resourced facilities. Parts of east and southern Africa are suffering from a dramatic shortage of health workers, particularly in rural areas (Equinet 2007, 143). There is a desperate need to train and retrain health care workers to ensure an effective health care system. Real wages need to be increased, and workers need to be provided with incentives such as professional development, meaningful career paths and improved working and living conditions. Beyond this, there are also social needs of frontline workers: transportation, housing, education for their families, electricity, and their own access to health care. Some research illustrates a problematic approach to labour issues in the context of public utility restructuring. A reduction in employees is automatically assumed to lead to an increase in efficiency, not recognizing that a higher-quality and more equitable service can sometimes take more time and require additional workers (Hall and Lobina 2006, 13). Positive results of efficiency are often expressed in ratios of workers per service-access point or connection, such as the *Perbadanan Bekalan Air Pulan Pinang* (PBA) water utility in Malaysia that boasts a ratio of workers to end users of 1:373 (Santiago 2005, 56). This type of quantitative analysis can have negative consequences on the health and safety of workers, as well as the quality of the service.

Labour is often perceived as a cost to be reduced or something to be made more efficient. There is an implicit assumption in some of the literature that workers try to "avoid" doing their job and need to be made more efficient. Whereas this may be the case in some situations, many frontline service workers go above and beyond what is required of them in their job and are strongly committed to the goals of the service. As Hall and Lobina argue, "the knowledge and commitment of workers, and the capacity of their unions to participate in restructuring and improvements, should be seen as key strengths to be encouraged" (2006, 12). In Colombia, the public water sector has followed the trend of privatization in outsourcing work and has imposed a flexible, precarious model of employment where workers lack security and stability (Velez 2005, 106). In the case of the publicly owned utility SANAA in Honduras, which underwent serious restructuring in 1996, reducing the workforce by 35% and instilling buzzwords of "dedication, enthusiasm, integrity and pride" were seen as positive outcomes. In the case of Sabesp, in Brazil, a state-owned water utility that underwent substantial restructuring, employment levels were reduced through "a moderate and one-off reduction" and costs were significantly reduced by 45% through outsourcing of ancillary operations (Lobina and Hall 2000, 48–49).

Hall and Lobina also note that the relationships between workers and the community are an important element that strengthens the delivery of the service (2006, 15). In a slum project in Ahmedabad, India, workers developed relationships with community members, creating a cycle of gratitude and pride, which deepened the workers' commitment to, and involvement in, the project. Similar experiences were reported in several projects in rural Pakistan. Pro-privatization pundits often characterize public sector workers as lazy and inefficient beneficiaries of state spending, creating tensions between workers and the community they serve. Alternative forms of service delivery must avoid these unnecessary, false, and counterproductive binaries.

Finally, it must be asked whether the benefits described above extend to all workers along gender, race, ethnic, age, and other demographic and socio-economic lines.

Sustainability

Alternative forms of service delivery should be sustainable over a reasonable period of time if they are to be considered successful (though short-lived examples can serve as indicators of what is possible and as lessons for future initiatives). Sustainability happens on many fronts.

In order for an alternative service delivery system to sustain itself financially, there must be adequate resources provided. Existing public alternatives utilize a great diversity of funding structures, with some receiving strong and sustained financial support from the state, while others practice some form of cost recovery from end users. This is a possible point of tension. Within the literature some view financial autonomy or independence from the state as a positive development, while others label this as a form of commercialization that forces public services to valorize finances and private-sector management principles.

A common constraint is finding funding outside of international financial institutions, many of which have stipulations about private sector involvement or may not be willing to support alternative models such as cooperatives. Balanyá et al note that there is a "desperate need for funding mechanisms that are without political conditions and that are oriented to serve societal goals instead of economic and ideological objective" (2005, 266). Relying on progressive donor funding may also prove to be a problem, however, as donor withdrawal could undermine the systems being developed.

Some alternative service models rely heavily on volunteers from the community, in the form of volunteer labour or in terms of time commitments necessary for the participation process. While it is often beneficial to have strong volunteer participation, consideration must be given to how this volunteerism affects community members and whether this level of involvement can be sustained. Also, is the model robust enough to deal with changing demographics and/or socio-economic conditions (e.g. xenophobia)? Are the processes internal to social movements and community organizations robust and democratic enough to sustain long-term interest and capacity building? Are there hidden costs of participation (e.g. do social movements lose "independence" and the ability to criticize if they join a participatory process)?

There is disagreement within the current literature on what the relationship should be between alternative public utilities and the state. Some researchers argue that having a supportive and involved state and government is crucial for the success of a public utility. In Hall et al's examination of PuPs in the health sector, the authors note that government policy played a significant role in supporting and/or facilitating partnerships (2005, 38). Local and national governments played a key role in public alternatives in the water sector in Porto Alegre, Kerala, and Caracas (Balanyá et al, 2005, 264). However, others argue that having independence and autonomy from the state is what is necessary to succeed. Murthy and Klugman assert that decentralization implies that leadership remains with people elected by community members not bureaucrats, and connect decentralization to a higher level of community participation, although decentralization can involve devolution of responsibility for delivery without necessary resources as well as capture of resources and provision by local elites (2004, 83). Reynoso (2000) contends that there are important benefits to local planning and management, as opposed to a top-down approach, which is unable to adapt to the specific context and issues of the state. However, Reynoso also argues that there is a need for a supportive state to help facilitate and oversee the objectives of the public alternative. Equinet views the state as playing a key role in establishing "people-centered" health systems, but they make a distinction between a strong state, and a domineering state, seeing the role of states to act "with" society, not in replacement of it (2007, 174).

Beyond the political climate at a local/national level, there is recognition of the need to have change at an international or global level to facilitate these alternatives. Balanyá et al conclude that real public alternatives cannot be achieved within the context of neoliberalism, that despite progress and individual victories there is a need for a more enabling environment:

> The cumulative impact of these neoliberal policies is a fundamental obstacle to the development of public provision of essential services. Lasting solutions, it seems, are only feasible if this model of development is replaced by a different model of globalization, one that facilitates progressive public solutions rather than hindering them. (2005, 264)

Environmental resources are another element that must be considered in an evaluation of alternatives. "Public" providers have been amongst the worst abusers of natural resources (Soviet electricity generation being but one example), and it is critical that we do not overlook questions of resource type and consumption rates simply because they are being done in the public domain. It may be that alternative sources/forms of resources are required, and it is incumbent upon public providers to ask and investigate the difficult resource questions that many private providers are loathe to query.

Similar responsibilities apply to choices of technology (e.g. coal-fired versus solar electricity), some of which can be determined by the momentum of previous delivery practices and ideologies. Determining the appropriate types of technologies is partly a question of the environmental resources available but also a question of the social, economic, and political factors associated with the objectives of the service delivery models that are chosen.

Finally, while some aspects of service delivery are inherently local, the resources required to provide them can be much broader in their reach. From tapping into regional watersheds to sourcing health products from overseas producers, it is important to determine the most appropriate and sustainable scale of resource procurement and distribution. In the electricity sector, for example, there is a growing debate over whether it is better to produce large transmission grids for regional distribution from large generating sites or to have small-scale decentralized production.

Solidarity

One of the main aims of building non-private systems is to create clusters of activity and "solidarity" between different sectors of society and synergies between service providers struggling to improve services in the public sector, be they government officials, frontline workers or community members involved in a project. Solidarity is a difficult concept to define, however, and with very different manifestations in political life. And yet there is something palpable about a service delivery system that generates bonds and commitments across space and scale, and this generalized phenomenon of bond making and knowledge sharing amongst non-private participants is important to understand.

Traditional social democratic and welfarist systems have been criticized for failing to produce real social solidarity (Williams 1989; Ignatieff 1995). Hall presents an interesting discussion of solidarity within public services, drawing on the notion of a "European Social Model", which espouses a commitment to income equality, progressive tax systems, public ownership, and political solidarity (2008, 17). He also describes financial solidarity, which has led to centrally financed development spending to help reduce inequalities between individual member states, including financing for infrastructure, retraining of workers and funds to help fight discrimination in the workplace. Whatever the definition, understanding the extent to which non-private service systems can overcome the individualizing and alienating effects of commercialization is an important aspect of evaluating and promoting alternative models of delivery.

Public ethos

Throughout the literature on alternatives to privatization there is an implicit assumption that these models have a greater degree of "public-ness" and "public ethos" than their privatized counterparts, but little is given by way of explicit definitions of what this means. Balanyá et al write that publicness involves commitments to "societal objectives, including democracy, environmental sustainability and human security" and further delineate a "progressive publicness", involving direct citizen participation in addition to the goal of serving public needs (2005, 260). In their notion of "public", they include a wide variety of not-for-profit management models, from cooperatives to municipal utilities to corporatized entities. Cann also offers a broad understanding of publicness as something that goes beyond formal public ownership and management. It is described as containing several elements pertaining to different actors within the system: taking pride in one's work (workers), valuing staff (management and users), transparency and accountability (policy makers), and community participation (2007, 8).

There is also the question of whether an alternative needs to be explicitly "anti-privatization" in its motivation and composition. Speaking to the question of public-public partnerships, Hall et al note that some PuPs can be seen as an explicit defence against privatization while others have actually been used to pave the way for privatization (or at least PPPs), bringing into question their commitment to a public ethos (2005, 10). This question is also of relevance to cooperative models and partnerships with non-governmental agencies, many of which act autonomously from the state and are not directly accountable to the public at large. In the case of health cooperatives in Costa Rica, Gauri et al perceive the latter as part of a broader trend towards the privatization of public services, intended to "increase private sector participation and to introduce market-like mechanisms in health care to enhance efficiency" (2004, 294).

As difficult as it is to define, public ethos looms large in the motivation for alternative service delivery models, making it all the more important to try and understand.

Transferability

Transferability is not an indicator of success, per se, but rather a way of understanding relationship with other alternatives in other sectors/places. A particular model of service delivery may work well in one place/sector but not in another. Geographical location, population size, political climate, available technologies, existing state and non-state institutions, and attitudes of citizens to the state are some of the many factors that will influence the ability of a particular model to start up and survive. An analysis of these considerations will also help to indicate the adaptability/ suitability of certain models to other contexts. For example, some argue that cooperatives are more efficient in population clusters of 50,000 or less (Munoz 2005, 101). A similar argument is often applied to participatory schemes. However, Balanyá et al argue that notable examples in Porto Alegre and Recife have shown that scale is not necessary an obstacle to participatory management (2005, 250). Should an alternative be considered more successful if it has greater potential to be reproduced elsewhere? No two options are ever going to be exactly alike, and although related in many ways through similar technology, solidarity, and support across scales, we must resist the idea that alternatives can be imposed from outside. Nevertheless, the extent to which lessons—practical or theoretical—can be learned from one model and adopted in another is a useful point to know.

CONCLUSION

The list of "criteria for success" provided here is a long and ambitious one, and it is important to reiterate that none of the sectoral/regional studies in this book looked at every one of these factors; nor were they expected to. The criteria are intended as reference points and guidelines—important screening tools for what has been a relatively unprogrammatic field of study to date. The more detailed case studies that will form the second stage of this research project will provide more fine-tuned analysis of these criteria, but even then it will only be possible to explore a limited number of factors in any detail given the complexity of concepts such as equity and accountability.

Our hope is that we have provided clearer and firmer parameters for the investigation of alternative service delivery mechanisms than has been offered to date and that they serve as a reasonable basis for comparing service models and experiences across regions and sectors. The proof of the pudding is in the eating, however, and we encourage readers to review as many of the chapters in this book as possible to get a fuller sense of the degree to which we have been able to provide such an analytical and comparative platform.

We particularly encourage people to read across sectors, with the aim of stimulating more dialogue between health, water, and electricity activists and researchers. For if we are to develop meaningful universal guidelines for "alternative" essential services, they must be as convincing across sectors as they are across place and culture.

NOTES

1. Special thanks to Amanda Wilson for her work on the literature review for the "criteria for success" section of this chapter.
2. See www.municipalservicesproject.org for more detail.

REFERENCES

Avrillier, R. 2005. A return to the source: Re-municipalisation of water services in Grenoble, France. In Balanyá, B., Brennan, B., Hoedeman, O., Kishimoto, S. and Terhorst, P. (Eds), *Reclaiming public water: Achievements, struggles and visions from around the world*, pp. 63–71. Amsterdam: Transnational Institute and Corporate Europe Observatory.
Balanyá, B., Brennan, B., Hoedeman, O., Kishimoto, S. and Terhorst, P. 2005. Empowering public water—Ways forward. In Balanyá, B., Brennan, B., Hoedeman, O., Kishimoto, S. and Terhorst, P. (Eds), *Reclaiming public water: Achievements, struggles and visions from around the world*, pp. 1–9. Amsterdam: Transnational Institute and Corporate Europe Observatory.
Boyd, C.M.J. 2009. Can a Marxist believe in human rights? *Critique* 37(4): 579–600.
Cann, V. 2007. Introduction. In World Development Movement (Ed), *Going public: Southern solutions to the global water crisis*, 7–14. London: WDM.
Clarke, T. 2005. *Inside the bottle: An exposé of the bottled water industry*. Ottawa: Polaris Institute.
Cleaver, F. 1998. Choice, complexity, and change: Gendered livelihoods and the management of water. *Agriculture and Human Values* (15): 293–299.
Dugard, J. 2009. Free basic electricity. In McDonald, D. (Ed), *Electric capitalism: Recolonising Africa on the power grid*, pp. 264–287. London: Earthscan.
Equinet. 2007. *Reclaiming the resources for health: A regional analysis of equity in health in east and southern Africa*. Uganda: Fountain Publishers.
Fine, B. 2001. *Social capital versus social theory: Political economy and social science at the turn of the millennium*. London: Routledge.
Gauri, V., Cercone, J. and Briceño, R. 2004. Separating financing from provision: Evidence from 10 years of partnership with health cooperatives in Costa Rica. *Health Policy Planning* 19(5): 292–301.
Gomez, L.S. and Terhorst, P. 2005. Cochabamba, Bolivia: Public-collective partnership after the Water Wars. In Balanyá, B., Brennan, B., Hoedeman, O., Kishimoto, S. and Terhorst, P. (Eds), *Reclaiming public water: Achievements, struggles and visions from around the world*, pp. 121–130. Amsterdam: Transnational Institute and Corporate Europe Observatory.
Hall, D. 2008. *Alternatives to PPPs: Positive action for in-house services*. Public Services International Research Unit, London: Unpublished Mimeo.
Hall, D., Lethbridge, J. and Lobina, E. 2005. *Public-public partnerships in health and essential services*. Municipal Services Project Occasional Paper No. 9. Cape Town: MSP.
Hall, D. and Lobina, E. 2006. Water as a public service. Public Services International Research Unit. 15 December. www.psiru.org/reports/2007–01-W-waaps.pdf.
Harriss, J. 2001. *Depoliticizing development: The World Bank and social capital*. London: Leftword Books.
Harvey, D. 1996. *Justice, nature and the geography of difference*. Oxford: Basil Blackwell.
———. 2000. *Spaces of hope*. Berkeley: University of California Press.

Ignatieff, M. 1995. The myth of citizenship. In Biener, R. (Ed), *Theorizing citizenship*, pp. 51–76. Albany: State University of New York Press.

Lobina, E. and Hall, D. 2000. Public sector alternatives to water supply and sewage privatization: Case studies. *Water Resources Development* 16(1): 35–55.

McIntyre, D. and Mooney, G. (Eds). 2007. *The economics of health equity*. Cambridge: Cambridge University Press.

Merrett, S. 2002. Willingness to pay—A review: Deconstructing households' willingness-to-pay for water in low-income countries. *Water Policy* 4(2): 157–172.

Montemayor, C.A. 2005. Possibilities for public water in Manila. In Balanyá, B., Brennan, B., Hoedeman, O., Kishimoto, S. and Terhorst, P. (Eds), *Reclaiming public water: Achievements, struggles and visions from around the world*, pp. 213–225. Amsterdam: Transnational Institute and Corporate Europe Observatory.

Munoz, A.D. 2005. Water cooperatives in Argentina. In Balanyá, B., Brennan, B., Hoedeman, O., Kishimoto, S. and Terhorst, P. (Eds), *Reclaiming public water: Achievements, struggles and visions from around the world*, pp. 95–101. Amsterdam: Transnational Institute and Corporate Europe Observatory.

Murthy, R. and Klugman, B. 2004. Service accountability and community participation in the context of health sector reforms in Asia: Implications for sexual and reproductive health services. *Health Policy and Planning* 19(2): 78–86.

Nakhooda, S., Dixit, S. and Dubash, N.K. 2007. *Empowering people: A governance analysis of electricity*. Washington, DC: World Resources Institute.

Reynoso, V.G. 2000. Towards a new water management practice experiences and proposals from Guanajuato state for a participatory and decentralized water management structure in Mexico. *Water Resources Development* 16(4): 571–588.

Ruiters, G. 2007. Contradictions in municipal services in contemporary South Africa: Disciplinary commodification and self-disconnections. *Critical Social Policy* 27(4): 243–262.

Santiago, C. 2005. Public-public partnership: An alternative strategy in water management in Malaysia. In Balanyá, B., Brennan, B., Hoedeman, O., Kishimoto, S. and Terhorst, P. (Eds), *Reclaiming public water: Achievements, struggles and visions from around the world*, pp. 55–61. Amsterdam: Transnational Institute and Corporate Europe Observatory.

Spronk, S. 2010. Water and sanitation utilities in the global South: Re-centering the debate on "efficiency". *Radical Review of Political Economics* 42(2): 156–174.

Velez, H. 2005. Public services in Colombia: A matter of democracy. In Balanyá, B., Brennan, B. Hoedeman, O., Kishimoto, S. and Terhorst, P. (Eds), *Reclaiming public water: Achievements, struggles and visions from around the world*, pp. 103–109. Amsterdam: Transnational Institute and Corporate Europe Observatory.

Wagstaff, A., Doorslaer, E. and Pierrella, P. 1991. Equity in finance and delivery of health care: Some tentative cross country comparisons. In Maquire, A., Fen, P. and Mayhew, K. (Eds), *Providing health care: The economics of alternative systems*, pp. 132–156. Oxford: Oxford University Press.

Whittington, D., Lauria, D.T. and Xinming, M. 1991. A study of water vending and willingness to pay for water in Onitsha, Nigeria. *World Development* 19(2/3): 179–198.

Williams, F. 1989. *Social policy—A critical introduction. Issues of race, gender, and class*. Cambridge: Policy Press.

World Bank. 1999. Annual World Bank Conference on Development in Latin America and the Caribbean: Decentralization and accountability of the public sector. Washington, DC: World Bank.

Part I

Actors, Issues and Ideologies

3   Terrains of Neoliberalism
Constraints and Opportunities for Alternative Models of Service Delivery

Ben Fine and David Hall

The purpose of this chapter is not so much to demonstrate that neoliberalism is suffering some degree of crisis of legitimacy, as it is to explain why, despite this crisis, the momentum behind alternatives to neoliberalism remains so weak. There are good reasons for this, reflecting the extent to which neoliberalism is not merely an ideology and a set of policies to be reversed but that it is systemically attached to developments across contemporary capitalism over the past 30 years that have been underpinned by, but cannot be reduced to, what has been termed "financialization".

We begin by giving an account of financialization—what it is, what are its effects and what challenges it poses to alternative policy making. Of course, to point to financialization is not to blame finance or the economy for all of the world's woes, even if this is in part an understandable reaction to the current crisis. For neoliberalism is not simply confined to economic imperatives but has also reflected, for example, responses to the collapse of the Soviet bloc, the erosion of the vitality and strength of trade unions and liberation struggles, and the perceived failings of the (welfare) state following the collapse of the post-war boom.

Financialization has, then, involved the excessive expansion and proliferation of financial markets and their penetration into, and influence over, almost every area of economic and social life. But this has occurred against a broader and deeper background of changes that have been systemically disadvantageous to public sector provision. The systemic hold of neoliberalism explains why proposals for public sector alternatives have been so thin on the ground and also why those that do prevail against the odds should be constrained from meeting wider goals than commercial viability. The institutional capacity to deliver public sector alternatives has been severely undermined so that even corresponding *proposals* remain limited, let alone *delivery in practice.*

As will be shown, these observations are borne out in acute form by the financial crisis that began in 2008 and the policy responses to it. The imperative to rescue the financial system from itself begs the question of "rescue it for what and how", and here there tends to be a yawning gap in real outcomes, especially in public provision, reflecting the extent to which policy has been geared towards supporting the private sector in general and finance in particular. This leads us to suggest that the building of public sector alternatives, on which the vast majority of the poorest in developing countries will continue to depend for provision of many of their basic needs into the foreseeable future, will have to dovetail with the building of broader policy initiatives and institutional capacity to deliver them. It is not, then, simply a matter of different policies and of a different politics that informs them. The most immediate, but far from final, task is one of placing finance at the service of delivery rather than the other way about.

But this is much simpler to say than to target and realize in practice as, even within the context of the global crisis for which finance is primarily responsible, its needs have commanded the deepest and prior claims on both resources and policy making. Whereas, for example, the rhetoric of reining in the speculation of, and rewards to, the financial system was prominent once its crisis broke, there has been an astonishing return to business as usual in the widest sense. As the Centre for Research on Socio-Cultural Change finds, those UK bodies reporting on the financial system, and how better to regulate it, drew upon a membership of "662 years of work experience and 75% of those years were spent in City [the London financial centre] occupations or servicing City needs" (CRESC 2009, 5). Further, "90% of its witnesses came from finance or consultancy with revenue links to finance".[1] Indeed, "Membership contained no non-financial businesses and their trade associations, no trade unions despite the unionisation of retail finance workers, no NGOs to represent consumers or press social justice agendas, no mainstream economists or heterodox intellectuals, very few politicians or civil servants" (CRESC 2009, 23). Significantly, even as witnesses, the representation of the public sector was notable for its absence.[2]

What is both striking and disturbing in these respects is the extent to which different constituencies other than those attached to finance have been marginalized or subordinated, almost as second nature, within both the institutions and processes of government. While CRESC (2009) has at least made this transparent in the case of reform and policy making in the UK, the dull weight of business as usual—or should that be unusual—is liable both to prevail and to go unnoticed in the developing world, with at most a necessary deference to more straitened circumstances as global recession hits. This is crucial both in understanding the fate of public sector alternatives in the past as well as in building their potential for the future. For the task is not only to build alternatives based on public sector provision but also to dig deeper into creating the conditions that allow them to emerge and to be sustained and to deliver the goods just as, putatively, neoliberalism has previously set about the same task on behalf of the private sector and finance with the current devastating results.

Our critical response begins in the third section of the chapter by addressing the nature of neoliberalism and how it has systematically, through financialization and otherwise, undermined the potential for public sector alternatives to emerge and prosper. The fourth section carries this further by reference to empirical developments around "public" service delivery and how the private sector has been promoted to be involved both directly and indirectly. The last section suggests that secure alternatives are only liable to be sustained by subordinating the role of finance and paying close attention to sector- and country-specific issues of provision within each of health, water and electricity, for example, without neglect of generic issues such as equity, labour market conditions, and participatory forms of governance.

FINANCIALIZATION

Financialization is a relatively new term and has its roots primarily in heterodox economics and Marxist political economy (Fine 2007, Goldstein 2009), although it is liable to be increasingly adopted by orthodoxy. It has also been understood in a number of different, distinct but connected and overlapping ways. First, at the most casual level, it refers to the astonishing expansion and proliferation of financial markets over the past 30 years, during which the ratio of global financial assets to global GDP has risen three times, from 1.5 to 4.5 (Palma 2009).[3] That this might be indicative of dysfunction—why do you need three times as many financial services proportionately to oil the economy than previously?—has previously been much overlooked precisely because of the market success of financialization in terms of growth and rewards. As the variously infamous former US Treasury Secretary, Chief Economist at the World Bank, Head of Harvard, and then Barack Obama's chief economic adviser Larry Summers has described the Efficient Market Hypothesis (as cited in Davidson 2008, 2, emphasis added):

> The ultimate social functions are spreading risks, guiding investment of scarce capital, and processing and disseminating the information possessed by diverse traders . . . *prices always reflect fundamental values.* . . . The logic of efficient markets is compelling.

The logic today is less compelling, not least to the bankers themselves who had previously deployed it to rationalize what is now being revealed to be a reality of inefficient, dysfunctional, and parasitical markets, with a rather different meaning materializing in the crisis to the notion of "spreading risks" than the intended reduction!

Second, financialization has been associated with the expansion of speculative assets at the expense of mobilizing and allocating investment for real activity. This is most notable in the *ex post* recognition of the lax regulation of the financial sector and corresponding calls to put the speculative *milch* cow back in the barn and reduce the contamination between speculative and real investments. That real investment itself is speculative, being contingent upon uncertain future returns, and that competition in financing depends upon expanding systemic risk by potential contagion at a greater rate than individual risk, are not necessarily overlooked. But greater restraint is called for between barn and field.

Third, this is because financialization has been understood as both the expansion *and* the proliferation of financial instruments and services. These have given birth to a whole range of financial institutions and markets and corresponding acronyms that are simply bewildering, quite apart from futures markets for trading in commodities yet to be produced (for which carbon is the most fetishized) and, most infamously of all, subprime mortgages. The expansion of the latter and their bundling into derivatives that were traded on and on ultimately had the effect of triggering the crisis, and is indicative of the previous two aspects.

Fourth, at a systemic level, financialization has been located in terms of the dominance of finance over industry. Empirically, this is not a matter of finance telling industry what to do, as recent trends have witnessed corporations relying less rather than more upon financial institutions to fund their operations as they have been able to raise funds on their own account. Yet, especially in the US, even non-financial corporations have necessarily been caught up in the process of financialization as they have increasingly derived profitability from their financial as opposed to their productive activities. As the leading *Financial Times* journalist Martin Wolf has put it:[4]

> The US itself looks almost like a giant hedge fund. The profits of financial companies jumped from below 5 per cent of total corporate profits, after tax, in 1982 to 41 per cent in 2007.

The corresponding implications for the level, pace and efficacy of productive activity have been highlighted by Rossman and Greenfield from a labour movement perspective:

> What is new is the drive for profit through the elimination of productive capacity and employment. . . . This reflects the way in which financialization has driven the management of non-financial companies to 'act more like financial market players'. (2006, 2)

More generally, Stockhammer (2004) has been at the forefront in arguing that financialization has been at the expense of real investment.

Fifth, for some, not least as a defining characteristic of neoliberalism itself, financialization is perceived to be a strategy for redistributing income to a class of rentiers (Palma 2009, but see Lapavitsas 2009 for a contrary view). Certainly, the rewards to finance systemically and individually have been astonishing not least, once more, in the US, where real incomes for the vast majority of the population have stagnated over the last 30 years and any productivity gains have accrued to the top 1% of earners whose share in GDP had risen from less than 10% to more than double this.

Sixth, though again with the US in the lead, consumption has been sustained by the extension of (consumer) credit, not least through the use of capital gains in housing as collateral. For some, this has been part and parcel of the leading role played by financialization in exploiting workers through provision of financial services at abnormally high levels of banking profits (dos Santos 2009, Lapavitsas 2009, but see Fine 2009d, 2010 for a critique). This is, however, a single element in the much broader system of financial arrangements at the global level that has witnessed huge balance of trade and payments deficits for the US, matched by a corresponding holding of US dollars as reserves by other countries (with dramatic increases for China in particular). This is a consequence of neoliberal policies to relax if not eliminate exchange controls, opening economies to vulnerability to capital movements and, thereby, requiring high levels of reserves as a safeguard. The paradox is that with all its deficits and minimal interest rates, the US dollar has not suffered a collapse despite failing to follow the neoliberal policy advice on such matters that it has sought to impose on other countries through the World Bank and IMF when similarly inflicted by deficits of lesser magnitudes. Previous crises elsewhere have been used to facilitate financialization by opening up financial markets to international, and especially US, participation.

However the term financialization is defined and used, it points to a complex amalgam of developments within global finance and in its interactions with, and consequences for, economic and social life more generally. For further, seventh, it is not merely the expansion and proliferation of (speculative) financial markets that are striking but also the penetration of such financing into a widening range of both economic and social reproduction: housing, pensions, health, and so on. This is, of course, of paramount significance for social and economic infrastructure and for the displacement of public by private sector provision, most notably in case of privatization, which can lead to proliferation of financial assets and consultancies.

Thus, different approaches and contributions to financialization may offer different emphases, but there is equally a need to locate it within a theory of finance itself. For this, there are as many competing candidates as there are forms of finance, ranging from the now discredited efficient market hypothesis to analyses of systemic financial fragility (most closely associated with economist Hyman Minsky). It is not possible to appraise these here and offer a synthesis other than in the form of a number of conclusions, namely that financialization:

- Reduces overall levels and efficacy of real investment as financial instruments and activities expand at its expense even if excessive investment does take place in particular sectors at particular times (as with the dotcom bubble of a decade ago).

- Prioritizes shareholder value, or financial worth, over other economic and social values.
- Pushes policies towards conservatism and commercialization in all respects.
- Extends influence more broadly, both directly and indirectly, over economic *and* social policy.
- Places more aspects of economic and social life at the risk of volatility from financial instability and, conversely, places the economy and social life at risk of crisis from triggers within particular markets (as with the food and energy crises that preceded the financial crisis).

Although financialization is a single word, it is attached to different forms and effects of finance. The discussion here has drawn much of its illustration from the US and the UK, and these have been in the forefront of financialization. Different countries have experienced financialization differently, and this is especially true of the developing world. It has, for example, been much less affected by international transmission mechanisms associated with toxic financial assets than through the slowdown in growth, corresponding export demand, and capital flows from direct foreign investment, aid, and migrant remittances. Nonetheless, financialization has been important in the developing world, with corresponding diversity of impacts on the way in which and the extent to which financial interests have been formed and have influenced policy. This has been especially important for social policy and provision of economic and social infrastructure generally conceived, not least through the influence of donor agencies. So, if financialization lies at the heart of neoliberalism, itself in crisis, what are future prospects?

NEOLIBERALISM IS DEAD? LONG LIVE . . .

A striking feature of the current global crisis is the speed and depth with which the legitimacy of neoliberalism has been discredited. While the last recession on this scale, following the collapse of the post-World War II boom, also witnessed the loss of its ideological underpinnings—those of Keynesianism—it did so much more slowly. Keynesianism itself only emerged over a decade or more in response to the Great Depression of the 1930s, with a world war intervening before it was established as the new conventional wisdom before its own demise. The monetarist counter-revolution that replaced it and initiated the era of neoliberalism, also took a decade to take hold, from the early 1970s. Today, though, the erstwhile peddlers of Tina ("there is no alternative" to neoliberalism) are understandably thin on the ground in the wake of the extraordinarily acute and systemic failure of what is the perfect market, or markets, those attached to finance.

To point to the crisis of neoliberalism does not in itself offer alternatives, and these also seem to be thin on the ground apart from the ad hoc appeals for stronger regulation of financial markets and particular Keynesian measures of demand management to temper the worst fall-out from the credit crunch. We return to alternatives later but first consider the ideology of neoliberalism beyond the simple nostrum of leaving as much as possible to what are presumed to be the efficient workings of markets. For the ideology runs much deeper than posing the market and the individual against the state and officialdom, with the presumption that individuals endlessly pursue self-interest—legitimately when done through the market but also illegitimately through the state as in rent seeking and corruption. The role of the state, therefore, has to be minimized because it provides opportunities for purely self-seeking actors. This has the effect of disparaging the role that can be played by collective action and of denying the possibility of a public sector ethos.

Indeed, one of the consequences of neoliberal ideology is to have corruption defined as something that only takes place within the state. As the Asian Development Bank puts it, "The succinct definition [of corruption] utilized by the World Bank is 'the abuse of *public* office for *private* gain'".[5] This conveniently excludes the extent to which corruption involves the private sector as one of its partners in crime. The corporate payer of bribes cannot, on this definition, be guilty of corruption—only the public sector receiver of the bribe can. And totally excluded are "corrupt" dealings entirely confined within the private sector for which the neoliberal expansion of the market allows for greater scope and, by no means, greater transparency.

Nor is neoliberal ideology a simple stance of being pro-market and anti-state, for it is only able to be so on the basis of gathering mutually inconsistent stances together. This is most apparent in terms of economic analysis, for appeal is made to mainstream neoclassical economics for the *static* efficiency that accrues from perfectly working markets. This depends upon taking preferences, resources, and technologies as given, and relying upon the market to allocate those resources efficiently to most desirable uses in the absence of the distortions and the rent seeking that would derive from the interventions of the state (and its self-seeking officials). Irrespective of the extraordinarily demanding conditions for the market to work in this way, even on the theory's own terms (no externalities, increasing returns to scale, oligopolies, etc), there is an alternative neoliberal rationale for reliance upon the market that is entirely different and incompatible with one based on static market efficiency. For the neo-Austrian strand of neoliberalism sees the market as the means by which imperfectly informed but innovative individuals can best bring about *dynamic* change, in major part relying upon the spontaneous emergence of the necessary institutions to support the market in this role (Denis 2004).

Such, in a nutshell, are the neoliberal arguments for *laissez-faire*, its stance on the economy. But the ideology does not rest there because it is generally recognized that the economy as market does not work in a vacuum and needs the state and other institutions, spontaneous or otherwise, as supports. Where these begin and end remains fuzzy, but the liberal veneer associated with the freedom of the individual within the market and the antipathy to the state is rapidly abandoned once it comes to the state's essential functions. We should recall that the first major experiment with neoliberalism was undertaken by the "Chicago boys" in Chile in the mid-1970s. Not surprisingly then, although democracy is now seen as an element of good governance, neoliberalism has previously been associated with authoritarianism, conservatism and the limitations on freedoms once stepping outside the market. This is especially so in the case of labour markets and the antipathy to trade unions although, markedly over the more recent period for reasons that will emerge, there is a more ambiguous stance on social movements (and civil society). These have the potential to be politically conservative, to be market conforming and correcting, and to serve as an alternative to campaigning for more and more secure provision through the state.

Complementing the ideology of neoliberalism has been an equally prominent and familiar set of policies, especially for the developing world, associated with the Washington Consensus. These have included both privatization and limits on government spending more generally, in deference to keeping a tight rein on budget deficits. But over the last decade or more, the Washington Consensus has given way to the post-Washington Consensus, which has, at least theoretically and rhetorically, distanced itself from neoliberalism. It presents itself as more state-friendly, as rejecting the notion that one (free-market) model fits all, and that both market and institutional imperfections offer a rationale in principle for a role for the state to make markets, and globalization, work better through piecemeal intervention to that end (Fine et al, 2001, Jomo and Fine 2006, Fine 2009b). Yet, policy advice, and aid conditionalities in practice, despite the emergence of Poverty Reduction Strategy Papers and Millennium Development Goals, have often been criticized for departing very little from those associated with the original Washington Consensus. Indeed, the so-called *augmented* Washington Consensus may even be seen to have broadened the imposition of neoliberal policies, adding more conditionalities to those such as free trade, privatization, deregulation, fiscal austerity, and so on. And, further compounding the potential confusion, there is the stance of John Williamson (2007), who is universally acknowledged as having originated the term Washington Consensus in the late 1980s. He explicitly distances it from neoliberalism as such and complains that the differences between the Washington Consensus and the post-Washington Consensus have been exaggerated by the supporters of the latter to garner higher profiles for themselves (see also Marangos 2007, 2008).

There is, then, considerable ambiguity if not confusion over exactly what constitutes neoliberalism in both ideological and policy terms. This is compounded once it is recognized that policies in practice are highly diverse across time, place, and area of application. This is so much so that some commentators have even questioned whether it is appropriate to talk about neoliberalism at all, not least because its ideological and policy content have been so diverse (Castree 2006 and Ferguson 2007, for example, but see also Hart [2002, 2008] for the need to take context into account in unravelling rather than rejecting neoliberalism [and globalization] as macroinfluences).

Such concerns over the conceptual viability of "neoliberalism" are likely to have been reinforced by the response to the current crisis. For it broke while President George W. Bush was still in office in 2008, and policy took the form of immediate and extensive intervention by the US and other states to support the financial system, even to the point of taking financial institutions and so-called toxic assets into public ownership. Yet, such measures still carried the scent of neoliberalism despite its loss of legitimacy and that of the financial system in particular. It was not simply guilt by association in that the leading neoliberals, such as Bush, were doing the rescuing, but what they were rescuing and have continued to rescue, have been the very financial markets and institutions that prided themselves on their efficiency and efficacy—until they needed massive state support and received it more or less on demand.

This paradox is readily resolved once it is recognized that neoliberalism has never, in practice, been about withdrawal or minimizing the state's economic role. On the contrary, neoliberalism has concerned state intervention to promote private capital. In this, though, it is not distinctive from the role of the state in the Keynesian period, where it is as well to remember that policy towards state-owned enterprises, for example, was often criticized for serving private capital at the expense of public provision. What does mark the neoliberal era of the past 40 years is the extent to which the interests of private capital in general have been identified with, if by no means reduced to, those of finance in particular.

Within the literature, this core feature of contemporary capitalism has been increasingly acknowledged by reference to the previously discussed notion of financialization (without necessarily recognizing its connection to neoliberalism; Fine 2007). The term has been deployed with a number of different meanings but, as indicated, it is most appropriate to be all-inclusive of these in order to incorporate not only the extraordinary expansion and proliferation of financial markets, derivatives, and instruments but also to acknowledge the extent to which these have penetrated into ever more areas of economic and social reproduction. At the forefront of these developments has been privatization in all of its forms. The point is not to suggest that privatization has simply been some sort of conspiracy on the part of finance to further its interests irrespective of those of others. Rather, as finance has increasingly come to the fore, so it has both promoted and benefited from privatization with the additional effect of undermining the potential for, and nature of, alternatives.

In short, before addressing this in more detail, it is as well to recognize that neoliberalism is characterized by two fundamental aspects. First, it combines a complex, shifting, and generally inconsistent amalgam of ideology, scholarship, and policy in practice. Second, while this is generally true of representations of capitalism for other periods, the process of financialization is what has given the current period of neoliberalism its own peculiar character. In addition, neoliberalism can be adjudged to have gone through two roughly delineated phases, with the early 1990s as a boundary between them. For the first "shock" phase, the promotion of private capital in general and of finance in particular have taken precedence, but it neither originated with, nor was confined to, eastern Europe, where it did take extreme forms. The second phase, however, has had two aspects. One has been to respond to the conflicts and dysfunctions of the first phase but, more important, the second has been to sustain the process of financialization itself with, in a sense, the response to the current crisis expressing this in extreme form.

That neoliberalism has gone through two phases of the sort we have identified is well-illustrated by the World Bank's shifting position on privatization. In the first phase of shock therapy, both rhetoric and policy conformed to one another with the explicit aim of promoting as much privatization as possible. The virtues of privatization were lavishly praised, with any number of microeconomic and macroeconomic benefits promised to result. Interestingly, the mainstream scholarship of the time was considerably more cautious, emphasizing that ownership as such does not matter as opposed to conditions of competition and regulation (Fine 1990). This was simply ignored and, not least from the privatization think tank run from Margaret Thatcher's Cabinet Office, we were told to "just do it", irrespective of the objections and potential stumbling blocks for which abstract theory was demonized. Exactly the same unthinking and dogmatic approach was taken by the World Bank.

Over the past decade the World Bank's position has changed dramatically, although with a significant lag of five or more years on the shift from Washington Consensus to post-Washington Consensus. The delay allowed as much privatization to be pushed through as possible after which the World Bank has gone through what it itself calls a "rethink", rejecting the idea that one model fits all. Perversely, it has even adopted the earlier academic wisdom that privatization needs to be wedded to closer consideration of regulation and competition and has added consideration of other conditions such as sources of finance, customer access and capacity to pay for vital services.

In practice, however, this does not represent a "rethink" at all, other than as a means to push through more participation of the private sector and, ultimately, full privatization itself (where possible, and otherwise drawing upon, for the private sector, risk-minimizing public-private partnerships [PPPs]). For the privatization programme of the first phase was already faltering by the mid-1990s, not entirely delivering on its promises in terms of levels of investment and performance. The easy and acceptable privatizations had already been pushed through, whether because of high levels of potential profitability or lack of effective popular resistance. The new strategy now involves the fuller use of the state's resources and capacities to incorporate the role of the private sector where previously it had been reluctant to engage. Significantly, the focus of World Bank strategy has been to shift aid for social and economic infrastructure from state to private or PPP provision, with a pecking order of telecommunications, energy, transport, and water as privatization and private sector participation becomes harder to achieve. In other words, the rethink is concerned to push the state even further in favouring the private sector because of the latter's failure otherwise to provide. While, especially for water, state provision remains the predominant source for an overwhelming majority of the population, policy continues to be directed at supporting the private sector, or preparing the public sector for it as much as possible through commercialization/corporatization and otherwise holding back the extension of the public sector.

NEOLIBERALISM IN ACTION

By specifying the nature of neoliberalism, a stronger perspective can be taken on policy in terms of what has materialized in the past and what are the prospects for the future. First and foremost, it should be emphasized that much more is involved than simply reversing the ideologies and policies of neoliberalism as if it were a tap that can be turned on and off. For the thrust of our analysis, now made explicit, is to suggest that neoliberalism goes far beyond ideology and policy insofar as neoliberalism is systemically rooted in contemporary capitalism as a whole in the age of globalization with financialization to the fore.

This has had profoundly negative implications for the extent to which we are able to draw upon recent experience for alternative models of public provision as ideal types since these have been crowded out and undermined. One useful way of recognizing this is in terms of the momentum behind what has been called the "evaluatory trap" associated with privatization and the commercialized forms of new public sector management more generally (Olson et al, 2001). Essentially, following upon privatization, it is found that outcomes are not as promised for investment levels, quality and access of service, and so on. This then places demands upon the state to regulate, make amends for those excluded from creaming off of most profitable delivery, renegotiate and monitor contracts, etc.

Here, there are three important points. First, if costs and benefits of such outcomes had been known and fully assessed in advance, the privatization would not have been seen to be so attractive and might not have been undertaken (as might now be anticipated in retrospect, on a grander scale, the extent to which finance has been deregulated). Second, the burdens upon the state to make privatization a success are far from negligible. It is not simply a matter of handing everything over to the "free" market. This too is costly, not least in use of the state's resources and capabilities. Indeed, to regulate the private sector sufficiently and successfully may involve greater demands than the state running things itself as wider goals and objectives are always resisted or being undermined by the pursuit of private profit. Third, also required is a qualitative shift in the nature and capabilities of the state itself as it has become increasingly oriented towards regulating and promoting the private sector as opposed to serving public provision.

This can be seen in the development of policies in support of PPPs since 2008. The central rationale for PPPs is that they provide direct investment by the private sector as an alternative to public finance, thus reducing the need for public finance through increased government debt. The most fundamental problem with PPPs, or any form of privatization, is that even in good times it is a more expensive way of financing capital than state borrowing (IMF 2004, OECD 2008). This extra cost is then carried by the state, which is the ultimate customer for public service PPPs such as hospitals or schools, or by users where the PPP is based on charges, such as toll roads or public transport, or some forms of water concessions. The state can manage this cost by providing guarantees of various kinds for the private loans, but at the expense of undermining the rationale: the "private" finance becomes in effect a public liability, which is why statisticians have begun insisting in the UK and elsewhere that PPPs should appear on government balance sheets (KPMG 2009).

The financial crisis has exacerbated this fundamental problem because the gap between interest rates paid by the private and public sector has widened, as companies have become unable to raise finance, thus increasing the relative costs of PPPs further. For existing PPPs needing to refinance their business, the problem has been even sharper. The response in a number of countries, including the UK, France, and India, has been to create special state financial agencies, which in effect borrow as the state and then lend it to private companies in PPPs. The International Finance Corporation (IFC) has created a similar "infrastructure crisis fund", aiming to use $1.2–10 billion of public finance from the IFC itself and donors (Hall 2009). These measures have been generally derided as an implausible attempt to maintain the fiction that the finance is raised by the private entities themselves.

The state/public sector, national and international, now provides layers of guarantees for companies, and the burden of these guarantees is often effectively transferred to governments of developing countries. If a project is partly financed by the IFC, it gains a much better credit rating for the whole project because the IFC is in practice a "preferred creditor", which always gets repaid (Bayliss 2009). The Multilateral Investment Guarantee Agency (MIGA)—a World Bank division—is dedicated to providing insurance for political risk, and when the now discredited Enron claimed successfully in respect of a power station project in Indonesia, abandoned after the dictatorship of Suharto was overthrown, MIGA insisted that the Indonesian government reimburse the entire amount. Export credits provided by northern countries to companies selling to developing countries have a similar effect. The loans are structured so that the company is paid upfront, and then the government of the importing state is liable for repaying the debt (Greenhill and Pettifor 2002).

The donor countries also use some of their aid budgets to finance private sector activity in developing countries. This is done partly through funds, which are dedicated to support private companies, such as Sweden's Swedfund International AB, France's *Société de Promotion et de Participation pour la Coopération Économique* (PROPARCO), and the Netherlands Development Finance Company (FMO), following the same principle as the IFC. The sectors covered include the full range of production industries, but the funds also support private activity in sectors such as telecoms, energy, health care, higher education, and waste management. They can be described as donor-state-owned private equity funds. At the end of 2007, these private equity funds of European donors stood at €15.1 billion, invested in 3,385 projects.[6] These funds could not invest in any project or service run directly by public authorities because they are only allowed to be invested in commercially viable operations involving a private company. As Swedfund states "Our decisions regarding investments are based solely on business principles".[7] Returns to private investors become the criterion of success. The Commonwealth Development Corporation (CDC), the UK government's private investment fund, more than doubled the value of its assets between 2004 and 2008 to a total of £2.7 billion, of which £1.4 billion remained in cash in the UK, and increased its chief executive's salary to £970,000 per year. This was regarded as a developmental success story: for the UK government, "financial performance is the principal indicator of CDC's development impact".[8]

International and national development banks have also adopted the role of "financier of last resort" for private ventures. When multinational corporation Bechtel insisted on leaving a water concession in Estonia, the European Bank for Reconstruction and Development (EBRD) stepped in to buy 25% of the equity, as a kind of "default private owner"; as PPPs became harder to finance in Europe in 2009, the European Investment Bank (EIB) agreed to finance over 50% of some schemes. The same role can be seen at the national level: in Brazil, for example, the national development bank, *Banco Nacional de Desenvolvimento Econômico e Social* (BNDES) was used to cofinance many of the privatizations of the 1990s as a partner to private companies. Following the election of the Lula government in 2002, BNDES was later used as a way of buying stakes in the same companies from multinationals as they left the projects.

Governments also provide implicit or explicit guarantees as purchasers, underpinning the returns on many forms of privatization. For example, power purchase agreements with private electricity generators will pledge that state-owned distributors will buy output under "take-or-pay" deals for periods of 20–30 years; water treatment plants are built under similar contractual terms of long-term purchases at prices that guarantee returns; hospitals, schools, and sometimes roads may all rely on similar government spending guarantees.

Regulatory systems often have the effect of providing a virtual guarantee of a minimum rate of return, which may be used as an indirect guarantee for raising corporate finance. Utilities were able to issue corporate bonds even in 2009, unlike most other companies, and were able to issue index-linked bonds before the credit crisis, thanks to this implicit guarantee underlying regulated industries. French water multinational Suez has issued a local bond in Indonesia to refinance its water concession in Jakarta, paying off a Euro loan; the Spanish electricity multinationals Endesa (now owned by Enel) and Iberdrola both reduced their equity stakes in electricity companies in Latin America by issuing bonds and raising loans in local currency.

Long-term contractual rights to public spending are typical of PPP and PFI (private finance initiative) schemes, with much longer contractual periods (25–30 years or more) than conventional service contracts (e.g. for refuse collection it is three to five years). The effect is thus larger than with ordinary outsourcing—switching public spending from direct employment to purchasing from a private company. As a result, the public good becomes subordinate to the imperatives of designing a commercially viable contract. This may involve restructuring of the service itself (e.g. the previously national Ghanaian water service was split, to ring-fence the profitable area of the capital Accra with the rest of the country served by a separate, financially disadvantaged, state company [Fuest and Haffner 2007]). In Estonia and Italy the basis for assessing the viability of PPPs has been restricted to examination of the potential profitability of schemes, with no reference to public policy objectives or effective comparison with public sector alternatives (Friedrich and Reiljan 2007, Barretta and Ruggiero 2008).

The effect persists during the long life of PPP contracts. The contractual obligations render them immune from being cut on policy grounds, for example, so that any reductions in public spending fall disproportionately on services provided by staff employed directly by public authorities, because these are not part of a contract with a private company that would require compensation if the payments by the public authority were reduced. The contracts may even explicitly protect companies against the consequences of democracy. Contracts for private road schemes in the US, for example, include clauses giving companies "the right to object to and receive compensation for legislative, administrative, and judicial decisions". Contracts have become standardized with as much as 70% identical content, reflecting the cumulative expertise of corporate lawyers, whereas the public authorities with which they deal often have little or none (Dannin 2009).

In this light, it is crucial to recognize how significant privatization is for the functioning of the neoliberal state and vice-versa, far beyond the selling off of state assets, the commercialization of public services, and the deregulation of public and private provision. For every element of policy is potentially involved, along the dimensions connecting macro to micro as well as more broadly. Macroeconomic policy, for example, has been geared towards globalization of financial markets which have long been recognized to press for excessive fiscal restraint, thereby reducing finance available for public investment.

One form of financial deregulation has been the relaxation of traditional restrictions on pension funds investments. These were typically restricted largely to investing in government debt, with extra incentives in the form of tax relief for the funds, which had multiple advantages in security and long-term assets to match their long-term liabilities, while offering the state a reliable source of demand for bonds and other government debt. Deregulation meant that funds were able to diversify into national and international equity investments, providing extra funds for private capital at the same time as governments were reducing their borrowing. One result has been that some of the largest pension funds have themselves become leading financiers of privatization in its various forms: in Chile, for example, one-third of the water companies and a major electricity distribution company, are now majority-owned by the Ontario Teachers Pension Plan (OTPP), a pension fund covering 284,000 active and retired elementary and secondary school teachers in the province of Ontario (Canada),[9] and in the UK, local government pension funds alone own as much as 3.5% of companies whose main business consists of contracted-out public service work, such as Serco and Capita.

The privatization of public-sector pension funds is another way in which pension contributions, made compulsory by the state, are diverted into private hands. Private funds can extract profits through administration fees, and invest solely on the basis of maximizing returns—by contrast with governments, which may use such funds for development purposes. Argentina, for example, was persuaded by the IMF in 1994 to reorganize its pensions by creating private pension funds to receive and manage the compulsory pension contributions, from which the private funds extracted large administration fees, which rapidly made them unpopular. But this process too is contested: in 2008, the government of Argentina renationalized the funds. This not only reduced the cost to pensioners of administering the funds, it also restored to the government a significant flow of revenue, in the form of pension contributions, and ownership of a strategic slice of the economy: the pension funds owned 13% of all shares on the stock market.[10] Not surprisingly, the rush to privatize pensions has now been caught short as stock markets have crashed. But the apparently more reasonable line of the international financial institutions of now shifting to a more mixed system of private, public, and safety nets is more a way of using the state's resources to restore whatever can be recovered for the private sector from the shambles in which it now finds itself (Fine 2009e).

The same neoliberal agenda is reflected in the mistrust of large state-run "sovereign wealth funds", especially those owned and run by governments of developing countries, which now have dominant shareholdings in some large US and European companies. These were feared to be using their power to pursue "political" objectives rather than simple profit maximization. This fear was substantially modified during the crisis in 2008 when the funds were welcomed for investing in US banks, precisely because of the political imperative to rescue the current financial system, with the US dollar at its pinnacle as a reserve currency (despite the huge external and domestic deficits and minimal interest rates that would have both brought down any other currency as well as severe conditionalities in return for the support enjoyed by the US).

The interception of state revenues, or compulsory social insurance contributions, is a recurrent theme in the framework of privatization. Public spending, or compulsory private spending, is legitimized as long as it is channelled through corporate entities. The US health care insurance companies, for example, lobbied the proposed health reforms by US President Barack Obama to insist that contributions required under the proposals be paid into a private scheme, not a public-sector health insurance scheme. Public borrowing for infrastructure investment is seen as irresponsible if it takes the form of direct government borrowing and an increased deficit but legitimate and welcome when it is channelled through PPPs.

More recently, the crisis has sharply revealed the extent of US international and domestic indebtedness, the counterpart to which is a corresponding burden carried by developing countries, by no means confined to China (Rodrik 2006). Capital accounts have been liberalized so that accumulated stocks of dollar reserves have been required to guard against short-term capital flight. At the macro level, neoliberalism has also been associated with increasing inequality within economies, not least arising out of, or trickling down from, the excessive rewards accruing to those attached to finance with negative benefits in terms of the mobilization and allocation of resources for investment.

Other areas of policy making, as with industrial and regional policy, health, education and welfare, research and development, and skills and training, have all been profoundly influenced by neoliberalism, quite apart from the pressure for "flexibility" in labour markets, signifying a race to the bottom in wages and working conditions. The priority assigned to private participation in delivery has both squeezed public sector alternatives and the rationale for, and capacity to deliver, them. As already suggested, the logic and practice is to push for what the private sector can deliver with limited regard to broader social and economic objectives or the presumption that these should be picked up by other compensating policy measures. Whether this ever happens is a moot point as opposed to journeying further down the "evaluatory trap". There is also significant reliance upon devolution and decentralization with the presumption of greater local and democratic participation, whereas this can often turn out to be the passing on of responsibility for delivery by an authoritarian central state without provision of support for necessary resources.

In short, neoliberalism is not just marked by policy and ideology favouring the private over the public sector, but this has itself been institutionalized within government capacity itself and the commercial pressures to which it responds. And this has been devastating for the potential for formulating and implementing alternative forms of public provision.

This institutionalization takes a number of forms at global, regional, and national levels. At the global level, the key role is played by the World Bank, and especially its arm dedicated to financing the private sector, the IFC. While the World Bank has included privatization conditionalities in many of its loans over the years, an increasingly high proportion of World Bank funds have been channelled through the IFC, effectively tying this flow of public money to the private sector. By the end of 2007, the IFC had committed over $10 billion for this, double the level of just four years earlier (Bayliss 2009). A special advisory unit, the Public-Private Infrastructure Advisory Facility (PPIAF) has promoted PPPs globally since 1999. Both agencies actively spend money on propaganda activities promoting PPPs: for example, the IFC allocated $500 million a year to investing in PPPs in India, including $20 million for "advisory services and support staff".[11]

The regional development banks, especially the African Development Bank and the Inter-American Development Bank (IDB), have also actively promoted various forms of privatization in their regions; the European Commission has promoted PPPs throughout Europe. The institutionalization of corporate interests can be seen even in UN bodies: UNESCO receives financing from the leading water multinational, Suez, and the United Nations Economic Commission for Europe (UNECE) now plays a leading role in promoting privatization and PPPs across the countries of eastern Europe and central Asia (Hall and Hoedeman 2006).

More generally, government and international policy making itself is subject to institutionalized corporate capture/influence through the extensive use of management consultants and business appointees. These consultancies are themselves made up of a small group of multinational firms—such as PriceWaterhouseCoopers, Deloitte, Ernst and Young—which act as a policy replication mechanism. Another form of this is the appointment of increasing numbers of businessmen and women to government policy positions, which would normally be held by career civil servants. The process can also be seen at an international level, most obviously in the collaboration between companies, donors and development banks over privatizations.

The institutionalization of these relationships can be seen as a generalized, if tacit, form of collusion, bordering upon corruption. For these individual acts occur as part of a systematic network between political parties and institutions on the one hand, and corporate interests on the other, regularly agreeing which policies to adopt, which companies get which contracts, and at what price (Della Porta and Vanucci 1999). The process includes not only bribes but also legal donations and other networks of influence, constituting effective "state capture" (Hellman et al, 2003). The operation of conditionalities by the development banks can also be recognized as tantamount to corruption, whereby money—in the form of finance for a socially and politically valuable project—is offered in exchange for a national government transferring assets and/or contracts to the corporate interests in the sector, through privatization or PPPs.

At the national level, in sectors which are privatized, neoliberal orthodoxy insists that regulators must be "independent" of government. Responsibility for public policy in these sectors is thus transferred from elected ministries to bureaucracies, which are not subject to direct political intervention. The UK service regulators, for example, are constitutionally "government departments without a minister", a neat summary of this combination of state power without democratic direction.[12] Such regulators are then subject to a well-recognized process of "capture" by the private corporations in the sector. This independence does not prevent corporate interests from continuing to lobby politicians to overrule inconvenient regulatory decisions, as happened in Argentina for example in the period of privatized water services in Buenos Aires (Lobina and Hall 2003).

Another form in which the role of the private sector is secured is through the creation by governments of special units, usually within finance ministries, to promote and manage PPPs. These units are dominated by business interests:

> In Egypt, for example, all PPP Unit members are from the private sector—this helps because the staff is already in a position to understand private stakeholders' concerns. Moreover, extensive training was undertaken with the help of in-house consultants and outside training. A key element is also to have a balanced staff composition, including legal advice, bankers, accountants, etc. (IFC 2009b, 16)

A key function is the (re)education of civil servants:

> A PPP Unit can help by providing a focal point for education and dissemination of knowledge, as well as driving the process. In India, for example, at the inception of the PPP Program, IDFC acted as a so-called 'secretariat of thoughts' to bridge the thinking between the private sector and public sector, change the mindset of government officials and their understanding of the value the private sector brings to the table, and to align incentives. This process, like any fundamental change, takes time. (IFC 2009b, 15)

There are now attempts to combine these global and national institutions into a wider international pressure group for PPPs. An international conference on PPPs in May 2009, involving the World Bank, the Asian Development Bank, UNECE, and various Asian governments, was presented with a lucidly expressed argument that the political conditions exist for an alternative based on a stronger role for the state (Hamilton 2009):

> Discontent, even outright hostility, among the general public against the capitalist system has gained ground during the crisis. . . . The "system" is mistrusted, and confidence in capitalism and its future is low . . . The crisis appears to have had its roots in the era of deregulation and is replaced by the growing role of the state in managing financial capitalism and exercising accountability previously absent in the system; . . . PPPs are equated with the now discredited privatisation and financial liberalisation.

This was not presented by a critic of PPPs, but by an official of UNECE, an extremely anxious supporter of this form of privatization. His conclusion was that there was a need for "tools to bring back the banks and new institutions able to articulate a pro-PPP policy in the crisis (and those in the future) . . . a global advocate to spread support and the message around the globe: an alliance of PPP units". Thus, the international financial institutions and national finance ministries—all public sector institutions sustained by public finance—would combine to act as a de facto international lobby group to protect PPPs and discourage a revival of direct state funding and provision of infrastructure. The objective is not, however, to cut or eliminate state expenditure. Hamilton (2009) also argued that the crisis brought opportunities for potential PPPs because of the economic, social, and environmental needs for public spending:

> The potential demand for social infrastructure such as public lighting, hospitals, and schools, is amplified in volatile times when financial and economic crisis negatively affect low-income people's life. The social infrastructure can not only serve as a safety net but also generate economic flow-on effects with increased human resource investment. . . . There are ongoing needs to restore and replace much of the existing physical infrastructures, to accommodate population growth and to deal with the threats of global warming in response to the call for sustainable development.

Similar rhetoric is present in other IFC documents. In a recent health care report, the IFC states that it aims to "help Africa address its health care challenges—including improving services to the poor"; that "the scale of the challenge has driven a reassessment of traditional approaches and a growing acceptance that the private sector should be a key part of the over-all health strategy". And so the IFC is creating a $400 million vehicle for equity investment, "[i]mproving the environment for private health care" and educating health workers through PPPs" (IFC-World Bank 2009). The solution to the health needs of Africans turns out to be placing hundreds of millions of public dollars at the disposal of private companies.

As a health strategy, it was rejected by Oxfam (2009, 1) in a compre-hensive critique, which concluded that prioritizing private sector delivery "is extremely unlikely to deliver health for poor people". Yet, the IFC "estimates that private sector entities have the potential to deliver between 45 and 70 percent of the needed increase in capacity" in the health sector, thereby rec-ommending that governments needing the support of the private sector to fund the expected growth in health care demand must create an environment "supportive of significant private sector investment" (IFC 2009a, 15).

In addition, the role of private donor agencies in health, with the Gates Foundation at the fore, has become extremely important. They now pro-vide levels of funding that are dominating official aid quantitatively and, to some extent, qualitatively. Not surprisingly, they are attuned towards non-state, if not necessarily private, forms of provision, and their ethos is geared more towards private and clinically driven provision as opposed to public provision of primary and preventive health care and the broader conditions necessary for good health. As McCoy comments on Gates's funding of the World Bank:

> More controversial is the award of two grants to the International Finance Corporation, whose mandate is to support private sector development. The reasons why the International Finance Corporation needs philanthropic funding are not clear, but this donation suggests that the Gates Foundation is keen to promote the growth of private health-care providers in low-income and middle-income countries, and is consistent with views that have been expressed by the foundation and the observation that private foundations generally view the public sector with scepticism and disinterest. (McCoy 2009, 1651)

It is also noteworthy that the World Bank's interventions into health have been at the expense of the World Health Organization, with "more than 80 per cent of WHO's funding . . . dependent on voluntary or so-called extra budgetary resources" (Koivusalo 2009, 289).

CONCLUSION

Where does this leave the promotion of alternative public sector provision into the future? Initially, we can draw two general lessons. First, there is a need to insulate public provision from financialization (the direct or indirect effects of turning provision into a financial asset however near or distant). Privatization incorporates finance directly into services, with provision becoming subject to the vagaries of stakeholder value on the stock market; subcontracting does it indirectly as the firms involved require their own financial imperatives to be observed. In short, finance needs to be placed in a subordinate not a dominant position. This is easier said than done not least because, prior to the crisis, this was said to be true of the financial system in terms of its efficient mobilization and allocation of funds for investment and its trading in risk. But financialization continues to impinge upon public provision in multifarious ways that can only be guarded against as opposed to being absolutely eliminated, at least for the foreseeable future.

Second, the vulnerability of public sector provision to erosion and distortion is a consequence of the absence of broader supportive institutions and policies in the wake of decades of neoliberalism. Alternative public sector provision and new, broader policy capacities, and corresponding means and sources of finance must be built in tandem.

Beyond these two generalities, we would emphasize the need to address the specificity of particular types and circumstances of public sector provision in terms of the diversity of causes, content, and consequences to which they are subject, but without losing grip of the bigger picture. In particular, our own approach has been to posit the notion of public sector systems of provision (PSSOP). Specificity is incorporated by understanding each element of public provision as attached to an integral and distinctive system—the health system, the education system, and so on. Each PSSOP should be addressed by reference to the structures, agencies, processes, power, and conflicts that are exercised in material provision itself, taking full account of the whole chain of activity bringing together production, distribution (and access) and use, and the conditions under which these occur.

Thus, the PSSOP approach has the advantage of potentially incorporating each and every relevant element in the process of provision, investigating how they interact with one another, as well as situating them in relation to more general systemic functioning. This allows for an appropriate mix of the general and the specific and, policy-wise and strategically, signals where provision is obstructed, why and how it might be remedied. This is in contrast to unduly focused approaches, those that emphasize mode of finance alone for example, as has been the case for housing both before and after its current crisis (as opposed to emphasis on who is building what, how, and for whom, with what means of access). At the opposite extreme are unduly universal approaches such as those that appeal to market and/ or institutional imperfections, and which accordingly fail to recognize that water provision is very different from housing provision in and of itself as well as in different contexts.

The PSSOP approach has been addressed in Fine (2002) for the welfare state, in Bayliss and Fine (2008) for electricity and water, and in Fine (2009a, 2009e) for social policy. We are not so much concerned here to develop, let alone impose, the PSSOP approach more fully as such for it is essential to see it as an approach that needs to be contextually driven rather than as a source of the ideal types or universal theory that characterizes, and even mars, much of the current literature (leave things to the market, or correct market and institutional imperfections). Indeed, the purpose is rather to persuade of the need for something akin to the PSSOP approach irrespective of the method and theory with which it is deployed, which will, no doubt, continue to be controversial, alongside the nature, depth, and breadth of economic and social transformation essential for any significant change in provision to be secure. In other words, there is something different about water and housing, just as there is something different about South Africa and India.

Further, though, this does allow for the results of existing studies to be incorporated into the PSSOP approach to the extent that they do identify, however partially, the factors involved in provision and how they interact with one another. Of course, in practice, sectorally grounded approaches by electricity, health, and water appear to be adopted as if by second nature. But this has not necessarily been so of how they are analytically broached, where sectoral and contextual sensitivity often gives way to universal prescription driven by the neoliberal fashion of the moment, whether privatization, user charges, or public-private partnerships. At the very least, the PSSOP approach offers a framework with which to address policy needs in light of provision deficiencies, broadly interpreted, as opposed to general models and blunt recipes drawing to the fullest extent upon the "market"—i.e. private capital and finance—in practice even when recognizing its deficiencies in principle.

In addition, as highlighted in earlier accounts of the approach, not only is each PSSOP uniquely and integrally organized in provision, by country and sector, each will also be attached to its own meaning and significance for those engaged with (or excluded by) it. For example, whether public provision is seen as household risk management against vulnerability or collective provision towards developmental goals is both cause and consequence of material provision itself and, equally, subject to debate (or not insofar as different approaches exist in parallel with one another according to context). As also argued in the approach, the cultural (in the widest sense) system attached to each PSSOP is also integral with material provision and is generated along and around that provision itself. Without going into details, the culture and meaning of public provision, thereby, becomes subject to what has been termed the 8Cs—Constructed, Contextual, Chaotic, Construed, Contradictory, Contested, Collective, and Closed (Fine 2009c). This is important for developing and understanding the meanings attached to public provision, not least in prizing them away from the negative stance attached to the neoliberal ideology of public provision.

One apparent weakness of the PSSOP approach, a consequence of its strength of examining provision comprehensively within sectors, is its distance, at least initially, from the synergies and interactions across sectors, as with the role of "horizontal" factors (as opposed to the "vertical") such as equity, labour conditions, and macroeconomic impacts. Arguably, however, these need to be addressed in their own right *and* in the context of particular sectors within which they are rooted. Indeed, as revealed in the sectoral and regional studies offered elsewhere in this book, the dialogue between generic and sectoral issues is vital in designing, promoting, and defending public sector alternatives.

NOTES

1. For the Bischoff and Darling (2009) and Wigley (2008) reports, respectively.
2. As is sarcastically remarked by CRESC of Wigley: "Of the 71 witnesses, some 49 came directly from finance and a further 15 came from consultancy activities which generally have revenue connections to finance. Quite remarkably, the public sector provided just one witness: presumably the knowledge and expertise of HM Treasury or Department of Business Enterprise Regulatory Reform were irrelevant to the story that Wigley told about the importance of defending this valuable activity" (2009, 25).
3. In absolute terms, global financial assets rose from $12 to somewhere between $196 and $241 trillion from 1980 to 2007 (Blankenberg and Palma 2009, 531).
4. *Financial Times.* 2008. Why It Is so Hard to Keep the Financial Sector Caged. 6 February.
5. Asian Development Bank. www.adb.org/Documents/Policies/Anticorruption/anticorrupt300.asp?p=policies.
6. www.edfi.be.
7. Swedfund International AB. www.swedfund.se/en/investments-and-new-markets/meet-the-entrepreneurs-who-have-already-invested/health-care-in-ethiopia.
8. UK Parliament Public Accounts Committe 2009. Eighteenth Report Investing for Development: the Department for International Development's oversight of CDC Group plc 30 April 2009 HC 94 2008–09. www.publications.parliament.uk/pa/cm200809/cmselect/cmpubacc/94/9402.htm.
9. See OTPP (Ontario Teachers Pension Plan). www.docs.otpp.com/Infrastructure_2008_9B.pdf.
10. *Economist.* 2008. Harvesting pensions. 27 November; *Financial Times.* 2008. Argentina moves to nationalise pension funds. 21 November; *Financial Times.* 2009. Telecom Italia contests Argentina ruling. 13 April.
11. *Financial Express.* 2007. IFC to invest $5bn in India, to set up PPP advocacy unit, 15 March 2007. http://www.financialexpress.com/printer/news/194057/
12. Department for Environment, Food and Rural Affairs (Defra). 2008. Statutory Social and Environmental Guidance to the Water Services Regulation Authority (Ofwat). www.defra.gov.uk/environment/quality/water/ . . . / ofwat-guidance080922.pdf.

REFERENCES

Barretta, A. and Ruggiero, P. 2008. Ex-ante evaluation of PFIs within the Italian health-care sector: What is the basis for this PPP? *Health Policy* 88(1): 15–24.
Bayliss, K. 2009. *Private sector participation in African infrastructure: Is it worth the risk?* UNDP IPC-IG Working Paper Number 55, May. www.ipc-undp.org/pub/IPCWorkingPaper55.pdf.

Bayliss, K. and Fine, B. (Eds). 2008. *Whither the privatisation experiment? Electricity and water sector reform in Sub-Saharan Africa.* Basingstoke: Palgrave MacMillan.

Bischoff, W. and Darling, A. 2009. *UK international financial services—The future: A report from UK based financial services leaders to the government.* London: HM Treasury.

Blankenberg, S. and Palma, G. 2009. Introduction: The global financial crisis. *Cambridge Journal of Economics* 33(4): 531–538.

Castree, N. 2006. Commentary. *Environment and Planning A* 38(1): 1–6.

CRESC. 2009. *An alternative report on UK banking reform.* ESRC Centre for Research on Socio Cultural Change, University of Manchester. www.cresc.ac.uk/publications/documents/AlternativereportonbankingV2.pdf.

Dannin, E. 2009. *Infrastructure privatization contracts and their effect on governance.* Penn State Legal Studies Research Paper No. 19. University Park, PA: Pennsylvania State University

Davidson, P. 2008. Securitization, liquidity and market failure. *Challenge* 51(3): 43–56.

Della Porta, D. and Vannucci, A. 1999. *Corrupt exchanges: actors, resources, and mechanisms of political corruption.* New York: Aldine Transaction.

Denis, A. 2004. Two rhetorical strategies of *laissez-faire. Journal of Economic Methodology* 11(3): 341–353.

dos Santos, P. 2009. On the content of banking in contemporary capitalism. *Historical Materialism* 17(2): 180–213.

Ferguson, J. 2007. Formalities of poverty: Thinking about social assistance in Neoliberal South Africa. *African Studies Review* 50(2): 71–86.

Fine, B. 1990. Scaling the commanding heights of public sector economics. *Cambridge Journal of Economics* 14(2): 127–142.

———. 2002. *The world of consumption: The material and cultural revisited.* London: Routledge.

———. 2007. Financialisation, poverty, and Marxist political economy, Paper presented at the Poverty and Capital Conference, University of Manchester, Manchester, United Kingdom, 2–4 July 2007. www.eprints.soas.ac.uk/5685/1/brooks.pdf.

———. 2008. The evolution of the anti-Washington Consensus debate: From "post-Washington Consensus" to "after the Washington Consensus". *Competition and Change* 12(3): 227–244.

———. 2009a. Social policy and the crisis of neoliberalism, Paper presented at the Conference on The Crisis of Neoliberalism in India: Challenges and Alternatives, Tata Institute of Social Sciences (TISS) Mumbai and International Development Economics Associates (IDEAs), Mumbai, India, 13–15 March. www.networkideas.org/ideasact/jan09/ia27_International_Conference.htm.

———. 2009b. Development as zombieconomics in the age of neoliberalism. *Third World Quarterly* 30(5): 885–904.

———. 2009c. Political economy for the rainbow nation: Dividing the spectrum? Paper presented at Making Sense of Borders: Identity, Citizenship and Power in South Africa, Annual Conference of the South African Sociological Association, Johannesburg, South Africa June/July.

———. 2009d. Financialisation, the value of labour power, the degree of separation, and exploitation by banking, Paper presented at the SOAS Research Students, Summer Seminar Series, 30 April. www.eprints.soas.ac.uk/7480.

———. 2009e. Financialisation and social policy, Paper prepared for Conference on Social and Political Dimensions of the Global Crisis: Implications for Developing Countries, UNRISD, Geneva, Switzerland, 12–13 November. www.eprints.soas.ac.uk/7984.

Fine, B. (2010). Locating financialisation. *Historical materialism* 18(2): 97–116.

Fine, B., Lapavitsas, C. and Pincus, J. (Eds). 2001. *Development policy in the twenty-first century: Beyond the post-Washington Consensus*. London: Routledge.

Friedrich, P. and Reiljan, J. 2007. An economic public sector comparator for public private partnership and public real estate management, Paper presented at the ASPE Conference, St Petersburg, Russia, 12 November.

Fuest, V. and Haffner, S.A. 2007. PPP—Policies, practices and problems in Ghana's urban water supply. *Water Policy* 9: 169–192.

Goldstein, J. 2009. Introduction: The political economy of financialization. *Review of Radical Political Economics* 41(4): 453–457.

Greenhill, R. and Petifor, A. 2002. Recommendations for the Export Credits Guarantee Department (ECGD) on debt and export credits. Cornerhouse Reports. www.thecornerhouse.org.uk/item.shtml?x=52009.

Hall, D. 2009. A crisis for public-private partnerships (PPPs)? www.psiru.org/reports/2009–01-crisis-2.doc.

Hall, D. and Hoedeman, O. 2006. Aquafed—Another pressure group for private water. PSIRU Special Report, March. www.psiru.org/reports/2006–03-W-Aquafed.doc.

Hamilton, G. 2009. Impact of the global financial crisis—What does it mean for PPPs in the short to medium term? Paper presented at the KDI/ADB/ADBI/WBI Conference Knowledge Sharing on Infrastructure Public-Private Partnerships in Asia, Seoul, Korea, 19–21 May. www.pima.kdi.re.kr/eng/new/event/090619/9–4.pdf.

Hart, G. 2002. *Disabling globalization: Places of power in post-apartheid South Africa*. Durban: University of Natal Press.

———. 2008. The 2007 Antipode AAG Lecture—The provocations of neoliberalism: Contesting the nation and liberation after apartheid. *Antipode* 40(4): 678–705.

Hellman, J., Jones, G. and Kaufmann, D. 2003. Seize the state, seize the day: State capture and influence in transition economies. *Journal of Comparative Economics* 31(4): 751–773.

IFC (International Finance Corporation). 2009a. The business of health in Africa. www.ifc.org/ifcext/healthinafrica.nsf/Content/FullReport.

———. 2009b. Public Private Partnerships Seminar April 2009: PPP fundamentals through roads sector experiences—Overview, assessment and recommendations for improvement. www.ifc.org/ifcext/psa.nsf/AttachmentsByTitle/PPPseminar_Report042009/$FILE/PPP+Seminar+Report_April+2009.pdf.

IFC-World Bank. 2009. Health in Africa initiative 2009. www.ifc.org/ifcext/fias.nsf/AttachmentsByTitle/DonnorMeeting2009HiA/$FILE/IIiAInitiative.pdf.

IMF (International Monetary Fund). 2004. Public-private partnerships. www.imf.org/external/np/fad/2004/pifp/eng/031204.pdf.

Jomo, K. and Fine, B. (Eds). 2006. *The new development economics: After the Washington Consensus*. London: Zed Press.

Koivusalo, M. 2009. The shaping of global health policy. In Panitch, L. and Leys, C. (Eds), *Morbid symptoms: Health under capitalism* 145–167. London: Merlin Press.

KPMG. 2009. Evidence to House of Lords Select Committee on Economic Affairs, October 13. KPMG.

Lapavitsas, C. 2009. Financialised capitalism: Crisis and financial expropriation. *Historical Materialism* 17(2): 114–148.

Lobina, E. and Hall, D. 2003. Problems with private water concessions: A review of experience PSIRU. www.psiru.org/reports/2003–06-W-over.doc.

Marangos, J. 2007. Was shock therapy consistent with the Washington Consensus? *Comparative Economic Studies* 49(1): 32–58.

McCoy, D. 2009. The Bill and Melinda Gates Foundation's grant-making programme for global health. *Lancet* 373(9675): 1645–1653.

OECD (Organization for Economic Co-operation and Development). 2008. Public-private partnerships: In pursuit of risk sharing and value for money. www.oecd.org/document/27/0,3343,en_2649_34141_40757595_1_1_1_1,00.html.

Olson, O., Humphrey, C. and Guthrie, J. 2001. Caught in an evaluatory trap: A dilemma for public services under NPFM. *The European Accounting Review* 10(3): 505–522.

Oxfam. 2009. *Blind optimism: Challenging the myths about private health*. www.oxfam.org.uk/resources/policy/health/bp125_blind_optimism.html.

Palma, G. 2009. The revenge of the market on the rentiers: Why neoliberal reports of the end of history turned out to be premature. *Cambridge Journal of Economics* 33(4): 829–869.

Rodrik, D. 2006. The social cost of foreign exchange reserves. *International Economic Journal* 20(3): 253–266.

Rossman, P. and Greenfield, G. 2006. Financialization: New routes to profit, new challenges for trade unions. *Labour Education, Quarterly Review of the ILO Bureau for Workers' Activities* 142. www.iufdocuments.org/www/documents/Financialization-e.pdf.

Stockhammer, E. 2004. Financialisation and the slowdown of accumulation. *Cambridge Journal of Economics* 28(5): 719–741.

Wigley, B. 2008. *London: Winning in a changing world*. London: Merrill Lynch Europe Limited.

Williamson, J. 2007. Shock therapy and the Washington Consensus: A comment. *Comparative Economic Studies* 49(1): 59–60.

4 Transformative Resistance
The Role of Labour and Trade Unions in Alternatives to Privatization

Hilary Wainwright

Proponents of privatization have presumed that there are no actors within the public sector able to drive improvement or change. The idea that public sector workers and their trade unions might be amongst the instigators of public service reform is quite beyond contemporary political orthodoxy. In the past decade, however, resistance to privatization has produced extensive evidence of public sector workers, and their unions, leading changes that make services more responsive to the needs of those who use them. Across the world, there are trade union organizations reacting to privatization as service users as well as providers, as workers, and as citizens. They use their distinctive organizing capacities and the detailed knowledge of their members to improve the quality of the service they deliver to their fellow citizens, as a necessary part of defending its public character. In the process, trade unions have worked alongside civic organizations, farmers and rural movements, and sometimes public sector managers and politicians.

One trade union leader of an exemplary struggle of this kind—Luis Isarra from the Federation of Unions of Water Workers of Peru (FENTAP) in the Peruvian city of Huancayo—summed up the civic-driven process of reform borne out of resistance to privatization as "modernization without privatization" (Terhorst 2008, Spronk 2009). Recently these developments have produced new kinds of partnerships across public institutions in different countries (public-public partnerships), sharing expertise and obtaining the finance to more than match the private sector from the perspective of public benefit (Hall et al, 2009).

The purpose of this chapter is to describe some of the dynamics involved in unions taking on a reforming role; to identify the distinctive contributions they make; and to explore the conditions that explain or make these dynamics possible (as well as the difficulties they face). This chapter thus explores a few cases in-depth—Brazil, Uruguay, and South Africa. It also draws on other experiences in the course of suggesting some generalizations and posing questions that could be the basis for further research. A wider mapping of labour or trade union involvement in the improvement of public services has yet to be done, although the reports of the Public

Services International (PSI) Research Unit (www.psiru.org) from 1998 onwards provide details of many union campaigns around alternatives to privatization. The examples in this chapter concern the water sector, where there is a wide range of experiences of the role of trade unions in such campaigns—involving both successes and limits. Such a focus enables us to develop hypotheses on the role of labour and trade unions that can be explored more widely, including in health and electricity, where there are considerable similarities in the role of labour in the struggle to create alternatives to privatization.

Examples of trade union-driven or co-driven reform of public services are still the exception to the ways in which trade unions tend to respond to privatization, however. More typically, public sector trade unions attempt to negotiate for the transfer of the same or similar wages, pensions, and employment conditions to the new privatized regime (Terry 2000). Alternatively, unions fight to defend the status quo of public provision. Examples here include the successful defensive campaign against water privatization in Nigeria (Hall et al, 2005), the unsuccessful trade union-led campaign against Margaret Thatcher's early privatization of water in the UK (Ogden 1991), and the successful defence of publicly owned railways in India. There are also experiences of a third kind, in the form of a worker cooperative, frequently independent of the state and striving to be economically viable without state subsidies, although the exact relations with the state vary (Hall et al, 2005).

The examples of "transformative resistance" that are the focus of this chapter are distinctive because they include a practical (and sometimes theoretical) vision of state-owned public services that are often very different than the status quo, involving, for example, new forms of worker and citizen participation. They are also under-reported and under-analyzed. Their future is uncertain too: they face the obstacles of hostile neoliberal policies (see Chapter 3, this volume), the structural conservatism of many trade union institutions (Patroni and Poitras 2002, Spronk 2009), and the weakness or absence of party political voices for the kind of social transformations they envisage.

In my analysis of these developments, I will suggest a conceptual framework to answer two main sets of questions. First, when trade unions become involved in developing alternative plans to privatization, they are defending members' jobs, but they are also moving beyond the conventional trade union focus on collective bargaining over wages and conditions and taking responsibility for the wider public benefit and, indeed, the very purpose of their members' labour. This involves, amongst other strategies, a radical widening of the agenda of collective bargaining. How do we understand and explain this move towards society-wide goals of day-to-day trade union activity? Are there any general points to be made about what is involved when unions self-consciously develop strategies that move significantly beyond their everyday routines and take responsibility, with others, for the future of the service?

The second set of questions stem from the fact that virtually all of the labour struggles for "transformative resistance" to privatization involve social movements beyond the workplace (see Chapter 6, this volume). What, if any, is the distinctive role of labour and of trade unions in these alliances? There is a further variation on this question: what is distinctive about trade unions—flowing from the nature of labour under capitalism—as compared to the political parties with which they are or have been associated? It is noticeable that parties associated with labour—in both the North and in parts of the South—have driven privatization or more or less acquiesced in the drive to privatize. Yet, in some—not all—circumstances, the unions historically allied with these parties have resisted, responding to the pressures of their members rather than the demands of party loyalty. What are the distinctive features of labour and trade unionism in such circumstances, and how do these dynamics feed into struggles for alternatives to privatization?

In an attempt to answer these questions, I focus my discussion on the efforts of trade unionists in Brazil, Uruguay, and South Africa to transform, as well as to defend, the public provision of water in creative, if sometimes tense, relations with a variety of social movements, non-governmental organizations (NGOs), and political parties. These are not necessarily representative of labour in the global South, but they are indicative of the kinds of challenges and successes that unions have met.

TRANSFORMATIVE LABOUR ACTION IN PRACTICE

Brazil: A multiscalar campaign

In Brazil, the story of labour's transformative resistance to privatization starts in 1996 with the attempt of the Cardoso government (1995–2003) to sell off the National Sanitation Company and to move responsibility for the management of water from a municipal to a regional level. This was part of a wider process of reorganizing public water companies to make them more attractive to private investors (de Oliveira Filho 2002). The move to regional responsibility would have meant the breakup of the well-established and frequently successful public companies in many municipalities where the political left was relatively strong (Hall et al, 2005).

From the mid-1990s, this attempt to make state and municipal water and sanitation companies more attractive to private investors had already meant large-scale layoffs. Resistance to these policies had been restricted to the isolated struggles of particular groups of workers. As preparations to privatize public companies accelerated, "the workers began to confront 'the war' more politically", reports Abelardo de Oliveira Filho, then Sanitation and Environment Secretary of the urban workers' union, *Federação Nacional dos Urbanitários* (FNU), an affiliate of the trade union federation, *Central*

Única dos Trabalhadores (CUT; Keck 1992). He explains how "it became necessary to expand the struggle beyond the unions and make society as a whole aware of the importance of defending such essential services; in other words, to become the Citizens' Union" (de Oliveira Filho 2002, 7).

This approach led the unions, notably FNU and CUT, to reach out to and help bring together all those with a shared commitment to the public management of sanitation and water as a public good and basic human right. The result was the founding of the *Frente Nacional pelo Saneamento Ambiental* (FNSA) in 1997. With 17 co-founding organizations, it was a powerful alliance of consumer organizations, NGOs involved in urban reform, public managers, the church, and social movements. Especially important was the participation of the National Association of Municipal Water and Sanitation Services (ASSEMAE). This organization of water managers played a key role in both the technical arguments against the government and—with workers and consumers—in plans for improving the management and delivery of municipal water companies, thereby making these public companies less vulnerable to the pressures to privatize. Several public water and sanitation companies joined the FNSA, including the Departments of Municipal Water and Sanitation in Porto Alegre and Santo Andre, near São Paulo. Both these cities were then under the leadership of the *Partido dos Trabalhadores* (PT, Workers' Party), which had pioneered the participatory principles of budget making and public management more generally.

FNU/CUT provided the organizational resources for coordinating the FNSA, including the executive secretary. Logistical help was also provided by the *Federação de Órgãos para Assistência Social e Educacional (Fase)*, a radical Brazil-wide NGO with a long history of popular education, campaigning, and research with popular movements for human rights, democracy, and environmental justice. FNSA was located at the Commission for Urban Development of the Chamber of Deputies in Brasilia. The combination of such core sources of support indicates the broad base of the alliance. It chose its name "National Front" to indicate this breadth and that it was not dominated by any one social group whether it be trade union, NGO, faith organization, or social movement.

A particular contribution of the trade unions was to provide well-organized and informed networks of politically conscious activists, experienced in organizing in their communities, right across Brazil's hugely differing regions. CUT had been a central organizing force in the struggle against the dictatorship less than 15 years earlier. It had established a strong legitimacy as a hub for the coordination of different autonomous movements with shared goals. For example, in 1983 CUT had created ANAMPOS (*Articulação Nacional dos Movimentos Populares e Sindicais*) as a means of coordinating social movements and trade unions when the need arose. In the struggle against the dictatorship, just over a decade earlier than the struggles over water privatization, a culture of mutual respect (although not without tensions) was nurtured among different kinds of movements, urban and rural, industrial and social, and religious and secular (author interview with Kjeld Jacobsen, past International Secretary CUT, October 2010).

The FNSA's framework of principles "for the universal guarantee of sanitation and water services to all citizens regardless of their economic and social condition" acted as the basis for a massive process of participation (quoted in de Oliveira Filho 2002, 4). Each constituent organization worked separately and together to develop proposals and strategies to resolve the still dire state of water supply in Brazil, to overcome endemic corruption, and to come up with coherent alternatives to privatization. It sought to generalize and apply the principles of participatory democracy developed in practice by the Brazilian left. This participatory process was combined with strategic and high-profile interventions in the parliamentary and judicial process. Interventions in Brasilia, for example, would always be accompanied by mass activities, demonstrations, or other high-impact events.

The international dimension to the campaign contributed to these high-profile interventions. At a key moment in the government's attempt to get its privatization proposals passed, the FNSA organized a well-publicized seminar in the Chamber of Deputies with speakers from South Africa, Canada, and the PSI trade union confederation. This documented the social and environmental costs of the corporations leading the process of privatization in Brazil and elsewhere and showcased alternative models of public improvement. "International help and exchange has been essential in our struggle", affirmed de Oliveira Filho (2002, 18). By 2000, this multilevel campaign had successfully challenged the constitutional legitimacy of shifting responsibility for the management of water from the municipal to the regional level and had defeated the government's proposal for the sale of the National Sanitation Company.

Following Lula's election in 2002, the success of the campaign was symbolized by de Oliveira Filho's appointment as Minister of Water. The proposal for wholesale privatization was dropped, but the government bowed to demands from international capital to enable public-private partnerships (PPPs) in public services, including water. Several municipalities also submitted to pressures from national capital for privatization of their water services (author telephone and e-mail interview with Sergio Baierle, coordinator of the Porto Alegre NGO *Cidade*, March 2011).

Uruguay: The trade union vertebrae of a popular movement

In Uruguay, the story began in 2002 with a newspaper leaking a letter of intent between the Colorado government of Jorge Batlle (2000–2005) and the International Monetary Fund (IMF), which set out a timetable for the privatization of Uruguay's national water company, *Obras Sanitarias del Estado* (OSE). It was the publication of this letter that led to the formation of a popular and effective alliance in defence of water as the source of life, the *Comisión Nacional en Defensa del Agua y de la Vida* (CNDAV; Taks 2008). CNDAV had its roots in an alliance involving the water workers' union, the Federation of State Employees of OSE (FFOSE), to resist initial moves towards privatization in the Maldonaldo region.

FFOSE, was part of the trade union federation *Plenario Intersindical de Trabajadores—Convención Nacional de Trabajadores* (PIT-CNT) which, like the Brazilian CUT, had played a key role in supporting resistance to the dictatorship (between 1973–1985) and thus had a high degree of popular legitimacy. The water workers had been part of that resistance too. In the struggle for water as a human right and a common good—widely seen as a continuation of the struggle for democracy—the union continued to play a central, supportive role. An activist describes the role of FFOSE as providing the "spinal vertebrae" of the CNDAV (author e-mail and phone interview with Carmen Sosa, a FFOSE organizer and representative on the CNDAV, July 2010).

FFOSE's initial concern, like that of the water workers in Brazil, was the interests of its members as jobs were frozen and their workload increased. But following a similar logic to the Brazilian FNV, FFOSE members' concerns soon went beyond their jobs. As staff of the national water company, which from the late 1990s had been threatened with breakup and privatization, they also felt a strong connection with the farmers and rural population whose livelihoods were dependent on the supply of water. "For us", explained Adriana Marquisio, president of FFOSE between 2004 and 2010, "the problems of water shortage in rural areas is very sensitive. There are staff of the public water company (OSE) in even the smallest rural towns. They grew up there, they live there, and they are part of the affected population. Water is too vital for the task of providing it to be carried out as just any other job" (author e-mail and phone interview with Adriana Marquisio, July 2010).

FFOSE and its partners in CNDAV believed that the strongest institutional defence against the IMF would be a constitutional one. They had to find a political route that outflanked the existing government. A previous success against privatization provided a solution. In 1992, 72% of the electorate voted against a law that would have opened up virtually all state enterprises to privatization (Chavez 2008). CNDAV, with FFOSE, followed this example and made the most of a clause in the constitution enabling citizens to call for a referendum if they could win the support of at least 300,000 people (more than 10% of registered voters). The referendum would be over an amendment to the constitution to include a reference to "access to water and . . . sanitation as constituting fundamental human rights" and to such a public good being provided "solely and directly by state legal persons" (Chavez 2008, 38). Within a year, the CNDAV gained the 300,000 signatures necessary for a referendum.

In Montevideo, NGOs and urban movements played a major role in CNDAV. Outside the capital it was mainly FFOSE, working with rural organizations that pushed the reform of the constitution. One FFOSE organizer describes how, "In 2004, the general secretary of FFOSE (with other *compañeros*) went round the country on horseback for 23 days, from village to village, to talk to people about the need for constitutional reform" (author e-mail interview with Carmen Sosa, July 2010). FFOSE also used its membership in PSI to organize international support. This included research and arguments—drawing especially on the international experience of privatization—that FFOSE could use to build support for the amendment.

The other side of FFOSE's commitment to water as a common good and its delivery as a public service has been its concern to make OSE an organization that is properly accountable for public money. The FFOSE members played a leading role in 2002 in ridding the Uruguayan water company of corruption and participating with management in its transformation into a model public utility. An important element of this model was a formal requirement, after the success of the referendum, that citizens and staff have an effective role in the running of the company. The process of making this a reality is still underway, but the level of citizen and NGO participation in CNDAV has prepared the way. "Citizens insisted on it", remembers Maria Selva Ortiz from REDES, "and as a result of the role citizens played in the campaign, we could not be refused" (author personal interview with Maria Selva Ortiz, November 2010).

South Africa: Blocked attempts at restructuring for public benefit

The South African experience, although not as "successful" as the ones above, is an important one because it demonstrates that public ownership is not a sufficient condition for the creation of "public services". I focus here on the experience of the South African Municipal Workers' Union (Samwu). Following the 1994 election of the African National Congress, the ruling party adopted neoliberal macroeconomic policies (Satgar 2008). In response, and to address the specific problems of dismantling the apartheid state, Samwu mobilized the skills and commitment of its members to develop a public capacity for restructuring public services without privatization to meet the needs of all. There were several other trade union-led attempts at similar democratic restructuring, variable in the extent of their success.

Samwu's initiatives have been part of an often divided but at times very militant opposition to privatization, as well as the corporatization, of public water and electricity utilities. Corporatization effectively means organizing a public utility as a separate financial entity and managing it as a market-oriented private enterprise. It confronts workers and service users with a common problem of an organization that is structurally oriented to reducing and recovering costs on a commercial model (Hall et al, 2002,

McDonald and Smith 2002). Opposition to corporatization has come from well-organized community movements as well as from the trade unions. But there have been tensions in the relationship. A good example of both a common front of resistance and of the tensions produced by the different immediate interests of the staff and of the service users is provided by the experience of the Anti-Privatization Forum (APF) in 2000.

The APF brought together community groups defending themselves against rises in service charges, cutoffs, eviction, and the other consequences of cost recovery with students and unions, especially Samwu, to resist two of the government's flagships of corporatization: the Igoli 2002 plan for the services of Johannesburg and the corporatization of Witwatersrand University (Van de Walt et al, 2001, Ngwane 2010). The tensions in the alliance arose from the fact that the unions won some concessions regarding the terms of Igoli 2000, and this helped to protect their members' jobs. Many community activists saw this as moving away from opposition, to negotiating simply around the terms on which it was to be introduced (author e-mail interview with Trevor Ngwane, one of the community leaders of the APF, and with Roger Ronnie, Samwu's General Secretary 1995–1999 and 2000–2007, December 2010). These, and other widespread resistance, have impeded the momentum of corporatization and privatization but have not halted it.

Samwu's post-apartheid strategy was to pursue a double track of "stopping the privatization of municipal services (in whatever form)", and "contributing to the transformation of the municipal services to allow for effective, accountable and equitable service delivery" (Samwu 2002). In other words, Samwu, like several other unions—most notably the transport union, Satawu (which faced the privatization of the railways and the ports)—engaged with restructuring with the aim of developing and demonstrating the public sector's capacity for a reorganization of state services on the basis of the social rights entrenched in South Africa's democratic Constitution.

In 1997, after a national campaign of demonstrations and extensive public argument, Samwu won agreement with the South Africa Local Government Association (Salga) on a protocol for how restructuring would take place. The key commitment, as far as the unions were concerned, was that the public sector would be the preferred option. Samwu made the most of the space this legal agreement provided for municipal workers and managers to develop alternatives with a chance of implementation. At every level its members initiated both emergency and longer-term plans for public reconstruction—from union members mending water pipes for their own communities in their own time to working with sympathetic municipal managers on overcoming the institutional legacy of apartheid.

One exemplary initiative over a two-year period beginning in 1996 was in the Hillstar area of Cape Town, where the union brought together staff and managers across townships to integrate what had been a fragmented water department. They massively improved the infrastructure so that water was piped to people's homes, valves opened up or reconstructed, and the poor received the 50 litres of free water per person per day as the ANC had originally promised in the Reconstruction and Development Plan of 1994 (RDP 1994). The Hillstar experience became a template for other larger scale attempts to reconstruct water services as well as being widely drawn on in Samwu's education programme for shop stewards.

Major attempts at union and community-led reconstruction, however, came up against the wider political context of the political party that led the struggle against apartheid (the ANC) becoming the same political party driving through privatization and neoliberal restrictions on public sector investment and local government finance (Bond 2002, Samwu 2002, Satgar 2008, von Holdt 2010). Efforts to develop the Hillstar model on a provincial level demonstrated that Samwu could not carry through plans for reconstruction on its own, in the face of the combined forces of water multinationals like Biwater, the government, and teams of largely US-trained consultants (Van Niekerk 1998).

The Congress of South African Trade Unions (Cosatu)—to which Samwu is affiliated—was the union's natural ally. In the early days of privatization, however, when Samwu passed a resolution at its 1995 Congress asserting that it would "implacably oppose the government's privatization policies, whatever they may be called", Cosatu argued for a case-by-case approach—although in all its statements and campaigning, it became highly critical of the government's neoliberal economics (Bayliss 2001). Even when its opposition to privatization has been most militant though, this powerful federation has been less concerted in its support for alternative, public restructuring (author telephone interviews with Roger Ronnie and Karl von Holdt, who had worked for National Labour, Economic and Development Institute (NALEDI), the strategic research and policy organization created by Cosatu, December 2010).

Common features?

For the purpose of this chapter, these experiences, with all their limitations, constitute exemplary initiatives whose distinctive features are the product of particular histories but have a wider importance. Understanding their innovations, the conditions that make them possible, and those that block their full realization might contribute to the development of hybrid models of state services that ameliorate the most negative aspects of capture by private capital while ensuring a more sustainable, equitable, and democratic form of services for all.

What do these experiences have in common that illustrates the potentially transformative role of labour in response to the challenge of privatization? I will group these common features into two categories. First, there are those that concern the consciousness of workers and their organizations regarding the *nature and purpose of labour.* As I have already stressed, all three experiences involve trade unions self-consciously moving beyond the defence of jobs and working conditions to taking responsibility, with citizens organizations, for both defending a public utility and changing the way it is managed. There is a common commitment across all cases to fully utilizing the skills of public service staff to identify the failings of the public sector as it is and to propose an alternative way of organizing the service on the basis of principles of equity, the creativity of labour, responsiveness to the community, and full accountability and transparency for public resources.

Related to this, all the trade unions involved were influenced by cultural and organizational traditions that understand workers not simply as wage earners but as knowing subjects. Whether coming from the commitment to participatory democracy characteristic of the Brazilian labour movement (Keck 1992), the syndicalism influential in the formation of Samwu (Mawbey 2007), or the radical social democratic traditions of civil and intellectual society in Uruguay, these trade unions are conscious of themselves as collective actors for social justice society-wide. From this understanding of their members as citizens as well as workers, followed the logic of building popular alliances to defend and develop what belongs to the people. With varying degrees of success, they were involved in creating sustained relationships or "deep coalitions" (Tattersall 2005, Spronk 2009) with services users and citizens more generally, rather than merely tactical and instrumental alliances.

These alliances and relationships had a dual purpose. On the one hand, they brought together sources of expertise—practical, expert, investigative—that were vital to transforming the organization of the service, its accessibility and its quality. The local and regional assemblies that developed alternatives in the Brazilian campaign, the plans for transforming the organization of the OSE, and the way the Hillstar process depended on the knowledge of local communities, all illustrate this process of building a counter knowledge. So too does the international collaboration, whether through the PSI or through direct transborder, sometimes regional, collaboration led to a sharing of information and strategic understanding, otherwise not available on a national basis. On the other hand, the success of these alliances—in countering the pressures of global corporate and financial power and acquiescence of the political system—depended on their ability to use a variety of sources of power and influence to win legitimacy and build political support for the public option.

This brings us to the second innovative feature that these experiences have in common, if not all the same success: the development of strategies and forms of organization to challenge the *power of capital beyond the workplace* and in the new circumstances of the globalization of the capitalist market. This includes the expanded power of finance, including its power over nation states, the role of international financial institutions (IFIs), the growth of globally dominant corporations, and the importance of the public sector in the emerging form of neoliberal capitalism, privatization, and marketization (Huws 2011).

In all three experiences, the trade unions were part of wider class and popular alliances or initiatives that sought to respond to the changing nature of capitalist power. None could depend on political parties to address these wider political issues. The ambitious initiatives of CNDAV in Uruguay and FNSA in Brazil to mobilize popular power over the political process were calculated to counter their governments' willing submission to pressures of the IFIs. The attempts by Samwu, through Cosatu and in direct interventions in the political process and in negotiations with the local government association, were similar, although generally unsuccessful, attempts to loosen the grip that IFIs and elite private interests had gained over the reconstruction of the South African political economy after apartheid. The new priority that the trade unions in these campaigns gave to close international collaboration was, in effect, part of this same attempt to build forms of international power and knowledge with which to counter and, if possible, pre-empt corporate capital's attempts to commodify public services (Keck and Sikkink 1998).

A less apparent feature of the wider significance of alliances like CNDAV concerns the relation between community and work. These alliances cannot accurately be understood in terms of connections between "work" and "community", as if they were separate worlds in the way that might have been true, especially in urban areas in the North, 20 years ago. These movements are now, in part, about building new forms of collectivity in the face of the disintegrative forces of the neoliberal economy—in particular, the casualization and precariousness of work and the erosion of traditional forms of trade union solidarity. Under these conditions the workplace is often the home or the streets and issues of community, family, education, and health, become inseparable from those of work—and lack of it.

A final point about these alliances is their relative autonomy from political parties, including those for which their members probably vote. It is an autonomy of perspective and knowledge as well as organization, underpinned by the independent resources and institutional capacity of the unions. On the basis of this independence, they establish strategic relationships with political parties, as we saw, for example, with the FNSA's interventions in the House of Deputies. At least this is the theory. In practice, relations with political parties have been complex and uneven depending, for example, on the timing of the electoral cycle.

THE DUAL NATURE OF LABOUR

To understand, and possibly generalize, from these examples of how trade union strategy changed priorities in response to the threat of privatization, it helps to draw on Karl Marx's understanding of the dual nature of labour under capitalism. On the one hand, argues Marx, labour is abstract labour, involved in producing commodities for the market, objectified as value, expressed in the exchange of commodities for money, from which capital extracts profit. On the other hand, labour is also involved in the production of use value, concrete labour, both individual and social. Under capitalism, the two forms of labour are, he argued, in constant tension with each other: creative, purposeful activity is subordinated to labour disciplined for the maximization of profits. Potentially, this tension is one of self-determining activity versus alienated labour (Elson 1979). In this tension lie a source of agency and the transformative potential of labour.

This distinction is very helpful for analyzing the shift we have observed to be triggered by the threat of privatization, from conventional defensive trade unionism to strategies based on taking responsibility for the use value of public sector labour. Before the pervasive spread of privatization, the taken-for-granted routines of trade unionism in the public sector generally appeared to be based on those of trade unionism in the private sector, with governments as the employer rather than capital (Terry 2000).

To be more specific, while public sector unions often deploy sources of bargaining power specific to the institutionally political nature of their members' employment contracts—mobilizing public opinion, using party union links, and so on—it has been exceptional for these unions to make the nature, organization and future of the service as such central to the content of their activities. Trade union strategies focusing on developing or radically reforming public services usually in close alliance with fellow citizens, began to appear in both Southern and Northern hemispheres in response to privatization and other forms of commodifying what had been out of, or partially out of, the capitalist market.

In contexts in which trade unions develop these strategies of radical reform, we observe a dynamic in which the struggle against privatization is not only about public versus private ownership but also about democratic control over the labour process and the purposes of labour, including the accessibility and quality of the service. In practice, this takes many different forms: a common one is that the need to justify opposition to privatization in a context in which the public utility is patently inefficient and/or corrupt in its management of public money leads unions to investigate why it is inefficient and use their combined knowledge as service providers to develop alternatives.

In the cases studied here, the unions effectively used their everyday organizing capacity to gather their collective knowledge of the production process in exactly this way, illustrating in practice a definition of public efficiency.

The focus on the dual nature of labour might seem a bit abstract, but I would suggest that it helps us to understand both trade union involvements in alternatives to privatization: they have extended their priority to struggling over use value, not just exchange value. It also helps to highlight the distinctive contribution of organized workers and knowledgeable producers in shaping, achieving, and sustaining these alternatives.

A full elaboration of the role of workers in developing and achieving alternatives is beyond the scope of this essay. The basic argument, however, is this: public services and utilities as non-market institutions created for social and political purposes are governed by an economic logic distinct from that of market-driven organizations (although in capitalist economies, the public sphere has also been subject to pressures and constraints set by capitalist markets and the priority of profit). For the past 40 years or so, North and South, movements and struggles of many kinds have tried to make this public economics more responsive to public needs and expectations. From the student, feminist, and urban movements of the 1960s and 1970s through to the experiments in participatory democracy in the 1980s and the environmental justice movements of the 21st century, there has been a growing pressure to make the actual, living, specific public—especially the poor and the subordinate parts of the public—a powerful presence in public decision making. But these movements rarely focused on the role of labour in the process of democratization. Understanding the struggle against privatization as potentially a struggle over use value helps us overcome this strategic limitation and draws attention to the potential importance of labour in this struggle for democracy.

Structurally at least, the partially decommodified nature of the public sphere opens up distinct possibilities for the struggle against alienated labour. In particular, it opens up the possibility for public service workers to express themselves through their labour, in the delivery of services to fellow citizens, as knowing, feeling people, rather than simply as workers selling their labour power or, in abstract terms, alienating their creativity as if it were a commodity. Of course, many workers in private, profit-maximizing enterprises try to do the same, but the partially decommodified sphere of public services enables this to take place and be struggled for on a more systematic basis.

As we have already implied, this possibility would always have been a struggle. Few, if any public sector institutions were designed to realize the creativity of labour in the process of serving their fellow citizens. But when trade unions struggle over privatization, this is exactly the possibility that comes to the fore. It is the workers' commitment to the purpose, the potential use of their labour, that underpins the move from a struggle simply to defend workers' livelihoods to a struggle over a service that should be for the benefit of all.

This points to a need to deepen models of participatory democracy to involve the worker as citizen in influencing the nature of the decisions about the use of their labour. Such participatory governance is therefore not only about the allocation of public money, it is also about the ways of managing to realize the creativity of service workers for the benefit of, and in collaboration with, their fellow citizens. Furthermore, the fundamental importance for high-quality services of valuing the creativity of labour, and working within a framework of goals set by extensive citizen participation, points to a notion of the division of labour and of discipline that is based on collaboration and motivation rather that a bureaucratic version of the discipline and divisions of the capitalist market.

As a development coming out of not only the unacceptability of privatization, but also the failure of the command state—social democratic as well as Soviet—these pioneering struggles of labour could be useful sources of insight for a logic of "socially efficient" public services (Spronk 2010). We will return to this in the conclusion as an issue for future research. First, however, let's catch at least a glimpse of how such a *democratized public benefit economics* is emerging in practice, including the difficulties and dilemmas it faces.

CAPITALIST POWER BEYOND THE WORKPLACE

Historically, in Europe in particular, the recognition of the power of capital beyond the workplace—in the appropriation and distribution as well as the production of surplus and the character of capital accumulation—has been a driving force behind the participation of trade unions in the creation of political parties of labour, social democratic, and communist persuasions (Sassoon 1996, Eley 2002). For most of the 20th century, the goal of social control, or overthrow of the power of capital was, in practice, understood by the dominant political traditions of the left in primarily national terms. Capture of national state institutions was seen as not only necessary but more or less sufficient for this purpose. The consequence of this model—the British Labour Party being the most classic example—has been a process, or indeed an institutional habit, of delegating political matters beyond the narrow agenda of industrial collective bargaining to the party and electoral politics (Miliband 1961).

In the countries that figure in this chapter, the institutions of liberal democratic nation states that underpinned this separation were never established for a significant length of time. By the time dictatorships, including apartheid, had been overthrown (1985 in Brazil and Uruguay; 1994 in South Africa), the unrestrained movement of capital had already begun to produce a new, multiscalar geography of capitalist power—in which state institutions at different levels played active, shaping roles but in which there was a significant denationalizing of state systems, upwards and downwards (Sassen 2006).

We have seen in Uruguay and Brazil how the traditions formed during the struggles against dictatorship, of alliance-building with a wide variety of social movements and the acute awareness of the limits of liberal political institutions, were clearly carried over into the struggles for alternatives to privatization. These unions retained a significant autonomy from the parties they helped to create to lead the political struggle for democracy—the PT and Frente Amplio. They saw themselves, amongst their other roles as guarantors, along with (and often in active alliance with) other social movements, of a radical democracy accountable to strong civil societies.

In South Africa, there was a similar tradition of alliance-building across social sectors in the struggle against apartheid. However, Cosatu's position in the alliance with the ANC and the South African Communist Party (SACP), their shared belief in the necessity of a stage of national liberation (bourgeois revolution) before any further radical transformation, the depth of the ANC's legitimacy as the party of the post-apartheid nation (Satgar 2008), meant that Cosatu's (and thereby to some extent Samwu's) position vis-à-vis the ANC was ambiguous, as we have seen, despite its official position of autonomy in relation to its alliance partners (author personal interview with Devan Pillay, January 2011).

To understand the particular role of trade unions in creating or trying to create alternatives to privatization, it is important to recognize the specific and ambiguous position of the trade unions. They cannot be understood in the same way as the (erstwhile) left-of-centre parties with which they have been in alliance. In general, trade unions are in a different structural position from political parties vis-à-vis their membership on the one hand and the institutions of the state on the other. Generally, the very existence of unions is rooted in workers' day-to-day antagonism to capital, which limits the extent of their integration into the neoliberal consensus. The conflict with capital is not necessarily explosive or political but if they abandon the daily battlefield over wages and conditions, and struggle for and defence of the social wage, members will protest and, depending on the degree of union democracy, this will put pressure on the leadership and, if that fails, membership will fall away (Anderson 1967).

Generally, unions depend on their members to an extent that parties do not. Parties are often integrated into state structures, receiving state funding or high salaries for elected representatives and their staff. Parties are also reliant on the media and have a highly mediated relation to the people (Mair 2006). At the same time as unions across the world are under more effective pressure to resist the transnational powers of capital, their strength and capacity is undermined by the deregulation of national labour markets. Increasingly, the majority of the economically active population is either unemployed, their work is casualized, or they are hired through labour brokers. The unions simply do not reach these precarious workers, other than through innovative social movement-influenced networks increasingly organizing in the informal sector.

At this stage, the shape of an alternative kind of relationship between trade unions and wider political and economic change is unformed, but certain features recur in the struggle for alternatives to privatization, as in the broader struggle against privatization. The approach developed by Novelli and Ferus-Comelo (2010) through reflecting on a wide range of case studies of struggles involving labour and other social movements resisting different aspects of neoliberal globalization provides a useful framework for identifying underlying tendencies in these struggles. They understand these strategies, and the forms of organization produced through, for and out of these struggles, as being an embedded process of learning and of producing counter-knowledge. This could also be put in terms of the development or renewal of new forms of capacity in the face of capital's contemporary forms of power. An important dimension of this is a growing knowledge of how to operate at different geographic levels: "transborderism".

TRANSFORMATIVE TRADE UNIONISM AND THE DEVELOPMENT OF KNOWLEDGE

A distinctive feature of the way trade unions struggle with others for alternatives to privatization is the emphasis on developing their shared knowledge and capacity for collaborative self-determination. This is understood as vital to effective strategy and is evident in a strong emphasis on, and demands for, worker education and professional training. This is a feature of all the unions mentioned in this chapter.

It is also evident in their international collaboration. For example, when water workers' leader Abelardo de Oliveira Filho says, "International help and exchange has been essential in our struggle", he is referring, amongst other work, to the investigations initiated by PSI in carrying out the mandate their members gave them to resist the privatization of water, to look into "how the privateers worked" (author interview with David Boys of PSI, June 2010). This, in turn, led to the creation of a dedicated Research Unit, the PSIRU, whose method—in line with the PSI's philosophy—brought together different forms of knowledge of activists, researchers, and civic organizations. As the movement against water privatization became increasingly global and radicalized by its encounters face-to-face with the privateers at the Global Water Forum, the PSI, the Transnational Institute (TNI), and others created a space, the Reclaiming Public Water (RPW) network, specifically for knowledge exchange, production, and dissemination on alternatives to privatization. The work of the RPW network, its books and seminars bringing together trade unions and civic organizations from 41 countries with a common commitment to alternatives to privatization to share experience as a resource for practice, is exemplary of the counter-knowledge about which Novelli and Ferus-Comelo (2010) write.

Central to the alternatives promoted by both PSI and the RPW network, and sometimes driven by trade unions on the frontline of resistance to privatization, are collaborations between public authorities. The impetus to improve public benefit and capacity has led to over 130 such public-public partnerships (PuPs) being forged in 70 different countries. Through these partnerships, public organizations are able to keep up the process of improvement, learning new technologies, gaining greater access to finance, practising better forms of management and training (Hall et al, 2009). Many of them are transnational or transborder partnerships, usually skipping the national level, and instead directly linking utility to utility. In Latin America, there is a concerted attempt by trade unions working on alternatives to privatization to develop PuPs across the continent on the basis of the principles of accountability and participation that they have developed locally. The important role of trade unions in pushing PuPs is an illustration of the multilevel character of emerging trade union strategies. At the same time, the process of working at this transnational level presents a serious challenge to unions whose strength in working for alternatives lies with the active support and evolving capacity of their members.

FFOSE from Uruguay had been one of the unions at the forefront of developing PuPs in Latin America. Adriana Marquisio reflects on how the unions bridge the local level of membership involvement and the often international level at which PuPs are negotiated: "PUPs are a distant issue from the day-to-day lives of the workers, so we have discussed this topic in our union structures, and we run workshops and conferences with the aim of incorporating this process into our organization". She's optimistic though: "In FFOSE today, we have a new generation that has taken up the issue with great interest" (as cited in Terhorst 2011, 3).

Here, then, are two distinct but related dynamics evident when labour and the trade unions have been involved in alternatives to privatization: on the one hand, a struggle to transform the management and labour process in the public sector to maximize public benefit and create mechanisms of accountability and on the other hand, strategies to build counter-power to the macroeconomic pressures exerted by capitalist power. They are distinct and not always in sync. The experiences observed here, corroborated by a wider range of experiences (Hall et al, 2005, von Holdt and Maserumule 2005, Terhorst 2008, Yesmin-Mannan 2009, Novelli 2010) indicate that both dynamics are necessary to successful alternatives but not sufficient on their own.

The importance of labour in reforming the management of public companies requires further elaboration. An investigation into the challenges facing the internal democratization of public water companies in two cities celebrated for their struggles over democratic control over water, Cochabamba and Porto Alegre, warns against overgeneralizing from the experiences of transformative resistance on the part of public sector trade unions and the conditions required for democratic public management.

LESSONS IN LABOUR: REFORMING PUBLIC COMPANIES

Cochabamba: Inside the company

Paradoxically, a negative example of the role of unions in the reform of public services emerges in the context of the historic victory of the citizens of Cochabamba, Bolivia, in ousting private water company Bechtel from taking over the public water company (Travis 2008). For in Cocha-bamba, the aim of transforming the newly secured public company into a company genuinely serving the city's citizens was effectively blocked by the water workers' union, which remained entrenched in a self-interested relationship with management, defending the status quo against popular pressure for change.

"Cochabamba" rightly evokes victory, the first victory in the war of those fighting for water as a commons against the multinationals driving the modern movement for enclosure (Tapia 2008). This struggle met every condition for success: a powerful local campaign, including a citywide strike and other popular protests; national and international collaboration to block the water multinationals; and, finally, a vision of democratic con-trol, which could answer the attempt to use the inefficiency of the public company SEMAPA to bolster the arguments for privatizing it. Oscar Oli-vera, one of the spokespeople from the Bolivian water justice movement and a leader of the local trade union movement (that included all unions *except* the water workers), summed it up thus: "The true opposite to priva-tization is the social re-appropriation of wealth by working-class society itself—self-organized in communal structures of management, in neigh-bourhood associations, in unions, and in the rank and file" (as quoted in Spronk 2009, 27).

Yet, a decade after the success, which could have been the basis for turn-ing that vision into reality, SEMAPA as a public company is still refusing to put the necessary resources into providing every resident with running water and is facing serious problems due to the continuing incompetence in which the union leadership seems to have been complicit. A struggle for reform within the unions is underway, however, led by activists radicalized by their participation in the *Coordinadora* (the community-labour coali-tion that defeated privatization).

The SEMAPA water workers joined in the coalition to defeat Bechtel, but they opposed attempts to democratize the running of SEMAPA. This was not just a loss of a powerful ally. It was more specific than that. With-out an internal dynamic of reforms, gathering inside knowledge through the workers about the working of company across the traditional division of labour and petty departmental empires and collaborating with the com-munity to work out practical alternatives, attempts to transform the com-pany would invariably falter.

The hidden dimension of the struggle for alternatives

This Bolivian experience points negatively to a vital, often hidden, dimen-sion of the struggle to create alternatives to privatization: the empowerment or self-empowerment of public sector workers as citizens to realize their capacity to contribute to the public benefit. The "empowerment" of com-munities is widely discussed. Sometimes, however, it is described as if the actors are simply "the citizens" and "the state". As if the state were simply a "structure" or an "institution". Human relations—including the relations of particular labour processes, particular organizations of labour—are effectively absent from the frame. Similarly, to open up what it means to realize the capacities of public service workers, it becomes important to understand state/public institutions as involving relationships, which can be more or less favourable to democratic control. The relations of management and the organization of labour "internal" to the state are a part of this complex of relationships, and are decisive to the flows of information, knowledge, and problem solving among staff and between staff and users. Ultimately, the combination is vital to achieving the goals, the measurements and dynamics of a different kind of economic logic.

The experiences of the water company DMAE in Porto Alegre, Brazil, and OSE, in Uruguay, illustrate forms of empowerment and self-empowerment through which labour for the state can be a (co)transformative actor, coming nearer to Olivera's vision of a "true opposite of privatization". In both cases, the trade unions have had a broadly positive commitment to popular control over the decisions of the public water company. And, in both cases, processes of genuine citizen power and collaboration with workers and managers have, in different ways, been vital to the relative success of these public companies as alternatives to privatization. The role of the trade unions was completely different in DMAE from their role in OSE. In DMAE, the water workers' union *qua* union had a really minimal direct involvement in the processes of management and purpose of the work. In OSE, the union, with citizens' organizations and REDES, took the initiative to restructure the company, to "modernize without privatization".

Different political histories, however, have produced quite distinct kinds of relationships between organized labour and citizens' power. The preliminary exploration of these differences opens up a rich seam of questions about the possible role and character of labour in the feasible utopia of democratic public services.

Porto Alegre: Labour and participatory budgeting

In Porto Alegre, the process of democratizing the public water company, DMAE, was well established by the time that the threat of privatization loomed—hence DMAE's leading role in the national movement against privatization in the late 1990s both in mobilizing the constituency of water technicians and in demonstrating a model of public competence (Maltz 2005). The driving force for this process was political, but through the participatory political culture of the PT, not through the institutions of exclusively representative politics.

The content, culture, and processes of the PT were initially a product of the radical and participatory movements that led the fight against the dictatorship. The radical independent trade unions, which were federated through the CUT were central to the process. The distinctive emphasis of the PT on participatory democracy—especially at a municipal level—stems from these origins in the movements. Indeed, some argue that this open, participatory approach to public finances was significantly influenced by the participatory forms of democracy through which CUT members, in local and regional assemblies, decided on the priorities of the whole organization.

The first decade and a half of the PT's history (it was founded in 1980) has involved a kind of relay process with the radical unions and other movements, beginning with the party incorporating, at least partially, organizing principles from the movements, then in office going back to the movements and opening up the process of governing on the basis of these same participatory principles. The Mayor of Santo Andre and early adviser to Lula was quite explicit: "When we won electoral victories, we went back to the movements from whence we came" (Selso Daniel, author interview, 1997). Thus, in a certain sense, labour didn't see itself as requiring a specific role in the participatory processes of PT municipalities. Possibly, they assumed that as citizens they were already part of the process.

To understand the consequences of this for the role of labour and the trade unions in DMAE, or any model of alternative to privatization based on it, we need to distinguish between the time when the PT was in office and participatory budgeting was at its most powerful as an autonomous source of democratic power (albeit not without problems; Chavez 2006) and the period from 2004 after the PT was defeated and the participatory budget was steadily marginalized.

In the earlier period, with the PT in government, the management of DMAE initiated an internal participatory budget process for determining how the company should carry out the projects that had been decided, in part, by the citywide participatory budget exercise. Carlos Todeschini, the General Manager of DMAE in that earlier period described how it worked:

> Management made a radical shift from a budget being drawn up by one man, behind closed doors, to a situation which started at the bottom with workers in every department discussing what could be done to improve the quality of their work, what equipment, what re-organization and so on. This was then discussed at other levels and decisions were made in which everyone had a say. It was all done through a deliberative, problem-solving way. It was very transparent. There was a general feeling of being part of the process, being heard, having your opinion and your work count for the common goal of improving DMAE's service. (author e-mail and telephone interview, February 2011)

Since the defeat of the PT in 2004, a coalition (re-elected under a new leadership in 2010) has governed, which is explicitly hostile to the PT. It has been unable to dismantle the participatory budgeting, but it has weakened its power. In the DMAE, the open budgeting process has stopped. As to the role of the union, the general municipal union SIMPA welcomed the opening up of the budget. Its members became involved, but SIMPA, as a union, did not. Now that the process is being dismantled, the union is not in a strong enough position to defend it.

Judging by the rise in public complaints in the media, the consequence has been a decline in efficiency and in DMAE's position as an exemplary alternative to privatization. Nevertheless, its history illustrates the possibilities of combining effective citizen participation with workplace democracy.

CONCLUSIONS

This chapter is a preliminary mapping of issues related to the role of labour and trade unions in the development of "alternatives to privatization". My conclusions are therefore intended as catalysts for further thought and research.

Labour as an agent of radical democratic reform

This essay has focused on a particular strategic phenomenon within the broader sphere of labour resistance to privatization: that is, instances where the defence of a public service has involved a refusal to accept the status quo and where labour, mainly through the trade unions and in alliance with others, has turned itself into an agent of radical reform. We are faced with an unusual phenomenon of public sector trade unionists—in an extraordinarily wide range, and in many dimensions contrasting contexts, of public companies in Brazil, Uruguay, and South Africa; in cities such as Cali in Colombia, Newcastle in the UK, Huancayo in Peru, and in municipalities across Norway, and many other locations that have not yet been studied—pursuing very similar strategies of resistance and reform. I have looked only at experiences from the water sector, but I am aware that there are other examples in which trade unions have played a similar reforming role in health, transport, electricity, and municipal services. Can we identify common or similar motor forces behind this new global phenomenon other than the pressures of capitalist globalization and the threat of privatization?

I would suggest, on the basis of the case studies presented here and research I have carried out in Northern Europe (Wainwright 2009, Wainwright and Little 2009), that what these experiences have in common is a leadership formed or greatly influenced by powerful struggles for radical democracy. Whether it was the participatory democracy of movements against the dictatorships in Latin America, the emphasis on workers' control and civic power in the grassroots resistance to apartheid in South Africa or the refusal of alienated labour and the emancipatory social struggles of the late 1960s and 1970s in Europe, formative influences on these leaderships were democratic political traditions that went beyond liberalism and the limits of representative democracy. In one sense, it is not surprising that the unions with such roots and influences are those involved in the practice of public service reform, which is, after all, essentially a process of deepening democratic control over public institutions, including the labour process.

But what explains why and how this democratizing impetus came to the fore? How significant is the nature and extent of union democracy? For example, are these same unions characterized by a high level of control by members who are embedded in the work of the public service as distinct from unions more dominated by full-time officials? How important is loyalty and identification with place and the association of the particular public body with the locality, region, or nation? How important are expanded levels of mass education, breaking subordinate cultures and raising expectations about workers' rights to be involved?

The democratization of the labour process

Participatory democracy, as a means of deepening democracy and overcoming the limits of representative democracy in the face of the pressures of mobile global capital, is in crisis. There are strong tendencies—whether in Latin America, South Africa, Europe, the US, or in the World Bank—towards a "participation lite" (Chavez 2006), in which participation is reduced to consultation or various forms of decentralization that legitimate or disguise the dismantling of public services. It is revealing that in the increasingly global discourse of these weak forms of participation references to labour are rare. When they do appear, it is only as "the vested interests of the trade unions". Civil society is evoked, but the organizations of labour are rarely referred to as part of civil society.

In retrospect, it is arguable that radical advocates and leaders of participatory democracy have paid insufficient attention to the role of labour. It could be argued, for example, that a lesson from Porto Alegre is that the weakening of participatory democracy was a result not only of political change but also of the minimal involvement of the unions. This meant that democracy was not embedded in the municipality's internal administration. This has often been reinforced by a lack of interest on the part of public sector trade unions. The reforming initiatives of trade unions in response to privatization point to an important opportunity for a strategic convergence between radical policies for citizens' participation and efforts to democratize public sector labour processes.

Corrupt vested interests or servants of the public?

Public managers figure in this chapter as either villains or fairy godmothers. We have not had the opportunity to study their varying roles and the conditions under which they could be allies of democratization and with what implications. This would help present a more subtle analysis. On the one hand, there are the managers of the public water company SEMAPA, who on several occasions had to be removed due to corruption. On the other hand, there are the managers organized through the ASSEMAE in Brazil, who played a central role in the campaign against privatization, the managers at DMAE in Porto Alegre who opened up the internal budget as part of the citywide participatory budget, and the middle-level managers in South Africa who collaborated with Samwu in trying to reorganize the country's apartheid-riven institutions to create public services for all.

Clearly, the role of public service managers depends on the context, including the moral and institutional strength of the processes that set their priorities and make them accountable. But what about their relation to unions? In a capitalist, profit-maximizing enterprise, management and labour are in a relationship of structural conflict over the share of value, while at the same time being required by the nature of production to be day-to-day cooperators. In theory, the goals of the public sector could mean a different, more fundamentally collaborative relationship even as unions maintain autonomy and the right to disengage when they feel the interests of their members as workers are threatened. Is workplace democracy backed by strong and autonomous unions a complementary means of holding management true to their public service mission? This, in turn, raises the question of how unions maintain their capacity and right to take militant industrial action, at the same time as working with management on reform. Their ability to hold management to account in this way—unique to trade unions—depends on exactly this capacity.

Changes in the nature of trade unions

From the research that has been done so far (Novelli 2004, Terhorst 2008, Spronk 2009), there are signs that, especially at a local or regional level, trade unions involved in resisting privatizations with campaigns for public service reform are themselves reforming. Several processes can be identified descriptively but need further research. First, unions taking the initiative in public service reform have recognized the importance of building lasting collaborative relationships with service users and communities. They have had to work hard to do so. In a context of high unemployment, public sector workers appear privileged and are often regarded with suspicion, seen to be interested only in their own welfare, however much they may claim otherwise. Unions have had to prove that they are committed to serving the wider public, rather than simply seeking instrumental alliances to save their own jobs.

Although research is developing on trade union-community alliances in general (Tattersall 2005), there is as little done specifically on struggles over public service reform, with some notable exceptions (Novelli 2004). Tattersall uses case studies of community-trade union coalitions in Canada and

Australia to draw up a list of conditions for success. One of these is that the trade union does not seek to control the alliance it enters. She describes the willingness to enter into an alliance with community and other civic organizations without being in control as representing a significant change for many unions.

Ferus-Camelo and Novelli (2008) document ways in which unions are learning new ways of participating in alliances with other kinds of organizations, whether social movements, NGOs, or initiatives and networks, and experimenting with new forms of communication and new ways of organizing and making decisions. The experiences described here, especially Brazil and Uruguay, show these unions acting more as resource for a variety of organizations, rather than asserting themselves as a singular leader or centre. Recent developments in Cosatu, as we have seen, indicate a similar trend is underway in South Africa.

The limits and potentials of trade unions

Privatization involves a seemingly systematic process of depoliticization of the questions and decisions about how public services should be delivered. The significance of the role of the trade unions co-organizing alliances defending water as a commons and access to it as human right has given voice to underlying beliefs, albeit vague, that otherwise have little organized political expression. They provide a set of counter-arguments that give confidence and a language to describe the instinctive recognition that water should not be treated as a commodity.

The campaigns we have described for alternatives to privatization all move issues—of ownership, sources of finance, the nature of contracting, measurements of efficiency and so on—from being neutral, technical, and opaque, if not entirely hidden by veils of commercial confidentiality, into the open, albeit conflictive, world of values, power, and debates over different goals and interests. In this sense, unions play a vital role in a process of *democratic politicization* of the means of service provision and delivery.

Most of the distinctive features of trade unions are ambivalent with regard to the distinctive contribution of unions to alternatives to privatization. Their consequences clearly depend on particular histories and contexts. Take, for example, their large, due-paying membership, providing regular revenue. Formally at any rate, unions have a popular reach unparalleled by political parties today. Only organized religion is still a serious competitor in this regard.

The question of dues should be separated from the question of mass membership. The regular dues come from large numbers of members who are mainly passive members and pay dues through check off system negotiated by the union with the employer. Nevertheless, if the union is a campaigning, activist union its potential popular reach is significant. It is *potentially* a source of unique practical and expert knowledge that through the organizational capacities of the union can be socialized and used as a basis for improving the social efficiency of services. This would draw on workers' dual role as citizens and public servants, activating the public service values that latently underpin their work. Its mass base can be a source of bargaining power too, including for a bargaining agenda, which concerns the quality or protection of service provision. Through the regular dues that members provide, unions can also be a material base for critical institutions of education, communication, research, and other ways of deploying resources or combining with other sources of an alternative hegemony—as we saw in Brazil and Uruguay and also internationally through the PSI in relation to water. Further, institutional stability, along with material or physical resources, can enable unions to be what FFOSE's Carmen Sosa described as the spinal cord of campaigns made up of more precarious, scattered civic forces.

On the other hand, these factors can all be the basis of quite opposite dynamics. A mass membership and institutional longevity can be a source of cautiousness, of a union leadership putting protection of the institution, or a short-term view of members' interests before a more transformative, but perhaps riskier approach.

Similarly, links with political parties can enable unions, from the autonomous political base of a campaigning alliance around alternatives to privatization, to exert political bargaining power to counter private elite pressures on political parties and require political institutions to open up to the alternatives—as we saw in Brazil and Uruguay. On the other hand, close links with political parties can be the basis for passiveness amongst union members once the party, which the union has spent time and money supporting, wins office. The widespread assumption then is that protecting, expanding, and improving public services can be left to the government. This has been a major problem in South Africa, for example, where unions originally invested much in the ANC government.

Given that the potential of trade union capacities and resources for democratic social change are so ambivalent, the challenge of privatization poses major questions for the future of public sector unions. Uruguay and Brazil illustrate the possibilities for unions as co-drivers of democratization, but the unions in those countries had a very particular history of struggle: producing a highly political and participatory kind of trade unionism. And even in those countries, it requires concerted organization and education to sustain these traditions over the generations. These positive experiences must be balanced by the hostile balance of forces faced by Samwu in the mid- to late 1990s, as the ANC submitted to the pressure of the global market. Samwu's predicament led Roger Ronnie to warn of the limits of trade unions as organizations always involved in negotiations as well as in militancy. "Sometimes", he said, reflecting on experiences working with militant community organizations, "too many hopes were projected onto SAMWU, as if it could provide solutions to problems that were more political than even a radical trade union could resolve" (author interview with Roger Ronnie, August 2010).

A useful focus for future work, then, would be to look at those collaborations between trade unions and others that have proven effective, to identify the complementarities between varied movements and different kinds of organizations, and to explore how the collaboration took account of the strengths and limits of each. It would also be important to recognize that increasingly we are not talking just about campaigning organizations but organizations that are also bringing about changes in the present, trying to remedy immediate problems and prefigure a desirable future.

ACKNOWLEDGEMENTS

Discussions with many people helped me to write this chapter. In addition to comments from the editors, feedback from Daniel Chavez, David Hall, and Susan Spronk on an earlier draft was very useful. Kenny Bell, Marco Berlinguer, Gonzalo Berron, Roy Bhaskar, Fiona Dove, Rolv Hanssen, Patrick Kane, Satoko Kishimoto, Martin McIvor, Steve Platt, Jane Shallice, and Michelle Wenderlich have also helped along the way. I want to dedicate this chapter to the memory of my mum, Joyce Wainwright, in whose greenhouse I did much of the work on this chapter and on whose telephone I conducted many of the interviews.

REFERENCES

Anderson, P. 1967. Limits and possibilities of trade union action. In Blackburn, R. and A Cockburn, A. (Eds), *The incompatibles: Trade union militancy and the consensus*, pp. 276–278. London: Penguin.

Bayliss, K. 2001. The World Bank and privatization: A flawed development tool. *Global Focus* 13(2): 95–103.

Bond, P. 2002. *Against global apartheid: South Africa meets the World Bank, IMF and International Finance*. Cape Town: University of Cape Town Press.

Chavez, D. 2006. Participation lite: the watering down of people power in Porto Alegre. Transnational Institute. www.tni.org/article/participation-lite-watering-down-people-power-porto-alegre (accessed 4 December 2011)

de Oliveira Filho, A. 2002. Brazil: Struggle against the privatization of water. www.psiru.org.

Eley, G. 2002. *Forging Democracy: The History of the Left in Europe, 1850-2000*. Oxford: Oxford University Press.

Elson, D. 1979. The value theory of labour. In Elson, D. (Ed), *Value: The representation of labour in capitalism*, pp. 127–180. London: CSE Books /Humanities Press.

Hall, D., Bayliss, K. and Lobina, E. 2002. *Water privatization in Africa*. PSIRU Report, University of Greenwich. London: PSIRU.

Hall, D., Lobina, E. and de La Motte, R. 2005. Public resistance to privatization in water and electricity. In Chavez, D. (Ed), *Beyond the market: The future of public services*, pp. 187–195. Amsterdam: Transnational Institute.

Hall, D., Lobina, E., Corral, V., Hoedeman, O., Terhorst, P., Pigeon, M. and Kishomoto, S. 2009. *Public-public partnerships (PUPs) in water*. Amsterdam: PSIRU, PSI, and TNI.

Huws, U. (in press). The 2008 crisis as opportunity: A new phase in capital accumulation based on the commodification of public services. *Socialist Register*.

Keck, M.E. 1992. *The workers party and democratisation in Brazil*. New Haven: Yale University Press.

Keck, M.E. and Sikkink, K. 1998. *Activists beyond borders: Advocacy networks in international politics*. Ithaca: Cornell University Press.

Mair, P. 2006. *Party system change: Approaches and interpretations*. Oxford: Oxford University Press.

Maltz, Hélio. 2005. El agua en Porto Alegre: Un bien público y universal. In Balanyá, B., Brennan, B., Hoedeman, O., Kishimoto, S. and Terhorst, P. (Eds), *Por un modelo público de agua: Triunfos, luchas y sueños*, pp. 33-40. Transnational Institute and Corporate Europe Observatory.

Mawbey, J. 2007. SAMWU and 20 years of municipal labour struggle. *Labour Bulletin* 31(4).

McDonald, D.A. and Smith, L. 2002. Privatizing Cape Town: Service delivery and policy reforms since 1996. Municipal Services Project Occasional Paper No 7. Cape Town: MSP.

Miliband, R. 1961. *Parliamentary socialism: A study of the politics of labor*. New York: Monthly Review Press.

Ngwane, T. 2010. Labour strikes and community protests: Is there a basis for unity in post-apartheid South Africa? Paper presented at the Decade of Dissent Symposium, University of Johannesburg, South Africa, 12–14 November.

Novelli, M. 2004. Globalisations, social movement unionism and new internationalisms: The role of strategic learning in the transformation of the municipal workers union of EMCALI. *Globalisation, Societies and Education* 2(2): 161–190.

———. 2010. Thinking through transnational solidarity: The case of SINTREAM-CALI in Colombia. In Bieler, A. and Lindberg, I. (Eds), *Global restructuring, labour and the challenges for transnational solidarity*, pp. 64–79. New York: Routledge.

Novelli, M. and Ferus-Comelo, A. 2010. *Globalisation, knowledge and labour: Education for solidarity within spaces of resistance*. New York: Routledge.

Ogden, S. 1991. The trade union campaign against water privatization: Industrial impotence or political maturity? *Industrial Relations Journal* 11(1): 20–35.

Patroni, V. and Poitras, M. 2002. Labour in neoliberal Latin America: An introduction. *Labour, Capital and Society* 35:2: 207–220.

Samwu. 2002. The Samwu fight against privatization and strategic engagement with the ANC. Discussion document. Samwu. Mimeo.

Sassen, S. 2006. *Territory, authority, rights: From medieval to global assemblages*. Princeton, NJ: Princeton University Press.

Sassoon, D. 1996. *One hundred years of socialism: The West European Left in the twentieth century*. New York: New Press.

Satgar, V. 2008. Neoliberalized South Africa: Labour and the roots of passive revolution. *Labour, Capital and Society* 41(2): 45–61.

Spronk, S. 2009. Water privatization and the prospects for trade union revitalization in the public sector: Case studies from Bolivia and Peru. *Just Labour: A Canadian Journal of Work and Society* 14: 164–176.

———. 2010. Water and sanitation utilities in the global South: Re-centering the debate on "efficiency". *Radical Review of Political Economics* 42(2): 156–174.

Taks, J. 2008. El agua es de todos/Water for all: Water resources and development in Uruguay. *Development* 51: 17–22.

Tapia, L. 2008. Constitution and Constitutional Reform in Bolivia. In Crabtree, J. and Whitehead, L. (Eds), *Unresolved tensions: Bolivia past and present*, pp. 160-171. Pittsburgh, PA: University of Pittsburgh Press.

Tattersall, A. 2005. There is power in coalition: A framework for assessing how and when union-community coalitions are effective and enhance union power. *Labour and Industry* 16(2): 97–112.

Terhorst, P. 2008. Huancayo: From resistance to public-public partnership. In Balanyá, B., Brennan, B., Hoedeman, O., Kishimoto, S. and Terhorst, P. (Eds),

Reclaiming public water: Achievements, struggles, and visions from around the world, pp. 32–41. Porto Alegre, Brazil: Transnational Institute and Corporate Europe Observatory.

———. 2011. Public community partnerships in Peru and Uruguay. Paper prepared for the Platform for Public Community Partnerships of the Americas Water Justice Group of the Reclaiming Public Water Network. www.tni.org/sites/www.tni.org/files/Water_interview%20on%20public-community%20partnerships%20in%20peru%20and%20uruguay.pdf.

Terry, M. (Ed). 2000. *Redefining public sector unionism.* New York: Routledge.

Travis, D. 2008. Collective management strategies and elite resistance in Cochabamba, Bolivia. *Development* 51: 89–95.

RDP (Reconstruction and Development Programme). 1994. RDP policy framework. Pretoria: Government of South Africa.

Van de Walt, L., Mokoena, D. and Sakhile, S. 2001. Cleaned out outsourcing at wits. *SA Labour Bulletin* 25(4): 12–15.

Van Niekerk, S. 1998. Privatization: A working alternative. *SA Labour Bulletin* 22(5): 24–27.

von Holdt, K. 2010. Institutionalisation, strike violence and local moral orders. *Transformation: Critical Perspectives on Southern Africa* 72: 127-151.

von Holdt, K. and Maserumule, B. 2005. After apartheid: Decay or reconstruction? Transition in a public hospital. In Webster, E. and Von Holdt, K. (Eds), *Beyond the apartheid workplace: Studies in transition.* Scottsville, South Africa: University of Kwazulu-Natal Press.

Yesmin-Mannan, F. 2009. Corporatizing Dhaka water supply and sewerage authority, Bangladesh. MA thesis. Queen's University, Kingston, Ontario, Canada.

Wainwright, H. 2009. *Reclaim the state, experiments in popular democracy.* London: Seagull.

Wainwright, H. and Little, M. 2009. *Public service reform, but not as we know it.* London: Picnic Books with UNISON.

INTERVIEWS

Adriana Marquisio, President of FFOSE, 2004–2010

Carmen Sosa, FFOSE organizer and representative on the CNDAV

Carlos Todeschini, General Direct DMAE and City Counselor, Porto Alegre, Brazil

David Boys, Utilities Officer at PSI

Devan Pillay, Professor Department of Sociology, University of the Witwatersrand, South Africa

Dan Gillin, Chair of the Global Labour Institute and past General Secretary of the International Union of Food Workers, 1968–1997

Guatam Moby, Coordinator, the New Trade Union Initiative, Delhi, India

Joao Avamileno, founder member of CUT and former PT Vice Mayor of Santo Andre

Karl von Holdt, formerly worked at NALEDI, a research unit linked to Cosatu, and now works for the Society, Work and Development Institute

Kjeld Jacobsen, Former International Secretary of CUT

Maria Selva Ortiz, REDES, Friends of the Earth Uruguay.

Pat Horne, Coordinator Streetnet, South Africa

Roger Ronnie, General Secretary, Samwu 1995–1997, 2000–2007

The late Selso Daniel, PT Mayor of Santo Andre, Brazil

Sergio Baerlie, Coordinator Cidade, Porto Alegre, Brazil

Trevor Ngwane, ex-ANC Councillor, helped to found the Anti-Privatization Forum and the Soweto Crisis Committee

5 Gendering Justice, Building Alternative Futures

Chandra Talpade Mohanty
and Sarah Miraglia

> We want guaranteed access to basic services such as telecommunications, energy, health and water. Moreover, we want to live in a world without war, with social justice, with equity, where men don't dominate women, where children don't have to work in cane fields or in factories, where children don't roam the streets without hope. With this desire, when our various organisations come together, we know this movement has a bright future. America is destined to be the continent of hope and life. And our struggles will show that, though we might not experience it in our lifetime, we will have added a grain of sand to the pile. (Reyes 2009, 18)

Erasto Reyes reminds us of a vision for social and economic justice that fuels continuing struggles for liberation in the 21st century. While neoliberal cultures inevitably place capitalist interests above the needs and hopes of people, it is people's movements (anti-colonial/anti-imperial, peasant, ecological, labour, women's, peace and justice, anti-globalization, etc) that have exposed the fault lines of neoliberal capitalism and placed questions of democracy, equity, and justice at the centre of struggles for emancipation. A decade into the 21st century, we face an unprecedented consolidation (and crisis) of social, economic, and political power fueled by the conjuncture of relentless neoliberalism, masculinist religious fundamentalisms, rampant militarisms, resurgent racisms, and the criminalization of minoritized populations in many countries. This chapter argues that gender equity and women's agency are core components of envisioning anti-capitalist struggles for social and economic justice, in general, and for enacting alternatives to privatization, in particular.

The first section interrogates the politics of economic restructuring, arguing that neoliberal reforms have effectively worked to reprivatize women through "empowerment" projects that entail the commodification of public services and participatory projects. The next section takes us *beyond* a critique of neoliberalism, developing an argument that counters the disempowering effects of commodified public services, suggesting that rather than seeking to "empower" women, alternatives need to focus on women's agency in struggles for social and economic justice. Our review of gender equity in "alternatives to privatization" highlights the complex nature of working in and through established governance structures and within institutional settings and argues for models of action that work to create the infrastructure necessary for women's strategic interests. Finally, we introduce an analytical framework that allows us to see women's agency through their struggles around the body, the environment, and diverse economies—through place-based struggles that originate in the lived experiences of women struggling against neoliberal reforms.

Feminist scholarship and activism in the last several decades has shown conclusively that gender is constitutive of economic and political structures of governance, that gender ideologies and representations consolidate hierarchical relations of rule globally, and that peoples' subjectivities and identities are profoundly gendered. Thus, any project that seeks to confront the hierarchical and unjust relations of rule embedded in processes of privatization and commercialization must engage with the everyday politics of gender. Fundamentally, a gendered analysis assumes attentiveness to unequal male/female power relations and a commitment to gender justice—i.e. strategies to eliminate the subordination and impoverishment of women. Gendered analysis does not assume that women are uniformly or universally subordinated or that women in different places, spaces, and cultures face identical challenges (Anzaldua and Moraga 1981, Davis 1985, Mohanty 1986, Jayawardena 1995). Class, caste, sexuality, religion, culture, ability, and race/ethnicity/indigeneity all intervene to position women in different *and* similar relationships to power and inequality. In addition, patriarchal histories of colonialism, racism, and capitalist exploitation position communities of women in the global South and North in different, yet comparable, relationships to each other, to the state, and to transnational governance structures. Women in the global South bear the brunt of the current economic order.

Speaking of the Americas, Beckman suggests that, while "'Old' forms of domination such as patriarchy, capitalism and racism remained in place . . . neoliberal economic and political arrangements have exacerbated the feminization of poverty across the region" (2001, 32). In other words, neoliberal economic policies further cheapen women's labour in the workplace, simultaneously increasing their labour in the home via the dismantling of social services in particular, and the welfare state in general. Privatization and commercialization constitute key aspects of neoliberal restructuring in the global South. Privatization recasts the principles of democratic governance, leading to the abdication of responsibility and shift in power and accountability from governments to private corporations, transforming the "structures of entitlements" (Elson 1995) in ways that are most injurious for the poor, especially poor women who subsidize the environmental costs of overconsumption. Power relations of gender, class, and race/ethnicity are reconfigured through the mechanism of feminization as devaluation. What many analysts refer to as the "feminization of labour" operates through a devalorization of the labour and skill involved in performing tasks, simultaneously reducing wages for jobs considered "feminized". The feminization of labour has led to the marginalization of men in the workforce, and this loss of a male income leaves households with very few resources for survival, pushing more families into poverty. Thus, gender analysis and questions of women's rights and agency remain central to envisioning and enacting alternatives to privatization in the global South

This chapter suggests a relational, complex understanding of gender. We speak of gender as, (i) a theoretical lens and an epistemological project (gender in relation to meaning systems—ideologies, theories, paradigms), (ii) an apparatus of governance embedded in institutions of rule (gendered structures, practices and forms of social reproduction), and (iii) as lived cultures—gendered subjectivities, self and collective identities (Marchand and Runyan 2000, Nagar and Writers 2006, Ahlers and Zwarteveen 2009). Our analysis is anchored in an anti-racist, materialist feminist framework that links everyday life and local gendered histories and ideologies to larger, transnational/global structures and ideologies of capitalism through a gendered "place-based" framework (Harcourt and Escobar 2005). This particular framework draws on historical materialism and centralizes a differentiated notion of gendered struggles anchored in the bodies, environments, and economies of the most marginalized communities of women—poor and indigenous women in affluent and neocolonial nations and women from the global South (Mohanty 2003). We suggest that an experiential and analytic grounding in the lives and struggles of marginalized communities of women (urban poor, working class, peasant, indigenous, etc) provides the most inclusive paradigm for advocating gender justice in the creation of alternatives to privatization.

We agree with Fine and Hall (see Chapter 3, this volume) in their call for public sector systems of provision that utilize an "approach that needs to be contextually driven rather than as a . . . universal theory". However, our call for a particularized framing is coupled with a vision of gender justice that is both expansive and universal. We envision a world that values and promotes gender justice within households and the larger polity; a world in which legacies of colonialism, violence, poverty, and deprivation are acknowledged and actively resisted. We work and struggle for a post-capitalist world, for what many people refer to as a "solidarity economy"—one that values cooperation and interdependency above profit and greed. Our work is dedicated to the feminist struggle for gender justice—to an expansive and universal vision, anchored in the differences and specificities of women's lives. In our discussion of alternatives to privatization, gender justice (the elimination of hierarchies and unequal power based on gender) is central to socio-economic practices and structural arrangements that value equity in access to resources, participation, leadership, and the politics of knowledge.

Some of the questions pertaining to a gendered analysis of privatization and commercialization include a *gendering* of the left critique of neoliberalism in Africa, Asia, and Latin America, a critique of global restructuring in terms of the gendered impact of policies/practices and implications for gender equity and finally, a focus on the ways in which women cope, adjust, resist, and advocate for their communities and on their own behalf (i.e. women's agency). In concrete terms, this gendering of the left critique includes a shift away from treating "the poor", "the worker", or "the peasant" as homogenous identity groups, to being attentive to the ways in which gender, race, ethnicity, and nation inflect and constitute each identity in ways that shape the opportunities and constraints faced by women and men positioned differentially in hierarchies of power, privilege, and exclusion utilizing an intersectional approach. For example, the particularities of poor, indigenous women's lives in Latin America are different from (and similar to) the lives and struggles of poor male peasants in South Asia. While each group may be "poor", the challenges faced by the different communities can only be understood if gender, race, and ethnic particularities are taken into account. These are some of the questions we address in what follows.

GENDERING NEOLIBERALISM

Colonial legacies, neoliberal frameworks

Colonial legacies and patriarchal structures, as well as ideologies and practices of masculinist, class, and race/caste supremacy, underlie social relations and institutions that constitute neoliberal economic and political orders. Legacies of colonialism include capitalist processes of recolonization that consolidate and exacerbate relations of domination and exploitation by making use of existing social divisions to further the goal of profit maximization (Alexander and Mohanty 1997, xvii). As Sen suggests, "Faced with intransigent social structures and rigid hierarchies such as those based on gender, race, or caste, the expansion of commerce builds on these hierarchies, altering and reshaping them in the process, and transforming the life experiences of those involved" (1996, 821). In fact it is colonial legacies of racialized patriarchies that underlie the division of labour in contemporary capitalist cultures. Maria Mies (1984) theorizes colonization and "housewifization" as linked processes of racialized gender that were instituted by colonial powers during the 18th and 19th century to extract maximum profit from women's labour in the colonies and at "home". Thus, while slave women's "productive" labour was valorized, and reproductive labour controlled because it led to loss of profit, bourgeois women in the metropole were subjected to a process of housewifization that valorized their reproductive roles, withdrawing them from the public sphere, simultaneously constructing gender regimes of public/private spheres. It is these very processes of race, class, and gender differentiation in the service of capital exploitation that traffic in the present. Since the 1970s, US feminist economists have critiqued the notion of "hegemonic economic man" (a self-made man: narrowly self-interested, competitive, individualistic, and motivated by greed) that developed historically in 19th-century Europe and the US. The "economic woman" required by this hegemonic notion of masculine personhood tended to be the full-time homemaker-wife, a racialized, class-specific, and heteronormative notion of womanhood (Matthaei 1982). However, while public/private distinctions have been the basis of gendered regimes since post-15th century colonialism, an intersectional approach that is attentive to race and class particularities suggests that women in the global South, and poor, immigrant and women of colour in the global North do not fall neatly into the homemaker-wife or "economic woman" designations.

Neoliberalized global restructuring has drawn on these colonial legacies to consolidate the current regime of international debt, development aid, and the so-called structural adjustment of the economies and governance structures of developing countries. Marchand and Runyan (2000) argue that global restructuring reworks practices and meanings of masculinity/femininity by shifting the boundaries and meanings of public/private, domestic/international, and local/global. Feminist scholars of global restructuring claim that the relations of domination and the economic and political hierarchies instituted by neoliberal cultures are profoundly gendered and could not be sustained without the gendered symbolism and metaphors that serve to "naturalize" the gendered division of labour that underlies processes of economic restructuring. The withdrawal of government responsibility for social welfare has resulted in the transfer of these obligations to women, a process that Babb (1996) refers to as women "absorbing the shocks" of adjusting economies. In essence, women subsidize processes of economic liberalization, both through unpaid labour in the home and paid labour in formal and informal work (Beneria 1999). It is erroneous, however, to construe public and private spaces as discrete spaces. As Pitkin and Bedoya suggest, "Production and reproduction overlap and often occupy the same space in women's lives" (1997, 47). Women's work in the home is increased in a number of ways that are often directly related to changes in the public sphere. They have to work harder to collect water, provide food, ensure health, and supplement household incomes due to cuts in health, education, and food subsidies and the privatization of water, which often has detrimental effects on the poorest women.

Over three decades of feminist activism and scholarship in the global South, from the early critiques of the impact of economic development on poor "Third World" women by DAWN (Sen and Grown 1987), to more recent analysis by the Feminist Initiative of Cartagena (2003), point to the profoundly negative effects of mainstream development policies, and SAPs (structural adjustment programmes) anchored in neoliberal paradigms. The 1980s to early 1990s witnessed the sustained engagement of development discourse by feminists via the United Nations (UN) world conferences on women and the entry of women's movement activists into international governing bodies and non-governmental organizations (NGOs) focusing on women's issues. Harcourt (2006) argues that this engagement of international governance structures by women's rights advocates resulted in a "professionalization" of development and a proliferation of NGOs on women's issues leading to a depoliticization of radical gender justice projects and the creation of a management apparatus of development. It is this particular development discourse, backed up by UN statistics, texts, case studies, and reports that partially fueled the managerial and bureaucratized neoliberal policies, in turn, discursively producing a generic, gendered female body with a particular set of needs and rights, thus potentially erasing differences among women. The radical feminist critiques of SAPs and privatization thus resulted at this time in an organizational focus on "gender mainstreaming" (as evidenced through static measures of gender parity in development plans and projects and/or women's participation in the private sphere), not gender justice (an analysis of gendered power hierarchies that unearth and destabilize the roots of gendered forms of inequality; a project often regarded as meddling in the "cultural" affairs of "other" nations).

From gender mainstreaming to women's empowerment: Reprivatizing women through health, water and electricity projects

Gender mainstreaming was agreed upon as the "global strategy for the promotion of gender equality" (Manase et al, 2003, Panda 2007) in the 1995 Beijing Platform for Action (the Fourth World Conference on Women). In some ways, gender mainstreaming represents the gains made through the persistence and struggle of thousands of women around the world whose activism and advocacy persuaded international organizations to rectify gendered silences and omissions in international policies. But it also represents ongoing negotiations and contestations between women-based/feminist groups and the members of the UN system and ostensibly the larger development industry (Mukhopadhyay 2004). While the goal of gender mainstreaming was to bring women's issues to the centre of development agendas and to move away from "the earlier 'add women and stir approach'" (Subrahmanian 2004, 89), it has fallen short of actually transforming gendered inequalities in development plans. As Mukhopadhyay argues, "feminist concerns with the political project of equality are being normalised in the development business as an ahistorical, apolitical, decontextualised and technical project that leaves the prevailing and unequal power relations intact" (2004, 100). Despite—and partly because of—the attempts to make gender politically viable within international organizations and NGOs, gender mainstreaming has more often than not failed to rectify gender inequalities, though it has spurred debates on methods and strategies. This policy dialectic—the relationship between activists, advocates, and planners—has generated a new/old paradigm emphasis on "women's empowerment" as a strategy for gendering development.

The empowerment approach, we argue, is gender mainstreaming adapted to a neoliberal ideological agenda. On the surface, women's empowerment is concerned with promoting equality of access to resources, and power in decision making for women, but in practice it works to conceal deep-seated social, political, and economic inequalities that need to be addressed to make real, meaningful change. Empowerment approaches tend to individualize gender equity, subject gendered interests to tests of market efficiency, and essentially *reprivatize* women through a marriage of "efficiency, productivity and empowerment" (Cleaver 1998, 294). This marriage of objectives is enacted on the ground through the commodification of resources and the decentralization of resource management, which also is a process of commodification as it relies on the "free labour" of community members to enact the project (Aguilar 2005; what Elson [1995] refers to as the "cash and committee" approach). The introduction of commodified public services, it was argued, would increase access for millions. On the whole, this prediction has not played out in practice. Billions continue to lack access to safe drinking water, sanitation, electricity, and health care. Worse yet, not only have women not gained access to these vital services, but also in many cases they have lost government subsidies for them and/or the total provision of them. The gap between what can be paid and what commodified services cost, and/or the loss of the service altogether, is filled in by women's labour. In very concrete ways, neoliberal policies have "privatized social reproduction" by reprivatizing women's labour (Roberts 2008). In the following, we highlight some of the problematics of this approach to gender and service delivery.

The costs of commodified public services

One means of commodification is the introduction of user fees and "full cost recovery" programmes into systems of public service delivery. Katz (2001, cited in Roberts 2008) identifies this process of commodification as one that moved from pricing schemes that valued "social equity" (paying what one could afford) to "economic equity" (users must pay for the full costs of the resource). Proponents of this system argue that user fees compel consumers to make judicious choices in their use of the good. What are not accounted for in these models are the consequences of an inability to pay. In the field of health care, for example, Nanda (2002) found that women's rates of utilization of health care decreased dramatically in several African nations after the introduction of user fees, thus jeopardizing women's health. Nanda similarly shows that maternal death rates increased by 56% in the Zaria region of Nigeria as a result of an inability to pay user fees.

In this case, women could not afford maternity care and thus suffered the consequences of unattended births. Commodified services have multiplicative effects as well. Brown's (2010) study of water privatization in Tanzania shows how an inability to pay for water makes HIV/AIDS care increasingly difficult, particularly in Tanzania, where home-based care for HIV/AIDS patients is policy. In this case, an inability to pay for water jeopardizes women's safety as at-home caregivers. Thus, not only is the patient's health put at risk, but so too is the health of the caregiver.

In the electricity sector, neoliberal reforms have had similarly detrimental effects because planners have tended to focus on supply-side concerns that value profit over equity and prioritize industrial consumption (Clancy 2000, UNESCAP 2003). The supply-side focus has marginalized the energy needs of women through a lack of policy attention to biomass fuels, which are largely used by the poor in both rural and urban settings (Clancy 2000, Batliwala and Reddy 2003). Women's health is put at risk by the lack of attention to biomass fuels; they are tasked with the responsibility of collecting biomass fuels and also with cooking responsibilities that have particularly adverse, though well-known health effects (Holdren and Smith 2000, Reddy 2000). The World Bank, for example, "classed indoor air pollution in LDCs [least developed countries] among the four most critical global environmental problems" (Cecelski 2000, 18). Beyond indoor pollution, the use of biomass fuels puts women at risk of injuries related to collecting firewood and inhibits school participation by young girls who often work alongside their mothers to collect biomass energy sources. In these ways, women's labour becomes a subsidy for supply-side electricity reforms.

The costs of supply-side reforms are often compounded by the rising costs of energy, and by the loss of government fuel subsidies (Clancy 2002). Taken together, these reforms work to further marginalize rural populations in poverty where electrification requires costly infrastructure that investors are unwilling to take on given low expectations for a return of profit (Zomers 2003). The gap between rural and urban electricity access is the greatest in Sub-Saharan Africa where Hall (2007) shows that 54% of households in urban areas have access, versus 8.3% access in rural areas. Though significant, the gap between rural and urban access is crosscut by race, class, and gender inequalities. For example, Annecke's research on the South African electricity sector notes that, "The 46% of households that are not yet electrified are usually those housing poor, black women in rural areas, further marginalized as a result of their lack of access to electric power" (2009, 291). Additionally, McDonald (2009) argues that although connections to the grid have been made possible, millions of South Africans continue to live without electricity because they are unable to afford the service under cost-reflexive pricing schemes. These findings suggest that increasing connections may work to bridge the rural/urban gap in service, but poor communities will continue to lack adequate access when economic efficiency is valued over social equity.

One of the primary arguments for the commodification and/or privatization of public services is that it will allow governments to save money. However, actual savings have been the exception rather than the rule. Such was the case in Buenos Aires when the International Finance Corporation (IFC) provided funding to distribution companies to reduce electricity theft by terminating "illegal" connections. The terminations resulted in lawsuits being brought against corporate distributors, which argued that privatization deprived people of basic services. The lawsuit ended with the government subsidizing the costs of hook-ups for the unserved populations (World Resources Institute 2002). As such, while the urban poor received electricity in Buenos Aires, it was the actions of the government—not the corporation—that ensured such access. As this case illustrates, government spending on energy has often increased rather than decreased leaving fewer resources available for the provision of basic welfare services (Bayliss 2001). In another example from the health sector, Bernal et al (1999) show budget cuts resulting from economic restructuring work to inhibit the provision of legalized access to abortion. Though Mexican political leaders have signed on to statements that call for greater access to reproductive health care, they are able to sidestep this controversial issue by arguing that they lack adequate funding to materialize that mandate.

Gender and politics of "community" participation

The participatory approach to resource management co-constitutes a process of donor-driven decentralization of governance and has become *sine qua non* for development agencies. Participation, it is argued, creates commitment to a project, ensures efficiency, accountability, and transparency, democratizing decision making through bottom-up processes, and enables empowerment for women and marginalized groups (Resurreccion et al, 2004, Beall 2005). The focus on decentralizing management, feminists hoped, would open the door for women to gain measures of control over natural resource management and, ostensibly, access to natural resources (Zwarteveen and Meinzen-Dick 2001). However, these hopes have not fleshed out in practice. Instead, feminist advocates and activists point out that women's relationships to water are essentialized according to a gendered division of labour, communities are conceptualized as homogenous in their interests, and households are treated as a congruent unit of interests. Finally, there are also critiques of the meaningfulness of participation, which can vary greatly from "nominal" to "empowering" (Agarwal 2001) with direct consequences for how a project is structured and to what degree it meets the needs of all community members.

Much of the development work on gender and water tends towards an essentialization of women's relationships to water and fails to problematize the socially constructed division of labour informing these roles (Meinzen-Dick and Zwarteveen 1998, Sultana 2009). In mainstream policy literature, women's uses of water are typically limited to their uses in the domestic sphere, including washing, cleaning, and reproductive work. The essentialization of women's uses of water casts their activities as predominately rooted in their "natural" role as caretakers (Cleaver 2000, 61). Taking for granted the idea that women primarily use water for domestic purposes fails to question the socially constructed division of labour. Zwarteveen and Meinzen-Dick (2001) provide a useful corrective, arguing that women's uses of water should not be seen as a product of their natural gender roles but as produced by a naturalization of gender inequality. They ask if policy makers would observe different uses of water for women if there were structures in place that allowed such uses. The essentialization of women's uses of water is representative of narrowly construed resource management schemes. These abstractions make it easier to design a universalized approach, but the flattening out of difference forecloses the potential for these projects to produce meaningful changes in women's lives.

Treating the community as a homogenous entity has serious consequences for the structure of a community-based group and the distribution of benefits. Without a nuanced approach to the community, privileged community members are more likely to become the primary contacts (referred to as "elite capture") for participatory projects (van Koppen 1998, Sultana 2009), perpetuating and/or exacerbating "naturalized" inequalities (Resurreccion et al, 2004, Boelens and Zwarteveen 2005, Karim 2006). For instance, in the Chhattis Mauja irrigation scheme in Nepal, a local woman leader volunteered to act as a village leader, called a *muktiyar*. Though she was given the position, she was forced to resign after five months because the villagers would not accept a woman in this position (IFAD 2006). In this example, the leadership position was made available to women, but the project planners did not account for male resistance to a woman in a leadership position. Beyond male/female gender inequalities, an intersectional approach further compels a consideration of relations between women. For example, Singh's (2006) study of village-level water management committees in rural India found that although the majority of women were vastly under-represented at the meetings, upper caste women were more likely to have their needs met because, unlike lower caste women, their interests were represented by male family members. The result was that in two different instances, hand pumps were located in places considered to be the province of upper caste members. The lack of accountability for the poorest members means that the benefits of community-based projects tend to accrue to more powerful members in a given community with gender being mediated by race/caste/class.

As with the water sector, energy sector projects treat communities and households as unitary in their goals and interests. As a UNESCAP report argues, "technologies and innovations that are actually targeted for women are based on perceptions and preferences of men" (2003, 21). Similarly, Annecke (2009) reports that even when the benefits of energy interventions are meant to accrue to women the unequal status of women permits male community and household members to reap the benefits of those projects. Cecelski (2000) and Skutsch (2005) add an intersectional dimension to this discussion by arguing that within groups of women, it is also necessary to give attention to the energy uses of various classes of women or women from different castes. As Cecelski (2000) notes, the benefits of rural electrification programmes tend to accrue to wealthier families, including, of course, women. In these ways, to homogenize groups of women, as mainstream development projects often do, is to miss opportunities to provide equitable services to those who need them most.

Community-based projects also operate at the household level where, similar to homogenization at the community level, an assumed "congruency of interests" (Upadhyay 2005) between men and women means that women's interests are not adequately represented in the project. Project planners are more likely to meet with male members of the household and are sometimes apt to not speak with women at all (Clancy 2000, Udas and Zwarteveen 2010). This model also assumes there is a male breadwinner in each family, which conceals a number of realities faced by women. In the agricultural sector, access to water is often dependent on ownership of property. However, many women are prohibited from land ownership, which by extension prohibits them from owning the water sources (natural or constructed) on that land. This, in turn, effectively erases the fact that women—as well as men—are also farmers, either by themselves or alongside husbands or children. Women are further marginalized when land ownership determines the selection of participants in community-based agricultural groups, as was the case in a project designed to optimize the scarce water supply in Llullucha, Peru (Delgado 2005). The project was organized by the *Instituto de Manejo de Agua y Medio Ambiente* (IMA; a government entity), which chose a participatory approach that engaged the local *comuneros*. The comuneros form a group of registered landowners and an all-male group. Through this focus, the IMA effectively excluded women from participation. The result was that women protested the irrigation system that did not allow water to flow into the waterholes that they used to care for livestock. As a consequence of women's protests, project planners were forced to alter their plans (Delgado 2005). Similarly, in the energy sector, the disenfranchisement of women at the household level has contributed to the devaluation of women's labour expenditures and the neglect of women's energy needs (Reddy 2000). For example, Clancy (2002) finds that male control over household funds often means that investments are not made in technologies that would make women's tasks easier or safer. As these examples make clear, energy policies are not gender neutral, as is assumed by energy experts. The failure of these experts to include gendered analyses reverberates in the reprivatization of women's labour.

Finally, participation can also be problematically construed solely as economic exchange. This approach to participation reprivatizes women (and men) in the form of consumer-citizens whose participation consists of market transactions rather than meaningful democratic participation. For example, in the water sector in Mexico, Castro argues that "[t]he prevailing notion of user participation is mostly limited in practice to the expectation that users would become obedient customers who pay their water bills punctually" (2007, 764). O'Reilly similarly highlights the role that gender plays in the making of a modernized citizen-consumer by focusing on a water project that invoked modernization as a justification for women's empowerment through the commodification of water in Rajasthan, India: "the promotion of modern water by project staff ran parallel to a marketing of modern womanhood and consumerism coded as 'women's participation'" (2006, 962). In these examples, the rhetoric of participation operates as a thin disguise for the imposition of commodified service delivery.

In each of these sectors—water, electricity, and health—the imbrications between gender and neoliberalism have produced perverse consequences that pay lip service to gender equality, while advancing projects that undermine that goal. Women's workloads have increased through the removal of government subsidies, and they are reprivatized through participatory projects that fail to meet their needs but require their participation. Empowerment through participation is often a pretense that furthers project goals, but conceals the fact that women actively negotiate access to resources in their everyday lives. An alternative approach to gendering resource management would be attentive to the practices that women already employ to gain access to resources. As argued by Pradhan, alternative models should work to "find out how or in what ways women influence decisions even under conditions of structural subordination" (2003, 54). Rather than impose an empowerment agenda, we argue that alternative models would do well to seek out what Miraftab calls "invented spaces of participation", or those spaces "characterized by defiance that directly challenges the status quo" (2004, 4). Like Miraftab, we argue for attention to women's agency in the context of gender justice and imagining alternative futures—not in defending a patriarchal status quo or in the service of conservative social movements. Starting with women's transformative agential practices is a "bottom-up process" that builds on and broadens the agency that women already express. In the following sections, we review projects that recognize and build on women's agency, as opposed to projects that seek to *give* empowerment.

GENDER EQUITY: IMAGINING ALTERNATIVE FUTURES

The previous sections briefly reviewed feminist scholarship on neoliberalism and global restructuring, and privatization and commercialization in the water, health, and electricity sectors in the global South. The remainder of this chapter focuses on "alternatives", taking up the question of envisioning and enacting alternatives to privatization (and commercialization) that centralize gender equity and gender justice.

Struggles against private incursions are galvanizing new social movements that join together the efforts of diverse communities. These movements draw on and build up processes of participatory democracy that compel state actors to take seriously their mandate to govern in a manner consistent with the needs of the people. In this way, processes of privatization and commercialization should also be regarded as processes of politicization (Naples 2002). Thus, as suggested earlier, engaging the perspectives and experiences of those most marginalized by capital provides a fuller understanding of how capital operates and points towards strategies of resistance that can fundamentally transform social inequalities from the ground up.

We have sought a variety of sources to inform our analysis of gendered alternatives but locating sources that systematically review gendered alternatives has not been easy. While there is a growing body of literature that documents the rise of social movements against commercialization (most notably in regard to water and sanitation), there are far fewer resources that explicitly address the role of gender, particularly as it relates to race, nation, ethnicity, class, and/or caste. Many of the reports and articles we found give gendered concerns only a passing mention, noting that women are deeply affected by neoliberal policies but fail to explicate how they might become agents in the process of constructing alternatives. Many of the feminist analyses of gender in relation to the restructuring of health, water, and electricity centre on critiques of processes associated with commercialization, not necessarily on creating alternatives. In most cases we do not see women presented as agents and change makers. Our work here pieces together the stories of resource management projects that include partnerships between community-based groups, NGOs, governments, and international organizations that have made specific efforts to confront inequalities based on gender, race/ethnicity, class/caste, and/or indigenous identities.

Writing about Empire in the neoliberal age, Roy (2004, 66) argues passionately that no act that confronts Empire is too small. She urges us to resist by identifying "it's working parts, and dismantle them one by one. No target is too small. No victory is insignificant". It is in this spirit that we craft our vision of gender justice in the context of neoliberalism, global restructuring, and privatization. Fundamental to this vision, is the recognition that women have been key to late 20th-century social movements— indigenous, feminist, anti-racist, anti-colonial, environmental, labour, peasant, lesbian, gay, bisexual, and transexual (LGBT), and anti-globalization, creating and cross-pollinating more just, democratic, and sustainable economic values, practices, and institutions that many see as the basis of a new "solidarity economy". Feminist economists have long argued that the values of a solidarity economy—cooperation, equity in all its dimensions, economic democracy, local and community control, and sustainability—are commensurate with global struggles for gender justice (Nelson 2006, Allard and Matthaei 2008). While place-based struggles and contextual approaches to women's resistance to privatization and commercialization are key to understanding larger struggles for gendered economic justice, it is the universal principles embodied in the right to equity and dignity in varied economic practices, the right to clean, sanitary and sustainable living arrangements, the right to develop relationships and households based on autonomous sexual choices, the right to bear children or not, and even the right to leisure for working class/poor women that constitute the broad parameters of our vision of gender justice. Thus, documenting forms of resistance and evidence of alternative visions in the terms we have laid out in this chapter is itself an important contribution. Our hope is that activists, scholars, advocates, and practitioners will take up the tactics and strategies outlined below in pursuit of this vision of gender equity and more just and democratic systems of governance.

Governance practice, institutional settings, and women's agency

From the Chipko Movement to protect the forests in Northern India to *Las Madres de la Plaza de Mayo* in Argentina (Safa 1990) to the Cochabamba "Water War", women have been a formidable source of power and protest, but women have also seen their victories usurped as protest movements take on formalized structures. Molyneux's (1985) analysis of "women's emancipation" as it was taken up by the Sandinista government after the Nicaraguan Revolution provides insight into the processes that give rise to the subordination of women's interests. Molyneux distinguishes between "practical gender interests" and "strategic gender interests". Practical gender interests ease the hardships for women struggling under conditions of poverty but do not subvert the systems of inequality that perpetuate their subordination. Challenging those systems requires the development of strategic gender interests, those based on an "analysis of women's subordination and from the formulation of an alternative, more satisfactory set of arrangements to those which exist" (Molyneux 1985, 232). Thus, strategic gender interests work towards undoing gendered divisions of labour, male violence, and unequal political representation.

In many ways commitments to gender and participation have been used as a charitable front for profitable endeavours. The necessary focus on women's experiences has been overlooked in the process of developing "toolboxes" of gender mainstreaming techniques designed to expedite and streamline the process of creating new markets for commercialized water, sanitation, health, and electricity services, and although there are clear critiques of the role of international financial institutions, the analysis is a bit murkier in regard to the work of the UN bodies and the international NGOs that have taken shape around issues of gender inequality. Speaking of the gendered health initiatives emerging through global platforms, such as the International Conference on Population and Development (ICPD), Harcourt notes the complexities of women's engagement with international bodies: "While such global processes open up new spaces for women's solidarity and network building with the new communication technologies and new economic resources, it is also pushing women into new forms of poverty" (2003, 6–7). Broad policy commitments do not easily lend themselves to concrete, practical actions and are made more tenuous by the predictable tensions between stated interests in gender equality, programmatic commitments to a market-based system of service provision, and (in the case of health care in particular) the rising power of fundamentalist religious authorities (Shiva 2005). Harcourt's observation suggests that meaningful change does not begin at the top, but must be generated from the ground up, at local levels of experience and organizing.

Beyond protest and critique, people's movements are beginning to construct alternative practices and paradigms for access to and management of resources. The struggles over access to water, health, and electricity are also struggles for creating inclusive models of democratic governance that empower people (Balanyá et al, 2005). The question for us is how and to what extent women and/or women-based groups have been or can be part of the process of imagining and creating alternatives. Though it is certainly the case that community-managed resources are more accountable to the needs of people, it is also the case that gender, class/caste, religious, and racial/ethnic relations inform processes at the community level. Laurie's (2011) analysis of the roles of women in the Cochabamba "Water War" illustrates the contradictory gender relations embedded in this iconic struggle. Laurie found that while women were active members of the Cochabamba protests, they were also solely responsible for the reproductive work that was necessary to maintain the protests—cooking, providing water, and attending to families. Thus, while women were centrally involved in the "Water War", gendered ideologies and expectations may remain unchanged.

Opening doors: Rethinking women's participation and decision making

> The challenge is how to open doors, doors and not windows, doors and hopefully big doors so we can take over decision-making spaces. That doesn't mean just being present; I am tired of that kind of tokenism in which women leaders are delegated to the same domestic role within the board of directors in the water organization as in the homes. It's not enough to say that women hold a leadership position. We must ask: what is the quality of this post or what kinds of decisions are they allowed to make? (Gomez 2009, 15)

Gomez calls attention to the necessity of an approach to gendering alternative movements that goes beyond formal statements and participatory quotas, beyond visibility to the power to make decisions. The larger question here is how to move from the politics of representation to a politics of equity and justice. We have argued that gendered assumptions are embedded in systems and institutions, naturalized into discourses, practices, and policies that structure access and resource management, and give shape to the presumed roles and alleged capabilities of women that are deeply ingrained in local, state, national, and international contexts. Because gender is so integral to these processes, gender inequalities cannot be undone by simply ensuring that women gain numerical parity with men. Instead, a feminist approach is one that challenges gender inequalities in a way that builds on and develops women's agency (Ahlers and Zwarteveen 2009). The examples we review take steps to not merely bring women to the table but to enhance the power they have over decisions that affect their lives.

Bringing women to the table in meaningful ways has been a major challenge for women-based groups and gender advocates. A particularly trenchant issue has been the resistance of male community members to the increased public presence of women. There are, however, examples of women's groups and project teams that have effectively stifled male resistance and even induced male appreciation for women's active roles in resource management. The work of SEWA, the Self-Employed Women's Association (India), has been invaluable in this respect. The struggles over women's meaningful participation were brought into sharp relief through SEWA's "Women, Water and Work" campaign, which later became the "Millennium Water Campaign". The campaign covers 11 districts in 500 villages and seeks to bring women into water projects as active participants in the locally operated water boards and committees. Women were initially hesitant to serve on these boards, and male villagers were even more resistant: "[Men] were critical of women entering the public domain on this issue, and several went so far as to say they would not drink water from a source created by women. Many threatened not to work on water harvesting structures that would be managed by women. Some men openly said women would make financial blunders and force them to mortgage their lands (as all land titles are in men's names) to repay their debts" (Panda 2005, 8). Regarding itself as a "militant" organization, SEWA continued to facilitate the inclusion of women on water user committees despite this resistance. SEWA's persistence worked to increase women's agency in the water project but also within communities and homes. As Panda (2005) reports, the spheres of activities that women engage in have broadened to include new women-based institutions with strong links to governance structures.

Male resistance to women's roles in public spaces is not unique to SEWA's experience, but in some cases it has been so strong as to require alternative sites for women's participation. Such was the case in a community-based water management committee in the Ghogha Region of Gujarat, India, where a women's "self-help group" (SHG) was created. Ahmed (2005, 76) looks at one example of a SHG in the Ghogha Region that was formed by *Utthan*, a local NGO that facilitates the participation of local communities in the construction and maintenance of water supply systems. The *Utthan* project facilitators explicitly sought to increase the role of women in decision-making realms but found that male resistance was quite formidable. In the village of Neswad, women reported that male attendees would complain to their husbands about their wives' participation, thus acting as a form of social control on women's participation. *Utthan* opted to form a SHG, which Ahmed asserts to "provide a 'safe' place for women to voice their priorities and articulate their opinions" (2005, 79). In this case, the SHG operated as a site for women to voice their concerns and a stage from which to launch concerted actions that benefited women in particular and the community in general.

A Rural Energy Development Programme (REDP) in Nepal, a joint effort between the Nepalese government and the United Nations Development Programme (UNDP), also wanted to increase the role of women but recognized that specific efforts would need to be made to sensitize men to women's increased presence in the public arena. The project focused on creating community organizations (COs) that formed the basis for the functional groups, which are the decision-making bodies in regard to community energy needs. The REDP project considered it important to organize gender differentiated COs in order to provide a space for women to voice their concerns, noting that "in mixed groups women only tend to nod their heads in unison rather than genuinely participate in discussions and decisions" (Winrock, n.d.). Women-only COs are drawn into decision-making processes through the functional groups, which require membership of both male and female COs. The results of this project suggest that women have made gains beyond greater access to energy sources. In several districts, women manage the microhydro schemes, and, in some cases, husbands watched the children while their wives participated in the training to become managers. While gains appear to have been made through this project, the focus on gender is not met with a necessary focus on the role of caste in the villages where, as the report notes, caste hierarchies exist. It is not clear how or if the project conceptualized gender in relation to class/caste.

In some cases, women have organized themselves in attempts to fill the gaps in service left by unresponsive governments. In Northeast Brazil, a group of women began to notice that the Olho d'Agua River, located in Santa Cruz da Baixa Verde, was drying up, largely due to the effects of large-scale irrigation projects. The river was a lifeline to the women who made their homes along its banks. The Rural Women Workers Movement of Sertao Central (MMTR) and the Rural Workers Labour Union (STR), a municipal-level union, began to organize themselves and the community in order to save the river from "dying" (Branco and Almeida, 2002). At the time of Branco's writing about the project, it was in its initial stages but included plans to contact each of the families affected as a mobilization strategy, conduct workshops with all members of the community with the assistance of gender and environment experts, and involve local authorities in the project once a broad-based coalition had been formed. Though the project began through the efforts of women, men also became involved in the activities believing that saving the river will contribute to the sustainability of the community. In 2002, the project planners also began to make alliances with the Federation of Agricultural Workers (FETAPE), a state-level union. This project illustrates the process of women forming activist groups at the community level, while also making strides to connect to broader political goals and organizations. This strategy allows community groups to make connections to large-scale political processes through a bottom-up process of collective action.

While beginning with women's everyday experiences is necessary to the process of creating alternatives that are accountable to women, the continued marginalization of women's interests compels partnerships with groups and organizations outside of the local context in order to obtain funding, access to media and technical assistance. Gender budgeting advocates, for example, take this approach to organizing for women's interests. Gender budgeting initiatives (GBI) draw from the contestatory framework of Latin American public budgeting (PB) programmes but build on them by denaturalizing the assumed gender neutrality of the budgeting process. PB is a model of economic governance that devolves power over financial decision making to local levels of governance, where communities and civic groups engage in setting budget priorities and overseeing expenditures. PB experiments began at the municipal level through the work of community leaders and the Brazilian Democratic Movement (MDB) in São Paulo and Santa Catarina within the context of an authoritarian Brazilian government (Souza 2001). In this context, facilitating the participation of the people served to put pressure on an unresponsive government and worked to create systems of governance that were responsive to the needs of people. PB thus emerged as a challenge to the absolute power of strong, centralized governments, and these early examples set the stage for future attempts at redressing unequal and unaccountable government budgets. While the value of PB has surely been demonstrated in the Latin American context, the assumption that budgets are gender-neutral instruments has largely remained in place in those initiatives (UNIFEM 2009).

Since the mid-1980s, a series of budget initiatives have been launched in over 60 countries that extend the critical and participatory elements of PB beyond the assumed gender neutrality of conventional budgeting practices (Budlender and Hewitt 2003). These initiatives are models of collective action that include the efforts of international organizations, national, state, and local governments and NGOs working at the grassroots level. Gender budgeting facilitates an analysis of budgets at multiple levels of governance but can also be used to analyze the spending priorities of non-governmental entities (Villagomez 2004). The implementation of gender-budgeting initiatives at local levels of governance has particular relevance because decentralization has meant that public services are often provided at these local levels (Budlender and Hewitt 2003). With regard to creating alternatives, gender budgeting can be used to pressure local governments to be accountable to agreements that have been made at the international level. For example, Khosla (2003) notes that feminist organizations in Mexico have made use of gender budgeting to illustrate the gaps created by unfunded mandates made by Mexican authorities through the ICPD. In this way, gender budgets deal "directly with the responsibility of governments to international commitments to women, namely equality in the distribution, access and funding of public resources" (Villagomez 2004, 4). The application of gender-budgeting processes to groups and organizations working to create alternatives can work to ensure that women's needs are met and that women's labour is properly accounted for by alternative systems.

What seems evident from the above review is the gap between international agreements on women's equality and national action on these agreements. However, gender justice activists continue to utilize these agreements in their work. The new (as of 2010) UN entity, UN Women, was created to address this precise gap, to pressure nation-states to address questions of gender equity in economic, political, social, and cultural arenas. What is also obvious is the existence of male resistance and patriarchal cultures at all levels in women's struggles for democratic and just alternatives. These structural issues and institutional cultures need to be addressed directly in imagining and enacting alternatives. Alternatives that are gender sensitive, that centralize women's experiences in the origin of the project, that define women's roles as leaders and decision makers, and defend this position through the life of the project are likely to be more effective than projects that are not attentive to these issues. Additionally, alternatives that provide women with economic assistance and security (as SEWA does), and those that provide women with skills, knowledge, and political education to mobilize their strategic interests are likely to have the most lasting impact in terms of gender justice.

Democratizing knowledge: Critical literacy and alternative pedagogies

At the heart of creating alternatives that are responsive to issues of equity and access for women is the question of knowledge production. How do we come to know what the best arrangements are for all women? Given that neoliberal policies assume a "generic and oppressed" Third World woman, the task for feminist research is to excavate the ideological basis of these assumptions and privilege the lived realities that are concealed by them. A productive and sustainable approach to gendering alternatives compels us to recognize that "knowledge *is* produced by activist and community-based political work—that some knowledge can *only emerge within these contexts and locations"* (Alexander and Mohanty 2010, 27, emphases added). This approach thus addresses the question of what gets to count as knowledge and who counts as knowledgeable and suggests a reprioritization of subaltern knowledges and experiences.

Mainstream development projects have focused their efforts on training communities and groups in the methods of resource management developed by academics and practitioners situated in the global North. This approach often valorizes Northern-centric models of resource management, obscures the biases with which development practice operates, "evades the question of whether 'modernity' is desirable . . . [and] neglects the issue of local, subjugated knowledges" (Wieringa 1994, 841). Whereas mainstream development projects assume an approach that is "universally rational and efficient" (Boelens and Zwarteveen 2005, 753), indigenous approaches are sensitive to local environmental conditions and have created complex modes of distribution that can accommodate the needs of diverse constituents (Adams et al, 1997). Trawick argues a similar point in his analysis of the problems associated with the privatization of water systems in Peru where water laws were based on "rational" use models that "failed to achieve an equitable and efficient distribution of the resource" (2003, 985). By contrast, he argues, the models that have been employed in the Andean region since precolonial times are models that are attentive to the local geographical terrain and the equity concerns that exist in the region. While we need to be careful to not romanticize the "equitable community", learning about indigenous methods of resource management provides a means of acquiring cultural competence in structuring alternatives.

Practitioners working in the health care field have similarly critiqued the top-down approach to knowledge production. Alternative approaches to health care have, in some cases, sought to remedy this situation in order to build sustainable systems of delivery that make sense for the communities in which they work. The Zimbabwean coalition Community Working Group on Health (CWGH) is an example of a health research, education, and advocacy project that works to undo the "one-way transfer of knowledge from technocrats to the community" in order to make health education more relevant to the local context (Chigudu 2007, 256). Their work takes on the gender neutrality of 'traditional' (meaning technocratic, top-down) information, education, and communication approaches to HIV/ AIDS education and awareness that do not address the "unequal gender power relations, and notions of masculinity and femininity that shape expectations [and] . . . erode women's and girls' ability to negotiate safe sex, make informed choices regarding reproduction, and enjoy control over their bodies" (Chigudu 2007, 263). By contrast, CWGH works extensively with men and women to bring issues of sex and sexuality to the fore in order to adequately address issues of power and inequality between men and women that endanger women's sexual health, freedom, and choice.

The CWGH also trains community members in the process of collecting local data that can then be used to advocate for themselves in the policy arena. It is the belief of CWGH that information generated by the community is more likely to be credible to the community, and this facilitates the advocacy efforts of the communities they work with. This is similar to the goal of the AMANITARE coalition in Africa, which works to "create a knowledgeable constituency that would act as a pressure group to influence health and legal professionals, political institutions and society at large" (Ochieng 2003, 41). The CWGH takes the research process one step further to include "report back sessions". During these sessions, the results of the research are discussed with community members, and resolutions may be made to address the concerns that arise in the project. For example, after hearing the stories of several women who made use of dangerous methods for abortion and listening to the reasons why they would seek an abortion, one community opted to campaign for the full legalization of abortion. These examples of efforts anchored in women's everyday lives and struggles provide models for the development of alternatives that embody women's strategic interests, focusing as they do on education, accountability, and women's leadership.

Similar efforts have been made by gender budget advocates who call attention and create resistance to the gendered impacts of macroeconomic policies related to trade, investment debt repayments, and market liberalization; policies largely regarded as gender neutral and/or policies that have been depoliticized by neoliberalism (Cagatay 2003). One such initiative is the Gender and Economic Reforms in Africa (GERA) programme. GERA began in 1996 and consists of African women researchers, advocates, and activists who are particularly concerned with extending gendered analyses of budgets beyond national budgetary processes. GERA is also concerned, however, with the process of knowledge production and thus works towards bringing women into the research process with the understanding that "research is an important means of empowering women and marginalised groups" (Randriamaro 2003, 45). Importantly, GERA's work moves beyond empowerment as the appropriation of women's experiences to coordinating women's voices and experiences into a cohesive source of opposition. "GERA advocates for African gender researchers and activists to re-claim the concept of gender mainstreaming, so that it plays the role of a political tool for women's empowerment, instead of a technical device for legitimising inequitable trade and economic policies" (Randriamaro 2003, 48). The GERA approach to reclaiming gender mainstreaming is to organize a pan-African network of active and engaged activists, researchers, policy makers, and scholars who can work together to transform economic policies and processes.

Gendering alternative, democratic structures of governance and resource management demand that alternative methods of presenting and sharing information also be developed. In an innovative example, a Handpump

Technology project in rural Costa Rica produced educational materials that explicitly strove to destabilize gender binaries (Aguilar 2005). The educational materials consisted of manuals that illustrated the process of building and maintaining hand pumps. In the manuals, women and men were each pictured in non-traditional gender roles (i.e. women were installing hand pumps, and men were caring for children), there was equal male/female representation throughout the manual, and gender-neutral language was also used. In addition to the strategic use of gendered images, the manuals were also created in a manner that allowed people who could not read to follow the steps necessary for building and repairing the hand pumps (Aguilar 2005, 129). In this way, the relatively simple task of producing educational materials becomes an important route to destabilizing gender binaries and educational hierarchies. Similarly, the South African Women's Budget Initiative (WBI) has employed strategies to democratize participation in gender budgeting exercises. What these examples show is that while resource and budget management has been construed as the realm of educated bureaucrats, these modes of management have worked to exclude laypersons from active participation in the legal and economic structures that affect their lives. But activist groups are deconstructing the mantle of bureaucratic authority that has stifled the participation of citizens. Such is the case in Ecuador where a coalition group of activists are in the process of drafting a new constitution: "What's been really important is that this new constitution has been created by a group of citizens, environmentalists, women, economists, architects, farmers, and social leaders. We've broken with the notion that the constitution is only for lawyers, only for constitutionalists" (Martines 2009, 27). For those groups that have sought to democratize resource management, knowledge has to be created by all and extended to all.

In all sectors a lack of gender-disaggregated data has been perhaps the greatest barrier to designing policies that are responsive to women's needs. This is true at both the macro and micro levels of policy making. As such, feminist researchers have sought new methods of data collection that work towards illuminating women's contributions. At the micro level, GBI worked to make visible women's unpaid labour in the home and in the community, to enumerate the extent to which their unpaid labour bolsters economies, and to quantify the impacts on women of the reductions in public services (Khosla 2003). Budlender et al (2006) have identified an approach to gender budgeting that allows for data collection at the micro level in order to fill the gaps created by the neglect of women's work in national indicators called Community-Based Monitoring System (CBMS). The CBMS approach facilitates the collection of disaggregated data at the level of the community and household and is conducted at the lowest administrative level of governance in order to provide the most detailed information to local-level government planners. The value of this approach is that it covers a relatively small area but captures data and information that is neglected by state and national surveys. In regard to gender budgeting, the CBMS approach facilitates a data-backed discussion of the productive and economic value of women's unpaid labour.

Whereas the CBMS approach does not appear to directly draw women into the process of negotiating budgetary priorities, a method identified as the "interpretive focus group" (IFG) may assist in that process. The IFG was developed by Dodson et al (2007) as a means of bridging the "interpretive" gap between researchers and participants of differing social locations and is a model of practice drawn from feminist participatory action research. Although the CBMS approach strives to make visible the economic contributions of women's unpaid labour, the gap between researcher and participant may work against the process. The IFG provides a means of overcoming this distance by involving participants in the analysis of their responses. Dodson et al (2007, 826) argue that IFGs have two central purposes: First, they include participants in the research process through the final stage, and second, they ensure the accuracy and appropriateness of the researchers' evaluation of the data. Thus, the CBMS approach in tandem with the IFG provides a methodological approach to acquiring gender-sensitive data that is also accountable to the differences between women. To further the relationships between women, the findings from the CBMS as analyzed through the IFG may also be shared amongst various groups of women in a process of knowledge sharing. These methods of research provide a model for building alternatives that are grounded in the needs of those groups that are marginalized by neoliberal development policy and discourse. They also work to train these groups in the process of advocating for what they want and need. In this way, alternative research practices create alternative models of citizenship and action that are necessary for building accountability into alternative models of resource management.

The value of knowledge sharing for the creation of alternatives is that it works to make connections across communities whether those communities are geographical or social. These knowledge-sharing exercises permit the cross-fertilization of understanding, both in terms of similarities of struggle but also in terms of strategies for resistance. SEWA's "Women, Water and Work" campaign, again, serves an instructive purpose here. The campaign included groups and organizations from 11 districts and 500 villages, and the vastness of the project meant that information sharing was an important part of the overall success of the programme. To facilitate this part of the project, SEWA organized monthly information meetings that were held in selected villages where the successful initiatives had occurred. As noted by Panda:

> This is essentially a lateral learning process between members providing them with opportunity to learn from each other as well as visit different parts of the state to get a first-hand knowledge of how water problems have been tackled by other women. Thus, this is not only an

exposure visit meant to build capacities of women, but also an empowering experience. (2005, 7)

We suggest that projects that frame gender equity as an epistemological project, in terms of the transformation of practices and institutions, and as lived culture are the most successful in addressing women's strategic interests. It is this framework of envisioning alternatives that emerges in the conceptualization of place-based struggles in the discussion that follows.

GENDER JUSTICE AND PLACE-BASED STRUGGLES

Our objective, even if it is unconscious, is to reactivate the processes of participation, to re-appropriate in our own hands our own resources of our own communities, contexts, territories: From the little, without the big. Related to 'the big', related to the general themes, to grand values, grand issues, universal struggles, but, within the dynamics of the small, of the quotidian. (interview, Porte Alegre 2003, cited in Osterweil 2005, 184)

The critique of the managerial and bureaucratized development apparatus, and of the NGOization of the women's movement, as discussed earlier, led to a distancing by some women's rights scholars and activists from the UN establishment. As many feminist activists have become disillusioned with the UN system, they have moved to a more effective, transformative gender justice strategy of place-based politics (Harcourt and Escobar 2005). This strategy grows organically out of women's struggles as they materialize in and through particular sites. In an effort to bring together these collective struggles under a framework that allows for cross-comparison and analysis, Harcourt and Escobar (2005) developed a "Women and the Politics of Place" (WPP) framework. The WPP framework argues that the place-based practices of women involved in social justice struggles invoke related transformations around the body (e.g. women's movements that involve sexual, productive, and reproductive rights), the environment (ecological and environmental justice movements), and the economy (social and economic justice movements). In other words, the WPP framework makes capacious use of "place". It refers not only to place as territorially based but also to place as a site of struggle for gender justice, particularly in relation to women's bodies, their environments, and their economic activities. Importantly, place is also attentive to difference, diversity, and specificity in relation to these struggles as well as to larger, global processes. It is to the imbrications between global processes and the politics of place that we now turn.

Place-based movements and activism should not be regarded as place-bound (Harcourt and Escobar 2005, 5). Instead, the framework suggests that places act as prisms that refract global economic and governance structures, bending and shaping them in ways that make sense within the politics of particular sites and in different communities; what Michal Osterweil calls a "place-based globalism" (2005). This is not to suggest that global processes exact a determined force on the ground. Rather, it is a recognition that global processes become part of the terrain upon which women struggle and this perspective compels us to see the ways that women are politicized and act through these changes. The defence of one's right to survive in the face of the overwhelming valorization of markets compels new strategies and modes of resistance that challenge left political organizing, as well as hegemonic development discourses and practices, and create new modes of globalized struggle. Recognizing the power of place privileges local and translocal modes of resistance to totalizing theories of global processes, and seeks to valorize those movements. As sites where global processes are materialized, the analytical value of a place-based framework lies in thinking through place as a unit of analysis.

The pertinence of a place-based framework is borne out by the scholarship on anti-privatization water movements and the creation of alternatives to privatization, which can be read as place-based, economic justice struggles—what others have called "territory based" (Spronk 2007) or livelihood struggles. For instance, Danilo Urea, a Colombian, says that water struggles lead not just to a re-appropriation of water sources but also their territories:

> We are told that 'territory' means the land, but really territory means the construction of a life profoundly rooted in our natural heritage. The river, the watershed, the mountain, all this forms part of what we mean by territory, and all of it is profoundly linked to culture. So for our communities, organisations, and movements in Latin America, the defence of territory is fundamental; protecting territory is protecting culture, and water runs through both. (2009, 7)

Similarly, Spronk (2007) discusses territorially based organizations versus class-based organizations in anti-privatization struggles in Bolivia, where membership is based on participation in daily struggles and the focus is on living conditions and neighbourhood issues, not just workers' rights. All of the above are examples of struggles that grow out of lived realities that draw on indigenous knowledge and participatory decision making in the context of larger struggles for equity and democracy.

As *Changing the Flow: Report on Water Movements in Latin America* (Bell et al, 2009) illustrates, the recent water wars engaged in place-based local and regional movements leading to a new vision of water democracy based on principles of equity and access in resource management, exchange in technical and indigenous knowledge across linguistic, cultural, and national borders, ecological, and environmental sustainability, and community participation founded on reciprocity and collective and inclusive recognition. Women are centrally involved in these struggles, although they tend to not be visible in leadership positions. As Marcela Olivera from Red Vida (Bolivia) states:

> It is true that the role of women is more invisible but that doesn't signify that it is less important in the element of water. Red Vida is a network propelled by women. It's a network where there's a diversity of organizations, everything from unions to non-profit organizations to grassroots organizations, but women are the driving force. I think it's rich that women have appropriated the defence of water. On our continent, at least, the face of the movement is the face of a woman. (2009, 34–35)

Envisioning alternatives to privatization that address questions of gender equity necessitates attentiveness to the ways in which women have organized around their own practical and strategic gender interests.

This model contrasts sharply with the formal leadership structure and official platforms generated by older forms of internationalism that required a centralized strategy of action detached from the specificities of place and gendered realities and suggests the need to shift to a model of organization embedded in what Rocheleau describes as "rooted networks" (2005, 84) of people involved in place-based politics anchored in vertical (class/race/gender hierarchies) and horizontal (cross-national/cultural/linguistic borders) resistance networks. These rooted networks signify a place-based globalism that Osterweil argues "is not simply a tactical or technological perspective for effectively reaching the global scale; it also constitutes an ethico-political vision, a basis for revisioning political practice at a global scale without succumbing to a totalizing or universalizing approach that ignores or negates difference and specificity" (2005, 186). Using the WPP framework of place-based globalism or the notion of rooted networks of people involved in anti-privatization struggles allows us to be attentive to gender in all the ways that we argued earlier constitute a materialist project: as knowledge/ideological frames, as institutional practices, and as lived culture. This feminist framing reorients our theoretical and methodological lenses allowing us to *see* women and to centralize their/our everyday lives so that the prisms through which we understand global economic processes are gendered.

What these cases illustrate is a move away from coalitions based on homogenized identity politics to coalitions rooted in place-based struggles that kaleidoscope difference and diversity into powerful social justice movements. This is illustrated by Brazil's National Environmental Sanitation Front, which brought together unions, public municipal sanitation workers, neighbourhood committees and peasants, an entire cross-class/gender/race coalition in defence of water (Melo 2009, 29). Similarly, in Ecuador, the constitutional "Human Right to Water" was written by a group of "citizens, environmentalists, women, economists, architects, farmers, and social leaders" (Martines 2009, 27). When we look specifically at the gendered aspects of place-based organizing, we can see a critique of the domestication of women in stereotypically gendered ways through the commodification of water, electricity, and health and the reconstitution of a public/private divide. In contrast, we argue that the politics of place offers a way to rethink and reconfigure alternatives that are accountable to women's struggles in access to and control over municipal services. Our approach centralizes the agency that women express in their everyday lives, which are not usually lived through the public/private binary that is assumed in neoliberal policies and practices. The structure of alternatives that we argue for would recognize and build on the agency that women enact through practices of survival and resistance and that often occur in places that are neither wholly public nor wholly private. Countering the reprivatization of women, then, calls for an imagining of new publics that work against the neoliberal model of atomizing resource management along the lines of a public/private divide, and through which women are able to exert autonomy and influence. Alternatives cannot be just technical projects; they must also be projects aimed at creating transformative publics.

POSTSCRIPT: TOWARDS GENDER EQUITY PROJECTS IN ALTERNATIVES TO PRIVATIZATION

As privatized and commercialized systems of service delivery fail to deliver on their promise of increased access, a new moment is opening up that is ripe for anti-privatization activists. The crisis of global capital is a moment of opportunity for its critics. Imagining and enacting alternatives that do not recreate race/class/caste/gender/indigenous inequalities means that women from marginalized groups must be at the centre of analysis. This approach is one that makes use of the framework of WPP to understand women's livelihood strategies. This is an epistemological project that seeks a nuanced understanding of women's practices of accessing health, water, and electricity services. This approach is open to traditional research methods so long as feminist methodological concerns shape the research process. In a very general sense, feminist researchers engage strategies that "excavate" women's experiences. This process of excavation is one that strives to "elicit accounts and produce descriptions . . . of practice and thought that are part of female consciousness but left out of dominant interpretive frames" (DeVault 1999, 65). Thus, it requires an approach that moves away from generalizations to specific accounts of the social divisions that mediate structures of access and distribution.

Concretely, there must be a commitment to including women in numbers that are either equal to or greater than men. Beyond numerical parity, however, there must be a commitment to advancing women's agency within these groups. We suggest the inclusion of a gender justice advocate as part of the project team who can mediate discussions in favour of women's active participation, someone who is willing to do the difficult work of redistributing power within male-dominated groups. There is also a need to accurately account for women's labour contributions in the health, water, and electricity sectors. One means of accounting for women's unaccounted activities is to employ a time-use study that is attentive to women's work in the household as well as their income-generating activities. In a similar approach, Elson (1995) argues for analyses of "waterpoints" that can illuminate the patterns of water usage by particular women. Time-use or waterpoint studies can work to illustrate the analytical value of a place-based approach by employing these methods in multiple settings in order to empirically understand the similarities and differences of women's lives in different context. More generally, seeking alternatives that are accountable to gendered inequalities requires coalitions with women's groups—the "invented spaces" of participation that emerge organically in response to threats to women's lives. Engaging with women and women's groups at multiple levels of social hierarchies entails a commitment to producing empirical studies of their activities, their goals, and their modes of resource use and management. We are advocating for a bottom-up process that recognizes and seeks to augment women's agency in order to create alternatives that are accountable to multiple constituencies. These are only a handful of options that may be employed for those seeking to document or conduct new studies on gendered alternatives to privatization. Given the lack of attention to women in resource management, the possibilities are virtually endless.

To conclude, this chapter suggests that women's experiences, specifically the experiences of women who have been reprivatized through the commodification of municipal services, should be the most basic unit of analysis when thinking through questions of equity and access with regard to alternatives. This involves a commitment of energy and resources to gain a deep understanding of the community that is intended to benefit from the alternative service, including attention to the relevant identity categories such as class/caste composition, wealth distribution (measured in local terms, i.e. land, income, etc), educational levels and disparities (by wealth and gender), gender composition, religious orientations, and race/ethnic divisions. We have argued that in terms of gender justice, alternatives to privatization and commercialization cannot be narrowly circumscribed but must be envisioned as part of a larger struggle for women's rights and economic and social justice. Women cannot be treated as a "special interest" group—economic gender justice and non-private service delivery systems are core aspects of a larger anti-capitalist struggle and of a universal vision for equity and freedom. Taking women's interests as central to building alternatives requires us to move beyond the liberal frame of "gender mainstreaming" and the neoliberal frame of "women's empowerment" to an approach that recognizes and builds on women's agency. This shift begins in the lives of women, learns from their perspective, and formulates policies that are attentive to local, place-based struggles as they exist within structures of privilege, power, and inequality.

ACKNOWLEDGEMENTS

Many thanks to Amanda Wilson for getting us started with an initial bibliography on gender and alternatives to privatization.

REFERENCES

Adams, W.M., Warren, E.E. and Mutiso, S.K. 1997. Water, rules and gender: Water rights in an indigenous irrigation system, Marakwet, Kenya. *Development and Change* 28: 707–730.

Agarwal, B. 2001. Participatory exclusions, community forestry, and gender: An analysis for South Asia and a conceptual framework. *World Development* 29(10): 1623–1648.

Aguilar, L. 2005. Water as a source of equity and empowerment in Costs Rica. In Bennett, V., Dávila-Pobelete, S. and Nieves Rico, M. (Eds), *Opposing currents: The politics of water and gender in Latin America*, pp. 123–134. Pittsburgh: University of Pittsburgh Press.

Ahlers, R. and Zwarteveen, M. 2009. The water question in feminism: Water control and gender inequities in a neo-liberal era. *Gender, Place and Culture* 16(4): 409–426.

Ahmed, S. 2005. Negotiating gender equity through decentralised water management in coastal Gujarat: The case of UTTHAN. In Ahmed, S. (Ed), *Flowing upstream: Empowering women through water management initiatives in India*, pp. 51–92. Ahmedabad: Foundation Books Pvt. Ltd.

Alexander, J.M. and Mohanty, C.T. (Eds). 1997. *Feminist genealogies, colonial legacies, democratic futures*. London: Routledge.

———. 2010. Cartographies of knowledge and power: Transnational feminism as radical praxis. In Lock Swarr, A. and Nagar, R. (Eds), *Critical transnational feminist praxis*, pp. 23–45. Albany: SUNY Press.

Allard, J. and Matthaei, J. 2008. Introduction. In Allard, J., Davidson, C. and Matthaei, J. (Eds), *Solidarity economy: Building alternatives for people and the planet*, pp. 1–18. Chicago: ChangeMaker Publications.

Annecke, W. 2009. Still in the shadows: Women and gender relations in the electricity sector in South Africa. In McDonald, D.A. (Ed), *Electric capitalism: Recolonising Africa on the power grid*, pp. 288–320. London: Earthscan.

Anzaldua, G. and Moraga, C. 1981. *This bridge called my back: Writings by radical women of colour*. San Francisco: Aunt Lute Press.

Babb, F. 1996. After the revolution: Neoliberal policy and gender in Nicaragua. *Latin American Perspectives* 23(1): 27–48.

Balanyá, B., Brennan, B., Huedeman, O., Kiguamoto, S. and Terharst, P. (Eds). 2005. *Reclaiming public water: Achievements, struggles and visions from around the world*. Porto Alegre, Brazil: Transnational Institute and Corporate Europe Observatory.

Batliwala, S. and Reddy, A.K.N. 2003. Energy for women and women for energy (engendering energy and empowering women). *Energy for Sustainable Development* 7(3): 33–43.

Bayliss, K. 2001. Privatisation of electricity distribution: Some economic, social and political perspectives. London: Public Services International Research Unit (PSIRU). www.psiru.org/publicationsindex.asp.

Beall, J. 2005. Decentralizing government and decentering gender: Lessons from local government reform in South Africa. *Politics and Society* 33: 253–276.

Beckman, E. 2001. The Eight Encuentro. *VACLA Report on the Americas* 34(5): 32–33.

Bell, B., Conant, J., Olivera, M., Pinkstaff, C. and Terhorst, P. (Eds). 2009. *Changing the flow: Water movements in Latin America.* Food and Water Watch, Other Worlds, Reclaiming Public Water, Red VIDA, and Transnational Institute.

Beneria, L. 1999. Structural adjustment policies. In Peterson, J. and Lewis, M. (Eds), *The Elgar Companion to Feminist Economics*, pp. 687–694. Northampton: Edward Elgar Publishing.

Bernal, G.E., Bissell, S. and Cortes, A. 1999. Effects of globalization on the efforts to decriminalize abortion in Mexico. *Development and Change* (42)4: 130–133.

Boelens, R. and Zwarteveen, M. 2005. Prices and politics in Andean water reforms. *Development and Change* 36(4): 735–758.

Branco, A. and Almeida, V. 2002. Women, mobilization and the revitalization of water resources: The case of Northeastern Brazil. Paper prepared for the Forum for Water in the Americas in the 21st Century, Mexico City, DF, February.

Brown, R. 2010. Unequal burden: Water privatisation and women's human rights in Tanzania. *Gender and Development* 18(1): 59–67.

Budlender, D. and Hewitt, G. 2003. *Engendering budgets: A practitioner's guide to understanding and implementing gender-responsive budgets.* London: Commonwealth Secretariat.

Budlender, D., Reyes, C. and Melesse, M. 2006. *Gender-responsive budgeting through the CBMS lens.* Discussion Paper Series No. 2006–17, Philippine Institute for Development Studies (PIDS). www.dirp4.pids.gov.ph/ris/dps/pidsdps0617.pdf.

Cagatay, N. 2003. Gender budgets and beyond: Feminist fiscal policy in the context of globalization. *Gender and Development* 11(1): 15–24.

Castro, J.E. 2007. Poverty and citizenship: Sociological perspectives on water services and public-private participation. *Geoforum* 38: 756–771.

Cecelski, E. 2000. Enabling equitable access to rural electrification: Current thinking and major activities in energy, poverty and gender. Briefing Paper prepared for Asia Alternative Energy Policy and Project Development Support: Emphasis on Poverty Alleviation and Women. The World Bank, January 2000. www.sarpn.org.za/genderenergy/resources/cecelski/energypovertygender.pdf

Chigudu, H. 2007. Deepening our understanding of community-based participatory research: Lessons from work around reproductive rights in Zimbabwe. *Gender and Development* 15(2): 259–270.

Clancy, J. 2000. *Policies, projects and the market empowering women? Some initial reactions to developments in the energy sector.* Working Paper Series Technology and Development Group No. 105. Enschede: University of Twente, Technology and Development Group.

———. 2002. *The gender-energy-poverty nexus: Finding the energy to address gender concerns in development.* DFID Project CNTR998521. London: DFID.

Cleaver, F. 1998. Choice, complexity, and change: Gendered livelihoods and the management of water. *Agriculture and Human Values* (15): 293–299.

———. 2000. Analyzing gender roles in community natural resource management. *IDS Bulletin* 31(2): 60–67.

Davis, A.Y. 1985. *Violence against women and the ongoing challenge to racism.* Latham: Kitchen Table Press.

Delgado, J.R.V. 2005. Irrigation management, the participatory approach, and equity in an Andean community. In Bennett, V., Dávila-Pobelete, S. and Nieves Rico, M. (Eds), *Opposing currents: The politics of water and gender in Latin America,* pp. 109–122. Pittsburgh: University of Pittsburgh Press.

DeVault, M. 1999. *Liberating method: Feminism and social research.* Philadelphia, Temple University Press.

Dodson, L., Piatelli, D. and Schmalzbauer, L. 2007. Researching inequality through interpretive collaborations: Shifting power and the unspoken contract. *Qualitative Inquiry* 13: 821–843.

Dubash, N.K. (Ed). 2002. *Power politics: Equity and environment in electricity reform.* Washington, DC: World Resources Institute.

Elson, D. 1995. Gender awareness in modelling structural adjustment. *World Development* 23(11): 1851–1868.

Feminist Initiative of Cartagena. 2003. In search of an alternative development paradigm: Feminist proposals from Latin America. *Gender and Development* 11(1): 52–58.

Gomez, A.E. 2009. A new definition of hope. In Bell, B., Conant, J., Olivera, M., Pinkstaff, C. and Terhorst, P. (Eds), *Changing the flow: Water movements in Latin America,* pp. 13–15. Food and Water Watch, Other Worlds, Reclaiming Public Water, Red Vida, and Transnational Institute.

Hall, D. 2007. *Energy privatization and reform in East Africa.* London: Public Services International Research Unit (PSIRU). www.publications.marsgroup-kenya.org/GAP_Report4_KPLC/PDFs/Energy_Privatisation_and_Reform_in_East_Africa.pdf.

Harcourt, W. 2003. Building alliances for women's empowerment, reproductive rights and health. *Development* 46(2): 6–12.

———. 2006. *The global women's rights movement: Power politics around the United Nations and the World Social Forum.* Civil Society and Social Movements Programme Paper Number 25. Geneva, Switzerland: United Nations Research Institute for Social Development.

Harcourt, W. and Escobar, A. (Eds). 2005. *Women and the politics of place.* Bloomfield, CT: Kumarian Press.

Holdren, J.P. and Smith, K.R. 2000. Energy, the environment, and health. In Goldemberg, J. (Ed), *The world energy assessment: Energy and the challenge of sustainability,* pp. 61–110. New York: UNDP.

IFAD (International Fund for Agricultural Development). 2006. *Gender and water: Securing water for improved rural livelihoods. The multiple uses system approach.* Rome: IFAD. Mimeo.

Jayawardena, K. 1995. *The white woman's other burden: Western women and South Asia during British rule.* London: Routledge.

Karim, R.K.M. 2006. Gendered social institutions and the management of underground irrigation water resources in a Bangladeshi village. *Gender Technology and Development* 10(1): 13–36.

Khosla, P. 2003. Water, equity and money: The need for gender-responsive budgeting in water and sanitation. The Netherlands Council for Women. Mimeo.

Laurie, N. 2011. Gender water networks: Femininity and masculinity in water politics in Bolivia. *International Journal of Urban and Regional Research* 35(1): 172–188.

Manase, G., Ndamba, J. and Makoni, F. 2003. Mainstreaming gender in integrated water resources management: The case of Zimbabwe. *Physics and Chemistry of the Earth* 28: 967–971.

Marchand, M. and Runyan, A. (Eds). 2000. *Gender and global restructuring: Sightings, sites and resistances.* New York: Routledge.

Martines, J.P. 2009. Keepers of Water. In Bell, B., Conant, J., Olivera, M., Pinkstaff, C. and Terhorst, P. (Eds), *Changing the flow: Water movements in Latin America*, pp. 27–28. Food and Water Watch, Other Worlds, Reclaiming Public Water, Red Vida, and Transnational Institute.

Matthaei, J. 1982. *An economic history of women in America: Women's work, the sexual division of labour, and the development of capitalism.* New York: Schocken Books.

McDonald, D.A. 2009. Electric capitalism: Conceptualising electricity and capital accumulation in (South) Africa. In McDonald, D.A. (Ed), *Electric capitalism: Recolonising Africa on the power grid*, pp. 1–49. London: Earthscan.

Meinzen-Dick, R. and Zwarteveen, M. 1998. Gendered participation in water management: Issues and illustrations from water users' associations in South Asia. *Agriculture and Human Values* 15: 337–345.

Melo, M. 2009. Alternatives for another, possible world. In Bell, B., Conant, J., Olivera, M., Pinkstaff, C. and Terhorst, P. (Eds), *Changing the flow: Water movements in Latin America*, pp. 29–30. Food and Water Watch, Other Worlds, Reclaiming Public Water, Red Vida, and Transnational Institute.

Mies, M. 1984. *Patriarchy and accumulation on a world scale: Women in the international division of labour.* New York and London: Zed Books, Ltd.

Miraftab, F. 2004. Invited and invented spaces of participation: Neoliberal citizenship and feminists' expanded notion of politics. *Wagadu* 1: 1–7.

Mohanty, C.T. 1986. Under Western eyes: Feminist scholarship and colonial discourses. *Feminist Review* 30: 61–88.

———. 2003. *Feminism without borders: Decolonizing theory, practicing solidarity.* Durham: Duke University.Press.

Molyneux, M. 1985. Mobilization without emancipation? Women's interests, the state, and revolution in Nicaragua. *Feminist Studies* 11(2): 227–254.

Mukhopadhyay, M. 2004. Mainstreaming gender or "streaming" gender away: Feminists marooned in the development business. *IDS Bulletin* 35(4): 95–103.

Nagar, R. and Writers, S. 2006. *Playing with fire: Feminist thought and activism through seven lives in India.* Minneapolis: University of Minnesota Press.

Nanda, P. 2002. Gender dimensions of user fees: Implications for women's utilization of health care. *Reproductive Health Matters* 10(20): 127–134.

Naples, N. 2002. Changing the terms: Community activism, globalization, and the dilemmas of transnational feminist praxis. In Naples, N.A. and Desai, M. (Eds), *Women's activism and globalization: Linking local struggles and transnational politics*, pp. 3–14. New York: Routledge.

Nelson, J. 2006. *Economics for humans.* Chicago: University of Chicago Press.

Ochieng, R.O. 2003. Supporting women and girls' sexual and reproductive health and rights: The Ugandan experience. *Development* 46(2): 38–44.

Olivera, M. 2009. A struggle for life. In Bell, B., Conant, J., Olivera, M., Pinkstaff, C. and Terhorst, P. (Eds), *Changing the flow: Water movements in Latin America*, pp. 33–35. Food and Water Watch, Other Worlds, Reclaiming Public Water, Red Vida, and Transnational Institute.

O'Reilly, K. 2006. "Traditional" women, "modern" water: Linking gender and commodification in Rajasthan, India. *Geoforum* 37: 958–972.

Osterweil, M. 2005. Place-based globalism: Locating women in the alternative globalization movement. In Harcourt, W. and Escobar, A. (Eds), *Women and the politics of place*, pp. 174–189. Bloomfield, CT: Kumarian Press.

Panda, S.M. 2005. Women's role in local water management: Insights from SEWA's Millenium Water Campaign in Gujarat (India). EMPOWERS Regional Symposium: End-Users Ownership and Involvement in IWRM. Cairo, Egypt, 13–17 November.

———. 2007. Mainstreaming gender in water management: A critical view. *Gender Technology and Development* 11(3): 321–338.

Pitkin, K. and Bedoya, R. 1997. Women's multiple roles in economic crisis: Constraints and adaptation. *Latin American Perspectives* 24(4): 34–49.

Pradhan, B. 2003. Measuring empowerment: A methodological approach. *Development* 46(2): 51–57.

Public Services International Research Unit (PSIRU). www.publications.marsgroupkenya.org/GAP_Report4_KPLC/PDFs/Energy_Privatisation_and_Reform_in_East_Africa.pdf.

Randriamaro, Z. 2003. African women challenging neo-liberal economic orthodoxy: The conception and mission of the GERA Programme. *Gender and Development* 11(1): 44–51.

Reddy, A.K.N. 2000. Energy and social issues. In Goldenberg, J. (Ed), *The World energy assessment: Energy and the challenge of sustainability*, pp. 39–60. New York: UNDP.

Resurreccion, B., Real, M.J. and Pantana, P. 2004. Officialising strategies: Participatory processes and gender in Thailand's water resources sector. *Development and Practice* 14(4): 521–533.

Reyes, E. 2009. The power that makes pitchers overflow and rivers flood their banks. In Bell, B., Conant, J., Olivera, M., Pinkstaff, C. and Terhorst, P. (Eds), *Changing the flow: Water movements in Latin America*, pp. 16–19. Food and Water Watch, Other Worlds, Reclaiming Public Water, Red Vida, and Transnational Institute.

Roberts, A. 2008. Privatizing social reproduction: The primitive accumulation of water in an era of neoliberalism. *Antipode* 40(4): 535–560.

Rocheleau, D. 2005. Political landscapes and ecologies of Zambrana-Chacuey: The legacy of Mama Tingo. In Harcourt, W. and Escobar, A. (Eds), *Women and the Politics of Place*, pp. 72–85. Bloomfield, CT: Kumarian Press.

Roy, A. 2004. *An ordinary person's guide to empire*. Cambridge, MA: South End Press.

Safa, H. 1990. Women's social movements in Latin America. *Gender and Society* 4(3): 354–369.

Sen, G. 1996. Gender, markets and states: A selective review and research agenda. *World Development* 24(5): 821–829.

Sen, G. and Grown, C. 1987. *Development, crises, and alternative visions*. New York: Monthly Review Press.

Shiva, V. 2005. *Earth democracy: Justice, sustainability, and peace*. Cambridge: South End Press.

Singh, N. 2006. Women's participation in local water governance: Understanding institutional contradictions. *Gender Technology and Development* 10(1): 61–76.

Skutsch, M.M. 2005. Gender analysis for energy projects and programmes. *Energy for Sustainable Development* 9(1): 37–52.

Souza, C. (2001). Participatory budgeting in Brazilian cities: Limits and possibilities in building democratic institutions. *Environment and Urbanization* 13(1): 159–184.

Spronk, S. 2007. Roots of resistance to urban water privatization in Bolivia: The "new working class", the crisis of neoliberalism, and public services. *International Labour and Working-Class History* 71: 8–28.

Subrahmanian, R. 2004. Making sense of gender in shifting institutional contexts: Some reflections on gender mainstreaming. *IDS Bulletin* 35(4): 89–94.

Sultana, F. 2009. Community and participation in water resources management: Gendering and naturing development debates from Bangladesh. *Transactions of the Institute of British Geographers* 34(3): 346–363.

Trawick, P. 2003. Against the privatization of water: An indigenous model for improving existing laws and successfully governing the commons. *World Development* 31(6): 977–996.

Udas, P.B. and Zwarteveen, M. 2010. Can water professionals meet gender goals? A case study of the Department of Irrigation in Nepal. *Gender and Development* 18(1): 87–97.

UNESCAP (United Nations Economic and Social Commission for Asia and the Pacific). 2003. Mainstreaming gender in energy and planning policies. Background paper for expert group meeting. UNESCAP Project on Capacity Building on Integration of Energy and Rural Development Planning. www.unescap.org/esd/energy/cap_building/integration/egm/documents/Soma_D_paper.pdf.

UNIFEM (United Nations Development Fund for Women). 2009. Gender responsive budgeting. Newsletter, Issue 3. New York: UNIFEM.

Upadhyay, B. 2005. Gendered livelihoods and multiple water use in North Gujarat. *Agriculture and Human Values* 22: 411–420.

Urea, D. 2009. Protecting territory, protecting culture. In Bell, B., Conant, J., Olivera, M., Pinkstaff, C. and Terhorst, P. (Eds), *Changing the flow: Water movements in Latin America*, 27–28. Food and Water Watch, Other Worlds, Reclaiming Public Water, Red Vida, and Transnational Institute.

van Koppen, B. 1998. Water rights, gender, and poverty alleviation. Inclusion and exclusion of women and men smallholders in public irrigation infrastructure development. *Agriculture and Human Values* 15: 361–374.

Villagomez, E. 2004. Gender responsive budgets: Issues, good practices and policy options. Paper presented at the Regional Symposium on Mainstreaming Gender into Economic Policies. Geneva, Switzerland, United Nations, 28–30 January. www.gender-budgets.org/uploads/user-S/Gender%20budgets%20-%20UNECE%20web%20draft.pdf.

Wieringa, S. 1994. Women's interests and empowerment: Gender planning reconsidered. *Development and Change* 25: 829–848.

Winrock International. n.d. Report on assessment of rural energy development program (REDP): Impacts and its contribution in achieving MDGs. Nepal: Winrock International. www.redp.org.np/phase2/pdf/impactsandcontricution.pdf.

Zomers, A. 2003. The challenge of rural electrification. *Energy for Sustainable Development* 7(1): 69–76.

Zwarteveen, M. 1997. Water: From basic need to commodity: A discussion on gender and water rights in the context of irrigation. *World Development* 25(8): 1335–1349.

Zwarteveen, M. and Meinzen-Dick, R.S. 2001. Gender and property rights in the commons: Examples of water rights in South Asia. *Agriculture and Human Values* 18(1): 11–25.

6 Social Movement Struggles for Public Services

Susan Spronk and Philipp Terhorst

In the context of widespread public sector crises engendered by neoliberal globalization, social movements have sought to resist the privatization of basic services such as water, electricity, and health care and to promote democratic development of public and community alternatives (Parliamentary Forum, WSF 2006). In contrast to literature on participatory governance in public service sectors that focus on how institutions work rather than how they come about, this chapter focuses on the role of social movements in advancing the development and implementation of "alternatives to privatization".

The first section reviews some of the main trends in social movement theory, arguing that Harvey's (2003) concept of "accumulation by dispossession" offers a useful analytical framework for assessing the strengths and limitations of the struggles for public services for all in the water, electricity, and health sectors. The second section analyzes the differences in social movement dynamics in these three sectors, drawing attention to the importance of their political economies on social movements' perceptions of these services as "commodities" and their abilities to draw links between the sectors. The third section begins with an analysis of the politics of coalition building among the main social movement organizations involved in struggles over service delivery: trade unions, non-governmental organizations (NGOs), and community-based organizations. It then examines the role of social movements in developing alternatives to privatization and explains the potential—as well as the limitations—that social movements have on influencing the paths of reform.

DEFINITIONS AND APPROACHES IN SOCIAL MOVEMENT THEORY

Given that the term "social movement" is used for phenomena as diverse as revolutions, religious sects, trade unions, and consumer campaigns, it comes as no surprise that the concept defies precise definition. Complications also arise from the fact that distinct traditions give prominence to different aspects of social movements (Armstrong and Bernstein 2008), as they pertain to rival ideological frameworks and concepts of social change, ranging from Marxism to liberalism. As Jelin notes: "Social movements are objects constructed by the researcher, which do not necessarily coincide with the empirical form of collective action. Seen from the outside, they may present a certain degree of unity, but internally they are always heterogeneous, diverse" (cited in Egan and Wafer 2004, 2).

At stake in the debate over the definition of social movements are scholars' different ideas of what constitutes the social order but also disagreements about which strategies and tactics are most effective to bring about social change. The contemporary debate has been coloured by the perceived decline of class-based movements such as labour, peasant, and socialist organizations that threatened the political order during the period of nascent industrialization in the late 19th and early 20th centuries. As Tilly (1978) explains, the early growth of social movements was connected to broad economic and political changes that accompanied the process of capitalist development— urbanization, industrialization, and proletarianization. The process of urbanization, which created large cities, facilitated social interaction between scores of people. Similarly, the process of industrialization, which gathered large masses of workers in the same region, was responsible for the fact that many of those early social movements addressed matters important to that social class, such as the lack of basic services (Hamlin 1998). Indeed, the labour and socialist movements that emerged in the industrial centres of the late 19th century were seen as prototypical social movements for most of the 20th century, by Marxists and non-Marxists (such as Tilly) alike. With deindustrialization in the North from the late 1950s onwards, the orthodox Marxist conception of revolution—centred as it was on the idea that the organized industrial working class was the privileged historical subject to bring about revolutionary social change—became increasingly criticized, accompanied by the rise of various anti-oppression struggles through the course of the 20th century that did not take the relationship between capital and labour as their main focus.

Beginning with the student mobilizations of May 1968 in urban centres as diverse as Mexico City and Paris, a body of literature describing "new social movements" (NSMs) emerged, which professed that old forms of "class organization" had waned in the context of the post-industrial society, particularly in continental Europe (Touraine 1969). Unlike labour and socialist movements of the past, the NSMs that emerged in the late 1960s—such as the civil rights movement, feminist movements, and gay movements—did not concentrate on the contradiction between capital and labour but on other forms of domination and violence, such as racism, sexism, and homophobia.

The supposed historical shift signalled by the rise of these "new" movements inspired the bifurcation of the mainstream academic literature into two theoretical paradigms that emerged on opposite sides of the Atlantic:

the "political process approach" of North American sociology and the "NSM approach" of continental Europe (Foweraker 1995, Canel 1997). These two schools of thought were not only reacting to historical events but also to the perceived shortcomings of different bodies of theory to interpret them. Specifically, the political process approach emerged as a response to earlier theories of social movements inspired by French sociologist Émile Durkheim, which saw protest either as a result of participants' pathologies or the destruction of community affiliations in mass society. By contrast, the NSM approach sought to overcome reductionist forms of Marxism, which assigned the working class (conceived narrowly as the industrial proletariat) a privileged place in the unfolding of history.

While much ink has been spilled about the superiority of one approach over the other, the supposed theoretical differences owe much to the fact that each approach examines social movements at different, but complementary, levels of analysis. The political process approach tends to focus on the public, outward manifestations of social movement activity (e.g. their relationships with the state), while NSM tends to focus on internal processes (e.g. identity formation amongst participants). Since the 1990s, the trend has been to seek convergence between the two approaches, as researchers from both paradigms aim to link considerations of microlevel analysis of the process of mobilization (the focus of the NSM school) with the macrolevel political and institutional context (the focus of the political process approach; Haber 1996). This rapprochement has encouraged scholars from the political process school to integrate "cultural" considerations into their analysis (Rao et al, 2000, McAdam et al, 2001), while NSM scholars have aimed to bridge debates about structure and agency through the analysis of networks (Diani and McAdam 2003).

The relevance of both of these approaches for understanding struggles for public services in the global South is, however, limited for several reasons. First, both schools emerged in an attempt to explain the significance of social movements in "post-industrial" societies, yet most parts of the global South lie on the periphery or semi-periphery of the capitalist world economy and therefore cannot be characterized as "industrial" let alone "post-industrial". Second, the political process approach was developed based on the experience of liberal, capitalist democracies and the concepts fit rather awkwardly in post-colonial contexts of the global South (Cook 1996, Almeida 2003). Third, while social movement struggles for health, water, and electricity are sometimes identified as "new" social movements because they focus on non-class forms of identity (Schonwalder 2004), these struggles are still very material in the sense that they place demands on spheres of reproduction, which coincide with the demands of the working classes (Castells 1977, Mainwaring 1987). Fourth, the literature on new social movements creates a division between "old" (read labour) movements and "new" movements that is shown to be false by the emergence of social movement unionism (Moody 1997), which has been an important phenomenon in struggles for public services. Fifth, contrary to the claim of NSM scholars that a defining feature of these "new" movements is their claims for autonomy from the state, most social movements in the water, electricity, and health sectors use a rights-based discourse, which implies demand making on the state (Nelson and Dorsey 2007, Dugard 2009).

Harvey (2003), a geographer who has written extensively on social movements, identity politics, and Marx's critique of political economy, gives us an alternative way to understand contemporary struggles for basic services in the global South that is sensitive to the concerns about identity raised by the NSM scholars, while paying attention to the historical context in which different social movements emerge. In his work on "new imperialism", Harvey draws our attention to changes in class formation affected by capitalist development that took place over the 20th century, arguing that the kinds of struggles that favoured the formation of trade unions at historical moments of expanding production in the 19th and first half of the 20th century have since been usurped by "insurgent movements against accumulation by dispossession" (2003, 166). These struggles, mainly taking place in the sphere of reproduction, such as the struggle of the Ogoni of Nigeria against Shell oil or the campaign for a universal health care system in the US, do not take place under a working class or trade union banner or with working class leadership identified as such. Rather, they draw from a broad spectrum of civil society groups that have in various ways been subject to dispossession, marginalization, and impoverishment. Given the wide range of social interests that participate in these struggles, Harvey posits that they aggregate in "a less focused political dynamic of social action" than the revolutionary socialist movements that emerged throughout the world during the early and mid-20th century. He warns, however, that amongst these movements a "danger lurks that a politics of nostalgia for that which has been lost will supersede the search for ways to better meet the material needs of impoverished and repressed populations" (2003, 168, 177).

Many of the contemporary social movements struggling for public services for all can be characterized as struggles against accumulation by dispossession (Bond 2005, McDonald and Ruiters 2005, Spronk and Webber 2007): they involve diverse constituencies, including the most marginalized members of society (the "poors"), middle-class professionals (NGOs) and public sector workers; the site of organizing tends to be a territory, neighbourhood or the city rather than the workplace; and they are fighting contemporary forms of capitalist enclosure, particularly evident when infrastructure such as public hospitals and water and electricity networks built over decades are transferred to the private, profit-seeking sector for next to nothing.

Most importantly, as Harvey's work highlights, contemporary struggles for basic services are one strong indication of the changes to class formation under neoliberalism. The historic role of trade unions as leaders of the working class struggle has been usurped by coalitions of social movement organizations dominated by informal workers. In the context of post-apartheid South Africa, for example, scholars have observed that class-based forms of struggles led by trade unions have been transformed into "struggles about direct relief for marginalized groupings" (Ballard et al, 2006, 8). As Nash similarly observes in the context of the social havoc caused by World Bank-sponsored structural adjustment policies in Bolivia, the primary concern of the majority of the working population on the margins of capitalist development during the neoliberal era became "the right to live in a world with a diminishing subsistence base" rather than "class struggle against exploitation defined in the workplace" (1994, 10). Indeed, as Olivera, a trade union activist and a spokesperson of the coalition of diverse civil society groups that formed to fight water privatization in Cochabamba, Bolivia, describes it, in the "new world of labour" social movements have increasingly focused on fighting for the "basic necessities of daily life" as a means by which to broaden the base of struggle for larger social transformation (2004, 126).

These contemporary social movements, however, still draw on social movement repertoires from the past. Barchiesi reminds us, for example, that despite the shift in the focus from production to reproduction, the "new generation of social movement politics in South Africa" have "organizational and ideological/discursive relationships with long standing experiences of working class organizing" (2006, 38). One of the central demands of social movements of past and present is the call for the "decommodification" of basic services, a term that was popularized in the academic literature by Esping-Andersen (1990). During the first half of the 20th century, the Scandinavian welfare state grew because urban-rural, worker-farmer alliances demanded that the elite extend social protection to the working class and small farmers to guard against the vagaries of employment, especially during periodic recessions, by building a social safety net of state-provided services. Over a period of decades, these social protections took the form of generous pensions, health care, and education, which were financed through the taxation system and provided by the state at no cost to the direct user, which, like childcare and eldercare, disproportionately support and liberate women. The goal of decommodification—taken up by contemporary social movements—is therefore to remove basic services, such as water, electricity, and health, from the market (Leys 2001), based upon the proposition that the decisions about the production and delivery of goods and services that are decided by the market are beyond the realm of democratic control.

GEOGRAPHIES OF SERVICE DELIVERY AND SOCIAL MOVEMENTS

During the neoliberal era, social movements fighting for the decommodification of basic health, water, and electricity services have challenged government privatization policies in Peru, South Africa, Thailand, and India, amongst many other states (McDonald and Ruiters 2005, Arce 2008, Hall 2010) and have even contributed towards political transition in countries such as Bolivia and Uruguay (Santos and Villareal 2006, Spronk 2007). There are also *transnational* social movement networks that operate across regions, particularly in the health and water sectors—making it possible to talk about *global* health and water movements—although this is not so in the electricity sector. At the local level, by contrast, the same people are often involved in struggles for water and electricity, while different coalitions of actors are involved in struggles for health.

Why do we observe these differences between social movements in the three sectors? Following Harvey's emphasis on the interconnections between capitalist development, geography, and struggle, we posit that the major differences amongst the sectors owe to the particular political economies and geographies of service provision, which affect social movements' perceptions of these services as commodities and open possibilities for making intersectoral links. First, all three sectors involve high levels of public investment but the electricity sector is the most capital intensive of the three, involving generation (e.g. dams), transmission, and distribution. On the other hand, while urban water and sanitation systems and advanced medical care facilities can certainly be technologically sophisticated, low-cost, "home-grown" alternatives exist. As the hundreds of thousands of rudimentary artisanal systems in the rural and peri-urban areas of the global South attest, water is a "gift from Nature" that can be extracted from the ground and distributed with basic technology. Health services can also involve capital-intensive technology such as medical resonance imaging machines, but in most cases, primary public health—the focus of most social movements—requires basic care and prevention rather than the promotion of costly pharmaceuticals and equipment. This is to say, the relations between citizen and electrical services have always been mediated by capital and/or the state, while the same is not true for water or health services, for which traditional, artisanal alternatives still exist.

Furthermore, the hierarchies of human needs make it easier for social movement leaders to argue that access to water and health are "human rights", facilitating the construction of global movements, while it is less common for demands to be framed this way in the electricity sector.[1] Water has no physiological substitute, making it the "essence of all life". It also has cultural importance since it has played a central role in the development of humanity (Illich 1985). Similarly, health care is primordial and, like the various meanings assigned to water, perceptions of "good health" tend to be culturally specific (Paulson and Bailey 2003). There are substitutes to "modern" health care—such as "traditional" systems—but these are increasingly integrated into formal health systems, particularly at the primary level. Many people employ more than one health care stream, making it difficult to separate demands for the different options. Electricity, on the other hand, is a recently constructed "need" and is not essential in the same way as health and water. Instead of cooking on the stove or turning on the light, it is possible to burn wood or light a candle (although, of course, these options may be more damaging to the environment and health than generator-provided electricity or cooking gas). In addition, the substitutes for electricity (wood, candles, etc) are organized on the level of the household and do not require the social organization of a community in the same way as a neighbourhood hand pump or a traditional health system. This is not to say that manifold protests of urban residents seeking connection to the electricity grid do not exist, but rather that such protests are not as likely to generate a social movement dynamic, as is the case in the water and health sectors. To date, the "need" for health and water has facilitated the mobilization of the rights discourse in these sectors compared to electricity where it is less present. For instance, there are international advocacy networks mobilized around rights in these latter sectors, but not in electricity (see Nelson and Dorsey 2007), although international organizing around climate change may change this scenario.

Second, the geography of service provision also leads social movement actors to make connections between water and electricity, but activists who defend public health care systems tend to be an entirely different group of people. Two factors help explain the former. First, as networked, infrastructure services, water and electricity services are often provided by the same level of government or the same utility. In the case of trade union organizations, workers in the water and electricity sectors are more likely to belong to the same trade union confederation. Furthermore, water and electricity services are subject to the same kinds of cost-recovery policies because of their similar point-of-consumption tariff structures. A good example of this synergy is the Soweto Electricity Crisis Committee, in South Africa, which sees as its principal task to "participate in wider struggles over water ('Operation Vulamanzi') and housing ('Operation Buyel'ekhaya')—in short '[w]hen the ANC government fails to deliver we must deliver where it is possible'" (Egan and Wafer 2004, 10). Second, links between the water and electricity sectors tend to be particularly strong in agricultural communities populated by small farmers who depend on electricity for pumping irrigation water. In the Andean region of Latin America, for example, coalitions of user groups, including urban consumers and peasant irrigating associations, have taken on the state to prevent the privatization of public water and electricity utilities, framing the struggle as a defence of national patrimony (Olivera 2004, Arce 2008).

Social movements in water services

It is widely accepted that the "global water justice movement" is composed by a multitude of social and political struggles at local and national levels in all continents, and organized in transnational networks (Balanyá et al, 2005). Fighting the trends of privatization, commercialization, and deregulation, water justice movements "went global" in the late 1990s (Hall et al, 2005). Acting in a field that is shaped by conflict, struggle and disruption, "activists from social movements, non-governmental organizations, and networks . . . struggle throughout the world in the defence of water and territory and for the commons" (International Forum in the Defense of Water 2006, 1).

Liberal analysts such as Morgan consider water movements primarily as "consumer movements" reacting against private sector participation and neoliberal global governance. For Morgan, water movements are largely disruptive, producing "fractious parallel trajectories of legislative change and social protest that occasionally intersect but largely co-exist in uneasy tension" (2006, 412). More radical scholars, on the other hand, understand water social movements as potentially counter-hegemonic forces that not only seek the immediate goal of securing "services for all" but in so doing also build challenges for participatory democracy, social justice, and ecological sustainability. In Bolivia and South Africa, social movement leaders from the water movement have articulated a socialist agenda, linking demands for democratization to transformation of the society and economy (Coetzee 2004, Olivera 2004). Although the water justice movement was born as a reaction to privatization policies, one of the central demands of the movement is the democratization of the social and property relations around water, as expressed in the discourse for "the commons" (Bakker 2007, Naidoo and Davidson-Harden 2007).

As Swyngedouw observes, "the water problem is not merely a question of management and technology, but rather, and perhaps in the first instance, a question of social power" (2004, 175). It is because water systems are embedded in broader socio-historical institutions shaped by struggles over resources that water movements face many challenges in meeting their own aspirations to develop and implement alternatives (Terhorst 2009). Nonetheless, there are a large number of successful campaigns across all continents: the numerous legal and constitutional affirmations of the human right to water that seek to prohibit privatization, especially in Latin America (Mychalejko 2008, Taks 2008, van Schaick 2009); a series of movement-sponsored reform processes in public water utilities designed to keep water in public hands (Balanyá et al, 2005); and various initiatives to promote public-public partnerships (PuPs; Hall et al, 2009). At the level of global governance, movement challenges have not only disrupted proceedings of the World Water Forums and challenged the corporate lobby within UN agencies, which has led to the inclusion of social movement representatives in the global governance bodies such as the United Nations Secretary General's Advisory Board (UNSGAB) and the Global Water Operators Partnership Alliance (GWOPA). But the water movements, especially the international NGOs such as the Council of Canadians, were also instrumental in securing a vote on July 28, 2010 at the General Assembly of the United Nations, introduced by the Bolivian government, in favour of a resolution on the human right to water and sanitation.

Social movements in health

According to a recent publication on health under capitalism (Panitch and Leys 2009), health presents a major field of the political economy that is determined by the struggle between forces of commercialization and popular forces that struggle to keep or make it a public service with equal access for all. Given the multidimensional nature of the determinants of public health, social movement organizations in the health sector tend to have broad goals, intervening on debates about the political, economic, and environmental issues, such as the importance of access to water, food and housing, amongst a myriad of issues (Zoller 2006). As noted in the *Civil Society Report to the World Health Organization's Commission on Social Determinants of Health*, "peoples' quest for health [is] inseparable from unjust social and political forces, both internal and external" (CSDH 2007, 195). Similar to water, struggles for health are often used as an "entry point" for social movements seeking radical transformation of the political-economic system.

While social movements on health-related issues have existed as early as the industrial revolution, when concerns over occupational health were of importance, the body of social movement theory has been applied only recently to health movements. As a consequence, the wide array of different movements and their strategies, tactics, and political approaches have not been sufficiently studied in depth or comparatively (Brown and Zavestoski 2004). Scholarly attention, especially in the North, has focused on social movements for occupational safety, the women's health movement, HIV/ AIDS activism, and environmental justice organizing, recognizing their significance for the history of medicine and health policy and politics. At the global level, Obrinski identifies a widening array of actors that form health social movements as driving "key changes in the discourse and practice of global health" (2007, 29). Examining the process of global health politics and governance, he concludes that health social movements are major forces that have redefined the conceptions of global health in the past.

Brown et al (2004) identify three types of health social movements, all of which can be found in the global South, although the first two tend to dominate given poor provision of primary health care. *Health access movements* seek equitable access to health care and improved provision of health care services, for example, through national health care reforms to push for primary health care or the extension of health insurance. *Constituency-based health movements*, such as the women or gay and lesbian health movements, address inequality and health inequity based on lines of social division such as race, gender, or class. *Embodied health movements* aim at the treatment and/or research of illnesses or diseases, which have hitherto been denied recognition, such as breast cancer due to environmental pollution and the movements that aim to have recognize the illnesses of health care workers at Ground Zero who attended to the victims of the attacks on the World Trade Centre in New York City on September 11, 2001.

One example of a health access movement is the People's Health Movement—with its central slogan "Health for All"—a transnational network of social actors that strive for the right to health care and politicize the debates about the social determinants of health (e.g. clean water, food security, etc). With its Global Right to Health Care Campaign, the network aims to document violations of health rights, assess the right to health care in different countries, and campaign for the fulfillment of the right to health from the national to the global level. Such a bottom-up, rights-based, and antagonistic movement on health addresses today's environment of policy making that is framed by economic and ideological globalization.

Social movements in electricity

As noted above, given that the electricity sector lends itself the least to a rights-based discourse, there appear to be fewer social movement struggles over electricity than in the other two sectors we have documented. And given the perception of electricity as a "commodity", social movement struggles emerging in this sector tend to be primarily local in nature and directed against punitive forms of neoliberalism, as illustrated by two well-known cases of social contestation in the electricity sector: Arequipa, Peru, and Cape Town, South Africa.

As Arce (2008) argues, the Arequipa uprising against the concession of two state-owned electricity companies, Egasa and Egesur, to a Belgian company by the Toledo administration in Peru in 2002, is an example of a massive social response to neoliberal reform measures. Similar to the 2000 Water War in Cochabamba, Bolivia, "[t]he protest was fuelled by the conviction that economic growth and increased prosperity had not been beneficial to the poorer layers of society" (Biekart 2005, 87). The Common Civic Front of Arequipa (*Frente Amplio Cívico de Arequipa*, FACA), which grouped together trade unions, popular organizations, transport unions, agricultural workers, unemployed workers, and left political parties, led protests which successfully blocked the sale of the companies. Two people lost their lives in the protests known as the *Arequipazo*.

In South Africa, residents from many cities in the country have taken matters into their own hands reconnecting electricity services by ripping out prepaid electricity meters and/or tapping "illegally" into electricity lines (Ruiters 2007, McDonald 2009). Articulated with the national Anti-Privatization Forum, the community movement represents a radical challenge to "disciplinary neoliberalism" and demonstrates the effectiveness of direct action tactics given the many concessions that have been won by these electricity social movements (such as a free basic allotment of electricity of 50 kWh per household per month).

The relative silence on social movement struggles in the electricity sector (compared to water and health), however, might also be related to the fact that trade unions rather than "civil society" organizations have tended to lead these struggles. As Hall argues, "[m]ost of the [anti-privatization] campaigns [in the electricity sector] have been led by trade unions". Electrical workers all over the world have opposed privatization, often in coalitions with political parties, environmental groups, community organizations, and consumer groups, "based on the clear economic interest of workers whose jobs and working conditions are threatened, but the unions have generally campaigned on wider issues of public interest, including prices and accountability" (2010, 192). In comparison to the electricity sector, trade unions in the health and water sectors have formed deep coalitions with other actors such as NGOs and community-based organizations, acting as lead organizations in these coalitions.

FROM MOVEMENT COALITIONS TO ALTERNATIVES

Social movement organizations and the politics of coalition-building

Social movement organizations (SMOs) are formal organizations that do not necessarily involve the majority of the participants of social movements but prepare the terrain for "episodes of contention", such as protests and campaigns. The distinction between social movements and SMOs is based on the observation that as organizations grow and become formalized structures, they also tend to become more bureaucratic and conservative (Zald and Ash 1966). In the contemporary water, electricity, and health sectors in the global South, the most important SMOs represent the producers and users of these services—trade unions, community-based organizations, and NGOs. Since these organizations involve such broad and diverse constituencies, it is not surprising that tensions, but also synergies, emerge among them.

Public sector trade unions have been a favourite target of attack in neoliberal reform. Governments facing fiscal pressures have sought to weaken or destroy the bargaining power of unions in order to claw back workers' wages and benefits by using arguments that these "privileged workers" are overpaid relative to the rest of the population. Unions that represent workers providing services in water, health, and electricity services have been no exception to the rule (Hall 2005). Indeed, in the global South, public sector unions find themselves in a particularly difficult political situation in highly segmented labour markets in which the majority of the working population is engaged in informal types of work. In such a context, public service workers tend to be viewed by other members of the public—even by their allies—as a privileged "labour aristocracy". Under such conditions, meeting citizens' rights to affordable services and workers' rights to decent wages, benefits, and working conditions within public utilities becomes a challenging political balancing act (Spronk 2010). For these reasons, joint political mobilization between trade unions and community-based organizations, often referred to as "social movement unionism", has been upheld as a way forward for organized labour in a neoliberal world economy (Moody 1997).

Trade unions have been at the head of coalitions to defend water and electricity utilities against privatization in Uruguay and Peru, assisted by international organizations that have provided crucial resources to the trade union leadership (Novelli 2004, Taks 2008, Spronk 2009). In a successful campaign to prevent the partial privatization of the public health care system in El Salvador, health care workers were the lead organizations in a coalition with peasant organizations and NGOs that brought 20,000 people to the streets of Salvador in a mass march for public health in 1999 (Almeida 2006). As discussed further below, however, in many situations in which trade unions have historical alliances with the political parties in office, they have colluded with privatization processes in order to preserve their jobs and benefits, as has been well documented in several cases in Latin America and India (Murillo 2001, Uba 2008). It is not very well known, for example, that in the case of the 2000 "Water War" in Cochabamba, Bolivia—a widely cited example of social movement unionism—the public water workers' union was notable for its absence, and it was the local manufacturing workers who played a leading role (Spronk 2009).

If trade unions are seen as the *bête noire* that impedes public service reform, civil society organizations such as NGOs and community-based organizations (CBOs) are often seen as the *cause célèbre* (see, for example, World Bank 2004). For neoliberal ideologues, NGOs are conceived as organizations that are driven by shared values rather than by the quest for economic or political power and thus are innovative private organizations with a "public" ethos that are more capable than the state or the market at promoting people-centred development (Cernea 1988). Such an idealistic view of NGOs ignores, however, two of the principal problems faced by these organizations. First, they purport to speak for "the poors" but lack formal accountability mechanisms to any constituency but their donors (Hulme and Edwards 1997). Second, in the context of state retrenchment, they tend to be staffed by middle-class professionals who have little in common with the public they purport to serve and represent (Pfeiffer 2004). As the title of a recent collection published by the INCITE! Women of Colour against Violence collective on the "non-profit industrial complex" suggests, "The Revolution will not be Funded" (2007).

Nonetheless, it is important not to paint all NGOs with the same brush. Many organizations are militant advocacy organizations that play a crucial role as facilitators and brokers in social movement struggles, providing research, expertise, and leadership in social movement networks (Baud and Rutten 2005). As the many examples scattered throughout this book attest, NGOs have also played a crucial role in defining and supporting the implementation of alternatives to privatization. Environmental NGOs and policy think tanks play a crucial role in defining alternatives in the energy sector (e.g. International Rivers). International NGO intervention in the field of health policy has been effective in securing access to anti-retroviral drugs for those living with HIV/AIDS (Nelson and Dorsey 2007). The intervention of international NGOs was also crucial to pressuring Bechtel to drop its controversial case against the Bolivian state for cancelling the water concession contract arising from the "Water War" in 2005 (Spronk and Crespo Flores 2008).

CBOs, in contrast to NGOs, are "mass organizations" that tend to be more representative of the constituencies that they represent. The positive and important role of CBOs in delivering health services, particularly in intervening in culturally sensitive areas of service delivery such as HIV/AIDS treatment and prevention, has been particularly well documented (see, *inter alia*, Chillag et al, 2002). The advantage that CBOs have in terms of (potential) representativeness and their sensitivities to local context does not mean, however, that they do not face the same problems as NGOs; they, too, are embedded in local power structures. A case study of NGO-CBO-state relations in efforts to reduce urban poverty and improve service delivery in three cities in India finds that "rather than being vehicles of empowerment and change, CBOs and their leadership often block progress, controlling or capturing benefits aimed at the poor and misusing them for private (political) interests" (de Wit and Berner 2009, 927). Indeed, breaking out of the clientelist logic often requires that CBOs become part of a broader social movement involved in militant, direct action. As Piven and Cloward's (1977) classic work on "poor people's movements" has demonstrated, disruption has historically been the most effective tactic to gain concessions from state authorities, especially because "the poor" exist in such large numbers.

Building coalitions between trade unions, NGOs, and CBOs might be necessary to pull together the large protests, which have proven effective in pressuring governments to reverse privatization (Olivera and Lewis 2004, Almeida 2006), but it is not always a straightforward task. A good example is the relationship between the South African Municipal Workers' Union (Samwu) and the Anti-Privatization Forum (APF) in South Africa. Social movement unionism was born in the context of apartheid when trade unions were independent, combative organizations that took on the structures of the apartheid state. In the early 1990s, Samwu took an oppositional stance to privatization, perceiving that as public sector workers they were caught in a "producer-worker squeeze" as "SAMWU members are not only depot workers whose working conditions and job security were under attack, but also community members threatened by service cut-offs and poor delivery" (Lier and Stokke 2006, 813). In November 2002, Samwu called an indefinite strike in solidarity with the APF, but as Barchiesi (2007) explains, its objectives quickly faltered due to the accommodating position of the trade union umbrella, the Congress of South African Trade Unions (Cosatu), which had renewed its allegiance to the ANC during the elections that were to take place the following month. When push came to shove, the local union's oppositional stance was compromised by its stronger loyalty to the workers' central, irrespective of the support for the APF within the rank and file of Samwu.

The impact of social movements on public sector alternatives

In the chapter thus far we have demonstrated that social movements and their organizations have been crucial actors in the struggle to defend public sector alternatives. During the neoliberal period, social movement campaigns have tended to be overwhelmingly "reactive", centred on defending actually-existing systems from perceived threats, rather than being proactive (i.e. proposing new alternatives that seek to overcome the perceived problems with the old systems). Yet over the past decade, as the neoliberal model has become increasingly discredited, social movements have built upon their victories by opening public dialogue on, and advancing political demands for, alternatives.

Given the victories of social movements against privatization in the water sector, it is here that the debates on alternatives tend to be the most advanced. While their international networks initially focused primarily on the defence against privatization and commercialization, over the last decade they have undergone a remarkable qualitative shift towards a constructive, positive challenge for public water alternatives (Terhorst 2009). As a representative from the Public Services International (PSI) put it during a water workshop in the World Social Forum of 2005 in Porto Alegre: "We are winning the privatization debate—and what now?", reminding participants that movements for "public services for all" are confronted with the challenge to advance alternatives because of their own achievements in defeating the privatization agenda.

The current discourse on alternatives takes up this challenge and argues for the protection, restoration, and promotion of public and community sector water management. Today, water movements aim for the revitalization and democratization of non-commercialized public and community water management that are appropriate for their local political, socioeconomic, and political-ecological contexts (International Forum in the Defense of Water 2006). Given the differences between the movements, some of which launch a strong anti-systematic critique of capitalism and liberal democracy while others seek improvements within the existing system, it is no surprise that there exist unresolved conceptual and political tensions in what exactly presents a desirable alternative. For example, there is a debate over whether social movements should promote the human right to water or endorse the idea of water as a commons, as it is feared that the former can serve the interests of corporations, while the latter presents a systemic alternative to capitalist social property relations (Bakker 2007). Nonetheless, different political tendencies within the movement share a common goal to universalize services, arguing that the democratization of institutions will depend on effective intervention of social movements at all levels, from local to global. Given the fact that water systems are embedded within the broader relations of production and reproduction and systemic barriers to change, the clarification of the who, how, and what of alternatives presents a formidable challenge for social movements. In the context of waning neoliberalism, the strategic political task of social movements today is to widen their organizations and repertoires so that they become proactive and constructive, but nevertheless still confrontational organizations that push for the reform of public service systems based on collective ownership and popular democracy.

The struggles for reform in the water sector in Peru, Bolivia, and Uruguay, and the Treatment Action Campaign to increase access to anti-retroviral drugs in South Africa, illustrate the point. The water struggles in the Peruvian regional capital of Huancayo that started in 2003 demonstrate how movement coalitions, which in the first instance are a defensive reaction against privatization, can develop proactive movement strategies towards public alternatives. The Regional Front for the Defence of Water and Life in Huancayo presents a "deep coalition" between citizens, users and organized civil society—such as market stall owners, pensioners, social welfare organizations, neighbourhood committees, and the water utility workers union (Tattersall 2005, Spronk 2009). In 2005, the Front successfully stalled a planned privatization of the municipal water utility, SEDAM Huancayo. Demonstrating how crucial alternatives are for movement strategies, the privatization was cancelled fully in 2006 only after a series of popular seminars developed, socialized, and politicized an alternative management plan for the modernization without privatization or commercialization of the local utility (Terhorst 2008).

In another example, the creation of the Uruguayan national water movement coalition (*Comisión Nacional en Defensa del Agua y la Vida*, CNDAV), composed of the water workers' union from the public utility, environmental, and human rights NGOs, which promoted a successful national referendum campaign in 2004, started off initially as a limited civic and union response to development plans for environmentally damaging waste water treatment and further privatizations of parts of the national utility, *Obras Sanitarias del Estado* (OSE). From the initially localized and limited social mobilization in one department of the country, there developed a national referendum campaign by a broad coalition of social forces that brought together an impressive range of social actors to develop a far-reaching constitutional reform proposal that included a series of substantial changes such as the human right to water, direct public control, participation of citizens in all areas and steps of water resource management, and an ecosystems approach.

Treatment Action Campaign (TAC) in South Africa is another example of how movement organizations not only develop resistance strategies but also intervene in the sector with constructive policy and institutional proposals.

TAC, launched in 1998, works for the rights of people living with HIV/ AIDS in poor urban townships and rural areas. It started to engage in service delivery work and advocacy for cheaper access to anti-retroviral drugs in South Africa. In 2001, TAC created a research committee and held workshops and conferences to develop a proposal and campaign for a "National Treatment Plan". After a successful case at the constitutional court for the socio-economic rights of people living with HIV/AIDS, TAC pressured the government through formal and informal channels to realize a rollout of anti-retroviral drugs in 2003 (Makino 2009). TAC is an important source of cultural innovation in the health sector of South Africa, highlighting that new organizational forms, values, and sector practices "are infused into social structures via political contestation" (Rao et al, 2000, 275).

These three examples demonstrate how movements seek and strategically strive for the transformation of public service through the radical transformation of the social relations of production, distribution, and consumption, thereby affecting the political ecology and political economy of these economic state apparatuses. But as Bond (2005, 353) argues for the South African context, "the challenge . . . as ever, is to establish the difference between 'reformist reforms' on the one hand, and reforms that advance a 'non-reformist' agenda on the other, allowing democratic control of social reproduction, of financial markets and ultimately of production itself".

Once the barricades come down, however, and the defensive struggle has been won, it is difficult to maintain the social energy required to shift the balance of power that would be required to create true "non-reformist" alternatives. Such has been the case in Bolivia and Uruguay. The struggle for alternatives began in Cochabamba, Bolivia, in 1999 with urban demands for the reduction of tariffs and demands from the powerful irrigator's association for the modification of the government's pro-privatization law. By the time the Bolivian government finally backed down, cancelling the privatization contract and modifying the national water law, the cycle of struggle had further expanded into a movement for the reappropriation of the municipal utility under the banner of participation, transparency, and social control. These demands turned the social movement organizations themselves into agents of change inside the utility board, as they occupied two of five seats in an interim utility board, but crucially, the most powerful actor in the coalition—the irrigator's association—moved onto other projects of greater relevance to their immediate interests. In the following years, the social activists who remained developed proposals and implemented mechanisms of social control and popular participation in the public water and sanitation utility, SEMAPA. However, these movement-induced changes did not reach the desired result of a well-functioning public utility (Sánchez Gómez and Terhorst 2005, Spronk 2008). The fact that SEMAPA today remains an ill-performing and badly governed utility only highlights the difficulties of social movement organizations in turning themselves into long-term agents of sector change, particularly in the absence of a transformation of the power relationships that characterize local politics.

In comparison, the campaign for constitutional reform in Uruguay was successful, but only in narrow terms. Under the constitution, water services and resources by law now have to be governed by a specific and centralized public body that has to insure the participation of citizens and workers. As a result, the government created the National Directorate for Water and Sanitation Services (DINASA) and its Advisory of Water and Sanitation (COASA) in 2007. These institutions, however, were not the far-reaching reforms that the movement had demanded and expected from the left-of-centre government that was elected in 2005. Instead, they represented a state-centric step in sector development that was strongly criticized at the time for its lack of radical change and exclusion of CNDAV from the parliamentary decision-making process (Santos and Valdomir 2005).

On a more positive note, the constitutional entrenchment of the human right to water has affected Uruguay's international negotiations, upsetting the organizers of the neoliberal World Water Forums. Also, the improvement of public sector management has been turned into a political priority and involved the movement members in formal and informal participation, especially the trade union FFOSE. At FFOSE's insistence, the public water and sanitation utility (OSE) has created a Social Office to implement amongst other things a social tariff policy and has developed an international solidarity strategy to support other public water operators in the region (Terhorst 2009). OSE is also one of the main organizers of a regional utilities forum proposed for 2010, which aims to create a regional network of non-commercialized public utilities through the promotion of PuPs. These institutional changes in OSE and in the union would have been inconceivable were it not for the constructive intervention of the social movements that started but, most importantly, did not end with the referendum campaign. CNDAV also stands out as an exceptionally positive example of how movement coalitions can involve social movement unionism, generate social capital, create resources, and take advantage of political opportunities. The example of CNDAV in Uruguay confirms Diani's argument that "the solidity of the linkages within the movement sector as well as—more crucially—of the bonds among movement actors, the social milieu in which they operate, and cultural and political elites" (1997, 129) increase the influence and impact of social movements on the reform of public institutions.

These two cases illustrate that it is easier for movements to generate procedural outcomes than it is to enforce substantive change. That is to say, it is relatively easy to create new channels of participation that include social movement actors but it is another matter altogether to actually implement the decisions they generate. In addition, social movements are more likely to be successful in a campaign to prevent a "public bad", for example, by preventing privatization, than in creating substantive movement outcomes that generate a new "public good", for example the reform of an ill-performing utility. Following Kriesi (1995), such positive substantive outcome requires that the state has both the capacity and the political will to put into operation movement demands. While the cancellation of a privatization contract does not require too many state resources, apart from the high financial costs that can be related to contract cancellations, the implementation of a new alternative path of development does. For example, although TAC won the case in the South African constitutional court and successfully exerted formal and informal pressure on the Health Ministry, which resulted in a policy decision for an anti-retroviral drug rollout scheme for people living with HIV/AIDS (Makino 2009), the actual implementation of such a policy decision depended on the state's capacity, political will, and resources. At the stage of policy implementation however, social movements have reduced power to influence as legal and institutional changes are processes that can take decades and are not easily influenced by social movements (Soule and King 2006). While TAC became a recognized actor with access to formal policy decision making within corporatist bodies of health policy making in South Africa, it also maintained its oppositional stance by using direct action tactics to confront the Health Ministry (Makino 2009) in order to compensate for a certain lack of strategic capacity within the policy implementation process.

Apart from these limitations that movements face in moving from procedural to substantive reforms and from defensive to proactive, the innovative power of social movements lies particularly in the diffusion of repertoires. One such example can be found in the water movement networks that diffuse and elaborate PuPs. The water movements, especially trade unions but also some international NGOs, have developed this mechanism on the basis of existing practices in the field of water management, such as twinning arrangements in the Baltic Sea, and have politicized and filled these neglected tools of exchange with renewed normative meaning and political impetus (Hall et al, 2009). A number of PuPs have developed "from below" in recent years at the initiative of trade unions and local social movement organizations (see Chapter 15, this volume, on the water sector in Latin America). They were facilitated through the networks of the global trade union confederation of Public Services International, the regional water network (*La Red Vida*), and the global Reclaiming Public Water Network. The Uruguayan utility OSE, for example, has in May 2010 signed a PuP pre-agreement with the municipal utility SEDACUSCO in Peru. Such bottom-up PuPs exemplify how water movements generate novel proposals for water management through their politicized participation in concrete policy and management decisions. They also show how a shift in norms, towards equal, not-for-profit strengthening of the public sector, can generate new forms of interaction between social movements, managers, and workers.

CONCLUSION

Bevington (2005) emphasizes the need for scholarship that prioritizes the relevance of research to social movements themselves and argues that this requires a turn away from the theoretical schisms that merely emphasize different variables instead of looking comprehensively at movements.

Accordingly, we have developed an account of the distinct characteristics, roles, and impacts of social movements that seek alternatives to "accumulation by dispossession" in the health, water, and electricity sectors and which avoids the schism between "old" and "new" social movements which has little relevance in analyzing struggles for basic services in the global South.

During the neoliberal period, social movement activity in the health, water, and electricity sectors has been primarily defensive in nature, focused on preventing or reversing the privatization of state services. Having won campaigns against this corporate agenda, social movement leaders face the question "now what?" and have increasingly turned their attention towards making proposals to remedy the perceived weaknesses of state-public and communal forms of management. These tasks involve the elaboration of a new set of social criteria by which to define what an alternative is and how to evaluate its "success" (hence the emphasis in this book on research methodology, as discussed in Chapter 2).

Despite several successful cases of social movements that have had an impact on the provision of health, electricity, and water services, our survey of social movements in these sectors confirms the findings of other scholars that collective action is less effective for achieving policy change than generally believed (Foweraker 2001, Burstein and Sausner 2005). While the coalition form of organizing has proven an effective way to rebuild the capacity for mobilization lost over the past three decades of neoliberal restructuring, it has been a challenge for social movement leaders to maintain the social energy required to move from single-issue, defensive campaigns towards the more complicated task of elaborating proposals for alternatives. In the case of multi-actor coalitions, the participation of key stakeholders—particularly public sector workers—is key, as demonstrated by the perceived failure of reform after the Bolivian Water War.

This survey also suggests that it tends to be easier for social movements to achieve procedural rather than substantive outcomes, as illustrated by the case of TAC that sought to expand access to anti-retroviral drugs in South Africa, and that continual pressure on the state is often necessary to transform policy into action. Furthermore, since political bargaining and negotiation with state authorities often requires compromise, initial policy decisions for radical reforms proposed by social movements are often watered down in the course of their execution by the state, as was the case with the Uruguay referendum for the right to water.

As the social movement slogan "another world is not only possible, it is necessary" suggests, however, the crisis of neoliberalism, and more recently the global financial crisis, have created new opportunities for public debate about alternatives to models that have dominated the policy agenda for the past three decades. Introducing ideas of transparency, democracy, participation, equality, and collective ownership, social movements struggling for "services for all" make an essential contribution not just to sectoral debates on service delivery but to much broader local and global debates on economic and social justice.

NOTES

1. South Africa because of its history of privatization after apartheid—particularly the unfulfilled promises to extend basic services made by the African National Congress (ANC) government—appears to be an exception. On a rights-based framework in electricity, see Ruiters (2007) and see Dugard (2009) on the movement to self-reconnect water and electricity services in defiance of prepaid meters.

REFERENCES

Almeida, P.D. 2003. After the revolution: Gender and democracy in El Salvador, Nicaragua, and Guatemala. *Contemporary Sociology: A Journal of Reviews* 32(2): 214–215.

Almeida, P.D. 2006. Social movement unionism, social movement partyism, and policy outcomes: Health care privatization in El Salvador. In Johnston, H. and Almeida, P.D. (Eds), *Latin American Social Movements*, pp. 57–73. Lanham: Rowman and Littlefield.

Arce, M. 2008. The repoliticization of collective action after neoliberalism in Peru. *Latin American Politics and Society* 50(3): 37–62.

Armstrong, E.A. and Bernstein, M. 2008. Culture, power, and institutions: A multi-institutional politics approach to social movements. *Sociological Theory* 26(1): 74–99.

Bakker, K. 2007. The "Commons" Versus the "Commodity": Alter-globalization, anti-privatization and the human right to water in the Global South. *Antipode* 39(3): 430–455.

Balanyá, B., Brennan, B., Hoedeman, O., Kishimoto, S. and Terhorst, P. (Eds). 2005. *Reclaiming public water: Achievements, struggles, and visions from around the world*. Porto Alegre, Brazil: Transnational Institute and Corporate Europe Observatory.

Ballard, R., Habib, A. and Valochia, I.. 2006. *Voices of protest: Social movements in post-apartheid South Africa*. Scottsville, South Africa: University of KwaZulu-Natal Press.

Barchiesi, F. 2006. Classes, multitudes and the politics of community movements in post-apartheid South Africa. In Gibson, N. (Ed), *Challenging hegemony. Social movements and the quest for a new humanism in South Africa*, pp. 161–194. Trenton: Africa World Press.

———. 2007. Privatization and the historical trajectory of "social movement unionism": A case study of municipal workers in Johannesburg, South Africa. *International Labour and Working-Class History* (71): 50–69.

Baud, M. and Rutten, R. (Eds). 2005. *Popular intellectuals and social movements: Framing protest in Asia, Africa, and Latin America*. Cambridge: Cambridge University Press.

Bevington, D. 2005. Movement-relevant theory: Rethinking social movement scholarship and activism. *Social Movement Studies* 4: 3185–3208.

Biekart, K. 2005. Seven theses on Latin American social movements and political change. *The European Review of Latin American and Caribbean Studies* 79: 85–94.

Bond, P. 2005. Globalisation/commodification or deglobalization/decommodification in urban South Africa. *Policy Studies* 26(3–4): 337–358.

Brown, P. and Zavestoski, S. 2004. Social movements in health: An introduction. *Sociology of Health and Illness* 26(6): 697–694.

Brown, P., Zavestoski, S., McCormick, S., Mayer, B., Morello-Frosch, R. and Gasior Altman, R. 2004. Embodied health movements: New approaches to social movements in health. *Sociology of Health and Illness* 26(1): 50–80.

Burstein, P. and Sausner, S. 2005. The incidence and impact of policy-oriented collective action: Competing views. *Sociological Forum* 20: 403–419.

Canel, E. 1997. New social movement theory and resource mobilization theory: The need of integration. IDRC. www.idrc.ca/en/ev-54446-201-1-DO_TOPIC. html (accessed on 29 June 2010).

Castells, M. 1977. *The urban question: A Marxist approach.* London: E. Arnold.

Cernea, M.M. 1988. *Non-governmental organizations and local development.* Washington: World Bank.

Chillag, K., Bartholow, K., Cordeiro, J., Swanson, S., Patterson, J., Stebbins, S., Woodside, C. and Sy, F.. 2002. Factors affecting the delivery of HIV/AIDS prevention programs by community-based organizations. *Aids Education and Prevention* 14(3): 27–37.

Coetzee, D. 2004. South Africa's new social movements. In Polet, F. (Ed), *Globalizing resistance: The state of struggle*, pp. 103–111. London: Pluto.

Cook, M.L. 1996. *Organizing dissent: Unions, the state, and the democratic teachers' movement in Mexico.* University Park, PA: Pennsylvania State University Press.

CSDH (Commission on the Social Determinants of Health). 2007. Civil Society Report to the Commission on Social Determinants of Health. *Social Medicine* 2(4): 192–211.

de Wit, J. and Berner, E. 2009. Progressive Patronage? Municipalities, NGOs, CBOs and the limits to slum dwellers' empowerment. *Development and Change* 40(5): 927–947.

Diani, M. 1997. Social movements and social capital: A network perspective on movement outcomes. *Mobilization* 2: 129–147.

Diani, M. and McAdam, D. 2003. *Social movements and networks: Relational approaches to collective action.* Oxford: Oxford University Press.

Dugard, J. 2009. Power to the people? A rights-based analysis of South Africa's electrical services. In McDonald, D.A. (Ed), *Electric capitalism: Recolonising Africa on the power grid*, pp. 264–287. London: Earthscan.

Egan, A. and Wafer, A. 2004. *The Soweto Electricity Crisis Committee.* Discussion Paper. Durban, South Africa, University of Kwazulu-Natal: Centre for Civil Society.

Esping-Andersen, G. 1990. *The three worlds of welfare capitalism.* Cambridge, UK: Polity Press.

Foweraker, J. 1995. *Theorizing social movements.* London: Pluto Press.

Foweraker, J. 2001. *Grassroots movements, political activism and social development in Latin America: A comparison of Chile and Brazil.* Geneva: United Nations Research Institute for Social Development.

Haber, P.L. 1996. Identity and political process: Recent trends in the study of Latin American social movements. *Latin American Research Review* 31(1): 171–189.

Hall, D. 2005. Electricity privatisation and restructuring in Latin America and the impact on workers, 2005. PSIRU. www.psiru.org (accessed 29 June 2010).

Hall, D. 2010. Struggles against privatization of electricity worldwide. In Abramsky, K. (Ed), *Sparking a worldwide energy revolution: Social struggles in the transition to a post-petrol world*, pp. 188–196. Edinburgh: AK Press.

Hall, D., Lobina, E. and de la Motte, R. 2005. Public resistance to privatisation in water and energy. *Development in Practice* 15(3–4): 286–301.

Hall, D., Lobina, E., Corral, V., Hoedeman, D., Terhorst, P., Pigeon, M. and Kishimoto, S. 2009. *Public-public partnerships (PUPs) in water.* Greenwich, UK: PSIRU.

154 *Susan Spronk and Philipp Terhorst*

Hamlin, C. 1998. *Public health and social justice in the age of Chadwick: Britain, 1800–1854.* Cambridge: Cambridge University Press.
Harvey, D. 2003. *The new imperialism.* Oxford and New York: Oxford University Press.
Hulme, D. and Edwards, M. 1997. *NGOs, states and donors: Too close for comfort?* New York: St. Martin's Press.
Illich, I. 1985. *H2O and the waters of forgetfulness: Reflections on the historicity of "stuff".* Dallas: Dallas Institute of Humanities and Culture.
Incite! Women of Colour against Violence. 2007. *The revolution will not be funded: Beyond the non-profit industrial complex.* Cambridge: South End Press.
International Forum on the Defense of Water. 2006. Joint declaration of the movements in defense of water. www.blueplanetproject.net/Movement/Declaration.html (accessed 20 July 2010).
Kriesi, H. 1995. The political opportunity structure of new social movements: Its impact on their motivation. In Jenkins, C. and Klandermans, B. (Eds), *The politics of social protest: Comparative perspectives on states and social movements*, pp. 167–198. Minneapolis: University of Minnesota Press.
Leys, C. 2001. *Market-driven politics: Neoliberal democracy and the public interest.* New York: Verso.
Lier, D.C. and Stokke, K. 2006. Maximum working class unity? Challenges to local social movement unionism in Cape Town. *Antipode* 38(4): 802–824.
Mainwaring, S. 1987. Urban popular movements, identity, and democratization in Brazil. *Comparative Political Studies* 20(2): 97–117.
Makino, K. 2009. Institutional conditions for social movements to engage in formal politics: The case of AIDS activism in post-apartheid South Africa. In Shigetomi, S. and Makino, K. (Eds), *Protest and social movements in the developing world*, pp. 110–133. Northampton: Edward Elgar.
McAdam, D., Tarrow, S. G. and Tully, C. 2001. *Dynamics of contention.* New York: Cambridge University Press.
McDonald, D.A. 2009. *Electric capitalism: Recolonising Africa on the power grid.* London: Earthscan.
McDonald, D.A. and Ruiters, G. (Eds). 2005. *The age of commodity: Water privatization in Southern Africa.* London: Earthscan.
Moody, K. 1997. Towards an international social-movement unionism. *New Left Review* (225): 52–72.
Morgan, B. 2006. Turning off the tap: Urban water service delivery and the social construction of global administrative law. *European Journal of International Law* 17(1): 215–246.
Murillo, M.V. 2001. *Labour unions, partisan coalitions and market reforms in Latin America.* Cambridge: Cambridge University Press.
Mychalejko, C. 2008. Ecuador's constitution gives rights to nature. Upsidedownworld. www.upsidedownworld.org/main/content/view/1494/1/ (accessed 29 June 2010).
Naidoo, A., Davidson-Harden, A. and Harden, A. 2000. The geopolitics of the water justice movement. *Peace, Conflict and Development* (11). http://www.peacestudiesjournal.uk
Nash, J.C. 1994. Global integration and subsistence insecurity. *American Anthropologist* 96(1): 7–30.
Nelson, P. and Dorsey, E. 2007. New rights advocacy in a global public domain. *European Journal of International Relations* 13(2): 187–216.
Novelli, M. 2004. Globalisations, social movement unionism and new internationalisms: The role of strategic learning in the transformation of the Municipal Workers Union of EMCALI. *Globalisation, Societies and Education* 2(2): 161–190.

Obrinski, J. 2007. Global health, social movements, and governance. In Cooper, A.F. (Ed), *Governing global health. Challenge, response, innovation,* pp. 29–40. Aldershot: Ashgate.

Olivera, O. 2004. A political thesis. In Olivera, O. and Lewis, T. (Eds), *Cochabamba! Water War in Bolivia,* pp. 117–128. Cambridge: South End Press.

Olivera, O. and Lewis, T. 2004. *Cochabamba!: Water War in Bolivia.* Cambridge: South End Press

Panitch, L. and Leys, C. (Eds). 2009. *Socialist Register 2010: Morbid symptoms–Health under capitalism.* London: Merlin Press.

Parliamentary Forum WSF. 2006. *Final declaration of the Sixth World Parliamentary Forum.* Caracas, Venezuela: World Social Forum.

Paulson, S. and Bailey, P. 2003. Culturally constructed relationships shape sexual and reproductive health in Bolivia. *Culture Health and Sexuality* 5(6): 483–498.

Pfeiffer, J. 2004. Civil society, NGOs, and the holy spirit in Mozambique. *Human Organization* 63(3): 359–372.

Piven, F.F. and Cloward, R.A. 1977. *Poor people's movements: Why they succeed, how they fail.* New York: Pantheon Books.

Rao, H., Morill, C. and Zald, M.N. 2000. Power plays, how social movements and collective action create new organizational forms. *Research in Organizational Behaviour* 22: 239–282.

Ruiters, G. 2007. Contradictions in municipal services in contemporary South Africa: Disciplinary commodification and self-disconnections. *Critical Social Policy* 27(4): 487–508.

Sánchez Gómez, L. and Terhorst, P. 2005. Cochabamba, Bolivia: Public-collective partnership after the Water War. In Balanyá, B., Brennan, B., Hoedeman, O., Kishimoto, S. and Terhorst, P. (Eds), *Reclaiming public water: Achievements, struggles, and visions from around the world,* pp. 121–130. Porto Alegre, Brazil: Transnational Institute and Corporate Europe Observatory.

Santos, C. and Valdomir, S. 2005. Agua, reforma y después: El largo camino hacia una política de aguas. *REDES—Amigos de la Tierra (Uruguay).* http://www.redes.org.uy/wp-content/uploads/2008/10/agua_informe_serpaj.pdf

Santos, C. and Villareal, A. 2006. Uruguay: La democracia directa en la defensa del derecho al agua. *Movimientos sociales y luchas por el derecho humano al agua en América Latina* 34: 171–179. ILSA. Bogotá, Colombia: Instituto Latinoaméricano de Servicios Legales Alternativos.

Schonwalder, G. 2004. *Linking civil society and the state: Urban popular movements, the left, and local government in Peru, 1980–1992.* Pittsburgh: Pennsylvania State University Press.

Soule, S.A. and King, B.G. 2006. The stages of the policy process and the Equal Rights Amendment, 1972–1982. *American Journal of Sociology* 111(6): 1871–1909.

Spronk, S. 2007. Roots of resistance to urban water privatization in Bolivia: The "new working class", the crisis of neoliberalism, and public services. *International Labour and Working-Class History* (71): 8–28.

———. 2008. After the Water Wars in Bolivia: The struggle for a "social-public" alternative. Upsidedownworld, www.upsidedownworld.org/main/content/view/1255/31/ (accessed 20 July 2010).

———. 2009. Water privatization and the prospects for trade union revitalization in the public sector: Case studies from Bolivia and Peru. *Just Labour: A Canadian Journal of Work and Society* 14: 164–176.

———. 2010. Water and sanitation utilities in the global South: Re-centering the debate on "efficiency". *Radical Review of Political Economics* 42(2): 156–174.

Spronk, S. and Crespo Flores, C. 2008. Water, national sovereignty and social resistance: Bilateral investment treaties and the struggles against multinational water companies in Cochabamba and El Alto, Bolivia. *Law, Social Justice and Global Development* (1). http://www2.warwick.ac.uk/fac/soc/law/elj/lgd/2008_1/spronk_crespo

Spronk, S. and Webber, J.R. 2007. Struggles against accumulation by dispossession in Bolivia—The political economy of natural resource contention. *Latin American Perspectives* 34(2): 31–47.

Swyngedouw, E. 2004. *Social power and the urbanization of water.* Oxford: Oxford University Press.

Taks, J. 2008. "El agua es de todos/Water for all": Water resources and development in Uruguay. *Development* 51: 17–22.

Tattersall, A. 2005. There is power in coalition: A framework for assessing how and when union-community coalitions are effective and enhance union power. *Labour and Industry* 16(2): 97–112.

Terhorst, P. 2008. Huancayo: From resistance to public-public partnership. In Balanyá, B., Brennan, B., Hoedeman, O., Kishimoto, S., and Terhorst, P. (Eds), *Reclaiming public water: Achievements, struggles, and visions from around the world.* Porto Alegre, Brazil: Transnational Institute and Corporate Europe Observatory.

———. 2009. The role of social movements in developing public alternatives in urban water services. PhD thesis. Loughborough University, Leicestershire, UK.

Tilly, C. 1978. *From mobilization to revolution.* Reading: Addison-Wesley.

Touraine, A. 1969. *La société post-industrielle.* Paris: Denoël.

Uba, K. 2008. Labour union resistance to economic liberalization in India: What can national and state level patterns of protests against privatization tell us? *Asian Survey* 48(5): 860–884.

van Schaick, A. 2009. Bolivia's new constitution. NACLA report on the Americas. www.nacla.org/node/5437 (accessed 29 June 2010).

World Bank. 2004. *Making services work for the poor: World Development Report 2004.* Washington, DC: World Bank.

Zald, M.N. and Ash, R. 1966. Social movement organizations: Growth, decay and change. *Social Forces* 44(3): 327–341.

Zoller, H.M. 2006. Health activism: Communication theory and action for social change. *Communication Theory* 15(4): 341–364.

7 Careful What You Ask For
State-Led Alternatives to Privatization

David A. McDonald and Greg Ruiters

In the search for alternatives to privatization one of the most commonly heard calls for action is to "bring the state (back) in". Strictly speaking, the state was never "out"—it authored and managed privatization—but scholars, activists, and policy makers alike have argued that a necessary part of countering the commercialization of public services is to defend and advance state-owned, state-funded and state-operated services such as municipal water providers, provincial electricity generators, and national health care agencies.

This is not simply a "left wing" narrative. Since the failure of much of the privatization agenda of the 1980s and 1990s, even the World Bank has begun a "rethink" of market fundamentalism and private sector involvement in essential services and now calls for a stronger presence of the state.

Nor is this a new narrative. Over a century ago, many private services were municipalized or nationalized, often by conservative governments looking to rationalize fragmented, corrupt, and inefficient private service delivery systems. Since that time, there has been a steady stream of calls to bring the state (back) in by nationalizing and municipalizing sectors as diverse as health care, car manufacturing and tourism, and from regimes as disparate as Mussolini's Italy to Evo Morales's Bolivia. In other words, calling for state-owned/managed services is neither institutionally novel nor ideologically uniform.

After World War II, a large number of state-owned enterprises were formed, and these became central to national development strategies in both "advanced" and "less developed" countries. They were a means to provide universal public services, promote social objectives, and build national identity in what were called "mixed economies". The Mexican government, for example, owned over 1,500 enterprises, from airlines to oil. Socialist-inclined governments moved beyond mixed economies towards more extensive nationalization. In the mid-1980s, however, most state enterprises ran aground: the state could no longer fund nationalized firms, service quality was poor, and corruption and persistent strikes by public sector workers led to large-scale public resentment. In response, neoliberal ideas and privatization became hegemonic, as evidenced by the election of popular conservatives such as Margaret Thatcher and Ronald Reagan in the late 1970s and early 1980s, and "social" neoliberals such as Bill Clinton, Thabo Mbeki, and Tony Blair in the 1990s.

In moving beyond neoliberalism, the variety of forms of state owner-ship and the difference between a Mussolini (fascist state) and a Morales (democratic movement) government are crucial. Property forms and state organizations cannot be evaluated independently of their contexts, and it cannot be assumed that all countries have followed the European path of state and civil society formation (Mamdani 1995).

It is equally important to see the debate about "bringing the state back in" in terms of historical specificity. State intervention that is motivated on the part of capital to save a system that has spiraled out of control (such as state-sponsored buyouts after the financial crisis of 2008) is very differ-ent from defending public systems with anti-capitalist objectives. Calls for bringing the state back in must therefore be conditional and clearly speci-fied, making it important to take an historical and contextual perspective on the role of the state in challenging privatization, and proposing "alterna-tives", as the very diverse record of state-led service delivery over the past 150 years has demonstrated. Unless it has been radically democratized, there may be little point in bringing the state back in since it can act as a crude instrument to reassert a neoliberal agenda and market ideology.

Our objective in this chapter is to critically investigate this history, with a focus on instances in which the state has explicitly attempted to reverse and/or resist privatization in the areas of water, electricity, and health care. The focus is on "modern" public services—i.e. industrialized networked service systems since the mid-1800s—with the aim of drawing lessons from these state-led service experiments: What were the reasons for state inter-vention? What did they look like institutionally and ideologically? Were they successful and why? What do these experiments tell us about state-led alternatives to privatization in the global South today?

The review raises important questions about the nature of the state, the meanings of citizenship, and how we define notions of "public" and good-quality services. It also suggests that we should avoid seeing the state as a bureaucratic set of institutions (as Weberians tend to do) endowed with its own capacity and suspended above society, but rather as a condensation of social relations (Mamdani 1995). The socio-political processes of ser-vice delivery are as important as the deliverables. These are complex and contentious issues, and we cannot expect to resolve them here, but we do hope to challenge some simplistic assumptions about the ability of states to alter commercialization trends simply through ownership, without political and social mobilization and without questioning the larger productive and distributional mechanisms of the economy.

We are largely supportive of state-owned and state-operated services, under democratic conditions, but our objective in this chapter is to highlight some of the tensions and limitations associated with this policy objective and to emphasize the very different practical and ideological tones it can take on. Calling for state-owned/managed services is of little value in and of itself without considering how state and social groups are interrelated and how "empowered democracy" and public ethics might be attained. It is the *type* of state, and the social, political, and economic *milieu* within which it operates that matter. We must, therefore, be careful what we ask for.

Our discussion ranges from 19th-century European efforts to municipalize water to contemporary experiences of renationalization in the global South. We look at a wide range of scalar and institutional state formations, from fascist dictatorships to socialist local governments. We do this intentionally to highlight the breadth of institutional formations and state ideologies that have explicitly challenged the privatization of services, and to demonstrate just how different state ownership and management of services can be.

THE STATE AND STATE OWNERSHIP

For heuristic purposes, we have divided our analysis of state intervention into two broad categories—capitalist states and socialist states—and look at the ways in which these two types of governments have argued for state ownership and management of basic services. The former is made up of states that are supportive of market economies but which have decided that state ownership of (certain) services is preferential to private ownership, at least at a particular moment in time. Socialist states, by contrast, are those opposed to marketized systems of production and distribution and generally in favour of state ownership and management of essential services.

These are crude characterizations, of course, but we have done this for two reasons. First, the overwhelming majority of states today are market-oriented, and any attempt to "bring the state back in" will necessarily be within a market context (locally or internationally). Understanding the variegated history of state engagement in services within capitalist systems helps us understand the possibilities and limitations of such state interventions in the future.

Second, some of the most interesting alternatives to privatization today are taking place in socialist-oriented states, notably in Latin America, and there remains an interest in the service delivery experience of former socialist countries. It is therefore important to understand what differentiates these socialist states from their market-oriented counterparts—as well as what makes them similar—and to try and decipher discernable patterns associated with state-led socialist service delivery systems.

The primary focus of the chapter is on capitalist states, however, in an attempt to throw critical light on what has (too often) become a naïve celebration of "publicly owned" services in market economies. This is not to suggest that state ownership of services should not continue to be a primary demand of anti-privatization activists—as noted above we are supportive of state ownership over private ownership of essential services—but we do feel it is important to challenge the notion that state ownership is inherently positive. Without such a critical lens, we are prone to promoting/accepting policy programmes that fail to address some of the underlying problems of commercialization. Both privatization and nationalization are strategies that have been deployed by capital at various moments. At the very least, we need to see state intervention as a characteristic and cyclical feature of capitalist state behaviour and not an altruistic move on the part of market-oriented decision makers. Nationalization is often a temporary bailout of failed capitalist enterprises, reversed when capital is stronger and desires to take them over again.

Our understanding of the reasons for state-led services in capitalist economies therefore depends in part on different perspectives of how and why these states intervene against privatization and what is termed "market failure". The mainstream pluralist perspective is one that sees the capitalist state as politically contested terrain with many different social forces competing for access and influence. These analysts see the state as having varying degrees of autonomy from these social formations, with decisions to take state control of a service away from the private sector to be a demonstration of the state's willingness and capacity to act *against* the interests of fractions of capital to preserve broader social stability and address issues of equity and sustainability (Evans et al, 1985). Democratic institutions are seen to be critical to the maintenance and management of these dynamic forms of governance.

A competing view is one that sees capitalist state institutions as inherently oriented to serving dominant class interests, because the state operates within circumstances beyond its control and has to prioritize economic growth, protect profits and social order, and defend private property. As Harvey writes, the role of the state is explained by the need for "capital to find ways to maintain a reserve army alive and in place by unemployment benefits, social security, welfare schemes and so on. Individual capitalists cannot easily assume such burdens which typically devolve upon the state" (1982, 382). Even the progressive welfare state and public health measures can be seen as characteristic of the state, which is the "general manager" of the capitalist class *as a whole,* and much of the social functions of the capitalist state can be explained by this rationale. The neoclassical notion of "public goods" intellectually expresses capitalism's inner workings rather than scientific concepts. Why, for example, do mainstream economists see food as a private good but water as a public good?

Seen from this perspective, capitalist services and infrastructure can be a double-edged sword. "Public" services such as roads and schools may bring benefits but can equally serve to exploit, pacify, integrate, and reconstitute subjects and cultures (Payer 1982, 90–91). Welfare states can help produce docile subjects. In order to extend its authority, the state needs routinized, everyday forms of surveillance and everyday incentives for integrating various strata into society. Statecraft occurs as a continuous but delicate process of social and cultural engineering by trial and error and through new institutional forms of rule and norms of routinized behaviour (Doornbos 1990, 80).

The conspiratorial view of the state as captive of economic elites is a weaker version of the Marxist theory that sees the state as internally heterogeneous with intra-elite struggles that illustrate how the state and capital are involved in processes of realignment in order to constitute stable ruling class alliances and partly incorporate the dominated classes through buying them off with concessions. However, the state's subjects are not passive, and the state is not all-powerful. Militant protests, strikes, and uprisings force the state to make concessions and reforms. For many on the left, the reforms and spaces won by the poor can be seen as necessary to further struggles for fundamental (socialist) change.

EXISTING VARIETIES OF STATES

These two perspectives (mainstream and left) impose very different conceptual lenses on interpreting the motivation for, and possible outcomes of, state intervention in essential services in capitalist economies. We associate ourselves broadly with the leftist perspective but also recognize that state involvement is complex and contested, and that some capitalist states are more powerful than others. The US, Uganda, and Slovenia are market-oriented states but possess very different capacities to realize and resist privatization. States are also marked by the conditions of their birth and the specific class configurations that gave rise to them. More advanced and powerful economies have more means to pursue co-option and hegemonic social inclusion and stability.

The welfare state in advanced economies produced labour aristocracies (and trade unions), which often defended their own privileges against countries of the South (Arrighi and Silver 1999). Authoritarian states often emerged because the economic basis for widespread social welfare and incorporation did not exist. In some cases limited co-option of some groups in corporatist structures emerged (e.g. Latin America has a history of authoritarian corporatist states in which a selected group of leaders representing social sectors formed part of the state). Furthermore, in Europe the development of liberal democratic states was a slow process, while in post-colonial states universal franchise often came about overnight in the context of unevenly developed state institutions and political parties. Civil war was often the result, leaving deep scars and blocking even a modicum of "stateness" in many parts of the world where state formation and consolidation is still in process. Notions of a coordinated capitalist interest have been hard to sustain in the face of centrifugal forces (Nigeria, the Democratic Republic of the Congo [DRC] and Sudan being good examples).

There is also the question of scales of stateness. As both supranational and subnational state entities have proliferated and become more powerful over the past 30 years, the notion of a centralized, omnipotent national state has been exploded (though reports of its death have most certainly been exaggerated!). Which scales of state now mediate on behalf of capital are exponentially more difficult to calculate and assess today, with multiple interventions often taking place at any one time (e.g. a World Bank loan might make water privatization a "conditionality" in a particular country, but this typically requires the involvement of national, regional, and/or local authorities, in conjunction with transnational and/or local capital).

Socialist states are also complex and diverse, but the literature on how and why socialist states have resisted/reversed the privatization of essential services is not nearly as large or as conceptually advanced as it is with regard to capitalist states (a point we return to below). Most socialist states have state-run water, health care, and electricity, but there is a dearth of critical literature on how and why these different models emerged, how they have differed across place and time, and whether they are appropriate for struggles against privatization today.

What we can say is that the dynamics of state-run services in socialist systems is typically very different than that of capitalist states. There may be little that binds the centralized service delivery systems of the Soviet bloc to the more localized initiatives of Hugo Chavez's "modern socialism" in Venezuela, but there is much that distinguishes them from their market-oriented cousins—most notably the absence of demands by the private sector for the state to intervene in services and infrastructure at times of economic crisis. It is the latter dynamic that shapes much of the debate over privatization in a market economy, and it is this point that we take up below in our review of state interventions in market systems.

Our argument, in short, is that state-run services in capitalist economies are never fully "public". Despite the well-meaning and often highly effective efforts of millions of public sector employees and anti-privatization activists around the world to preserve and enhance these state services, the accumulation demands of the private sector and the boom-bust cycles of the market have invariably led to an unequal distribution of state resources (even at the height of welfarism) and eventually to pressures to (re)privatize services. There have been important gains along the way—particularly when compared to the more *laissez-faire* forms of privatization that have often preceded state intervention—but nowhere have market-oriented states been able to sustain truly equitable and democratic service provision in the face of market pressures, and nowhere have these localized systems managed to escape the productive demands of the market or systematically share these gains with the most needy parts of the world.

Once again, this is not to say that we should abandon efforts to push for more progressive state ownership of services in market economies. Nor do we agree with some anarchist theories of the state that reject *all* forms of state intervention as inherently oppressive and unequal. Equally, we do not want to argue that socialist states have offered magic alternatives—compromised as many have been by cronyism, a lack of transparency, and blind attempts to "catch up" to the perceived productivity and modernity of their capitalist competitors. In the end, there may be no "ideal" state-led models that we can point to but it is important that we understand the different rationales and *modus operandi* of what has existed to date and how this might affect our choices in the future. For states are the only actors large enough to affect the scale of change required for basic service delivery around the world today, and they will need to be central to any serious effort to resist and reverse privatization trends and to develop sustainable "public" alternatives. Our review is more negative than affirmative in this regard but is intended as constructive criticism for what has become a somewhat populist and sanguine call for state-led service delivery on the part of anti-privatization advocates.

STATE OWNERSHIP OF SERVICES IN CAPITALIST ECONOMIES

Pre-Keynesian "rationalization"

Much of what we consider to be modern services today—reticulated water supplies, household sanitation, electricity—were begun by the private sector in the 1800s. As towns, cities, and industries expanded across Europe (and in some colonial regions), the demand for mass service delivery increased, creating opportunities for private firms to meet growing productive and consumptive needs (Goubert 1989). Many of these service entities remained highly localized, but there were opportunities for expansion into new geographical and sectoral areas for profit-making early on—including transnational operations (Clifton et al, 2007a)—giving birth to many of the large private service delivery firms that still dominate the market today (e.g. the precursor to *Suez Lyonnaise des Eaux* was founded in 1880, while the *Compagnie Générale des Eaux*, the precursor to Violea, was founded in 1853). The emergence of these private service providers was encouraged by governments that were ideologically committed to reducing public spending, while at the same time creating market opportunities for an increasingly restless capitalist class (Kellet 1978, Jone 1983, Johnson 2000, Harvey 2006).

A lack of regulatory capacity and laws soon led to a patchwork of inefficient and irrational private service systems. However, with growing public health problems such as cholera that cut across geographic and class lines

(Lewis 1952), there were public outcries and complaints from industrial and business interests about the "sanitary syndrome" that threatened the health and welfare of the bourgeoisie (not to mention the impact on profits due to absenteeism and the unpredictable costs of service delivery) that soon led to calls for reform. In London, private companies had partitioned the water supply amongst themselves in what became a "nine-headed monopoly", with none of these firms supplying water for non-paying purposes such as fire-fighting, street cleaning, or flushing sewers. John Stuart Mill, one of the leading liberal thinkers of the time, criticized the byzantine inefficiencies of this balkanized private sector supply, arguing that great savings in labour:

> would be obtained if London were supplied by a single gas or water company instead of the existing plurality. While there are even as many as two, this implies double establishments of all sorts, when one only, with a small increase, could probably perform the whole operation equally well; double sets of machinery and works, when the whole of the gas or water required could generally be produced by one set only; even double sets of pipes, if the companies did not prevent this need-less expense by agreeing upon a division of the territory. Were there only one establishment, it could make lower charges, consistently with obtaining the rate of profit now realized. (Mill 1872, 88)

It was an error, he argued, to believe that competition among utility companies actually kept prices down. Collusion was the inevitable result, he said, not cheaper prices:

> Where competitors are so few, they always end by agreeing not to compete. They may run a race of cheapness to ruin a new candidate, but as soon as he has established his footing they come to terms with him. When, therefore, a business of real public importance can only be carried on advantageously upon so large a scale as to render the liberty of competition almost illusory . . . it is much better to treat it at once as a public function. (Mill 1872, 88–89)

Water was not the only service deemed more efficiently provided by a single supplier. According to Mill:

> The cases to which the water-supply of towns bears most analogy are the making of roads and bridges, the paving, lighting, and cleansing of streets. The nearest analogy of all is the drainage of towns, with which the supply of water has a natural connexion. Of all these operations it may reasonably be affirmed to be the duty of Government, not necessarily to perform them itself, but to ensure their being adequately performed. (Mill 1967)

It was an uphill battle for such reformers initially, but in the end it was the bourgeois fear of contagion, "enlightened" self-interest, and the need for insulation from the working classes that forced the rich, and political elites, to tolerate the idea that services should be universal and public (Hardy 1993). The state increasingly imposed rationality of a certain kind upon an atomized capitalist class, which lacked a broader vision, but other social forces played a role in forcing the state to act against segments of capital—in this case private service delivery companies.

Similar developments took place in the US where, by the late 1870s, water supply was seen as "the first important public utility" and the "first municipal service that demonstrated a city's commitment to growth":

> City officials and urban boosters, such as chambers of commerce, boards of trade, and commercial clubs, promoted a variety of downtown improvements in competition with rival communities. In concert with sanitarians and municipal engineers they supported sanitary services to improve health conditions and to secure bragging rights about the cleanliness of their cities (Melosi 2000, 119).

In 1870 less than half of the waterworks in the US were state-owned. By 1924, 70% were state-owned (Melosi 2000, 120). The emergence of national bond markets for public takeovers of services was a catalyst here, emerging alongside the growth of investment banking at the time.

Otto von Bismarck's Prussia of the 1870s–1880s is also emblematic of this proto-welfare state. As the first national government to introduce basic social security to workers (health, accident, and old age insurance), Bismarck's policies were explicitly market-oriented and introduced in the hopes that they would be an antidote to revolutionary socialism (Taylor 1996; and given that he set the age of retirement at 70, some 25 years after the average Prussian's life expectancy, it did not much to run). These were not the sophisticated Keynesian welfare policies that were to be developed by capitalist states after the Depression of the 1930s, but they served the same basic purpose with regard to essential services by attempting to ensure a reliable, affordable, and (nearly) universal supply of certain public goods with the intent of supporting and expanding capitalist growth. To provide and maintain adequate "public goods" and social solidarity, moderate socialists (the Fabians) embellished the idea of "the state as a public servant, total commitment to parliamentary democracy, unequivocal support for the welfare state, notion of the state and a neutral embodiment of the general will, moral collectivism", and so on (Taylor 1996, 164). In other words, these were capitalist states intervening in service delivery to enhance capital accumulation, not hinder it, and to ultimately promote market ideologies and market growth, not to challenge them.

This practice was not limited to the metropole. Although many colonial governments initially allowed private companies to establish and run many (if not most) services, there were many cases of reversal, with colonial governments intervening to republicize and/or prevent further private sector service delivery expansion (Floyd 1984). In some cases colonial governments decided early on to keep key services in state hands for accumulation purposes. As Jomo and Tan explain in the Malaysian context:

> [British] colonial authorities recognized the need to develop utilities and other infrastructure so crucial to profit making in the colonial economy. Hence, public enterprise or state-owned enterprise (SOE) emerged during Malaysia's colonial era to provide the public goods and services needed by British private enterprise to secure profits from their control of tin mining, plantation agriculture and international commerce. (2006, 2)

These early interventions against privatization by the state capture the essence of "public" services in a capitalist economy. The motivation for state ownership and management is primarily one of protecting the interests of (particular factions of) capital and re-establishing a platform for growth, not necessarily for improving the broader public good. The form and language of intervention was to change over the years—as we shall see in subsequent sections—but the essence of market-oriented state intervention has remained largely the same.

Keynesian stimulus states

The high watermark for state intervention in public services in market economies—intellectually and practically—was post-World War II Keynesianism in western Europe. State involvement in essential services was particularly strong and "considerably decommodified the daily lives of the population" (Keane, as cited in Offe 1984, 18). Huge numbers of services were either municipalized, nationalized, or built from scratch by the state, partly in response to post-war reconstruction efforts in Europe, and partly to contain the ongoing threats of socialist and communist parties demanding more equitable control and allocation of resources. State-owned services allowed some of these demands to be met while at the same time providing stimulus spending in areas deemed critical to renewed capital growth after the Depression and war (roads, electricity, airports, etc).

Far from being socialist in their orientation, the rationale for state intervention was to stimulate a "capitalist spirit" through the incorporation of a wide swath of humanity into mass consumption societies (Toninelli and Vasta 2007, 45). Keynes himself made it clear that one of his primary motivations for writing his General Theory was to combat the rise of socialism in Europe, noting that "the class war will find me on the side of the educated bourgeoisie" (as quoted in Moggridge 1992, 453). As Offe notes, the social policies that accompanied Keynesian-era, state-sponsored social rights were intended to maintain the reproduction of the working class. The "flanking sub-systems" of services necessary for the incorporation of labour power into the labour market—composed of specialist institutions such as the family, school, health care facilities and urban water supply—ensured that the working class had the "cultural motivation" to become productive wage-labourers. In short, the state's intervention in the delivery of essential services was both a reaction to the "problem" of the strong working class after World War II *and* the need to reconstitute the working class, with the most decisive function of state social policy being its regulation of the process of proletarianization (Offe 1984, 94–99).

But whereas pre-1940s' rationalization was related to orderly urbanization, the post-World War II period was driven geographically by massive suburbanization, extensification of housing developments, transport systems, and private automobiles (Harvey 1982). These spatial expansions required a scaling up of state intervention as well, with national and international-level authorities becoming predominant vehicles for state-led service delivery (as compared to the municipal-level interventions in services in the 19th century), with the creation, for example, of regional water planning boards, national health care systems, and interstate electricity authorities. The scope and size of state intervention cannot be overemphasized, and most large "public" service systems in the capitalist West today originate from this period.

There is much to celebrate from this time, of course, with major gains in public health, education, and welfare, not to mention labour laws and regulatory frameworks, many of which remain in place today. But it is equally important to see the underlying rationale for state intervention in the Keynesian era as one driven by assisting capital accumulation, not hindering it, and one of re-establishing capital's strength (in general) by investing in services and infrastructure (in particular). That there should be a clawing back of such state involvement from the 1970s onwards—sometimes by the same people/parties responsible for state intervention in the first place—is less of an ideological *volte-face* than an inherent feature of Keynesian boom/bust management: move the state in when the system is in crisis; move the state out when capital is ready to stand more on its own feet. In this regard, Keynesianism and neoliberalism can be seen more as a continuum of each other than as ideological opposites—as mainstream analysts tend to portray them—with formal policies on state ownership and management being more a product of the inherently cyclical nature of the market economy than philosophical commitments to individualism or communitarianism.

Finally, it should be noted that Keynesianist welfare states were typically constituted as professional bureaucracies, which were benevolent but top-down and depoliticizing. The citizen was incorporated as a beneficiary and demobilized. It is questionable how much social solidarity and commitment to public interests was built by the welfare systems, even at their best. Republican ideals of citizenship, such as the political citizen who both governs and respects the laws, were less important to welfare states (Ignatieff 1995, 54–55), with the norms being solidly male and family-centred.

Post-colonial nationalist states

Some of the biggest post-war service and infrastructure deficits were in Africa, Asia, and Latin America, and the role of the state in public service delivery in these post-colonial entities is worthy of separate discussion. The colonial legacy had left highly uneven physical, economic, and social infrastructures: roads and railways were designed to extract minerals not connect people or build state authority, and water and health facilities were designed to serve a colonial elite not assist local populations.

Addressing these deficits was the first task of many post-colonial governments, with most regimes emulating their erstwhile masters, broadly following the Keynesian pattern of state-led service delivery under the labels of "national planning" or "import substitution industrialization". In many cases it was a matter of nationalizing foreign-owned corporations; relatively easy and popular targets for newly minted independent governments wanting to make a political statement, particularly some of the more charismatic nationalist leaders such as Getulio Vargas in Brazil (1930–1945 and 1951–1954), Lázaro Cárdenas in Mexico (1934–1940), and Juan Domingo Perón in Argentina (1946–1955), with Asia and Africa seeing similar bursts of nationalization with their post-independence restructurings.

But "the state" in the global South after World War II was seen by mainstream analysts as "underdeveloped" and weak compared to Europe, with uneven capacity to exercise control, collect taxes, and maintain the service systems required for large-scale capital accumulation. Africa fared the worst. Despite early efforts at economic nationalism and striving to build cohesive state systems, many states remained internally weak. In the 1960s and 1970s Zambia, Tanzania, Mozambique, and others encouraged extensive state ownership and "Africanization" to capture the "commanding heights" of the economy, but although highly visible politically, the state-owned enterprises that emerged more often than not created patronage networks, rewarded connected political elites, and failed to provide a basis for social citizenship, let alone sustained capital accumulation or improved welfare for residents.

Authoritarian regimes in Asia and Latin America fared better in this regard—typically bolstered by massive economic and military support from the US—using strategic investments in key infrastructures and services to build national industries and jump-start a domestic capitalist class. In some cases (e.g. Singapore), sustained state spending eventually contributed to a welfare system more akin to that of Europe, but most market-oriented "developmental states" in the South have resulted in highly polarized societies with state-subsidized services tending to benefit a small middle-class and elite, largely in urban areas.

That many of these so-called "inefficient" states were subsequently the target of privatization agendas is another indication of the inherent limitations of such Keynesian strategies. Having served to help build and expand networks of capital penetration—or at least having helped keep a lid on demands for greater equality—the need for direct state intervention was no longer as great by the 1980s, with privatization seen to promise even greater rewards for domestic and transnational capital. That this too was to fail, and fuel another round of calls for direct state intervention, is the basis of our current round of "social" or "third way" neoliberalism, throughout most of the North and the South.

"THIRD WAY" STATES

The 1970s and 1980s saw aggressive attacks on Keynesian state-led models of delivery. The initial phases of neoliberalism of this time saw wholesale privatizations of everything from airlines to water systems to hospitals. Blocs of capital that had once called for state intervention were now howling for its removal, demanding the right to own and/or manage virtually every state service on offer. There were windfall gains for many factions of capital, but as with earlier experiences with privatization concerns with efficiency, reliability, and public health began to surface over the zealous and under-regulated sell-offs and outsourcing of essential services, giving birth to another round of calls for state intervention in the 1990s and 2000s.

But instead of the Keynesian-era models of direct ownership and control, the response was one of "social" neoliberalism, using residual or safety net approaches to social delivery alongside public-private partnerships and commercialized public services. The role of the state is to ensure that services are "targeted" at the poor (as opposed to expensive universal entitlements of citizenship) and to offer new forms of "public management" such as corporatization, which incorporate private sector management techniques and some private sector outsourcing and "partnerships", as opposed to full-blown privatization. The objective has been one of better controlling the flow of public resources to areas deemed most critical to the (ever changing) needs of capital accumulation and to better manage the demands of an un(der)employed consuming class through new monitoring and disciplining techniques such as prepaid water meters, differential user fees, geographically defined development zones such as "business improvement districts", and so on; ideological tools that "encourage people to see themselves as individualized and active subjects responsible for enhancing their own well-being" (Larner 2000, 13; see also Brenner and Theodore 2002, Harvey 2005, Peck 2007). On a larger scale, loan conditionalities from the

World Bank, the International Monetary Fund (IMF), and some bilateral donors contained privatization and commercialization clauses, serving as a lever for capital penetration from the North into the "emerging" markets of the South (Amenga-Etego and Grusky 2005).

We need not detain ourselves here with this well-known story of commercialization by stealth since the 1990s except to say that the state (at increasingly diversified scales) has been a critical actor in, and author of, this form of neoliberalization (Harvey 2005). Efforts to "bring the state back in" must therefore be cognizant of the ideological and institutional construct of much of what exists under contemporary forms of neoliberalism, with heavily commercialized notions of the "public good" having penetrated all levels of decision making in market economies in the North and the South.

As noted at the outset of this chapter, unless contemporary market-oriented states have been radically democratized, there may be little point in bringing them back in, as they may simply reassert a neoliberal agenda and market ideology, under the guise of being "public". Even democratic initiatives such as participatory budgeting are increasingly being captured by neoliberal ideals, serving to contain demands for social and economic justice rather than expanding them (Wampler 2007, Barrett et al, 2008, Geddes 2010).

Authoritarian states

Finally, we look briefly at some of the fascist, military, and dictatorial regimes of the 20th century that promoted state-led service delivery, if for no other reason than to demonstrate how diverse and problematic the call for state intervention in services has been in market economies. Recent neoconservative reactions to the individualism and "amoralism" of unbridled capitalism also provide interesting material for understanding how an interventionist state might work to "restore social values" (Harvey 2005, 82–84). Ridiculed as chauvinistic and irrationally megalomaniacal, it is often forgotten that many fascist regimes—particularly those in Europe— came to power on an explicitly anti-market, anti-liberalization rhetoric, arguing that capitalism would erode the moral, productive, and racial character of a country (with *Nazi* being short for "national socialism").

In Italy, Mussolini created the *Istituto per la Ricostruzione Industriale* (Institute for Industrial Reconstruction), which, "as of the late 1930s . . . led to the Italian state owning a bigger share in the economy than in any other country except the USSR" (Baker 2006, 229). Hitler took similar initiatives in Germany, building an expanded range of new state-run public services intended to improve "the folk" and boost public welfare (at least for those deemed sufficiently "Germanic"). The state was argued to be the only institution capable of seeing the moral obligations of public service and was regarded as essential to the generation and protection of a disciplined and good society.

Much of this anti-market rhetoric was hollow in the end—with Mussolini and Hitler both embracing big capital to boost strategic industries (Guérin 1938) and with the Nazis beginning to privatize in the late 1930s due to fiscal pressures (Schweitzer 1946, Bel 2009)—but there was considerable emphasis put on nationalization of services long before it became Keynesian mantra in liberal-democratic states, revealing once again the temporal, crisis-management nature of state intervention in market-driven economies that serves to strengthen, not weaken, the private sector.

Notably, this nationalization trend began to fade with longer-lasting—and less capitalist—European dictatorships, such as those in Greece, Spain, and Portugal, which "fail[ed] to develop either a strong welfare state or significant SOEs [state-owned enterprises] in public services" (Bela Nunes et al, 2007, Clifton et al, 2007b, 92). By the 1970s the trend had come full circle, epitomized by the Pinochet regime of Chile, which, from the mid-1970s, became the standard bearer for a privatizing state and a testing ground for newly emerging doctrines of neoliberalism introduced by the technocrats known as the "Chicago boys" (Skidmore and Smith 1997, 142).

STATE OWNERSHIP OF SERVICES IN SOCIALIST ECONOMIES

Socialist states have not been immune to these dictatorial tendencies. Nor have they been all that different from capitalist states when it comes to seeing services such as water, electricity, and health care as central to the building of a "modern" productivist economy, best kept out of the hands of a self-serving private oligopoly. There is much that binds the economistic mind.

What does differentiate socialist states from market states in this regard is the lack of pressure associated with capital accumulation. There have, to be sure, been "special" demands from political and military elites that have skewed resource distribution in socialist economies, but the motivation for—and the necessity of—using services and their related infrastructure to try and fix crises of capital accumulation does not factor into service delivery decisions in countries that have eliminated or drastically reduced private ownership of the means of production. In socialist economies the locus of decision making around services has moved away from the boom-bust cycles of the market towards politically determined priorities, be it an attempt to ensure universal access to a service to correct injustices of the past (e.g. the introduction of free water services for all residents in post-revolutionary Cuba), as a strategy to diversify the productive base of an economy (e.g. the nationalization of electricity in Bolivia since 2004), or narrower, narcissistic efforts to immortalize a political leader (such as the investments in Stalingrad in the 1930s or Pyongyang today).

Our argument here is a simple but important one. Capitalist states have taken on state ownership and management of key services in the past largely because they have been forced to by economic crises. They alter their pro/anti-privatization rhetoric depending on the scale and stage of accumulation problems and the capacity of a given state to intervene. Socialist states, on the other hand, are not bound by these "laws" of the market, with decisions over service delivery being more ideological in nature. As Thomas notes of the vigorous urban planning debates that took place in the early years of the Soviet Union, planners asked complex questions about the nature of urban infrastructure and services that had little to do with market logics: How does communist ideology express itself in infrastructure and services? What is the relationship between physical form and political thought? At what speed and at what cost was communist society to be created? What use was to be made of the experience of the rest of the world (Thomas 1978, 269)?

In short, socialist service delivery planners have been able to think beyond the demands of capital accumulation cycles. They may make wise, efficient, and consultative decisions that meet the real needs of citizens, or they may make ill-conceived, autocratic, and wasteful decisions that expose the empty promises of an undemocratic regime. Either way, without the pressures of private capital accumulation, socialist state ownership and management of essential services are much less predictable than that of capitalist states.

As a result, they are also more politicized and volatile, all of which makes an understanding of the decision making around state intervention in service delivery in socialist societies critical. As with capitalist states, we need to ask what motivations there have there been for state-run services, how these have differed across socialist countries, what kinds of technical and ideological debates have taken place in different sectors at different times, what level of state has been deemed most appropriate, and what role, if any, citizens have played in decision making.

Unfortunately, there is little literature that discusses these questions or provides details on the specifics of service delivery in particular socialist countries, in particular sectors, at particular times. Much of the contemporary writing on the subject compares socialist and post-socialist service delivery, with a focus on what has been lost/gained as a result of liberalization since the 1990s (e.g. Vinogradov 1996, World Bank 1999, Anex 2002, Williams and Dubash 2004, Wang et al, 2009). The historical reviews in this literature tend to be broad and cursory, and although much of it argues that socialist states generally offered good-quality, universal, and affordable services in the past, there is a tendency to either dismiss these systems out of hand as too hierarchical, non-transparent, and inefficient (e.g. Deason and Daane 1998, World Bank 1999, Komives et al, 2005) or to uncritically celebrate them with little analysis as to how (and if) they could be reproduced today.

There was a substantial contemporaneous literature (in English) that explored Soviet, Chinese and, to a lesser extent, other Asian, African, and Latin American socialist service systems, while they were in operation in the 20th century, but this writing (as with so much scholarship of the time) tended to be tainted by Cold War overtones, offering limited insights into the specifics of service delivery that could assist in understanding how and why particular systems emerged (e.g. Micklin 1987, 1988). There is, no doubt, much more written in Russian, Mandarin, and other languages by scholars situated in various socialist countries, but this literature has been insufficiently mined by academics, activists, and policy makers engaged in the search for alternatives to privatization today (the current authors included).[1]

As a result we have an insufficient understanding of the various motivations for, and debates around, state-led delivery in specific service sectors in socialist countries, and even less in the way of critical writing on how these lessons might help in the current struggle for alternatives to privatization in the global South. When compared to the vast literature on privatization (whether pro or anti), or the relatively sophisticated understanding we have about the motivations for state-led service delivery in capitalist economies (as discussed above), the dearth of careful historical research on the rich and complex debates and practice of state-led service delivery in socialist countries is notable. The growing literature examining more contemporary efforts to create "socialist" services in such places as Venezuela and Bolivia is a useful correction, but there is a vast vault of historical knowledge that remains largely untapped.

Nevertheless, it is possible to make some general observations on the motivations for, and outcomes of, state interventions in service delivery in socialist systems. These broad observations are not intended as a typology of state formations of the kind provided above for capitalist states, but they do serve to highlight some of the decision-making architecture that has informed socialist state interventions in essential services in the past—be it 1920s USSR, 1970s Angola, or Venezuela today. Despite the very different scales, levels of industrialization and balances of political forces that have animated the theory and practice of socialism in different countries, there are some important common themes.

The most obvious and pertinent point to note is the desire on the part of socialist states to rapidly address massive service inequalities. The degree to which services actually existed, or were privatized, prior to a particular socialist regime varies, but virtually all socialist governments have inherited service systems that were radically unequal—be it the quasi-feudal arrangements of Tsarist Russia, the sabotaged remnants of colonial service provision in Mozambique, or the impacts of shock therapy privatization in contemporary Bolivia. Revolutionary governments came to power at least in part on the promise that they would make essential services more widely available, and it was inconceivable that this responsibility would be handed over to the private sector (though China's more recent forays into privatization under the name of "socialism" deviate from this theme, as do some of Cuba's private sector "joint ventures").

Making services affordable has also been a priority. In some cases services have been provided for free as part of a package of state services offered to most, if not all, citizens. Socialist states have also tended to target the most needy/vulnerable with heavily subsidized services (such as water and electricity in the former Soviet Union [Deason and Daane 1998]). In some cases industry subsidized residential consumption, in part because the former was by far the largest service user (Zaidi et al, 2009), a far cry from the tax breaks and subsidization of services for industry in market economies at the expense of (low-income) households. The objective has often been to provide universal coverage at affordable/free rates. The fact that this would make for a more "productive" workforce was central to much of this thinking, but it was a decision motivated more by long-term state planning rather than short-term reactions to market crises.

Socialist state services have also tended to be highly centralized and "modernized", in part because this was deemed the fastest way to roll out services on a massive scale, in part because it was seen as necessary for industrialization, and in part because of a "keeping up with the Joneses" complex that saw many socialist states attempting to accomplish what capitalist states had done, only faster and better. The result has largely been highly technicized and hierarchical systems of service delivery, though there have been some notable exceptions, such as the decentralized system of health care in Kerala (Elamon et al, 2004, Suchitra 2009), and more recent efforts in Venezuela and Bolivia to create decentralized systems of provision in services such as water and sanitation (see Chapter 15, this volume).

In terms of outcomes, the quality and quantity of services generally improved dramatically over presocialist systems, and most socialist countries attained equal or superior quality and quantity of service provision when compared to their market-oriented peers (such as Cuba's widely vaunted health system relative to other Latin American countries [see Chapter 14, this volume]). As Zoidze et al note of the *Semashko* health model developed by the Soviets, it provided:

> universal or close to universal entitlement to free health care. . . . [and there were] few financial barriers to accessing services. . . . From 1950 to 1970, many of the [Soviet bloc] countries experienced a dramatic fall in early mortality and enjoyed better health outcomes than other countries with a similar level of average income. (2006, 29)

Less positively, there have been widespread criticisms of socialist service delivery systems as top-down, undemocratic, inflexible and environmentally destructive (to name but a few of the complaints). As Zoidze et al note of the Semashko model, it was "not without flaws", tending to be "inefficient and unresponsive to patients' demands and needs" (2006, 29). It is not just anti-socialist ideologues that have made these criticisms, and it is not just the Soviets who suffered from these difficulties.

"Third World" socialisms struggled with the additional challenges of neocolonial drag—including heavy intervention and exploitation at the hands of their Soviet or Chinese "friends"—and they often lacked sufficient numbers of technical and managerial skills and funds for infrastructure to roll out modern services on a large scale. As a result there was a trend towards an urban bias in service delivery in many post-colonial socialist states and a growing nepotism in decision making bolstered by commodity resource booms and busts.

Not all socialist service systems have fallen victim to these problems, and there have been lessons learned and applied within, and across, socialist states over place and time. Current efforts to introduce "modern socialism" in Venezuela and Bolivia are shaped in part by this history, though, as noted above, it is not clear that we have a sufficient understanding of the role that states played in service delivery in socialist systems in the past to say that this is a suitably rich source of information.

What we can say is that the absence of internal market pressures has freed socialist states to pursue a more egalitarian-oriented approach to service delivery should they choose; one that is based more on the use value of services for citizens than exchange value for private capital. The extent to which states have succeeded in pursuing and achieving these goals has varied from place to place, with some notable successes and some spectacular failures, but the lack of private sector pressures creates a very different environment for state ownership of services in non-capitalist systems.

WHERE TO IN THE FUTURE?

The single most important message from this discussion is that we must not too readily accept "state ownership" as a positive alternative to privatization. In recognizing that the state can be a site of contested forms of class rule and that there are different forms and types of state, it is important that we are both "in" and "against" the state. Needs, the role of experts in service delivery, and community/citizenship are major issues for democratic negotiation. We therefore stress that *horizontal* relations between citizens or communities and the various forms of sociality and collectivism they produce should take precedence over technocratic approaches to state-led service delivery. The negotiation across, between, and within particular collectivities about services and needs raises crucial issues around universalism and values such as solidarity. The *vertical* relation between citizens and the state needs to be de-emphasized (Pateman 1985).

We also stress that popular movements and projects that dissolve the state-society boundary need to be considered. Citizens or communities can become self-acting states. Each society can adopt forms of social-political and ecological organization that makes sense culturally and historically rather than following blueprints, though some form of "universal norms" in terms of service outcomes should inform any evaluation of the success or failure of a particular state project (see Chapter 2, this volume, for an extended discussion of the need to see universalisms and particularisms in service debates).

As we have seen from this historical review, state ownership in market economies is often a means for directing public resources that implement market-friendly policies in the name of "public" services (e.g. "new public management"). It is essential that we recognize the inherently cyclical nature of these state interventions and how they fit with the boom-bust cycles of capitalism. In an increasingly neoliberal world, where decisions on ownership can make enormous differences to people's daily lives—life and death for many—we must be sophisticated as well as pragmatic in our thinking and action, evaluating the pros and cons of particular state interventions and pushing for meaningful people's participation in decision making, equitable pricing, environmentally oriented services, and so on. It should be taken as a given that the private sector and neoliberal bureaucrats will use "public" language rhetoric to create an impression of universality and democracy, while working behind the scenes to redirect resources to market ends, and perhaps even preparing the ground for a future round of privatization, as has been the case with much of the trend towards the "corporatization" of state services.

Monitoring and challenging neoliberal discourse and action requires technical and political knowledge, organizational capacity, and resources. Public sector unions are perhaps best equipped to play a central role in this regard given their frontline understanding of services, their skills, and global coordination, but any serious attempt to monitor/manage state-owned services must include social movements, community organizations, and other non-profit agents if we are to avoid the kinds of overly centralized, bureaucratic, and technocratic state service agencies we have seen in capitalist economies in the past. Doing so will expand the horizontal relations of stateness and create better awareness about "good" and "bad" public management.

And finally, we must continuously remind ourselves that the formal capacity for state-led services in the global North remains significantly stronger than that in the global South. Yet the impetus for community and people-driven transformation is greater in the South. It is important to celebrate victories in the North such as the "Model Municipalities" programme in Norway[2] and the remunicipalization of water in Paris in 2010, but as long as these state-led services benefit only a localized population and continue to reflect a North-South disparity in service delivery, they are but a partial victory. Preserving state-owned universal public health care in Canada is valuable, but when two million people a year in the South die from diarrhea-related illnesses due to a lack of water and sanitation, the success is necessarily limited. Positive advances in "public" state services in the North are important, but they cannot distract us from the larger, global task at hand.

Nevertheless, local victories can provide inspiration and set precedents for advances elsewhere, providing valuable insights into successes and failures across regions and sectors. It is here that state-led service activities of socialist states may be of most value. With the triumphal "end of history" discourse about the superiority of markets finally waning, there is renewed interest in learning from historical and contemporary models of socialist service delivery. Notwithstanding serious mistakes, the Soviets, the Chinese, the Tanzanians, the Sandinistas, Frelimo, and a myriad of other socialist states made massive gains in public health and welfare with state-led service delivery in the past, while the Cubans and the governments of Venezuela and Bolivia continue to push socialist service delivery agendas forward today. There may be limited scope for creating new socialist states, but learning from the successes and failures of these experiments are as important as learning from the circumscribed gains made within market economies.

There will be no single state-led (or public- or community-led) model that meets all the complex and differentiated challenges of transformative service delivery, but gains made in specific places can act as beacons and catalysts elsewhere and may contribute to the development of hybrid models of state services that ameliorate the most negative aspects of capture by private capital, while ensuring a more sustainable, equitable, and democratic form of services for all. Central to this will be a less top-down approach to state decisions. Following Unger, we would argue that "the use of coercive state power to impose alternatives without grass-roots participation is likely to backfire", while grassroots innovations and self-mobilization can be consolidated and widened through state support (1997, 268–269). As movements grow stronger, so do their senses of possibility. Whether this means "breaking off parts of the state and using these 'floating' levers to reinforce social mobilization" (Unger 1997, 274) is a matter of debate, but such positions are suggestive of the kinds of practical and theoretical discussions that are required when asking to "bring the state back in".

NOTES

1. The difficulty of such undertakings should not be underestimated, however, as research by one of the authors into decision making on water reforms in revolutionary Cuba demonstrates (Cocq and McDonald 2010). Getting access to documents and decision makers in Cuba was challenging, taking many years, and there was no coordinated record keeping or critical secondary literature on the subject in Spanish.
2. For information, see www.qpsconference.org/content/co-operation-not-co-option.

REFERENCES

Amenga-Etego, R.N. and Grusky, S. 2005. The new face of conditionalities: The World Bank and privatization in Ghana. In McDonald, D.A. and Ruiters, G.

(Eds), *The age of commodity: Water privatization in Southern Africa*. London: Earthscan Press.

Anex, R.P. 2002. Restructuring and privatizing electricity industries in the Commonwealth of Independent States. *Energy Policy* 30(5): 397–408.

Arrighi, G. and Silver, B.J. 1999. *Chaos and governance in the modern world system*. Minneapolis: University of Minnesota Press.

Baker, D. 2006. The political economy of fascism: Myth or reality, or myth and reality? *New Political Economy* 11(2): 227–250.

Barrett, P.D., Chavez, D. and Rodriguez-Garavito, C. (Eds). 2008. *The new Latin American left: Utopia reborn*. Pluto Press: London.

Bel, G. 2009. Against the mainstream: Nazi privatization in 1930s Germany. *Economic History Review* 63(1): 34–55.

Bela Nunes, A., Bastien, C. and Valério, N. 2007. Privatisation and transnationalisation of network services in Portugal, 1980–2005. In Clifton, J., Comin, F. and Diaz-Fuentes, D. (Eds), *Transforming public service enterprises in Europe and North America: Networks, integration and transnationalisation*, pp. 128–144. New York: Palgrave.

Brenner, N. and Theodore, N. 2002. Cities and the geographies of "actually existing neoliberalism". *Antipode* 34(3): 349–379.

Clifton J., Comin, F. and Diaz-Fuentes, D. (Eds). 2007a. *Transforming public service enterprises in Europe and North America: Networks, integration and transnationalisation*, pp. 54–74. New York: Palgrave.

———. 2007b. Transforming network services in Spain. In Clifton, J., Comin, F. and Diaz-Fuentes, D. (Eds), *Transforming public service enterprises in Europe and North America: Networks, integration and transnationalisation*, pp. 1–28. New York: Palgrave.

Cocq, K. and McDonald, D.A. 2010. Minding the undertow: Assessing water "privatization" in Cuba. *Antipode: A Radical Journal of Geography* 42(1): 6–45.

Deason, J. and Daane, R. 1998. Water meeting policies in the former Soviet Union: Lessons from Lviv. *Ukraine Environmental Engineering and Policy* 1(2): 75–80.

Doornbos, M. 1990. The African state in academic debate: Retrospect and prospect. *Journal of Modern African Studies* 28(2): 179–198.

Elamon, J., Franke, R. and Ekbal, B. 2004. Decentralization of health services: The Kerala People's Campaign. *International Journal of Health Services* 34(4): 681–708.

Evans, P., Rueschemeyer, D. and Skocpol, T. 1985. *Bringing the state back in*. New York: Cambridge University Press.

Floyd, R.H. 1984. Some topical issues concerning public enterprises. In Floyd, R.H., Gray, C.S. and Short, R.F. (Eds), *Public enterprise in mixed economics*, pp. 36–71. Washington, DC: International Monetary Fund.

Geddes, M. 2010. Building and contesting neoliberalism at the local level: Reflections on the symposium and on recent experience in Bolivia. *International Journal of Urban and Regional Research* 34(1): 163–173.

Goubert, P. 1989. *The conquest of water*. Princeton: Princeton University Press.

Guérin, D. 1938. Fascism and big business. *New International* 4(10): 297–300.

Hardy, A. 1993. *The epidemic streets: Infectious disease and the rise of preventive medicine, 1856–1900*. Oxford: Oxford University Press.

Harvey, D. 1982. *The limits to capital*. Oxford: Blackwell.

———. 2005. *A brief history of neoliberalism*. Oxford: Oxford University Press.

———. 2006. *Paris, city of modernity*. New York: Routledge.

Ignatieff, M. 1995. The myth of citizenship. In Biener, R. (Ed), *Theorising citizenship*, pp. 51–76. Albany: SUNY Press.

Johnson, D.J. 2000. No make-believe class struggle: The socialist municipal campaign in Los Angeles, 1911. *Labour History* 41(1): 25–45.

Jone, L.J. 1983. Public pursuit or private profit?: Liberal businessmen and municipal politics in Birmingham, 1865–1900. *Business History* 25(3): 242–245.

Jomo, K.S. and Tan, W.S. 2006. *Privatization and renationalization in Malaysia: A survey.* www.unpan1.un.org/intradoc/groups/public/documents/UN/UNPAN021546.pdf (accessed 15 June 2010).

Kellett, J.R. 1978. Municipal socialism, enterprise and trading in the Victorian city. *Urban History* 5: 36–45.

Komives, K., Foster, V., Halpern, J. and Wodon, Q. (Eds). 2005. *Water, electricity, and the poor: Who benefits from utility subsidies?* Washington, DC: World Bank.

Larner, W. 2000. Neo-Liberalism: Policy, ideology and governmentality. *Studies in Political Economy* 63: 5–25.

Lewis, R.A. 1952. *Edwin Chadwick and the public health movement.* London: Longmans Green.

Mamdani, M. 1995. A critique of the state and civil society paradigm in Africanist studies. In Mamdani, M. and Wamba-dia-Wamba, E. (Eds), *African studies in social movements and democracy*, pp. 602–621. Dakar: Codesria.

Melosi, M.V. 2000. *The sanitary city: Urban infrastructure in America from colonial times to the present.* Baltimore: Johns Hopkins University Press.

Micklin, P.P. 1987. The fate of "Sibaral": Soviet water politics in the Gorbachev era. *Central Asian Survey* 6(2): 67–88.

———. 1988. Desiccation of the Aral Sea: A water management disaster in the Soviet Union". *Science* 241: 1170–1176.

Mill, J.S. 1872. *The principles of political economy with some of their applications to social philosophy.* Boston: Lee and Shepard.

Mill, J.S. 1967. The regulation of the London water supply 1851. Reproduced in Robson, J.M. (Ed), *The collected works of John Stuart Mill, Volume 5—Essays on economics and society Part II.* Toronto: University of Toronto Press.

Moggridge, D.E. 1992. *Maynard Keynes: An economist's biography.* New York: Routledge.

Offe, C. 1984. *Contradictions of the welfare state.* London: Hutchinson.

Pateman, C. 1985. *The problem of political obligation: A critique of liberal theory.* London: John Wiley and Son.

Payer, C. 1982. *The World Bank: A critical analysis.* New York: Monthly Review Press.

Peck J. 2007. Neoliberalization at work: The long transition from welfare to workfare. In Wood, G. and James, P. (Eds), *Institutions, production, and working life*, pp. 315–331. Oxford: Oxford University Press.

Schweitzer, A. 1946. Big business and private property under the Nazis. *The Journal of Business* 19(2): 99–126.

Skidmore, T. and Smith, P. 1997. *Modern Latin America.* Oxford: Oxford University Press.

Suchitra, M. 2009. Kerala spearheads community-care health revolution. *Appropriate Technology* 36(2): 49–51.

Taylor, G. 1996. OFWAT and the regulation of change. In Braddon, D. and Foster, D. (Eds), *Privatization, social science themes and perspectives*, pp. 135–159. Dartmouth: Aldershot.

Thomas, M.J. 1978. City planning in Soviet Russia (1917–1932). *Geoforum* 9(4–5): 269–277.

Toninelli, P.A. and Vasta, M. 2007. Public enterprise and public networks in Italy 1952–2001: A quantitative profile. In Clifton, J., Comin, F. and Diaz-Fuentes, D. (Eds), *Transforming public service enterprises in Europe and North America: Networks, integration and transnationalisation*, pp. 75–94. New York: Palgrave.

Unger, R .1997. *The politics: The central texts.* New York: Verso.

Vinogradov, S. 1996. Transboundary water resources in the former Soviet Union: Between conflict and cooperation. *Natural Resources Journal* 36(2): 393–416.

Wampler, B. 2007. *Participatory budgeting in Brazil: Contestation, cooperation and accountability.* Pittsburgh: Pennsylvania State University Press.

Wang, N., Gericke, C. and Huixin, S. 2009. Comparison of health care financing schemes before and after market reforms in China's urban areas. *Frontiers of Economics in China* 4(2): 179–191.

Williams, J.H. and Dubash, N.K. 2004. Asian electricity reform in historical perspective. *Pacific Affairs* 77(3): 411–436.

World Bank. 1999. *Non-payment in the electricity sector in Eastern Europe and the former Soviet Union.* World Bank Technical Paper No. 423. Washington, DC: World Bank.

Zaidi, S, Alam, A. and Mitra, P.K. 2009. *Satisfaction with life and service delivery in Eastern Europe and the former Soviet Union.* World Bank Working Paper No. 162. Washington, DC: World Bank.

Zoidze, A., Gotsadze, G., and Cameron, S. 2006. *An overview of health in the transition countries.* International Hospital Federation Reference Book (2006–2007). Geneva: IHF.

Part II

Sectoral and Regional Reviews

Asia
Regional Overview

Jenina Joy Chavez

Asia is a very diverse region. In terms of history, political economy, endowments, growth patterns, and current development, different subregions of Asia exhibit wide disparities. This diversity makes for an interesting study of how Asia responds to economic and political challenges and how alternative ideas are given space.

This regional introduction focuses on the three subregions of East, Southeast, and South Asia. Home to approximately 3.5 billion people, or more than half of humanity (ADB 2010), these subregions also host two of the oldest civilizations in the world, China and India, both of which are considered the biggest emerging economies today.

Income inequalities are sharp in the subregions. Southeast Asia has wider income gaps than South Asia: the highest per capita income (Singapore US$48,893) was 31 times that of the lowest (Myanmar US$1,596) in 2008 "purchasing power parity" (ppp) terms, whereas in South Asia it was only fourfold (Afghanistan US$1,419 "ppp" versus the Maldives US$5,408 "ppp") in the same year. However, South Asia has higher incidence of and deeper poverty, as well as ranks lower in terms of human development (UNDP 2010).

DEVELOPMENT PATTERNS AND TRENDS

Of the most industrialized regions in the world, East Asia was a latecomer but industrialized the fastest. Japanese business, under the administrative guidance of a "developmental state", paved the way for the country's industrialization (Bello 2009). In the 1970s, facing rising costs at home and in search of markets, Japan relocated production to its former colonies, Taiwan and South Korea, and much later to Singapore and Hong Kong, in a fashion described by economists as the "flying geese" model of development and gave rise to the newly industrializing countries (NICs; Chavez 2007). China until then was consolidating its productive capacity under communist state planning, applying a "gradualist approach", and starting in the 1990s has begun engaging foreign markets and slowly established itself as an economic giant (Prokopenko 2000).

Notwithstanding differences in their current political-security status—both emerging from years of colonialism—independence was the biggest challenge for Southeast Asia and South Asia. Territorial divisions artificially drawn up by departing colonial powers created tensions within and amongst neighbouring countries, strong manifestations of which persisted for decades and remain to this day. Southeast Asia has largely neutralized these tensions and prevented conflicts in the subregion, but South Asia continues to be weighed down by long-standing conflicts, particularly between India and Pakistan, on broad political issues, and between Bangladesh and India, particularly on issues of migration and water. Internal conflicts also plague countries of both subregions (Chavez 2009).

Singapore developed its economy closer to the time of Taiwan and South Korea and is considered an original NIC. Equally strong states such as Thailand, Indonesia, and Malaysia replicated the "flying geese model" by hosting relocated production of the original NICs, making use of market instruments in much the same way the original NICs had, embarking on export-oriented industrialization guided by national priorities, and graduating into the second-generation NICs. Strong inflows of foreign direct investment (FDI) propelled these three countries, capturing 44% of FDI flows to Southeast Asia by 1990 (a figure that jumps to 90% if Singapore is taken out of the picture; ADB·2010).

Cambodia, Laos, and Vietnam remain centrally planned socialist economies but opened up their markets in the 1990s. Called the Southeast Asian "transition economies", the emergence of these countries was facilitated by substantial foreign aid, and, especially in the case of Vietnam, foreign investments and introduction to new markets. Cambodia, Laos, and Vietnam have been the fastest growing in the subregion, growing at an average 7.5% in the last decade (2000–2009). Myanmar remains under a military dictatorship, giving rise to human rights and democracy issues but has managed to build up its economy, growing twice the average for the region (12.4% versus 6%; ADB 2010).

The Philippines, having enjoyed good prospects in the 1970s, has lagged behind economically. The country was captured in the structural adjustment web of the World Bank as early as the 1980s (Bello 2009) and hence failed to "take off" like its neighbours. A huge army of overseas Filipino workers sending remittances now contributes more than a 10th of the country's GDP (BSP 2010), serving as a floater that prevents another 1980s-like balance of payment crisis.

South Asia has taken a growth path that is substantially different from that taken by the two other subregions. Post-independence, the subregion's capacity for industrialization has been weakened, and its compulsion to export has not developed as highly as it had in East and Southeast Asia—and certainly not as early. Countries in South Asia shared an "apparent synchronicity of policies and processes across the region, despite very differing social and political pressures", with "import-substituting industrialisation strategies for the first few decades after independence, with the attendant development of some industry and associated dualism in the economy, as well as regulation of much economic activity" (Ghosh 2004). Responding to historical pressure from "domestic political and economic dynamics" (Dash 1996), domestic demand propelled the subregion's growth (ADB 2006). Export orientation came late and somewhat haltingly in the 1980s and 1990s. Still, with its big internal markets, and with the eventual rise of India and aided by the high growth of the services sector and foreign direct investments, South Asia has grown steadily, especially after the East Asian crisis (which it largely escaped), eclipsing subregional growth by 2005 (7.6% versus 8.1%) and significantly outpacing global output (ADB 2006).

Today, developing Asia hosts one of the most robust productive capacities worldwide; its growth was estimated at 9.4%, almost double global growth (4.8%) in 2010. The estimate for Japan was a slower 2.8%, but this was after several years of negative growth (IMF 2010).

NEOLIBERAL REFORMS AND RESTRUCTURING

Asia's relative economic prosperity and stability enabled it to build internal capacities for infrastructure and running state-assisted essential services. These capacities were, however, uneven across and within countries; and continue to be threatened as the region is swept by waves of neoliberal reforms. While most of the subregions were in the reform path by the mid-1990s, the timing and pacing of reforms also exhibited wide variations.

East and Southeast Asia's dependence on foreign markets and investments made them susceptible to international economic fluctuations, and vulnerable to the herd behaviour of capital. The financial crisis of 1997 debilitated the economies of Thailand, Indonesia, and South Korea and started a contagion that spread throughout the subregions. This paved the way for harsh stabilization and structural adjustment policies monitored by the International Monetary Fund (IMF) and led to the introduction of foreign equity and dilution of once-exclusive East Asian capital (Bello 1997).

The Philippines was an early structural adjustment experiment by the IMF and the World Bank that followed most prescriptions to the letter: removing most trade restrictions, deregulating its oil and electricity sectors, privatizing many state-owned and controlled enterprises, and removing most subsidies. The transition economies meanwhile have taken in reforms faster than the flexibilities offered them.

The restructuring process in South Asia started when Sri Lanka dismantled its universal food security system in the late 1970s. By the 1990s, with the exception of Nepal, the subregion embarked on "comprehensive policies of internal and external liberalisation, reduction of direct state responsibility for a range of goods and services and privatisation" (Ghosh 2004).

The reform process also ushered in great interest in the region's infrastructure and essential services. Developing Asia is seen as a region of great infrastructure backlog. Electricity generation was only 1,181.4 kWh per capita in 2004, less than half the global average and merely a 10th of the average for industrialized countries. In the same year, only 45% of the region's population had access to sanitation services (ADB 2007). Together with a strong population growth and recovering incomes, the region is a substantial market. Asia has been attractive to foreign capital and a target of restructuring for many decades, the results of which have been as varied as the multiplicity of government and community responses.

The public, private, and community responses to the commercialization of essential services discussed in this chapter reflect the diversity of Asia's context. Innovative provisioning systems offer hope that public and community alternatives abound and need only be cultivated.

REFERENCES

ADB (Asian Development Bank). 2006. *South Asia economic report*. Manila: ADB.

ADB. 2007. *ADB's infrastructure operations: Responding to client needs*. Manila: ADB.

ADB. 2010. *Key indicators for Asia and the Pacific*. Manila: ADB.

Bello, W. 1997. Addicted to capital: The ten-year high and present-day withdrawal trauma of Southeast Asia's economies. *Focus Papers*. Bangkok: Focus on the Global South.

Bello, W. 2009. States and markets, states versus markets: The developmental state debate as the distinctive East Asian contribution to internal political economy. In Blyth, M. (Ed), *Routledge handbook on international political economy (IPE): IPE as a global conversation*, pp. 180–200. Oxon: Routledge.

BSP (Bangko Sentral ng Pilipinas). 2010. 2009 OF Remittances exceed 4% growth forecast. www.bsp.gov.ph/publications/media.asp?id=2269.

Chavez, J.J. 2007. Regionalism beyond an elite project: The challenge of building responsive sub-regional economic communities. In Curley, M. and Thomas, N. (Eds), *Advancing East Asian regionalism*, pp. 158–178. London and New York: Routledge.

Chavez, J.J. 2009. Regional social policies in Asia: prospects and challenges from the ASEAN and SAARC experiences. In Deacon, B., Macovei, M.C., Langenhove, L.V. and Yeates, N. (Eds), *World-regional social policy and global governance: New research and policy agendas in Africa, Asia, Europe and Latin America*, pp. 140–161. London and New York: Routledge.

Dash. K. 1996. The political economy of regional cooperation in South Asia. *Pacific Affairs* 69(2): 1–24.

Ghosh, Jayati. 2004. Neo-liberal reforms. *South Asian Journal* 4: 35–47.

IMF (International Monetary Fund). 2010. World economic outlook update: Recovery, risk and rebalancing. Washington, DC: IMF.

Prokopenko, Joseph. 2000. *Privatization: Lessons from Russia and China*. ILO Enterprise and Management Development Working Paper—MD/24/E. Geneva: International Labour Office.

UNDP (United Nations Development Programme). 2010. *Human development report*. New York: UNDP.

8 Creating, Reclaiming, Defending

Non-Commercialized Alternatives in the Health Sector in Asia

Amit Sengupta

The health sector encompasses a very large canvas, including not just health care services but also allied services that contribute to health, such as water supply and sanitation, as well as determinants of health such as food security, secure employment, gender equity, education, housing, and a clean environment. However, for the purposes of this chapter, we limit ourselves to health care services in order to focus the analysis on the ownership and management systems that operate them and the extent to which these systems can be considered "alternatives to privatization".

A scrutiny of health care provision and health systems in Asia needs to be located in the prevailing economic framework of the region. Like other parts of the world, the neoliberal framework of public policy formulation has permeated Asia over the past three decades. A typical feature that has characterized neoliberal policies is a clear position against the pursuance of policies designed to promote welfare. This has translated into progressive abolition of welfare rights related to economic security, health services, and education. Similar to other regions of the world, policies pursued by most states in the region have imposed wide-ranging cuts on welfare programmes, such as anti-poverty initiatives, food and agricultural subsidies, and free or subsidized public sector services (Haque 2008). In the health sector, it is ironic that this shift in public policy was set in motion even before the ink was dry on the resolution on Primary Health Care (PHC) that was adopted in Alma-Ata in 1978.[1]

There is no single "Asian reality", however, given that Asia is home to 60% of humanity and includes countries with very diverse histories, political systems, and social conditions. But it is remarkable nonetheless that in the last three decades virtually the entire continent has adopted a neoliberal framework while "reforming" the health care sector. Such reforms are evident, for example, in the two largest countries of the world—China and India. China's Gini coefficient (a standard measure of income inequality) was a low 29 in 1981 but reached 41 in 1995, similar to the US. The rural-urban divide increased, regional disparities widened, and access to opportunities became less equal during the 1990s. Only the incomes of the richest quintile of the Chinese population grew faster than the national average—again remarkably similar to the US. The government share of health expenditures fell by over half between 1980 and 1998, almost tripling the portion paid by families (People's Health Movement et al, 2006, 11–51). In India, while elements of neoliberal policies were introduced in the 1980s, formal structural adjustment measures for the economy were introduced relatively late, in 1991. The immediate fallout was a savage cut in budgetary support to the health sector. The cuts were severe in the first two years of the reform process, followed by some (but not complete) restoration in the following years. Indonesia, Thailand, and the Philippines were forced to undergo neoliberal reforms to access International Monetary Fund (IMF) loans in the midst of the Asian economic crisis in the 1990s. Cambodia, Laos, and Vietnam turned to the IMF/World Bank for funding and advice in the 1980s, while attempting to build their war ravaged economies (McGregor 2008). In Vietnam, in the process of economic restructuring in the 1980s, more than a million workers and over 20,000 public employees (of whom the majority were health workers and teachers) were laid off. The agreement signed with the IMF prohibited the state from providing budget support either to the state-owned economy or to an incipient private sector.

OVERVIEW OF COUNTRY SITUATIONS

We have discussed above the broad macroeconomic framework that informs the situation as regards health care services provisioning. We now turn to look at more specific trends in different countries in the region. The analysis is limited to a select list of countries—Bangladesh, China, India, Iran, Laos, Malaysia, Nepal, Sri Lanka, and Thailand. The above comprise a fairly good representation of the Asian region—i.e. West Asia (Iran), South Asia (India, Sri Lanka, Bangladesh, Nepal), Southeast Asia (Thailand and Malaysia), Indo-China (Laos), and China. These countries represent broad trends in the specific subregions in Asia and can be seen to provide a macropicture of important trends in the region.

Table 8.1 provides an overview of some important indicators of health service provision, as well as broader determinants of health. Of the four countries from the South Asian region, Sri Lanka stands out as a positive exception. The other three countries (India, Bangladesh, and Nepal) show similar patterns in terms of prevalence of high child mortality and malnutrition rates and poor public expenditure on health. Sri Lanka's performance is discussed later in our analysis of the public health system of the country. The other interesting insight is that some of India's indicators are actually worse than those of Nepal and Bangladesh, which needs to be seen in the context of the hype about India (along with China) being the latest "poster boy" of neoliberal reforms!

Table 8.1 Overview of Country Situation in Health—Asia

	ppp* per capita income (US $)	Under five mortality rate (per 1,000 live births)	Life expectancy at birth		Health expenditure as % GDP (2004)		Human development index (HDI)	Prevalence of child malnutrition (2000–2007)	Access to safe delivery (% of total births)
			M	F	Public	Private			
Bangladesh	1340	69	63	65	0.9	2.2	140	39.2	20
China	5370	24	70	74	1.8	2.9	81	6.8	98
India	2740	76	63	66	0.9	4.1	128	43.5	47
Iran	10800	34	69	72	3.2	3.4	94	–	90
Laos	1940	75	63	65	0.8	3.1	130	36.4	19
Malaysia	13570	12	72	76	2.2	1.6	63	–	98
Nepal	1040	59	63	64	1.5	4.1	142	38.8	19
Sri Lanka	4210	13	72	78	2.0	2.3	99	22.8	96
Thailand	7880	8	66	75	2.3	1.2	78	7.0	97

* (ppp = purchasing power parity); Source: World Bank 2009, UNDP 2008.

If we disregard the data on public health expenditure, China would be seen to be performing remarkably well. The data, however, hides regional, rural-urban, and income-based inequities that have been widely commented upon, including by Chinese government officials. The income ratio of urban residents over rural residents increased from 2.2 in 1990 to 2.9 in 2003. The National Health Survey in China indicates that nearly 30% of patients in that country did not use in-patient care when they were advised by doctors to be hospitalized. The predominant reason for not accessing in-patient care was affordability (70%)—54.1% in urban areas and 75.4% in rural areas. The survey also revealed that in rural counties, the proportion of health expenditures in total non-food expenditures was 28.9% for the lowest-income families, while it was 17.6% for highest-income families (CHSI 2004).

Southeast Asia, represented by Malaysia and Thailand, presents a contrast. Identified as part of the "East Asian Tigers" even before the present phase of neoliberal reforms, their indicators approach those of developed nations. There are divergences in the two countries, however, which we will examine later.

Laos is somewhat typical of the three countries—Vietnam, Cambodia, and Laos—in the "Indo-China" region. They embarked on "reforms" in the mid-1980s after a period of promoting a socialized pattern of development. In this region, and particularly in Vietnam (the largest country in the region), public health was considered a state responsibility implemented by a centralized, hierarchical five-tier health care system. Health services were provided free of charge throughout the country's provinces, districts, and over 10,000 communes—extending occasionally down to the brigade level. Services were financed entirely from state finances generated at the commune, provincial, and central levels. Health care coverage was extensive and mostly equitable, and the density of hospital beds and doctors in Vietnam was among the highest in Asia (Sida 1994). The collapse of the commune-based social welfare system led to the collapse of the fiscal base of social programmes. Services were withdrawn, privatized, or supported by user charges. The data on Laos indicates the fairly clear trajectory and consequences related to the dismantling of public systems. The data, for example, shows that relative private sector participation is next only to what is seen in India and that public expenditure (as a percent of GDP) is the lowest of all the countries we examined (Laos, along with India, ranks in the bottom five globally in this respect).

Finally, Iran presents a specific context. Expenditure data shows high public as well as private participation. Iran's ability to maintain its public system in the face of the constraints of US-led sanctions is laudable. But it should also be noted that Iran's economic performance continues to be better than most countries in Asia, so Iran does have the internal resources to develop its public systems, supported largely by oil and gas exports, which contribute 60% of government revenue. The relatively high child mortality figures in Iran in spite of better economic performance and a functioning public health system, however, stand out as a cause for concern and deeper investigation.

Table 8.2   Selected Indicators of Health Services

	% Births attended by trained personnel		% Infants fully immunized (measles + DPT)		Oral rehydration therapy use in diarrhea (%)	Anti-retroviral drug coverage (%)
	1990–1999	2000–2008	1990	2007	2000–2007	2007
Bangladesh	14	18	65	88	70.1	7
China	89	98	97	93	NA	19
India	42	47	56	62	26	NA
Iran	NA	97	85	97	NA	5
Laos	7	20	18	40	50.5	95
Malaysia	81	100	70	90	NA	35
Nepal	9	19	43	81	29.3	7
Sri Lanka	NA	99	80	98	NA	NA
Thailand	85	97	80	96	68.3	71.5

Source: WHO 2009, 72–79.

The comparative data on indicators of health services (Table 8.2) reinforces what was discussed earlier. The poor performance of countries in South Asia (with the remarkable exception of Sri Lanka) and of Laos (except for anti-retroviral coverage for HIV/AIDS) is striking. Of significance is the laudable performance by Bangladesh regarding usage of oral rehydration therapy (ORT) for treatment of diarrhea. ORT is often held up as one of the most important public health measures to have been introduced in modern times and is believed to be responsible for saving millions of lives each year. The fact that its use is still far from universal in most settings is an indicator of how health systems often obstinately resist introduction of low-cost technologies in spite of overwhelming evidence of efficacy (Werner and Sanders 1997). Bangladesh is an example of large scale adoption of such technology. While most countries have shown a significant rise in immunization coverage, the coverage in India has stagnated, and in the case of China, coverage has actually come down. This is an indicator of the faltering public systems in the two largest countries of the world.

We turn now to examine some indicators of broader determinants of health. Of note in Table 8.3 is the very high prevalence of malnutrition in South Asia. Also striking is the fact that India is worse off in this area than even its much poorer South Asian neighbours. It has been postulated that this phenomenon, termed as the "South Asian enigma", has its roots in the much larger levels of gender inequity present in the region (Ramalingaswami et al, 1996). We point this out to underline that while in our analysis we limit ourselves largely to health services, other determinants often have a very significant impact on the health status of communities.

Differences also exist across the countries under analysis as regards availability and deployment of health personnel. Table 8.4 provides comparative data. Of particular significance is a fairly clear picture (irrespective of the absolute numbers) of the higher ratio of nurses/midwives to doctors in most countries with better performing public health systems (such as Thailand, Sri Lanka, and Malaysia in contrast with India, China and Bangladesh). The finding should not come as a surprise, as private systems rely inordinately on personnel with more specialized training (e.g. physicians rather than health workers), specialists rather than general physicians, and so on. Private systems, thus, rely on health personnel with a narrower and more specialized focus of expertise, each designed to treat very specific patient groups. There is no evidence, however, that this leads to any significant advance in outcomes. In some settings the converse is true. India's reliance on highly trained personnel, for example, translates into large areas in poorer regions being denied medical facilities as personnel with higher levels of training (doctors) are reluctant to serve there. This may be contrasted with the situation in Thailand, with a much better performing public system, where the density of doctors is lower than in India, but the density of health workers is much higher.

Table 8.3   Determinants of Health—Drinking Water and Nutrition

	% of population with access to drinking water		% of children under five that are underweight	
	1990	2006	1990–1999	2000–2007
Bangladesh	78	80	52	39.8
China	67	88	NA	6.8
India	71	89	44.4	43.5
Iran	92	95	NA	NA
Laos	NA	60	NA	36.4
Malaysia	98	99	NA	NA
Nepal	72	89	38.2	38.8
Sri Lanka	67	82	NA	22.8
Thailand	95	98	NA	7

Source: WHO 2009, 83–94.

Table 8.4   Availability and Deployment of Health Personnel

Country	Physician per 10,000 population 2000–2007	Nurse/midwife per 10,000 population 2000–2007	Ratio of physicians to nurses/midwives
Bangladesh	3	3	1:1.0
China	14	10	1:0.7
India	6	13	1:2.2
Iran	9	16	1:1.8
Laos	4	10	1:2.5
Malaysia	7	18	1:2.6
Nepal	2	5	1:2.5
Sri Lanka	6	17	1:2.8
Thailand	4	28	1:7.0

Source: WHO 2009, 95–106.

Table 8.5 Financing of Health

	Total health expenditure as % GDP		Public expenditure on health as % GDP		Private expenditure as % total expenditure		Out-of-pocket expenditure as % of private expenditure	
	2000	*2006*	*2000*	*2006*	*2000*	*2006*	*2000*	*2006*
Bangladesh	3.3	3.2	0.9	1.0	73.5	68.2	88.1	88.3
China	4.6	4.6	1.8	1.9	61.7	59.3	95.6	83.1
India	4.3	3.6	0.9	0.9	78.2	75.0	92.1	91.4
Iran	5.9	6.8	2.2	3.4	63.0	49.3	95.9	94.8
Laos	3.2	4.0	1.0	0.7	67.5	81.4	91.8	76.1
Malaysia	3.2	4.3	1.7	1.9	47.6	55.4	75.4	73.2
Nepal	5.1	5.1	1.3	1.6	75.1	69.5	91.2	85.2
Sri Lanka	3.6	4.2	1.7	2.0	52.1	52.5	83.3	86.7
Thailand	3.4	3.5	1.9	2.3	43.9	35.5	76.9	76.6

Source: WHO 2009, 107–118.

Table 8.6 Out-of-pocket (OOP) Payments in Public Services in the Year 2000

Country	OOP as % of total expenditure on health	Percentage of total OOP on public sector care
Bangladesh	64.85	0.50
India	80.00	25.61
Malaysia	40.20	7.17
Sri Lanka	45.59	0.86
Thailand	32.74	34.93

Source: van Doorslaer et al, 2005, 33.

Table 8.7   Per Capita Public Expenditure on Health

Country	Per capita government expenditure on health (in "purchasing power parity" US dollars)	
	2000	*2006*
Bangladesh	7	12
China	42	88
India	14	22
Iran	143	344
Laos	13	15
Malaysia	151	242
Nepal	10	16
Sri Lanka	47	81
Thailand	97	170

Source: WHO 2009, 107–118.

How health care services are financed is a major determinant of access and equity. Table 8.5 provides data on the large variations in health care financing. It is generally accepted by public health advocates, as well as within the World Health Organization (WHO), that public health expenditure should be at least 5% of a country's GDP.[2] By that count all the countries studied lag behind significantly, with only Iran approaching anywhere near the benchmark (at 3.4%). India and Laos stand out as the worst performers with 0.9% and 0.7% of GDP public spending on health. Importantly, in all cases private expenditure is significant, and in all countries (except Thailand) outstrips public expenditure. This clearly suggests that in most countries of the region the dominant mode of provision of health services is through the private sector.

It is also important to understand that when public facilities are available they are not necessarily free. Users of public facilities often need to pay, in the form of user fees for facilities. Public facilities also entail out-of-pocket expenses when users are required to purchase medicines prescribed—a prominent cause of expense in the public sector in many countries. Table 8.6 provides data from some countries regarding out-of-pocket expenses in the public sector. While data is not readily available for all countries under analysis, similar trends are discernible. In China, for example, earlier studies estimate that income from user fees is 36% of total expenditure on the public system (Dezhi 1992).

It is significant that in all the countries examined per capita public health expenditure (as purchasing power parity in US dollars) has increased between 2000 and 2006 (see Table 8.7). This is a positive trend, though in some cases the increase is marginal. What is cause for concern is the fact that of the three countries where private expenditure has expanded faster than public expenditure, two are countries that historically have had better performing public systems (Malaysia and Sri Lanka). Another data set that merits comment is the extent of out-of-pocket expenses in the case of private expenditure, which indicates the limited penetration of private health insurance, even in situations in which the private sector is the major provider of health services.

SEEKING ALTERNATIVES

Having provided a survey of the current state of public/private PHC provision, we turn now to a discussion of instances of service delivery that does not involve the participation of the private, for-profit sector. Essential information regarding these various initiatives are consolidated below and analyzed based on a range of predefined "criteria for success". This "mapping exercise" is seen as a step towards identifying health care practices, in the Asian context, that can be leveraged upon to suggest alternative strategies for health systems that are in the public domain, are sustainable, and advance health equity.

Methodology

The research was carried out by first identifying possible initiatives that needed to be documented, predominantly through literature reviews. The process was augmented by sending out requests to contacts in different parts of the region to provide information about interesting initiatives that fit the criteria of "alternatives to privatization" (see Chapter 2 for a fuller account of research methodology). Additional information was also obtained from available documentation of the Health Systems Knowledge Network of the Commission on Social Determinants of Health (Gilson et al, 2007).

Based on the above, examples of "alternatives to privatization" were short listed for more detailed analysis. These initiatives were researched further using information received from respondents in different countries, published reports and papers, and through material available on the Internet.

Typologies of "alternatives"

The word "alternatives" is intentionally placed in quotation marks. Some of the cases identified and discussed do not fit an ideal notion of alternative (as contradistinctive to the present trend towards privatization and commercialization of health care and delivery mechanisms). However, as the short narratives provided below attempt to make clear, many of these initiatives are important because they do bring out the tension between the neoliberal ethos on one hand and the designed intent of addressing issues of inequity related to health and access to health care. Nevertheless, although none of the cases discussed have an overt agenda to promote privatization, the prevalence of an ideological mindset that is unable to visualize a system of health care delivery that is entirely publicly owned and financed is evident in many of the cases identified.

Below, we discuss some of the important features of the identified alternatives within different typologies. There is a degree of overlap, and we have, for example, grouped together NGO and government programmes, which address a specific aspect of access to health services.

The initiatives we have mapped can be classified as follows:

- Large national initiatives by governments that aim to provide comprehensive access to health services
- Primary care initiatives by not-for-profit non-governmental organizations, which have a large span of coverage
- Primary care initiatives, which have a limited span of coverage but are useful models to take note of
- Initiatives that address a specific aspect of access to health services, such as access to medicines, HIV treatment, etc

LARGE NATIONAL INITIATIVES BY GOVERNMENTS

China: New Rural Cooperative Medical Scheme (NCMS)

NCMS was introduced in China in July 2003. It is a consequence of the Chinese government's stated effort to restructure health services, with a larger focus on improvement of equity in health and health care (Meng 2007, 1–3). The scheme is the result of a large consultative process and aims to remedy the visible decline in access to health care services in China since the economic reforms initiated in the 1970s. The decollectivization of agriculture resulted in a decrease in support for the collective welfare system, of which health care was part. In 1984, surveys showed that only 40–45% of the rural population was covered by an organized cooperative medical system, as compared with 80–90% in 1979. Specifically, the NCMS aims to reverse this situation and target the problems related to catastrophic out-of-pocket expenditures incurred by people to take care of medical expenses.

The scheme started operating in 2003, and by 2008 over 800 million people in China's rural areas were covered by it. The premium under the NCMS is paid by three sources. In 2003, Chinese national and local authorities each contributed 10 yuan per person, while individuals contributed at least 10 yuan. By the end of 2009, the total annual premium was targeted to be raised to 100 yuan, of which 80 yuan will come from the central and local governments and individual payments will be 20 yuan (Wang 2009, 245).

Review of the programme shows that the scheme has led to some increase in access to in-patient care for vulnerable populations, but out-of-pocket expenses continue to be a major issue. Reimbursement of expenses for in-patient care is still low (but expanding), at approximately 30% of total costs (Parry and Weiyuan 2008, 822–825). The scheme envisages that by 2020, it will help achieve its goal of "safe, effective, convenient, and low-cost" medical care for the entire population. Higher-end treatment will continue to be available, although funded only through private insurance schemes. A more detailed implementation plan for the three years until 2011 is being developed and is expected to receive 850 billion yuan (124 billion US dollars) for the reform in three years. This is the largest and most sustained initiative in post-liberalization in China to reverse the trend of privatization and inequity in health care and access. The programme is designed to provide comprehensive coverage by 2020, and its importance is immense as it seeks to reverse a three-decade trend of rolling back public support for health services. Over the last five years, there has been significant expansion, and there seems to be a political will to sustain the momentum (Wang 2009).

Iran: PHC through "health houses"

The Iranian "health houses", conceived and introduced during the 1980–1988 war with Iraq, lie at the core of the PHC system in Iran. The system relies on the following components: (i) establishing health houses in remote and sparsely populated villages; (ii) staffing health houses with health workers, known as *behvarzan,* recruited from local communities; (iii) developing a simple but well-integrated health information system; and (iv) a referral system linking with rural and urban health centres and hospitals (Sadrizadeh 2004).

The health house is the most basic unit of the Iranian PHC network. Located in individual villages, it is designed to cover a target population of about 1,500. The distance between the village in which the health house is located and the satellite villages served by it, is typically no more than a one-hour walk. The health houses refer patients to rural health centres, which cover about 6,000 to 10,000 people, and have up to two physicians and several health technicians. These centres are responsible for elective and emergency case management, supporting the health houses, and supervising both the health technicians and the *behvarzan* (meaning "good skills" in Farsi*),* or community health workers (Abbas 2007).

One male and one or more female health workers run each rural health house. The health workers are chosen among local people familiar with the households in the village. Training occurs at the district level; students receive free training and financial support throughout the two-year training period. In return, they are formally obliged to remain and serve at the village health house for a minimum of four years after completing their study. Almost 30,000 community health workers are working in these health houses, more than 16,000 of them are women. The minimum age for male and female health workers is 20 and 16, respectively.

The system is funded entirely by the national government. Challenges now faced include sustaining financial support in the face of sanctions that are imposed on Iran, the need to strengthen the referral system, the need to better address non-communicable diseases and the need to strengthen secondary and tertiary levels of care (Tavasolli 2008).

The system is perhaps the most comprehensive of all the alternatives discussed here—both in terms of service coverage and the range of services offered. The primary care elements are better organized than secondary and tertiary care, but overall its sustenance and expansion appears to be an integral part of public policy. As a result, it may be argued that there is merit in not being part of the global economic architecture (even though forced, as in the case of Iran!).

Malaysia: PHC system

PHC is seen as the thrust and foundation of the public health system in Malaysia. It is a two-tier system comprised of health clinics, which cater to a population of 15,000–20,000, and community clinics that cater to 2,000–4,000 people. It is a nationwide programme funded by the country's national budget. Health clinics provide eight identified essential services, as well as dental and mental health care. Community clinics provide maternal and child health services and outpatient care for minor ailments. The system is comprised of about 900 health clinics and 2,000 community clinics across the country. The health clinics are linked to public hospitals by a referral system (Awin 2002).

The system caters to the bulk of the population (about 65%) but is served by just 45% of all registered doctors, and even fewer specialists (25%–30%). Patients pay only nominal fees for access to outpatient and hospitalization services. Medical and surgical emergencies are also adequately provided for, with a government-managed fleet of ambulances, including airlift capacities for more remote sites.

Doctors, nurses, pharmacists, dentists, and other allied health care workers are employed and deployed by the Ministry of Health to various health care centres: from rural clinics to district hospitals to tertiary specialist hospitals throughout the country. The distribution of these resources is based on the size, need, and population of the various districts and states. However, in rural and more mountainous or remote regions, the deployment of facilities as well as manpower is uneven, and there remains great disparity and inequitable distribution of health care personnel, especially doctors.

There appears to be a covert—if unannounced—shift in thinking that eventual corporatization of the public sector facilities and services should be allowed to unfold in Malaysia, where market forces dictate the price, extent, and quality of the services offered. However, public dissent has ensured that over the past 20 years, or so, there have been only sporadic and partially successful attempts to privatize or corporatize various components of the public health sector—e.g. the government's drug procurement and distribution centre, and the divestment of its support services (cleaning, linen, laundry, clinical waste management, biomedical engineering maintenance). Nevertheless, commercialization trends remain a concern, with a shortage of trained personnel and some specialty services being purchased by the public system from the for-profit private sector (Chee Khoon 2010).

Thailand: Universal health care coverage scheme

Thailand's National Health Insurance Bill was enacted in 2002, creating the Universal Health Care Coverage scheme (UC; formerly known as the "30-baht scheme", in reference to the Thai currency). The UC scheme shifted away from a means-tested health care coverage insurance program for low-income patients, to a comprehensive health care plan that provides universal coverage. Originally, participants in the UC scheme were charged a co-payment of 30 baht (approximately US$1 in 2002), but this co-payment was later abolished. The UC scheme focuses on providing PHC services to Thais who were left out of the health care system prior to 2002. Thais joining the UC scheme receive a "gold card", which allows them to access services in their health district and to be referred to a specialist if necessary. The scheme is administered by the Thai National Health Security Office and is primarily funded by the government, based on a budget calculated on a per capita rate. At present the scheme covers an estimated 46.95 million Thais (out of a total population of 62 million; Tangcharoensathien et al, 2007).

One of the key elements of the programme is that reimbursement of expenses to public hospitals by the government is based on enrolled populations in the hospitals' service areas. The system is geographically structured, and hospitals have fixed revenues based on the local population and financial viability depends on an ability to control costs (Wibulpolprasert and Thaiprayoon 2008).

The Thai public health system is of more recent vintage as compared to Malaysia but has seen an opposite trajectory. Before introduction of the scheme, public health insurance covered only 9% of the population. There has been progressive strengthening of the system in recent years, in spite of overall economic liberalization programmes pursued by the government. Among all the alternatives that we analyze here, the Thai UC scheme appears to have had the fastest trajectory in transforming a largely private health care system into a robust publicly funded system.

Sri Lanka: Public health system

The public health system in Sri Lanka, unlike other countries in the South Asian region, dates back to its pre-independence (1948) period, with free health care subsequently being introduced in 1953. In spite of political changes, the public system has survived and expanded, with the public health system comprising a network of medical institutions (larger, intermediate, and smaller peripheral institutions) and health units. As of 2008 there were 258 health unit areas with populations ranging from 40,000 to 60,000 (Rannan-Eliya and Sikurajapathy 2008).

The health unit area is a clearly defined region congruent with the administrative divisions of the country. Health units are managed by Medical Officers and are supported by a team of public health personnel comprising one or two Public Health Nursing Sisters, four to six Public Health Inspectors, one or two Supervising Public Health Midwives, and 20–25 Public Health Midwives. Each health unit area is subdivided into Public Health Midwife areas, which constitute the smallest working units in the public system. Each Public Health Midwife has a well-defined area consisting of a population ranging from 2,000–4,000 (Perera 2007).

Of the total ambulatory care market, 50% is serviced by the private sector, although 95% of in-patient care is still provided by the public sector. Although all Sri Lankans have this entitlement, those who can afford to can choose to use private sector services. The private health sector only began to develop in earnest during the 1960s. It focuses particularly on ambulatory care in the form of general practitioners. Although there are some full-time private general practitioners, most private provision takes the form of dual practice by doctors who are employed in the public health sector and have a limited private practice outside of official working hours (Rannan-Eliya and Sikurajapathy 2008).

Problems with this system include lower utilization of peripheral facilities and overcrowding in secondary and tertiary facilities. New challenges to the system are emerging in the form of policies related to the overall neoliberal thrust of the economy, although the health system is still relatively secure. Challenges are also being faced with the entry of the corporate private sector (often imported from India).

The Sri Lankan system is often discussed as one of the "success stories" of a public system. There is considerable merit in these arguments given that the country has consistently performed in a situation in which its other South Asian neighbours have floundered. There are several historical reasons why this has been so. The development path followed by Sri Lanka has been described as "support-led security", in which public provision and funding of health and other social services has promoted social progress. Even before independence in 1948, there was a rapid expansion of public investment in education and health facilities in the 1930s and 1940s. Free education was introduced in 1947 and free health care in 1953. Along with strong support for publicly funded social services, the commitment to social justice, with particular emphasis on addressing the needs of the worst off, was a key feature of state policy. Despite having low income levels and only gradual economic growth, as well as relatively low levels of spending on health (with public health care expenditure only being equivalent to 2% of GDP), Sri Lanka has achieved remarkably good health status and a high literacy rate. These achievements are testimony to the effectiveness of sustained public spending on social services and the consistent commitment to equity and social justice, which is also borne out by the relatively equitable distribution of income (with a Gini index of only 33; McIntyre 2006).

Similar to the Malaysian situation, Sri Lanka's system faces the threat of reforms that seek to align it with the neoliberal ethos of commercialization. The attempted reforms have been less sustained than in Malaysia but do pose a threat. The unfolding of the dynamics would be useful to study in detail, especially given that public investment in social infrastructure in Sri Lanka has enjoyed such a large consensus across the political spectrum for decades.

India: National Rural Health Mission

The National Rural Health Mission (NRHM) was launched in April 2005, as a response to a large body of criticism regarding the performance of the public health system in India. The NRHM is designed to strengthen the existing public health system, which is a three-tiered system offering primary care linked to a network of secondary and tertiary public health facilities. The primary care system is an extensive network comprising subcentres (covering population areas of between 3,000–5,000), Primary Health Centres (covering 20,000–30,000 people), and Community Health Centres (covering a population of 100,000). Across the country, as of 2007, there were a total of 145,272 subcentres, 22,370 Primary Health Centres, and 4,045 Community Health Centres. While impressive on paper, in large parts of the country, the network barely functions as a consequence of poor resourcing and maintenance. Shortage of personnel and material resources plague the system (Rao 2009).

Some of the important strategies that form part of the NRHM include:

- Access to health care at household level through trained Accredited Social Health Activists (ASHA). The programme targets the training and deployment of one activist in each village (i.e. about 550,000 trained activists across the country). ASHA trainees should have a minimum of middle school level education and are provided a three-month long training module. They are required to be chosen from the community and remunerated based on services performed, e.g. facilitating family planning, safe deliveries, etc.
- Architectural correction of the health system to enable it to effectively handle increased allocations and policies to strengthen public health management and service delivery.
- Effective integration of health concerns through decentralized management at district level.
- Health Plan for each village through village health committees.
- Strengthening of the different tiers of the public system.
- Promotion of public-private partnerships for achieving public health goals.
- Regulation of private sector to ensure quality service.
- Reorientation of medical education to support rural health issues.
- Risk pooling and social health insurance. (Government of India 2009)

In 2008–2009 the allocation by the central government for the programme was Rs107.9 billion (approximately US$2.4 billion). This is augmented by funding from state governments (Government of India 2010).

The achievements have been modest. There has been a perceptible advance towards some strengthening of the public system, but the impact is still fragmented and inadequate to prevent a high dependence of patients on the private for-profit sector. The flagship programme of the mission is the training and deployment of ASHAs. While a massive drive towards this has been initiated, the impact is still limited. This is due, in part, to the fact that the ASHA is not conceived as a full-fledged and fully remunerated health worker but rather as a health "assistant" who is remunerated for services delivered. However, some states are moving towards providing a fixed honorarium for ASHAs. Although strengthening of the primary care facilities is taking place, the pace is still too slow to address current needs. Public-private partnerships are being pursued at the secondary and tertiary level of care, and remain an issue of concern as they lend to private infrastructure creation and strengthening. There are also trends towards privatization in the form of outsourcing of auxiliary services such as ambulance and laundry services. The promise of the programme was to increase public spending to 2–3% of GDP, but this has stagnated at around 1%. A major part of the shortfall is a result of state governments being unable to mobilize resources to support the programme, a consequence of fiscal measures in the last two decades which have starved state governments of finances due to a sharp fall in the tax to GDP ratio (People's Rural Health Watch 2008).

In ways similar to China, the "alternative" being discussed here is the first cogent response of the government in India to growing health inequities in the neoliberal era. India, of course, differs from China in that it has always had a flourishing private sector in health and a relatively weak public sector. The imbalance has worsened since the early 1990s. Given this background the Rural Health Mission merits a close look as it unfolds. Parts of it continue to be informed by the neoliberal ethos, e.g. its stated intent to promote public-private partnerships in the secondary and tertiary sectors, some attempts to promote user fees, and so on. However, the initiative is important because it is an attempt to go against the overall trend of neoliberal reforms in other sectors.

PRIMARY CARE INITIATIVES WITH LARGE SPAN OF COVERAGE

Bangladesh: Integrated Rural Health Care (Gonoshasthya Kendra)

At the time of the liberation war of Bangladesh in 1971, a group of Bengali expatriate doctors working in London organized the Bangladesh Medical Association. Two of the doctors, Dr. Zafrullah Chowdhury and Dr. M.A. Mobin visited the frontlines of the war and began treating wounded soldiers who were fighting a guerrilla war against the Pakistan army. With the help of the Bangladesh government in exile in Calcutta, they established a 480-bed makeshift hospital on the eastern border of Bangladesh. After the independence of Bangladesh in December 1971, some of the volunteers of Bangladesh Field Hospital formed an NGO called *Gonoshasthaya Kendra* (GK, "people's health centre") to provide health care to rural communities as part of the national effort to rebuild the war-torn country (Upham 2004).

GK has come a long way since this time, both in terms of programme coverage and achievements. During the last three and a half decades, it has increased its basic health care coverage, including reproductive and child health care, from serving about 50,000 people in 50 villages in 1972 to now over 1.2 million people in 592 villages geographically spread across the country in 31 unions of 17 *upazilas* in 15 districts. Presently, GK runs two 150-bed hospitals—one in Savar and another in the Dhanmondi area of Dhaka city. GK has two other rural hospitals with 30 beds each, and all other centres run by GK have five hospital beds where patients with severe diarrhea, respiratory infections, simple fractures, abortion complications, and difficult delivery are admitted (Gonoshashthya Kendra, 2009).

GK provides an integrated package of health services, through its village/community-based health workers and secondary and tertiary level care through strong referral linkages to both GK and government hospitals. GK also offers a locally organized *Gonoshasthaya Bima,* a community-based cooperative health insurance scheme, and runs a continuing training programme for Traditional Birth Attendants (TBAs) to upgrade their skills to become trained TBAs. GK health workers link with the TBAs to ensure an effective referral system. GK is known for its advocacy role on many issues and its innovations to promote gender equity (Huda and Chowdhury 2008).

GK is explicit in stating that it is not in competition with the government of Bangladesh, arguing that its role is to supplement the public health system. GK's primary focus is to work with the state so that its innovative schemes, if found result yielding, can be adopted by the public sector. Many activities are self-supporting (e.g. the hospitals, pharmaceutical unit, medical college), but a large annual subsidy (20–30% of the overall budget, largely sourced from donor agencies such as the French Support Committee to GK-Savar, Medicos, Germany, etc) is still necessary to continue the programme.[3] Major challenges being faced include problems in retaining trained personnel who are lured away by the growing private sector (as well as better-funded NGOs), the need to constantly seek donor funding, and the paucity of a robust second-line leadership. The hospital in Dhaka also faces difficulty in competing with the private hospitals that have emerged in the city.

The GK alternative is an important initiative that has attracted attention in the South Asian region, partly because of its early association with the country's liberation struggle. The organization also played host to the first People's Health Assembly in 2000, out of which developed the global People's Health Movement.[4] The important aspect of the "alternative" is the purposive links that have been forged with the programme and political campaigns on access to health and medicines. Also of importance is the strong focus on gender issues and gender empowerment.

Bangladesh: Essential health care by BRAC

Also in Bangladesh, the Bangladesh Rural Advancement Committee (BRAC) started its activities in 1972 in the district of Sylhet, as a relief and rehabilitation project to help returning war refugees after the Liberation War of 1971. Currently BRAC is present in all 64 districts of the country, with over 7 million microfinance group members, 37,500 non-formal primary schools, and more than 70,000 health volunteers. BRAC employs over 120,000 people, the majority of whom are women. BRAC has also diversified its activities outside Bangladesh and operates different programmes such as those in microfinance and education in nine countries across Asia and Africa. The organization is 80% self-funded through a number of commercial enterprises that include a dairy and food project and a chain of retail handicraft stores called *Aarong* (BRAC[5]).

In 1979, BRAC began working on health issues through the nationwide Oral Therapy Extension Programme, a campaign to combat diarrhea, the leading cause of the high child mortality rate in Bangladesh. Over a 10-year period, 1,200 BRAC workers went door-to-door to teach 12 million mothers the preparation of homemade ORS. Since 2002, all of BRAC's health interventions have been incorporated under the BRAC Health Programme. The maternal, neonatal, and child health programmes currently target 8 million urban slum dwellers and 11 million rural people. The tuberculosis control programme has already reached 86 million people in 42 districts. Some 70,000 community health volunteers and 18,000 health workers have been trained and mobilized by BRAC to deliver door-to-door health care services to the rural poor. It has established 37 static health centres and a Limb and Brace Fitting Centre that provides low-cost devices and services for the physically disabled. Until 2006, the programme provided health support to the members of BRAC's village organizations. In 2007, there was a shift in operations towards a more community-centred approach, meaning that everyone in the community was offered BRAC's essential health care services.

Perhaps no discussion of NGO initiatives is complete without a discussion of some aspects of BRAC's work in Bangladesh, if for no other reason than BRAC operates the world's largest NGO programme and is the second largest employer in Bangladesh after the state! The health programme has been scaled up to the extent that it is an alternate structure to the government's public health system. To be fair, the two often collaborate and work together, though governance systems remain fairly distinct. The growth of such large NGO-led programmes is also related to large donors putting their faith in NGOs rather than country governments, as the former are often perceived as more honest, responsive to community needs and more efficient (Green and Matthias 1995). What is also interesting is to contrast the trajectories of the GK health programme and that of BRAC's. While the former is also large, BRAC has scaled up much faster and is by far the larger programme. This has occurred in a situation in which BRAC has focused more on expanding its operational activities and has not been as upfront about linkages to ideological movements and its own positions regarding inequity and access. It may be argued that this has made it easier for integration and collaboration with public systems. Another important aspect of BRAC's work is its practice of cross-subsidizing its developmental work through incomes from its commercial activities, raising questions about just how non-commercial their health initiatives really are.

PRIMARY CARE INITIATIVES WITH LIMITED SPAN OF COVERAGE

Laos: Comprehensive PHC project in Sayaboury Province

In partnership with the Ministry of Public Health and with funding support from AusAID, a comprehensive PHC project began in 1992 in Sayaboury

Province in Laos with Save the Children Australia (SCA) and the Sayaboury Department of Health. Project activities have gradually extended to cover the entire province, with 10 districts and 547 villages, with a population of 307,086 comprised of many ethnic minority groups. The programme has been carried out in four phases, each phase spanning three years and building on its predecessor's successes (Perks et al, 2006).

The first phase focused on strengthening the management and training skills of the provincial management team, which conducted in-service training for district teams and dispensary staff. During the second phase, the programme expanded into four additional districts and was geared towards integrating PHC activities at all levels. The third phase expanded into four newly created districts in the north that were quite remote. The International Fund for Agricultural Development constructed dispensaries, augmenting the construction programme instituted by SCA and expanding access to first-line health services. The fourth phase aimed to strengthen the skills of health workers, with an emphasis on those in the northern districts. The Integrated Management of Childhood Illness strategy was adopted in all districts.

The Sayaboury programme has shown significant successes, at the very affordable rate of only US$1 per person each year, or US$4 million over a 12-year period. The district's maternal mortality ratio fell from 218 per 100,000 live births in 1998 to 110 in 2003. The median age at which infants received complementary foods increased from 2.8 months in 1999 to 3.7 months in 2001, while the rate of exclusive breastfeeding for the first four months rose from 28% in 1999 to 66.2% in 2004. Vaccination coverage remained inadequate, however, with only 50% of children under one year of age receiving three or more doses of the vaccine for diphtheria, pertussis, and tetanus in 2007. The project is seen as a model for the country and efforts are underway to upscale the programme in other provinces (SCA[6]).

As we saw earlier in the chapter, Laos has very poor health indicators and a high incidence of private expenditure on health. In such a situation the present initiative to extend primary health coverage in one province is important to examine, especially given that the initiative is now being scaled up in other provinces of the country.

India: "Public-private partnership"[7] for PHC (Karuna Trust)

Karuna Trust, a leading NGO in India working to provide PHC services, was tasked with the responsibility of managing the Gumballi PHC Centre, in the state of Karnataka, in 1996. This was part of an experiment by the Government of Karnataka to outsource the running of some Primary Health Centres to non-government entities. A Primary Health Centre, within the public health infrastructure of India, is the second tier of the three-tier system designed to provide primary care. Each centre covers a population of about 30,000 people and provides outpatient care, basic in-patient services, and coordinates preventive and promotive services such as antenatal and post-natal care, immunization, etc. While Primary Health Centres are the hub of the primary care system, a large majority of them function suboptimally. In a majority of cases, in-patient services are not available, and in a significant number the centre is reduced to a dispensary that functions for just two to three hours a day. This is the context in which the Karnataka government chose to outsource the running of the Primary Health Centre to an NGO (Karuna Trust[8]).

Karuna Trust integrated the activities of all national health programmes, including reproductive and child health into the activities of the centre. It ensured that, under its management, it would provide round-the-clock emergency and casualty services, outpatient facilities six days a week, a 10-bed in-patient department, and 24-hour labour and essential obstetric facilities. Additionally, the Karuna Trust has introduced innovations such as integration of mental health services, eye care, and specialist services at primary care level. The Primary Health Centre provides services to 47 surrounding villages, with a population of around 39,000 people. There have been significant improvements as regards a number of indicators in the area covered by the Gumballi Primary Health Centre, in comparison to indicators in the state of Karnataka (e.g. Infant Mortality Rate is 23.6 in the project area in contrast to.48.01 for the state).

The success of the Gumballi Primary Health Centre and its impact as a "model" have strengthened the idea of public-private partnerships as a viable model among policy makers. Its success has led the Karnataka government to issue a formal policy on public private partnerships in 2000. Today the model has been upscaled and Karuna Trust runs 26 such centres in all the districts of the state of Karnataka and nine more in the north-eastern state of Arunachal Pradesh, covering a population of approximately 1.2 million people. The initiative has been a subject of considerable debate within the country. The Trust sees itself as building "models", and does not see the initiative as an alternative to the state taking the responsibility in managing and maintaining the public health care system. Its experience in managing the Primary Health Centres indicates that success is variable and depends crucially on strong support from the local public health department.

India's public health system, especially at the primary level of care, has been perennially plagued with problems, including issues regarding inability to attract human resources, inefficiency, poor infrastructure, and corruption. A way out is sought in outsourcing primary care facilities, especially in resource poor areas, to private entities. The Karuna Trust alternative examines one of the largest such ventures involving a not-for-profit trust that has been promoting primary care through its own programmes. While the outsourcing of public facilities is an issue that is a cause for a larger debate, the apparent initial success of the initiative merits further investigation (Ghanshyam 2008).

India: Comprehensive Rural Health Project (CRHP) in Jamkhed, Maharashtra

The Comprehensive Rural Health Project, Jamkhed (CRHP), was founded in 1970. The extremely poor and drought-prone area of Jamkhed, India, was plagued by high rates of malnutrition, infectious diseases, maternal deaths, and occupational injuries. Social injustices such as the low status of women and caste-based prejudices contributed significantly to this chronic state of ill health. Initially covering eight villages with a combined population of 10,000, the project rapidly expanded in its early years reaching out to a larger number of village communities. By 1980 CRHP expanded to cover a total of 70 villages with a combined population of 100,000. By 1985, a total of 250,000 people in 250 villages in Karjat and Jamkhed *talukas* were working with CRHP. Eventually over 300 villages with a combined population of 500,000 were participating with CRHP through the selection, training, and support of Village Health Workers (VHWs) and through the formation of community-based organizations (CBOs) such as farmers' clubs, women's clubs (*Mahila Vikas Mandals*), and self-help groups (SHGs; Jamkhed[9]).

The trained VHW acts as the local agent of positive health and social change. She is selected by her community and receives training in health, community development and organization, communication skills, and personal development from CRHP. Her primary role is to freely share the knowledge she obtains with everyone in the community, to organize community groups and to facilitate action, especially among women, the poor, and marginalized. At the outset, many of these VHWs were often illiterate women from the "untouchable" (Dalit) caste. The VHWs, working entirely as volunteers, became empowered by learning skills with which to earn a living through microenterprise.

The impact of the programme is visible. The number of leprosy cases in the project area declined from 157 in 1988 to just six in 2006. Similarly, new tuberculosis cases have declined from 592 in 1988 to six in 2006. The infant mortality rate, which was 176 in 1971, has come down to 24 (against a national average of 62 per 1,000 live births). Child malnutrition rates are less than 5% against a national average of 47%, and 99% of women receive antenatal care and a similar proportion have access to safe delivery.

Unlike many other NGO-led programmes in the region, the Jamkhed project has resolutely resisted the temptation to scale up. In fact, the present reach of the project is lower than in the 1990s; it currently works in 120 villages and the mobile team actively visits 45 of them. However, scaling up can be seen in a different way—small programmes all over the world, from Nepal to Brazil, use Jamkhed's principles. The Indian government also sends its own officials for orientation and training to Jamkhed. The project is financed (the annual budget is about US$500,000) through fees (which are very reasonable and sought only from those who can pay) from a small hospital that is run in Jamkhed and individual donations from people across the world.

The Jamkhed project has been held up, globally, as a true example of a community-based and community-owned primary care programme, and one that has been in existence for over four decades. Also interesting to learn from are the community mobilization and health worker training methodologies used in the programme (Rosenberg 2008).

INITIATIVES ADDRESSING A SPECIFIC
ASPECT OF ACCESS TO HEALTH SERVICES

India: Home-Based Neonatal Care (HBNC) in Gadchiroli, Maharashtra

This programme was initiated by the Society for Education Action and Research in Community Health (SEARCH), a non-profit NGO set up by a husband and wife team of doctors in 1986. They identified the main causes for infant mortality in the region and devised a strategy of home-based neonatal care to address them. Gadchiroli District, in Maharashtra, had an infant mortality rate of 121 per 1,000 births when the programme started. This has been brought down to less than 30 per 1,000 (SEARCH et al, 2011).

The programme hinges around trained community health workers (CHWs), or *arogyadu,* who are at the centre of the efforts to reduce neonatal and infant morbidity and mortality. SEARCH recruited village women with a minimum of four years schooling and trained them to provide care for women during pregnancy and for their babies after birth. The CHWs visit pregnant women to provide information on care for themselves during pregnancy, and recognition of danger signs, which may indicate that there are complications. CHWs' work is complementary to that of the traditional birth attendants; their focus is on newborns, and the roles are kept distinct. After the birth, they visit the mother and baby at home eight times during the first month (or 12 times if the baby is at high risk).

Among the types of preventive care they can offer are examining the baby, checking weight, temperature, and respiratory rate, and administering vitamin K. The CHWs also advise mothers on caring for the newborn, including breastfeeding, prevention of hypothermia, and recognizing danger signs. They can diagnose asphyxia, sepsis, low birth weight, and breastfeeding problems using simple, standardized criteria. Simple treatment is carried out on sick newborns at home by following standard practices learned during training. Many innovations have been introduced to provide support to the programme. One such innovation is the design and local fabrication of "breath counters" that are used by CHWs in place of stethoscopes.

The programme operates in 42 villages, and around 80 village health workers and 120 traditional midwives have learned to diagnose and treat major killers such as neonatal sepsis and infant pneumonia. An evaluation of the work of CHWs showed that there was a 62% reduction in the neonatal mortality rate, 71% reduction in the perinatal mortality rate, and 49% reduction in incidence of neonatal illnesses. In addition, the fatality rate in cases of sepsis/pneumonia fell from 16.6% to 2.8%, and the fatality rate among premature newborns and/or newborns with low birth weight went down by 60% (Bang et al, 2001, 956). The incidence of postpartum maternal illness was reduced by 51%. The positive findings from the Gadchiroli project have resulted in trials to upscale the programme, including some by the government's health department in its National Rural Health Mission.

Although this is not an alternative to commercialization that covers the entire spectrum of health services, the programme nonetheless dovetails with primary care systems. Of interest are moves to scale up the programme through adoption in the country's public system. Innovations used in training and training materials are useful to take note of, especially in the context of fairly high success rates reported in controlling childhood mortality and morbidity.

India: Sonagachi HIV/AIDS International Project (SHIP)

In 1992 the All India Institute of Hygiene and Public Health (AIIHPH) initiated a conventional sexually transmitted infections treatment and prevention programme in Sonagachi, the principal red-light district of Kolkata, home to over 7,000 sex workers. The Sonagachi HIV/AIDS International Project (SHIP) was implemented through an intersectoral partnership of the WHO, AIIHPH, the British Council, and a number of ministries and local NGOs. The project quickly moved beyond traditional treatment and education modalities to focus on the empowerment of the sex workers. Key interventions during the first five years included vaccination and treatment services for the sex workers' children, literacy classes for the women, political activism and advocacy, microcredit schemes, and cultural programmes (Jana and Singh 1995).

The sex workers created their own membership organization, the *Durbar Mahila Samanwaya Committee* (DMSC) that successfully negotiated for better treatment by madams, landlords, and local authorities. In 1999, the DMSC took over the management of SHIP, and has since expanded it to include 40 red-light districts across West Bengal, including a community of around 65,000 male, female, and transgendered sex workers based in brothels, streets, and hotels. DSMC's work includes struggle against extortion and harassment by local hooligans and police, fighting against eviction of individual sex workers from their homes, running a HIV helpline, and action against forcible HIV/AIDS surveillance. DMSC's efforts have resulted in the creation of a self-regulatory board that, whenever a new girl/woman arrives in Sonagachi, scans legal issues such as her age and whether she is willingly entering this sector of work. The initiative receives support from the Ford Foundation, the United Nations Development Programme (UNDP), Action Aid, and the National Aids Control Organization (NACO) of the government of India (Smarajit 2004).

Efforts to empower people with knowledge and tools for health are at the centre of this programme. Peer educators provide sexual health and HIV education to sex workers and madams and distribute condoms. To support non-formal education efforts, 29 educational centres in and around Sonagachi have been set up. To foster economic security, sex workers seeking financial credit are encouraged to become members of a community-lending cooperative that provides affordable loans. As part of its empowerment strategy, the Sonagachi Project also promotes the various talents of sex workers through a cultural wing—the *Komal Gandhar*. In addition, an anti-trafficking unit, controlled by self-regulatory boards, works across West Bengal to protect children; two homes are also in operation to provide a safe shelter for children in distress.

Evidence suggests that the project has had a major impact. In 1992, rates of consistent condom use with clients in the previous two months was a mere 1%. By 2001, that figure had increased to 65%. Prevalence of syphilis dropped during that period from 25% to 8.76%. The programme has attracted substantial attention as an example of healthy sector intervention that is premised on community involvement and organization. Of particular importance is the fact that the community of sex workers is one of the most marginalized. Within such a context, it is useful to examine the success of the alternative to provide a political voice to the community and to combine it with programmes that address several determinants of good health in the sex-worker community. The expansion of the initiative and its proposed adoption within the public health system are also areas that merit further scrutiny.

Nepal: Community-based Management of Childhood Pneumonia

Pneumonia is a leading cause of mortality of children aged under five in Nepal. Female community health volunteers (FCHV) were selected to manage childhood pneumonia at community level using oral antibiotics. A technical working group composed of government officials, local experts, and donor partners embarked on a process to develop a strategy to pilot the approach and expand it nationally. Community-based management of pneumonia doubled the total number of cases treated compared with districts with facility-based treatment only. Over half of the cases were treated by the female community health volunteers. The programme was phased in over 14 years and now 69% of Nepal's under five population has access to pneumonia treatment (Dawson et al, 2008, 341).

The female community health volunteers were selected by the communities and trained by the Ministry of Health. The WHO, United Nations Children's Fund (UNICEF), and United States Agency for International Development (USAID) supported the development of technical guidelines for programme implementation. UNICEF conducted a focused ethnographic study to understand community-perceived danger signs of pneumonia and care-seeking practices. Training and behaviour-change communications materials were developed by members of the technical working group. To address the low literacy level of some FCHVs, extensive effort was given to developing pictorial training manuals, educational materials, and reporting booklets. This preparation phase took place in 1993–1994.

Training began in June 1995 involving role play and practical skills development. FCHV supervisors were included in training to strengthen their links with the FCHVs for future follow-up and field monitoring. Four districts were selected for the pilot intervention, two "treatment" and two "referral", with a total of 1,497 FCHVs and 525 health facility staff trained. In all four districts, health facility staff were trained in both pneumonia case treatment and programme management to ensure that FCHVs received necessary supportive supervision, feedback, and replenishment of supplies. District health office staff were trained on monitoring and supervision for follow-up and documentation. Mothers' groups and village leader orientations were held in all villages to encourage prompt care seeking and local support. In 1997, the two "referral" districts were converted to "treatment" and the programme gradually expanded. By 2007, 42 of Nepal's 75 districts were included, where 69% of the population of children aged less than five years reside. Quality of care provided by the FCHVs is regularly monitored by district and partner staff and remains high. Standardized checklists are used and immediate feedback given. Community-based pneumonia treatment data are part of the government's routine Health Monitoring Information System. An estimated 6,000 lives are currently saved each year through this intervention in Nepal (Dawson et al, 2008, 340–342).

Nepal is one of the poorest countries in Asia and has suffered the consequences of political turmoil and devastation through natural disasters in recent decades. What has gone largely unnoticed, however, is some remarkable progress in Nepal in recent years in terms of reduction in mortality and morbidity indicators. Some commentators have ascribed this to the success of focused, donor agency-supported programmes that have been successful in harvesting the "low hanging fruits" of PHC. While such an analysis has some merit, it would be interesting to examine such programmes, such as the one described above. The initiative is also interesting to follow as it addresses one of the key downstream causes of childhood mortality. Also of interest is the impressive scale up of the programme as evident from the fact that more than half of Nepal's expected pneumonia cases (56%) in 42 programme districts (of 75 districts) currently receive treatment, and community management of pneumonia provides over half of that treatment (Dawson et al, 2008).

India: Affordable drugs for everyone (Locost)

Low Cost Standard Therapeutics, or Locost, was set up to enable all Indians, even the poor in remote areas, to access quality medicines at affordable prices. Locost was founded in 1983 as a non-profit charitable trust registered in Baroda, Gujarat. Locost's medicine prices are significantly lower than those of other manufacturers. For example, Atenolol, a drug used to treat high blood pressure available at retail stores for Rs20–25 a strip, is sold by Locost at Rs3 per strip. A strip of paracetamol from Locost costs Rs2, while proprietary brands cost Rs9 per strip (1 Rs is approximately US$0.02; Locost[11]).

Locost's small-scale manufacturing unit makes over 60 essential medicines in 80 formulations (liquid, capsule, tablet). Locost buys the active pharmaceutical ingredient from bulk drug manufacturers and then manufactures its own formulations. Locost also pays its workers more than the regular wages; its wage scales are, in fact, the highest among the small-scale industries. Despite all the expenses that go into maintaining a high standard, Locost is able to sell its drugs at one-fourth to one-tenth of the price of drugs being sold in the retail market. With such competitive prices, Locost makes a profit of about 10% on annual sales, which it ploughs back to scale up its production volumes.[12]

Locost has been supplying drugs to over 100 civil society and charitable organizations. The idea of making the Locost drugs available at various retail outlets is, however, a relatively new concept. Besides its manufacturing unit in Baroda, Locost has a retail store in Vadodara, a depot in Karnataka (Bangalore) and the Northeast (Guwahati), and small retail outlets in various parts of Maharashtra.

Locost also has an education cell that focuses on issues related to education and training for rational use of medicines. It brings out a Gujarati language monthly, *Apnu Swasthya*, and other publications for the general public, the latest being the Gujarati version of the famous classic, *Where There Is No Doctor;* and *A Lay Person's Guide to Medicine, A Guide on the Use and Political Economy of Medicines.* Locost is also active in pharmaceutical policy advocacy at regional and national levels. Its partnership, as respondent, in an ongoing case in the Supreme Court has resulted in the elimination of several categories of harmful and irrational drugs.

India's generic pharmaceutical industry has been called the "Pharmacy of the South" because of its ability to supply low-cost medicines to a large number of poor countries across the globe. However, within India, access to medicines is still a big issue, and the major constraint continues to be the prices of medicines. An estimated 50–80% of people in India do not have access to essential medicines. The "alternative" presented here addresses this issue by making available medicines at low prices to community health programmes. It is an alternative to commercial pharmaceutical production and distribution that has the potential for replication in many resource-poor settings.

EVALUATION OF ALTERNATIVES

It would be inappropriate to suggest overly specific trends or make broad generalizations based on the limited evidence contained in the alternatives to commercialization presented here. There are, however, some general developments that can be commented upon, divided into two areas: those relating to the public sector and those related to the private not-for-profit sector.

Public sector

There is an interest and some urgency among governments that have followed neoliberal reforms and dismantled public systems (e.g. China, India, Laos) to attempt to remedy the negative impacts of these reforms through some strengthening of public systems. Unfortunately, most public initiatives continue to be informed by, and located in, an understanding that public strengthening must go hand in hand with partnerships with the private sector.

- Neoliberal ideologies permeate the thinking on health systems even in countries in which public systems are acknowledged to have produced laudable results (e.g. Sri Lanka and Malaysia). However, proposed commercialization reforms face popular opposition and have not proceeded at the pace projected by the neoliberal lobby.
- The presence of a growing private sector impacts on the ability of the public system to thrive and expand by drawing away technical and human resources.
- Generally, "reform" ideology is prominent in the secondary and tertiary health care sectors, for the good reason that the for-profit private sector is not interested in the primary level of care. This is creating a move towards the bifurcation of health systems, where the primary sector is seen as the domain of public systems and the secondary/tertiary sectors are opened up to the private sector.

Not-for-profit sector

- Several alternatives are being developed and implemented by the not-for-profit sector, which have the potential for adoption within public systems. A systematic analysis of these can inform many public initiatives.
- CBOs implementing alternatives find it difficult to scale up when they need to reach out to regions that are outside their immediate geographical area of work.
- There appears to be a trade-off between ability (and intent) to scale up and engagement with issues of solidarity and ideological commitments to a public ethos. This adds an element of dilemma, whereby larger programmes may need to "compromise" more with basic principles of community mobilization, solidarity, ownership, and empowerment.
- The role of donor agencies in supporting programmes by not-for-profit organizations, in preference to government programmes, needs to be analyzed.
- The dividing line between a "contractor" of services for the government and a community mobilizer is often blurred. Some criteria need to be developed to examine programmes that involve partnerships between government and not-for-profit organizations.

WAYS FORWARD

The "public" has virtually disappeared from health care systems in many parts of the world. It is therefore necessary to address wrong perceptions and blatant untruths about the public sector, particularly given the systematic attempts to portray the private sector as more "efficient" and to argue that market-based competition and incentives lead to better care and more choices. Such arguments turn a blind eye to the fact that the public sector has played the major role in almost all situations in which health outcomes have improved significantly. Health systems that have depended on the public sector have been the norm, rather than the exception, even in wealthy countries. The success stories of health system development in the global South (e.g. Sri Lanka, Costa Rica, and Cuba) are success stories of public sector health systems. But the success of the public sector is not limited to health care systems. Publicly funded research in national institutes of science and universities has laid the foundations for many, if not most, developments in the medical sciences.

Public systems are desired because they promote equity. This is perhaps the most important reason why the public sector needs to play a leading role in health care systems—no matter which part of the world we are talking about. People have a right to health care in an equitable manner, not dependent on their ability to pay. Governments, not markets, can ensure that health systems address the needs of the poorest and the most marginalized. It is also, however, true that there needs to be conscious elements within public systems that promote equity. The mere fact that a system is funded through public funds does not mean that it necessarily promotes equity. There are various elements that come into play, including for example, how such a system targets those who need health services the most. This does not mean that public health services are "poor services for poor people". They should be seen as attempts to provide the best services possible to all, while addressing the special needs of those most vulnerable.

An equitable and efficient health care system requires planning that is based on local conditions. It is impossible for a profit-driven, fragmented system with multiple (often contradictory) objectives, to do so. For such a system to work optimally, it needs to regularly connect with peoples' needs and priorities. This is best achieved when popular participation ensures that the public is not just a recipient of public health care but is also involved in its planning and execution. It is only through the operationalization of an adequately financed public service that the link between the income of health care providers and the delivery of health care can be broken. Unethical behaviour of health care providers is directly linked with the fact that if care is linked to profit, more ill health means more profit!

Public initiatives that need to be reclaimed

The alternatives discussed above indicate some ways of moving forward and suggest that there is a genuine concern in many countries of the region that the marginalization of the public sector needs to be reversed. Some of this interest may be more practical than ideological, however, suggesting an ongoing tension between the neoliberal ethos of "new public management" and the practical evidence that commercialized health care systems are failing to deliver. Many neoliberal economists now admit this and have even taken recourse in coining the phrase "market failure" to explain away the fundamental flaw in neoliberal economics towards welfare programmes (People's Health Movement 2006, 11–51). However, especially in the Indian case, there is still hesitation to go "all the way", and methods are being sought to still find a significant role for the private sector.

Within the public systems discussed here that of Thailand merits special mention. For countries in the region, there is a strong case to study the Thai system and to draw appropriate lessons for emulation.

Public initiatives that need to be defended

We have consciously chosen also to discuss public systems that exhibit tendencies towards undermining the public ethos, e.g. the cases of Malaysia and

Sri Lanka. Of importance in these cases is the fact that while public policy in some sectors has shown a faster trajectory towards liberalization, public scrutiny and resistance have slowed down intended reforms in the health care sector. This indicates a strong case for promoting civil society scrutiny and mobilization around the issue of public provision of health services.

Innovations and alternatives: Models for adoption

The alternatives in the not-for-profit sector raised a different set of issues to inform future directions. It would be incorrect to dub any of these as alternatives that can transform the entire health care system. However, these programmes carry innovations that public systems can nurture and scale up. Importantly, these alternatives often keep alive the notions of public provisioning, community participation, comprehensive care, etc—notions that were at the core of the Alma-Ata Declaration in 1978 but which governments worldwide have failed to take forward.

Finally, notwithstanding short-term and intermediate-term tactics, public systems can survive and grow only at the expense of the private sector. This is a central message that we need to take forward. An analysis of many of the alternatives in the health sector in Asia shows that the private sector is a pernicious influence that erodes public systems. The future battle, in situations in which public systems are being resurrected, is to ensure that they are built at the expense of the private sector and not to complement the private sector.

NOTES

1. *Inter alia*, the Alma-Ata Declaration, issued at the conclusion of the "International Conference on Primary Health Care", Alma-Ata, USSR, 6–12 September 1978, stated "Governments have a responsibility for the health of their people which can be fulfilled only by the provision of adequate health and social measures. A main social target of governments, international organizations and the whole world community in the coming decades should be the attainment by all peoples of the world by the year 2000 of a level of health that will permit them to lead a socially and economically productive life" (Article V).
2. While the recommendation that at least 5% of GDP should be spent on health has never been formally adopted by the World Health Organization (WHO), the figure is extensively quoted in WHO documents. For an explanation of its genesis, see Savedoff 2003, 9–11.
3. Based on personal communications between the author and Dr. Zafarulah Chowdhury, one of the founders of GK, a face-to-face meeting 26 August 2009 and several visits by the author to GK before 2007.
4. For more information on the People's Health Movement, see www.phmovement.org.
5. BRAC. www.brac.net.
6. SCA. www.savethechildren.net/australia/where_we_work/lao_pdr/primary_health.html (accessed 3 October 2010).
7. While we describe a partnership between a not-for-profit NGO and government, it is termed as a public-private partnership, as this is the nomenclature

used by the Indian government regarding initiatives in which individual PHC centres are given out to NGOs to administer and provide services.

8. Karuna Trust. www.karunatrust.com/.
9. Jamkhed. www.jamkhed.org/.
10. Locost. www.locostindia.com/.
11. Information based on personal communication of the author with founder and director of Locost, S. Srinivasan, July 2009.

REFERENCES

Abbas Motevalian, S. 2007. *A case study on intersectoral action for health in I.R. of Iran: Community-based initiatives experience.* Teheran: WHO. www.who. int/social_determinants/resources/isa_community_initiatives_irn.pdf

Awin, N. 2002. *A review of primary health care in Malaysia.* Manila: WHO, Western Pacific Region.

Bang, A.T., Bang, R.A., Baitule, S.B., Reddy, M.H. and Deshmukh, M.M. 2001. Burden of morbidities and the unmet need for health care in rural neonates: A prospective observational study in Gadchiroli, India. *Indian Pediatrics* 38: 952–965.

Chee Khoon, C. 2010. Re-inventing the welfarist state? The Malaysian health system in transition. *Journal of Contemporary Asia* 40(3): 444–465.

CHSI (Centre for Health Statistics and Information, Ministry of Health, China). 2004. *An analysis report of national health services survey in 2003.* Beijing: Union Medical University Press.

Dawson, P., Pradhan, Y.V., Houston, R., Karki, S., Poudel, D. and Hodgins, S. 2008. From research to national expansion: 20 years' experience of community-based management of childhood pneumonia in Nepal. *Bulletin of the WHO* 86(5): 339–343.

Dezhi, Y. 1992. *Changes in health care financing and health status: The case of China in the 1980s.* Occasional Paper No 34. Florence: Innocenti.

Ghanshyam, B. 2008. Can public-private partnerships improve health in India? *The Lancet* 372(9642): 878–879. www.thelancet.com/journals/lancet/issue/vol372no9642/PIIS0140–6736%2808%29X6039–8.

Gilson, L., Doherty, J., Loewenson, R. and Francis, V. 2007. Challenging inequity through health systems. Final Report, Knowledge Network on Health Systems. WHO Commission on Social Determinants of Health. www.who.int/social_determinants/resources/csdh_media/hskn_final_2007_en.pdf.

Gonoshashthya Kendra. 2009. www.gkbd.org/aboutus.htm (accessed 31 May 2009).

Government of India. 2009. *Annual Report 2008–2009.* New Delhi: Ministry of Health and Family Welfare.

———. 2010. Website of national rural health mission, Ministry of Health. www.mohfw.nic.in/NRHM.htm.

Green, A. and Matthias, A. 1995. NGOs—A policy panacea for the next millennium? *Journal of International Development* 7(3): 565–573.

Haque, M.S. 2008. Global rise of neoliberal state and its impact on citizenship: Experiences in developing nations. *Asian Journal of Social Science* 36: 11–34.

Huda, C.R. and Chowdhury, Z. 2008. Maternal mortality in rural Bangladesh: Lessons learned from Gonoshasthaya Kendra programme villages. *Asia-Pacific Population Journal* 23: 55–78.

Jana, S. and Singh, S. 1995. Beyond medical model of STD intervention—Lessons from Sonagachi. *Indian Journal of Public Health* 39(3): 125–131.

McGregor, A. 2008. *Southeast Asian development.* New York: Routledge.

McIntyre, D. 2006. *Country case study: Universal tax funded health system in Sri Lanka.* Cape Town: Health Economics Unit, University of Cape Town. www. uct-heu.s3.amazonaws.com/14FinancingSriLanka.pdf.

Meng, Q. 2007. Developing and implementing equity-promoting health care policies in China. Health Systems Knowledge Network of the Commission on Social Determinants of Health. www.who.int/social_determinants/resources/ csdh_media/equity_health_china_2007_en.pdf.

Parry, J. and Weiyuan, C. 2008. Making health care affordable in China. *Bulletin of the WHO* 86(11): 822–825. www.who.int/bulletin/volumes/86/11/08–011108. pdf.

People's Health Movement, Medact, and Global Equity Gauge Alliance. 2006. *Global health watch 2005–2006: An alternative world health report.* New York: Zed Books.

People's Rural Health Watch—Jan Swasthya Abhiyan. 2008. Health services and the national rural health mission. New Delhi: People's Health Movement. www.phm-india.org/index.php?option=com_docman&task=cat_view&gid=54&Itemid=15.

Perera, M. 2006. *Intersectoral action for health in Sri Lanka.* Health Systems Knowledge Network, WHO's Commission on Social Determinants of Health. http://www.who.int/social_determinants/resources/csdh_media/ intersectoral_action_sri_lanka_2007_en.pdf

Perks, C.T., Michael, J. and Phouthonsy, K. 2006. District health programmes and health-sector reform: Case study in the Lao People's Democratic Republic. *Bulletin of the WHO* 84(2): 132–138.

Ramalingaswami, V. and Jonsson, U. and Rohde, J. 1996. The Asian enigma. Progress of Nations. 1996. UNICEF. http://www.unicef.org/pon96/nuenigma.htm

Rannan-Eliya, R.P. and Sikurajapathy, L. 2008. "Good practice" in expanding health care coverage in Sri Lanka. In Gottret, P., Schieber, G. and Waters, H. (Eds), *Good practice in health financing: Lessons from reforms in low and middle-income countries,* pp. 311–354. Washington, DC: World Bank.

Rao, M. 2009. Health for all and neoliberal globalization: An Indian rope trick. In Panitch, L. and Leys, C. (Eds), *Morbid symptoms: Health under capitalism,* pp. 262–278. New Delhi: Leftword Books.

Rosenberg, T. 2008. Necessary angels. *National Geographic Magazine* 214: 66–85.

Sadrizadeh, B. 2004. Primary health care experience in Iran. *Medical Journal of the Iranian Red Crescent* 7(1): 79–90.

Savedoff, W. 2003. *How much should countries spend on health?* Discussion Paper, Department of Health System Financing, Expenditure and Resource Allocation. Geneva: WHO.

SEARCH. Rani and Abhay Bang—pioneers of health care in rural India, www. searchgadchiroli.org/media%20stories/Lancot%20profile.pdf (accessed 3 June 2009).

Sida (Swedish International Development Assistance). 1994. Economic reform in Vietnam: Achievements and prospects. Series of Reports for International Seminar. Stockholm, Sweden: Sida.

Smarajit, J. 2004. The Sonagachi Project: A sustainable community intervention program. *AIDS Education and Prevention* 16 (5): 405–414.

Tangcharoensathien, V., Prakongsai, P., Limwattananon, S., Patcharanarumol, W. and Jongudomsuk, P. 2007. *Achieving universal coverage in Thailand: What lessons do we learn?* Thailand: Health Systems Knowledge Network, WHO Commission on Social Determinants of Health.

Tavassoli, M. 2008. Iranian health houses open the door to primary care. *Bulletin of the WHO* 86(8): 577–656. www.who.int/bulletin/volumes/86/8/en/.

UNDP (United Nations Development Programme). 2008. *Human Development Report*. Geneva: UNDP.

Upham, N. 2004. *Making health care work for the poor, review of the NGO experiences in selected Asian countries*. Background document: WHO Asian Civil Society Conference on Macroeconomics and Health, 27–28 April, pp. 16. Colombo, Sri Lanka. http://www.who.int/macrohealth/action/en/ngo_paper_sri_lanka.pdf.

van Doorslaer, E., O'Donnell, O. and Somanathan, A. 2005. *Paying out-of-pocket for health care in Asia: Catastrophic and poverty impact*. Equitap Working Paper No. 2. Equitap. http://www.equitap.org/publications/docs/EquitapWP2.pdf.

Wang, S. 2009. China's double movement in health care. In Panitch, L. and Leys, C. (Eds), *Morbid symptoms: Health under capitalism*, pp. 240–261. New Delhi: Leftword Books.

Werner, D. and Sanders, D. 1997. *Questioning the solution: The politics of primary health care and child survival with an in-depth critique of oral rehydration therapy*. Palo Alto, CA: Health Wrights.

WHO (World Health Organization). 2009. *World Health Statistics 2009*. Geneva: WHO.

Wibulpolprasert, S. and Thaiprayoon, S. 2008. Thailand: Good practice in expanding health coverage—Lessons from the Thai health care reforms. In Gottret, P., Schieber, G. and Waters, H. (Eds), *Good practice in health financing: Lessons from reforms in low and middle-income countries*, pp. 355–383. Washington, DC: World Bank.

World Bank. 2009. *World Development Report*. Washington, DC: World Bank.

9 Springs of Hope

Alternatives to Commercialization of Water Resources and Services in Asia

Buenaventura Dargantes, Cheryl Batistel and Mary Ann Manahan

Asia is well endowed with water resources, but monsoon cycles can induce large interseasonal variations in river flows, and there are significant variations across the four subregions (Central, South, Southeast, and East). With some 60% of the world's population, the amount of water per capita also varies, with Central, East, and South Asia typically recording levels lower than the global average. Southeast Asia, on the other hand, has more than twice the world average (WRI 2005, 1).

Hydrological cycles aside, much of the debate about water in Asia today revolves around water treatment and distribution and who provides these services. The Millennium Development Goals (MDGs) provide Asian countries with a quantitative framework for dealing with the challenge of water service provision, with MDG 7 Target 10 calling on nations to halve the proportion of people without sustainable access to safe drinking water and improved sanitation by 2015. Although 10–14% of Asians still did not have access to safe supplies as of 2006, many parts of the region met and surpassed their targets. In East Asia alone, over 400 million people were reported to have gained access to improved drinking water sources as of 2006 or an increase in coverage by 20% over the 1990 figures (UN 2008).

Aside from the MDGs, the Association of Southeast Asian Nations (Asean) Strategic Plan of Action on the Environment (1994–1998) provided that member states respond to specific recommendations of the United Nations (UN) Agenda 21, requiring that "adequate supplies of water of good quality are maintained for the entire population while preserving the hydrological, biological and chemical functions of ecosystems, adapting human activities within the capacity limits of nature and combating vectors of water-related diseases". The accord further recognized that "innovative technologies, including the improvement of indigenous technologies, are needed to fully utilize limited water resources and to safeguard those resources against pollution" (UN 1993, Section 2, Chapter 18).

In South Asia, part of the effort to ensure water security is embodied in the proposal of the United Nations Environment Programme (UNEP) and Development Alternatives (DA; a social enterprise whose mission is to create sustainable livelihoods on a large scale by delivering market-based technologies and institutions) for the adoption of the recommendations of the Human Development Report of 2006 with emphasis on making water a human right. UNEP and DA further advocate that "governments go beyond vague constitutional principles in enabling legislation to secure the human right to a secure, accessible, and affordable supply of water" (2008, 79).

Although there might have been no intention to dichotomize the prioritization, the increasing scarcity of water has renewed debates on the inclusiveness of the "water-for-all" agenda. Whereas some water activists have argued for the prioritization of human basic needs within the water-for-all framework, others have posited that the guarantee should apply to all life forms and to ecosystems themselves. The significance of the water-for-all-life-forms argument is highlighted when juxtaposed with the thrust to commoditize water and/or to privatize water services. As Naqvi points out, "According to World Bank philosophy, religious places, helpless poor, birds and animals—all are consumers" (n.d., 7).

Other recommendations embodied in Agenda 21 were for states to "support water-users groups to optimize local water resources management" and to develop and strengthen "cooperation at all levels . . . including the decentralization of government services to local authorities, private enterprises and communities" (UN 1993, Section 2, Chapter 18). With many states unable to provide centralized government services, these recommendations allowed communities and village-level associations, as well as local governments, to continue performing their role as water service providers (WSPs) to their respective constituencies, thereby increasing the variety of management models for water service delivery.

Foremost of these models are the centralized water utilities being managed by state or metropolitan water boards and water districts providing services mainly to capital cities, highly urbanized centres, and peri-urban communities. In some areas, water service delivery is being managed by municipal governments or by some other local government unit (e.g. province, city, town, or village). Areas not served by water boards, water districts or local governments are being covered by water supply enterprises as diverse as village-based water and sanitation associations, water service cooperatives, and homeowners' water associations. Isolated households or neighbourhood clusters mainly depend on stand-alone water sources such as springs, streams, and/or water pumps.

LEVELS OF WATER SERVICES IN ASIA

Although MDG 7 Target 10 calls for the reduction of the proportion of the population without sustainable access to safe water supply, the *Asia Water Watch 2015* report notes that safe water supply has been extremely difficult to assure (2006). In view of this, the phrase "improved water supply" has been proposed as a substitute after having been adjudged to be "the best measurable standard" to indicate that "water is more accessible, and some measures have been taken to protect the water sources from contamination".

Based on this phraseology, *Asia Water Watch 2015* reported that from 1990 to 2002, water supply coverage in the region improved from 82–84%, but the increase was not uniform (ADB et al, 2006). East and South Asia reported increases of five and six percentage points, respectively, but coverage declined in Southeast Asia mainly due to the deterioration of existing facilities and service delivery systems coupled with rapid population growth. Although an additional 100 million persons were provided with improved water supply between 1990 and 2002, such increase in coverage was less than the population growth of Southeast Asia during that period (Table 9.1).

Asia Water Watch 2015 predicted that WSPs in Asia would cover a total of 3.7 billion people, or 89% of the projected population of the region by 2015 (ADB et al, 2006). South Asia is predicted to achieve the highest coverage in terms of nominal population (90%), followed by East Asia (87%). Southeast Asia, despite its relatively high level of per capita water availability, is projected to only have 88% of its 2015 population covered by improved water supply. Central Asia, which faces a very low level of per capita water availability, is expected to maintain its 91% coverage mainly because of its relatively low population growth.

By 2006, Asia as a whole surpassed the 2015 MDG target for population with access to improved drinking water source (IDWS), 86% versus the actual 87%. This level of access reflected a tremendous improvement over that of 2004, during which Asia was reporting only 78% of its population with access to IDWS. The 2004 level was even a regression over the 1990 level of 80% access (Table 9.2).

Table 9.1   Profile of Population Served by Improved Water Supply

Subregion	Total population served as of 1990 (millions)	% Coverage of total population as of 1990	Total population served as of 2002 (millions)	% Coverage of total population as of 2002	Projected total population served by 2015 (millions)	% Coverage of projected population by 2015
Central Asia	34.339	91	37.734	91	42.223	91
East Asia	985.171	81	1,193.722	86	1.476.209	87
South Asia	822.188	79	1,242.036	84	1.699.788	90
Southeast Asia	305.927	76	405.098	75	494.228	88
Asia Total	2,147.625	82	2,878.590	84	3,712.448	89

Sources: ADB et al, 2006, 12-13).

Table 9.2   Profile of Access to Improved Drinking Water Sources in Asia

Subregion	% of 1990 population with access to IDWS	% of 2004 population with access to IDWS	% of 2006 population with access to IDWS	MDG 7 Target 10 to be attained by 2015 (%)
Central Asia	86	66	NA	NA
East Asia	83	84	88	84
South Asia	69	80	87	87
Southeast Asia	82	81	86	87
Asia Total	80	78	87	86

Sources: WHO and UNICEF 2004, 24–31, UN 2008, 42.

PUBLIC VERSUS PRIVATE WATER SERVICES

In an effort to map the degree of public versus private sector service delivery in Asia, we conducted a survey of 646 listed water utilities, of which 171 (24%) provided information on the number of service connections and the number of people serviced. This is a large and broadly characteristic sample, we believe, but it should be noted that it is not statistically representative due to data collection limitations, foremost of which was language (see next section). Those included in the list from Central and South Asia were large, centralized utilities. In Central Asia, an average water utility would have 103,000 service connections covering more than 1.2 million people. In South Asia, a utility would have an average of 320,000 service connections serving 3.7 million individuals. Those in East Asia have a little less than 1 million service connections serving an average of 5 million people. The water utilities in the list in Southeast Asia also covered smaller water districts in the Philippines. They have an average of 62,000 service connections providing water to 240,000 people (see Table 9.3).

Most of the utilities listed are public in nature—either as state-sponsored agencies or as municipal corporations. Although our research found only two private water corporations in the Philippines (Manila Water Company, Inc. [MWCI] and Maynilad Water Services, Inc. [MWSI]) and two in Indonesia (PT Pam Lyonnaise Jaya and PT Thames Pam Jaya), online information indicated that some private corporations worked for the development of sources of water supply and for the acquisition of rights or entitlements to the water they were able to produce from their projects. Endowed with legal entitlements for the abstraction of water, these corporations then enter into bulk water supply arrangements with the public sector or non-profit utilities.

Table 9.3   Water Utilities in Asia

Subregion	Number of water utilities listed	Number of utilities with data	Average number of connections	Average number of people served
Central Asia	3	3	103,056	1,238,865
East Asia	8	8	961,361	5,052,414
South Asia	13	13	320,590	3,685,044
Southeast Asia	622	147	61,731	243,046
Asia Total	646	171	12,4963	799,881

Source: Authors' surveys.

THE SEARCH FOR ALTERNATIVES

Countries covered by the study and limitations in their selection

Our survey of WSPs in Asia initially only covered South and Southeast Asia. Central and East Asia were included later. But because our research capacity is strongest in India and the Philippines, more detailed datasheets on service providers were generated for these countries. We relied mainly on desktop research to gather data on possible "alternatives to privatization" in Hong Kong, Indonesia, Pakistan, Bangladesh, Thailand, Nepal, and Cambodia. Data obtained through Internet searches were further substantiated in regional validation workshops in Bangkok, Thailand. Research collaborators from the Hong Kong-based Globalization Monitor provided additional information on China. Language difficulty was one of the biggest constraints in the research; many materials on East, Central, and Southeast Asia are not written in English.

Data collection methods

In addition to Internet reviews, the researchers reviewed relevant secondary literature, consulted with research associates of other research and activist organizations, and conducted face-to-face interviews with management and labour representatives of water utilities, civil society representatives, and community leaders working on water issues.

Desktop data collection was limited by two problems: (i) national/local websites did not always carry English translations and (ii) the use of local terminologies (for governance entities, measurement units, currencies, and community practices) made it difficult to make comparisons across the region. Priority was thus given to English-language websites, many of which were set up by international agencies. Materials from websites were sifted and cross-checked with other references as they rarely provide operational details.

In terms of operations, the prospective alternatives identified in the research varied in scope from village-level systems to initiatives undertaken by state-level water boards and by national-level association of WSPs. Among WSPs, the alternatives took on a variety of forms: from targeting service provision to the poor to providing service for all.

The following sections outline our findings according to the organizational typologies of "alternatives to privatization" outlined in Chapter 2 of this volume.

ALTERNATIVES TO PRIVATIZATION ACCORDING TO ORGANIZATIONAL TYPOLOGIES

Public/non-profit partnerships

Public-non-profit partnerships (PuNP) were the most common alternative service delivery mechanism identified in our mapping. It was particularly prevalent in South Asia. PuNPs are arrangements wherein one or more public sector agency works with one or more civil society or community-based organization (CBO) to deliver water services (see Table 9.4 for a summary of the different numbers of typologies found, by subregion). This typology is exemplified by the Tamil Nadu Rural Water Sector Programme

Table 9.4 Types of Alternatives by Organizational Typologies

	Type of alternative	*Number of examples found*
East Asia	Public/Non-profit Partnership	2
	Single Public Sector Agency	2
South Asia	Public/Non-profit Partnership	5
	Non-profit/Non-profit Partnership	4
	Single Non-profit Agency	4
	Single Public Sector Agency	3
Southeast Asia	Public-Public Partnership	6
	Public/Non-profit Partnership	4
	Single Public Sector Agency	2
	Single Non-profit Agency	1
Asia Total	Public/Non-profit Partnership	11
	Single Public Sector Agency	7
	Public-Public Partnership	6
	Single Non-profit Agency	4
	Non-profit-Non-profit Partnership	4
Total		33

(TNRWSP) implemented by the Tamil Nadu Water Supply and Drainage Board (TWAD) in India. Under this programme, a partnership was forged between local communities and the water utility for the joint management of water services based on equity, resource management, reduction of water consumption, improvement of reliability, and reduction in operating and maintenance costs.

Another dimension of these partnerships is demonstrated by the Convergence Experiment conducted in the state of Tamil Nadu. The experiment enabled various line departments to coordinate and cooperate with each other to provide irrigation water to the farms of more than 1 million families and showed the viability of PuNPs in different contexts. Based on the partnership, individual water users, community-based groups, and the water utility organization as a whole were able to align their perceptions and commitments so that the necessary change efforts could be identified and initiated. According to Nayar et al (n.d., 26), the change in perspective has led engineers to assume the larger role of "Managers of the Commons" and gave impetus to the emergence of a vision that articulated the current concerns of local farming communities, as well as future generations.

In urban settings, PuNPs were exemplified by the cooperation between the Dhaka Water and Sewerage Authority of Bangladesh and a local non-governmental organization (NGO), the *Dushtha Shashtya Kendra* (DSK), and between the Residents Association of Tinagong Paraiso, a local NGO, and the Bacolod City Water District (BACIWA) of the Philippines. Through such partnerships, communal water points were provided to residents of slum communities, thereby improving access to clean water among informal settlers and urban poor. In the Philippines, the community tap stands were even directly managed and maintained by the Association.

PuNPs also came in the form of collaboration between village and municipal governments, NGOs, academic institutions, community-based water users, and WSPs. These partnerships took on such tasks as the delineation of watershed boundaries, inventory of biophysical resources and assessment of socio-economic conditions of watersheds and development planning for sustainable water supply. In the Philippines, a project like this was collaboratively implemented by Plan Philippines and the Environmental Legal Assistance Centre, by universities (particularly the Eastern Samar State University and the Visayas State University), and by the village and municipal governments of Salcedo, Eastern Samar. Similarly, local WSPs, NGOs, village and municipal governments, and academic institutions used PuNPs as a mechanism to implement a multi-agency initiative to estimate the benefits of watershed protection to justify opposition to mining applications within the Sibalom Natural Park of Antique, Philippines. A PuNP also provided an avenue for local NGOs, communities located along the Ping River of Thailand, Hang Dong farmers, and members of the Hmong Hill Tribe to negotiate an acceptable system of water allocation for household, agricultural, tourism, and industrial uses.

The PuNP between community members, faculty members of the Bengal Engineering and Science University (BESU), and the NGO Water for People, an affiliate of the American Water Works Association, facilitated the installation of arsenic removal equipment in the well heads of pumps installed in rural villages of West Bengal.

Single public sector agency

The second most reported category of alternative service delivery mechanism was what we have called single public sector agency (SiP) initiatives. This mechanism usually involved a public sector water utility working on its own to continue the delivery of water as a public service or to improve the quality of the service delivery system itself. For example, the Water Supplies Department of the Hong Kong Special Administrative Regional Government (HKSARG) continues to provide drinking water as a basic human right, while retaining the water supply system as a public utility. Pressure to reduce public investments in the water system and to minimize its operational costs pushed HKSARG to consider privatizing the service. However, the department's good track record in managing water resources and delivery systems and maintaining water quality has earned the support of property owners, taxpayers, and citizens. Moreover, by adopting a "social tariff" structure, the department was able to generate funds from high-usage charges to cross-subsidize low-usage households, which were usually composed of the elderly and low-income families.

Such exemplary management of public waterworks was also demonstrated by the Hydraulic Department of the Municipal Corporation of Greater Mumbai that supplies water to 13 million people at a very low cost. Similarly, the Phnom Penh Water Supply Authority (PPWSA), after Cambodia's 20-year civil war and after the Khmer Rouge destroyed much of the city infrastructure, strengthened management capacity, rehabilitated its decrepit water distribution system, and worked to minimize unregistered or unmetered service connections in slum areas or among informal settlers. And by implementing a system of hydraulic isolation of operation zones and district metering areas, the *Maharashtra Jeevan Pradhikan* (MJP) in India was able to supply water 24 hours a day, seven days a week to eight (out of 34) wards of the city, without going into a partnership with private entities.

Alternatives undertaken by SiPs also took the form of village-level implementation of decisions and programmes. This was demonstrated by the Indian village Panchayat of Hivre Bazar, which implemented a ban on unlimited grazing and felling of trees, undertook watershed development on forest lands, constructed water harvesting structures, and regulated the utilization of water that was available to the community. Such community-level decision making was also practiced by the village council of Paulba, Ligao City, Albay, Philippines, when it decided to establish and manage a piped water system using funds from an Asian Development Bank (ADB) loan of the Philippine Government, initially intended for the development of irrigation facilities.

Public-public partnerships

Collaboration among public sector agencies has been reported as a significant mechanism in preventing privatization of water utilities and the commercialization of water resources and services (Chiong 2008). For example, the public-public partnership (PuP) between the Alliance of Government Workers in the Water Sector (AGWWAS), the Visayas State University, the Public Services International Research Unit (PSIRU) and several water districts, facilitated the firming up of positions to oppose privatization of financially viable water districts in the Philippines. Moreover, the partnership provided an opportunity for representatives of labour and management of Philippine water districts to work together to enhance their capabilities to implement performance benchmarking and to develop a set of benchmarks to be used by their respective water districts. The cooperation of labour and management facilitated the identification of technical, financial, socio-economic, and environmental indicators that considered the viability of the water district (AGWWAS et al, 2008, 2).

In India, the state government of the National Capital Territory of Delhi entered into a PuP with the local government of New Delhi when it planned to implement a tertiary-level treatment of waste water. Under the partnership, the state government would process up to 5 million gallons of urban waste in its sewage treatment plant and make the treated water available to the local government for distribution to non-domestic users. Target users included transport companies that use water for washing buses, institutions that need water for flushing toilets, and construction companies that use large volumes of water for concrete mixing. Under this mechanism, demand for water from the piped water system could be reduced (conversely making more water available to domestic users) and ameliorate the effluent load of the sewage system.

At a community level, officials of the villages of Guadalupe and Patag of Baybay, Leyte, Philippines, negotiated with officials of the Visayas State University for access to what they perceived as excess water use of the university. They observed that the university was releasing water through outlets in its pipelines or was allowing water to overflow from its swimming pool. They wanted to use this water to supplement water supply to poor informal settlers in their respective villages.

Similarly, the village councils of Patag and Gabas formed a PuP and negotiated with the Baybay Water District (BWD) in the Philippines for access to water from a spring, to which BWD holds the water right, as well as for the turnover of water district facilities within the village. Under the proposed terms of reference, the village governments would manage the water source and the on-site distribution facilities to provide safe drinking water to their constituents. In return, they would undertake watershed conservation and protection of facilities installed by the water district.

Single non-profit agencies

During the mapping exercise, some NGOs—categorized here as single non-profit agencies (SiNs)—were found to have the capacity to develop non-commercialized water systems. For example, the Sehgal Foundation established water harvesting structures and check dams that allowed pockets of fresh water to form underground in the village of Ghaghas in the Mewat District of Gurgao, Haryana, India. Carried out in conjunction with community education programmes on water conservation, the project proved that integrated water resources management (IWRM) need not be too cost-intensive or too long drawn in terms of time.

For its part, the Yenepoya Medical and Dental College (YMDC) located in the Dakshina Kannada district of Karnataka, India, implemented a rainwater harvesting project on its campus and in its neighbouring communities. Through such interventions, the college administration was able to directly service an additional 2,000 students, while pointing to a water management model that addresses severe water scarcity and reduces the abstraction of groundwater.

As alternatives to commercialized water service delivery organizations, community-based SiNs demonstrated that they too could implement water system improvement projects. The Self-Employed Women's Association (SEWA), a trade union and community-based movement of poor and self-employed women workers in the state of Gujarat, India, was able to establish, operate and maintain a system that provided safe potable water to its members. Similarly, CBOs in the province of Punjab, Pakistan, participated in the planning and construction of water system projects funded by an ADB loan. Their experience gave them the confidence to take on the greater responsibility of operating and maintaining the distribution pipelines, drains, and oxidation ponds.

Even urban-based organizations of water users, exemplified by the Bagong Silang Community Water Service Cooperative (BSCWSC) of Caloocan City, Philippines, used their consumer-owned utility to secure dependable water supply from third-party bulk providers at reduced transaction costs. This particular cooperative negotiated with financial institutions to generate funds for the establishment of improved water supply and distribution systems. Democratic control, peer-level monitoring, and enforcement of rules, which are inherent characteristics of cooperatives and associations, drastically reduced management cost and eventually relieved the pressure to commercialize the service.

ALTERNATIVES TO COMMERCIALIZATION
ACCORDING TO POLITICAL CRITERIA

Innovative models of public service delivery

Five types of alternatives to the commercialization of water services according to political criteria were identified during the mapping exercise (see Chapter 1, this volume, for a description of these categories). The most common type involved alternatives that were found to be new and/or innovative models of water service delivery that were neither private nor "old-style" public (see Table 9.5). Examples of such innovative models were reported in India, particularly the Change Management initiatives of TWAD. Under these initiatives, water supply to 60 million people of Tamil Nadu and the delivery of irrigation water to the farms of more than 1 million families were undertaken in conjunction with the management of attitudinal change, shifts in perspective, and transformation of the institutional culture of water engineers using a process-oriented participatory training methodology based on the traditional practice of *Koodam*, a Tamil word for gathering and social space, and for consensus that implies harmony, diversity, equality, and justice. The transformation of the institutional culture of water engineers and the changes in perspectives and relations between local communities and the water utility facilitated the implementation of the joint management of water resources. As an official-to-official transfer of ideas and experiences, the change in perspective gained during the workshops helped transform the engineers into becoming "managers of the commons".

Another innovative mechanism was implemented in Thailand through the river-basin-wide negotiations between local NGOs, upstream and downstream communities of the Ping River, Hang Dong farmers, and members of the Hmong Hill Tribe to settle competing demands for water for household, agricultural, tourism, and industrial uses. It demonstrated that conflicting claims to water resources based on geographic proximity to the resource, perceived traditional and/or preferential entitlements to the resource, purported economic significance of the activity being supported by the water resource base, and the human right to water could actually be discussed and settled through public negotiations.

Confronted with various threats to their water supplies and distribution systems, communities in India had to devise and implement innovative ways to improve service delivery. Residents of rural villages in West Bengal collaborated with faculty members of the Bengal Engineering and Science University and with the NGO Water for People, in the installation of arsenic removal equipment in the well heads of local water pumps. Despite initial reservations that the highly technical solution would encounter problems during village-level implementation, project reports did not indicate any major difficulty that villagers faced with respect to comprehending the underlying principles of operating the water treatment units.

Table 9.5   Types of Alternatives by Political Criteria

Subregion	Political criteria	Number of examples
East Asia	Innovative models of public service delivery	3
	Model of public service delivery deemed to be good and thus defended against commercialization	1
South Asia	Innovative models of public service delivery	8
	Model of public service delivery deemed to be good and thus defended against commercialization	4
	Model moving towards reinvigorating the delivery of public services	2
	Alternatives towards reclaiming public services	1
	Model of public service delivery that is still being proposed or discussed for implementation	1
Southeast Asia	Innovative models of public service delivery	6
	Model moving towards reinvigorating the delivery of public services	3
	Model of public service delivery that is still being proposed or discussed for implementation	2
	Alternatives towards reclaiming public services	1
	Model of public service delivery deemed to be good and thus defended against commercialization	1
Total Asia	Innovative models of public service delivery	17
	Model of public service delivery defended against commercialization	6
	Models geared towards reinvigorating public water services	5
	Model of public service delivery that is still being proposed or discussed for implementation	3
	Alternatives towards reclaiming public services	2

In the Indian village of Ghaghas, where water was inadequate and contained high levels of nitrates and fluorides, the Sehgal Foundation worked with the community to build check dams to raise the water table and to accumulate freshwater underground. In addition to these innovative engineering interventions, the Foundation initiated community education programmes on water conservation in an effort to reduce the rate of groundwater depletion. The two-pronged approach allowed the aquifer to recharge without restricting water availability for essential uses. Improved resource availability eventually reduced the pressure to use tariffs as a regulator of utilization.

Another innovative mechanism involved the partnership between the *Gram Panchayat* of 185 villages in the districts of East Godavari, Guntur, Krishna, Ranga Reddy, Visakhapatnam, and West Godavari in Andhra Pradesh, India, the community and the Byrraju Foundation. Under this partnership, the *Gram Panchayat* would provide raw water and land and supply power at concessional rates. The community would pay 50% of equipment costs, construct the building, supervise the operation of the treatment plant, and distribute the water. The Byrraju Foundation would select the equipment, bear 50% of equipment costs, provide technical support in the operation of the treatment plant, and test the quality of the water. Through the cost-sharing mechanism, water treatment plants were set up in various locations thereby improving access to safe drinking water. Without the treatment plants, water supply would continue to be contaminated by coliform, by chlorides, and by other chemical impurities in excess of permissible levels.

In the Philippines, when mining companies applied to mine inside the Sibalom watershed, community-based water users, village and municipal governments, WSPs and NGOs banded together to oppose the approval of the applications. They also invited researchers to conduct studies to estimate the benefits of watershed protection as a means of opposing mining applications within the watershed area. In doing so, the major beneficiaries of the Sibalom watershed were able to gain deeper insights into the non-use and bequeath values of the ecosystem.

The YMDC located in the Dakshina Kannada district of Karnataka used to spend Rs6 million (more than US$130,000) per month to truck its water requirements into its campus. The high level of water use by the school contributed to groundwater depletion and to a general water shortage in the neighbourhood. By digging 1.2-ha ponds on campus, the college was able to collect 30 million litres of rainwater, which was enough to serve some 2,000 students.

Defending the public sector against commercialization

The second most prevalent reason used to resist commercialization in the water sector in Asia involved defending good quality existing public services. A notable example is the Water Services Department of Hong Kong (HKWSD). While contemplating ways to reduce investments and operational costs, the Hong Kong Special Administrative Region Government (HKSARG) considered the following options: (i) contracting out part of the services to private business; (ii) "corporatization", which is often seen as a transition to privatization; or (iii) complete privatization. According to the Government Waterworks Professionals Association, all these suggestions were strongly opposed by Hong Kong civil servants. The majority of the public also did not support the proposal for fear that the changes would lower the quality of water supply and increase fees (2007, 19).

In 2003, HKSARG proposed the use of a public-private partnership (PPP) as the mode of renovation and operation of the potable water treatment in Hong Kong. In 2004, the PPP feasibility study was expanded to cover water distribution, effectively affecting 3 million citizens. The PPP model was seen as a means to reduce investments in water supply services and as a mechanism to enhance control, efficiency, and productivity in the water sector. However, the civil servants in HKWSD strongly opposed the proposal. During the May 2004 meeting of the Panel on Environment, Planning, Lands and Works, the panel members also expressed opposition to the PPP approach. The panel then recommended to HKSARG to revisit the feasibility study and to conduct public consultations regarding the proposal.

Over the past 150 years, HKSARG had the responsibility of providing drinking water to the public as a basic human right, despite severe water shortage and the rapid expansion of the economy. It had shown its capability to invest resources and to introduce new technologies in order to maintain a world-class water supply system that benefits Hong Kong citizens and its economy. HKWSD has been continually introducing innovations to enhance water supply services. Over the years, it has produced a team of trustworthy professionals in the public sector who can provide outstanding water supply service that is comparable to what any private organization can deliver (Government Waterworks Professionals Association 2007, 19). In the end, the exemplary performance of HKWSD helped convince the general public and HKSARG to forego the PPP proposal.

In India, the water system managed by the Hydraulic Department of the Municipal Corporation of Greater Mumbai (MCGM) proved that a large state sector water utility, despite being seen as unwieldy and unviable, could provide basic water supply to a large and rapidly growing population at very low cost (ADB 2007). The utility adheres to a welfare state model, which started during the colonial times. Despite functional constraints (e.g. more than 1,500 unfilled vacancies in the water department and the rotation of engineers between the various departments of MCGM, leading to the lack of skilled engineers and waterworks and to difficulties in leadership and succession planning), citizen groups together with the waterworks employees' union have conceptualized a public-public management system. The proposed participatory management model would retain operations and management under local public control, help save money, reward employees, and ensure improved water quality. To disseminate the concept, the Mumbai *Paani*, an initiative of concerned citizens and groups, has called public meetings with local residents, MCGM corporators, unionists, and senior citizens in order to start the process of forging PuPs.

MJP in India was also able to deliver good public service when it implemented hydraulic isolation of operation zones and district metering areas. Through the application of such hydraulic interventions, MJP showed its capability to improve water supply delivery (Dahasahashra 2008, 13–15).

The improvements were facilitated by a mechanism institutionalized by the Kulgaon-Badlapur Municipal Council wherein feedback from the water users (e.g. replacement of non-working meters) provided the impetus for the utility to make the water system more effective.

In the Philippines, the AGWWAS and the Philippine Association of Water Districts separately firmed up their respective positions opposing the official policy to privatize financially viable water districts (Chiong 2007, 58). Both organizations believed that water districts, as public entities, were still the best option in the delivery of water services. Moreover, through a series of trainings aimed at enhancing the capabilities of labour and management, participating water districts started to evolve a set of performance benchmarks for their own use. The information derived from the initial benchmarking exercises provided both labour and management with insights into their respective financial and operational status, which further strengthened their resolve to retain water districts in the public domain.

Attempts to impede the commercialization of water services also occurred at the village level. For example, the management of a water system improvement project by SEWA allowed the community to maintain control over water service delivery (ADB 2007). Based on personal interviews, the implementation of village-level decisions in Hirve Bazar to regulate the utilization of available water not only retained control over the allocation of water in public hands but also placed the management of the resource base directly under the community's jurisdiction.

Reinvigorating public water services

There were also instances wherein existing public modes of water service delivery were no longer appropriate for the service area, for reasons such as population growth and increases in the number of informal settlers, depletion of water sources, and deteriorating infrastructure. Even in cases where a water utility was not directly threatened by privatization or commercialization, maintaining the status quo could mean serious implications for its performance and could eventually lead to possible calls for the privatization or commercialization of its services. Under such circumstances, some utilities embarked on alternatives geared towards reinvigorating and improving the delivery of services of their respective public water systems rather than simply relying on the status quo.

The Dhaka Water and Sewerage Authority, for example, was legally constrained from providing service connections to slum communities because the residents usually did not have tenure to the land they were living on. By entering into cooperative arrangements with the NGO DSK, the water utility was able to establish communal water points, which improved access to clean water among informal settlers and urban poor. Adhering to the status quo could have perpetuated the exclusion of such residents from the service coverage of the water system.

The Phnom Penh Water Supply Authority faced a similar challenge when it inherited a decrepit water distribution system. By strengthening management, it succeeded in rehabilitating the system, allowing it to embark on initiatives to minimize unregistered or unmetered service connection in slum areas. Although the initiative was financed by the ADB, the case illustrated that business as usual is not the only option for the public sector.

In India, in cases in which public agencies vested with the mandate to manage water resources disregarded or neglected to perform their functions, actions initiated by the NGO *Tapas* could provide an alternative model. Land-owning government agencies that neglected to safeguard Delhi's water bodies prompted *Tapas* to file Public Interest Litigations (PILs). These PILs initiated the process to protect Delhi's water resource base, stop the lowering of groundwater levels, establish reservoirs for rainwater storage, and preserve traditional water recharge structures. Through the cases filed in the courts, various government agencies became legally bound to take on the responsibility to revive, rejuvenate, and safeguard 629 water bodies. With the government agencies working on storing rainwater, aquifers were recharged, floods were minimized, and water was made available for domestic use.

The defence of sources of water supply, however, need not reach the courts. This was demonstrated by the actions of village and municipal governments, NGOs, and academic institutions when they embarked on the delineation of the boundary of the watershed in Salcedo, Eastern Samar, Philippines. Through their joint efforts, the village and municipal councils were able to pass appropriate legislation proclaiming the watershed as a protected area. The local legislation equipped the village and the municipal governments with the legal mandate to formulate and implement programmes to ensure sustainable water supply.

Reclaiming public water

In this research we were unable to find cases in which water services that had been privatized were either renationalized or remunicipalized, as has been occurring in other parts of the world (see www.remunicipalisation. org). There was an opportunity to renationalize the MWSI in the Philippines in 2006 when it declared bankruptcy, and its former owners, the Lopez family, signalled their intention to return the private concession back to the state. But despite this intent and campaigns by civil society and public interest groups for renationalization, the Philippine government maintained its position to have the utility operated by a private corporation. There are also ongoing discussions about the possibility of remunicipalizing water services in Jakarta, Indonesia, but these were still at the very early stages of negotiations at the time of writing.

What the mapping exercise did manage to identify were community initiatives geared towards ensuring that water services remain in the public domain. Such alternatives, although not directly engaged in legally reclaiming public services, established mechanisms for retaining water systems within community control. In the Philippines, this type of alternative was implemented by the Residents Association of Tinagong Paraiso, in cooperation with a local NGO, and BACIWA. By establishing community tap stands, and by having these managed and maintained by the Association, access to safe drinking water reverted to community control instead of being operated by private concessionaries of the water district, who charged high prices for retailing the water to slum residents.

Similarly, the Bagong Silang Community Water Service Cooperative of Caloocan City, Philippines, a utility owned by water users, managed to secure dependable water supply from MWSI, a private, third-party bulk water supplier. Through the cooperative, democratic control, and peer-level monitoring and enforcement of rules in the establishment of improved water supply and distribution systems was ensured.

In the province of Punjab, Pakistan, CBOs participated in the planning and construction of water facilities under the ADB-financed Rural Water Supply and Sanitation Sector Project. Upon completion, the CBOs assumed the responsibility of operating, maintaining, and managing the water system. Through this, the communities were able to gain control over access to and availability of water supply.

Future alternatives

Some alternative models of public service delivery systems that surfaced during the research were still being proposed or discussed for implementation. One of these involved the treatment of 5 million gallons of waste water to be undertaken by the state government of the National Capital Territory of Delhi, India. Under the scheme, the treated water would be made available for distribution to non-domestic users in New Delhi for washing buses, flushing toilets, or mixing with concrete for construction works. Although the scheme would commercialize the output of the treatment process, it was conceptualized as a way of reducing utilization of potable water from the piped distribution system. By providing an alternative source of water for non-domestic uses, the state expects to improve the equity in access to potable water among household users.

At the community level, the village councils of Patag and Gabas of Baybay, Philippines, had initiated negotiations with the BWD to allow both communities to source water from a spring, to which the water district holds a water right. Moreover, the village councils proposed that one of the reservoirs, the pipelines, and other facilities found within the village be turned over to the village government for management. In return, the village would undertake watershed conservation in the catchment that serves as a source of water supply and protect the facilities installed by the water district for the production, treatment, and distribution of water to the municipality of Baybay, Leyte, Philippines. If implemented, such arrangements could point to ways of addressing a major paradox, that of communities inside important source watersheds not being served by the water utility. Moreover, the arrangement could provide detailed mechanisms for strengthening partnerships between village governments and water utilities, especially with respect to watershed management by host communities.

SUCCESSES AND FAILURES OF ALTERNATIVES

Participation

As a major determinant of success, participation could be assessed from dimensions of depth or meaningfulness, scope or sufficiency, and appropriateness of scale. The interplay of these dimensions of participation could be discerned in the democratization of water management in the Public Sector Reform of the TNRWSP. Implemented by TWAD, the programme worked for the transformation of the attitudes of water users, water engineers, community-based WSPs, and village governments. The democratization process adopted the practice of *Koodam*, which recreates a traditional cultural and social space wherein members would relate to each other as individuals without distinctions of age, status, or hierarchy, where sharing was transparent, experiential, and self-critical, and where learning was built on values of democracy, consensual decision making, and collective ownership. By institutionalizing the traditional practice of *Koodam*, intersectoral and inter-hierarchical participation was assured, resulting in a more responsive programme.

Meaningfulness, sufficiency, and appropriateness of the scale of participation could also be inferred from the dynamics involved in the river basin-wide negotiations on the allocation of water from the Ping River. Water allocation is a highly contested issue and makes the thorough involvement of various water user groups necessary to reach a settlement that can be acceptable to all parties concerned. By allowing claimants to come together and discuss their respective requirements vis-à-vis the availability of water, various water groups were able to agree on certain quantitative allocations or entitlements to the water resource. Another important dimension was the possibility of coming together to discuss and renegotiate possible changes in the terms and conditions of the agreed-upon allocations.

Meaningful and sufficient participation was also provided by community residents and local government officials when they embarked on a management and development planning process for the watersheds of Salcedo, Eastern Samar, Philippines. Active community participation in the delineation of watershed boundaries provided a common physical framework for making competing land uses compatible for purposes of creating reliable sources of domestic water supply. Similarly, by participating in the conduct of resource inventories, community members were able to identify livelihood options that matched the resource endowments of the watersheds.

Other success indicators—e.g. the empowerment of marginalized and vulnerable groups, and the fair selection of members that reflect the diversity of a population—were highlighted by community groups that directly managed and controlled village-level water systems. For example, SEWA in Gujarat, India, took on the task of maintaining the system that provided them with safe potable water by digging water canals, laying down pipelines, and chlorinating the water supply. For their part, the Residents Association of Tinagong Paraiso in the Philippines negotiated with BACIWA the installation of community tap stands and assumed direct management and maintenance of the water service.

Another form of direct action was implemented in the village of Hivre Bazar in Maharashtra, India. Faced by persistent water scarcity punctuated by drought during certain years, the village assembly decided to pursue a two-pronged approach to water resource management. The first action was to ban destructive practices such as unfettered grazing, felling of trees, cultivation of crops that require a lot of water, and digging of bore wells. The second involved the construction of earthen or stone bunds and check dams as rainwater harvesting structures, the adoption of drip irrigation methods to conserve water, and use of cow dung as fertilizer to maintain water quality. Participation in activities requiring community action came in the form of labour contribution by the residents.

Equity

Fairness in access to, and availability of, water for all is a major determinant of the success of an alternative. In Hong Kong, the principle of equity came as a built-in feature of providing safe drinking water to citizens as a basic human right. Equity also served as a decision criterion in the formulation and adoption of a "social tariff". As a tool for enhancing equitable access, the tariff structure mandated the collection of high-usage charges with the revenues used to cross-subsidize low-usage households. As an economic regulatory mechanism, the tariff put in place a water conservation incentive mechanism, which facilitated the availability of water to users regardless of levels of consumption.

In northern Thailand, the issue of equitable access and availability was confronted head on by the Ping River Basin Committee when it brought water users together to seek a common ground for sharing and protecting the Ping River. Through discussions and negotiations, the competing demands for water from the river were placed within a context of equitable resource allocation. Although some participants in the negotiations had reservations regarding the agreed-upon quantitative allocations, there seemed to be no major adverse criticism of the framework that was adhered to during the negotiations.

Equitable access and availability were apparently in the minds of residents of the villages of Pangasugan, Patag, and Guadalupe in Baybay, Leyte, Philippines, when they experienced inadequate water supply. The village officials initiated negotiations with the Visayas State University to gain access to what they perceived as excess water usage by the university. The village officials argued that allocating the excess volume for use by residents would make access more equitable and the utilization of the water less wasteful.

Efficiency

In most of Asia, the performance of water utilities is typically assessed on technical and financial efficiency of their respective operations. In the Philippines for example, Board Resolution No. 4 (Series of 1994) of the National Economic Development Authority (NEDA) mandated the Local Water Utilities Administration (LWUA), a national water agency tasked to financially regulate water districts, to implement only financially viable projects. This gave the impression that (i) commercially viable service areas should be turned over to private corporations and (ii) LWUA should keep its hands off projects that were not financially viable. Considering that LWUA is a quasi-lending institution for water utilities the policy provided an "interesting" platform for reducing subsidies to the poor, while increasing subsidies to the private sector through concessional loans and sovereign guarantees to water financing (Dargantes and Dargantes 2007, 54).

In counterpoint, the Capability Building Programme on Performance Benchmarking of Philippine Water Districts provided an opportunity for management and labour to jointly look at the technical and financial indicators of their respective utilities in an effort to find ways to improve the efficiency of water service delivery. Although labour was initially reluctant to participate in the program, the opportunity enabled labour representatives to develop a greater appreciation of the implications of financial indicators on their operational efficiency vis-à-vis the privatization of their respective water districts. As a form of feedback, the efficiency indicators further provided labour and management with not only common points of reference for performance improvement but also with sound decision points to support their separate positions to oppose the privatization of their water districts.

To address conditions of inadequate and irregular water supply, and of increasing demand among residents of Bagong Silang, Caloocan City, Philippines, residents organized a water system that consumers owned. The cooperative was able to demonstrate its capability to attain financial efficiency by securing water supply from third party bulk suppliers at reduced transaction costs. Apparently, it was also able to convince sources of capital that it was financially viable by obtaining a loan to cover the costs of establishing distribution lines.

Among large utilities, financial efficiency has been seen to go hand-in-hand with technical efficiency. In Cambodia, for example, PPWSA achieved financial viability, such that it could forego its planned tariff increase, by rehabilitating its distribution system and minimizing illegal connections. MJP in India was also able to achieve financial efficiency, recovering up to 99% of expenditures, through the introduction of hydraulic isolation of operation zones and district metering areas. The technical interventions facilitated the achievement of water resource efficiency as water users shifted availment strategies from household-level storage to non-storage due to improved pressure and balanced distribution. Coupled with improvements in meter reading, billing, and revenue collection, MJP attained high levels of efficiency in terms of water resources allocation and use, operational performance, and financial management.

Efficiency in making water resources available to users could also be inferred from the retention of the Hong Kong WSD under public control. Despite pressures to reduce investments and operational costs for water supply, prudent financial management enabled the utility to continue to generate public funding for it to bring the supply and distribution system to near perfect levels, while maintaining excellent water quality. With a high level of support from the citizenry, the WSD was able to maintain adequate levels of public investments, for the maintenance of its facilities and the continuous upgrading of its workforce.

Quality

The viability of an alternative can be directly ascertained by the quality or safety of the water provided and by the overall standards of service that a water system is expected to adhere to. The former was demonstrated by the villagers of West Bengal, in partnership with faculty members of BESU, and support from the NGO Water for People, who installed arsenic removal equipment in well heads, leading to the elimination of threats to people's health. The latter was also shown in Badlapur City wherein the implementation by the MJP of hydraulic isolation of operation zones and district metering areas resulted in continuous water supply to eight wards of the city, while maintaining water quality at safe drinking levels.

In the Philippines, the water systems in Bagong Silang and Tinagong Paraiso showed that dependable water supply and distribution could be viably provided by consumer-owned and controlled utilities. In Bagong Silang, democratic control of the cooperative allowed the consumers to give direct operational feedback, which facilitated improvements in allocation and distribution. For the Tinagong Paraiso residents, having a direct hand in operations and maintenance ensured that water quality was up to standard and that availability was responsive to the needs of the consumers.

For members of SEWA, taking over the management of the water service not only ensured potability but also availability. By undertaking chlorination, water quality improved tremendously in comparison to the water that used to be collected from the earthen reservoirs. By taking direct responsibility over pipeline maintenance and/or repairs, including distribution and allocation, the association improved the availability of water. Improvement in the quality of service, moreover, gave women in particular more time to devote to their means of livelihood.

Accountability

Policy makers at various levels of bureaucracy, as well as managers of water utilities, usually establish lines of communication or define relationships with water users. Major determinants of the success or failure of such lines of communication or relationships would be the trustworthiness of the source of explanation or justification, the understandability of the message, and the verifiability and veracity of the facts and information being provided. Considering that the vigour of accountability mechanisms would depend, to a large extent, on the enforceability of rules, the more direct the pressure that water users would have on policy makers and/or on the management of water utilities in obtaining satisfactory answers, explanations or justifications for policies, programmes, and projects, the broader the scope and the higher the quality of accountability would be.

In the Tamil Nadu experiment, accountability of TWAD reached deep down into the level of the communities. With the water engineers themselves becoming part of the line of communication, the trustworthiness of the source could then be directly assessed by the water users. Through the *Koodam*, the understandability of the programme was enhanced, especially given that information used for decisions could be openly discussed, verified, and validated.

Training on performance benchmarking in the Philippines, on the other hand, strengthened the accountability mechanism between management and labour through the sharing of verifiable operational data and information. Although the benchmarks were to be used in reviewing the financial, technical, social, and environmental indicators to improve water services, the process provided the opportunity for management to explain the basis for policy decisions and for labour to justify performance levels. With the institutionalization of labour-management cooperation, such accountability mechanisms could then be formally operationalized within participating utilities.

In Nepal, accountability in the management of the Panchakanya irrigation water distribution system was transferred by the national government to the Water Users' Associations at the community level. Although the transfer gave the water users greater operational control, it also allowed the national government to shift part of the accountability for the water distribution system to the users themselves. Thus, the mechanism was able to simulate direct accountability for community-level management, but it became a structure to reduce transparency for the national government.

Transparency

Through clear accountability mechanisms, information pertaining to decisions and performance levels could also be made readily available to the public. In the Panchakanya case, greater transparency could have been achieved by the devolution of management—but only up to the operational level. Transparency pertaining to the decisions on system design as well as the financial transactions could have been reduced by the transfer of responsibility.

For the Tamil Nadu experiment, detailed discussions on costs and tariffs enhanced the awareness of consumers regarding the need for water conservation and different rationales for setting water fees. Diligent maintenance of records on pumping hours, water supply hours, electricity meter readings, and linking these aspects to the water supply costs served to spread awareness regarding water tariffs.

Transparency could likewise be deduced from the operations of the BSCWSC. As a community-based, water-user-owned utility, the operational performance of the cooperative could readily be assessed by its members. The mandated reportorial mechanisms, on the other hand, would allow members to seek explanations for policy decisions or for financial transactions. Through activities such as continuing education, as well as mandatory periodic reporting on the state of operations, information pertaining to policy decisions, operational mandates, organizational structures, and financial status became available not only to the water user-cum-owner but also to the general public.

The context of the Capability Building Programme on Performance Benchmarking for Philippine Water Districts was that management and workers of water utilities had signified their commitment to the same goal: to deliver high-quality and efficient public services. By the very nature of labour-management cooperation, managers and workers had to exercise transparency as they identify and look for the key features to ensure better water service delivery services to consumers. Through this joint effort, management would be able not only to provide the logical and theoretical bases for policies but also to get feedback on the operational implications of its decisions. Labour, on the other hand, would be able to share experience-based and practical operational details to make policies work.

Workplace

The Capability Building Programme on Performance Benchmarking, moreover, allowed management of some PWDs to understand the roles of rank-and-file workers in the improvement of water systems. As persons close to the production process, workers would possess knowledge from a workplace level on the types of services that work and on what services needed to be improved or created.

On the part of labour, the programme gave workers a better appreciation of the importance of adhering to the prescribed number of work hours and of observing occupational health and safety regulations. The exercise, likewise, enabled workers to relate employees' compensation, work leaves and social insurance to the technical and financial performance of their respective water districts. It even provided initial insights into the implications of compliance or non-compliance to core labour standards on forced labour, child labour, discrimination and equal remuneration, freedom of association, right to collective bargaining, and of providing continuous staff development.

Sustainability

The ability of a utility to continue to operate in view of its current and future financial position depends, to a large extent, on its sources of funds for maintenance and operating expenses and capital outlays. Sources, which range from full state support to full cost recovery mechanisms, could also, over time, and depending on political and economic conditions, increase or decrease their respective contributions to the financial requirements of utilities.

As governments contend with increasing financial costs for the delivery of a wide range of basic social services, utilities, in turn, have to face the possibility of reduced state spending for the sector. For example, in Cambodia, as the state struggled to rebuild a war-torn nation, the PPWSA endeavoured to install water meters for all connections, set up an inspection team, revise and improve its consumer files, embark on a programme to educate the public on the importance of paying water bills, and increase the water tariff to cover the costs, which the state could no longer provide for. To avoid a huge jump in water tariffs, a three-step increase over a seven-year period was contemplated. As collections improved and revenues fully covered costs and as non-revenue water dropped from 72% in 1993 to 6% in 2006, the third increase was eventually scrapped. Although such management interventions manifested numerous aspects of commercialization, prudent revenue generation measures aimed at raising funds to improve, or at least maintain, levels of operational performance—as opposed to profit maximization—could help at a strategic level in the retention of public control over the utility.

In Hong Kong, on the other hand, the Asian financial crisis brought pressure upon the government to reduce investments and cut back on expenditures for water supply. The impeccable performance of the WSD in providing water services to support the transformation of Hong Kong into a world-class metropolis gave it the leverage to continue operating as a public utility and to continually access government subsidies, through land rates, as a source of funds to cover more than half of its costs. This demonstrated that operational efficiency could provide a utility ample political capital to remain in the public domain.

The relationship between operational and technical efficiency and financial sustainability was also demonstrated by the adoption of appropriate technology options such as timely maintenance activities in Tamil Nadu. These technological interventions helped reduce potentially expensive repairs and replacements of parts, regulated hours of pumping, and maintained both quality and quantity of water. By reducing operations and maintenance expenditures while improving revenue generation, financial sustainability of the system was enhanced.

The Capability Building Programme on Performance Benchmarking was designed to enhance the appreciation of managers and workers not only of technical and financial efficiency parameters but also the sustainability of social (e.g. adherence to core labour standards and improvement of customer relations) and environmental aspects (e.g. including watershed protection, integrated water resources management, and sanitation). By promoting closer collaboration among public institutions based on equality and mutual benefit, the exchange of strategic and practical information, especially pertaining to practices in well-performing water utilities, through peer-to-peer learning, strengthened social cohesion among workers and among participating water district managers.

Whereas the pursuit of financial viability would usually take in some aspects of commercialized operations, the sustainability of social engagement would depend, to a large extent, on the level of publicness of participation in decision making and operations of a utility. In the Philippines, for example, the residents of Tinagong Paraiso having successfully petitioned their landowner to grant them property rights then raised and borrowed money and convinced the BACIWA to install a piped connection, which they collectively owned and managed as a community. The BSCWSC enhanced its financial viability by reducing transaction costs when it secured dependable water supply from third-party bulk water suppliers or when it borrowed capital to build a water distribution system. The cooperative also minimized management costs and enforced subscription rules through democratic controls and peer monitoring, thereby mitigating the impact of water tariffs. In Gujarat, India, SEWA formed a village committee to address the acute water shortage and the absence of livelihood options. Members met regularly to decide on water management issues and supervise the work that had to be done. Through their direct management of the water system, SEWA not only ensured operational sustainability but also set into place a mechanism for enhancing financial viability.

Environmental sustainability was another major concern in the overall effort of ensuring water for all. Most of the cases included in the mapping exercise implemented variations of two major strategies. The first involved the protection of watersheds as a source of water supply. Activities under this strategy could be as direct as the planting of thousands of saplings in identified watershed areas similar to what was done in Tamil Nadu and Hivre Bazar in Maharashtra. Other initiatives to ensure watershed sustainability included the conducting of consultative planning workshops to identify local conditions affecting the watershed, and the formulation of municipal- and village-level watershed management development action plans such as those undertaken in Salcedo, Eastern Samar, Philippines. Activities also took the form of agro-forestry development and watershed rehabilitation and protection.

Another strategy involved setting up physical structures to capture, store, and preserve water. Examples included the construction of rainwater harvesting structures like those managed by the village Panchayat of Hirve Bazar, establishment of check dams by the Sehgal Foundation, which led to rising water tables in the Mewat region of Haryana, and the digging of ponds by the YMDC to catch run-off in the campus.

A prominent example that would straddle both strategies would be the rejuvenation of water bodies. Through PILs filed to safeguard essential water recharge structures, which were dying due to administrative apathy, the Delhi High Court directed different government authorities to protect and beautify all natural water bodies so that people or civic agencies would not encroach upon them. The Court ordered 629 water bodies rejuvenated in an effort to sustain its water resource base. As planned, the National Capital Territory of Delhi would develop green cover along the rejuvenated water bodies to maintain ecological balance.

Solidarity

With PuPs as the guiding framework for the implementation of the Capability Building Programme on Performance Benchmarking, labour, management, and regulatory agencies such as the National Water Regulation Board (NWRB), international organizations like the PSIRU, and the Transnational Institute, and academia cooperated not only in defending Philippine water districts as public utilities but also in improving their service delivery performance. Civil society organizations like Focus on the Global South and Jubilee South Asia Pacific Movement for Debt and Development supported the workers in evolving a set of performance benchmarks and in developing PuPs among water districts and other water stakeholders.

For the Tamil Nadu experiment, the water engineers manifested their solidarity with the villagers through regular participation in meetings, interacting with them, and making a special effort to increase awareness among women and household members beyond the call of official duty. This solidarity also extended to workers in other government line agencies providing water services to the communities. At the national level, the Change Management Group (CMG) received manifestations of solidarity from the federal government and other state governments of India. Internationally, water utilities in Egypt and some countries of South America have already signified their interest in collaborating with TWAD in the introduction of change management practices in their respective jurisdictions.

Public ethos

For more than 150 years, Hong Kong demonstrated that a publicly operated water supply system could be successful in providing the water required by a rapidly changing city. By increasing the availability of water resources, by bringing the supply system to near perfect operational efficiency, and by maintaining excellent water quality, the citizens of Hong Kong were convinced that the services should remain publicly operated. With such confidence, civil servants in the WSD, members of the Panel on Environment, Planning, Lands and Works under the Hong Kong Legislative Council, and the water users themselves strongly objected the proposal to privatize the water system.

The Capability Building Programme on Performance Benchmarking, on the other hand, led to a realization among water districts managers and workers of the lack of merit of the official policy of turning over to the private sector those utilities that were financially viable. Through a better understanding of the implications of technical and financial indicators, both management and labour were able to put into a better context their respective resolutions opposing the privatization of their utilities. They then expressed their collective opinion that water districts should remain publicly operated water systems.

Transferability

A major methodological exercise to test, even on an *ex ante* basis, the "transferability" of an alternative to another location involves matching local resource endowments, knowledge, and skills possessed by management and labour and levels and direction of political support with the water service requirements of the utilities. Taking the Tamil Nadu water management democratization experiment as an example, the adoption of the concept by the federal government of India, and, reportedly, by UNICEF at the national level, would indicate a higher degree of convergence of resource endowments, knowledge, and skills levels and political support, mainly due to similarities in existing local conditions and of institutional arrangements at the state and district levels. This resulted in the formation of the National Level Change Management Forum to pioneer reforms in other state utilities. The *Koodam*, a major component of the experiment, would also be compatible with the general socio-cultural conditions of India. Internationally, there had been expressions of interest from water utilities of other countries to collaborate with the CMG of the TWAD. In the adaptation of the experiment, however, the cultural dimension of the *Koodam* would need to be adequately assessed to determine compatibility with local practices.

LESSONS LEARNED

A vote for public

The findings of this mapping exercise highlight several issues. First, while there is no perfect alternative, an enabling institutional and policy environment—at appropriate levels—is important for an alternative to develop and flourish. Second, articulating and building alternatives are collective processes, most successful when inclusive, gender just, transparent, and participatory. The alternatives mapped out in this chapter emphasize that partnerships between people and communities who have suffered from lack of access to water and sanitation, and water agencies, whether state-level or municipal, that believe in democratic functioning, can ensure safe, equitable and adequate water service provision and sustainable water resource management. This is universal, regardless of the type of alternatives. Finally, what underpins these alternatives are principles of "good water governance", which include (i) water justice—ensuring that all communities have equal and equitable access to safe, affordable, and sustainable water for drinking, fishing, recreational, and cultural uses. At the heart of the issue is the concept of democracy and democratization, of ensuring that everyone, especially the poor and marginalized, have a say on how they want their water governed; (ii) water is part of the commons and a human right: water is life, a gift of nature, and its nurturing remains the responsibility of everyone for the survival of the planet in the present and for the future. This nurturing is rooted in the respect of all living cultures, values, and traditions that sustain the global water commons; and (iii) these rights can be allocated, framed, protected, and realized in an equitable and sustainable way, as long as those who are historically marginalized and poor are part of the process.

Decentralization trends in water service delivery

In the Philippines, the Neda Board Resolution No. 4 (Series of 1994) ruled that local government units (LGUs) were allowed to implement all levels of water supply projects consistent with the decentralization and devolution process. This ruling gave the impression that commercially non-viable water projects were the responsibility of the LGUs. Data for 2005, however, revealed that 43% of the 1,639 WSPs listed in the Philippines were operated by LGUs. Another 30% were managed by users or communities (Dargantes and Dargantes 2007, 54). These figures indicate that a large majority of the WSPs were operationally decentralized and geographically dispersed. These utilities might not be operating at optimum technical and financial efficiency, but they would definitely have addressed some pressing need for water among populations not served by water districts.

Importance of finance in infrastructure

The generation of funds to finance the construction of water infrastructure is one of the challenges in realizing the development of water systems. Typically, financial support would be provided by the state or international organizations. Among the cases included in this mapping exercise, most of the large-scale central utilities remain state funded. Considering, however, that governments were usually not in a financial position to adequately address the capital requirements of water supply systems, they then turned to multilateral international financial institutions (IFIs) and to private sources of funds for their requirements. As borrowing for water infrastructure would involve large amounts the tendency was to avail of loans from IFIs.

In other instances, governments would consolidate the funding requirements of smaller systems in order to avail of lending from IFIs. Although such arrangements would give a semblance of fund adequacy to cover the capitalization needs of utilities, the consolidation process could lead to the formulation and confirmation of loan conditionalities, which might not be part of project plans submitted by the concerned utility or WSP. Fortunately, the alternatives included in this research were generally given flexibility by the IFIs to implement their respective projects.

In certain instances, the state might even promulgate policies to constrain its own agencies from exercising flexibility options. For example in the Philippines, LWUA—a specialized lending institution created to promote, develop, and finance local water utilities with powers to prescribe standards and regulations, provide technical assistance and personnel training, monitor and evaluate water standards, and effect system integration, annexation and deannexation—had been mandated to finance only creditworthy and semicreditworthy water districts. Those deemed to be not creditworthy were expected to seek financing from other sources.

This situation brings in another dimension of the relationship between borrower-state and international financial institutions. IFIs might impose loan conditionalities, but the borrower could opt not to conform to the impositions. This has been the case of the Tamil Nadu democratization experiment, which was financed through a World Bank loan. Of course, there would be limits as to what conditionalities to reject. And these limits would serve as the starting point for the search for alternative sources of financing or for the redesign of projects or project components to make them amenable to combinations of funding modalities.

In the village of Tian-xin, China, for example, the construction of water reservoirs both for irrigation and domestic uses were expected to be a state responsibility. But in order for the village to be able to provide water free of charge to 2,000 people, the village head introduced counterpart funding as an alternative way to finance the project. By generating half of the amount required for the construction of a reservoir largely from contributions of migrant workers and successful businessmen in Tian-xin, Guangdong Province, the head of the village and the local community found it easier to ask for supplementary funding for the project than to depend entirely on the government for resources.

Lessons for/from the private sector

Private corporations and other forms of enterprises (including privatized water utilities) have realized that for them to remain socially relevant (or, as some claim, to soothe their social conscience), they should not only engage in responsible business behaviour but also voluntarily or consciously accede to humanitarian norms and standards. Such practice, usually referred to as part of corporate social responsibility (CSR), encompasses divergent elements of respect for human rights, implementation of environmental laws, rules, and regulations, adherence to accepted labour standards and consumer safeguards, and provision of aid to disadvantaged sectors or relief to victims of disasters.

In the Philippines and China, CSR projects provided examples of how water service delivery could be undertaken without embarking on a path of privatization. The *Tubig Para sa Barangay* (TPSB) or Water for the Poor Programme, a CSR project of the MWCI private corporation that took over the erstwhile public operations of the Manila Waterworks and Sewerage Services used funds from the World Bank to subsidize the cost of connection fees of customers living in low-income communities or communities with poor water service and of informal settlers.

A variant of the CSR alternative was likewise being applied to the villages in the Guangdong province. Reportedly, the state had officially encouraged for-profit companies to manage infrastructure in the villages of their choice. Whereas the company was responsible for the cost of the water system infrastructure, the village would take over the management of the system once the construction phase was finished. Apparently, this could also be classified as a state-sponsored or state-mandated CSR initiative.

Considering that such practices were carried out by for-profit corporations or by non-profit agencies that were using funds derived from corporate profits, the dimension of publicness of these options has to be closely examined. Under the TPSB programme, the involvement of the communities lent a certain degree of publicness to the service delivery mechanism. Moreover, the cross-subsidy to cover the cost of connection fees gave a non-commercialization flavour to the programme. Under the state-mandated CSR programme in China, the partnership between profit companies and the community as a non-profit recipient of corporate funds and community-based implementer gave the water project an aura of publicness. As a free-of-charge service, the project could perhaps be characterized as a non-(or lesser-) commercialized operation.

Role of bureaucrats in enhancing accountability

Good governance of water resources and services, an important component of poverty reduction efforts, would require two major characteristics of the government entities responsible for water management: namely, accountability and competence. Policy makers, regulators, and utility managers should establish a system of communication with water users in order to arrive at a common understanding of the goals, policies, programmes, and activities of the utility. The communication process should primarily serve as an avenue wherein management decisions or indecisions would be articulated, explained, and justified. Moreover, it should promote change based on the water users' feedback regarding essential measures for improving service delivery.

A major determinant of success or failure of the communication system would be the credibility of the source of information. Credibility, as a reflection of the value given by the audience, could be gained by the source of the information through different ways such as being able to accomplish tasks efficiently and being honest and fair. Whereas honesty and fairness would basically be personal attributes of members of the bureaucracy, competence could be directly addressed by relevant staff development programmes.

WAYS FORWARD

Research on alternatives

The next steps for research on alternatives to commercialization of water resources and services in Asia should include more detailed and thorough characterization of possible options to determine the relationship between organizational typologies and the determinants of success/failure. Case studies should look at the context by which certain political criteria would eventually become determinants of success/failure. During this mapping exercise the process of coming up with operational definitions of alternatives, organizational typologies, political criteria, and determinants of success/failure was mainly hampered by the inadequacy of available secondary information. Future research should endeavour to collate, integrate, and analyze various data sets from different primary sources to characterize alternatives using techniques that would allow the simultaneous analysis of environmental attributes together with socio-economic variables. This process could create a core group of researchers and practitioners who could promote inter- and multidisciplinary work and data sharing for water resources and services development.

The systematic collection of data on alternatives, organizational typologies, political criteria, and the determinants of success/failure would be useful to sector planners, local governments, and regulators, as the information would highlight the constraints of alternatives and help set realistic operational targets for improvement. More importantly, studies could dig up actual operational experiences of WSPs that would be shared within the sector for possible scaling-up or for application under specific socio-economic conditions and policy environments. Additionally, case studies should provide an initial glimpse at the practicability of generating and analyzing time series or multiyear data on the alternatives.

Advocacy for alternatives

Advocating for alternatives can be done in various arenas and through different mechanisms. One way forward is through institutional and policy reforms—including legislative reform. With an enabling environment, alternatives to commercialization of water resources and services can thrive.

Policy and institutional reforms become even more relevant when combined with on-the-ground problem solving. As exemplified above, pushing for reforms includes creating platforms, spaces, and processes in which various stakeholders, including water activists and water justice movements, can come together to promote and advance alternatives.

Advocacy for alternatives in the water sector should also include case studies that can be used as course content for diploma and/or graduate programmes specializing in water resources and services management. This would allow students to gain actual experience and acquire factual evidence and eventually enhance the level of appreciation of the alternatives being implemented. Students could then identify factors of success or failure and determine ways to improve the alternatives to make these useful to WSPs and other stakeholders working in the water sector.

Likewise, identified alternatives could be discussed during development planning for the water and sanitation sectors being undertaken by local governments, civil society organizations, and community-based WSPs. This would provide a mechanism whereby stakeholders could identify, review, and/or define/redefine their respective roles, functions, and organizational processes and could agree on institutional arrangements. The discussion could also incorporate non-formal education and capability building opportunities on community-based water resources and services management and participatory and democratic governance in the water and sanitation sector for community organizations, NGOs, local governments, and regional and inter-regional committees. Furthermore, it would encourage the participation of community organizations and NGOs and the incorporation of IWRM approaches in the local and regional development processes.

Another way of advancing advocacy for alternatives is via civil society organizations in donor countries. These organizations can enlighten their respective governments, including international aid agencies, of the impacts of funded projects on local communities and populations from the perspective of water consumers. This mechanism would provide excellent opportunities for local utilities and communities to show existing water resources and services management practices that conform to local conditions.

Lastly, Asian utilities and water sector advocates should encourage more study visits among and between water consumers, WSPs, NGO workers, and members of academia to strengthen mechanisms for multifaceted analyses of alternatives. The resulting discourses could serve as a counterbalance to the predominance of neoliberal frameworks without necessarily rejecting them in a knee-jerk fashion and hopefully introducing alternative perspectives into the sector.

Advancing the practice of alternatives

Some governments have been examining alternative ways of providing water but may be holding back due to what they see as potential drawbacks. For example, alternative water systems could generate additional costs, particularly when these were not integrated in the initial plans for service provision and building construction. Water being more than just an infrastructure project needing huge investments, financing, and technology would require alternative modes of governance that respond to changing physical conditions as well as socio-economic realities and policy environments. Increasing the capability of water sector managers and workers to address the significant factors that could influence success or failure would be an important component of the overall effort to advance water governance. Enacting legislation to address unfavourable socio-economic conditions and iniquitous policies could eventually expand service coverage and improve service delivery.

Another aspect of water governance that needs to be vigorously pursued would involve the management of transboundary water. As water flows across state boundaries, its management would then require new forms of interstate water governance mechanisms. Considering that water divides might not conform to politico-administrative boundaries, there might be a need for new forms of delineations requiring a new set of transnational policies and management arrangements. In effect, the governance of transboundary water could redefine regional affiliations and necessitate alternative forms of regionalism to address the inadequacy of state frameworks.

ACKNOWLEDGEMENTS

The authors would like to thank the following individuals for their assistance in gathering data for this chapter: Afsar Jafri (Senior Associate, Focus on the Global South India Programme, Delhi), Meena Menon (Senior Associate, Focus on the Global South, Mumbai), Dr. V. Suresh (Director, Centre for Law, Policy and Human Rights Studies and Adviser to the Supreme Court on Food Security, Chennai, India), Nila Ardhianie (Director, Amrta Institute for Water Literacy, Indonesia), S.A. Naqvi (President, STEPS Research Foundation; President, Water Workers Alliance; and Co-convener, Citizens Front for Water Democracy, New Delhi), Sofia Chu (Globalization Monitor, Hong Kong), Victor Chiong (President, Alliance of Government Workers in the Water Sector, Cebu City, Philippines), and Violeta P. Coral (Public Services International Research Unit, Asia-Pacific Region).

REFERENCES

ADB (Asian Development Bank). 2007. *Asian water development outlook 2007: Achieving water security for Asia.* Manila, Philippines: ADB. www.adb.org/Documents/Books/AWDO/2007/AWDO.pdf.

ADB (Asian Development Bank), UNDP (United Nations Development Programme), UNESCAP (United Nations Economic and Social Commission for Asia and the Pacific(, and World Health Organization (WHO). 2006. *Asia Water Watch 2015.* Manila; ADB.

AGWWAS (Alliance of Government Workers in the Water Sector), MCWD (Metro Cebu Water District), Public Services International Research Unit (PSIRU) and Visayas State University (VSU). 2008. Public-public partnership (PUP): Training on performance benchmarking for Philippine water districts. 21–24 October 2008. Cebu City, Philippines: Metro Cebu Water District (MCWD) Regional Training Center. www.api.ning.com/files/BChojgJ3nYy8H4mzrZRqOwAHL-medldGzGSfQrj6kO6i1QcNfFt7cVdijCP5a5w2oc863o8HOjQXh4lAgTCQR-vAV1t-tK6TNO/bmwdstrainingreport_vpcnov08.pdf.

Chiong, V. 2008. "Expression of commitment", in documentation report on capability-building program on performance benchmarking of Philippine water districts in the Philippines. Cebu City, Philippines: MCWD-RTC. Mimeo.

Dahasahashra, S.V. 2008. Maharashtra Jeevan Pradhikaran: From intermittent to continuous water supply in Kulgaon-Badlapur. In Ramachandran, M. and Mehta, A.K. (Eds), *National Urban Water Awards 2008: Compendium of good initiatives,* pp. 13–15. www.waterawards.in/compendium-2008.pdf.

Dargantes, B.B. and Dargantes, M.A.L. 2007. Philippine experiences in alternatives to privatization of water services. In Manahan, M.A., Yamamoto, N. and Hoederman, O. (Eds), *Water democracy: Reclaiming public water in Asia,* pp. 53–57. Focus on the Global South and Transnational Institute. www.focusweb. org/water-democracy-reclaiming-public-water-in-asia.html?Itemid=115.

Government Waterworks Professionals Association. 2007. Hong Kong: A role model of public-operated water supply services. In Manahan, M.A., Yamamoto, N. and Hoederman, O. (Eds), *Water democracy: Reclaiming public water services in Asia,* pp. 19–20. Focus on the Global South and Transnational Institute. www.focusweb.org/water-democracy-reclaiming-public-water-in-asia. html?Itemid=115.

Naqvi, S.A. n.d. Business of water, loot in business. In *Water for life, not for profit.* Campaign Paper, Series 4. Mimeo.

Nayar, V., Suresh, V. and Raveendran, V.A. n.d. *Democratization and water: Trysts with change in water sector in Tamil Nadu, India 2003–09.* Change Maganement Group, Tamil Nadu, India.

UN (United Nations). 1993. *Earth Summit Agenda 21: The United Nations programme of action from Rio.* New York: United Nations Department of Economic and Social Affairs (UN-DESA). www.un.org/esa/dsd/agenda21/res_agenda21_18.shtml.

———. 2008. *The Millennium Development Goals report 2008.* New York: United Nations Department of Economic and Social Affairs (UN-DESA). www.un.org/millenniumgoals/pdf/The%20Millennium%20Development%20 Goals%20Report%202008.pdf.

UNEP and DA (United Nations Environment Programme and Development Alternatives). 2008. *South Asia Environment Outlook 2009.* Kenya: UNEP, SAARC, and DA. www.roap.UNEP.org/publications/SAEO%202009.pdf.

World Health Organization (WHO) and United Nations' Children's Fund (UNICEF). 2004. *Meeting the MDG drinking water and sanitation target: A midterm assessment of progress.* Switzerland and New York: WHO and UNICEF. www.unicef.org/publications/files/who_unicef_watsan_midterm_rev.pdf.

WRI (World Resources Institute). 2005. *Freshwater resources 2005.* Washington, DC: WRI. www.earthtrends.wri.org/pdf_library/data_tables/wat2_2005.pdf.

10 The Public in Asia Power

Nepomuceno Malaluan

Electricity provision by governments in Asia grew meteorically from post-World War II to the 1980s, only to be challenged by a strong push for privatization from the late 1980s. This trajectory for electricity was underpinned by major shifts in the dominant development paradigm, particularly with respect to the role ascribed to the state in development.

The paradigm shifts were a product of complex issues. Financing, efficiency, equity, and sustainability have been key topics of the policy debates at the national and international levels. Less overt have been the various motive forces behind policy positions, including the foreign policies of world superpowers, often on behalf of the interests of their business and finance sectors. How a particular country responded depended on the power relations obtained in the country. But even as Asian countries introduced privatization in the 1990s and early 2000s, it would be wrong to conclude that public provision of electricity has been decimated. While private sector participation increased in scope, the transformation of the sector into systems fully in private hands is far from seeing fruition.

This chapter locates the "public" in historical and present electricity provision in selected countries from East, Southeast, and South Asia. By "public" we mean primarily entities that are owned, managed, and financed by the state and subject to political control and oversight. However, we also consider as public those arrangements whereby non-state, non-commercial organizations operating on a non-profit basis play a role in one or more aspects of the service delivery.

The first section of the chapter provides a description of the electricity sector in Asia, with an overview of its development and present state. This is followed by a description of the research approach used to explore "alternatives to privatization" in the sector, including the limitations met in the process. The third section enumerates the alternatives found in selected countries, while section four provides insights on how the identified typologies measure up to our predetermined "criteria for success". The final section provides the author's perspective in imagining an alternative for an electricity sector in

Asia, drawing lessons from the research output and identifying other factors that need to be considered in constructing alternatives.

ELECTRICITY IN EAST, SOUTHEAST, AND SOUTH ASIA

In the late 1900s a number of practical uses of electricity, such as for lighting and communications, were invented. Thus, technologies for generating electric power and for transporting it to the intended site of use (transmission and distribution) were also developed. The reality of being able to provide electricity in large and continuous supply spurred the development of more applications, such as electric motors, heating, refrigeration, electronics, and computing. Electricity became the backbone of modern industrialization and of multiplying household conveniences.

From its seat in the US and Europe in the early 1900s, electricity technology and its various uses were introduced to the rest of the world, including Asia, through colonial policy as well as through investments. Still, electricity generation in Asia grew little in the first half of the 20th century, except for industrializing Japan. It was from 1950 onwards that electricity provision in Asia took off (see Table 10.1).

At the centre of power sector growth in Asia was the state. From private origins, most electricity provision in Asia came under state consolidation after the end of World War II. But by the late 1980s, and intensifying in the 1990s, power sector provisioning came under very strong pressure to restructure, particularly from the World Bank and the Asian Development Bank (ADB) in their role as lenders and gatekeepers of foreign capital.

Table 10.1   Electricity Generation in Selected Asian Countries in 1929, 1950, 1980, and 1990 (Billion Kilowatt Hours)

Country	1929	1950	1980	1990
China	2.1	4.3	285	590
India	1.2	5.1	119	275
Korea	1.5	0.4	34	98
Thailand	0.0	0.1	14	44
Japan	13.3	44.9	547	813
Malaysia	0.2	0.9	10	24
Indonesia	0.2	0.4	13	43
Philippines	0.1	0.6	17	24

Source: Williams and Dubash 2004, US Energy Information Administration. www.tonto.eia. doe.gov/cfapps/ipdbproject/IEDIndex3.cfm?tid=2&pid=2&aid=12.

In January 1993, the World Bank released a policy paper entitled "The World Bank's Role in the Electric Power Sector: Policies for Effective Institutional, Regulatory, and Financial Reform". It spelled out key elements of the country policy reforms that the Bank required for its intervention in the electricity sector. These included:

- Regulatory change—The bank will require countries to set up transparent regulatory processes that are independent of power suppliers and that avoid government interference in day-to-day power company operations.
- Importation of services—The bank will push twinning arrangements or contracting out selected sector services to foreign entities.
- Commercialization and corporatization—Power utilities must begin to operate as commercial businesses, earning commercial rates of return on equity capital, and being responsible for their own budgets.
- Private investment—The policies and institutions will be aimed at attracting greater private sector participation in electricity provision. The bank also committed to deploying a wide range of private sector financing tools and techniques to assist the process (World Bank 1993, 14–18).

Following this lead, the ADB released its own policy paper, "The Bank's Policy Initiatives for the Energy Sector" (ADB 1995). Its policy on sector intervention did not depart much from that of the World Bank. Concretely, it advocated power sector restructuring in the medium term involving unbundling of generation, transmission, and distribution to enable greater private sector participation and introduce elements of competition. In the short term, it called for the corporatization and commercialization of government-owned utilities as a prelude to their privatization and the entry of private sector through various private build-operate options.

To amplify their influence, World Bank and ADB policies both required commitment lending. The World Bank resolved to focus lending to countries that showed commitment to its policy prescriptions, denying finance to utility projects in countries in which the government was unwilling to carry out fundamental structural reforms. When a country, with the Bank's analytical support, decided to step up privatization, it would put together a comprehensive sector work programme to put in place the necessary legal and regulatory frameworks. Like the World Bank, the ADB also conditioned its lending and technical assistance on government willingness to restructure their power sector towards its preferred direction.

From 1990 to 2001, the World Bank approved US$22.2 billion in lending to electric power projects throughout the world. Of this, 65.4% related to private sector development. Of the 154 total electric power projects from 1990 to 1999, East Asia and Pacific countries accounted for 35, while South Asia accounted for 20, or 55 projects in all (Manibog et al, 2003). For its part, the ADB, from 1995 to 1999, approved US$4.83 billion in lending to

40 energy projects. It also approved US$74.1 million in technical assistance for the same period. These projects included six rural electrification projects in Bangladesh, Bhutan, Lao People's Democratic Republic (Lao PDR), Nepal, and Thailand; two programme loans and a technical assistance loan supported power subsector restructuring in Indonesia and the Philippines, including consulting services; a renewable energy loan to India; six loans financed thermal and hydropower projects in China, Lao PDR, Nepal, and Pakistan; and four loans for power transmission and distribution. In addition, the Private Sector Group provided direct assistance to four energy sector projects developed by the private sector in China, India, Nepal, and Pakistan with ADB assistance and complementary loans (ADB 2000).

In total, World Bank- and ADB-sponsored restructuring initiatives in the electricity sector led to 552 private sector participation projects in Asia from 1990 to 2008, of which 381 were in East Asia and Pacific countries and the remaining in South Asia. This mobilized a total of US$153.9 billion in private investments to the electricity sector for the same period, of which East Asia and Pacific countries accounted for US$98.26 billion and South Asia countries accounted for US$55.67 billion (data generated from World Bank Private Participation in Infrastructure Database at www.ppi.worldbank.org).

One common experience in private sector participation was contracting with independent power producers (IPPs). Typically, an IPP contract involves the contracting by a government electricity utility with a project sponsor under a build-operate-transfer, or variant, arrangement. The project sponsor is often a company created specifically for the project, generally by a private company or consortium of private companies, local or foreign. For the consideration of a long-term power purchase agreement (15 to 25 years) by the government electricity utility, the project sponsor agrees to put up a power plant and operate it for the duration of the contract term. Building the power plant means mobilizing finance through a combination of equity and borrowing and procuring its construction. The project sponsor retains ownership of the asset until the end of the contract term, at which time ownership of the asset, assuming it has not exhausted its useful life, is transferred to the government utility. IPP contracts make up the bulk of the growth in private investment in electricity from 1991 and up to its peaking levels in 1996 and 1997.

The 1997 Asian financial crisis, however, exposed the risks associated with IPP contracting. IPPs demand generous protection from market risk (guaranteed capacity off-take), financial risk (exchange rate guarantee), and operational risk (fuel price guarantees). This reduced risk for the private sector, sometimes coupled with corruption in the contracting process, provides incentives to overcontract/overbuild. When the financial crisis struck, therefore, government utilities were faced with overcapacity and huge power purchase escalation that put even greater pressure on their financial bottom line. Many utilities were forced to increase electricity rates or to book greater losses and indebtedness. Some IPP contracts became the subject of disputes. Overall, IPP contracting significantly lost its luster after the Asian financial crisis.

Alongside contracting with IPPs was the introduction of deeper sectoral restructuring in many Asian countries. No doubt the restructuring model pushed by the ADB and World Bank heavily influenced the restructuring design. This model involved the vertical unbundling of the system, with an unambiguous objective of transferring the system into private hands. Unbundling, under the World Bank and ADB model, is a means to separate the parts that in their analysis can accommodate competition—particularly electricity generation—and the parts that remain a natural monopoly, particularly transmission and distribution. Generation is broken into a number of generation companies that compete in a power market. Transmission and distribution utilities are obliged to allow the transport of electricity to end users for a fee. While distribution utilities are allowed to retail electricity, they are subjected to competition by allowing high-capacity consumers and small consumer aggregators to buy power directly from generation companies. In addition to competition, the concentration of market power is sought to be prevented by a legal framework that limits cross-ownership. It also involves the creation of an independent regulatory agency to regulate pricing and service of the natural monopoly segments of transmission and distribution. Under this model, except for the regulator, all segments are envisioned to be sold off or contracted out to the private sector.

However, the World Bank's and ADB's strategic objectives of transforming the sector into an unbundled system, fully in private hands, is far from being realized. Still, given the intrusion of IPPs and restructuring, in many countries involving divestments, the sector can be best described as mixed from a public-private standpoint. Nevertheless, given the resilience of state roles in many countries, the ultimate trajectory of each system remains uncertain.

RESEARCH APPROACH

In attempting to locate the "public" within electricity provision in Asia, we confined the initial target coverage to the subregions of East (China, Japan, North Korea, South Korea), Southeast (Brunei, Cambodia, Indonesia, Laos, Malaysia, Myanmar, Philippines, Singapore, Thailand, Vietnam), and South Asia (Afghanistan, Bangladesh, Bhutan, India, Nepal, Pakistan, Sri Lanka). Owing to an absence of resources for country visits, we proceeded mainly with online data gathering and secondary literature on country electricity provision, focusing on the present state of service delivery, historical development, and sector reforms, while looking for information on the various "criteria for success" being used to evaluate the performance of these "public" electricity entities (see Chapter 2, this volume, for a fuller discussion of the research methodologies employed). The websites of many utilities were helpful in providing technical data, while secondary literature from academics, industry experts, researchers, and consultants were useful in providing narratives on historical development and reform. The online library services of the International Development Research Centre provided valuable assistance in making available a number of titles not otherwise retrievable from open sources.

Certain countries in the original target scope yielded very little online information and had to be omitted from closer study. These are Brunei, Cambodia, Laos, Myanmar, North Korea, Afghanistan, and Maldives. Other countries, while yielding appreciable data and literature, have gaps that make it difficult to construct a full picture. They were Pakistan, Bangladesh, Nepal, Sri Lanka, Japan, Singapore, and Vietnam.

The study delved deeper into the remaining countries with substantial available information. These were China, India, Indonesia, Malaysia, Philippines, South Korea, and Thailand. These countries provided a good mix of cases. South Korea is an industrialized country. China and India are two countries with very large populations (each with more than 1 billion people) and fast growing economies. Indonesia, Malaysia, Thailand, and the Philippines are middle-income countries with diverse histories, cultures, and development strategies.

For "alternatives" outside the main electricity system, we looked at Thailand and the Philippines for examples. The choice was based on resource availability, as the primary researcher is based in the Philippines and has a strong working partnership with an industry expert in Thailand.

What was particularly challenging was to find consistent, comparable, and substantial information on the various criteria for success. These often required in-depth study not supported by the resources of the research and also involved areas not traditionally studied by sector analysts. Also, where information may be available, it might not match the time element for the alternative. Thus, we were confined to evaluating each identified typology against selected criteria, as they may be applicable.

The research was also informed by a research methodology workshop and a regional validation workshop on alternatives for Asia, both in Bangkok, Thailand, which included participation by Asia sector researchers and selected experts who provided comments and insights on methodology and preliminary findings.

TYPOLOGY AND OBJECTIVES OF IDENTIFIED ALTERNATIVES

Single public sector—Historical models

As mentioned above, most electricity provision in Asia began under state consolidation after World War II. One variant of such consolidation is through a *vertically integrated monopoly under a state agency or a state-owned corporate body*. Vertically integrated means that a single entity owns and operates the generation, transmission, and distribution aspects of the system.

In terms of organization of the operator, it can be through a state agency that forms part of the bureaucracy. Others are organized as a state-owned corporate body; that is, the operator is given a legal personality independent from the central or local government. It must be noted, however, that such corporate organization does not necessarily mean losing state control and oversight. Strategic planning, budgeting, and other major decisions are often still done through the relevant line agency (such as a department or ministry of energy). What this setup does, however, is to provide the operator an independent legal personality enjoying corporate powers, including the capacity to own property, to enter into contracts, and to sue and be sued. This gives the operator flexibility in dealing with operational transactions, such as procurement, without the more tedious administrative requirements of a state agency setup.

Falling under this category are the following:

- China—In 1949, the Chinese Communist Party confiscated electricity assets and placed them under central planning through the State Planning Committee, Ministry of Electric Power and Bureau of Electric Power, with the operations implemented through state-owned enterprises at both central and provincial levels (Yang 2006).
- South Korea—In 1961, the military government of General Park Chung-Hee, installed by a coup, grouped together three existing regional electric companies to form a single nationally operating electric power entity. The resulting structure was a vertically integrated monopoly under the Korea Electric Company (KECO), later renamed Korean Electric Power Corporation (KEPCO; Funding Universe 2009).
- India—The Constituent Assembly (after independence in 1947), passed the Electricity (Supply) Act of 1948, providing for the creation of State Electricity Boards as well as of a Central Electricity Authority. The State Electricity Boards operated vertically integrated systems within states, alongside various national generation corporations and grid corporations, under combined central and state planning. Whereas at the start, there was flexibility to honour existing private licenses, in 1956 an Industrial Policy Resolution was adopted reserving production of power to the public sector (Kale 2004).
- Indonesia—In 1950, after Indonesia gained independence, the Indonesian government established the National Electric Power Company or the *Perusahaan Umum Listrik Negara* (PLN). PLN operated a vertically integrated system under oversight by the Ministry of State-Owned Enterprises, Ministry of Energy and Mineral Resources, and Ministry of Finance (Seymour and Sari 2002).
- Malaysia—Public consolidation started in 1949 when the British authority, after the Japanese occupation, established state-owned enterprises for development in an effort to foil communist insurgency. The Central Electricity Board of the Federation of Malaya was formed. The consolidation intensified after independence in 1957,

with the *Malayanization* policy. The Central Electricity Board of the Federation of Malaya became the National Electricity Board of the States of Malaya in 1965, operating a vertically integrated monopoly in peninsular Malaysia. Two other state monopolies provide the service in Sarawak and Sabah (Jomo and Tan 2003, TNB[1]).

Another variant is a *partially integrated system*, where there is integrated generation and transmission but separate distribution. Falling under this setup were the following:

- Philippines—Public sector participation in generation started in 1936 through the creation of the National Power Corporation (NPC) with the obligation to develop hydro power. In 1972 at the onset of Martial Law, President Ferdinand Marcos issued Presidential Decree 40, instituting an NPC monopoly over transmission and on-grid new generation. From then on, it progressively took over private plants and operated a monopoly over generation and transmission. Distribution was given to regulated private distribution utilities, cooperatives, local government units, and other authorized entities over a specific franchise area (Malaluan 2003).
- Thailand—In 1969, generation previously undertaken by three generation authorities was combined into the Electricity Generating Authority of Thailand (EGAT). EGAT operates as a state-owned company involved in generation and transmission throughout Thailand, selling wholesale power to the state-owned Metropolitan Electricity Authority for distribution in Bangkok and Provincial Electricity Authority for distribution throughout the country (Greacen and Greacen 2004, Funding Universe 2009).

Public/non-profit partnership

We found examples of partnerships between the state and non-state entities operating on a non-profit basis that helped secure public objectives in electricity provision. As the first two examples below illustrate, participation by the non-state, non-profit sector are confined to small initiatives but can be embedded in the overall structure. The other form of partnership extends beyond the physical provisioning and goes into other important aspects of the sector, particularly planning. In many countries, the people's drive to make the sector accountable results in institutional mechanisms for people's participation, as our third set of examples shows:

- Rayong City Biogas project—In Rayong City, Thailand, there is a 1-megawatt biogas plant that supplies electricity to the grid. There are plans to increase its capacity to 4 megawatts. It is a project of the Rayong local government, with cooperation from a non-profit organization, the Energy for Environment Foundation (HPPF 2010).

- Electric cooperatives in the Philippines—As mentioned earlier, in the historical public consolidation of electricity provisioning in the Philippines, distribution was not integrated with generation and transmission. Among the entities allowed to perform the distribution function are electric cooperatives. The formation of electric cooperatives is governed by a 1969 law (Republic Act 6038) declaring total electrification of the country a state policy and identifying electric cooperatives as a central mechanism for such. These cooperatives are non-stock, non-profit membership corporations, with membership open to consumers served. Knowing the start-up cost required for a distribution utility to be able to operate, the same law created the National Electrification Administration tasked with assisting cooperatives through lending and technical assistance. The number of electric cooperatives has grown to 119.

- Initiatives for public participation in state planning and regulation—Outside of the physical provisioning of electricity, there has also been a push in certain areas for stronger public participation in electricity planning to protect community interest. In Thailand, some environmental groups are advocating the adoption of an Integrated Resources Planning framework. In contrast to conventional power supply planning by government, this approach integrates demand-side management into the demand and supply determination and also expands the cost considerations to include environmental and social costs. One key element in the process is greater transparency and public participation in the planning process (Bijoor et al, 2007). In the Philippines, the Regional Development Council (a government mechanism for participatory planning) in one of its regions passed a resolution in 2004 calling for a Multi-Stakeholder Power Development Planning (MSPDP) for Panay, a Philippine island comprising four provinces. The initiative was a response to the clamour of local organizations for greater understanding of the planning and decision process in local electricity and to questions over the power rates, power demand forecasts, and concerns over the environmental impact of power plants. The local organizations see the initiative as a way to give people a voice in the setting of local priorities, the identification of problems, and the search for solutions. The organizations are looking to the challenge of bringing the initiative into the mainstream of the planning process of the Department of Energy, and replicated in other provinces and regions (FDC 2008). In India, the non-governmental, non-profit organization *Prayas*, is actively intervening in electricity regulation in the state of Maharashtra. Since 1999, it has been nominated by the Maharashtra Electricity Regulatory Commission (MERC) as a Consumer Representative. Prayas is also recognized as a member of the Advisory Committee of MERC. In these capacities, Prayas participates in all key regulatory initiatives. It has also initiated regulatory cases and intervened significantly in all major regulatory cases (Prayas, n.d.).

Non-profit/non-profit partnership

In off-grid areas in which there are significant barriers to linking with the grid, the need for electricity coupled with the absence of private commercial interest drive communities, non-profit organizations, and governments to find non-commercial alternatives to providing electricity:

- Microsystems—An illustrative initiative is one led by *Sibol ng Agham at Teknolohiya* or SIBAT (translated, Sprout of Science and Technology) in the Philippines. SIBAT is a network of non-governmental organizations and people's organizations promoting appropriate technology through its core programs in sustainable agriculture and renewable energy development. Since 1994, it has facilitated the setting up of community-based, small power supply systems in remote, upland, and marginal communities. From 1994 to 2007, it has either installed or is in the process of installing Microhydro Power Facilities (capacity ranges between 5–40 kW) in 20 localities, benefiting more than 1,000 households (SIBAT, 2005).

Single public sector—Defending/revising the status quo

Amidst strong pressure to adopt the unbundling/privatization model of restructuring, a number of state entities have worked to fend off privatization, either by selling the merits of what they provide (defending the status quo) or through internal restructuring to improve public service delivery. In other instances, even as the governments have already made a policy shift towards privatization, implementation is halted or prevented by public opposition, including through judicial action. We provide several illustrative examples below. More often, the adjustments and transitions still result in the introduction of private elements, making the identification of these cases as "public alternatives" perhaps controversial. This matter will be addressed in the succeeding section as we discuss the identified cases in relation to the predetermined "criteria for success".

- China: Taking Unbundling towards a Different Route—In 1997, the State Council of China (its highest administrative organ) created the State Power Company of China. It took over most electricity assets and operation from the Ministry of Electric Power. Parallel corporatization was also done for generation assets controlled by provinces (Zhang and Parsons 2008). In 2002 the State Council launched deeper reforms intended to prepare the sector for the introduction of competition through regional wholesale power markets and exchange of power among regions. Part of the reform process was the setting up of an independent regulatory agency, the State Electricity Regulatory Commission. The State Power Company was split into several corporate entities. Transmission was assigned to two companies, the State Grid Corporation of China and the China Southern Power Grid Corporation. The State Grid Corporation is further broken down into five regional grid companies of North China, Northeast China, East China, Central China, and Northwest China. Generation assets, in turn, were assigned to five generation corporations: the China Huaneng Group, the China Datang Group, the China Huadian Corporation, the China GuoDian Corporation, and the China Power Investment Corporation. The corporatized enterprises remain under state ownership (CSP, n.d.). Beginning in 2004, a number of pilot trials were done in several regional wholesale electricity markets, particularly in Northeast China, the East Region, and the South Region. However, it does not appear that such power markets have continued.

- South Korea: Retreat from Privatization—In South Korea, the Korean Electric Power Corporation (KEPCO) was listed on the Korea Stock Exchange in 1989, and 21% of its shares were offered by government to the public. In 1994, KEPCO shares were also listed on the New York Stock Exchange, where American Depositary Receipts (ADRs) amounting to US$300 million were issued. These partial privatization initiatives were intended to raise capital for the corporation, but the listing also brought the company into commercial scrutiny. When the country was hit by the Asian financial crisis in 1997, and in the face of strong pressure to privatize coming from the International Monetary Fund, the government initiated planning for deeper restructuring. This culminated in the release of the Basic Plan for Restructuring the Electric Power Industry in 1999. The restructuring was to be phased from 2001 to 2009. Phase one involves spinning off KEPCO's generation assets into six subsidiaries. Competition in generation will be introduced by setting up a power pool, with KEPCO remaining a single buyer. The generation companies will be privatized through a combination of negotiated sale and initial public offering in the stock market. Phase two involves spinning off the distribution assets into several companies and privatization similar to the generation companies. Large consumers will be allowed to purchase in the power pool. The transmission sector shall remain with KEPCO. It will allow open access to all market participants under regulated transmission charges. The final phase involves full retail competition, with generation companies, consumers, and other market participants having open access to transmission and distribution. Implementation of the plan began in 2000, with the passage of a law authorizing the separation of KEPCO's generation assets into several companies. In 2001, six generation subsidiaries were established. Another legislation mandated the setting up of the

Korea Power Exchange and a regulatory body called the Korea Electricity Commission. The privatization component, however, met strong opposition from the public. Privatization was suspended following a change in government in 2003, and more definitely halted in 2004. Today KEPCO remains owned by government in majority (51.07%) and retains full ownership of the spun-off generation subsidiaries. It also has considerable investment interests in related businesses in the country and overseas (Mun 2002, KEPCO[2]).

- Judicial challenge in Thailand and Indonesia—In Indonesia, the seeds of restructuring started with Law No. 15/1985 allowing private sector participation in electricity generation. But for this law to be implemented it requires corresponding executive instruments. This came during the inception of the IPP wave, with the issuance of Presidential Decree No. 37/1992, or the Private Power Decree, coupled with the corporatization of PLN in 1994 through Decree No. 23/1994. These implementing decrees facilitated PLN's contracting with IPPs (Sari· 2001). Sections of generation were also spun-off into two subsidiary companies, the PLN *Pembangkitan Java-Bali I*, and *Pembangkitan Java-Bali II*. Hit hard by the Asian financial crisis in 1997, the government committed to multilateral agencies even deeper restructuring of the power sector. This culminated in the Parliament passing Electricity Law No. 20/2002. This law called for the establishment of an electricity regulatory commission within one year from passage of the law and the designation of at least one area for free competition in generation. Government will retain ownership and control of transmission and distribution. Licensing of generation companies will be decentralized, allowing local governments to issue licenses to private companies within their jurisdiction (Tumiwa 2002). Opposition to the restructuring challenged the law before the Constitutional Court. In December 2004, the said court declared Electricity Law 20/2002 to be contrary to the Constitution. The court held in part that as electricity is a commodity vital to the people, it should remain under the full control of the state and only allowing partnerships with private companies. The industry should also remain an integrated business.

Thailand experimented with a different mode of involving the private sector in the 1990s and early 2000. In May 1992 it formed the Electricity Generating Company (EGCO) to which it assigned two power plants (120-mW Rayong Power Plant and 750-mW Khanom Power Plant). EGCO then sold 60% of its shares through initial public offering (IPO) in the Stock Exchange of Thailand in November 1994. In 1997 it sold more shares to strategic investors, bringing its interest further down to 25.8%. The same strategy was pursued in EGAT's Ratchaburi Power Plant Complex, by forming the Ratchaburi Electricity Generating Holding Co. Ltd. in March 2000. It retained 45% interest, offered 40% to the public through the stock market, and assigned 15%

to EGAT employees and the EGAT Provident Fund. These initiatives were intended to be part of a comprehensive sector restructuring along the unbundling and privatization model, as approved by the cabinet in July 2000. The plan called for the further spinning off of the generation assets of EGAT into more generation companies for privatization and retaining with EGAT mainly the transmission assets. A power pool operated by an independent system operator will be established, where the spun-off generation companies and other private generation companies will compete for the sale and dispatch of their generated electricity. The distribution business of the Metropolitan Electricity Authority (MEA) and the Provincial Electricity Authority (PEA) will be subject to competition by allowing private unregulated retail companies to operate and compete for electricity consumers. There were also proposals to break MEA and PEA up into several distribution companies. Finally, an independent regulator will be set up to regulate the natural monopoly businesses of transmission and distribution (NEPO 2000). The plan, however, was abandoned by the government of Thaksin Shinawatra who won the elections in 2001. Instead, Thaksin proposed to reform Thailand's biggest state-owned enterprises by corporatizing and publicly listing them and offering minority shares to the public. The idea was to increase stock market capitalization and raise funds for the enterprises, while retaining state majority ownership (Greacen and Greacen 2004). Following this shift, EGAT was corporatized in June 2005 into EGAT PLC. Preparations were made for the offer of 25% interest in the company to the public for US$753 million. However, members of the Confederation of Consumer Organizations in Thailand filed a case before the Supreme Administrative Court questioning the validity of the planned sale. On March 23, 2006, the court declared the privatization illegal. Among the grounds were the lack of consultation and the illegality of allowing private ownership of an entity that retains a right to expropriate, which is reserved for the state.

• Malaysia corporatization—In Malaysia, the Electricity Supply Act of 1990 corporatized the National Electricity Board into *Tenaga Nasional Berhad*. Although it was publicly listed, there was no intention to let go of controlling interest by government. The government retains majority interest through its investment holding arm as well as the Employees Provident Fund under the Ministry of Finance.

ASSESSING PUBLIC ALTERNATIVES AGAINST "CRITERIA FOR SUCCESS"

How do these public electricity service providers stand up to performance scrutiny? We have evaluated them using a predetermined set of "criteria for success" (see Chapter 2, this volume, for an extended discussion), as follows.

Equity

One indicator of equity in electricity is access rates in urban versus rural areas. Access is particularly challenging in rural areas that are often characterized by lower levels of consumer capacity to pay and wide geographic dispersion, making cost of provision high and relative demand low. It is thus an accomplishment for developing countries to be able to provide high access rates for rural areas or at least to be able to provide relatively close access levels between rural and urban areas.

Among the countries identified as having strong historical state provision of electricity, China, South Korea, Malaysia, and Thailand have near universal access rates. Of the lower performers, the Philippines has relatively high total access, with respectable urban to rural comparisons. The poor performers were India and Indonesia (see Table 10.2).

Table 10.2   Electricity Access in Southeast, East, and South Asia (2008)

Country	Electrification rate (%)			Population without electricity (millions)
	Total	Urban	Rural	
Southeast Asia				
Brunei	99.7	100.0	98.6	>0.1
Cambodia	24.0	66.0	12.5	11.2
Indonesia	64.5	94.0	32.0	81.1
Laos	55.0	84.0	42.0	2.7
Malaysia	99.4	100.0	98.0	0.2
Myanmar (Burma)	13.0	19.0	10.0	42.8
Philippines	86.0	97.0	65.0	12.5
Singapore	100.0	100.0	100.0	0.0
Thailand	99.3	100.0	99.0	0.4
Vietnam	89.0	99.6	85.0	9.5
East Asia				
China	99.4	100.0	99.0	8.0
Japan	100.0	100.0	100.0	0.0
North Korea	26.0	36.0	10.0	17.7
South Korea	100.0	100.0	100.0	0.0
South Asia				
Afghanistan	14.4	22.0	12.0	23.3
Bangladesh	41.0	76.0	28.0	94.9
India	64.5	93.1	52.5	404.5
Nepal	43.6	89.7	34.0	16.1
Pakistan	57.6	78.0	46.0	70.4
Sri Lanka	76.6	85.8	75.0	4.7

Source: International Energy Agency (IEA). www.iea.org/weo/database_electricity/electricity_access_database.htm.

It is interesting to compare the performance of the two poor performers with similarly situated high performers. India compares to China in terms of its large population and vast geographical territory, but China far outstrips India in terms of providing access for the rural sector. Indonesia compares to the Philippines in terms of its archipelagic territory, but the Philippines far outstrips Indonesia in terms of providing access for the rural sector.

One explanation is the effective combination of central and decentralized approaches in China and the Philippines to achieve more equitable access. In China, Yeh and Lewis (2004) describe the electricity development approach during the Maoist period of 1949 to 1977 as "walking on two legs". One leg was the construction of large scale, centralized projects, and the other was decentralized rural electrification. China promoted self-reliance and learning by doing, with assistance through small subsidies and technical support. The result was significant small-scale, decentralized systems (especially in hydropower) with high domestic technology content. In the Philippines, there was centralization and integration of generation and transmission, but the rural electrification drive was decentralized through the promotion and support for electric cooperatives as described in the previous section.

Participation

The Prayas intervention in electricity regulation in the state of Maharashtra in India is already showing very positive and sustained results. Their intervention in tariff and generation and power purchase regulatory issues and disputes, either as principal party or as intervener by way of comments and submissions, has articulated public interest perspectives and also won concrete decisions (see documentation of Prayas Maharashtra intervention at www.prayaspune.org). Part of the success stems from the institutionalization of the regulatory participation of Prayas. As mentioned earlier, Prayas has been nominated by MERC as a Consumer Representative since 1999 and is also recognized as a member of the Advisory Committee of MERC. No doubt such institutionalization was something Prayas itself worked for, partly through building credibility and expertise in dealing with regulatory issues.

The off-grid microsystem initiative of SIBAT also shows high levels of participation. Over the course of its experience, SIBAT has developed an approach or methodology for its projects, one aspect of which is a participatory project development process. It begins with planning that evolves together with community members. In contrast to commercial activities that simply regard the community as a market, the project schedule incorporates community participation in all phases, such as civil works and determination of technology appropriateness.

Of the initiatives for public participation in state planning and regulation identified, the examples from Thailand (Integrated Resources Planning framework) and the Philippines (MSPDP) are still new initiatives, and there is as yet no clear indication of their effectiveness in practice.

Efficiency

Table 10.3 gives some indicators of sector performance that show public systems can achieve high levels of efficiency. This is very clear from Korea, China, and Thailand with strong performance in bringing down system losses. Philippines and Malaysia also show respectable control of system losses. South Korea achieved very high levels of labour productivity as shown by its consumers-to-worker ratio. China also did very well, while Malaysia and Thailand should benefit from improvements. All these were accomplished while maintaining good rates of return, except for China.

The poor performer was India (along with Bangladesh), with very high system losses and poor rates of return. Although these figures are stark, care should still be exercised in cross-referring these indicators with other possible explanatory variables, such as high subsidy rates. In other words, there could be trade-offs with equity objectives.

Table 10.3   Electricity Sector Performance Indicators in Selected Asian Countries, 1987

Country	Generation per capita (kWh)	Total system losses (%)	End users per employee	Rate of return on investment (%)
Korea	1906	6	292	15
Malaysia	983	16	84	10
Thailand	567	10	92	11
China	465	9	118	6
Philippines	408	17	NA	10
India	273	24	NA	4
Pakistan	227	25	38	12
Sri Lanka	165	16	51	8
Bangladesh	56	37	39	2

Source: Williams and Dubash 2004, citing Jose R. Escay, Summary Data Sheet of 1987 Power and Commercial Energy Statistics for 100 Developing Countries (Washington, DC: World Bank, March 1990).

Accountability and transparency

It was difficult to find literature on these aspects of the electricity sector for many countries. There is, however, a study led by the World Resources Institute and Prayas that analyzed the electricity governance in India, Indonesia, Philippines, and Thailand in terms of transparency, public participation, and accountability (Nakhooda et al, 2007). One limitation of using this study for the purpose of this chapter is that the data were gathered at the point in which structural reforms in the sector were ongoing and therefore difficult to apply to the time element of our identified typologies. Still, the summary of key findings of the study is worth sharing:

- In terms of electricity policy and planning, in general little information about the basis for new policy initiatives is shared with the public.
- Opportunities for public participation in policy processes remain quite limited, and when consultations are conducted, input received is not always recorded or seriously considered by policy makers.
- The integrity and capabilities of executive agencies need to be improved, particularly in terms of addressing conflicts of interest and political interference.
- Planning processes can help mainstream environmental and social considerations. It was noted that independent planning agencies such as the Energy Policy and Planning Office in Thailand and the Central Electricity Authority in India, have significant technical capacity but lack credibility and resources, although in Thailand, there are efforts to conduct strategic environmental impact assessments for electricity.
- There are significant legal provisions for transparency, public participation, and accountability in independent regulatory bodies in India and the Philippines, but these rules need to be effectively operationalized.
- Public interests such as environmental sustainability and social equity are seldom included in the mandates of electricity regulators, even as civil society organizations in the countries studied showed interest in engaging in electricity governance although constrained by financial, human resource, and technical expertise limitations.

Quality of the workplace

This is another understudied area in the electricity sector in Asia. We can only make inferences on unionism as a facet of quality of the workplace from the countries studied. Particularly in the cases of South Korea, Indonesia, and Thailand, we can deduce the presence of a strong public sector union in the electricity sector of these countries, where the unions played a considerable role in the opposition to restructuring and privatization initiatives. Such strong unionism is possible not just through union organizing success but no doubt also thrives in a work environment that is open to such union activities.

Sustainability

The illustrative example for microsystems in off-grid areas—SIBAT—shows high levels of environmental and social sustainability. In addition to the participatory methods discussed earlier, project sustainability is made greater by requiring a people's organization to represent the community, with organizational track record in being able to mobilize the community to contribute materials and labour, with willingness to seek the necessary outside help (such as from the local government), and with capacity to manage the project after installation. SIBAT provides technology assistance and helps in the social preparation of the community. It also sources grants to provide a one-time subsidy, after which the people's organization takes over to ensure the operation, maintenance, and replacement of parts. The technologies used are also environment-friendly.

The Rayong City Biogas project provides an example of an on-grid environmentally sustainable initiative. The plant is not only addressed to electricity needs but also to waste management. It responds to the challenge of dealing with the ever-increasing quantity of municipal waste. Rayong City was among the first local governments to implement the biogas system using organic waste to generate electricity. The use of organic waste for biogas electricity generation is environmentally cleaner than alternative disposal, such as incineration (HPPF 2010).

Solidarity

In terms of the big systems, the decentralized components of the electricity development strategy of China and the Philippines showed strong elements of solidarity. These combined state support with local community power in developing smaller local systems for China and the decentralized electricity distribution through cooperatives in the Philippines.

Strong community solidarity was also shown in the retreat of privatization in Korea and the judicial interventions in Thailand and Indonesia. In South Korea, the labour unions were the first to oppose the restructuring agenda. The Korean National Electrical Workers Union opposed restructuring primarily from a job security perspective and reached compromise with KEPCO management on the first stage of the restructuring, which was to separate generation. This caused a split in the union, with the workers in the generation sector still opposed to the restructuring and forming the Korean Power Plant Industry union. It was this latter formation that evolved from opposition only based on job security to broader policy concerns including the stability in electricity supply, pricing, and foreign ownership (Mun 2004). On the part of the environmentalists, they were initially more open to the unbundling model. Coming from an anti-nuclear advocacy, many environmentalists saw some opening in the unbundling model to break up the monopoly of KEPCO, which they hoped would facilitate the reduction in reliance on nuclear power. As the restructuring plan unfolded, however, the environmentalists realized that the unbundling model never sought to address their environmental concerns. This precipitated an interest in dialogue with the labour unions and other civil society groups, which in March 2002 resulted in a joint declaration calling for the suspension of the restructuring programme and to undertake deeper consultation to forge social consensus. This proved instrumental in the eventual government decision to halt the implementation of the restructuring plan in 2004 (Byrne et al, 2004, Mun 2004).

The evolution of sector union-civil society solidarity in Thailand and Indonesia followed a pattern similar to that of South Korea. In Thailand, the first main opposition to the restructuring agenda came from the EGAT labour union, which put up a determined campaign alongside unions in other government-owned enterprises. While the unions were able to strongly engage the privatization proponents, they were seen by other organized sectors as only promoting their vested interests. The environmental and consumer movements instead focused their campaigns on electricity pricing as well as opposition to the construction of some power plants for environmental and social concerns (Nuntavorakarn 2002).

After Thai Prime Minister Thaksin Shinawatra changed enterprise reform from one of full privatization to a strategy in which state enterprises would be listed and partially privatized, the EGAT union members still continued their opposition. They staged protests in 2004 at the time when the new privatization plan was being finalized. The union got stronger alliance from other movements, particularly the environmental and consumer groups that were calling for the establishment of an independent regulator, a reform aspect present in the former unbundling model but absent in the Thaksin approach. Still, the plan proceeded but was finally stopped in March 2006 through court action by the Confederation of Consumer Organizations. No doubt the strong opposition added pressure to the decision of the court.

In Indonesia, the main opposition to the restructuring and privatization agenda came from the PLN Labour Union, again principally on job security concerns. But as the reform legislation was being taken up by Parliament in 2001, a broader formation, the NGO Working Group on Power Sector Restructuring (WG-PSR) was convened. This even expanded its reach by initiating a broad coalition of NGOs, academics, labour unions, and ex-PLN employees into the Civil Society Coalition for Electricity Crisis. Alongside mass campaigning, it undertook research and analysis and intervened in the legislative process (Tumiwa 2004). After the passage of the act, it shifted its focus to the judicial review of the act before the Constitutional

Court, culminating in striking down of the said act in December 2004 for being contrary to the Constitution.

Public ethos

A government's public ethos in terms of how it views the role of the state in securing social or public objectives comes into play in determining how its electricity sector is organized. This was very clear in the historical public consolidation of electricity provision in Asia. For countries that suffered destruction from World War II, reconstruction was a major objective. For other countries there was the dimension of gaining independence from a colonial power, of winning a communist revolution, or of the coming into power of governments characterized by strong leaders with developmental orientation. These countries all imposed upon the state a central role in developing infrastructure, with critical emphasis on providing for the electricity needs of nascent industry, of growing urban centres, and of the marginalized countryside.

At the present juncture, how a government's public ethos has evolved determines how it reacts to the pressure to undertake deep restructuring in the direction of full privatization of electricity provisioning. The two sample countries where restructuring took an independent path, China and Malaysia, both have a history of independent national and foreign policy and strong state intervention in the economy. While Communist China introduced market reforms in the 1990s, it did not mean blanket privatization. A closer look at the progression of China restructuring reveals that privatization was not the ultimate objective. Rather, corporatization was intended to separate governmental administrative function from government commercial or business activity or enterprise. Even the introduction of competition was not intended to facilitate the shift to private provision but rather was part of the internal reform in state enterprises to subject them to market forces.

The socialist market economy model of China emphasized the role of public ownership in corporatized state-owned enterprises. More specifically, in its programme of industrial structural adjustment of November 2001, enterprises were categorized into the following: (i) core sectors of national defence and military industries, where government retains absolute control; (ii) strategic enterprises supplying critical public goods and services, and sectors of natural monopoly, such as electricity, water services, and energy industries, along with enterprises of national economic strength, such as petrochemical and automobile, where state capital retains a controlling position; and (iii) key high-tech industries where government provides funding for basic and applied research (Nakaya 2006). It was on this basis that the electricity restructuring of China modified the unbundling model of the World Bank and the ADB to remain consistent with its public ownership and public goals perspective.

For Malaysia, it was proceeding from a historical strategy of a developmental state framework. As mentioned earlier, while its power utility was publicly listed, there was no intention to let go of controlling interest by government. The listing and partial divestment were intended to expand the capitalization of its stock market as well as to continue the redistribution of wealth to increase indigenous Malay (*Bumiputera*) ownership and entrepreneurship (Gomez, 2009).

South Korea comes from the tradition of a developmental state, with the government working in close coordination with business conglomerates in pursuit of its industrial policy. The initial push for the privatization of Korea's electricity sector came from the conglomerates, with the Federation of Korean Industry proposing to the government's Regulatory Reform Committee the opening of the sector to accommodate independent power producers and self-generators into the system (Mun 2004). The stronger pressure, however, came in the wake of the 1997 financial crisis. The International Monetary Fund (IMF) conditioned its bailout package on deep market reforms in the economy. KEPCO was a principal target for privatization, being the state-owned enterprise with the highest level of international debt. At that time, the Korean government was also in transition politically, with Kim Dae-Jung winning the December 1997 elections. Kim came from a background of opposition to the former military governments and a platform of political democratization. One could speculate that Kim's acceptance of the IMF economic reform conditionalities also proceeds from a rejection of the developmental state model of the military governments. Strong public opposition had indeed precipitated the retreat in the full implementation of the Korea electricity restructuring. But the Korean National Electrical Workers Union (KNEWU, n.d.) itself recognized that the election of Rho Mu-hyun, which it regarded as having a more progressive standpoint, helped provide a new foundation for the review of the restructuring and privatization plan.

In Thailand, Greacen and Greacen (2004) observe that business-friendly prime ministers in power from 1980 to the 1990s facilitated the growing clout of pro-market reformers in the Thai bureaucracy. For the energy sector, they identify Dr Piyasvasti Amranand, an economist trained at the London School Economics and appointed director of the National Energy Policy Office in 1986, as having played a key role, with technical assistance from the World Bank and foreign consulting firms, in planning the restructuring of the Thai power sector. But the election in January 2001, when the Thai Rak Thai party won majority seats in Parliament and its leader Thaksin Shinawatra became prime minister, signalled a change in state ideology. With the experience of the Asian financial crisis still fresh in the people's mind, Thaksin took a critical stance against the IMF stabilization programme and postponed sector reforms. This included changing enterprise reform from one of full privatization, to a strategy in which state enterprises will be listed and partially privatized, but remain state-owned and controlled to achieve strategic economic objectives, and called "national champions". Piyasvati was stripped of his erstwhile pre-eminent role in the reform process.

Transferability

Elements of the alternatives identified in the electricity sector in Asia can be argued to be replicable in other areas with compatible conditions. In Asian countries with low rural electricity access rates (or even low access rates overall for some) such as Cambodia, Indonesia, Laos, Myanmar, North Korea, Afghanistan, Bangladesh, India, Nepal, and Pakistan, the centralized/decentralized approach of China and the Philippines are worth considering. For urban centres, environmentally sustainable approaches such as the Rayong City, Thailand biogas project would be a good project to follow. For off-grid areas, sustainable microsystems such as the SIBAT initiative should be easy to replicate. In fact, developing microsystems even in areas linked to the grid should be considered.

The solidarity approaches for galvanizing public opposition to privatization and restructuring is instructive for countries in the process of considering or in the process of implementing reforms. In Indonesia, for example, after the court case invalidating the electricity restructuring was won in 2004, the Parliament again passed a new law in September 2009 (Electricity Act 30/2009). This law introduces adjusted restructuring initiatives in the electricity sector. Avoiding the constitutional questions, the new law does not introduce unbundling and competitive market in generation. However, it relaxes the monopoly (with allowable partnership with private sector) of the state in engaging in electricity supply business. Private enterprises will be allowed to engage in power supply business, provided only that state enterprises are given first priority to provide the power supply business, and subject to regulation. It remains to be seen how the government will implement the law. The public sector union has again questioned the law before the constitutional court. It will be a setback if the coalition of forces that characterized previous advocacy is not united in their position on the current law.

IMAGINING AN ALTERNATIVE ELECTRICITY SECTOR

From the results of the study, we draw general lessons that we believe can inform the construction of holistic alternatives to privatization in the electricity sector in Asia (and beyond).

Public electricity systems work

The fact that public electricity systems work has clearly been shown by the historical state consolidation of electricity provision in Asia. The experiences of South Korea, China, Thailand, Malaysia, and even the Philippines, show that efficiency and equity objectives are achievable, and lessons can be emulated by poorer performers. After all, the viability of public electricity provision is inherent in the nature of this service. For one, mass electricity provision, from power generation to its delivery to end consumers, is a large, complex, and interdependent system that is compatible with centralized day-to-day operations and strategic planning. The interrelated decision and planning areas include forecasting demand, deciding the optimal generation mix based on plant construction costs, operating costs, and fuel availability and security, the optimal use/dispatch of the available generation mix at any given time, the response to unforeseen system failures, and the level of interconnectedness of the system. In addition to efficiencies from centralization, the state is also better suited to address important objectives in electricity provision that competing private firms can be expected to ignore. These include social objectives (such as equity), national security, and environmental sustainability, among others.

The "public ethos" of government is crucial to securing public electricity systems

As discussed earlier, public ethos was a key determinant in the historical consolidation of the sector, as well as in its defence or public-oriented restructuring. On the other hand, the erosion of public ethos results in a privatization trajectory for the sector. The latter is what happened in the Philippines, which adopted the unbundling/full privatization model. While the external influence from the ADB and the World Bank was at work, there was at the same time a progression of a hegemonic shift in government ideology that came with the overthrow of the Marcos dictatorship. At that point of transition, the popular mandate for political democratization was clear, but this was not the case for what economic agenda would be implemented. This provided an opening for an informal coalition of academics, government bureaucrats, and the private sector to push for a programme of radical market reforms. In a way, this reform agenda provided the incoming government with an economic perspective and concrete programme that contrasted with the Marcos regime. Since the growth of government enterprises and the heavy government regulations during the Marcos period were demonized as having fostered corruption and consolidation of political power, the programme of privatization, deregulation, and scaling back of government gained legitimacy.

The Philippines went full steam with industry restructuring by passing into law in June 2001 the Republic Act 9136, or the Electric Power Industry Reform Act (EPIRA). This law unbundled the electric power industry into generation, transmission, distribution, and supply. It declared that generation is not a public utility operation, thereby carving it out from the constitutional requirements of franchise and nationality limitations on ownership. It required that all of the National Power Corporation's generation assets and contracts with independent power producers be privatized and stripped the National Power Corporation of authority to build new capacity or enter into new supply contracts. EPIRA also created the National Transmission Company (TRANSCO) also expressly required by the law to be privatized. The implication of the importance of public ethos in government is that this is a major arena for political battle in the fight for public alternatives.

Unions should strive for solidarity with the community

The experience of electricity unions in Thailand, South Korea, and Indonesia was that their opposition to restructuring and privatization were met with distrust from other groups. Eventually, however, it was demonstrated that a unified position can be forged. It would be best for electricity unions to develop solidarity with different sectors of the community at the onset (and not only during critical moments of crisis), for the union to internalize broader-based public objectives in addition to their private interests.

Financing is a major constraint

Electricity projects, particularly in generation and transmission, are characterized by very large start-up costs, with returns coming in over a long period of useful asset life. This makes project financing an inherently challenging characteristic of electricity projects. As borrowing is not always ideal, other alternatives introduce dilemmas to a public system. For example, while an IPP contract erodes the public in electricity provision, it can be a tempting option for a government utility facing power shortages, depressed financial capacity, pressure from international institutions, and willing project sponsors. It is easy for a government utility to regard IPP contracting as a no-other-option financing choice, especially if there is asset transfer from the IPP to the government utility at the end of the contract term. Here it is the contracting terms (allocation of market, exchange rate, and fuel price risks) that become crucial.

Another approach is the conversion to a stock corporation for partial privatization to raise funds. Such corporatization with divestment dilutes government ownership. Furthermore, the introduction of private ownership increases the need to conform to commercial standards, thereby limiting management flexibility to promote non-commercial objectives. However, by retaining majority interest, the government can retain control over management and keep a measure of political control and oversight. Also, partial divestment can be a strategy to in fact strengthen government electricity provision by facilitating financing, new investment, and strategic partnership. Clearly, however, a vote for public ownership necessitates developing more public-friendly modes of financing. Possible strategies are through strategic partnerships/cooperation with like-minded countries and reasonable use of government financial institutions.

Radical demand-side management and energy planning is a must

In the face of urgent environmental concerns and the financial burdens of ever-increasing electricity systems, there needs to be aggressive regulation of the use of electricity by households and businesses. We should face the collective challenge of drawing the line between reasonable needs and excess, and between productive and wasteful use.

The role of an independent regulator needs to be re-examined

India represents an interesting case. With traditionally strong left-wing political parties and social movements, it makes one wonder how the ADB and World Bank unbundling models were carried forward, beginning in 1995, and sustained until it culminated in the national level electricity law in 2003. Kale (2004) explains the turn of events as having to do with the severe macroeconomic crisis that India had to deal with in the early 1990s, along with a growing section of economists and policy makers inspired by the global market reforms and questioning the Nehru-era policies of centralization and state ownership. Industrialists were also beginning to demand less state intervention in the sector.

But perhaps a facet of the unbundling model that has cushioned opposition of the privatization aspect was the element of introducing an independent regulatory agency. Similar to the dilemma faced by the environmentalists in South Korea and Thailand (where unbundling was envisioned to emasculate an environmentally destructive monopoly by allowing entry of decentralized non-renewable systems), the setting up of an independent regulatory agency was seen by some public interest advocates as an improvement in the system of governance by allowing greater transparency, participation by the public, and accountability. The problem, however, is that an independent regulator has been designed mainly to meet the requirements of a privatized system. For public models, public participation, transparency, and accountability mechanisms can take the place of an independent regulator.

Alternatives must be able to deal with trade-offs

As we seek alternatives, we will not always be faced with neat answers. The forces opposing public alternatives often raise the reality of trade-offs with other public interest objectives to question their feasibility or reasonability. These questions must be met squarely, rather than avoided or overlooked. For example, if we propose a radical change to demand side management in electricity, we have to spell out how we will deal with the possible loss of employment this could entail. If we push for decentralization in certain aspects of electricity provision, we should be able to show how we address possible losses in economies of scale and their resulting impact on the cost of electricity. If we advocate price subsidies, we need to explain how we can secure financial viability or fiscal capacity.

To conclude, electricity provision can be made to work under public ownership in an efficient, socially responsible, equitable, and environmentally sustainable manner. There is a choice. The challenge is to build social movements that will defend the public in everyday government policy and ultimately defend or reclaim the public ethos in government. This becomes plausible if labour groups, consumer groups, environmental advocates, progressive academics and scientists, and other public interest forces are able to work together to evolve a credible and politically powerful agenda for public electricity provision.

NOTES

1. TNB. www.tnb.com.my.
2. KEPCO. www.kepco.co.kr/eng.

REFERENCES

ADB (Asian Development Bank). 1995. *The bank's policy initiatives for the energy sector.* Manila, Philippines: ADB.

―――2000. *Energy 2000: Review of the energy sector policy of the Asian Development Bank.* Manila, Philippines: ADB.

Bijoor, S., Greacen, C. and Greacen, C.S. 2007. Citizen-oriented power sector reform in Thailand. In Integrated Environmental Policy Packages in the GMS Workshop, pp.1–22. Bangkok, Thailand, 11–13 July, www.palangthai.org/docs/PowerSectorReformThailand-BlueMoon-Palang-Thai.pdf.

Byrne, J., Glover, L., Lee, H., Wang, Y. and Yu, J. 2004. Electricity reform at a crossroads: Problems in South Korea's power liberalization strategy. *Pacific Affairs* 77(3): 493–516.

CSP (China State Power). n.d. Power reform—Brief Information. www.sp-china.com/powerReform/bi.html (accessed 21 April 2010).

FDC (Freedom from Debt Coalition). 2008. National study session: The quest for an alternative power industry reform programme in the Philippines. Quezon City, Philippines: FDC.

Funding Universe. 2009. Company history: Electricity generating authority of Thailand. www.fundinguniverse.com/company-histories/Electricity-Generating-Authority-of-Thailand-EGAT-Company-History.html (accessed 21 April 2010).

―――. 2009. Company history: Korea Electric Power Corporation. www.fundinguniverse.com/company-histories/Korea-Electric-Power-Corporation-Kepco-Company-History.html (accessed 21 April 2010).

Gomez, E.T. 2009. The rise and fall of capital: Corporate Malaysia in historical perspective. *Journal of Contemporary Asia* 39(3): 345–381.

Greacen, C.S. and Greacen, C. 2004. Thailand's electricity reforms: Privatization of benefits and socialization of costs and risks. *Pacific Affairs* 77(3): 517–541.

HPPF (Healthy Public Policy Foundation). 2010. MSP survey data on electricity alternatives in Thailand. Mimeo.

IEA (International Energy Agency). 2010. Electricity access database. www.iea. org/weo/database_electricity/electricity_access_database.htm (accessed 22 September 2010).

Jomo, K.S. and Tan, W.S. 2003. Privatization and re-nationalization in Malaysia: A survey. Working paper. Kuala Lumpur, Malaysia: University of Malaya. www.unpan1.un.org/intradoc/groups/public/documents/un/unpan021546.pdf.

Kale, S.S. 2004. Current reforms: The politics of policy change in India's electricity sector. *Pacific Affairs* 77(3): 467–491.

KNEWU (Korean National Electrical Workers Union). n.d. Special report of KNEWU. Mimeo.

Malaluan, N.A. 2003. *The Philippine electric power industry reform: A tragedy of ADB and World Bank private sector fundamentalism and unaccountable government.* Quezon City, Philippines: AER (Action for Economic Reforms).

Manibog, F., Dominguez, R. and Wegner, S. 2003. *Power for development: A review of the World Bank Group's experience with private participation in the electricity sector.* Washington, DC: World Bank.

Mun, Y. 2002. Power sector reform in South Korea. In Asia Power Sector Reforms Workshop 2002, pp. 96–112. Chulalongkorn University Campus, Bangkok, www.prayaspune.org/energy/41_07korea.pdf.

Nakaya, N. 2006. China's socialist market economy and the reconstitution of state-owned enterprises. In JACSM (Japan Association for Comparative Studies of Management (Ed), *Business and society: New perspective for comparative studies of management*, pp. 28–41. Kyoto, Japan: Bunrikaku.

Nakhooda, S., Dixit, S. and Dubash, N. K. 2007. *Empowering people: A governance analysis of electricity.* Washington, DC: WRI (World Resources Institute).

NEPO (National Energy Policy Office—Thailand). 2000. Electricity supply industry reform and Thailand power pool. www.eppo.go.th/power/FF-E/pw-reform-1-main-E.html (accessed 29 March 2010).

Nuntavorakarn, S. 2002. The reform of the electricity sector in Thailand: A civil society perspective. In Electricity Sector Reforms in Asia Workshop: Experiences and Strategies. World Social Forum, Mumbai, India, 19 January. www. prayaspune.org/energy/41_05thai.pdf.

Prayas. n.d. Maharashtra Intervention. www.prayaspune.org/peg/energy_pbl. php?cat_id=3&sub_cat_id=5&child_cat_id=1&#links (accessed 31 March 2010).

Sari, A.P. 2001 Power sector restructuring and public benefits. Word Resources Institute (WRI). www.pdf.wri.org/power_politics/indonesia.pdf.

Seymour, F. and Sari, A.P. 2002. Indonesia: Electricity reform under economic crisis. In Dubash, N.K. (Ed), *Power politics: Equity and environment in electricity reform*, pp. 75–95. Washington, DC: WRI (World Resources Institute).

SIBAT (Sibol ng Agham at Teknolohiya). 2005. *Lessons from the field: An assessment of SIBAT experiences on community-based microhydro power systems.* Quezon City, Philippines: SIBAT.

TNB (Tenaga Nasional Berhad). n.d. About TNB: History. www.tnb.com.my/ about-tnb/history.html (accessed 15 March 2010).

Tumiwa, F. 2002. Power sector restructuring in Indonesia: Viable solution or recipe for disaster? In Asian Power Reform Workshops 2002. www.prayaspune. org/energy/41_03indo.pdf (accessed 31 March 2010).

US Energy Information Administration. International energy statistics. www. tonto.eia.doe.gov/cfapps/ipdbproject/IEDIndex3.cfm?tid=2&pid=2&aid=12 (accessed 8 September 2010).

Williams, J.H. and Dubash, N.K. 2004. Asian electricity reform in historical perspective. *Pacific Affairs* 77(3): 411–436.

World Bank. 1993. *The World Bank's role in the electric power sector: Policies for effective institutional, regulatory, and financial reform*. Washington, DC: World Bank.

———. Private participation in infrastructure database: Subsector data for Energy—Electricity.   www.ppi.worldbank.org/explore/ppi_exploreSubSector.aspx?SubSectorID=3 (accessed 15 March 2010).

Yang, H. 2006. *Overview of the Chinese electricity industry and its current issues*. Cambridge Working Papers in Economics 0617. Cambridge, UK: Faculty of Economics, University of Cambridge. www.ideas.repec.org/p/cam/camdae/0617.html.

Yeh, E.T. and Lewis, J.I. 2004. State power and the logic of reform in China's electricity sector. *Pacific Affairs* 77(3): 437–465.

Zhang, X. and Parsons, J.E. 2008. *Market power and electricity market reform in Northeast China*. Cambridge, MA: CEEPR (Center for Energy and Environmental Policy Research).

Africa
Regional Overview

Greg Ruiters

Africa is often portrayed as a lost cause—cursed by geography (the world's largest desert, untold varieties of insects, and lethal illnesses), topography (deep valleys but few navigable rivers), and too many resources that invite predators and stir up conflicts (oil, diamonds). Its treatment by Europe's barbaric transatlantic slave traders knows no equal in history (Rodney 1972). Wars of dispossession turned Africans into refugees, and up until the 1960s, forced labour was widely practiced by the Belgians, the Portuguese, and the South African white minority regime. In the 1990s, the majority of Africa's population were peasants and agricultural workers; it had half the world's refugees and displaced persons; external repayments on debt exceeded total resource flows into the continent (Cheru 1994, 61). The continent is described as "tragic", with Africans either dying of HIV/AIDS or slaughtering each other. Despite receiving significant foreign aid from the benevolent West, Africa shows little progress for the largess of its former tormentors (for this view see, for example, Guest 2004).

Many scholars dismiss the African post-colonial state as bloated and criminal, while at the same time denouncing it as weak and lacking in capacity to plan and implement basic policies (Mkandawire 2005). Alongside the relative absence of the state have emerged donors, non-governmental organizations (NGOs) and churches, which are celebrated as a civil society alternative. In the health sector, for example, mission hospitals are often the only reliable service available; in water, NGOs have helped with rural water schemes; and in electricity many who can afford it buy their own generators (Cheru 1994, Olukoju 2004). The wealthy rely on privatized services, while poor people rely on informal private providers or poor state services if they are lucky to get access, and peasants bypass the state, "whom they regard as their number one enemy" (Cheru 1994, 64). Proponents of private sector expansion in health care continue to argue that those who can afford it should buy their own health care in the private sector and governments should contract private providers to serve those who cannot. This approach is promoted as a matter of common sense. In Africa, however the term "private" sector can be misleading, for it includes the myriad of unregulated, informal small-scale suppliers of services (water vendors, spaza shops) and private corporations and faith-based organizations, which do not fall under state/public administration. Those trying to reform the state through civil service codes of conduct and rewards for good governance invariably do so "to arrest profound struggles and transformations taking place in Africa" (Zeleza 1997, 125).

Urban services in African cities are poorly planned and maintained and are compromised by what is seen as disorderly cities in permanent "crisis-mode" (Gandy 2006). In a self-fulfilling prophecy and partly to ensure that the private sector "alternative" would be hegemonic, in the 1980s the World Bank insisted that the numbers of public sector personnel and programmes be cut so the state could be lean and services be run by the private sector. In the wake of state retrenchment, on order of the international financial institutions (IFIs), the extremity of "disorder" found in cities such as Lagos is a major impediment (Gandy 2006, 252), but other scholars see the "self-service city" as a virtue and as an "alternative" (Simone 2005). But since water, food, and energy are "women's work", women carry the burdens of infrastructural problems facing African towns and cities (Schytler and Zhou 1995). Whatever one's view, the "problem" is compounded by the largest wave of urbanization in human history with millions of people moving into cities, which already have "terminally overstretched infrastructure" (UN-Habitat 2003, Davis 2006). Rural areas, meanwhile, have been left to languish as the idea of state national planning took a back seat in the last 20 years under structural adjustment programmes.

The situation gets worse as many academics argue that it is not only the state that is dysfunctional but "society" as well. The "state-society school" (Chazan 1988) argues that African societies are plagued by patronage, which has strong "society roots", meaning that the European style of rational-legal bureaucratic norms for bureaucracy cannot apply in Africa. For Chabal and Daloz (1999, 243), the continent's rooted "neopatrimonial" political systems do not depend on development in the Western sense, and elites find ways to translate social disorder into patronage resources that "shore up the loyalty of their client networks". Another version of this is that Africans did not want development in the first place; it was a Eurocentric idea of the development industry; developmentalism invented by the West (see Escobar 1995, Sachs 1993) and used by the elites to string the masses along a path doomed to fail.

With this kind of "Afro-pessimism", nothing positive could happen on the continent (Mamdani 1996, Arrighi 2002). As Zeleza (1997, 127) notes, "Afro-pessimism represented a discursive closure against conceptions of different futures for Africa outside of the prescriptions of the hegemonic neoliberal developmentalism".

And yet, there are counter-narratives. One, formulated by neoliberal institutions such as the World Bank, has it that Africa is the new investment frontier and is ripe for a 21st century economic "take off"—a continent full of "entrepreneurs" just waiting for bits of finance and infrastructure to allow them to build a robust "small and medium enterprise" economy. Combined with a wealth of natural resources, and efforts to promote "good governance", the continent is seen as a (potential) success story for big and small scale capital for the first time in decades.

However, there are those who take "development" seriously by insisting that issues such as equity, civil society and human rights, gender, and identity be incorporated into critiques of colonial forms of development and Euro-centric versions of progress. They also insist that we cannot understand uneven development in Africa without a larger picture of regions and world development and turbulence over the last 50 years (Arrighi 2002, Mkandawire 2005).

Yet another narrative is equally positive. Anti-neoliberal and people centred, it proposes a range of appropriate "alternatives" that are both home-grown *and* international, involving democratizing the state and building popular participation in service delivery, capable of drawing solidarity and lessons from other places. A host of NGOs opposing privatization of health and water have taken this line.

But while the obstacles are still considerable, new opportunities are emerging. In the 1960s and early 1970s, considerable progress was made in health, water, and energy, sustained by economic growth based on export earnings. With the oil shock from the mid-1970s, this changed dramatically. Deteriorating terms of trade was dramatic as earnings fell from US$90 billion to US$50 billion between 1980 and 1986 alone. The two decades from 1980 to 2000 saw the debt to GDP ratio rise from 23% to 66%. Thus the 1980s was described as the "lost decade" as external debt grew and governments were told to privatize and cut back social spending under structural adjustment programmes. Africa was effectively redlined as investment dried up and the foreign banks demanded payment on loans. With 10% of the world's population in 1996, Africa garnered only 3% of world trade.

In this context, the objective need for alternatives became manifest in the 1990s with the widespread failure of the neoliberal model. A new crop of leaders, untainted by narrow nationalism, emerged. Buoyed by civil society and "third wave" democracy, these leaders embraced privatization, did not respect borders, and became involved in cross-border wars. For this kind of conduct, Museveni of Uganda, Kagame of Rwanda, and Zenawi of Ethiopia stood out in this period (Mkandawire 2005, 14).

In thinking about "alternatives to privatization", therefore, we cannot ignore the particularity of Africa's insertion into the global economy and its international salience, which has shifted from the Cold War period to the post-1990s. During the former, the USSR and Cuba played a key role in Africa. Since the 1990s, Africa's resources have become more important to the now 'BRIC' countries. China's trade with Africa increased tenfold as China seeks to secure oil and mineral supplies from the continent. This new "scramble" for resources is different from earlier versions, however. In 2000, for example, China voluntarily waived $1.2 billion in sovereign African debt (*The Economist,* November 3, 2006). As Arrighi (2009, 207) argues, China invests where no Western power will and provides development assistance with no strings attached. Still, the almost complete absence of intra-African trade between countries— recently at less than 5%—remains a disturbing feature of these still extro-verted economies.

In addition, the liberation of South Africa in 1994 saw South African companies "re-colonize" the rest of the continent, invoking Thabo Mbeki's "African Renaissance" (Miller 2005). In the early 2000s, South Africa accounted for more than 40% of new investments on the conti-nent, moving into first place ahead of the US and UK, although China has also become a major investor and is now a key trade and investment competitor. In particular, South Africa dominates the Southern Afri-can Development Community (SADC) region, accounting for 71% of regional GDP, and foreign investors see South Africa as a conduit into the region.

But Africa needs to be seen on its own terms, not as a continent try-ing to imitate or catch up with others at a "higher stage of development". The pursuit of mega-projects (dams, stadiums, luxury hotels) has proved a disaster for social justice and people-centred development (Cheru 1994, 61). In our thinking of African "alternatives", then, we follow Mamdani (1996) in rejecting ahistorical and teleological comparisons with the rest of the world. But to particularize Africa as completely exceptional is to com-mit the opposite error, where solidarities and similarities between Africa and other places in the global South are erased and differences fetishized. Africans are very much part of a global economy, labour migrations and culture (often involuntary and sometimes on request).

Moreover, Africa as a "late entrant" has the opportunity to learn from others' mistakes. African states can also learn from each other and from the continent's past. We also need to look towards opening up the imagi-native space for incorporating the strengths of the past (especially values developed in precolonial communal life).

The issue of scale is also critical. Whereas we cannot bypass the sov-ereignty of the 54 states on the continent, it is sometimes better to scale up by organizing resources regionally. Health, water, and energy can be cross-border processes. Yet, in many cases, small-scale projects might also be suitable. The urban bias of development projects and elites tends to ignore the peasant and small-scale farmer in favour of luxury export goods and cash crops (Cheru 1994). In addition, in reclaiming and rebuild-ing accountable nation states, imaginative South-South cooperation along the lines of a "new Bandung" can radically change development prospects (Arrighi 2009).

In the course of doing alternatives dialogically—from below, above and regionally—better ones will arise. Frontline workers and professionals committed to community vocation should be accorded local and national respect. The notion of national and public interests and public services and solidarity should be operationalized at many scales (not only the parochial).

In principle Africans, not Europeans or Chinese, must develop Africa, while solidarity and advice are to be welcomed (Onimode 1994, 163). Self-reliance and diversification need to be promoted as solutions to external dependency. Finally, even if we recognize failures in African states compared to Asian states, it must be accepted that African elites and social movements promoted development as an ideal. To concede, this is an important starting point for more detailed consideration of alternatives.

REFERENCES

Arrighi, G. 2002. The African crisis: world systemic and regional aspects. *New Left Review* 15: 1–38.

Arrrighi, G. 2009. The winding paths of capital: Interviews with David Harvey. *New Left Review* 56: 61–94.

Chabal, P. and Daloz, J. 1999. *Africa works: Disorder as a political instrument.* Bloomington: Indiana University Press.

Chazan, N. 1988. State and society in Africa, images and challenges. In Rothchild, D. and Chazan, N. (Eds), *The precarious balance, state and society in Africa,* pp. 325–342. Boulder, CO: Westview.

Cheru, F. 1994. Renewing and restoring democracy in Africa. In Coetzee, S., Turok, B. and Beukes, E. (Eds), *Transition to democracy, breaking out of apartheid,* pp. 135–147. Johannesburg: IFAA (Institute for African Alternatives).

Davis, M. 2006. *Planet of slums.* New York: Verso.

Gandy, M. 2006. Planning, anti-planning and the infrastructure crisis facing metropolitan Lagos. In Murray, M. and Myers, G. (Eds), *Cities in contemporary Africa,* pp. 247–264. New York: Palgrave.

Guest, R. 2004. *The shackled continent, Africa's past present and future.* London: McMillan.

Mamdani, M. 1996. *Citizen and subject.* Princeton: Princeton University Press.

Mkandawire, T. 2005. *African intellectuals.* Dakar: Codesria Books.

Miller, D. 2005. New regional imaginaries in post-apartheid Southern Africa. Retail workers at a mall in Zambia. *Journal of Southern African Studies* 31(19): 67–72.

Olukoju, A. 2004. "Never expect power always": Electricity consumers' response to monopoly, corruption and insufficient services in Nigeria. *African Affairs* 103: 51–71.

Onimode, B. 1994. African perspectives on adjustment strategies and alternative development strategies. In Coetzee, S., Turok, B. and Beukes, E. (Eds), *Transition to democracy, breaking out of apartheid,* pp. 124–139. Johannesburg: IFAA.

Rodney, W. 1972. *How Europe underdeveloped Africa.* London: Bugle-L'Ouverture Publications and Dar Salaam: Tanzania Publishing House.

Sachs, W. 1993. The development dictionary. Johannesburg: Witwatersrand University Press.

Schlyter, A. and Zhou, A. 1995. *Gendered research on urbanisation, planning, housing and everyday life*. Harare: Zimbabwe Women's Resource Centre.

Simone, M. 2005. *Urban Africa, changing contours of survival in the city*. Dakar: Codesria Books.

The Economist. 2006. China and Africa, 3 November. http://www.economist.com/agenda/displaystory.cfm?story-id=8126261 (accessed 9 December 2009).

UN-Habitat. 2003. *The challenge of slums: Global report on human settlements*. UNHSP (United Nations Human Settlements Programme). London, Sterling, VA.: Earthscan Publications.

Zeleza, P. 1997. *Manufacturing African studies and crises*. Dakar: Codesria Books.

11 African Triage

Assessing Alternatives to Health Care Privatization South of the Sahara

Yoswa M. Dambisya and
Hyacinth Eme Ichoku

Health plays a central role in human development. In recognition of this fact, the United Nations adopted the Millennium Declaration, with eight Millennium Development Goals (MDGs), three of which are directly health related. Primary health care (PHC) is the cornerstone of the health systems of many countries in Africa and elsewhere. The nature of services provided through PHC, in accordance with the WHO and UNICEF definition is:

> Essential health care based on practical, scientifically sound and socially acceptable methods and technology made universally accessible to individuals and families in the community through their full participation and at a cost that community and country can afford to maintain at every stage of their development in the spirit of self-determination. (1978, Article VI)

PHC is an approach to health care that is not only primary (first contact) or curative but also comprehensive (WHO 2008). The PHC approach to health care is especially relevant in the Sub-Saharan African (SSA) context given the high burden of disease, much of which is attributable to infectious diseases that can be controlled through improvements in education, the economy, the physical environment, agriculture, and general and social development—all of which are encompassed by PHC. It is estimated that about 65% of deaths in SSA result from communicable diseases, including malaria, tuberculosis and human immunodeficiency virus/acquired immune deficiency syndrome (HIV/AIDS), perinatal and maternal, and nutritional disorders (Wurthwein et al, 2001).

The subregion has poor health indicators, with high maternal mortality ratios (MMR), high infant mortality rates (IMR), and high under five mortality rates. Life expectancy in the region varies from 74 years in Seychelles and Mauritius to 39 years in Zimbabwe (WHOSIS 2009). There is a high prevalence of HIV/AIDS in many SSA countries—with Swaziland (38.8%), Lesotho (28.9%), and Zimbabwe (24.6%) being the hardest hit—and AIDS is among the main causes of death (UNGASS and UNAIDS 2008).

There is also increasing concern about the rising morbidity and mortality due to non-communicable diseases (NCDs) such as diabetes mellitus, hypertension, cancer, endocrine disorders, and cardiovascular disorders following urbanization and the adoption of a Western lifestyle by many in the region (Turshen 1977, Unwin et al, 2001, BeLue et al, 2009). Indeed, there is evidence that NCDs are responsible for 15–25% of annual deaths in Tanzania for the 15–59 age groups and that the prevalence rate of diabetes mellitus in urban areas in Tanzania and townships in South Africa is 5–8%, while the prevalence rate for hypertension is 20–33%.

In many developed countries with far fewer disease burdens than SSA, health expenditure is more than 15% of the total state budget. Africa spends about 5% of its GDP on health as against the global average of 8.69%, and relative to other regions, a higher fraction of SSA's total health expenditure (10.7%) is accounted for by external assistance. SSA's average per capita health expenditure ($111) is far below the global average ($790). Similarly, the average government contribution to the health system per capita is $52, which, though higher than Southeast Asia ($28), falls much lower than the global average ($455). A large number of SSA countries included in this study spend less than $50 per capita as compared to $6,719 in the US, or even the $315 and $355 achieved by Algeria and Tunisia, respectively (WHO 2008).

Various studies have estimated that the informal health sector, despite its many shortcomings in terms of quality of service, provides treatment for 15–83% of childhood illnesses in Africa (Snow et al, 1992, Molyneux et al, 1999, Goodman et al, 2007). But as Mackintosh (2003, 2006) observed, the uncontrolled expansion of the informal sector is a striking aspect of privatization and commercialization of the health sector.

The above characteristics—high disease burden, poor macroeconomic environment, expansive and deepening household poverty, and the development of a large informal health market in the region—are critical for considering viable alternatives to privatization and commercialization in the subregion because they determine the nature and texture of possible alternatives to conventional public provision of health services. Following the economic crises of the 1980s, many SSA countries experienced social and economic upheavals, and the public health systems of most countries of the subregion started to wobble very badly.

DEFINING "ALTERNATIVES" IN THE SUB-SAHARAN AFRICAN CONTEXT

We refer to "alternatives" in this study as health systems, which are neither privatized nor commercialized. The former refers to all forms of private sector participation in service delivery. Commercialization, on the other hand, can refer to public service entities that operate much like private providers, characterized by: increased provision of health services through market relations and based on ability to pay even if such service is provided by or operated by the state; investment in the production of health services for the purpose of making profit; and expansion of health care financing based on individual payment or private insurance (Mackintosh 2003).

Hence, the critical elements of both commercialization and privatization of health services are market-oriented, profit-motivated financing and provision of health services whether by individual entrepreneurs or state corporations. In particular, privatization involves the devolution of health care responsibilities of the state to statutory quasi-autonomous non-governmental organizations (QUANGOs) or authorities, which then control and manage health services on behalf of the state as a corporation. Thus, state ownership does not necessarily mean non-market or non-profit; and private ownership or control does not necessarily imply the opposite.

The most obvious models of "alternative" health care provision are therefore the non-corporatized, state and non-state not-for-profit health care providers. Thus, alternatives considered here assume non-corporatized, non-commercialized state-provided health services and different variations of it as the bedrock of the health system, while other non-state alternatives are considered supplementary to this.

The private sector is wide and varied in terms of both its typology and the range of activities. Private health providers include traditional healers, community-managed health facilities, faith-based and other non-governmental organizations (NGOs) owned or managed health facilities, and private for-profit and not-for-profit facilities. Any institution or organization that provides an alternative model to market-oriented provision of services, private sector investment, or private financing of health services, will be considered, *prima facie,* to qualify as an alternative. Its viability and sustainability as an alternative will be assessed using a set of specified parameters, including equity, efficiency, quality, sustainability, participation, and accountability (see Chapter 2, this volume, for details on research methodology). Approaches that address the substantive business of health service provision, provide non-market-oriented investment options, or provide non-private financing of health care are therefore considered alternatives to privatization and commercialization.

THE SCOPE OF THE RESEARCH AND METHOD

This study is periscopic in intent as it does not aim to provide in-depth details about identified alternatives but rather to cover as many alternatives as possible within SSA, irrespective of the country where found. Since examples of alternatives are difficult to come by, or are not located in every country in SSA, the focus is on those countries that offer feasible alternatives.

Our review made use of secondary data generated through a thorough search of relevant databases for SSA as well as interviews and literature reviews as follows:

- The identification of key informants in different parts of SSA, particularly those engaged in health-related professional activities either as researchers, professional caregivers, and implementers of health policies.
- Questionnaire interviews: a number of individuals and institutions identified in different countries in the subregion were interviewed through e-mail. The e-mail interview enabled us to identify possible alternatives to commercialization and privatization in the different countries.
- Colleagues at different academic conferences and meetings were solicited for information on alternatives to privatization and commercialization in the health sector in their regions and countries.
- A search for regional and country-specific initiatives was undertaken for documentation related to new initiatives in health provision, health financing, and methods of provider remunerations that are new and that offer viable alternatives to privatization and commercialization in the region.
- Internet search (including WHO database, United Nations Development Programme [UNDP] database, World Bank database, Google, and Google Scholar search engines), using different combinations of search terms such as health insurance, mutual health organizations, mission hospitals, faith-based organizations, and community-based health insurance (CBHI) schemes. We also searched for information specific to all SSA countries, through ministries of health websites.
- Journal articles on the subject matter relating to SSA were reviewed.
- Official reports, such as those commissioned by Partners for Health Reform Plus, and the United States Agency for International Development (USAID), were also reviewed.

Every effort was made to ensure that comprehensive information was obtained and analyzed about all the viable alternatives that are available in the region. We are mindful of the fact, however, that some initiatives have been undocumented and are therefore inaccessible, and we may have missed others. Nonetheless, we believe that this report represents a good coverage of such initiatives within the SSA region.

IDENTIFIED ALTERNATIVES

In this study, three types of alternatives to privatization and commercialization were identified, namely:

- CBHI, also known as mutual health organizations (MHOs)
- National health insurance schemes (NHISs), and regional ones
- Faith- or church-based health organizations (FBOs)

CBHI and NHIS are to some degree directed at addressing challenges of health financing both from the supply and demand sides and tend to have as one of their aims equitable health care financing and/or financial risk protection for the poor, though there is an increasing number of CBHI schemes that also provide health services (Ndiaye et al, 2007). FBOs, on the other hand generally focus on health delivery although they have also, in some instances, motivated community-based financing for systems affiliated to them (Atim 1998). These alternatives are discussed, in turn, with examples and brief evaluations of their pros and cons.

COMMUNITY-BASED HEALTH INSURANCE

CBHI, also referred to as MHOs or *mutuelles de santé* (*mutuelles*), aims to extend the benefits of insurance to populations that have been excluded from traditional social protection schemes, which in most cases means rural populations and those working in the urban informal sector (Atim 2009). Atim defines the MHO as a "voluntary, non-profit insurance scheme, formed on the basis of an ethic of mutual aid, solidarity and collective pooling of risks, in which the members participate effectively in its management and functioning".

The potential benefits of CBHI schemes include resource mobilization for health, financial protection from catastrophic health costs, and negotiation for quality gains in health services for their members (Ekman 2004, Atim 2009). According to the Africa Union, CBHI schemes have tended to grow where user fees are high, good quality health care is available, solidarity networks or bonds are strong, and a tradition of self-help and organization exists (Atim 2009).

Atim (1998) identified the main types of MHOs as including:

- Traditional social solidarity networks which tend to bring urban migrants of the same ethnic and cultural origins together to foster their welfare through solidarities in times of sickness, burials, births, marriages, and other significant events
- MHO solidarity movements—based on rural or urban communities, trade unions, religious associations, professional organizations
- Community financing health insurance or low community participation model of community health financing which is usually motivated, organized and managed by the health facility with minimum participation of the community in the management of the scheme

- Co-managed or high participation community model that is usually motivated and managed by the community but with a negotiated arrangement with the facility that provides health services
- Medical Aid Associations—the most advanced form of MHOs based on formal insurance principles and regulations

MHOs have become a common feature of health care arrangements in many SSA countries. They are also identified with decentralized health care systems, following the inability of governments in the region to adequately fund health services and given the relative success of community-based microfinance systems in many SSA countries.

Table 11.1 illustrates the number of schemes and population covered in some countries of West Africa, but MHOs are not limited to West African countries, as the selected case studies will reveal. Table 11.1 also shows that only very small percentages of the population in each country have been covered. However, as case studies of the Rwanda *Mutuelles de santé* and the Ghana Community Health Planning (CHP) models indicate, community-based schemes can easily be leveraged into national health programmes through appropriate national policies and financial support. In fact, it has been suggested that the MHOs can serve as a learning model for fund administrators and social solidarity (Bänighausen and Suaerborn 2002). The Ugandan and Tanzanian models illustrate the motivations and the facilitation roles of ministries of health and donor agencies in the emergence of some of the schemes. They also illustrate the many problems these schemes face.

The typology of CBHI/MHO schemes using the framework developed for this research is single non-profit sector (SiNP), though some could be classified as non-profit/non-profit partnerships (NPNPP). An example of the latter is provider-based MHOs, which are driven by the need for cost recovery

Table 11.1 Coverage of MHOs in West Africa

Country	No. of schemes	Population covered	% Population covered
Mali	80	198,006	1.46
Côte d'Ivoire	40	235,280	1.30
Senegal	149	119,300	1.02
Niger	19	48,700	0.35
Ghana	45	61,600	0.28
Togo	25	16,325	0.27
Guinea	111	23,844	0.25

Source: Vialle-Valentin et al, 2008.

by the service provider (Derriennic et al, 2005). As is the case for Rwanda, there is also a partnership between government and the MHOs, and so the arrangement is that of a public/non-profit partnership (PuNPP).

Example 1—Mutuelles de santé in Rwanda

Rwanda presents one of the most dramatic recent experiences of CBHI in Sub-Saharan Africa, with wide population coverage. From the 1960s, health care was provided for free in Rwanda, with public subsidies through infrastructure, equipment, personnel, drugs, and other supplies. The economic problems of the 1980s and 1990s led to a dilapidated system, with poor quality of care. In 1992, the government introduced community participation for financing and management of health care, based on the Bamako Initiative (Sekabaraga 2008). By October 2007, the schemes had reportedly covered 6,702,391 beneficiaries or 75% of the population of the country, while by 2009 Rwanda boasted of being the only country in Africa with a 85% participation rate in MHOs.

To support the growth of the schemes, the government has created a special solidarity or risk-pooling fund, into which transfers from the Ministry of Finance via the Ministry of Health (MOH) are made to cover the costs of indigents and people living with HIV/AIDS. The Global Fund is providing financial support for five years to cover the government subsidy.

The MHOs are backed by government policy, which sets out the scope and regulation of MHOs. According to the official policy document: "The general objective of the policy is to assist grassroots communities and Districts to establish health insurance systems that will promote improvement of their financial accessibility to health care, protection of households against financial risks associated with diseases and strengthening of social inclusion in health" (MOH, Rwanda 2004, 10).

The scheme covers a Minimum Package of Activities, including prenatal consultation, postnatal consultation, vaccination, family planning, nutritional service, curative consultations, hospitalization, simple childbirth, essential and generic drugs, laboratory analyses, minor surgical operations, health education, and transportation of the patient to the district hospital. The hospitals offer a Complementary Package of Activities, which covers, *inter alia*, consultation by a doctor, hospitalization, caesarean operations, minor and major surgical operation, referred serious malaria, all diseases of children from 0–5 years, medical imaging, and laboratory analyses.

The mutuelles are, however, confronted with challenges that are organizational, technical, and operational. At the organizational level:

- The voluntary nature of subscription to mutual insurance leads to low levels of subscription. People who frequently fall sick are more likely to subscribe to *mutuelles*, resulting in an adverse selection that threatens financial sustainability.

- *Mutuelles* do not cover major risks like surgery.
- Premiums are fixed, not according to the real costs of care, but rather the contributing capacity of the population.
- There is a lack of a specific legal framework guaranteeing their moral and legal status, their independence, and autonomy.

At the technical and operational level the problems are:

- Over-utilization of the services by subscribers who hastily solicit health care services.
- Non-coverage of health care costs by partner health facilities due, on the one hand, to the low level of contributions and inadequate number of subscribers, and, on the other hand, the low level of risk sharing between sick people and healthy people.
- Abusive prescription of drugs by some health facilities.
- Poor quality of the care provided in some health facilities.
- Over-invoicing of mutual health insurance by some health facilities.
- Low management capacities of some mutual health committees.
- Benevolent nature of membership of mutual health committees.
- Lack of grants to mutual health insurance, in general, and, particularly, for bearing the cost of treatment in hospitals.

Example 2—Community health fund (CHF) initiative in Tanzania

The CHF was conceived by the government of Tanzania in collaboration with the World Bank's International Development Association and other donors as an approach to improve the financial sustainability in the health sector and to increase access to health services. CHF is a prepayment insurance scheme for rural people, based on the concept of risk sharing and empowering communities in health care decisions, while also promoting cost sharing through local participation (Baraldes and Carreras 2003).

CHF was piloted in 1996 in one district (Igunga) and later expanded to other areas with the intention of covering the whole country. By the end of 2006, CHF was operating in 69 of the 92 councils (Mtei and Mulligan 2007). The scheme aimed to grant access to basic health care services to poor and vulnerable populations in the rural areas and the informal sector in the country, rather than to raise additional funds.

The Community Health Fund Act of 2001 sets the objectives of the CHF as following:

- Mobilize financial resources from the community in order to provide health care services for members
- Provide quality and affordable health care services through sustainable financial mechanisms

- Improve health care services management in the communities through decentralization by empowering the communities in making decisions and by contributing on matters affecting their health. (CHF 2001, 5)

CHF membership contributions are decided at the council level, and each household contributes the same amount of fee, which varies between councils from Tshs5,000 (about US$4) to Tshs10,000 per year (MOH, Tanzania 2005). For that contribution, households receive access to care for the whole year, while households that do not participate in CHF are required to pay a user fee at the health facilities.

Revenues from members' contributions are matched by a 100% grant from the government (commonly known as *tele kwa tele*). The CHF Act provides for user fees paid at public health centres and dispensaries to be used as a source of funding to the CHF (CHF 2001). Other sources of funds include grants from councils, organizations, and donors. CHF contribution to Tanzanian health sector financing is rather modest, accounting for about 15% of total revenue, while user fees at primary facilities account for 85% (MOHSW 2006, Mtei et al, 2007).

CHF faces the challenge of low enrollment rates and early drop outs in membership; in many schemes, enrollment has dropped where it was once relatively high (Chee et al, 2002, Shaw 2002, Msuya et al, 2004, Musau 2004, Mhina 2005). Chee et al (2002) in their assessment of the CHF in Hanang district found that membership reached a peak of 23% in 1999, then dropped in 2001 to around 3% of total households, and this fell further to 2.2% in 2003 (Musau 2004).

Shaw (2002) argues that one of the reasons for low enrollment rates could be the small user fees set in public facilities because they give little incentive for community members to join an alternative financing system like the CHF. User fees in some councils are set at Tshs1,000 per visit at health centre level, and many community members are more willing to pay the user fee rather than pay the higher CHF premium (Mhina 2005). Similarly, high CHF membership fees set by some councils are also likely to be a barrier to enrollment (Mtei et al, 2007).

The barriers to higher enrollment in the scheme are summarized in Table 11.2. Notwithstanding these limitations, CHF has improved access to health facilities for the poor. Being a CHF member improved the chance of seeking health care from formal health care providers, compared to non-members, and CHF membership also reduced the use of alternative medical care such as self-medication and traditional healers especially for the poor (Msuya et al, 2004). Moreover, membership in the CHF reduces the risk of households selling their assets for the sake of getting money for treatment during a disease outbreak.

Whereas CHF schemes have great potential to improve access for poorer groups, by removing payment at the point of use and allowing members to

Table 11.2   Reasons for Low Enrollment in CHF, Tanzania

Reason for low enrollment	Source
Low public sector user fees vs. higher CHF premiums	Shaw 2002, Mhina 2005
High CHF membership fees	Mtei et al, 2007
Inability of the poor to pay membership contributions	Kamuzora and Gilson 2007
Poor quality of care, lack of trust in CHF manager	Bonu et al, 2003, Kamuzora and Gilson 2007
Lack of trust in CHF managers (average and wealthy community members)	Kamuzora and Gilson 2007
No need to protect against risk of illness (average and wealthy community members)	Kamuzora and Gilson 2007
Poor sensitization, lack of information	Msuya et al, 2004
Lack of information on CHF from district managers	Kamuzora and Gilson 2007
Top-down approach to CHF	Mtei et al, 2007
Low income and income unreliability among community members	Msuya et al, 2004
Introduction of NHIF, which removed the public servants	Mwendo 2001, Mhina 2005
Non-coverage of referral care	Mwendo 2001, Mhina 2005
Poor staff attitudes	Mwendo 2001, Mhina 2005
Broad exemption policies, which leave a limited number of people contributing to CHF	Mhina 2005, MOH, Tanzania 2006

pay when they can afford to (flexibility in contribution), in practice even relatively small contributions may be too high for the poorest to pay (Bennett et al, 2004). The MOH itself is concerned about weaknesses in management and accountability. There may not be the required financial and management capacity to handle the fund, in addition to delivering services to patients (MOH, Tanzania 2006). Districts are not clear on CHF management rules and procedures, and there reportedly was mismanagement of CHF funds in about 27% of CHF implementers. In other instances, CHF funds were not utilized and hence remained idle at the district level. An assessment by the MOH showed that not all councils conducted regular audits or reported to community members (MOH, Tanzania 2003, Mtei et al, 2007).

Example 3—Community-based health planning and services initiative in Ghana

Another CBHI scheme that has been used effectively to foster health care utilization and overcome barriers posed by scarce resources is the community-based health planning and service (CHPS) initiative developed at the Navrongo Research Centre in Ghana in the 1990s. This is a public-community partnership. The development of this project is documented by Binka et al (1995) and Nyonator et al (2005), among others.

This initiative aims to reduce barriers to geographical access to health services encountered by large populations in SSA, using the social structures of community organization. Some of these structures are lineage and kinship networks, the chieftaincy institution that is a central pillar in African community organization and social solidarity. The second dimension of CHPS is the community health nurse who is introduced into the community to improve service accessibility. A critical part of the CHPS is that instead of a community health worker that visits the community from a designated district health centre, the health worker lives within the community.

Community involvement in the scheme includes the donation of land, materials, labour, and other·resources required to make operational a "community health compound" constructed from local materials and resources. A committee is established to oversee the functioning of the community scheme, the requisite operational resources (including motor-cycle and logistics) are provided by the district health management teams, and the community health officer is introduced into the community. Thus, the introduction of CHPS into a community involves extensive planning and community dialogue (Nyonator et al, 2005).

The community health officer visits households to provide primary health services including immunization, family planning, antenatal care, supervision of delivery, postnatal services, treatment of minor ailments, and health education. On average, a community officer oversees a catchment area of about 3,000 individuals. The community health officers are supported by community volunteers in the mobilization and registration of community participants.

CHPS enhances access to PHC services for communities. Evaluation reports to date indicate that the programme has cut down child and maternal mortalities by 33% in communities where it has been adopted and has therefore become a national health policy in Ghana (Nyonator et al, 2005). The rating of this alternative as "successful" is based largely on its empirical success in Ghana, where it was designed and implemented. It subsequently became an electioneering and political instrument for national election campaigns as communities demanded of political parties the establishment of CHPS in their communities in return for their votes.

Evaluation of CBHI initiatives

Equity: A strong point of CBHI/MHO models as alternatives to privatization are their promotion of equity through cross-subsidization and equal access. As with formal health insurance, the theoretical expectation is that the wealthy would subsidize the poor, the employed subsidize the unemployed, the young subsidize the old, and so on. However, in many cases the full potential of cross-subsidization is often not realized as those in higher socio-economic status often exclude themselves, which leaves the schemes prone to adverse selection. The very poor are also often excluded because they cannot afford the premiums required for coverage as the preceding case studies in Uganda and Tanzania clearly demonstrate.

The equity dimension of these schemes is that benefits are not usually related to how much the beneficiary contributed to the scheme and that the poor are protected against impoverishment and catastrophic effects of financing health care out-of-pocket, and thus it also reduces the tendency to dispose of valuable assets to finance health needs.

The geographic equity gains from MHOs are clearly illustrated with the CHPS in Ghana, where the rural communities are the key drivers of the scheme, and in Rwanda, where the *mutuelles* originally targeted rural communities. The presence of community health workers in Ghana, for example, removes the access barrier, which is very critical in SSA countries. Furthermore, CHPS exemplifies a strong case of emphasis on PHC, which is known to have more equitable effects than curative care (WHO 2008).

There are potential vertical equity gains from MHO schemes that are not fully realized due to their tendency to rely on flat contributions rather than calibrated contribution that consider the socio-economic status of the members. Although it may be expected that income-dependent contribution would be easy to operationalize in the context of community-based schemes since the communities are usually small and that it would be easy to identify the socio-economic status of members within such contexts (Hargreaves et al, 2007, Rew et al, 2007), this is not the case in most instances because it is difficult to establish income levels or because of lack of consciousness of equity in the design of the schemes.

Democratic participation: The CBHI/MHO schemes improve democratic participation and social solidarity, and this is one of their underlying social benefits. However, even this important quality of the schemes is often compromised. Franco et al (2006), for example, report that participation was quite extensive across the MHOs in Senegal, although they also observed that several of them had difficulties convening general assembly meetings, which are a key mechanism for social participation. The Tanzanian case study also made the point that lack of participation was a major threat to the sustainability of the schemes. De Allegri et al (2006) observed that

MHOs often fail to attain their full potential because of inadequate participation. In the Rwandan example, however, democratic participation by the
community is built in, and may partly explain the success of the *mutuelles*
in that country.

Efficiency: The efficiency of the schemes is best assessed by their organizational efficiency, including administrative and cost effectiveness in collecting premiums. Cost effectiveness is usually enhanced for people in the
formal sector where deduction is made at source, but this is more difficult
for people in the informal sector. The lack of formal income implies that
the transaction costs of collecting premiums are high through searching
for information about and locating points of payment, transportation, and
logistics of paying the designated individuals or institutions and the additional secretarial administrative work. This may be particularly significant
for small, frequent premiums.

Furthermore, the realization of the goal of efficiency varies among
MHOs, depending on how the scheme is designed. For example, if the benefit package encourages more intensive use of PHC relative to the more
expensive secondary care as evident from the Tanzanian case study, then
the MHOs contribute to efficient use and conservation of national health
resources. Several reports show that MHOs contribute to improved technical and allocative efficiency of health systems through proper negotiation and cost reductions by the providers (Atim 1998). Some of the MHOs
are able to reduce moral hazard through social control and some others
through imposing co-payments and deductibles (Sekabaraga 2008).

Sustainability: This is a key issue with MHOs. There are indications of dwin-
dling membership due to low income and poor quality of service by selected
facilities (Criel and Waelkens 2003). For instance, one of the challenges in
the Tanzanian scheme was falling membership after the pilot phase of the
community-based scheme (Mtei and Mulligan, 2007). And yet MHOs have
had strong impacts on improving health care utilization among the poor and
represent strong coping mechanisms in low-income countries (Ndiaye et al,
2007) According to Tabor (2005), MHOs should be regarded as a complement to, not as a substitute for, strong government involvement in health care
financing and risk management related to the cost of illness. Government,
and its development partners, can support the growth of CBHI by ensuring
that there is a satisfactory supply of appropriate health services, by subsidizing start-up costs and the premium costs of the poor, by assisting CBHI to
build technical and managerial competence, by helping to foster development
of CBHI networks, and by assisting CBHI in establishing and strengthening
links with formal financial institutions and health care providers to better
manage covariate shocks and catastrophic health risks.

Quality: While, in some cases, MHOs have been able to control certain
aspects of quality of care such as long waiting times, lack of drugs, and

discourteous staff attitude towards their patients, a majority of MHOs lack the capacity to deal with critical quality issues such as drug prescription by doctors (Atim 1998). However, the schemes provide a framework for demanding improvements in quality of care.

Accountability: Accountability is the means by which individuals and organizations are externally answerable for their actions and through which they are internally responsible for shaping the goal and aspirations of the organization (Ebrahim 2003). Atim (1998) notes that most MHOs have standardized organizational structures for involving members in decision making and demanding accountability from their leaders. This is often accomplished through annual general meetings, which also generally elect the board members periodically.

Integration into health systems: The MHOs are easily integrated with the national health systems. The Rwanda, Tanzania, and Ghana case studies clearly demonstrate that these schemes can easily transmute into national policies. In Ghana, for example, the Navrongo experiment was scaled up to a national policy. Similarly, the Rwanda scheme transmuted into a bottom-up approach to national health insurance. The facility-based schemes in Uganda were designed as part of the facilities at which they operated, though such integration is then limited to participating facilities. However, if autonomy becomes the overriding consideration for the MHOs, it could pose a problem towards their integration into national health policy.

NATIONAL HEALTH INSURANCE SCHEMES

NHISs have been operating in industrialized countries for over a century but are now emerging as an important public health financing option in policy discussions in SSA. A number of countries, including Ghana, Nigeria, Kenya, and South Africa, either have started or are planning to start NHISs.

NHISs are more formal than community-based schemes, usually backed by legislative acts. The core concept is based on the pooling of risks using a particular group of people drawing on epidemiological and actuarial trends. In this manner, people that do not fall ill pay for those that are ill, and those who are ill and those who are not ill will change over time (McIntyre and van den Heever 2007). While they are usually supported by government budgetary subsidies, the main source of funding for NHISs is mandatory contributions from members and employers. The objective of these schemes is to pool risks of ill health and facilitate cross-subsidization among large national or regional populations that are covered by the scheme.

The NHIS tends to generate a lot of political interest through building national consensus and fundamental shifts in the way resources are mobilized and benefits are distributed in the health sector for large segments of the population. Issues involved include: the design of the scheme, calibration of contributions, the way in which contributions are made, who is to make the contributions, what roles for the state and its agencies and other stakeholders, accreditation of facilities and modes of reimbursement, who is covered first and how fast the scheme moves to universal coverage, eligibility conditions and what specific health packages are to be covered by the scheme, and the enactment of enabling laws, among others. These issues take a long time to iron out, and so the process involves lengthy political dialogue with all shades of interest groups.

Ghana's NHIS was conceived in the 1980s but only started in 2003 as the materialization of the electoral promise of the New Patriot Party made in its 2000 election manifesto, in which it proposed the abolition of user fees and cost recovery policy of the previous government. Within two years, the NHIS was able to cover one third of the population (Rajkotia 2007) and by 2009 the scheme had covered two-thirds of the population. It is now moving towards universal coverage.

The NHIS option was adopted by the Nigerian Ministry of Health in 1996 and formally promulgated into law through Decree 35 of 1999, which took effect in June 2005 after many years of debate, dialogue, and consultations. It was designed for the incremental expansion towards universal coverage beginning with those in the formal sector of the economy, similar to the pattern followed in the development of the German health insurance scheme (Bärnighausen and Sauerborn 2002). By 2008, the scheme had covered over 5 million employees of the federal government and their household members. The scheme has now shifted to covering the employees of subnational governments—state and local governments. There are, however, concerns that the scheme is not moving fast enough to cover the most vulnerable populations.

The State of Bayelsa, Nigeria, with a population of about 2 million, initiated a social health insurance policy in 2001 to pool resources across the country's population and to provide quality health care services for the citizens of the state (Ichoku et al, 2006). Enrollment requires a monthly premium of about US$1.5 per month, and this entitles the member to cover four other household members less than 18 years of age. It covers all treatment that can be obtained within the hospitals in the state.

The ideal of universal coverage has become the goal of the health financing system across both developed and developing countries. In Latin America, where there is a long tradition of national health insurance schemes, the rate of movement towards universal coverage has varied across countries ranging from 10% in the Dominican Republic to 80% in Costa Rica (Bärnighausen and Sauerborn 2002).

Typologically, NHISs could be classified as public-private partnerships (PPP) insofar as participating MHOs are private, as are most health care providers and employers of labour, while government is public. However, to the extent that a NHIS aims to raise funds for the public health sector through public health sources, such as public employers (including government), it may be seen as a form of public-public partnership (PuP). The typology gets more involved when one considers the above possibility plus that of getting services from the private, not-for-profit sector: effectively a public-public-private-not-for-profit partnership.

Example 1—South Africa

In South Africa, the debate about a national health insurance scheme has been going on for a long time. The objective is to address the wrongs of current (private) medical aid schemes and improve public access to affordable and decent health care. While the private insurance markets have been insufficiently developed or inaccessible to many individuals, large segments of populations have no access to any health insurance system mainly because of the high costs of contributions to the schemes. The problem with medical aid schemes is that they are selective in a sense that those with the greatest risk of illness are more likely than relatively healthy individuals to join.

Government direction on this issue was articulated by the former minister of health in South Africa, Manto Tshabala-Msimang, to a colloquium on "Health within a Comprehensive System of Social Security: Is NHI an Appropriate Response?" in which she indicated that:

> the idea of an NHI was a policy idea that was initially adopted by the African National Congress (ANC) prior to 1994. The NHI would be seen to address the crises in the medical aid sector and would be based on the principle of solidarity. This would then mean, amongst other things, that the NHI in South Africa would be compulsory and that current medical aid schemes could form the basis of the NHI, provided they met with specified statutory conditions governing the NHI system (cited in Botha and Hendircks 2008).

According to McIntyre and van den Heever (2007), the concept has failed in South Africa because it is perceived as complex, which has limited constructive engagement among key stakeholders and the extent to which consensus can be achieved. Additional resistance has come from the private sector, which sees the introduction of the NHIS as undermining quality of care, and employees who fear that they will miss their benefits under current private medical insurance schemes or else have to pay for both the NHIS and the private schemes to maintain the current level of care. Government, however, has been unwavering in its determination to see the introduction of the NHIS. How this develops remains to be seen, but it provides an opportunity for the country to merge the public and private health systems into one, to improve funding for the public sector, and expand access to health care for indigent populations.

Evaluations of NHIS

Equity: NHIS with comprehensive coverage equalizes financial access to most health services (Lu and Hsiao 2003), although equal financial access may not necessarily translate into equal overall access, because unequal geographical distances may create other forms of inequity because of misdistribution of health facilities, particularly between urban and rural areas in SSA. However, as in the case of MHO schemes, the achievement of financial equity may be enhanced or compromised, depending on the design of the scheme. If NHIS contributions are designed to spread financing burden according to ability to pay, and benefits according to need, then it is likely to achieve the goal of equity to a large extent. However, a major problem in realizing this critical objective is that in most cases the schemes begin with those employed in the formal sector, and those in the informal sector are the last to be covered (Donaldson and Gerard 1993).

This implies that public health resources finance the health of the well-off at the initial stages, which raises serious questions about social justice. Worse still, the scheme may lead to the displacement of the poor and those employed in the informal sector from public health facilities as most of the better equipped public health facilities are accredited and used to run the NHIS. However, when the scheme advances to universal coverage, the objectives of equity and equal access are achieved. In many situations, the solution to this equity problem is to cover the poor who cannot be enrolled through public tax revenue or through exemption schemes that enable them to use facilities without payment, as is the case in the Ghana NHIS. Furthermore, if payments are fixed and not varied by income level, it may lead to regressive contributions to the health system, thus defeating the goal of equity (Lu and Hsiao 2003).

Efficiency: NHIS generally tends to increase the amount of spending on health (Lu and Hsiao 2003), but whether that translates into a more effective health system depends largely on effective and efficient management of increased funds. Several efficiency issues arise in respect of efficiency of NHIS. Some of these include questions around heavy administrative costs, moral hazard, and adverse selection. For example, it has been noted that administrative costs alone take up about 20% of insurance costs in the US (Lu and Hsiao 2003). Some inefficiency problems are sometimes countered by requiring co-payments at point of use, referral systems, and compulsory enrollment for all members of the group to be covered to avoid adverse selection. Scale efficiency in the operation of the schemes often entails a centralized rather than multiple small schemes.

Quality: Quality of care has not yet been evaluated for any of the NHISs operating in SSA. However, evidence from Nigeria indicates that quality has improved significantly in the accredited hospitals (Ichoku et al, 2006). Evidence from elsewhere also suggests that NHIS is usually associated with improvements in quality of health care. For example, Szilagyi et al (2004) noted large and significant improvements in important indicators of quality of pediatric health services in the State Children's Health Insurance Programme in New York State.

Accountability: No systematic and detailed assessment has yet been undertaken about the level of accountability prevailing in the four operational NHISs in the subregion. However, in an environment of endemic corruption and grinding poverty, it is difficult to isolate the scheme from such social malaise. For example, reports of cheating, fraud, and overuse have already been identified as major problems threatening the Ghana NHIS.[1] Indeed, initiatives on national health insurance in Uganda have repeatedly been unsuccessful due to fear of corruption, and the same situation obtained in the 1980s and 1990s in Zimbabwe.

Sustainability: A study commissioned by USAID to assess the Ghana scheme noted with regard to its financial sustainability that because the premiums charged were too low, many regional branches of the scheme were already in financial distress, and some had to increase premiums illegally in order to sustain their operation. Sustainability problems also arise in times of economic hardship with high unemployment rates and reduced fiscal space, thus making social solidarity difficult to achieve.

Solidarity: Solidarity is a key factor in establishing the NHISs. The key consideration is the principle of cross-subsidization by which the rich subsidize the poor, those employed subsidize the unemployed, and those who are well subsidize those who are sick.

Integration into health systems: NHIS is usually integrated within national health systems. In Ghana and Nigeria, the ministries of health directly supervise the schemes. The health care providers are also the government-owned and government-accredited private health facilities in the countries. Referral from a lower to a higher level of care is encouraged. The NHIS envisaged in South Africa will lead to the merging of the public and private sectors through a single funding mechanism and equal access by all the population to either sector.

FAITH-BASED HEALTH ORGANIZATIONS

Mission-based organizations or FBOs represent a third type of alternative to privatization and commercialization in SSA. They are distinct from MHOs and NHISs in that they are direct health care providers (not simply financing mechanisms for other providers). FBOs have a long history of active involvement in the provision of health services in SSA, with their origin generally traced to the efforts of the European Christian missionaries who followed colonizing expeditionists by establishing hospitals and schools as instruments of their evangelizing work (Barthel 1985). While the role of European missionaries diminished with attainment of independence by African states, the indigenous clergy and religious supporters who replaced them have continued with the tradition of building schools and hospitals as part of their vision of "holistic" development.

FBO health systems or church hospitals are usually SiNP organizations, run on a non-profit basis. The size and relative contribution of FBO providers varies across the subcontinent, but they constitute the largest single health care provider outside of government in most of the subregion (World Bank 1993, Green et al, 2002). It is estimated that the Christian Health Association of Ghana (CHAG), which is the umbrella organization for all the Christian hospitals in that country, accounts for about 40% of health facilities in Ghana (CHAG 2008). USAID and FMOH (2009) report that the Christian Health Association of Nigeria (CHAN), an umbrella organization for missionary health facilities, operates 3,500 health facilities across the country.

A study undertaken by Medicus Mundi International (2009) on the health care situation in Cameroon, Chad, Tanzania, and Uganda shows similar levels of faith-based activity. At the time of its independence in 1961, half of the health services in Tanzania were provided by Christian missions, and more recent statistics for 2000 to 2005 indicate that 41% of all hospitals and about 21% of all health centres in Tanzania are owned by FBOs. In Uganda, about 30% of health facilities are owned by private, not-for-profit groups, the majority being FBOs. In Chad where the missionaries gained entry only after World War II, mission-owned health facilities have grown rapidly and now account for 20% of all health facilities in that country. Similarly, FBOs deliver about 25% of all health care provided in Kenya (Marek et al, 2005).

There has been a gradual recognition of the critical input of FBOs into the health sector. In Tanzania, the Democratic Republic of Congo (DRC), and Malawi, governments have collaborated with church-run hospitals and delegated to them responsibility for underserved regions (Gill and Carlough 2008). In Zimbabwe, the state funded the expansion of some mission hospitals that have been designated as district hospitals to serve rural people. In Tanzania, Cameroon, Lesotho, and Ghana, FBOs are seen as complementary to the public effort and are therefore sometimes subsidized by the state. In particular, since most FBO facilities tend to be located in rural and hard-to-reach areas, some countries have contracted out certain health services to rural populations through them (Green et al, 2002, Medicus Mundi International 2009). In Tanzania, some FBO hospitals are designated as district hospitals: they receive funding and staff from government, and, in turn, they render services to the districts where they are located. Typologically, this arrangement is that of a PuNPP.

In Lesotho, many development partners and donors continue to support the government's health sector. There has since been a move to harmonize and align donor support with national plans to make aid more effective. As a result, a sector-wide approach mechanism has been put in place, with major partners including member churches of the Christian Health Council of Lesotho (CHAL), comprising denominations such as the Catholic, Lutheran, and Seventh Day Adventists, among others. CHAL affiliates are committed to the provision of quality health services to Lesotho particularly in hard-to-reach places around the country. There are nine CHAL general hospitals (each serving a large geographical area) and more than 70 health centres, clinics, and outposts (mainly in rural areas). These FBO facilities serve areas that would otherwise have no health service coverage.

There are equally successful partnerships between government and FBOs in Malawi, through the Christian Health Association of Malawi (CHAM) and in Zambia through the Christian Health Association of Zambia (CHAZ). In each of these countries, Christian mission hospitals make up a third of clinical health services (Gill and Carlough 2008). In Uganda, major religious denominations have coordinating structures for the health service networks they run all over the country. These are the Uganda Catholic Medical Bureau, the Uganda Protestant Medical Bureau, and the Uganda Islamic Medical Bureau. Through the various bureaus, the FBO sector has been able to negotiate partnerships with government, whereby, for example government seconds staff and provides drugs and other supplies to FBO facilities. One area in which the FBO sector in Uganda has made tremendous contributions has been in the training of health professionals, especially the nurses who are the backbone of the health sector.

Evaluation of FBOs

Sources of funds: Mission hospitals usually collect funds generated from health care services and external donors. They rely on user charges to sustain their services (Green et al, 2002). Sometimes, because of their affiliation to other international bodies, they are better able to obtain the services of expatriates that are paid from abroad (Gill and Carlough 2008) or equipment donated to them by charity organizations.

Participation: Mission hospitals are usually owned and managed by Christian bodies. This implies that democratic participation of the public in management decisions is usually limited to the authorities of the church. However, in many instances broad-based advisory committees, usually including medical and health care management experts, are set up to advise the authorities on critical management issues.

Equity: FBOs charge user fees to sustain their operations, but they also have limited exemption schemes for those who are unable to afford payment for treatment received. As Green et al note, "Some church providers have demonstrated a particular concern for the poor" (2002, 349). A study by Levin et al (2000) in three anglophone African countries found that many aspects of mission health services cost less than public health services, and their services are of better quality. However, a similar study by Ndeso-Atanga (2003) in Cameroon found costs of services to be cheaper in public health facilities. This suggests that the comparative cost advantage of mission hospitals over public ones may differ from country to country.

Efficiency: The culture and ethics that govern the management of church organizations is usually different from that which prevails in the public and other private health facilities, although there may be internal differences in the management culture of the different church organizations. Unlike in government hospitals where proactive management is often absent, most mission hospitals, because they are independent and less encumbered by procedures and civil service hierarchies, seem better able to take management initiatives (Green et al, 2002, Gill and Carlough 2008). Their efficiency is also enhanced by the decentralized nature of decision making. Procurement and supply tend to be more efficient. For example, Gilson et al (1995) found that in Tanzania the probability of a mission dispensary stocking chloroquine, a popular malaria drug, was 90% as against 50% by government dispensary. Similarly, the likelihood of a mission dispensary stocking penicillin antibiotic was 70% against 20% for a public dispensary. Decentralized procurement systems also enable facility managers to negotiate supplies directly with vendors and to obtain competitive market prices. For example, in Kenya, Uganda, Tanzania, and Malawi, formulary committees of mission health facilities regularly meet with the representatives of the Essential Drug Programme to review and update drug list and treatment guidelines based on new epidemiological evidence (Gill and Carlough 2008).

Quality: The quality of care in mission hospitals is generally acknowledged to be higher than in both private for-profit and government hospitals (Green et al, 2002, Ndeso-Atanga 2003). According to Gill and Carlough (2008), mission hospitals have values that encourage compassionate services even at the expense of personal comfort and career enhancement. They reported that in Uganda religious not-for-profit health care facilities, qualified medical staff earn less than their counterparts from other providers, yet they were more likely to render services with elements of "public good". Similarly, Bowling (2004) reports that in Malawi, staff attitude towards service delivery improved remarkably when they joined the mission hospitals. Gill and Carlough (2008) attribute the relatively high quality of services in mission hospitals partly to closer supervision and to the fact that responsibility for hiring and firing of staff resides with on-site management rather than remote civil service hierarchy. Levin et al (2003) explain the reliable flow of pharmaceutical supplies in mission hospitals in terms of better management and efficient use of resources, all of which contribute to greater patient satisfaction with mission hospitals relative to other providers (Gilson et al, 1995).

Accountability: Accountability is often based on internal checks and balances within the Christian denomination that owns the health facility. Since they are usually independent of government funding, their managements are accountable to the church hierarchies that are the proprietors of such organizations. Without detailed case study evidence, it is difficult to comment on the extent of accountability within FBOs.

Sustainability and public ethos: The mission hospitals have endured over time. They have been part of churches that own them. Because they have often been supportive of government programmes, they are in some countries subsidized by government. Their ethos is typically guided by Christian beliefs and practices that discourage materialistic tendencies. Ethical difficulties arise, however, when health care provision is used as a forum for proselytizing. It is, for example, considered unethical to use the opportunity of someone's sickness to sway him or her to a particular religious faith.

Integration into health systems: The relatively large size of the contribution of FBO facilities to the health systems of different countries in Africa demands the attention of health policy makers, as they have often been ignored by MOHs, which sometimes consider them as rivals (Green et al, 2002). The formation of national associations of Christian health institutions in some countries in SSA provides important opportunity for their integration within the national health system without necessarily being absorbed into it. It also gives them a strong voice in influencing national health policies. As discussed above, integration of FBO services into national health systems is happening in countries such as Tanzania, Lesotho, Cameroon, and Ghana.

THE CHALLENGES AND OPPORTUNITIES
OF "PUBLIC" PARTNERSHIPS

Partnerships by governments with other organizations represent a strong current in the health sector. Countries such as Mozambique have benefited significantly from NGOs that have partnered with government to provide basic and essential services. For example, *Médecins sans Frontières* (MSF)—an international medical humanitarian NGO—first worked in Mozambique in 1984 and has now established long-term projects to support the government's response to the HIV/AIDS epidemic. MSF activities include treatment of people living with HIV/AIDS and provide voluntary counselling and testing, child and maternal health, and prevention of mother-to-child transmission of HIV through clinics, hospitals, and home visits.

One way external influences have tended to sway health policies has been through pushing for contracting out health services to non-profit or for-profit providers in order to attain health sector goals. The services contracted out may be clinical or non-clinical. Several schemes have been initiated under such programmes as the Community Nutrition Project in Senegal and Madagascar and faith-based NGOs in Cameroon, Chad, Tanzania, and Uganda. Marek et al (2005) document instances of the use of vouchers in purchasing insecticide-treated nets in Tanzania, delivering emergency contraception in Zambia and providing reproductive services in Kenya. Franchising, which involves a firm (the franchisor) offering a blueprint of how to sell its product to a local firm (franchisee) in a specified geographical area, has been used in a number of countries including Kenya (LaVake 2003). Marie Stopes International in collaboration with its local implementing partner, Marie Stopes Kenya and with funding from KFW (*Kreditanstalt für Wiederaufbau*)—the German Development Bank—has been working with the Kenyan ministries responsible for health to coordinate a network of socially franchised private providers. The network targets poor, underserved populations in Kenya, borrowing from franchising models in the commercial sector to increase access to health benefits for rural and urban poor. The aim is to increase access to affordable, high-quality reproductive health and family planning in rural and major urban slums in three administrative provinces of western Kenya.

There have, however, been a number of criticisms against the partnership paradigm in the provision of health services (Buse and Walt 2000a, 2000b, Buse and Waxman 2001, Richter 2004). It is argued that partnerships with for-profit firms are a slippery route to privatization and commercialization as the state's regulatory authority may easily be compromised. It is also argued that such partnerships lead to the state abdicating the responsibility of protecting the health of their citizens, corroding essential values of equity, fairness, and universal access. We have therefore not included examples of traditional PPPs in our discussion as they are often a prelude to deeper commercialization of health services.

LOOKING AHEAD

McIntyre et al (2006) and Mackintosh (2003) emphasize how powerful global ideological movements are in shaping events that influence health policies. The alternatives identified above represent new forms of health service delivery or innovations on existing structures to extend health services to reach greater segments of the populations of the region, without direct involvement of the for-profit private sector. Some of the emerging alternatives are aimed at expanding access and reducing barriers and complementing, rather than substituting, existing models of public health care service delivery and financing. For example, the emergence of MHOs was necessitated by the need to increase access to health services by reducing financial barriers that impeded access among the poor and rural communities, often building upon existing social and traditional community structures, as exemplified by the *mutuelles* in Rwanda. NHIS represents a global trend towards providing equal access and offering financial risk protection to all. On the other hand, Christian mission health services have been part of the health systems that complement state provision of health services in Sub-Saharan Africa for many decades.

It is also very likely that the development of NHIS will be a major health policy focus in many SSA countries in the near future. The recent success of this model in Ghana, as well as its modest gains in Nigeria and pending adoption in South Africa, two of Africa's largest and most influential economies, may lead to its adoption by other SSA countries. This could result in the expansion of health providers, particularly not-for-profit providers, who are willing to provide services at government-determined rates. Another likely implication of the expansion and deepening of NHIS is the integration of MHOs into the NHIS as is already happening in Rwanda and Ghana. A natural development would be that after MHOs have served critical roles in providing access and hedging poor populations against catastrophic financing, they fizzle out in the end giving way to NHIS and universal coverage.

It is expected that in the future in SSA, the question of how to finance the health of the population will assume more importance than the question of who provides it. In this context, the role of non-profit health care providers becomes important. As our analysis above indicates, the FBOs represent a viable middle ground between government and private, for-profit health providers. It would seem that they represent an opportunity for public/

non-profit collaboration in ensuring that, at least in the medium term, those left behind by forces of privatization receive quality health care.

ACKNOWLEDGEMENTS

The authors would like to thank Sehlapelo Irene Mokgoatsane, Ladislaus K. Mdee, and Mangaabane Gorden Mohlala—all from the Health Systems Research Group, Department of Pharmacy, University of Limpopo, South Africa—for their valuable assistance with the research for this chapter.

NOTES

1. These problems were identified in a report of the functioning of the Ghana NHIS presented during the first AFEA Congress in Accra, Ghana, 18–22 April 2009. See also *The Daily IIJ*, Ghana: National Health Insurance Scheme uncovers massive fraud at three hospitals. http://inwent-iij-lab.org/Weblog/2009/08/19/ghana-national-health-insurance-scheme-uncovers-massive-fraud-at-three-hospitals/ (accessed 14 October 2011).

REFERENCES

African Union. 2009. Health Financing in Africa: Challenges and Opportunities for Expanding Access to Quality Health Care. In Fourth session of the African Union conference of Ministers of Health, pp.iii-45. Addis Ababa, Ethiopia, 4-8 May.

Atim, C. 1998. *The contribution of mutual health organizations to financing, delivery and access to health care: Synthesis of research in nine West and Central African countries.* Bethesda, MD: Partnerships for Health Reform Project, ABT Associates Inc.

Baraldes, C. and Carreras, L. 2003. *Willingness to pay for community health fund card in Mwara rural health district, Tanzania.* Spain: Médecins Sans Frontières Spain.

Bärnighausen, T. and Sauerborn, R. 2002. One hundred and eighteen years of the German health insurance system: Are there any lessons for middle- and low-income countries? *Social Science and Medicine* 54: 1559–1587.

Barthel, D. 1985. Women's educational experience under colonialism: Toward a diachronic model. *Journal of Women in Culture and Society* 11(1): 137–153.

BeLue, R., Okoror, T., Iwelunmor, J., Taylor, K.D., Degboe, A.N., Agyemang, C. and Ogedegbe, C. 2009. An overview of cardiovascular risk factor burden in sub-Saharan African countries: A socio-cultural perspective. *Globalization and Health* 5: 10.

Bennett, S., Kelley, A.G. and Ly, S. 2004. *21 Questions on CBHF: An overview of community-based health financing.* Bethesda, Maryland: PHR Plus (Partners for Health Reform Plus).

Binka, F., Nazzar, A. and Phillips, J. 1995. The Navrongo community health and family planning project. *Studies in Family Planning* 26: 121–139.

Bonu, S., Rani, M. and Bishai, D. 2003. Using willingness to pay to investigate regressiveness of user fees in health facilities in Tanzania. *Health Policy and Planning* 18: 370–382.

Botha, C. and Hendricks, M. 2009. Financing South Africa's national health insurance: Possibliities and challenges—Colloquium Proceedings. HSRC South Africa: HSRC Press. http://www.hsrc.ac.za/document-2623.phtml (accessed 6 October 2011).

Bowling, A. 2004. *Measuring health: A review of quality of life measurement scales.* UK: Open University Press.

Buse, K. and Walt, G. 2000a. Global public-private partnerships for health: Part I—A new development in health? *Bulletin of the WHO* 78(5): 549–561.

———. 2000b. Global public-private partnerships: Part II—What are the health issues for global governance? *Bulletin of the WHO* 78(5): 699–709.

Buse, K. and Waxman, A. 2001. Public-private health partnerships: A strategy for WHO. *Bulletin of the WHO* 79(8): 748–754.

CHAG (Christian Health Association of Ghana). 2008. Comprehensive Annual Work Plan 2008 Annual Report. CHAG. www.chagghana.org/chag/assets/files/CHAGAnnualREport2008.pdf.

Chee, G., Smith, K. and Kapinga A. 2002. *Assessment of the community health fund in Hanang District, Tanzania.* Dar es Salaam: PHR Plus.

CHF (Community Health Fund). 2001. The Community Health Fund Act. Dar es Salaam: Government of the United Republic of Tanzania. www.bunge.go.tz/Polis/PAMS/Docs/1–2001.pdf (accessed 22 July 2009).

Criel, B. and Waelkens, M.P. 2003. Declining subscriptions to the Maliando Mutual Health Organization in Guinea-Conakry (West Africa): What is going wrong? *Social Science and Medicine* 57: 1205–1219.

De Allegri, M., Kouyaté, B., Becher, H., Gbangou, A., Pokhrel, S., Sanon, M. and Sauerborn, R. 2006. Understanding enrolment in community health insurance in sub-Saharan Africa: A population-based case-control study in rural Burkina Faso. *Bulletin of the WHO* 84(11): 852–858.

Derriennic, Y., Wolf, K. and Kiwanuka-Mukiibi, P. 2005. *An assessment of community-based health financing activities in Uganda.* Bethesda, MD: The Partners for Health Reform Plus Project, Abt Associates Inc.

Donaldson, C. Gerard, K.1993. *Economics of health care financing: The visible hand.* New York: St. Martin's Press.

Ebrahim, A. 2003. Making sense of accountability: Conceptual perspectives for northern and southern non-profits. *Non-profit Management Leadership* 14: 191–212.

Ekman, B. 2004. Community-based health insurance in low-income countries: A systematic review of evidence. *Health Policy and Planning* 19(5): 249–270.

Franco, L., Simpara, C., Sidibé, O., Kelley, A., Diop, F., Makinen, M., Ba, A. and Burgert, C. 2006. *Equity initiative in Mali: Evaluation of the impact of mutual health organizations on utilization of high impact services in Bla and Sikasso districts in Mali.* Bethesda, MD: PHR Plus.

Gill, Z. and Carlough, M. 2008. Do mission hospitals have a role in achieving Millennium Development Goal 5? *International Journal of Gynecology and Obstetrics* 102: 198–202.

Gilson, L., Magomi, M. and Mkangaa, E. 1995. The structural quality of Tanzanian primary health facilities. *Bulletin of the WHO* 73(1): 105–114.

Goodman, C., Brieger, B., Unwin, A., Mills, A., Meek, S. and Greer, G. 2007. Medicine sellers and malaria treatment in Sub-Saharan Africa: What do they do and how can their practice be improved? *American Journal of Tropical Medicine and Hygiene* 77(6): 203–218.

Green, A., Shaw, J., Dimmock, F. and Conn, C. 2002. A shared mission? Changing relationships between government and church health services in Africa. *International Journal of Health Planning and Management* 17: 333–353.

Hargreaves, J.R., Morison, L.A., Gear, J.S.S., Makhubele, M.B., Porter, J.D.H., Busza, J., Watts, C., Kim, J.C. and Pronyk, P.M. 2007. Hearing the voices of the poor: Assigning poverty lines on the basis of local perceptions of poverty.

A quantitative analysis of qualitative data from participatory wealth ranking in rural South Africa. *World Development* 35: 212–229.

Him, C. 2009. Health financing in Africa: Challenges as opportunities for expanding access to quality healthcare. In Fourth session of the African Union Conference of Ministries of Health, pp. iii–45. Addis Abada, Ethiopia, 4–8 May.

Ichoku, H.E., Useh, G. and Attahiru, A. 2006. A field survey report of health financing practices in Bayelsa and Edo states. Presented to the Technical Committee on the Drafting of National Policy on Health Financing, Government of Nigeria.

Kamuzora, P. and Gilson, L. 2007. Factors influencing implementation of the Community Health Fund in Tanzania. *Health Policy and Planning* 22: 95–102.

LaVake, S.D. 2003. *Applying social franchising techniques to youth reproductive health/HIV services.* Youth Issues Paper 2. Arlington, VA: Family Health International.

Levin, A., McEuen, M., Dymatraczenko, T., Ssengooba, F., Mangani, R. and Van Dyck, G. 2003. *Costs of maternal health care services in three anglophone African countries.* Bethesda-Maryland: Partnership for Health Reform.

Lu, J-F.R. and Hsiao, W.C. 2003. Does universal health insurance make health care unaffordable? Lessons from Taiwan. *Health Affairs* 22(3): 77–88.

Mackintosh, M. 2003. *Health care commercialization and the embedding of inequality.* Health Research Project Synthesis Paper. Geneva: RUIG/UNRISD (United Nations Research Institute for Social Development).

Mackintosh, M. 2006. Commercialisation, inequality and the limits to transition in health care: A Polanyian framework for policy analysis. *Journal of International Development* 18: 393–406.

Marek, T., O'Farrel, C., Yamamoto, C. and Zable, I. 2005. *Trends and opportunities in public-private partnerships to improve health services delivery in Africa.* Africa Region Human Development Working Paper Series No. 33646. Washington, DC: The World Bank.

McIntyre, D., Thiede, M., Dahlgren, G. and Whitehead, M. 2006. What are the economic consequences for households of illness and of paying for health care in low- and middle-income country contexts? *Social Science and Medicine* 62: 858–865.

McIntyre, D. and van den Heever, A. 2007. *Social or national health insurance.* Cape Town, Republic of South Africa: Health Economics Unit.

Medicus Mundi International. 2009. *Contracting between faith-based and public health sector in Sub-Saharan Africa: A continuing crisis?* Switzerland: Medicus Mundi International.

Mhina, L.G. 2005. *Factors contributing to high drop-out of CHF members in Nzega District.* Master of Public Health Thesis. University of Dar es Salaam, United Republic of Tanzania.

MOH (Ministry of Health), Tanzania. 2003. *Assessment of CHF in Tanzania: Factors affecting enrolment and coverage.* Dar es Salaam, United Republic of Tanzania: MOH.

———. 2005. Health sector public expenditure review for 2005. Dar es Salaam, United Republic of Tanzania: MOH.

———. 2006. The community health fund facilitative supervision report. Dar es Salaam, Ministry of Health, United Republic of Tanzania.

MOH (Ministry of Health), Rwanda. 2004. Mutual health insurance policy in Rwanda. Kigali, Republic of Rwanda: MOH.

MOHSW (Ministry of Health and Social Welfare), Tanzania. 2006. *Annual health statistical abstract.* Dar es Salaam, United Republic of Tanzania: MOHSW.

Molyneux, C.S., Mung'Ala-Odera, V., Harpham, T. and Snow, R.W. 1999. Maternal responses to childhood fevers: A comparison of rural and urban residents in coastal Kenya. *Tropical Medicine and International Health* 4: 836–845.

Mtei, G.J. and Mulligan, J.A. 2007. Community health funds in Tanzania: A literature review. Tanzania: Consortium for Researchon Equity in Health Systems, Ifakara Health Institute. www.crehs.lshtm.ac.uk/downloads/publications/Community%20health%20funds%20in%20Tanzania.pdf .

Mtei, G.J., Mulligan, J.A., Palmer, N., Kamuzora, P., Ally, M. and Mills, A. 2007. An assessment of the health financing system in Tanzania: Implications for equity and social health insurance: Report on shield work package 1. In Proceedings of the iHEA 2007 6th World Congress: Explorations in Health Economics Paper.

Msuya, J.M., Jutting, J.P. and Abay, A. 2004. Impacts of community health insurance schemes on health care provision in rural Tanzania. Bonn: ZEF Center for Development Research. www.zef.de/fileadmin/webfiles/downloads/zef_dp/zef_dp82.pdf.

Musau, S. 2004. *The community health fund: Assessing implementation of new management procedures in Hanang District, Tanzania*. Bethesda: The PHR Plus Project.

Mwendo, H.M. 2001. *Accessibility and sustainability of health services Iramba District: Three years after community health fund implementation*. Master of Public Health Thesis. University of Dar es Salaam, Tanzania.

Ndeso-Atanga, S. 2003. Health care quality and the choice of care providers: Cameroon II, global, area, and international archive. www.escholarship.org/uc/item/7643c49c (accessed 4 December 2009).

Ndiaye, P., Soors, W. and Criel, B. 2007. A view from beneath: Community Health Insurance in Africa. *Tropical Medicine and International Health* 12(2): 157–161.

Nyonator, F.K., Awoonor-Williams, J.K., Philips, J.F., Jones, T. and Miller, R.A. 2005. The Ghana community-based health planning and services initiative for scaling up service delivery innovation. *Health Policy and Planning* 20(1): 25–34.

Rajkotia, Y. 2007. *The political development of the Ghanaian national health insurance system: Lessons in health governance*. Bethesda, MD: Health Systems 20/20 project.

Rew, A., Khan, S. and Rew, M. 2007. "P3 > Q2" in Northern Orissa: An example of integrating "combined methods" (Q2) through a "platform for probing poverties" (P3). *World Development* 35(2): 281–295.

Richter, J. 2004. Public-private partnerships for health: A trend with no alternatives? *Development* 47(2): 43–48.

Sekabaraga, C. 2008. Subsidised community health insurances for universal access to health care in Rwanda. In Proceedings of the Public Health Association Annual Meeting, 25–29 October. http://gtz-rhp.com/conferences/gtz_ilo_kigali07/Presentations/2nd_Block/Workshops/Sekarabaga_SUBSIDIZED_COMMUNITY_HEALTH_INSURANCES_FOR_UNIVERSAL_ACCESS_TO_HEALTH_CARE_IN_RWANDA.ppt

Shaw, R.P. 2002. *Tanzania's community health fund: Prepayment as an alternative to user fees*. Tanzania: CHF (Community Health Fund).

Snow, R.W., Peshu, N., Forster, D., Mwenesi, H. and Marsh, K. 1992. The role of shops in the treatment and prevention of childhood malaria on the coast of Kenya. *Royal Society for Tropical Medicine and Hygiene* 86: 237–239.

Szilagyi, P.G., Dick, A.W., Klein, J.D., Shone, L.P., Zwanziger, J. and McInnerny, T. 2004. Improved access and quality of care after enrolment in the New York State Children's Health Insurance Program (SCHIP). *Pediatrics* 113(5): 395–404.

Tabor, S.R. 2005. *Community-based health insurance and social protection policy*. Social Protection Discussion Paper Series No. 0503. Washington, DC: World Bank.

Turshen, M. 1977. The impact of colonialism on health and health services in Tanzania. *International Journal of Health Services* 7(1): 7–35.

UNGASS (UN General Assembly on the Declaration of Commitment on HIV/AIDS) and UNAIDS (Joint United Nations Programme on HIV/AIDS). 2008. *Report of the UN Secretary General to the General Assembly on the Declaration of Commitment on HIV/AIDS*. Geneva: UNAIDS. www.data.unaids.org/pub/report/2008/20080429_sg_progress-report-en.pdf.

Unwin, N., Setel, P., Rashid, S., Mugusi, F., Mbanya, J-C., Kitange, H., Hayes, L., Edwards, R., Aspray, T. and Alberti, K.G.M.M. 2001. Non-communicable diseases in sub-Saharan Africa: Where do they feature in the health research agenda? *Bulletin of the WHO* 79(10): 947–953.

USAID (United States Agency for International Development) and FMOH (Federal Ministry of Health) of Nigeria. 2009. *Nigeria health system assessment 2008*. Abuja: USAID and FMOH.

Vialle-Valentin, C.E., Ross-Degnan, D., Ntaganira, J. and Wagner, A.K. 2008. Medicines coverage and community-based health insurance in low-income countries. *Health Research Policy and Systems* 6(11): 11.

WHO (World Health Organization). 2008. *World Health Report 2008*. Geneva: WHO.

WHO and UNICEF. 1978. Declaration of Alma-Ata, International conference on primary Health care, Alma-Ata, USSR 6–12 September. www.who.int/hpr/NPH/docs/declaration_almaata.pdf.

WHOSIS (World Health Organization Statistical Information System). 2009. World Health Organization Statistical Information System. Geneva: WHO.

World Bank. 1993. *World development report 1993: Investing in health*. Washington, DC: The World Bank.

Wurthwein, R., Ghangou, A., Sauerborn, R. and Schmidt, C.M. 2001. Measuring the local burden of disease. *International Journal of Epidemiology* 30: 501–508.

12 Where Have All the Alternatives Gone?

The Shrinking of African Water Policy Options

Kate Bayliss and Al-Hassan Adam

This chapter documents findings from research designed to identify successful alternatives to privatization and commercialization in the delivery of water and sanitation in Africa. Despite extensive efforts, our research found no examples of truly robust alternatives in Sub-Saharan Africa (SSA), although more diverse and promising examples can be found in North Africa. What cases are in evidence are dominated by commercialization and operate largely as private firms (i.e. corporatization) rather than in a spirit of public sector solidarity. We found even fewer alternatives in the delivery of sanitation. As a result, our discussion centres on water.

The chapter begins with an overview of the background to water provision across the continent. In SSA, water services in urban areas are characterized by low rates of access, crumbling infrastructure, heavy reliance on donors in the context of major financing shortfalls, and growing numbers living in urban slums outside the reach of formal water service providers. This is in contrast with North Africa where rates of access to both water and sanitation comfortably exceed those of other developing regions.

With this context in mind, the chapter sets out our research approach, which aimed to cast a wide net to encompass alternatives across the region at utility and municipality level as well as cases of community organization and activism. Although privatization has not been widespread in Africa, there has been a substantial policy shift towards marketization throughout the region. The cases that met efficiency criteria were less successful in terms of social inclusion and equity in SSA. However, cases from North Africa—Morocco and Tunisia in particular—offered relevant comparative case studies.

The following section of the chapter highlights the successes and failures of the cases, which are grouped according to the type of alternative. The Emerging Issues in African Water section provides a review of some of the key issues that have shaped water delivery in the region, including the impact and changing nature of engagement with the private sector, the roles of different stakeholders, and the major challenge of finance. The chapter closes with an assessment of key areas for further research.

A limitation of our research is that it is largely desktop and therefore reliant on secondary sources (though enhanced via our close connections with the continent-wide Africa Water Network[1]). It may be that our findings reflect a bias in the literature and that other cases exist that have not been documented (especially given that this is an area that has received such little research attention to date). Alternatively, our findings may reflect a reality in the region that SSA is far behind the rest of the world in terms of the existence of robust alternatives to commercialized and privatized water provision (see the chapters on Asia and Latin America in this volume for comparisons). Even more disheartening is that our research examines cases that have been celebrated as good examples of public provision but upon closer inspection are only successful in terms of efficiency and not because they meet the needs of citizens.

THE STATE OF WATER DELIVERY IN AFRICA

Rates of access to water and sanitation in SSA lag far behind those of most other regions. Furthermore, improvements since 1990 have been modest at best (Table 12.1). According to the Millennium Development Goals (MDGs), the aim is to "halve, by 2015, the proportion of the population without sustainable access to safe drinking water and basic sanitation" (MDG 7 Target 3).[2] For SSA, these targets are relatively low at just 75% coverage for water

Table 12.1   Regional Coverage Rates for Water and Sanitation (1990 and 2008)

	Drinking water coverage (% of population)		Sanitation coverage (% of population)	
	1990	*2008*	*1990*	*2008*
Western Asia	86	90	80	85
Latin America and Caribbean	85	93	69	80
Southeastern Asia	72	86	46	69
Eastern Asia	69	89	48	65
Commonwealth of independent states	92	94	89	89
Oceania	51	50	55	53
Southern Asia	74	87	25	36
North Africa	88	92	72	89
Sub-Saharan Africa	49	60	28	31
Developing regions	71	84	41	52
Developed regions	99	100	99	99
World	77	87	54	61

Source: Joint Monitoring Programme 2010.

and 50% for sanitation by 2015, but they are unlikely to be achieved. Meanwhile, North Africa is set to achieve goals of access rates of 81% coverage for sanitation and 94% for safe drinking water (JMP 2008).

The data presented in Table 12.1 are provided by the Joint Monitoring Programme (JMP), which was established by the United Nations Children's Fund (UNICEF) and the World Health Organization (WHO) to monitor progress towards the MDGs. The information is useful for general comparisons, but figures may be misstated. A safe drinking water source is defined as one, which by nature of its construction and design, is likely to protect the water source from outside contamination, in particular from fecal matter. Such sources are, for JMP classification purposes, piped water into dwelling, plot, or yard, public tap/standpipe, tube well/borehole, protected dug well, protected spring, and rain water collection (JMP 2010, 34).

To estimate the proportion of the population that has access to improved sources, the JMP collates data and information from national statistics offices and other relevant institutions through household surveys and national censuses. These reports present information on survey responses to questions regarding household water source. For example, in Ghana, the 2006 Multiple Indicator Cluster Survey (MICS) report provides survey information based on a sample of 6,302 households nationwide (Stats-Ghana 2006). In the survey, household representatives are asked to state their source of water. Translating this into the JMP, it is only users of "improved" drinking water sources that are defined as having access.

This approach has limitations. First, just because people pay a price for water, it may not be "affordable", as such usage may mean that they go without other essential items. Where households may say they have access, many may underconsume because of cost. Second, the MDGs and JMP data fail to incorporate the time taken to obtain water. Research indicates that water consumption remains fairly constant when the time taken to collect water is less than 30 minutes for the round trip but falls when collection takes longer than this (JMP 2008). According to the Ghana 2003 Demographic and Health Survey, nearly two out of 10 households in urban areas have to travel more than 15 minutes each way to access water. These people would be classified as having access according to the information in Table 12.1, even though the distance travelled to collect it is likely to mean that consumption is dangerously low.

In addition, there is a gender dimension to water collection. According to the MICS report in Ghana, adult women are more likely to be responsible for fetching drinking water than men and children. In households with better-educated heads, men play a relatively larger role in water collection than in households with less-educated heads (StatsGhana 2006). So, even though a respondent in a survey sample may be classified as having access, these data may disguise an onerous burden for women who travel long distances to collect water with adverse health implications as a result of carrying heavy loads, or inadequate consumption. The burden is greatest on women in households with the least education.

Notwithstanding weaknesses in the data, Table 12.2 provides more detail on coverage in SSA. Whereas progress has been made in reducing the *proportion* of the population without safe access since 1990 (this has fallen from 51% to 42%), improvements have failed to keep up with population growth so that the *absolute numbers* of those unserved have increased. In 2006, 331 million people in the region still did not have access to an improved drinking water source. In North Africa, the figure was approximately 8 million.

The data in Table 12.2 suggest that safe drinking water is unfairly distributed, with much lower rates of access in rural areas, but the percentage and number of people that lack safe access in urban areas is increasing. The overall proportion of the urban population served has stayed constant at 83%. The number of unserved has increased from 24.6 million to 51.7 million—a rise of 109%. North Africa also saw an increase in the absolute numbers of the urban population that lacked access to water by around 800,000—an increase of 20% (authors' calculations derived from JMP 2010 data).

Statistics fail to capture the full extent of deprivation in urban areas of SSA. For many living in cities, the quality and quantity of water is not sufficient. Hundreds of thousands of people who supposedly have access to water only have access to communal pipes with intermittent water supply shared by many. In lower income areas, people pay more for water, and there are additional costs associated with lack of access to safe water. For example, in SSA, people living in poverty spend at least one-third of their incomes on treatment of water-borne and water-related diseases such as diarrhea and malaria (UN-Habitat 2006).

SSA has the highest rate of urban growth in the world (4.58%). Overall it is estimated that around 30% of the population lives in urban areas, and this proportion is rapidly increasing and is expected to reach more than 60% by 2050 (UNDESA 2007). Urban growth in SSA typically goes hand in hand with increases in urban slums. SSA has the highest prevalence of

Table 12.2   Proportion of the Population of Sub-Saharan Africa with Access to Improved Water Source

	1990				2008			
	Population (millions)	*% served*	*Population unserved (millions)*	*% unserved*	*Population (millions)*	*% served*	*Population unserved (millions)*	*% unserved*
Urban	145,029	83	24,655	17	304,301	83	51,731	17
Rural	372,932	36	238,676	64	518,135	47	274,611	53
Total	517,961	49	264,160	51	822,436	60	328,974	40

Source: Joint Monitoring Programme 2010.

slums in the world with 71.8% of its urban population living in such areas. In the last 15 years, the number of slum dwellers in the region has almost doubled from 101 million in 1990 to 199 million in 2005 and is expected to reach nearly 400 million in 2020. High rates of inequality prevail within some cities, particularly in countries such as South Africa, Namibia and Angola (UN-Habitat 2008a). Slum cities (i.e. where the prevalence of slums is dramatically high so that they are the common form of human settlement) are prevalent throughout SSA where poor households experience multiple shelter deprivations. In such circumstances, the lack of access to water is intertwined with unplanned growth, so the lack of basic services is not just attributable to the informality of the settlements but is rather "an outgrowth of inadequate planning, construction and social services" (UN-Habitat 2008a, 113).

While deprivation occurs even in planned communities, municipal authorities often refuse outright to extend essential services to unplanned neighbourhoods putting thousands of families at risk. In some cases, settlements qualify as cities simply on account of the size of the population, but they lack the infrastructure and economic activities required to make the cities viable (UN-Habitat 2008a, 109). Rapid urbanization has meant that many residents are outside the scope of the piped network and depend on alternative water sources, which include private wells, small-scale private sector providers, community organized provision, or unsafe water sources.

In much of SSA, the water system is characterized by aging infrastructure that is in need of repair and replacement, let alone extension to unserved areas. Recent research into infrastructure spending needs, carried out by the Africa Infrastructure Country Diagnostic (AICD) indicates a substantial financing gap. The authors of the AICD study estimate the required spending figure for water supply and sanitation (WSS) to be about US$21.9 billion a year. Current spending in the region is US$7.6 billion (Foster and Briceño-Garmendia 2010). The scope for increasing revenue from user fees is slim, given that average tariffs for the region are high—at between US$0.86–6.56/m³. This is higher than in other developing regions where the average tariff is between US$0.03–0.6/m³, and not far off OECD countries where average water tariffs are roughly US$1/m³ (Foster and Briceño-Garmendia 2010).

Donor funding is far more significant in SSA than in other regions, and in water and sanitation than in other types of infrastructure. For the region as a whole, around 27% of capital expenditure is financed by donors and this rises to 35% for fragile states (Foster and Briceño-Garmendia 2010). However, other evidence suggests that the level of donor dependence is much higher. Research by WaterAid in Ghana indicates that between 2004 and 2010 around 85% of total planned investment in urban water was financed by donors (WaterAid 2005).

Privatization to large companies has not been widespread in SSA as compared with other regions, and the proportion of infrastructure spending that has come from the private sector for investment in water and sanitation in SSA is virtually zero. Some long-term concessions are still in operation in Côte d'Ivoire, Senegal, South Africa, Niger, and Mozambique, but no new concessions have been signed in the past 10 years (although the contract in Senegal has been extended). With long-term concessions in decline, methods for engaging with the private sector have metamorphosed. There has been a greater focus on short-term management contracts. Despite relatively low levels of privatization, many countries—with extensive donor involvement— have implemented some kind of commercialization in the water sector. As a result, public sector provision is often dominated by commercialized priori- ties leading to a blurring of the distinction between the two. Commercializa- tion often paves the way for the introduction of the private sector at some future stage. This is summarized by McDonald and Ruiters:

> The majority of water services in the region may still be in public hands—therefore allowing liberal analysts to argue that water has not been privatized in the region—but the reality is that virtually all water systems in Southern Africa have been fundamentally transformed by the (growing) pressures of commodification, as evidenced by the increasing number of public–private partnerships and the running of public water services like a private business. (2005, 23)

To summarize, the water delivery system is dominated by low access and poorly maintained infrastructure in dire need of investment in a context of rapid urbanization and growing slum prevalence. Large proportions of the urban population fall outside the scope of the formal piped water network. In such a context, efforts to privatize have brought little or no investment but have shaped policy frameworks within most countries, establishing commercialized utilities with a focus on efficiency and financial sustain- ability. Meanwhile, pressing concerns such as equity and social provision continue to be largely unaddressed.

LOOKING FOR "ALTERNATIVES"

Our aim was to identify alternatives to privatization and commercializa- tion in Africa that were effective in terms of social justice and equity and not just according to narrow criteria of economic efficiency. There were three broad themes on which we searched for cases: effective public sec- tor providers (as an alternative to privatized utilities), effective community provision (as an alternative to the domestic small-scale private sector), and examples of activism in response to privatization.

Initially our focus was on Sub-Saharan Africa, and we started with an A–Z list of 44 countries in this region. Our process of information gathering took the form of an ongoing Internet search and literature review, pursuing contacts from research and activist networks, such as trade unions and academics, development and research institutions. When cases appeared to be of interest, we pursued strands of investigation, following up with more detailed research to find out more details where possible. We identified the main water provider in each country. Key web sources included World Bank websites for information on programmes completed, ongoing, or in the pipeline. The International Benchmarking database (www.ib-net.org) and data provided by the Global Water Operators' Partnership Alliance (GWOPA) provided some kind of overview of utility performance.

As this process evolved, some cases began to firm up while others fell by the wayside. From our original list, we began to exclude those where we knew that the main water utility had been privatized (Côte d'Ivoire, Senegal, Gabon, Mozambique, Ghana, Cameroon). We also excluded countries in crisis (Somalia) or where our initial enquiries indicated that the performance of the water sector has been abysmal or non-existent (such as Chad) when it became clear that these were unlikely to offer inspirational examples of public service delivery, or at least examples that had been documented (although we kept an open mind regarding community provision).

It became clear that the extent of neoliberal reforms in the water sector is particularly pervasive in SSA, even if privatization has only been achieved in a few locations. Nigeria, for example, introduced a World Bank-sponsored Urban Water Sector Reform Project in 2004 with a view to encouraging full-scale privatization. Although privatization has not been achieved, it is clearly on the agenda and is shaping sector policy. Some countries are emerging from conflict and donors have been supporting reconstruction with infrastructure funding and promoting sector reform efforts including public sector partnerships (e.g. Sierra Leone, the Democratic Republic of the Congo [DRC], Burundi, the Central African Republic, Angola). After some initial enquiries, we expanded our geographical region to include North Africa when it emerged that Morocco and Tunisia would present suitable cases for our research and could be useful comparisons for those in SSA. This, then, is how our country selection was shaped.

In addition to exploring the activities of public utilities, we searched for evidence of smaller-scale service provision at the community level in each of the remaining countries. We also looked at activism and the effects of protests against neoliberal water sector policies. Our work in this area was less systematic, making enquiries of other academics and activists working in this field and exploring links and connections.

Despite the extensive reach of our research, detail is often lacking. We have largely had to rely on the work of others due to the scale of our task. Hence, what we have is a "mapping" of what has been documented about public and community provision of water in Africa. Our research is representative of the region as far as information is available. There may be other alternatives that have not yet been researched, for example in smaller African countries such as Togo (where the utility, TdE, comes eighth in a list of best performers in non-revenue water (NRW; composed of unbilled consumption, apparent losses [e.g. non-payment and metering inaccuracies], and real losses) and Benin (where the utility, SONEB scores highly on some efficiency measures [World Bank 2009, 59]). From discussions it appears that the water utility in Mauritius, CWA, has strong performance, although there is little documented on this. There may also be successful subnational municipal providers that have not been researched, for example in Tanzania and Botswana, and there are probably numerous additional community water systems across the region. The cases are representative of alternatives in the region as far as is generally known, but this is not a widely researched field.

Furthermore, the secondary information that is available is often clouded by a commercialization perspective. Hence, the vast majority of performance indicators are in terms of "efficiency". This has meant that public sector utilities are measured by how much they are like the private sector, with a heavy emphasis on financial performance. For example, a literature review of the impact of reforms in Uganda, Tanzania, and Kenya would suggest that they are all successful because of improvements in commercial, financial, and technical performance. This is attributed to autonomy, incentives, and accountability (Mugisha and Berg 2007). It has proved extremely difficult to obtain data on social aspects of delivery such as labour standards or access for the poor. In addition, any meaningful analysis on the extent of genuine participation and public sector ethos is difficult to gauge without conducting detailed fieldwork.

Notwithstanding these constraints, our research is a major advance in collating the disparate literature on public and community alternatives to private provision in the region. Our cases demonstrate capacity and support for public and community provision that are the start of a positive engagement and of promotion of alternatives to privatization. They should also be seen in relation to the other regions and sectors covered in this book.

Classifying alternatives

Our research has identified public providers and community systems that are classified and evaluated according to predetermined typologies and "success" criteria, as summarized in Table 12.3 (see Chapter 2, this volume, for a fuller discussion of research methodology). In addition, we have noted some successful community-managed systems of provision. These have been typically stimulated by an international NGO providing resources and impetus to local communities. These are numerous in the region in response to the failings of the dominant system of state-led provision to reach the urban poor. The findings from our research tentatively suggest that community-based organizations (CBOs) are more effective, however, when they operate in some kind of partnership with a public utility rather than in isolation.

Our findings fall into two organizational categories: single public sector agencies working alone to deliver a service (SiPs); and single

Table 12.3 African Water Alternatives

Country	Type	Name	Area served	Population served
Public provision				
Morocco	SiP	ONEP	National rural and urban—excluding some private concessions	27 million
Tunisia	SiP	SONEDE	National provider of drinking water	8.2 million
Uganda	SiP	NWSC	23 large towns	2.6 million
Burkina Faso	SiP	ONEA	42 cities	2.8 million
South Africa	SiP	Durban water, eThekwini Municipality	District—rural and urban	3.1 million
South Africa	SiP	Ugu	District— predominantly rural	700,000
Community provision				
Angola	SiNP/ PuNP	Development Workshop	73 standposts in Luanda	74,000
Ghana	SiNP	Savelugu		20,000
Ethiopia	SiNP	Hitosa	Villages and small towns	100,000
Zambia	SiNP/ PuNP	Lusaka water trusts		600,000
Tanzania	SiNP	Temeke	Peri-urban (Dar es Salaam)	43,000

non-profit agencies working alone to deliver a service (with no significant involvement by the state) (SiNPs). The typologies were blurred to some extent where, for example, public water utilities from one country were operating a management contract in another jurisdiction (as, for example, with publicly owned Rand Water from South Africa operating the Ghana Water Company Limited in Accra). While on one level this could be regarded as a public-public partnership (PuP), we have classified it as a form of privatization on the grounds that the consortium was awarded the contract in a commercial tender competing against private companies (van Rooyen and Hall 2007).

Some of the utilities in our list have always been in the public sector. Two of these cases, Morocco (ONEP) and Tunisia (SONEDE) were established over 30 years ago and do not appear to be under threat of privatization. Other SiPs were formed more recently in the wave of sectoral reform that has been experienced across the region since the 1990s and have had private sector participation to some degree and have been subject to commercialization to some degree (ONEA in Burkina Faso and National Water and Sewerage Corporation [NWSC] in Uganda).

The SiNP cases are smaller than state utilities. These are typically communities that have mobilized (or been mobilized by others) to address poor service delivery. While they are not a substitute for SiPs, they are an important alternative to the domestic private sector as a means to provide water to poor households, and some present innovative practices that could be replicated by state agencies. Whereas we have categorized these as single non-profit agencies, our research tentatively indicates that they are typically more successful when they have the support of a state utility.

Our research also uncovered various types of protest against privatization. Evidence from other regions indicates that social movement activism is a prelude to social change on a wider scale (see Chapter 6, this volume). The two countries that have demonstrated most resistance to privatization are Ghana and South Africa. These are discussed in more detail below.

SUCCESSES AND FAILURES OF ALTERNATIVES

Our discussion of successes and failures centres on alternative public utilities, of which we identified two in North Africa and two in SSA. We also discuss two municipal alternatives from South Africa and cases we have identified of community provision. The cases from North Africa are more robust, while the cases from SSA are heavily commercialized, yet these are the best available public water system alternatives that we could identify in the subregion. Most countries in SSA have strong donor input into sector finance and policy design. The similarities of the policies of commercialization and marketization—if not actual privatization—across SSA are striking.

SiPs I: Morocco and Tunisia

These state-owned water providers have income levels that are higher than several countries in the SSA region. The delivery of water in both is the responsibility of a public authority established in the late 1960s or early 1970s, and they have high rates of access and operate progressive tariff structures.

The water utility in Morocco, the National Office for Potable Water (ONEP), is an autonomous national public utility founded in 1972 and provides water to 27 million people with a staff of 6,800. ONEP is responsible for 99% of the water production and 70% of the distribution. Access rates for water are high (100% for urban water), although less so for sanitation (72% overall). ONEP is financially robust and has received no government subsidy since 1995, although it has received loans from donors, including the European Investment Bank and *Agence Française de Développement* (AFD). ONEP operates a progressive tariff structure, which aims to allow for solidarity between different regions to generate equality across the country as well as access for the poorest. ONEP is committed to public service delivery, has the right to water for all as a core value, and has a long-term vision (Bensaid 2008).

There was a movement towards privatization in Morocco in the late 1990s. Two long-term lease contracts were signed with French companies for the distribution of water in Casablanca and Rabat. Now, according to Samir Bensaid, Director for Cooperation and Communication at ONEP, a key obstacle to the development of public service is the privatization dogma along with frequent inappropriate technological choices and other dogmatic views, for example those regarding desalination. Internal obstacles to service improvement include bureaucracy, autocratic relationships with users, and lack of transparency (Bensaid 2008). ONEP is involved in two collaborative arrangements with water utilities in other SSA countries—namely, SNDE in Mauritania and SNEC in Cameroon.

In Tunisia, the national water distribution utility, *Société Nationale d'Exploitation et de Distribution des Eaux* (SONEDE) was created in 1968 under the supervision of the *Ministère de l'Agriculture et des Ressources Hydrauliques* (MARH). SONEDE is responsible for the delivery of water in both rural and urban areas. Water coverage is 99% in urban areas and 89% in rural areas. Unaccounted for water is at 20% (WSP and PPIAF 2009).

SONEDE is publicly owned and operated with a board of 12 directors. These are state agents or other government employees, one of which is a trade union representative. At the end of 2006, SONEDE employed 6,017 permanent staff. The law does not permit private sector participation in the form of leasing, build-operate-transfer, or disposition of financial assets, although SONEDE has introduced elements of the private sector over time.

SONEDE raises funds through user fees. The company is reported to have a strong technical performance but less good customer service. Tunisia has several national social programmes relating to water supply and sanitation for the poor, including Presidential Programmes and a National Solidarity Fund (FSN) that aim to increase public service delivery in underprivileged urban and rural areas. These programmes are financed from the state budget, external loans, and donations. Cross-subsidies are implemented—for example, a water connection loan is offered by SONEDE, which is repayable over a period of between five and eight years at 11% interest as a surcharge on the quarterly water bill. Surpluses from user fees enable the utility to cover all operation and maintenance costs as well as contribute an average 40% of financing for new projects with the rest from medium- and long-term loans. SONEDE borrows mostly on domestic markets and seeks concessionary loans for larger infrastructure projects (WSP and PPIAF 2009).

The extent to which these water operators will be affected by the democratic uprisings and changes taking place in the region in 2011 remains to be seen but may bring further transparency and equity orientation to both.

SiPs II: Uganda and Burkina Faso

Two national public water and sanitation utilities, NWSC in Uganda and ONEA in Burkina Faso, are regularly cited as examples of successful public provision in SSA (for example, Baietti et al, 2006). They are both operating in the context of very low incomes with extensive input from donors. NWSC in Uganda now provides consultancy to other water utilities in the region and the "Ugandan model" has been adopted elsewhere (for example in Tanzania).

Although publicly owned and operated, these utilities have all undergone restructuring along neoliberal lines (i.e. corporatized). Both cases have been associated with privatization to some degree as part of World Bank-sponsored reforms. In Burkina Faso, privatization was a condition for the provision of donor investment funds. Donors were pressing the government of Burkina Faso to introduce a form of private sector participation similar to the long-term lease contracts adopted in Senegal and Niger, but the state insisted on a less invasive form of privatization. ONEA signed a management contract with French multinational Veolia between 2001 and 2007. The private operator was appointed only to address financial aspects of utility management (World Bank 2008). In Uganda, NWSC had a three-year management contract with JBG Gauff (1997–2001), followed by a second management contract with Ondeo (2002–2004). These were considered a prelude to more far-reaching privatization, although this did not occur largely because of a marked improvement in the performance of NWSC as well as a downturn in investor interest in the African water sector (Watasa 2009). Thus these alternatives have emerged in the context of the need for donor finance and donor support for privatization.

The improvements that have taken place in these utilities are attributed to the introduction of performance contracts between the utility and the government. In Burkina Faso, three-year contract plans were introduced in 1993 between ONEA and the government of Burkina Faso that set targets for financial and commercial performance with targets for 34 indicators (WSP 2009a). In Uganda, the performance of NWSC was extremely poor in 1998 when a new board and CEO were appointed. The performance has improved dramatically according to key indicators. In addition to a performance contract with the government, the utility established a series of Internally Delegated Area Management Contracts—IDAMCs. Under these, an area manager has to meet agreed targets, which typically include working ratio, cash operating margin, non-revenue water, collection efficiency, and connection ratio measured by reporting systems as well as unannounced visits from "checkers". If targets are met, the manager earns a bonus, which can be as much as 120% of base salary. If targets are not met, a penalty is paid (Muhairwe 2009a).

Tables 12.4 and 12.5 show some key performance indicators for NWSC and ONEA. While there has been a dramatic turnaround in NWSC, the tables show that ONEA was performing well before the start of the management contract.

The data in these tables are from presentations developed to demonstrate the strength of performance of these utilities, but this is virtually always in terms of productive efficiency. In Burkina Faso, the World Bank

Table 12.4 National Water and Sewerage Corporation (NWSC), Uganda, performance comparisons in 1998 and 2008

	1998	*2008*
Service coverage	48%	72%
Network coverage	Increased by >50%	NA
Total connections	50,826	202,559
Staff per 1,000 connections	36	7
NRW	60%	32.5%
Turnover (US$)	21 million	84 million

Source: Muhairwe 2009b.

Table 12.5 ONEA, Burkina Faso, Performance Comparisons in 2001 and 2007

	2001	*2007*
Access to piped water	71%	76%
Number of customers	75,150	145,650
Staff per 1000 connections	8	5
UFW (% of production)	—	18
UFW (m³/km/day)	5.5	4.8
Turnover (US$)	25 million	45 million

UFW = unaccounted for water losses; Sources: Fall 2009, World Bank 2008 (Burkina Faso project evaluation).

2008 project evaluation report stated that "The financial equilibrium of the urban water sector was restored in 2006" (World Bank 2008, 10). This means that, according to the report, ONEA is fully able to cover its operational and maintenance costs and the debt service associated to its capital expenditures programmes without government subsidies.

In Uganda, NWSC can now cover operations and maintenance costs, as well as depreciation, through tariffs. However, despite substantial gains, according to the CEO, tariffs will not be sufficient to cover investment needs: "Full cost recovery tariffs remain a myth in most developing countries" because the tariff required would be unaffordable (Muhairwe 2009b). Alternative financing options are being explored. NWSC recently benefited from a debt-equity swap and is exploring the possibility of a local bond issue to raise funds for capital investment (Muhairwe 2008). This is potentially an innovative source of financing, but it is still in the planning stage. ONEA does not currently access local markets to finance capital infrastructure. While it is legally autonomous, ONEA struggles to collect payment from public sector customers (WSP and PPIAF 2009).

While the above indicators suggest that the performance of these utilities has been impressive, social policy has not featured strongly in reforms. There is now a "pro-poor" unit within NWSC, but the utility management has no incentive to serve poor households as they buy at the "social tariff", consume small amounts, and are less consistent payers. NWSC therefore applied to development agencies to help finance connections for poor households (Berg and Mugisha 2010).

According to Kouanda and Moudassir (2007), equity has deteriorated in Burkina Faso with the adoption of neoliberal reforms. Before the introduction of the management contract, water pricing was based on need and incomes from the profitable centres (the two biggest cities—Ouagadougou and Bobo), which were able to compensate for less profitable performance in other centres. Pricing objectives were aimed at achieving overall financial balance with cross-subsidy from different types of consumers. This was reportedly dismantled by Veolia, which, in the 2004 Contract Plan, stipulated that extension of network services will be dependent on financial profitability as well as size of the recipient community. The authors describe this as "a major turning point in ONEA's water supply policy" (Kouanda and Moudassir 2007, 17).

A different story is told by Matar Fall, the Lead Water and Sanitation Specialist at the World Bank, who presents a pre-reform case of low access and low productivity as well as an "inappropriate" tariff policy—i.e. one that is not based on cost recovery. The aim of the management contract was to restore "financial equilibrium" (Fall 2009, 27). According to Kouanda and Moudassir (2007), this has meant reducing charges to large volume consumers and increasing charges to small volume consumers.

In terms of pricing, both utilities have a progressive tariff policy with domestic users charged less than high-volume commercial users. The tariff structure is such that larger customers subsidize access for small consumers and large centres in the service area support small centres that are in deficit although the extent of this has reportedly been weakened in Burkina Faso (see above). Billing and collection rates for ONEA are hampered by non-payment by public institutions (WSP and PPIAF 2009).

In Uganda, NWSC water and sewerage rates are subject to annual indexation based on the domestic price index, exchange rate, foreign price indices, and electricity tariffs. As a result, the average tariff increased by 9.7% in 2008/2009, although the increase for large industrial users was only adjusted by 6%.[3]

There is concern about the amount of discretion of NWSC and the lack of adequate monitoring of the new mode of management (Watasa 2009). There is no independent regulator, and all reports are generated from within NWSC. The separation of roles (asset holding, regulation, and service provision), which was intended to create the institutional space for regulation still has not happened. Some regulatory instruments are provided for and some exist but their effectiveness is questionable. While the institutional arrangements seem to offer a good foundation for regulation, this is not the case in practice due to fragmentation (Water Dialogues 2007).

To conclude, then, these cases demonstrate that effective public provision is possible in the region—but the emphasis is clearly on a public utility that closely resembles the private sector. In a 2009 interview, the CEO of NWSC states that "We must run this business as if it were a private entity",[4] and this model is being extended to other countries in the region.

As the examples show, the way in which "success" of "public" service provision in Africa is interpreted is extremely narrow. The fact that these models are not participatory is never discussed. Some have policies in place for "customer" feedback, but these do not offer genuine forms of democratic participation. Nor have the concerns of CBOs been listened to (Watasa 2009). Similarly, the commercialized SiPs identified above are not necessarily equitable. Their coverage performance is usually in terms of access, without reference to who is getting access, and there is little incentive to serve poor households when performance is measured in terms of productivity and financial efficiency.

In Uganda, specific measures were taken to improve staff motivation and incentives, and the union was involved in efforts to improve staff performance. The workforce was halved, reportedly with no complaint from unions, and according to the Deputy Secretary General of the Uganda Public Employees Union, the union was closely involved in the restructuring process. Staff now work harder but for more money, and unions from other countries are benchmarking with NWSC on how to work best with management (Werikhe 2006).

These systems are sustainable where they provide water to reliable customers, but without an effective cross-subsidy system, service for poor households will be at the whim of donors, which seems to be the case in Uganda. Sustainability is therefore questionable due to the precarious financial situation of these utilities. Progress has been made, but large investments are required to reach the many end users who live in poverty.

Municipal-level services

There exists a wide array of institutional arrangements for the delivery of water in SSA. Some countries, such as Uganda and Ghana, have a national utility that provides water to major urban areas with different arrangements for rural areas. Elsewhere, there is a bulk water provider, which produces water and then distributes it to intermediaries (such as local or district municipalities) that are responsible for delivery to end users (as in Namibia and in some parts of South Africa). Elsewhere, municipalities are responsible for all aspects of service delivery, including abstraction and distribution (such as Tanzania).

There are therefore hundreds of municipal water providers in the region, and there has been little systematic research into how these operate. While some are listed in the data provided by GWOPA, these bald figures shed little light on how successful these utilities may be according to other criteria. Often these are established as part of programmes of decentralization and with support from the World Bank, and the information that is available is typically in terms of efficiency. Hence, we know for example that there are four "Category A" municipal providers in Tanzania (Arusha, Moshi, Tanga, and Mwanza), which means they are able to cover operation, maintenance, and staffing costs, but we could find little data on how effective they are at this, let alone on other aspects of performance such as support for poor households. Whereas some municipalities may perform well on an individual level, often the transfer of responsibility to the local level is part of a wider programme of decentralization, which reduces the scope for cross-subsidy at the national level, as for example in Namibia (Bayliss 2008), thus perpetuating regional inequity.

This section discusses two South African municipal providers, Durban and Ugu District Municipalities, which meet some of the success criteria defined for this research. In Durban, the eThekwini Water and Sanitation (eTWS) unit of the eThekwini Municipality (ETM) is responsible for the provision of water and sanitation services to all customers in the municipality. The ETM water and sanitation unit is a ring-fenced municipal department serving 3.1 million people with 394,000 connections. Water coverage is estimated to be around 50%. ETM is described by some observers as one of the strongest water providers in SSA (WSP and PPIAF 2009, 35).

ETM is pursuing social objectives, implementing a Basic Water and Sanitation Programme in the rural and peri-urban areas within its jurisdiction.[5] The aim of this programme is to provide an acceptable basic level of water and sanitation to all households in the eThekwini municipality by 2010. Priority is given to places at risk of water-borne disease. The project is funded in part by the national government's Municipal Infrastructure Grant.

ETM has received international acclaim. In 2007, the municipality won a United Nations Public Service Award for its Water and Sanitation Debt Relief Programme.[6] This was a scheme established to provide support for those who have difficulty paying their water bill, with a debt relief scheme that gives those with accumulated arrears a chance to write these off by signing a contract where they commit to pay the bill in full over a period of 20 months. Under the debt relief scheme, customers in arrears can choose to have a flow limiter installed to limit consumption to 200 litres a day. The ETM water and sanitation programme is also listed under the UN 2006 Best Practices database (www.unhabitat.org/bestpractices/2006).

However, while achievements have been made, there are concerns about the situation of poor households, a situation acknowledged even by ETM's own commissioned research, which found that "customer satisfaction" was lowest in poorest households (Hemson and Kvalsvig 2005). ETM provides different levels of service for different income levels. They provided a tank for the poorest, but they changed this to a flow limiter, which has been designed to restrict the flow of water to those that cannot pay their bills. These have been extremely problematic and heavily criticized. The programme in Durban has, on the one hand, meant that some have access to clean water for the first time in their lives, but for others bills have escalated while the amount of water provided is restricted to a level barely enough to survive (Loftus 2005). After the "free basic water" amount (25 litres per person per day), prices increase steeply. Evidence shows that the average per person consumption for low-income consumers actually fell from 22 kilolitres/household/month in 1997 to 15 kilolitres/household/month in 2003 (Bond and Dugard 2008). So while the scheme provides water, it also depends on limiting the amount of water that is available to the poor and then helping them to pay. In addition, it provides only the most basic level of service to poor households. An alternative would be a pricing structure that was more skewed to higher volume consumption rather than trying to get more money out of the poorest (Bond and Dugard 2008).

Also in South Africa, Ugu District Municipality serves about 700,000 people in the province of KwaZulu-Natal. The majority of the population (84%) lives in rural areas. The unemployment rate is about 30% and is higher in rural areas. Despite these constraints, Ugu District Municipality is performing well relative to other municipalities according to official benchmarking. Ugu was found to have the highest rate of payment collection, the lowest proportion of water quality sample failures and an encouraging rate of eliminating backlogs—between 6% and 10% a year for water—although the rate for sanitation is just 2% a year (Water Dialogues 2008).

Ugu is regarded as financially sound with high revenue collection and accurate billing. Unaccounted for water is around 35%. Connection charges for rural areas are subsidized by those for urban areas although prices still remain high. Consumption charges are also high. The Water Dialogues report cites evidence to show that:

> a household using 50 kilolitres per month will pay R6,704.54 (US$857) per year whilst a rural household using 10 kilolitres per month would have to pay R1,094.16 (US$140) per year excluding water rates (if rates are included this increases to R2,184.86 (US$279) per year). Even at R1,094.16 per year, it equates to close on R100.00 (US$13) per month—not an inconsiderable cost for a low-income household. (Zybrands cited in Water Dialogues 2008, 29)

While prices for water consumption are regarded as expensive, there is a surprisingly high payment rate (96%), although some people access water from standpipes or rivers and thus do not pay for their water. For those with metered connections, costs are dear, and there is a question as to whether they even receive their free basic water allocation.

The biggest challenge for Ugu is increasing access. Around 40% of the population still does not have access to potable water, and 70% lacks access to basic sanitation, although these are not spread evenly, with urban coastal areas receiving far better services than inland rural communities. Whereas this is in part due to historical inequities, there still seems to be a bias towards improving services for towns (Water Dialogues 2008). The utility operates well but struggles financially to make a dent in the long backlogs. Despite a very high payment rate, Ugu DM carries a considerable amount of debt.

Ugu employs 645 staff. They are 100% unionized, and the utility has a good retention rate, but, in common with ETM in Durban, there are severe shortages in key skilled areas, and many positions, particularly in middle and upper management, are left unfilled for significant periods. It is reported that the workload has been increasing with increased infrastructure development. In talking to communities themselves, the Water Dialogues (2008) research found that communities dug their own trenches as the municipality will only dig to the end of the municipal pipeline.

There are concerns about accountability and monitoring of Ugu as well as water quality. There is a threat of pollution from industry and agriculture, but recent benchmarking showed that Ugu had low rates of failure of water quality samples. CBOs were not successful in Ugu. Originally they dominated delivery in rural areas, but the municipality chose to disband them and absorb the employees into the water company. CBOs tended to run up debts and lacked capacity. However, according to the Water Dialogues (2008) report, there is a gap in provision in rural areas, which could go some way to being filled by CBOs.

Although these cases of municipal provision are flawed, they show some innovative practices in reaching poorer communities and have made this a priority rather than just focusing on financial sustainability. There has been very little documented about municipal provision in the region, and there are probably many other relevant cases. A key element in these two cases is that investment is not financed by user charges but by a national fund. These municipalities are therefore not limited to being financially self-sufficient but can access national reserves to finance capital investment.

Community provision

As noted earlier, some African cities have very high rates of slum prevalence. In Angola, over 86% of the urban population lives in slum areas (UN-Habitat 2008b). Many of these areas are not reached by public (or private) water utilities. Those that do have a piped connection often do not have water flowing through them. To fill such gaps in service provision people turn to alternative means of accessing water. This can be through small-scale private providers, NGOs, or CBOs—or alternative unsafe sources. Faith-based organizations have also filled this gap. It is not unusual to find communities organizing around water provision.

Effective public delivery to all households is a very long way off for most African urban areas. Service provision outside the limits of the utility is an element of water policy that has long been neglected, while attention has focused on improving the performance of the formal provider. Yet most poor households access water through such informal systems. These are not arrangements that are alternatives to the utility but must be considered in parallel.

Lack of formal water access has given rise to a range of private sector water entrepreneurs from sachet sellers to tanker trucks. These providers display all the entrepreneurial agility that is considered lacking in the public sector (customer care, no debts, threat of bankruptcy for poor performance). However, there is no reason to suggest that such providers would be anything but opportunistic and predatory, and anecdotal evidence suggests that this is the case in many situations. Community provision, although far from ideal, nevertheless presents an alternative model to domestic private provision.

This section considers successes and failures of five community managed water systems: Hitosa (Ethiopia), Development Workshop (Angola), Savelugu (Ghana), Lusaka Water Trust (Zambia), and Temeke District (Tanzania). Each of these was established with support from an international donor or NGO. WaterAid, Development Workshop, UNICEF, Global 2000, Tearfund, CARE International, and the UK Department for International Development (DFID) were all involved in one or more of these.

The CBOs were established on a small scale initially. The smallest of these, in Savelugu, Ghana, is a small-town community system, which is ultimately a distribution system. Unlike other community-managed schemes in Ghana, the Savelugu community accesses its water from the national utility, Ghana Water Company Limited (GWCL; Adam 2005). Temeke in Tanzania began by serving 11 streets in three wards, but eventually this has been extended to 72 standposts covering a population of 43,000. Similarly the Development Workshop project in Angola has evolved over a 15-year period to now serve over 70,000 people (Cain and Mulenga 2009). The biggest of these CBOs is the Lusaka Water Trust, which serves around 600,000 in peri-urban settlements (WSP 2009b).

These systems are basic—they are typically concerned with a system for managing kiosks and standposts. The communities have organized (or been organized by others) into a hierarchy of water committees and water associations with different levels of decision-making powers. The management appoints a tap attendant or kiosk manager. Before these community systems were in place, local residents were paying high prices for water from secondary providers, travelling long distances, and/or using unsafe water. Each of these cases also involves the local water utility to some degree; for example, in Lusaka the utility provides maintenance for the Water Trust system and the local council is represented on the board (Mwanamwambwa et al, 2005). In Ghana the community buys water from the utility.

Community providers are often outside the realm of utility financing and are usually self-financing. To this extent, they fit the mould of neoliberal cost recovery practices. On a practical level, experience from Angola shows that it is unrealistic to rely on funds from the state budget (Cain and Mulenga 2009). However, evidence from Tanzania indicates that the performance of these CBOs depends on resources and some have been successful in getting substantial donor funding (Dill 2010).

These community systems are far more participatory than the SiPs listed above. Key to their operation is elected officials and Water User Associations, but whether this has a genuine impact on outcomes is not yet known. While the institutional framework may be accountable and transparent, real decision making may take place behind the scenes. However, although the management system may not represent the interests of the most marginalized, this is an improvement on other options, which are typically paying a higher price to a private provider or use of unsafe sources. The impact on quality is uncertain, but it is clear that in some cases (Angola for example), the water sold by private providers is of dubious quality and inferior to that provided by the community (Cain and Mulenga 2009).

In terms of labour conditions, many of the staff of water user associations are volunteers. Similarly, some of the construction of infrastructure is done by volunteers. This typically takes the labour of the poorest and most disadvantaged. In community provision, labour standards are non-existent, and work is low-skilled, although skills are acquired on the job. This environment does not encourage unionization. Some solidarity has been built with other social networks, for example, with South Africa's Homeless People's Federation and Zimbabwe's Dialogue on Shelter networking with Temeke District community managed water (Glöckner et al, 2004).

Community organizations—like public utilities—encompass numerous different organizational structures. Community management is no guarantee of equitable management and some operate almost as private enterprises even if they are run on a not-for-profit basis. Whereas it is debatable whether such community-managed systems are sustainable, ultimately they need to be seen as a stop-gap, a temporary means of alleviating the challenges of service delivery holes. They are no substitute for public provision. The risk with advocating such community systems is that the level of need will be overlooked; a crucial component has to be scaling up to reach the point of effective advocacy for improved public provision, as has happened in South Africa. Community-managed systems can be supported to be agents for social change when empowered to demand better public services.

Activism for public services

There has been surprisingly little resistance to privatization in Africa outside South Africa and Ghana, which has created effective resistance movements (Prempeh 2006, Bond 2007). The relatively low levels of activism in relation to water in Africa has largely come about as a result of co-option of civil society groups into service provision, whose lifeline is patronage from the state and donor agencies. In some countries, the high handedness of dictatorial regimes contributed to the culture of silence. Advocating against neoliberal policies means either being starved of funding or facing state repression. Another factor is the marriage of convenience between civil society and political parties. In such circumstances, civil society is hesitant to criticize government policies (Bond 2007).

This situation is beginning to change as more and more people are challenging the dictators, and popular democracy is taking root in Africa (Prempeh 2006, Bond 2007), with events in North Africa in 2011 perhaps heralding a shift in public service delivery as well. Also, some of the donors and international organizations have come to realize that citizens' advocacy is more effective in promoting transparency and improving service delivery. The World Bank, DFID, the Danish International Development Agency (DANIDA), and the other major donors are setting up funds to support advocacy, although the ideological orientation of such activism may serve to reinforce rather than challenge privatization.

There are some progressive networks beginning to form across the continent, however, notably through the Africa Water Network (AWN). This platform has a membership of 24 African countries, whose members come from very different backgrounds. There are three main categories of membership, namely trade unions (predominantly from Public Services International affiliates), social movements, and NGOs, with some academics affiliated to the network. The formation of AWN has extended the reach of water activism on the continent (Pambazuka 2009), with AWN being key in initiating solidarity action across and within countries.

In November 2007, AWN organized a solidarity protest in Soweto, South Africa, against prepaid meters during its 2007 annual general meeting. AWN has also taken a stance against state-sponsored violence on water activism. In 2008, Malian police shot on a crowd protesting against water privatization. One protester was shot dead (*AFP* 2008), and AWN organized a global signature campaign, which was delivered to all Malian embassies from the Americas to Africa. The reach of AWN is expanding gradually and also in a diverse way. AWN has not only been protesting but also engaging bodies such as the African Union and the United Nations. In January 2009, AWN was elected to the UN-coordinated Steering Committee of the GWOPA to represent the interests of "civil society organizations".

A number of labour unions (Global Water Intelligence 2001, Hall et al, 2005) in Africa are also at the forefront of the struggle against water liberalization and privatization. The South African Municipal Workers Union (Samwu), the Ghana Trade Union Congress (GTUC), the Amalgamated Union Public Corporation Civil Service Technical and Recreational Employees (AUPCCSTRE), the Kenyan Local Government Workers Union,

Water Employees Trade Union of Malawi (WETUM), and the Tunisia *Syndicat Général des Eaux* (SGE) are the most active in these struggles, and these unions are also members of AWN.

South Africa

There are regular demonstrations and protests in South Africa over the poor state of service delivery and the treatment of low-income households. The Coalition against Water Privatization (CAWP) was formed in 2003 bringing together a range of social movements and progressive NGOs (McKinley 2006). CAWP has been active in organizing protests throughout South Africa against poor service delivery and the introduction of prepaid meters, including bringing in the gender dimension with demonstrations from Women for Water.

A key development in the social movement was a legal challenge on the basis of the right to water. The Centre for Applied Legal Studies (CALS)—a human rights research, advocacy and public interest litigation unit attached to the law school at the University of the Witwatersrand (Johannesburg)—together with CAWP and the Anti-Privatization Forum (APF) constructed a water rights case against disconnections, the installation of prepaid meters, as well as the low amount of Free Basic Water (FBW) provided by the government, focusing on the impoverished suburb of Phiri, in Soweto. The case was launched in the Johannesburg High Court in July 2006. After appeals, the final judgment was announced in October 2009, with the judge ruling that the installation of prepayment meters in Phiri was in fact lawful. Despite the setback, activism against water commercialization—and the push for effective "public" service delivery—continues apace in the country, with one of the most vibrant networks on the continent.

Ghana

The National Coalition against Privatization of Water (NCAP) was launched in May 2001 in Accra (Prempeh 2006). This initiative was taken by civil society (trade unions, NGOs, CBOs, student unions, and think tanks) to stop the privatization of the Ghana Water Company Limited. According to historians (Bohman 2010), Ghanaian civil society has been active in protesting against harsh water policies since 1934 when the then colonial administration introduced water rates.

Although the campaign by NCAP has not been entirely successful, it can be said that the impact of the campaign was the change of the private sector contract from lease option to service management contract, a less extensive private arrangement. The coalition relied on media campaigns, community mobilizations, solidarity with international water activists, and fact-finding missions to influence the process. NCAP has continued with its campaign even when the contract was changed to a service management contract with

Aqua Vitens Rand Limited (AVRL). Within three years of the management contract, AVRL has been summoned to parliament to answer questions on service standards, and two managing directors and one operations manager have been fired. These developments are a result of the public pressure generated by NCAP due to poor services. NCAP recently petitioned the serious fraud office to investigate the performance of AVRL vis-à-vis the contract performance benchmarks.

The campaign in Ghana has been a motivating factor for other countries on the continent to pick up the fight against privatization and NCAP has been instrumental in the formation of AWN. Within Ghana, NCAP has established a network including the following coalitions and platforms: National Coalition of Mining, Network for Women's Right, Essential Service Platform, and Freedom of Information Bill Coalition. Being part of such a network of civil society groups makes it easier to popularize and mobilize national opinion for its advocacy for public water services.

EMERGING ISSUES IN AFRICAN WATER

This section highlights some of the main themes that emerged in the course of our mapping exercise and some of the constraints to the development of strong alternatives in the region. There are three strands to this analysis. We consider the changing face of privatization in SSA, the role of different stakeholders (donors, governments, CBOs), and the issue of finance. A key message that underlies our findings is the importance of context and the need for water policy to be integrated into addressing wider issues of deprivation. The delivery of urban water and sanitation cannot be considered in isolation from ongoing rapid urbanization. Many of the problems in the region stem from inherited tenure and administration systems that cannot cope with rapid urban growth.

The changing face of privatization

Whereas privatization was a core policy for many countries, only a handful of long-term concessions are still in place in the water sector today (Côte d'Ivoire, Senegal, Gabon, Niger, and Mozambique), largely with French companies (Saur, Veolia). According to Briceño-Garmendia et al (2008), there have been 26 "private participation in infrastructure" transactions in water in SSA, but many have been controversial and problematic, with 40% of these cancelled before completion. Setting aside the extensive public sector and donor resources that were diverted to supporting privatization, times have changed, and three main features dominate the post-privatization institutional landscape.

First, while the extent of privatization may be limited, many more countries have voiced commitment to private sector participation and have introduced sector reforms that are designed to enable it. Many have taken measures to introduce commercialization such as establishing a corporation or similar entity for the delivery of water with a focus on full cost recovery. Some countries have spent years trying to privatize, such as Malawi, which initially began trying to sell Blantyre and Lilongwe water boards in 1996 before finally agreeing to a management contract with Vitens in 2009, some 13 years later—and even this was only achieved with finance from the EU and the European Investment Bank. Sector policy in SSA has been dominated by the push to attract the private sector. This contrasts with utilities in North Africa, whose cases outlined above demonstrate that public utilities in Morocco and Tunisia have been effective providers for decades.

The failure to achieve or sustain privatization has meant that public providers are operating in a policy framework designed for the private sector. In Tanzania, for example, the privatization contract collapsed after just 18 months when, despite extensive efforts—not to mention finance—the contract made the situation for the poor even worse (de Waal and Cooksey 2008). The utility has since been renationalized, but the state provider that stepped in to fill the gap left by City Water (DAWASCO) has taken on the same contractual framework as the private contractor. So, even if privatization has not been that far-reaching in terms of contracts signed, its influence has been far more penetrating in the design of policy frameworks, and the scope for alternative approaches has been weakened.

As a result, there is a mismatch between the institutional reality and the policy framework. For example, vast amounts have been spent on consultants for such activities as writing legislation to enable private sector involvement and to establish independent regulators. Now, however, it emerges that the water sector in countries with an independent regulator perform no better than those without one (Foster and Briceño-Garmendia 2010). Although a number of countries have only recently created independent regulators, it seems they are irrelevant.

Similarly, countries have separated the ownership of infrastructure assets from the management of service delivery. This was designed to enable the private sector to step in with low-risk exposure so that the more risky activity of owning infrastructure remained with the state. However, if privatization is not achieved, the benefit of creating two public sector bodies with similar but institutionally separate functions is not clear.

Second, expectations have been modified so that the private sector is no longer expected to provide finance or be exposed to any kind of risk but just to provide expertise in the form of management contracts. A report from the PPIAF indicates that it was a mistake to expect the private sector to bring finance and in fact it should only be expected to generate efficiency, but using public sector investment:

A new generation of water PPP projects already has been gradually emerging, as these elements were being internalized by the market. . .

More and more countries are adopting a PPP model in which investment is largely funded by public money with the private operator focusing on improving service and operational efficiency. (Marin 2009, 8)

Some of the examples of "successful" public sector utilities discussed
above have had short-term private management contracts (Burkina Faso
and Uganda). More recently, management contracts have been established
that have been awarded to external public utilities rather than the private
sector—for example, the management contract in Ghana is with Vitens
and Rand Water, Dutch and South African public utilities, respectively.
Similarly the management contract in Cameroon was awarded to ONEP,
the Moroccan public utility. Hence we are seeing an increasing blurring of
the divide between public and private as public utilities have been "privatized" in the past but are now public again, while some public providers are
operating in a similar vein to the private sector.

In a further twist, privatizations with management contracts have
increasingly taken the form of South-South collaboration, for example,
with the Moroccan utility ONEP winning contracts in Cameroon and
Mauritania. The Ugandan water utility, NWSC, is now operating in several
countries, and this has generated revenue for the corporation. It operates as
a consultancy and bids for tenders in the same way as private companies.
In 2008 NWSC won contracts to provide services to utilities in Rwanda
(Electrogaz), to the Zanzibar water authority, to DAWASA/DAWASCO in
Tanzania and Kenya (NWSC 2008). NWSC also provided in-house training, as in June 2009, for civil servants from the water utility in Harar in
Ethiopia. This is another mechanism for rolling out the Ugandan model
with an emphasis (in the course training manual) on reducing non-revenue
water, identifying "illegal" water use, improving billing, and how to provide good customer care. There is no reference to how to reach those most
in need or how to identify when a household cannot pay or how to finance
extensions to poor areas (NWSC 2009).

While collaboration between public utilities is vital, more research is
needed to determine how to make best use of such capacity. For example, where a state provider is operating as a private company, financing their domestic operations with services to other African utilities,
there is a lack of solidarity and dilution of the public sector ethos. Even
when the "consultancies" are financed by donors, these costs have some
opportunity value in that these are resources that could have been spent
on some other component of donor support. While public sector workers should be compensated for time and expertise devoted to advising
other providers, and this is on commercial terms, it is no different to the
private sector.

An alternative means of collaboration is promoted by GWOPA, which
aims to facilitate cooperation between public providers via the sharing
of expertise rather than competing for tenders on a commercial basis.

GWOPA is a UN initiative launched in August 2007 in Stockholm and formally constituted in January 2009 in Nairobi. The focus is on "political, financial and technical support to make Water Operators' Partnerships a more effective and systematic way of building capacity for utilities" (UN-Habitat 2009). Although GWOPA is a novelty, and some water activists are enthused about it, currently there is divergence about the use of a "quarantine" period against private sector companies who participate in the GWOPA. CSO representatives on the steering committee are arguing for 10 years quarantine for any private company who is engaged in the GWOPA, but this has not been agreed by the private sector. Furthermore, support for GWOPA has been based in part on what may be an overly consensual concept of "public" that includes entities that are underpinned by extensive commercialization (Boag and McDonald 2010).

Third, given the lack of interest from the international private sector, attention is turning to the domestic private sector. In urban areas of SSA, around half the population is outside the remit of the local water utility, obtaining water from alternative sources (small-scale private providers, NGOs, community organizations, or unsafe sources). This is more significant than in Latin America and East Asia, where about a quarter of the urban population obtains water from such sources. The operations of "water entrepreneurs" are attracting increasing attention (Marin 2009). This is a kind of privatization by default in response to the failings of other forms of service delivery.

The role of donors, governments, and CBOs

The extent to which the World Bank agenda has permeated water sector policy throughout the region is difficult to overstate. Other donors also have been strong supporters of marketization and corporatization (for example, the British aid agency DFID). The reach of these donors goes beyond policy conditionality to incorporate a dominance of available literature plus a stranglehold on funding for "independent" consultants and policy advisers. Hence, throughout the region countries have adopted policy measures designed to suit the private sector.

However, not all donors have the same perspective. For example, while the World Bank is promoting marketization and full cost recovery, UN-Habitat has championed GWOPA to strengthen capacity and spread knowledge in an extensive network of utility partners (UN-Habitat 2009). UN-Habitat underlines the need for an urban governance system that promotes the ownership of development strategies by local communities and incorporates principles of inclusiveness, sustainability, equity, and human rights (Moretto 2005). There is also considerable diversity in the funding sources outlined in the cases discussed above. Greater awareness of the underlying policy perspective of funders could support public utilities in identifying supportive donor partners.

The political elite in Sub-Saharan Africa are often closely allied with donors, be they ruling or in opposition. Their policies are generally geared towards pleasing the whims and caprice of donors. The case in point is the Ghana water sector reforms in 1999 when the World Bank was critical of the ruling government's implementation of the reforms and issued a threat:

> The Bank will be compelled to withdraw from this sector, as the Government plans to award a major contract under this program in a non-transparent manner. If this occurs, the Government has been informed that the allocated funds in the proposed lending program (FY2001), US$100 million, would be cancelled from the proposed three-year program. (World Bank 2000)

The Bank also makes a point of targeting political parties before they are elected: "Political will to carry out reform and to support its objectives has to be clearly expressed and manifested at the highest political level usually through a cabinet decision and a Letter of Sector Policy. . . Support of political opposition sought ahead of election (Ghana)" (World Bank 2002, 20).

This is in contrast with the political situation in Latin America, where the wave reviving leftist politics has had a positive effect on civil society as well as the organization of public utilities who are experimenting with all manner of social management and open space managements (see Chapters 14, 15, and 16, this volume).

CBOs in service delivery have emerged, but they need help to scale up, and ultimately the aim should be for these to be replaced by the public sector. CBOs are not necessarily an antidote to privatization and, unwittingly, community provision can reinforce the neoliberal policy framework by assuming responsibility for service delivery to the poorest and the more difficult to reach. This then eases demands on the utility that can then focus on provision for more attractive customers that are high volume, wealthy ones. In addition, community provision can often fail to recognize the interests of the most marginalized and can serve as a means to support the vested interests in the community. Page (2002a, 486) demonstrates how the presentation of community management is shaped to suit the tastes of international donors, glossing over internal social divisions and tensions, based on a case in Kumbo, Cameroon, where he describes "the invention of community".

It has also been demonstrated that gender-based discrimination can be more powerful at the community level. A review of decentralization and gender by Beall (2005) reveals that, while locally based decision making might be expected to be empowering for women, in practice the local government was more infused with customary practices, orchestrated by traditional authorities, which had a negative impact on women's prospects for democratic inclusion. She indicates that women are better able to participate in national rather than local administrations because local government is more open to informal systems that undermine or bypass formal rules and procedures. Women are less able to make use of informal structures.

There is some evidence to indicate that community provision cannot be sustained or scaled up without collaborating with the utility. Dill (2010) demonstrates in a review of different CBOs in Tanzania that they need public sector support to provide services on the scale required. However, this may also serve political ends. CBOs are not a threat to the government's sense of its own authority if it is allied to local government representatives, as demonstrated in Page's account of Cameroon (2002b). Whereas CBOs may be a stop-gap in the face of the massive gaps in urban service delivery, they need to become advocacy movements for a universal public service.

Finance

As noted at the outset of this paper, water delivery in Africa is crippled by lack of finance. Even in the relatively positive cases discussed above, Burkina Faso and Uganda, cost recovery tariffs can only cover operations and maintenance. One policy response has been to cut consumption subsidies to increase available revenue. However, tariffs are already high by developing country standards and the recommended tariff is close to that of OECD countries. Furthermore, it is not clear that additional revenue from removing subsidies will be simply translated into improving access. Many utilities provide only intermittent supply, which, aside from welfare implications, places a strain on the infrastructure. Regular supply to the existing network is often beyond existing capacity so additional finance is likely to be invested in strengthening bulk water supply, which will improve services for those with existing connections.

The World Bank's response to this challenge is increasing the time frame over which the MDG targets are set and aiming for lower cost technology (Foster and Briceño-Garmendia 2010, 83). But this approach is simply about lowering expectations, and hence cost, to reduce the funding gap, and is not about sources of finance.

Some more innovative approaches to address the financing gap are emerging in the region, although they have yet to be tested. In Uganda NWSC will issue a local bond, according to its CEO. It is envisaged that the bond will entail a Medium Term Note of about Shs100 billion (US$60 million), which will be disbursed in tranches of about Shs30 billion (US$18 million) per annum over three years. It may be that an institutional investor (such as National Social Security Fund—NSSF) takes up 60% of the bond (Muhairwe 2009a). Alternatively, water and sanitation, which typically attract only a small proportion of domestic public funding, could be awarded more substantial budget allocation. Other possibilities include radically revising tariff structures, so they are skewed more to higher volume consumption, while avoiding penalizing high-density households.

Other sources of finance include a stepping up in donor finance but without attachment to policy conditionality. As mentioned earlier, the financing gap is around US$13 billion a year. This is substantial for the economies involved but appears feasible for donor country governments that have spent many times this amount bailing out financial institutions in the 2008–2009 financial crisis.

There is potentially a tension between financial independence and social provision as utilities will be attracted to high volume consumers that are regular payers if performance is measured in financial terms. The World Bank has been behind a drive towards financial sustainability for utilities, so it comes as no surprise that social policy has been neglected. This is raised in a supporting paper for the AICD: "The culture of many utilities, particularly those without incentives aligned to broader policies of expanding access, tends to center around technical aspects of service delivery, and meeting financial performance targets" (Keener at al, 2009, 37). Although finance is needed, so is a change in ethos so that access for all, rather than revenue, becomes the policy goal.

CONCLUSION AND WAYS FORWARD

This chapter attempts to bring together findings on alternatives to commercialization in the water sector in Sub-Saharan Africa. The extent of alternatives is thin at this stage but is the result of both far-reaching neoliberal policies as well as a research agenda that has so far perpetuated these policies so that policy and research are closely linked (see Bayliss 2011). Far more research is required, particularly along three key themes. First and foremost, more investigation is required both with the cases cited above—in terms of their social and equitable approach beyond their financial performance—and into other potential alternatives. Promising cases that have emerged include Botswana and Tanzania municipalities (including Zanzibar) as well as Togo and Benin. More in-depth research also needs to consider the ways in which water features in social provision, exploring such issues as the linkages that exist with housing and health services as well as slum upgrading.

Second, in terms of future policy directions, the scope for cooperation between public providers is important, and key to this would be to understand the different terms of engagement for partnerships between public operators. A suitable starting point would be an evaluation of the different relationships in current collaborative arrangements—between ONEP (Morocco) working in Cameroon and Mauritania compared with NWSC (Uganda) working in Tanzania and Kenya, and Rand Water (South Africa) working in Ghana. This research would feed into understanding how to make best use of public utilities in the region and strengthen solidarity.

Third, additional research should also investigate the role and approach of donors in the region to identify differences in ethos and approach and to determine how donors can best support water delivery in the region to create accountable, equitable, participatory, sustainable systems of *public* provision.

To advance advocacy, we need to highlight the successes that have emerged while acknowledging their limitations. By global standards, there are no examples of "successes" in the delivery of water and sanitation in SSA that satisfactorily meet the baseline criteria established for this research project. Those that are considered a relative success in the regional context would be sorely lacking when compared with examples from elsewhere. The dilemma is whether to lower the bar because of the regional lack of good examples. Our cases from SSA are not robust but show some promise. We would argue that there is a need to engage with the weaker success examples in SSA as well as the cases from Morocco and Tunisia.

The cases presented here are far more imbued with neoliberalism than those in Latin America, which presents more vigorous alternatives. However, in terms of advocacy, our view is that we need to work within existing frameworks rather than aiming to bring in an alternative model wholesale from another region. We would argue that the historical and political context has shaped the existing pattern of delivery in Africa and will continue to do so. Thus, a push for change will be more effective by working with what is already in existence rather than aiming to supplant current frameworks with models that may be too contextually dependent to be effective in the African context.

Finally, our research needs to have broad reach to be of practical relevance and to have policy impact. We would therefore aim to support organizations working with alternatives. We would, for example, anticipate working with GWOPA to explore and establish concrete ways in which public utilities can support each other, as well as with trade unions promoting public provision. We would also recommend providing support at the community level to promote alternatives to the domestic private sector and direct support to include advocacy to put pressure on governments to provide services and to encourage scaling up. The reach and influence of such research would depend on the production of easily accessible and widely disseminated information, which would be vital in challenging the dominance of information provided by donor organizations.

NOTES

1. See www.africawaternetwork.org.
2. UN (United Nations). www.un.org/millenniumgoals/environ.shtml.
3. NWSC. www.nwsc.co.ug/index10.php (accessed 15 December 2009).
4. NWSC press release, "2009 NWSC Marks 35 Years in Existence" (posted on 1 February 2009).

5. www.durban.gov.za/durban/services/water_and_sanitation.
6. www.unpan1.un.org/intradoc/groups/public/documents/UN/UNPAN026042.
   pdf (accessed 19 January 2010).

REFERENCES

Adam, A. 2005. Against the current: Community-controlled water delivery in Save uGu, Ghana. In Balanyá, B., Brennan, B., Hoedeman, O., Kishimoto, S. and Terhorst, P. (Eds), *Reclaiming public water achievements, struggles and visions from around the world*, pp. 139–147. Transnational Institute and Corporate Europe Observatory.

AFP (Agence France-Presse). 2008. One dead, five hurt after Mali authorities open fire on protest. 10 November. www.afp.google.com/article/ALeqM5hA40p1aCePt_eyliWfiOeq1wH1Qg.

Baietti, A., Kingdom, W. and van Ginneken, M. 2006. *Characteristics of well-performing public water utilities*. Water Supply and Sanitation Working Notes No. 9. Washington, DC: World Bank.

Bayliss, K. 2008. Namibia: Lessons from commercialisation. In Bayliss, K. and Fine, B. (Eds), *Privatization and alternative public sector reform in Sub-Saharan Africa: Delivering on electricity and water*. Basingstoke, UK: Palgrave Macmlllan.

Bayliss, K. 2011. A cup half full: The World Bank's assessment of water privatisation. In Fine, B., van Waeyenberge, E. and Bayliss, K. (Eds), *The political economy of development: The World Bank, neoliberalism and development research*. London: Pluto Press.

Beall, J. 2005. *Decentralizing government and centralizing gender in Southern Africa: Lessons from the South African experience*. Occasional Paper 8. Geneva: UNRISD (United National Research Institute on Social Development).

Berg, S. and Mugisha, S. 2010. Pro-poor water service strategies in developing countries: Promoting justice in Uganda's urban project. *Water Policy* 12(4): 589–601.

Bensaid, S. 2008. *An efficient public service: A key option for expanding access to drinking water and sanitation*. In Proceedings of the International Conference on Water Governance in the MENA Region: From Analysis to Action. Marrakech, Morocco, 9–13 June. www.*gc21.inwent.org/ibt/en/site/mena/ibt/down/Bensaid_Samir_E.ppt* (accessed 21 October 2009).

Boag, G. and McDonald, D.A. 2010. A critical review of public-public partnerships in water services. *Water Alternatives* 3(1): 25.

Bohman, A. 2010. Framing the water and sanitation challenge: A history of urban water supply and sanitation in Ghana 1909–2005. PhD Thesis. Umeä University, Sweden.

Bond, P. 2007. *Looting Africa: The economics of exploitation*. London: Zed.

Bond, P. and Dugard, J. 2008. Water, human rights and social conflict: South African experiences. *Law, Social Justice and Global Development Journal* (LGD) 1. www.go.warwick.ac.uk/elj/lgd/2008_1/bond_dugard.

Briceño-Garmendia, C., Smits, K. and Foster, V. 2008, *Financing public infrastructure in Sub-Saharan Africa: Patterns and emerging issues*. Washington, DC: World Bank.

Cain, A. and Mulenga, M. 2009. *Water service provision for the peri-urban poor in post-conflict Angola*. Human Settlements Series, Water 6. London: International Institute for Environment and Development.

de Waal, D. and Cooksey, B. 2008. *Why did City Water fail? The rise and fall of private sector participation in Dar es Salaam's water supply*. London: WaterAid.

Dill, B. 2010. Public–public partnerships in urban water provision: The case of Dar Es Salaam. *Journal of International Development* 22(5): 611–624.

Fall, M. 2009. Improving performance, the role of governance: The case of Burkina Faso. In Proceedings of Water Week, World Bank, Washington, DC, 17–19 February 2009.

Foster, V. and Briceño-Garmendia, C. (Eds). 2010. *Africa's infrastructure: A time for transformation.* Washington, DC: IBRD.

Global Water Intelligence. 2001. The politics of PSP. *Global Water Intelligence* 2 (12). www.globalwaterintel.com/archive/2/12/general/the-politics-of-psp.html.

Glöckner, H., Mkanga, M. and Ndezi, T. 2004. Local empowerment through community mapping for water and sanitation in Dar es Salaam. *Environment and Urbanization* 16: 185.

Hall, D., Lobina, E. and De la Motte, R. 2005. Public resistance to privatization in water and energy. *Development in Practice* 15(3–4): 286–301.

Hemson, D. and Kvalsvig, J. 2005. *eThekwini Water customer service project report.* Human Sciences Research Council. South Africa: HSRC Press.

JMP (Joint Monitoring Programme). 2008. *Joint Monitoring Programme progress report on drinking water and sanitation.* UNICEF and WHO.

———. 2010. *Joint Monitoring Programme progress report on sanitation and drinking water.* UNICEF and WHO. .

Keener, S., Muengo, M. and Banerjee, S. 2009. *Provision of water to the poor in Africa experience with water standposts and the informal water sector.* Working Paper 13. Washington, DC: IBRD (International Bank for Reconstruction and Development).

Kouanda, I. and Moudassir, M. 2007. Social policies and private sector participation in water supply—The case of Burkina Faso. In Prasad, N. (Ed), *Social policies and private sector participation in water supply: Beyond regulation.* Geneva: UNRISD (United National Research Institute on Social Development).

Loftus, A. 2005 "Free water" as commodity: The paradoxes of Durban's water service transformations. In McDonald, D. and Ruiters, G. (Eds), *The age of commodity water privatization in Southern Africa,* pp. 190–204. London: Earthscan.

Marin, P. 2009. *Public-private partnerships for urban water utilities.* Washington, DC: World Bank/PPIAF. www.ppiaf.org/ppiaf/sites/ppiaf.org/files/FINAL-PPPsforUrbanWaterUtilities-PhMarin.pdf (accessed 4 December 2011).

McDonald, D. and Ruiters, G. (Eds). 2005. *The age of commodity water privatization in Southern Africa.* London: Earthscan.

McKinley, D. 2006. The struggle against water privatisation in South Africa. In Balanyá, B., Brennan, B., Hoedeman, O., Kishimoto, S. and Terhorst, P. (Eds), *Reclaiming public water achievements, struggles and visions from around the world,* pp. 181–189. Transnational Institute and Corporate Europe Observatory.

Moretto, L. 2005. *Urban governance and informal water supply systems: Different guiding principles amongst multilateral organisations.* In Proceedings of Conference on the Human Dimension of Global Environmental Governance, International Organizations and Global Environmental Governance. Berlin, Germany, 2–3 December 2005.

Mugisha, S. and Berg, S.V. 2007. Turning around struggling state-owned enterprises in developing countries: The case of NWSC-Uganda. In *Going public: Southern solutions to the global water crisis,* pp. 15–25. London: World Development Movement.

Muhairwe, W. 2008. Market finance for large service providers. Presentation by Managing Director of Ugandan Water Utility. www.wsp.org/userfiles/file/pa_2_wm_uganda_dpsp.pdf (accessed 15 July 2010).

————. 2009a. Fostering improved performance through internal contractualisation. In Proceedings of World Bank Water Week. Washington, DC, 18 February.

————. 2009b. Financing options for water and sanitation utilities: NWSC's experience. In Proceedings of World Water Week. Stockholm, August.

Mwanamwambwa, C., Nkoloma, H. and Kayaga, S. 2005. Linking community to policy level support: The CARE-Zambia trust model. In Proceedings of the 31st WEDC International Conference, Maximizing the Benefits from Water and Environmental Sanitation. Kampala, Uganda, October 2005.

NWSC (National Water and Sewerage Corporation). 2009. Capacity building for change agents from Harar Water Supply and Sewerage Authority. Training Report, Lake Victoria Water and Sanitation Initiative, Utility Management 15–20 June 2009. Kampala, Uganda: NWSC External Services Unit.

Page, B. 2002a. Communities as the agents for commodification: The Kumbo Water Authority in Northwest Cameroon. *Geoforum* 34: 483–498.

————. 2002b. Accumulation by dispossession: Communities and water privatization in Cameroon. In Proceedings of PRINWASS Conference. University of Oxford, United Kingdom, 24–25 April.

Pambazuka. 2009. Ghanaians deserve better water services. 6 November. www.pambazuka.org/en/category/advocacy/56909 (accessed 15 July 2010).

Prempeh, E.O.K. 2006. *Against global capitalism: Africa social movements confront neoliberal globalization.* London: Ashgate.

StatsGhana. 2006. *Multiple Indicator Cluster Survey (MICS).* Ghana Statistical Service, Office of the President. www.statsghana.gov.gh/nada/index.php/ddi-browser/15 (accessed 4 December 2011).

UN-Habitat. 2006. The state of the world's cities 2006/7: The Millennium Development Goals and urban sustainability. 30 years of shaping the habitat agenda. Nairobi: UN-Habitat.

————. 2008a. *The state of African cities: A framework for addressing urban challenges in Africa.* Nairobi: UN-Habitat.

————. 2008b. *The state of the world's cities 2008/2009: Harmonious cities.* Nairobi: UN-Habitat.

————. 2009. Water operators partnerships: Building WOPs for sustainable development in water and sanitation. Nairobi: UN-Habitat and IWA. www.unhabitat.org/pmss/listItemDetails.aspx?publicationID=2851

UNDESA (United Nations Department of Economic and Social Affairs). 2007. *World urbanization prospects: The 2007 revision.* New York: UNDESA.

van Rooyen, C. and Hall, D. 2007. *Public is as private does: The confused case of Rand Water in South Africa.* Occasional Paper 15. Kingston: Municipal Services Project.

Watasa, S. 2009. *Civil society organization involvement in urban water sector reform.* London: WaterAid.

WaterAid. 2005. *Ghana: National water sector assessment.* London: WaterAid.

Water Dialogues. 2007. Water and sanitation modes of supply in Uganda. Uganda: Water Dialogues. www.waterdialogues.org/documents/WaterandSanitation.pdf.

————. 2008. *Ugu case study.* Uganda: Water Dialogues.

Werikhe, P. 2006. Union reform process in Uganda Public Employees Union. A case study. In Proceedings of NWSC Uganda, 4th World Water Forum. Mexico, 16–22 March. www.bvsde.paho.org/bvsacg/e/foro4/19%20marzo/improving/union.pdf (accessed 15 July 2010).

World Bank. 2009. *Water operators partnerships Africa utility performance assessment.* Nairobi: Water and Sanitation Programme.

————. 2000. Memorandum of the President of the International Development Association and the International Finance Corporation to the Executive

Directors on a country assistance strategy of the World Bank Group for the Republic of Ghana June 29, 2000. Report No. 20185-GH. Washington, DC: World Bank.

———. 2002. Private sector participation in water supply and sanitation services in Sub-Saharan Africa. In Decision Markers Workshop. Dakar, Senegal, 13–15 February.

———. 2008. Implementation Completion and Results Report (Ida-34760 Ida-3476a) on a credit in the amount of SDR 55 Million (US$ 70 million equivalent) to Burkina Faso for the Ouagadougou Water Supply Project Report. No: ICR0000705. Washington, DC: World Bank.

WSP (Water and Sanitation Programme). 2009a. *Enhancing water services through performance agreements performance improvement planning.* May 2009 Field Note. Washington, DC: WSP.

———. 2009b. *Guidance notes on services for the urban poor: A practical guide for improving water supply and sanitation.* Washington, DC: WSP.

WSP and PPIAF (Public-Private Infrastructure Advisory Facility). 2009. Water utilities in Africa: Case studies of transformation and market access. Inputs to the Regional Practitioners' Workshop on Market Finance for African Water Utilities. Pretoria, South Africa: WSP and PPIAF.

13 Electrifying Africa
Turning a Continental Challenge into a People's Opportunity

Terri Hathaway

In 2004, 14-year-old William Kamkwamba electrified his family's home in rural Malawi. William's story—of how he worked tirelessly, using pictures of a windmill he found in a small, rural library—was chronicled by local media and has since travelled the world via cyberspace. His story has inspired a book and forthcoming documentary and influential leaders such as Al Gore have used William's story to personify the possibilities in Africa (*BBC News* 2009, Kamkwamba and Mealer, 2009).

William's remarkable story demonstrates the vast potential for indigenous knowledge and appropriate technology innovations to bring electricity to Africa's rural areas. Like William, two-thirds of Africans live in the continent's rural areas, where only 19% of people have access to electricity. With the right policies and investments in place, William's innovation could be scaled up to achieve much higher rates of rural electrification and at a fraction of the usual connection costs. It could spark rural economic development, local energy security, and reduce vulnerability to climate change.

Yet most electricity-sector planning and investments in Africa overlook the rural majority and instead focus on big cities—home to roughly one-third of Africans—including their commercial enterprises and industries that rely on power grids to deliver electricity for work, home life, and leisure. This more visible part of Africa's energy sector relies on centralized power grids that need more power than can be provided by small-scale wind turbines. At their best, power grids offer the most economical, reliable, and widespread access to electricity. Africa's best example in this regard is—arguably—Mauritius. This island nation of 1.3 million people invested in a public rural grid electrification programme in the 1980s, and was the first—and for many years, the only—African country with near-universal access to electricity. Mauritius remains one of only a handful of the continent's countries with an access rate greater than 50%.

However, at their worst, power grids can be costly and ineffective instruments for achieving development. Billions of dollars have been spent on energy systems in Africa that, by and large, have fallen victim to mismanagement, corruption, and unequal distribution of benefits. Poor-quality service and high costs to consumers are too often the result. A recent study (Foster and Briceño-Garmendia, 2010) found that Africa's power costs an average of US$0.18 per kilowatt hour (kWh) to produce, about twice that found in other developing countries, and expensive backup generators used during frequent power outages can cost up to $0.40 per kWh. Decades of investments notwithstanding, the electrification of Africa—public or private—is failing.

Despite the success of Mauritius and the risks encountered in many other African energy sectors, the World Bank—Africa's most influential energy lender—suggests that the way forward for Africa's energy sector is developing regional power systems based on large power supplies and long transmission lines. The World Bank's 2010 report *African Infrastructure: A Time for Transformation* suggests that Africa needs to spend $41 billion a year on energy infrastructure and regional power trading schemes (Foster and Briceño-Garmendia, 2010). Yet, to date, regional planning has been marked by opaque processes that promote large infrastructure projects prone to corruption.

This chapter provides an overview of electricity provision in Africa with a focus on "alternatives to privatization". Although effective "alternatives" are still few and far between on the continent—due largely to the corruption and unaccountability of state actors as well as policy reforms to enable privatization and disable public provision—there are innovative examples of public sector electricity provision, sometimes in collaboration with civic organizations. In some cases, such as South Africa, these public sector reforms are contentious, with ongoing opposition to what many see as a commercialization of the public sector, but this opposition is itself a sign of the desire for change, with inventive proposals emerging from resistance groups for more democratic, equitable, and sustainable systems of electricity provision. The scope of change required is daunting, however, as is the size of the electricity deficit on the continent, as outlined in the following sections.

ELECTRICITY IN AFRICA: AN OVERVIEW

The story of electricity in Africa is a story of access, or rather, a *lack* of access. More than half a billion people in Africa do not have access to electricity. Proportionally, electrification in Africa lags behind every other region in the world: only 38% of all Africans—and only 26% of Sub-Saharan Africans—have access to electricity, compared to 52% in South Asia, 78% in the Middle East, 89% in China and Southeast Asia, and 90% in Latin America (OECD and IEA 2006, 567).

As shown in Table 13.1, only seven countries have attained access to electricity for over 90% of their populations; five of these are in northern Africa, and two are small island states. Only three more countries—Cape Verde, Ghana, and South Africa—register rates above 50%. An additional nine countries in Sub-Saharan Africa have access rates above one-third, while the majority of countries register electrification levels well below

Table 13.1 African Countries with National Rates of Access to Electricity above One-third of the Population (of 54 Countries in Total)

Country	Overall access rate	Population	GDP per capita	Rural access rate
Libya	100.0%	6.3 million	$14,802	99.0%
Tunisia	99.5%	10.3 million	$3,903	98.5%
Mauritius	99.4%	1.3 million	$7,345	99.0%
Algeria	99.3%	34.4 million	$4,845	98.0%
Egypt	99.0%	81.5 million	$1,991	99.0%
Morocco	97.0%	31.6 million	$2,812	96.0%
Seychelles	96.0%	0.1 million	$9,580	NA
South Africa	75.0%	48.7 million	$5,678	55.0%
Cape Verde	70.4%	0.5 million	$3,193	44.9%
Ghana	54.0%	23.4 million	$713	23.0%
Djibouti	49.0%	0.8 million	$1,030	10.2%
Sao Tome and Principe	48.5%	0.2 million	$1,090	33.7%
Côte d'Ivoire	47.0%	20.6 million	$1,137	18.0%
Nigeria	47.0%	151.2 million	$1,370	26.0%
Botswana	45.4%	1.9 million	$6,982	12.0%
Senegal	42.0%	12.2 million	$1,087	18.0%
Comoros	40.1%	0.6 million	$824	NA
Gabon	37.0%	10.0 million	$10,037	18.0%
Namibia	34.0%	2.1 million	$4,149	13.0%

Sources: Legros et al, 2009; World Bank 2008

30%. By looking at population and gross domestic product (GDP) per capita data alongside access rates, it is clear that each African country is experiencing a unique development path and that some anticipated patterns are not present. For example, Morocco has a GDP per capita lower than South Africa, Botswana, Gabon, or Namibia but has attained near-universal electricity access, while the other four nations lag behind. Tunisia has roughly the same population size as Gabon, and just one-third its GDP per capita, but more than twice the electricity access rate.

Africa's access crisis is most acute in its rural areas, where two-thirds of the continent's population lives (see Table 13.2). Only 19% of Africa's rural population has access to electricity, compared to 68% of the urban population. Excluding North Africa, only 8% of rural Sub-Saharan Africans have access to electricity. More than 444 million rural Africans are waiting for access to electricity, roughly four times more than the number of urban Africans without access.

Table 13.2   Status of Rural Electrification in Africa

Region	Rural population (and as % of total)	Rural electricity access	Rural population without electricity
Africa	548 million (61.2%)	18.9%	444.6 million
North	71 million (46.4%)	91.8%	5.8 million
Sub-Saharan	477 million (64.3%)	8.0%	438.8 million

Source: OECD and IEA 2006, 567.

Africa is the only region in the world where the number of people without access to electricity is expected to increase over the next two decades (see Figure 13.1). The population growth rate continues to outpace connection rates in most countries; twice as many households are formed each year as those that receive new power connections. While the *proportion* of Africans *with access* is expected to increase in the next two decades, the *absolute number* of Africans *without access* will grow to 584 million by 2030 (OECD and IEA 2004).

Africa's centralized grid systems have been the traditional focus for energy development and are the electric lifeline for much of the continent's industrial sector and non-poor urban population. Many of these systems are today in serious crisis: starved of investment, facing growing demands, and experiencing poor management of existing infrastructure and finances. Massive investment is needed for grid systems of many African countries after years of poor maintenance and insufficient expansion. Experts estimate that Africa needs to quadruple its installed capacity—an

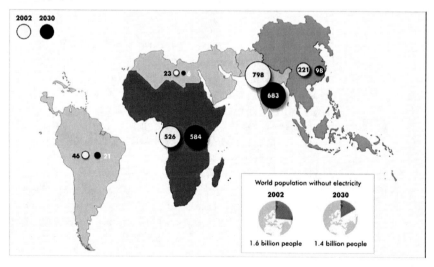

Figure 13.1   World population without electricity, in millions.

additional 270 gigawatts (GW)—and locate a staggering amount of investment by 2030, between $484 billion (OECD and IEA 2006, 148) and $563 billion (*Bloomberg* 2009). According to the World Bank, this translates to $41 billion of energy sector investments each year (Foster and Briceño-Garmendia 2010).

As planned, however, new investments in electricity infrastructure may not increase electricity access rates. Whereas energy experts suggest that at least half of electricity industry investments should be earmarked for transmission and distribution networks (OECD and IEA 2006, 95), the greatest proportion of energy investments needed in Africa is by far in distribution. The *2004 World Energy Outlook* (OECD and IEA 2004, 208) demonstrates that the investment needed in this subsector—$271 billion—is nearly equal to the *combined* investment needed in its generation and transmission—$292 billion. Yet major investments in energy infrastructure are currently targeted for high-voltage transmission lines to interconnect national grid systems to share supplies between existing consumers, and to rationalize extra-large supply plants, often large hydropower such as the massive Inga dams planned for the Democratic Republic of Congo (DRC). While major donors like the World Bank are focused on new generation and regional transmission, prioritizing distribution needs is often left to national governments, with very limited external support.

Governments often target new energy supplies that can help lure energy-intensive industries (e.g. aluminum smelters) or industries that can boost GDP (e.g. oil, mining, and timber). Governments may find it more profitable to connect large power consumers than to invest adequately in distribution systems that could expand the grid. They may also neglect to develop smaller, decentralized power sources that could help expand the reach of the grid or better serve communities too far from it.

African governments play two important roles in the energy sector. First, they create the policy and regulatory framework through which electricity provision is governed. At best, such frameworks can proactively create an *enabling* environment for effective service provision that supports the economic and social development needs of the people. At the very least, the framework should not create a *disabling* environment, in which the government creates barriers that unnecessarily block the development of people. Unfortunately, the history of African governance is one of often failed and fragile states, and, too often, of disabling environments for effective energy development.

The second role that African governments play is as service provider. The majority of today's electricity provision is supplied by government-owned utilities. African power utilities have traditionally been set up as unregulated or poorly regulated monopolies, an institutional arrangement that has contributed to the sector's poor status today. Corruption and poor management, enabled by non-transparency and poorly structured institutions, have reduced the quality and expansion of services.

In 1992, the World Bank introduced a new power sector policy that stressed the commercialization of power utilities and inherently de-emphasized access to electricity by disadvantaged groups (Covarrubias 1996). In 1997, the bank went a step further, indicating that it would not lend for electricity projects without a clear government commitment to sectoral reform. While few would argue against the need for reform to improve public provision of services, the World Bank's aims were to reduce state intervention in the energy sector to two narrow actions: unbundling and privatization. Bank-recommended reforms mainly address improvements in the financial and technical performance of power utilities and to date have focused primarily on enabling private-sector engagement rather than expansion of public service for the poor. Between 1990 and 2001, however, investment in power sector projects involving private participation totalled a mere $3.1 billion, spread across 22 countries (World Bank 2003). Across most of Africa, private sector involvement did not arrive as expected, leaving Africa's energy sector starved for capital (Bayliss 2008).

While continuing to promote privatization, the World Bank has been focusing much of its power-sector lending to Africa on developing interconnected regional power grids. Significant attention and funding is being put towards the institutional and infrastructure development of regional power trading systems. However, reforms that can improve accountability and promote the expansion of electrification—particularly to rural communities and the urban poor—should be seen as equally important.

The reforms adopted so far have had virtually no impact on increasing access to electricity. Power-sector reforms have failed to address exploits by private companies under poor government oversight, corrupt business practices between private companies and government, and improved civil society participation. In other words, there has been little effort to improve public sector electricity providers.

Other lenders play a role as well. The African Development Bank is increasingly important in financing infrastructure projects, and Chinese investment in African infrastructure—much of it in the energy sector—has exploded in recent years. A Frost & Sullivan (2009) report valued Chinese and other Asian commitments in the Sub-Saharan Africa electricity sector at $4.44 billion and projects they could grow by an additional $2 billion by 2014. European bilateral donor agencies in countries such as France, Germany, and Sweden have given funding priorities to the African energy sector. Other emerging economies—including India and Brazil—are beginning to invest in the sector. The expansion of rural electrification agencies and initiatives in recent years has seen a variety of multilateral and bilateral support, although activities are often a drop in the energy development bucket. In many African countries, religious organizations may play a more significant role than government in developing pockets of rural electrification. This could lead religious groups to play an increasing role in prioritizing access to energy services in Africa's rural regions.

RESEARCHING PUBLIC SECTOR PROVISION

In an attempt to map out the scope and character of non-commercialized service provision in the electricity sector in Africa, several research methods were employed. I began by collecting data on the status of electricity provision and power sector reforms in all countries of the continent where basic data on state-owned utilities were available. National public utilities were researched online due to time and logistical constraints. Additional information was supplemented with secondary literature, where it existed, supplemented with follow-up on specific cases by telephone and e-mail. Academic and non-academic literature searches were conducted and a variety of experts, and practitioners were identified and interviewed by e-mail, phone, or in person to provide further information and observations.

Due to the dearth of critical literature on the power sector in Africa, the scope of research on advancing "public" utilities was primarily defined by case studies, as well as the opinions of experts and practitioners. It is possible that data have been produced by the World Bank but are not publicly available. Additionally, many of the African government electricity departments approached for data were unresponsive to e-mail and phone queries. Examples from Francophone and Lusophone Africa may be underrepresented due to language barriers in the collection of data. Moreover, much of the data collected for this study does not critically assess the implementation of identified targets, policies, and programmes. This would be important for future work.

Although the state of neglect in Africa's power sector is well known, it may be more difficult to see progress and limitations in more recent years, and over shorter spans of time. Like most statistics in Africa, data on access to electricity may be less reliable than in other world regions. Official data may be influenced by a number of factors, including political interests. Electricity statistics may be based on data collected many years previous, and comparative analyses often use data collected at different times and using different methods.

Despite these limitations, this chapter presents the first attempt to systematically and comprehensively review "alternatives to privatization" in the electricity sector in Africa and advances our understanding of the scope and character of these developments.

NON-COMMERCIALIZED ELECTRICITY PROVISION IN AFRICA

Despite the significant push from the World Bank to enable private-sector financing and participation in the African electricity sector, the majority of provision remains in the public and non-profit arenas. Roughly 90% of infrastructural needs will continue to be funded by or through the state into the foreseeable future, making the state's role one of the most important

(Bayliss 2007). However, the quantity and quality of electricity provision—particularly in Sub-Saharan African countries—remains in a fragile state.

Because the African electricity sector is characterized by low rates of access, the research is focused not just on service provision but also on the state's role in providing an enabling environment for successful service provision. The legal and policy framework provided by the state for its energy sector sets the tone under which service providers must conduct their activities. The current and historical failings of state-owned utilities can often be directly linked to the policy environment in which they operated. The policy environment has also been responsible for disabling other opportunities for the state to meet its goals of electricity provision. The state also sets the tone for the kind of development that the power sector will support.

For this research, non-commercialized service providers are categorized into four types: state-owned utilities; state-based rural electrification programmes; community initiatives; and single-institution providers.

State-owned utilities

This category covers by far the majority of public electricity supply in Africa and has the overall largest number of customers. However, most state-owned utilities have been corporatized and commercialized following sector reforms undertaken in recent years. Many have undergone some type of commercialized change and others are in the process of, or predicted to, undergo similar reforms. Few have been successful in attaining high rates of access to electricity or rapid growth in access rates.

About half of all African countries have retained a vertically integrated state-owned power utility monopoly (see Table 13.3). A few countries, such as Mozambique and Namibia, operate a state-owned system with more than one institutional provider but do not currently have private sector ownership. Twelve countries—including Egypt, Ghana, and Zambia—have both state and non-state service providers. At least 10 countries are engaged in long-term contracts and/or have sold off some or all of their assets. Several countries, including Ghana, Egypt, Namibia, and South Africa, have set up regional power distributors. Many countries, including Egypt, Guinea, Mali, and Rwanda, have undergone privatization, only to be reclaimed by state ownership. Several countries underwent management contracts that ended and reverted to state management. Some utilities, such as the Zimbabwe Electricity Supply Authority, were restructured for sale but have failed to attract investors.

African power utilities have traditionally been set up as unregulated or poorly regulated monopolies, an institutional arrangement that has contributed to the current poor status of the sector. Most have failed to address electrification for the poor, with only nine African countries registering access rates above 70%. These systems largely obtained their high access rates prior to power-sector reforms in which state-owned utilities were commercialized. Some of these utilities are described briefly below.

Table 13.3　African Countries by State and Non-state Provision of Electricity
Services

Countries with fully state-owned systems (monopoly or multiple providers)	Benin, Botswana, Burkina Faso, Burundi, Central African Republic, Chad, Democratic Republic of Congo,* Equatorial Guinea, Eritrea, Ethiopia, The Gambia, Guinea, Guinea-Bissau,** Lesotho, Liberia, Libya, Madagascar,** Malawi, Mauritania,** Mozambique, Namibia, Niger,* Rwanda,** Seychelles, Sudan, Swaziland*, Tunisia, Zambia, Zimbabwe*
Countries with state and non-state providers	Algeria, Angola, Egypt,** Ghana, Kenya, Mauritius, Morocco, Nigeria,* Senegal, South Africa, Tanzania, Zambia
Full or partial control of electricity sector assets by non-state actors	Cameroon, Côte d'Ivoire, Gabon, Kenya, Mali, Morocco, Republic of Congo, Reunion, Sierra Leone, Uganda, Zimbabwe

* prepared for privatization; ** state control regained after non-state engagement.
Source: Lists based on author's research of energy sector by country.

North Africa has managed to obtain near-universal access levels in recent years. In Libya, the General Electricity Company of Libya (GECOL) is responsible for generation, transportation, and distribution of electric power in the whole country. Libya is the only African country with 100% electricity access rate. The state's objective has been to electrify all Libyan towns and cities with the lowest possible operating cost and with an acceptable level of continuity and quality of electricity supply. GECOL has an installed capacity of 6,284 MW and 1.2 million customers.

Before its utility was commercialized in 2002, Algeria already had 5,930 MW of installed capacity, exporting surplus power to Morocco and Tunisia. State-owned Sonelgaz—which controls electricity generation, transmission, and distribution—was converted into a private company in 2002, although the Algerian government continues to hold all of the company's shares. The 2002 law also created the Electricity and Gas Regulatory Commission to oversee the newly opened industry. Algeria aims to eventually split Sonelgaz into separate generation, transmission, and distribution companies, although those plans have faced domestic opposition from organized labour. Since the opening of the sector in 2002, there has been considerable private investment in new electricity generating capacity.

In Tunisia, the *Société Tunisienne de l'Électricité et du Gaz* (STEG) maintains a monopoly on electricity supply, transmission, and distribution. As of 2009, STEG operated a total power supply of 3,465 MW and had over 3 million customers. According to Practical Action Consulting's (2007) technical brief on grid connection, Tunisia's decision to adopt a lower-cost distribution technology is the single most important reason for the country's success in rural electrification. (It remains to be seen what effect the political changes in Tunisia, and elsewhere in North Africa in 2011, will have on these services but may serve to democratize state services further.)

Approximately 40 African countries operate small power grids with a capacity of less than 1,000 MW each. Arguably the most successful of these utilities in terms of access rate is the Central Electricity Board (CEB) in Mauritius, which was established in 1952 and completed its rural electrification programme in 1981. As of 2008, CEB operated a system with an installed capacity of 733 MW, although peak demand is only 378 MW (CEB 2008). CEB restructured in 2004 to become a vertically integrated utility. An independent regulator was created for the electricity industry and an external contractor was brought in to assist in CEB's management. CEB generates 40% of the country's total power requirements and purchases the remaining 60% from independent power producers that generate *bagasse*, an energy supply using agricultural waste from the sugar industry. CEB is the sole organization responsible for the transmission and distribution of electricity to the population. Mauritius has one of the highest GDP per capita in Africa.

In South Africa, Eskom is the state-owned utility that has long dominated the country's and the region's energy sector. Eskom is one of the world's largest power companies and produces nearly half of Africa's total electricity. When the African National Congress (ANC) came to power in 1994, an electrification target of 2.5 million new connections by 2000 (450,000 per year) was set, far larger than the maximum 25,000 connections per year provided in the waning days of apartheid (Greenberg 2009). Funding was provided by Eskom's internal funds, but a combination of corporatization and increasing costs per connection—as lower cost connections were completed first—led to a sharp decline in connections after 2003.

For 58 years, Eskom was mandated to "render, by the provision of power without profit, a worthy and ever-increasing contribution onto the development of South Africa and the welfare of her peoples" (Gentle 2009). In 1948, South Africa's power sector already possessed 2,378 MW, more than double the size of most African power systems today. Prior to the end of apartheid, Eskom had achieved near-universal electricity access for its white population, while funding of basic services for the country's majority non-white population had systematically been neglected. While the power sector of the racist apartheid era was grossly inequitable, it does speak to the capacity of a state-owned system in a non-commercialized setting to achieve the goals it has set out to accomplish.

South Africa's post-apartheid electrification programme has achieved some success but is falling short of anticipated goals. At the same time, the country's Free Basic Electricity Programme has been hindered by implementation barriers, resulting in a situation where very few of those who most need it are benefiting from the programme. When promises to provide free basic services were not kept, communities and activists organized political struggles using civil disobedience (Ruiters 2009).

State-based rural electrification programmes

State-based rural electrification programmes have been much less successful than their urban counterparts in Africa. Where they do exist, rural agencies are generally tasked with increasing connection rates but may not be considered a long-term service provider. Many are separate institutions, but some countries have created a department within the main power utility. The programmes are often financed through a levy on electricity services provided by state utilities with supplemental funding from development banks and other donors. The agency may connect new communities to the national power grid serviced by the utility, develop a minigrid for rural communities, or provide individual household systems. There is very limited research available that evaluates the progress of state-based rural electrification programmes on the continent.

Rural electrification in Africa has been impeded by the high financial costs of connecting Africa's sparsely populated rural areas to the centralized grid. In Kenya, for example, the average cost of a new connection for a rural home is seven times the national per capita income (REN21 2008). The high cost may also indicate a lack of political will to drive alternative initiatives, despite the fact that African households and small businesses spend upwards of $17 billion annually—30% of disposable income—on kerosene and other fuel-based lighting (Lighting Africa 2008).

Most national rural electrification agencies began in Africa in the 1990s as part of power sector reforms (Mostert 2008). These agencies were created to address the dismal rates of rural electricity services and spur new sources of funding to address the needs. Such agencies were often poorly integrated into reforms, which prioritized urban services, and were typically introduced at a late stage in the preparatory process. Despite the hope that reforms would lead to additional funds for rural electrification, rural connections remain dismal. Private investors in the electricity industry have tended to target lucrative urban and industrial consumers.

A 2004 study by the Global Network on Energy for Sustainable Development (GNESD 2004) identified several factors that contributed to the success of rural electrification programmes in Mauritius, Morocco, and Tunisia. Most importantly, the funds raised by levies were ring-fenced, meaning they used transparent planning and project selection processes and closely monitored the use of dedicated funds for rural areas. The governments in all three countries demonstrated great political will to accomplish rural electrification through financial contributions and by planning connections across all socio-economic groups without prioritizing less expensive communities. Rural communities participated in the decision-making bodies, making contributions towards the electrification of villages and in the selection of the schemes to be electrified.

Other rural electrification programmes have been less successful. In Kenya and Zambia, the rural electrification levies were not ring-fenced, allowing the funds to easily be mixed with other utility or national revenues, without being used to expand access (Karakezi and Kimani 2002). In Kenya, despite a rural electrification levy in place for 30 years, only 1% of the rural population has access to electricity (see Table 13.4).

Some government electrification programmes provide financial incentives for unelectrified communities that meet certain criteria to fast-track new electricity services. Often the communities are encouraged to participate either through financing the connection or providing community labour towards the construction of physical infrastructure. Some African countries have supported the use of electric cooperatives to connect rural communities. In Burkina Faso and Ethiopia—where cooperative ownership solutions enjoy political support—community cooperatives are encouraged to help organize new community connections as part of their respective rural electrification programmes.

In Morocco, the *Office National de l'Électricité* (ONE) was created in 1963 to meet the electricity requirements of the country. It remains a state-run company with 9,000 staff and approximately 3.5 million customers. In 1997, when 45% of Moroccans lived in rural areas, but only 18% had access to electricity, the Moroccan government implemented the Global Rural Electrification Programme with the goal of 100% rural electrification within 10 years. Between 1997 and 2008, ONE connected 4,000 communities per year, and Morocco's rural electrification programme has succeeded in increasing Morocco's access rate to 99%. Most new connections were provided by grid extension, while 7% were provided by decentralized electrification, namely solar PV kits.

Table 13.4   Rural Electrification Programmes in Four Countries

Country	Morocco	Tunisia	Mauritius	Kenya
Duration of programme	27 years	32 years	37 years	31 years
Estimated total investment on capital cost (US$ millions)	$4,050	$585	$22	$103
Estimated number of connections	5,375,000	609,000	737,000	93,080
Rural electrification rate	72%	96%	100%	1%
Average cost per connection	$753.49	$960.59	$29.85	$1,106.57

Source: GNESD 2004, 9.

In 1989, the government of Ghana launched the National Electrification Scheme (NES) and the complementary Self-Help Electrification Programme (SHEP) as a rolling electrification programme. The goal was to connect all communities with more than 500 people to the national grid by 2020. When the NES was launched in 1989, Ghana had 3,743 target communities. By 2004, the NES and SHEP had managed to electrify over 3,000 communities (Mostert 2008).

Communities located within 20 kilometres from the grid but not scheduled for immediate connection can apply for SHEP funds to fast-track electrification, but they must first meet additional requirements. They must procure a required number of poles for the distribution network and have at least 30% of the households wired for service as soon as electricity supply is connected. An interested community is required to set up a village electrification committee that has several responsibilities, including mobilizing funds to purchase low voltage poles, assisting in acquisition and clearing of right-of-ways, and providing public information and awareness on wiring homes.

In Burkina Faso, community cooperatives called *coopel* are used to develop rural electrification schemes. For isolated minigrids, the coopel owns all assets. For grid-connected projects, the coopel owns the distribution system and transformer. It has two committees: the grid committee for decisions on grid extensions and connections and the management and control committee for management, tariff setting, and accounting issues. A management consultant from the National Federation of Cooperatives provides assistance during the first two years of operation. However, *coopels* are required to tender a construction and five-year operation and management contract for the implementation of their project. The private manager-operator is responsible for system operation, system safety, billing, securing payment of bills, connecting new customers, and extending the distribution grid. The operator receives a monthly fee proportional to the number of customers (Mostert 2008).

In Ethiopia, more than 200 electricity cooperatives have been registered. The rural electrification fund uses regional energy bureaus, regional cooperative offices, and debt financing from the Ethiopia Development Bank to support the development of electricity cooperatives. Although Ethiopia's national utility subsidizes tariffs in its diesel-based community grids, systems developed under the rural electrification fund are not subsidized, causing a greater financial burden to members of electricity cooperatives. Fuel costs have continued to rise faster than tariffs, and many cooperative systems have reduced their operating hours to compensate. New cooperatives under design have been downsized and barred energy-intensive uses (Mostert 2008).

References to a small number of existing and planned electric consumer cooperatives in rural areas were also found in Kenya, Sudan, and Tanzania and are planned in Uganda.

Community initiatives

Community initiatives provide electricity for households and institutions within one or more nearby communities. Electricity is generally supplied by one local energy source or a combination of sources, also known as a hybrid system. Hybrid systems may rely on a combination of microhydro, wind, solar, and/or diesel.

Electric consumer cooperatives, where consumers are members and collectively own the system, were found in four countries. In all, 49 examples of existing community systems were found across 16 countries, although more research would be needed to determine the current status and sustainability of each system. The Global Environment Fund (GEF) has helped finance 18 of these systems.[1] The systems are supplied by a variety of renewable and non-renewable sources, as seen in Table 13.5.

Despite the vastness of the African continent, there are relatively few cases of community electrification systems that have been initiated by and remain under community management. Historically, most community electricity systems were supplied by diesel generators. As fuel prices have risen and other technologies have received more attention, there are increasing examples of community electricity powered by microhydro, wind, and solar. Limited financing options for infrastructure is often a constraint to scaling up community systems.

In Cameroon, a local NGO, *Action pour un Développement Équitable, Intégré et Durable* (ADEID), has assisted three communities in constructing village electricity systems using microhydro projects; two more are under construction but not yet operational (see Table 13.6; Nkeng 2009). Local engineering and materials are used to manufacture the power system, and

Table 13.5 Examples of Decentralized Grids in Africa

Type of power supply	Total examples found
Solar	6
Microhydro	17
Wind	6
Diesel	5
Biogas	2
Methane	1
Jatropha	2
Hybrid	5
Unknown	4

Source: Author's research.

Table 13.6   Microhydro Electrification Projects by ADEID, Cameroon

Community	System size	Customers	Availability
Bellah Nganga Fontem	7.5 kW 3-km transmission	1 health center 60 households	24 hrs/day, all year
Nefolem-Baleng	5 kW 2-km transmission	1 health post 1 school 25 households	12 hrs/day, 10 months
Tongou-Baleng	6 kW 2-km transmission	1 school 50 households	12 hrs/day, 10 months
Quibeku Fontem	10 kW 3-km transmission	1 school, 1 church 70 households	24 hrs/day, all year

Source: Nkeng 2009.

ADEID has assisted each community in developing a local management system. Systems have been financed partially by grants and partially by loans from international private funders. Each village has set up a management committee, but results have been mixed.

In The Gambia, the non-governmental organization German Association for Rural Electrification (*Dorfelektrik in Gambian E.v*) initiated a minigrid to electrify the village of Batokunku. In 1999, a six kilometer transmission line was connected to an overhead grid line that had previously bypassed the village. About 50 households and a community water pumping system began to receive electricity. In 2000, a 150-KVA wind converter with a total height of 41 meters was received from Denmark where it had previously been in operation. The community founded Batokunku Wind Power, which is overseen by an elected committee. In May 2008, a power purchase agreement between Batokunku Wind Power and the National Water and Electricity Company (NAWEC) was signed that defines the terms of agreement between the two parties as a non-profit pilot project for green energy in The Gambia. The village applied for a license from The Gambia Public Utilities Regulatory Authority (PURA). After deducting the operating costs, surplus revenues are either reinvested into the network to connect new citizens or into other village social projects. Batokunku Wind Power could eventually serve a network of about 1,000 villagers.

In Kenya, at least four community-owned microhydro systems are operational, and it is believed that up to three megawatts of microhydro could be generated across the country (Legros et al, 2009). Each system in operation is owned by an electricity users association that must register with the government's Department of Social Services in order to obtain a permit for abstracting water for electricity generation (Kirubi 2009). At each site, monthly membership fees of about US$3, equivalent to the local daily wage, are set and collected by the relevant association. Each user association implemented the advice to set tariffs and monitoring systems by maximum demand rather than by power consumption. A mechanism for allocating power was developed that uses "light packages" to determine household demand. Each light package is equivalent to 10 watts, and a household can choose how many light packages it will pay for on a monthly basis. Exceeding the limit is monitored by a load limiter that instantly disconnects the household if the amount is exceeded. To regain supply, the user has to unplug certain loads.

In Zambia, the North West Zambia Development Trust owns and operates Zengamina Power, a 750-kW hydropower station and 35-kilometer distribution network system. The system was built to help replace costly diesel generation at Kalene Mission Hospital and to promote rural development in the surrounding communities by providing electricity to farms, businesses, and rural households. Planning began in 2003, though previous studies were done as early as 1964. Fundraising and construction began in 2004. The system became operational in 2007 and currently supplies electricity to two towns, one large farm, one school, two mobile phone towers, and 130 private customers. Power demand is only about 20% of supply, but operators expect that demand could rise to 40% as the existing customer base increases their reliance on electricity. Zengamina's operators anticipate that it could support up to 1,000 customers in the future, reaching full capacity within 10 years. The $2.9 million project cost was funded through donations and a $25,000 subsidy from the Zambian Rural Electrification Authority. Zengamina Power employs 10 people full-time and another 10 part-time when electricity poles are being erected (Rea 2009).

While outside the scope of this chapter's research, there is one very innovative project tackling a controversial subject: *jatropha*, an alien plant species whose seeds produce oil for biofuel. In Mali, the village of Garolo has married together *jatropha* cultivation and a local electricity service using biodiesel, while trying to avoid harming local food security (Practical Action Consulting 2009). The 300-kW electric minigrid has 247 customers and engages 326 farmers who grow *jatropha* on lands that do not compete with local food crops. The power grid is owned and operated by a local private company that is an offshoot of a local NGO, Mali Folkcenter. The system was implemented with support from the national rural electrification agency and technical assistance from a German NGO. Project developers believe it has the potential to benefit more than 10,000 inhabitants through improved social services and income generation activities (Morris and Kirubi 2009).

Clarifying and reducing the regulatory obligations for small systems can help make the difference between encouraging or discouraging community systems. Some countries have changed the regulatory framework to better enable community initiatives:

- In Mali, no authorization is required for isolated grid projects involving less than 20 kW of power supply.
- In Burkina Faso, systems with capacities lower than 10 kW need no authorization; systems between 10 kW and 35 kW need an authorization; and systems larger than 35 kW require a concession.
- In Tanzania, the 2008 Electricity Act enables community electricity systems to sell excess power back to the grid.
- Kenya's revised Energy Act of 2006 ended the state utility's monopoly for power distribution by permitting private generation and distribution of electricity, enabling community initiatives to operate.

Another innovative community power system is the Multi-Functional Platform (MFP), in which a platform is built around a diesel engine that can power various tools, such as a cereal mill, husker, alternator, battery charger, pump, welding, and carpentry equipment, and generate electricity for lighting and pumping water. MFPs can be found in Benin, Burkina Faso, Ghana, Guinea, Mali, and Senegal; more than 450 MFPs have been installed in Mali alone, where the Malian Agency for Household Energy and Rural Electrification (AMADER) subsidizes up to 80% of the cost for each platform. MFPs can be installed and run using local management and local engineering. Often, a women's management committee is created to operate the MFP. New tools can be added to the MFP over time as the team acquires the capacity to finance new equipment. Typically, a grid up to three kilometers long can be attached to the platform, connecting 80% of the households that live within its service area. MFPs have an average lifespan of up to four years. Installation of an MFP usually occurs after conducting a feasibility study. The total cost, including installation, is approximately $7,000, while up to $5,000 in additional support for capacity and management development may be provided.

In Burkina Faso, the government has cofinanced 46% of the MFP installations, with another 10% coming from the United Nations Development Programme (UNDP), 9% from beneficiaries, and 35% from other donors. Financing is facilitated through an arrangement between the NGOs implementing the projects, the network of local credit and savings cooperatives, and the Regional Solidarity Bank. The government and UNDP have been responsible for developing the beneficiaries' capacity and monitoring and evaluating the MFP enterprises' performance. The Regional Solidarity Bank lends to the credit and savings cooperatives, which then provide small-scale finance to individuals with enterprises enabled by energy services provided by an MFP, such as welding and grain milling (Morris and Kirubi 2009). MFPs are credited with creating nearly 2,500 jobs in eight regions, in addition to saving about two hours per day of women's labour. The government of Burkina Faso would like to roll out the MFP programme to 13 more regions.

Another unique model for community electrification comes from the Barefoot College based in India. Since 2004, the Barefoot College has trained 110 rural African women, mostly grandmothers, as solar engineers. As a result, these women have solar electrified 5,500 remote rural houses in 15 African countries.[2] The training centre works on the premise that the very poor have the right to have, own, and access the most sophisticated technologies to improve their own lives. By design, the Barefoot College accepts only illiterate and semiliterate middle-aged women for their training because these women have a vested interest to stay in their villages. Selected trainees are invited to the centre in India for six months of training. Trainings are conducted by previous trainees; no written materials are used. After returning to their villages, the women are able to fabricate, install, maintain and repair residential solar lighting systems.

Before a village is solar electrified under this programme, a Village Energy and Environment Committee (VEEC) is formed. The VEEC is responsible for determining the household tariff structure and for selecting a woman from the village to be trained as a Barefoot Solar Engineer. Once the village is electrified, the VEEC continues to monitor funds and the performance of the Barefoot Solar Engineer. Households paying into the village solar system receive up to four hours of electric light every night.

Single-institution providers

This final category refers to non-commercialized service providers created to generate electricity for a single user, and is broken into two subcategories: institutional (such as a hospital or school) and household. Institutional systems are typically set up to run a single community service without expanding the service for community use, often for health care or educational institutions. Such systems are often run by non-profit organizations.

As decentralized energy systems become more available, better known, and less expensive, individual demand for private household systems is increasing. Demand for these services will likely come primarily from higher-income rural households and will be installed for domestic use or entrepreneurial activities conducted from the home, or both. Such systems can provide a rare opportunity to develop local livelihoods for builders (e.g. microhydro and small wind turbines), distributors (e.g. solar photovoltaic) and maintenance technicians. They can also provide badly needed electricity for regular household use, as in the case of William Kamkwamba outlined at the start of this chapter.

Churches and faith-based groups have contributed significantly to integrating electricity supplies for rural hospitals, schools, and other social service institutions (similar to their involvement in the health care sector in Africa, as discussed in Chapter 11, this volume). These types of installations are generally provided to services managed by the church organization and do not usually involve community-wide electrification. In Uganda, for example, the Solar Light for the Churches of Africa project was a $6-million, faith-based initiative established to electrify 5,000 individual churches, schools, health clinics, community centres, and homes over 20 years (US Department of Energy 2002). The initiative was financed by the Church of Uganda and a US-based foundation. Installation and maintenance are provided by Solar Energy for Uganda, Ltd. In the DRC, numerous mission-run clinics and hospitals are operating their own power systems (Boyd 2010).

Likewise, individual household provision of electricity accounts for an increasingly important part of electricity access and consumption in Africa. Households in particular may rely on local entrepreneurs who sell the products and provide maintenance. Often, the local markets that sell these goods have been or are supported by government or non-profit initiatives to develop consumer awareness of the goods.

Solar home systems are one of the most common forms of individual electricity systems in Africa. South Africa's solar PV installation is estimated at 8 MW. In the Eastern Cape province, there is a plan to install 50,000 solar home systems and a million homes could eventually use these types of systems. About 2,000 systems have been installed in schools and 200 in rural clinics (Ward 2002, 24). In Kenya, 30,000 PV systems are sold annually, making it a global leader, per capita, in sales of residential renewable energy systems (Kammen and Jacobson 2005).

Solar PV has come under criticism due to a high rate of poorly maintained installments, however. Solar PV installations are generally limited to lighting and other small power demands. The inability to run domestic appliances with higher loads has helped give solar PV a stigma as inferior to grid-based electricity. In South Africa's Eastern Cape, households have declined solar home systems offered by the government because they believe it will reduce their chance to be connected to the public grid. Rural solar PV installations have also been criticized because supplies are static and do not permit growth of consumption.

Diesel generators have long provided individual access to electricity. One of Africa's most notorious examples is Nigeria, where chronic power outages and unreliability of the national power grid has driven the use of individual generators. According to a 2008 report, Nigerians spend US$140 billion annually on fuelling private generators in the country, including almost US$67 billion for residential use and US$13 billion for commercial use (*Vanguard News* 2008).

Car batteries also serve as a relatively accessible, though costly, source of electricity. In Mozambique, there are an estimated 25,000 car batteries sold for the purpose of home electrification. A car battery is carried—often significant distances—to a location where it can be recharged for a fee; power at the charging station is usually provided by a diesel generator or from grid electricity supply. The small amount of power in the battery is then typically used for lighting or to run a television and radio. Electricity from a car battery can cost up to US$5 per kWh (Greenpeace and ITDG 2002, 60).

LESSONS LEARNED

Engaging civil society

Africa's electricity sector has largely failed Africa's poor majority and will continue to face enormous obstacles for decades to come. In the face of relatively low levels of political will, one of the most important factors to fast-track public electricity connection in Africa will be participation, advocacy, and monitoring by communities and civil society.

Although seldom mentioned in recent critical literature, civil society engagement in the power sector is working to ensure government accountability, pro-poor planning, and the development of community-level electricity services. In 2003, a worldwide network of NGOs formed the Citizens United for Renewable Energy and Sustainability (CURES) to monitor the energy-related international processes, which had resulted from the 2002 World Summit on Sustainable Development. CURES prepared a declaration as the common position of this group to influence the 2004 international conference on renewables held in Bonn, Germany (CURES 2003). There is currently an active Southern Africa CURES network, as well as a West African CURES network. In 2003, the African Rivers Network was formed to bring together communities and NGOs engaged in struggles against large dams, mainly hydropower dams. In 2006, the network published a booklet of case studies related to social and environmental impacts of hydropower dams in Africa (ARN 2006). Another strong civil society group is the South Africa Energy Caucus.

Some countries, such as Tanzania and Cameroon, have seen public protests against negative impacts on service provision due to privatization. Trade unions in Algeria, Nigeria, and South Africa have also opposed privatization of energy services. Light Up Nigeria, a grassroots advocacy movement for improved power supply, began in August 2009. The founders drafted a power bill that would incorporate their demands to the Nigerian government for a sustainable power service. By using the web-based social networking tool Facebook, Light Up Nigeria has attracted over 28,000 members.

Perhaps the best known case of civil society engagement in the African power sector is the collective struggles of South African townships to resist paying for electricity and other basic services, both during and after apartheid. As part of the anti-apartheid struggle, many townships engaged in boycotts against the provision of poor and unequal services, including electricity provision. When the ANC came to power in 1994, its Reconstruction and Development Programme promised "free basic services" for all. However, by 2000, the public South African utility Eskom began a serious campaign to disconnect households that were not paying for service and/or owed large amounts to the utility. Up to 20,000 households were being disconnected each month in the Soweto township alone (Naidoo and Veriava

2009, 324), with hundreds of thousands more being disconnected by public, municipal-level electricity distributors (McDonald and Pape 2002).

The Soweto Electricity Crisis Committee organized collective resistance that used illegal reconnections as a political tool. This organized resistance led to three achievements. In October 2001, Eskom announced a moratorium on cut-offs in Soweto. A month later, Eskom announced it would cancel 50% of residents' arrears, reform the billing process, and give amnesty to those reporting illegal connections. In May 2003, Eskom cancelled all arrears in Soweto and other nearby townships. But these wins were followed by the implementation of prepaid electricity meters, a move many South African groups have criticized for disempowering consumers (Naidoo and Veriava 2009), and cut-offs continue.

Electrification targets

In order to not backslide, African utilities must add new connections faster than new households are created. Without special public policies to address the need of underserved rural populations, the electricity gap will not only continue to grow but so too will the equity gap between those with and without electricity access. For the majority of African countries, this has remained a major challenge and they are only slowly beginning to set targets for new connections in order to catch up (see Table 13.7). In 2001, Mozambique's utility EdM had 279,000 customers. By 2006, EdM had increased its number of clients to 387,000.

Some attention has also slowly begun to focus on regional initiatives to expand access to electricity and energy in Africa. In 2002, the World Summit on Sustainable Development called upon the international community "to improve access to reliable and affordable energy services for sustainable development sufficient to facilitate the achievement of the Millennium Development Goals (MDGs) . . . bearing in mind that access to energy facilitates the eradication of poverty" (WSSD 2002, 5). By 2005, a

Table 13.7   Selected Examples of National Electricity Access Targets

Country	Current overall access	National target	Rural target
DRC	11.0%	67% by 2025	50% by 2025
Ghana	54.0%	100% by 2020	100% by 2020
Mali	17.4%	20% by 2011	8% by 2011
South Africa	75.0%	100% by 2012	100% by 2012
Togo	20.0%	66% by 2016	40% by 2016
Zambia	19.0%	41.8% by 2016	15% by 2016

Source: Legros et al, 2009.

UN strategy to "energize the MDGs" had been outlined, and the Forum of Energy Ministers for Africa (FEMA) committed to three serious targets for ramping up access to energy but at an underestimated cost: 50% of Africans living in rural areas should have access to modern energy services such as improved cook stoves; 50% of the urban and peri-urban poor should have access to reliable and affordable modern energy services; 50% of schools, clinics, and community centres should have access to modern electricity services for provision of lighting, refrigeration, information, and communication technology (Bbumba 2005). Since 2006, the EU Energy Initiative has led efforts to develop energy access strategies at the subregional level in Sub-Saharan Africa. This effort is currently expressed through the three-year Africa Electrification Initiative (2009–2011).

In 2006, the Economic Community of West African States (ECOWAS) determined that $52 billion must be invested by 2015 to energize the region to meet its Millennium Development Goals (ECOWAS 2006). For that price, the region could bring modern cooking fuels to everyone, increase electricity access in cities to 100%, and in rural areas to 33%, and make electricity and mechanical energy available to two-thirds of rural communities. With a regional population of 300 million people, the required investment is $16 per person per year. While other African regions are tackling the same issues, ECOWAS has made the most progress in calculating required investments. Based on ECOWAS' work, Sub-Saharan Africa would require $12 billion a year in energy service investments in order to halve the region's poverty as defined under the Millennium Development Goals, about one-third of the $41 billion annual investment assessed by Foster and Briceño-Garmendia (2010). This aligns with estimates published in the *World Energy Outlook 2006*, that an annual investment of $35 billion a year until 2030 could achieve universal access to electricity (OECD and IEA 2006).

Households within grid-electrified regions may still not have access to electricity, or may limit their usage. Poor households are challenged in two ways. First, connection fees charged by the utility can be too high for a household to pay all at once. Second, housing must often be of a certain standard for connection, barring those living in the poorest housing structures from accessing electricity. As a consequence, only about 10% of the households in electrified, rural communities in Tanzania are actually connected, even a decade after their rural electrification programme began. The investment required for an electric stove and appropriate cooking utensils remains an obstacle to electric cooking, even for electrified households (Kjellstrom 1994).

Effective policies

Improving energy sector policies is a prerequisite for building an effective environment for non-privatized electricity services. In recent years, a body of literature critical of power-sector reforms has emerged, with important implications for improved public-sector service provision. Important policies include:

- Autonomy and authority in regulatory boards
- Utility performance evaluations and license renewals based on technical performance and meeting connection targets
- Provision of targeted subsidies for poor households that minimize or eliminate connection fees and fixed charges
- Least-cost electrification options and appropriate technologies
- Improved oversight of state-owned enterprises
- New approaches to attack system losses, raise collection rates, and improve customer service

While much of this language has been used to promote private sector investment and participation in electrification in the past, or to push for the commercialization of public utilities, it can be equally valid to apply these principles, and even modify them, to non-commercialized public electricity entities in Africa, most of which would benefit from better management and transparency. It is important, for example, that "least-cost" electricity options do not mean substandard provision for the poor and that electricity users be seen as participative members of an electrification system rather than just passive "customers". Without addressing some of these policy and institutional factors, barriers to effective public service provision will remain, and services will not be able to flourish.

Community management

Hundreds of defunct demonstration and village power projects across Africa have proven the need for sustainable management beyond the setup of the power supply. Financial and technical oversight of any shared power system is essential. Two excellent guidebooks could help communities navigate how to setup ongoing management: *Guides for Electric Cooperative Development and Rural Electrification* (NRECA International, n.d.) and *Electricity Services in Remote Rural Communities* (Sanchez 2006). These guides help identify best practice for tariffs, contracts, and system oversight within the rural context of developing countries and with the aim of promoting the broader public good in energy provision.

Financial sustainability

Cost recovery and subsidies are key debates in Africa's electricity provision. Decades of subsidies to the power sector in Sub-Saharan Africa have failed to make electricity accessible or affordable, largely because access to service is almost entirely confined to the wealthier segments of society.

Appropriate subsidies can increase access rates, ensure that electricity costs are affordable to poor communities, inhibit inefficient use, and ensure that industrial users are not disproportionately benefiting from the system. Ending power subsidies for higher-income groups could allow resources to be reallocated to subsidize the expansion of power networks to serve lower-income rural and peri-urban communities.

The poor are often caught in the middle, with no access to modern energy services and limited options for financing to purchase such services. Recent research also suggests that it is the infrastructure—not the monthly use charges—that is the most prohibitive for low-income users. Subsidies that target connections and up-front costs will reach poor consumers better than subsidized tariffs. After studying examples in Burkina Faso, Kenya, and Tanzania, Morris and Kirubi (2009) found that access to modern energy services can be increased if small-scale finance options are available, and that the government can play a catalytic role in putting the pieces into place.

High-cost technologies are also an inhibitor. Adoption of low-cost technologies in electrifying rural areas was another important measure used successfully in Tunisia, Morocco, and Mauritius. Standards that could help to ensure cost effectiveness include "single-wire earth return" and transformer locations that are determined on a line-by-line basis depending on current and future demand growth (GNESD, see www.gnesd.org).

In South Africa, the Free Basic Electricity policy entitles poor households to receive a minimum amount of 50 kWh of electricity per month for free. Lifeline tariffs such as this one have largely been criticized by the World Bank and other institutions engaged in sectoral reforms as undermining the financial sustainability of state utilities, leaving them largely unable to cover expenses or maintain—let alone expand—their system. However, targeted subsidies that are well implemented can allow the state to meet its welfare goals. Increased rates paid by higher-consumption users can accomplish multiple goals; they can provide funds to help cover the costs for more connections, and they can cross-subsidize the costs for the poorest—often lower-consumption—users. Higher rates can also motivate users to become more energy efficient.

For community systems, Kirubi has argued that the design of the tariff system depends on whether the systems' variable and fixed costs are high or low:

> A system with high variable costs (e.g. a diesel system) demands reasonably precise monitoring of energy consumed so that users are billed for each unit of energy used. Such a tariff is commonly referred to as an energy-based tariff. In contrast, when a system has low variable costs and high fixed costs (e.g. microhydro), a capacity-based tariff makes much more sense because the marginal cost of consumption is insignificant. (2009, 57)

Community-based grids in rural areas in particular can benefit from load-limiting devices such as electrical ready boards. These devices can be used to enforce capacity-based tariffs, designed to limit the maximum power consumed.

Revenue collection is a legitimate issue. While emphasis in some countries has been put on residential collection and enforcement measures such as controversial prepaid meters, government institutions are also often delinquent, with far less chance for enforcement. In the DRC, public companies owed the state power company US$500 million. In 2005, Zimbabwe's utility, ZESA, owed US$110 million in arrears to power utilities in neighbouring countries, including: US$27 million to Mozambique; US$11 million to South Africa; and US$5 million to DRC and Zambia (*The Independent* 2005). Despite halving the arrears in 2006, the amount owed to neighbouring countries had again grown to US$100 million (*Chronicle* 2010).

"No regrets" planning

Countless African countries have faced unexpected power shortages in recent years. Some outages have been due to hydropower shortages during drought, while others have been due to imported fuel shortages driven by price hikes. Degraded power stations and slow-paced expansions have also been culprits of shortages. These crises have brought greater attention to the need for forward planning of a low risk—or "no regrets"—national power sector to ensure that national planners address new risks—particularly climate change—as well as risks that have been historically overlooked. "No regrets" energy planning would identify project long-term risks and prioritize low-risk projects within the scope of the commonly used least-cost energy planning. The financial burden of fossil fuel imports and new attention to carbon emissions have helped many countries recognize the benefits of developing indigenous energy sources and diversifying their sources of energy supply. A diverse energy portfolio is an important way to hedge the risks of any one power supply.

This is particularly true for large-scale hydropower. Already, 11 African countries are more than 80% dependent on hydropower (EIA 2006). Countries including Cameroon, Ethiopia, Ghana, Kenya, Malawi, Tanzania, Uganda, Zambia, and Zimbabwe have all witnessed power shortages in recent years caused by droughts that reduced hydropower supplies (UNECA 2007). Such power crises have caused countries to sign expensive short-term agreements for diesel generators. However, significant pressure to develop large-scale hydropower projects as "least-cost supply", including for regional use, remains influential in Africa's overall energy planning. This attempt to exploit Africa's hydro potential is blind to several risks that could ultimately undermine the cost-effectiveness of these choices, namely, energy portfolio overdependency on hydropower and the impacts of climate change—regardless of whether they are public or private. These projects also face the ongoing risks of corruption and mismanagement.

Renewable energy

Setting national targets for renewable energy can indicate a country's proactive vision for a diversified and sustainable power sector. National targets for renewable energy have been set by at least 13 African countries, although these targets may include large hydro: Algeria, Egypt, Kenya, Madagascar, Mali, Morocco, Nigeria, Rwanda, Senegal, South Africa, Tunisia, and Uganda. Egypt has a target to generate 20% of its energy from renewables by the year 2020. In 1994, the country's New and Renewable Energy Authority introduced the Bulk Renewable Energy Electricity Production Programme to target large-scale solar and wind power development. Egypt operates a 5 MW demonstration wind farm, with two 60 MW wind farms under construction.

A feed-in tariff can be one of the most dramatic catalysts to drive renewable energy projects. A feed-in tariff typically obliges grid utilities to purchase renewable electricity supplies from eligible projects and guarantees to the renewable supplier: grid access for the renewable energy supply; long-term power purchase contracts from the renewable project; and an equitable purchase price. The first African country to introduce a feed-in tariff was Mauritius, followed by Algeria in 2002, Uganda in 2007, Kenya in 2008, and South Africa in 2009. Egypt and Nigeria are both in the process of developing feed-in tariffs. Today, Mauritius generates 40% of the country's power from *bagasse*—agricultural wastes from its sugar industry—in part due to these policies.

The extent to which public electricity utilities are better placed to provide renewable energy sources than the private sector is a matter that has not been debated in any sustained way in the African context but should be a central part of any serious efforts to create "alternatives to privatization" on the continent.

Energy efficiency

Investing in more efficient use of energy supplies could lead to significant cost savings and delay construction of costly new supplies. Initiatives for energy efficiency and demand-side management are increasing in popularity but are far from reaching their full potential in Africa. In 2008, CEB in Mauritius wrote that, "Clearly, the most environmentally sound, inexpensive and reliable power plant is the one we do not have to build because we have helped our customers to save energy" (2008, 4).

The electricity supply industry in Africa is also characterized by high system losses—power produced but lost during transmission and distribution. Compared with the international target of about 10%–12% some of the power systems in Africa record figures as high as 30% (Karekezi and Kimani 2002). Some of the best improvements in efficiency would be reduced load losses, often through maintenance and upgrading of the grid. There's no reason to invest in a new power source when an equivalent amount of power could be "found" by decreasing existing system losses by public service providers.

Electric lighting consumes more than 19% of the world's electricity and accounts for up to 10% of energy consumption. Aggressively replacing incandescent light bulbs with compact fluorescent lamps (CFLs) could reduce energy demand from lighting by nearly 40%. The World Bank, which promotes bulk procurement and distribution of CFLs, has helped finance distribution of 2 million CFLs in Ethiopia, Rwanda, and Uganda, in order to cut each country's peak demand by 100 MW, while the government of Ghana distributed 6 million CFLs on its own (World Bank 2008, 52). A World Bank emergency loan to the Central African Republic, where electricity access is limited almost exclusively to the capital, includes US$300,000 for dissemination of 80,000 CFLs for an estimated savings of 2 MW. The Southern African Development Community has undertaken a three-year CFL dissemination programme with member utilities to disseminate over 40 million CFLs leading to 1,750 MW of avoided supply (SAPP 2009). Once again, public service providers can take the lead in energy efficiency.

Job creation

According to the International Labour Organization (ILO 2007), 37% of all Africans live in extreme poverty, down only 1% from a decade ago. In absolute terms, the number of Africans living in extreme poverty has actually grown by 55 million people during this time. There is strong consensus that sufficient, decent work opportunities across Africa are not being generated. Instead, more than 80% of Africa's workers remain in marginalized livelihoods, primarily in subsistence agriculture and the informal economy. Africa's youth—15 to 24 years—is also growing much faster than jobs are being created. African youth unemployment averages 20%, double that of the overall average unemployment. Africa will need to create 11 million jobs every year until 2015 simply to achieve unemployment rates that match the global average of about 6%.

Much of the energy sector development to date has reflected the energy needs of commodity-based industrial development, which continues to drive economic growth in many African countries. However, high economic growth often narrowly reflects high prices and/or increased sales of commodity exports but with few jobs and limited benefits to the rest of the population. Too often, though, the energy sector does not respond to development goals for job creation or direct poverty alleviation.

New end-use industries are not the only way that energy plans influence job creation. The ILO also noted that the development of infrastructure can optimize local job creation: "Ensuring strong linkages between infrastructure projects and local economies requires an equal investment in better social infrastructure facilities like support for rural micro, small and medium enterprises and cooperatives" (2007, 3). The ILO has also suggested that the march towards universal access to basic services creates jobs in the energy sector and beyond. But key opportunities are still being missed. In South Africa, a 2006 study by the International Development Corporation found that a significant portion of Eskom investments, including the use of public funds, was used to purchase imports, missing a key opportunity to use the investments to jumpstart local manufacturing (UNECA 2007).

Many experts agree that the renewable energy sector, particularly energy efficiency, generates more jobs than in fossil fuels (*San Francisco Chronicle* 2004, ILO 2008). In South Africa, one study found that renewable energy sources would create three times as many jobs as relying on fossil fuels (AGAMA Energy 2003).

Smaller-scale, decentralized electricity systems can also create more manufacturing and maintenance jobs for local people. Two enterprises in Kenya have pioneered the local manufacturing of wind pumps and wind generators in the country: Bobs Harries Engineering Limited manufactures wind pumps for water pumping, and Craftskills Enterprises manufactures wind turbines designed to utilize less-powerful wind gusts. An estimated 90% of the materials used to manufacture the turbines are sourced locally; recycled metals are used to make the machines, and the only imported components are magnets (GTZ n.d.). Craftskills provides regular technical maintenance and a hotline support desk for immediate problems. Companies like Deng Limited in Ghana and Zara Solar in Tanzania are local leaders in selling, installing, and maintaining solar PV systems and have received prestigious international awards for their accomplishments in sustainable energy (Ashden Awards 2007a, 2007b).

Building local capacity to analyze energy options and policy is also important to promote long-term sustainable provision. UNEP's Global Network on Energy for Sustainable Development (GNESD) has identified three "centres of excellence" in Africa—the African Energy and Policy Research Network based in Nairobi, Kenya; *Environnement et Développement du Tiers Monde* in Dakar, Senegal; and the Energy Research Centre at the University of Cape Town, South Africa. In West Africa, ECOWAS plans to set up a Regional Centre for Renewable Energy and Energy Efficiency. The government of Kenya also intends to set up a Centre for Energy Efficiency and Conservation.

Although no research exists as to the potential for job creation in renewables in the public versus the private sectors in electricity in Africa, it is arguable that coordinated public sector investment would create more jobs than ad hoc private sector investment.

Modern energy services for development

While this chapter is intended to focus on provision of electricity, the provision of other modern forms of energy can be equally vital to human and economic development in Africa and to the search for innovative public service provision. Energy needs for domestic use and for income-generating activities for Africa's rural majority are too often overlooked by state utilities and financiers focused on the electricity grid. In November 2009, the United Nations (UN) released a comprehensive review of targets set by African governments for access to electricity and other modern energy services, including access to mechanical power, modern cooking fuels, and improved cookstoves (Legros et al, 2009). These forms of energy services regularly lose out to electrification initiatives in the competition for scarce donor funds.

Even when electricity is available, it often does not displace traditional biomass use for cooking and heating. Approximately 579 million Africans—76% of the rural population and 47% of urban Africans—rely on wood, charcoal, and dung as their primary sources of cooking energy (OECD and IEA 2006). Instead of switching energy use entirely to electricity as it becomes available, households add fuels in a process of "fuel stacking":

> Modern forms of energy are usually applied sparingly at first and for particular services rather than completely supplanting an existing form of energy that already supplies a service adequately. The most energy-consuming activities in the household—cooking and heating—are the last to switch. Use of multiple fuels provides a sense of energy security, since complete dependence on a single fuel or technology leaves households vulnerable to price variations and unreliable service. Some reluctance to discontinue cooking with fuelwood may also be due to taste preferences and the familiarity of cooking with traditional technologies. (OECD and IEA 2006, 422)

Using traditional biomass for household energy is a significant health issue. Pollution concentrations in rural African homes can be as much as 100 times higher than those observed in the urban areas of many industrialized nations (Kammen and Jacobson 2005). The World Health Organization (WHO) estimates that about 1.5 million people die each year from indoor air pollution caused by cooking with traditional biomass energy, with the heaviest proportion in Sub-Saharan Africa. The lack of efficient energy sources also impacts health systems in the region (Enskat and Liptow 2008). Improved cookstoves are one form of modern energy service that could increase fuel efficiency and smoke departure of traditional biomass, thereby reducing both the demand for traditional biomass and health impacts.

The use of traditional biomass—primarily wood fuel and charcoal—is a significant source of environmental problems. As forest resources disappear a "fuelwood gap" is emerging. In Mozambique, for example, estimated total wood fuel consumption is about 640 m^3 per person per year. Illegal logging to supply the urban charcoal demand is still widespread despite heavy fines (Greenpeace and ITDG 2002, 60). This "traditional" energy source is seldom given high priority in energy policies or poverty alleviation strategies; there are few comprehensive national strategies for the traditional use of biomass in the energy sector (EUEI and GTZ 2008).

At least one-third of African countries have programmes for improved biomass cookstoves, and many more have pledged to help develop the technology, spread information, foster projects, and generally promote access to modern cooking energy for rural populations currently using traditional biomass. More than 8 million improved stoves are believed to be in circulation. Kenya has been the leader, where the Kenya Ceramic Jiko stove is found in more than half of urban homes and roughly 20% of rural homes. A significant number of improved cookstoves are also reported in Burkina Faso, Eritrea, Ethiopia, Ghana, Niger, Senegal, South Africa, Tanzania, Uganda, and Zimbabwe (REN21 2008). A number of African countries have set targets for increasing access to modern cooking fuels and improved cookstoves.

Solar PV and wind power for pumping both irrigation and drinking water are gaining widespread acceptance, and many more projects and investments are occurring. Large numbers of wind pumps for water are being used in Africa, including 300,000 in South Africa, 30,000 in Namibia, 800 in Cape Verde, 650 in Zimbabwe, and roughly 2,000 more across several other countries. There are an estimated 1,000 solar water pumps in use in West Africa. Donor programmes for PV-powered drinking water have appeared in Namibia, Niger, Tunisia, and Zimbabwe (REN21 2008).

THE WAY FORWARD

Africa remains the world's most concentrated population lacking access to electricity. This chapter provides a framework and some examples that demonstrate how public, community, and other non-commercialized systems will be fundamental for providing widespread access to electricity on the continent. A rethinking of the power sector reforms that have guided the unsuccessful shift towards privatization is necessary, and a review of the social welfare goals—particularly encased in the Millennium Development Goals—will be important. How many more creative minds like William Kamkwamba could be empowered to make energy innovations with local resources? What needs to be done to tap into this drive to bring electricity to communities, schools, and homes? How can this be done without relying on privatization and commercialization?

Based on the information presented in this chapter, the following actions are suggested:

- Given the history of poor service, state provision of electricity cannot be successful without holding governments and utilities accountable and ensuring that they create an enabling environment for successful public and community provision. Greater transparency of state-based electricity systems, targets, finances, and planning processes will allow greater accountability by communities and civil society, as well as by the donor community. As states increase their engagement

in regional energy planning, they should ensure civil society participation in regional planning and public accountability of decisions.

- Power sector reforms should be pro-poor as well as improve technical and financial management. Structures and mechanisms to address
rural electrification should be prioritized prior to privatization, or else
rural electrification may not be addressed at all. Reforms should also
adopt innovative approaches to meet electrification targets.

- National Electricity Acts should establish autonomous oversight for
rural electrification funds.

- Data collected on access to energy should be standardized and include
sufficient data to allow analysis of socio-economic factors. For example,
data collected on new connections should differentiate between rural
and urban households. Evaluations of utilities and rural electrification
agencies should reflect data on the number of new connections.

- Economic development in Africa needs to be pro-jobs and pro-poor.
Successful electricity provision should reflect national energy strategies that support industries that create decent jobs, build community
resilience, and do not threaten food security; this should be prioritized for local communities in both urban and rural areas. Focus
should include the agricultural value chain and manufacturing. Local
production of energy inputs and systems using local materials and
local technical knowledge should also be prioritized.

- Empowering and enabling communities to be active participants in the
electrification process is one of the greatest oversights to date. Communities can and should take action towards electrification. States
should publicize their targets and involve the public in monitoring
progress. States should reduce regulatory barriers for communities
and enable state financial support for communities.

- African energy ministers have provided a great gift: time-based targets for electrification. Civil society should use these government-
generated targets to hold their officials accountable and to work with
government and donors to ensure that resources are well allocated for
these targets.

- In many identified community experiences, a common challenge has
been creating and maintaining a management system for the electricity
service provider. Many examples identified some form of an elected
consumer committee responsible for technical and financial operations.
There is a particular need to create ways to share information across
community experiences and generate greater awareness for existing
examples. Building a knowledge base of examples and experts is an
effective way to share information between countries and communities.
The Internet and social networking offer a myriad of ways to gather
data, share experiences, and monitor government targets.

- Political will to electrify African communities is lacking. Africans
will need to generate political will through public action. Sharing

stories of successful community systems and building networks of activists and technicians can strengthen public and community movements towards energy development and help demonstrate the endless possibilities of community-driven power. To advance advocacy, more education is needed around national energy planning and institutions, understanding targets, advocating to national regional and continental institutes, and financiers.

- Renewable energy sources will be an important part of the solution to diversify Africa's energy portfolio. An effort led by the African Union to produce a continent-wide African Energy Vision 2030 is underway. This could be a key place to promote renewable energy targets. Developing a range of power sources of different scales can also help hedge risks and bring power sources closer to the people, enhancing the "public" nature of service provision.

NOTES

1. GEF is an intergovernmental funding initiative established to improve the global environment. Since 1991, the GEF has allocated $8.8 billion for more than 2,400 projects. The 18 systems noted here were funded through GEF's Small Grants Programme, which has made more than 10,000 small grants to non-governmental and community organizations (GEF, www.thegef.org/gef/whatisgef).
2. Barefoot College. www.barefootcollege.org/sol_work.asp (accessed 15 September 2010).

REFERENCES

AGAMA Energy. 2003. *Employment potential of renewable energy in South Africa*. Johannesburg, South Africa: Earthlife Africa.
ARN (African Rivers Network). 2006. *Voices from the ground: Case studies of hydro power and dams in Africa*. Pretoria, South Africa: ARN.
Ashden Awards. 2007a. Affordable solar energy for the rural poor. Deng Ltd, Ghana. www.ashdenawards.org/winners/deng (accessed 1 July 2010).
———. 2007b. Affordable solar energy for the rural poor: Zara Solar Ltd, Tanzania. www.ashdenawards.org/winners/zara (accessed 1 July 1 2010).
Bayliss, K. 2007. Water and electricity in Sub-Saharan Africa. In Bayliss, K. and Fine, B. (Eds), *Privatization and alternative public sector reform in Sub-Saharan Africa: Delivering on electricity and water*. Basingstoke: Palgrave Macmillan.
BBC News. 2009. Malawi windmill boy with big fans. 1 October.
Bbumba, S. 2005. Fema position paper: Energy and the MDGs. Heads of state dinner UN—Millennium Summit, New York. 14 September.
Bloomberg. 2009. Sub-Saharan Africa needs $563 billion spent on power generation. May 12.
Boyd. J. 2010. Personal communication. By e-mail. 9 April 2009.
CEB (Central Electricity Board). 2008. *Annual report*. Port Louis, Mauritius: CEB.
Chronicle. 2010. ZESA needs US$383m to import power. March 12.

Covarrubias, A.J. 1996. *Lending for electric power in Sub-Saharan Africa.* World Bank Operations Evaluation Study. Washington, DC: World Bank.

CURES (Citizens United for Renewable Energy and Sustainability). 2003. The future is renewable: Declaration for the International Conference for Renewable Energies (Renewables 2004). Bad Honnef, Germany, 5–8 October. www. cures-network.org/docs/dec_engl181103_lay.pdf.

ECOWAS *(Economic Community of West African States).* 2006. A white paper for a regional policy geared towards increasing access to energy services for rural and peri-urban populations in order to achieve the Millennium Development Goals. Abuja, Nigeria: Ecowas.

EIA (Energy Information Administration). 2006. World electricity installed capacity by type. International Energy Annual 2005 Table 6.4. www.eia.gov/iea/elec. html.

Enskat, M. and Liptow, H. 2008. Energy in Africa—Facing a double challenge energising sustainable development concepts and projects. GTZ (Gesellschaft für Technische Zusammenarbeit). www2.gtz.de/dokumente/bib/07–0294.pdf (accessed 1 July 2010).

EUEI (European Union Energy Initiative) and GTZ. 2008. The BEST initiative: Biomass energy strategies for African countries. Eschborn, Germany: EUEI and GTZ.

Foster, V. and Briceño-Garmendia, C. (Eds). 2010. *Africa's infrastructure: A time for transformation.* Washington, DC: World Bank.

Frost & Sullivan. 2009. *The Asian influence in the Sub-Saharan African electricity industry.* Dublin, Ireland: Research and Markets.

Gentle, L. 2009. Escom to Eskom: From racial Keynesian capitalism to neo-liberalism (1910–1994). In McDonald, D.A. (Ed), *Electric capitalism*, pp. 50–72. London: Earthscan.

GNESD (Global Network on Energy and Development). 2004. Energy access: Making power sector reform work for the poor (summary for policymakers). www.gnesd.org/Downloadables/Energy_Access_III/PowerSectorReformSpm. pdf (accessed 1 July 2010).

Greenberg, S. 2009. Market liberalisation and continental expansion: The repositioning of Eskom in post-apartheid South Africa. In McDonald, D. (Ed), *Electric capitalism*, pp. 73–108. London: Earthscan.

Greenpeace and ITDG (International Technology Development Group). 2002. Sustainable energy for poverty reduction: An action plan. www.greenpeace.org/ international/en/publications/reports/sustainable-energy-for-poverty/.

GTZ. n.d. Local manufacture of wind energy systems, Kenya. Best practice—Wind. Eastern Africa regional energy resource base. www.regionalenergy-net. com/index.php?option=com_content&task=view&id=104&Itemid=117.

ILO (International Labour Organization). 2007. Conclusions of the 11th African regional meeting. In Proceedings of the Eleventh African Regional Meeting, pp. 2–3. Addis Ababa, Ethiopia, 24–27 April.

———. 2008. Green jobs initiative: Facts and figures. Switzerland: ILO. www.ilo. org/global/resources/WCMS_098484/lang—en/index.htm.

Kammen, D. and Jacobson, A. 2005. Science and engineering research that values the planet. *The Bridge* 35(1): 11–17.

Kamkwamba, W. and Mealer, B. 2009. *The boy who harnessed the wind.* New York: HarperCollins Publishers.

Karekezi, S. and Kimani, J. 2002. *Status of power sector reform in Africa: Impact on the poor.* Nairobi, Kenya: Afrepren.

Kirubi, C.G. 2009. *Expanding access to off-grid rural electrification in Africa: An analysis of community-based micro-grids in Kenya.* PhD thesis. University of California, Berkeley.

Kjellstrom, B. 1994. Rural electrification in Tanzania. *Energy for the household* 32. www.hedon.info/RuralElectrificationInTanzania.

Legros, G., Havet, I., Bruce, N. and Bonjour, S. 2009. *The energy access situation in developing countries: A review focusing on the least developed countries and sub-Saharan Africa.* Geneva, Switzerland: UNDP (United Nations Development Programme) and WHO (World Health Organization).

Lighting Africa. 2008. About us. World Bank. www.lightingafrica.org/node/23 (accessed 15 March 2010).

McDonald, D.A., and Pape, J. (Eds). 2002. *Cost recovery and the crisis of service delivery in South Africa.* London: Zed Press.

Morris, E. and Kirubi, G. 2009. *Bringing small-scale finance to the poor for modern energy services: What is the role of government?* New York: UNDP (United Nations Development Program).

Mostert, W. 2008. *Review of experiences with rural electrification agencies: Lessons for Africa.* Washington, DC: EUEI-PDF (EU Energy Initiative Partnership Dialogue Facility). Mimeo.

Naidoo, P. and Veriava, A. 2009. From local to global (and back again?): Anti-commodification struggles of the Soweto electricity crisis committee. In McDonald, D. (Ed), *Electric capitalism*, pp. 321–337. London: Earthscan.

Nkeng, C. 2009. Personal communication. By telephone. 20 March 2009.

NRECA (National Rural Electric Cooperatives of America) International. n.d. *Guides for electric cooperative development and rural electrification.* Arlington, VA: NRECA International, Ltd.

OECD (Organization for Economic Co-operation and Development) and IEA (International Energy Agency). 2004. *World Energy Outlook 2004.* Paris: OECD and IEA.

———. 2006. *World Energy Outlook 2006.* Paris: OECD and IEA.

Practical Action. 2007. Grid connection. Rome. www.practicalaction.org/practicalanswers/product_info.php?cPath=21&products_id=293&attrib=.

Practical Action Consulting. 2009. *Small-scale bioenergy initiatives: Brief description and preliminary lessons on livelihood impacts from case studies in Asia, Latin America and Africa.* Practical Action Consulting.

Rea, C. 2009. Personal communication. By e-mail. 19 September 2009.

REN21 (Renewable Energy Policy Network for the 21st Century). 2008. *Renewables 2007 Global Status Report.* Paris: REN21 Secretariat and Washington, DC: Worldwatch Institute.

Ruiters, G. 2009. Free basic electricity in South Africa: A strategy for helping or containing the poor? In McDonald, D. (Ed), *Electric capitalism*, pp. 248–263. London: Earthscan.

Sanchez, T. 2006. *Electricity services in remote rural communities.* Rugby, Warwickshire, UK: Practical Action.

San Francisco Chronicle. 2004. Plan to junk oil, add jobs/New coalition pushes renewables. 14 April.

SAPP (Southern Africa Power Pool). 2009. A SADC Residential Compact Fluorescent Lamps Rollout Programme by Southern African Power Pool (SAPP). www.sapp.co.zw.

The Independent. 2003. ZESA arrears climb to US$110m. 19 June.

UNDESA (United Nations Department of Economic and Social Affairs), Population Division. 2006. Urban and rural areas dataset. In *World urbanization prospects: The 2005 revision*, pp. 46–75. New York: United Nations.

UNECA (United Nations Economic Commission for Africa). 2007. *Making Africa's power sector sustainable: An analysis of power sector reforms in Africa.* Addis Ababa, Ethiopia: UNECA and UNEP (UN-Energy/Africa).

US Department of Energy. 2002. Uganda: Solar Light for the Churches of Africa (SLCA). In *Energy and water for sustainable living: A compendium of energy and water success stories*, pp. 96–97. Washington, D.C. www.pi.energy.gov/documents/EWSLuganda_slca.pdf.

Vanguard News. 2008. Nigerians spend N16.408 trillion on fuelling generators. 28 January.

Ward, S. 2002. *The energy book for urban development in South Africa.* Cape Town, South Africa: Sustainable Energy Africa.

World Bank. 2003. *Private participation in infrastructure: Trends in developing countries.* Washington, DC: World Bank.

———. 2008. *Development and climate change: A strategic framework for the World Bank Group.* Washington, DC: World Bank. www.beta.worldbank.org/overview/phase-ii-development-and-climate-change-strategic-framework.

WSSD (World Summit on Sustainable Development). 2002. *Poverty eradication: implementation plan.* New York: United Nations.

Latin America and the Caribbean
Regional Overview

Susan Spronk

> *Latin America is the region of open veins. Everything, from the discovery until our times, has been transmuted into European—or later United States—capital, and as such has accumulated in distant centres of power.*
>
> Eduardo Galeano, Uruguayan writer and activist (1973, 12)

Citizens of Latin America and the Caribbean (LAC) face two serious challenges as they struggle to meet the needs of their communities. First, the LAC region as a whole has the greatest inequalities of income and wealth in the world so that an extreme concentration of resources and power yields deep and widespread poverty. Second, during the 1980s public services in Latin America became the most rapidly privatized in the world. Since then, however, there have been successful social movement struggles to return basic services to public hands, particularly in the water and electricity sectors in the countries of the "New Left", such as Bolivia, Brazil, Argentina, Uruguay, and Venezuela.

Although Africa, Asia, and the LAC region share a common history of colonialism, the latter is distinguished by its early independence and its long history of revolution and struggle. The Americas were home to many indigenous peoples and advanced civilizations, including the Aztec, Maya, and Inca. The islands that now form Cuba were invaded by Spanish explorers in 1492, while Portuguese explorers landed on the east coast of contemporary Brazil around 1500. Due to European colonization, only 10% of the estimated original population remained by the close of the 16th century (Galeano 1973). Lacking personnel to work the plantations that populated the Caribbean islands and the coastal areas of South America, it has been estimated that about 5 million slaves were imported to the LAC region from Africa between the 15th and 17th centuries (Curtin 1969), leading to the region's mixed "racial" heritage.

The legacy of racist and class exclusion engendered by colonialism gave rise to continued political turmoil in the 19th and 20th centuries. The first successful slave revolt established the Republic of Haiti in 1804. The rest of Latin America and the Caribbean achieved independence between 1810 and 1825 (except for Cuba, which remained an American colony until 1898, and Puerto Rico, which remains a US protectorate to this day). Although early independence leaders were inspired by the liberal ideas of the French Revolution, these newly minted republics remained highly segregated societies based upon rigid social hierarchies based on caste and the exploitation of indigenous and black labour, leading to more social turmoil and revolution. The first modern-day revolution in the Americas took place in Mexico in 1910, followed by the national-popular revolution of Bolivia in 1952, the Cuban Revolution in 1959, and the Sandinista Revolution in Nicaragua in 1979.

The middle decades of the 20th century were characterized by a state-led development project inspired by economists from the UN Economic Commission on Latin America and the Caribbean, known as "import substitution industrialization" (ISI), as states sought to "modernize" their economies to overcome the legacy of dependency and underdevelopment (Cardoso and Faletto 1979). Under ISI policies, central governments increasingly centralized control over basic services such as water, electricity, and health care. The expansion of the public sector arose from the decisions of governments and international institutions that decisive government intervention in the economy was required to maximize economic welfare through economic growth. In line with the Keynesian thinking of the time, basic infrastructure and service provision were seen as essential to maintain capital accumulation, to assist in the reproduction of labour, and to help maintain social consensus. The political pressure on the state exerted by the working class organizations pushed the state to spend more on basic needs, leading to improvements to the quality of life for the working population (Weisbrot et al, 2002).

Despite these gains, the state-led development strategy produced mixed results. First, ISI policies could not overcome the persistent race and class inequality that has pervaded Latin America since colonial times (Thorp 1998). Second, ISI sponsored rapid, chaotic urbanization and uneven development: by 1980, 65% of the region's population lived in urban areas, while rural workers bore the burden of producing cheap foodstuffs for urban workers but never had the same access to basic services (Lefeber 1980). To this day, there is a backlog in service delivery, particularly in the peri-urban and rural areas of the LAC region.

The most important legacies of ISI are authoritarianism and external debt. The "easy" phase had exhausted itself already by the late 1950s. The consequence was a cycle of state-sponsored violence against the civilian population. The first military coup took place in Brazil in 1964, and by the end of the following decade, 18 of 21 countries of Latin America were ruled by non-constitutional governments. Unaccountable to the public and supported by American imperialism, these authoritarian governments contracted large amounts of external debt from public and private sources of capital, which later put governments at the mercy of the international financial institutions (McMichael 2008).

First implemented at the bayonet of a gun following the Pinochet coup in Chile in 1972, the neoliberal policies implemented in the 1980s and 1990s fundamentally altered political and economic relations in the LAC region, reversing many of the gains of the previous era. Markets were opened to international private capital, land markets were liberalized, state enterprises were privatized, and social subsidies on basic services and foodstuffs were cut dramatically. Poverty rates worsened between 1980 and 1990, jumping from 40.5% to 48.3%. The problem of poverty is more serious in the rural areas; in 2005 rural poverty was 58.8% compared to 34.1% in the urban areas (ECLAC 2008, 52).

Given its relative wealth and highly urbanized population, the LAC region has traditionally had higher rates of access to improved water sources and sanitation than Asia and Africa. As of 2008, only 9% of the population remained without water services, and 21% did not have access to sanitation (WHO and UNICEF 2000). It is for precisely this reason, however, that the LAC region was particularly attractive to private water companies, which flooded into the region under the wing of World Bank-sponsored privatization policies. In the wake of currency devaluations and social mobilizations, however, flagship privatization contracts in Buenos Aires, Argentina, and La Paz-El Alto, Bolivia, have been cancelled, returning water to public control and opening the space for debate on real alternatives.

Similar to water privatization, the wave of privatization in the electricity sector began in Chile in the early 1980s. Distribution and generating companies that were privatized in the 1990s soon became unprofitable, though, leading to a restructuring of the sector in the past decade. Due to flagging profitability, the wave of privatization has since ebbed, followed by the trend of renationalization in countries such as Venezuela and Bolivia. Even in Colombia, where privatization made the most inroads, more than half of the holdings in the electricity sector remain in public hands (Hall 2007).

With respect to health care, the ISI model permitted the creation of incomplete welfare states in the 1960s and 1970s, which promoted the creation of social security and medical care institutions that only covered workers in the formal sector. This system excluded that majority of the population in many countries who are engaged in informal activities, in both rural and urban areas (Fleury et al, 2000). Cuba and Costa Rica, two countries with universal access to health services, were exceptions. Under structural adjustment policies of the 1980s and 1990s, the majority of countries adopted measures to reduce social spending, especially in health and education, simultaneously promoting the growth of the private sector. In this manner, public funds were increasingly channelled to the private sector through the introduction of prepaid medical insurance schemes and subrogation, among other actions.

In sum, the debate on alternatives in Latin America and the Caribbean in basic services must be understood in the context of the region's history of colonialism, authoritarianism, and exclusionary forms of capitalist development. The hard-fought social movement victories that returned the region to constitutional rule in the 1980s and 1990s have also deeply influenced debates on alternatives in the region. In some social movement sectors, distrust of state institutions runs deep, leading to an emphasis on democracy, accountability, and transparency in public management. While LAC is a highly urbanized region, the resurgence of indigenous social movements has also placed non-state alternatives on the political agenda.

ACKNOWLEDGEMENTS

Thanks to Luis Ortiz Hernández, Iliana Camacho Cuapio, Catalina Eibenschutz Hartman, and Silvia Tamez González for input on this overview.

REFERENCES

Cardoso, F.H. and Faletto, E. 1979. *Dependency and development in Latin America*. Berkeley: University of California Press.

Curtin, P.D. 1969. *The Atlantic slave trade*. Madison: The University of Wisconsin Press.

ECLAC (Economic Commission for Latin America and the Caribbean). 2008. *Social panorama of Latin America 2007*. Santiago, Chile: ECLAC.

Fleury, S., Belmartino, S. and Baris, E. (Eds). 2000. *Reshaping health care in Latin America: A comparative analysis of health care reform in Argentina, Brazil and Mexico*. Ottawa: International Development Research Centre.

Galeano, E.H. 1973. *Open veins of Latin America Five centuries of the pillage of a continent*. New York: Monthly Review Press.

Hall, D. 2007. Electricity companies in Latin America 2007. Public Services International Research Unit. http://gala.gre.ac.uk/2936/1/2007–10-E-Latam.pdf (accessed 28 July 2010).

Lefeber, L. 1980. Spatial population distribution: Urban and rural development. In Lefeber, L. and North, L. (Eds), *Democracy and development in Latin America*, pp. 58–76. Toronto: CERLAC-LARU.

McMichael, P. 2008. *Development and social change: A global perspective. 4th ed, Sociology for a new century series*. Los Angeles: Pine Forge Press.

Thorp, R. 1998. *Progress, poverty and exclusion: An economic history of Latin America in the 20th century*. Washington, DC: Inter-American Development Bank.

Weisbrot, M., Baker, D., Kraev, E. and Chen, J. 2002. The scorecard on globalization 1980–2000: Its consequences for economic and social well-being. *International Journal of Health Services* 32(2): 229–253.

WHO and UNICEF (World Health Organization and United Nations Children's Fund). 2000. *Global water supply and sanitation assessment 2000 report*. Geneva, Switzerland, and New York: WHO and UNICEF.

14 Progressive Alternatives in Primary Health Care in Latin America

Luis Ortiz Hernández, Iliana Camacho Cuapio, Catalina Eibenschutz Hartman and Silvia Tamez González

The history of primary health care (PHC) in Latin America is a complex one that has been deeply impacted by the introduction of neoliberal policies from the 1970s onwards. Country-level success stories are rare, and although there are progressive pilot programmes still in operation in some parts of the region, these initiatives have had little or no national-level support and have not been very effective at resisting commercialization trends in the sector.

This chapter explores four settings in the region where PHC services are in public hands, have been well funded by governments, and have been integrated into a broader set of social and economic policy making and practice. At a country level, Cuba and Costa Rica stand out as having national health programmes that prioritize PHC and which have explicitly aimed to remove or keep out private sector health operators. They have also been in place for many decades, providing useful historical records on the requirements for realizing "alternatives to privatization" in the PHC sector and the challenges of operating these systems in a neoliberal era.

More recently, Venezuela and the Federal District of Mexico City have introduced non-commercialized PHC initiatives with a more localized focus, in part driven by a desire to integrate these into local participatory management systems (in the case of Venezuela) and in part because of the ideological and fiscal constraints of collaboration with higher levels of government (in the case of Mexico City).

The summaries offered here are far from comprehensive, but they do provide an overview of the key successes (and failures) of these initiatives and attempt to place them within a broader set of social, economic, and political norms operating in the region. What is clear in each case is that without strong and committed support from the state—ideally in combination with participatory engagement with citizens and health care providers and users—it is difficult, if not impossible, to create and sustain effective public PHC delivery.

Background information is provided for each of the cases, followed by a discussion of how "successful" they have been. The latter discussion is informed in part by the "criteria for success" developed for all of the studies in this book (see Chapter 2, this volume, for a detailed discussion of methodology). We focus specifically on issues of *participation, equity, quality,* and *efficiency.* What is evident in our review is that none of the cases are successful on every success criterion, and there are inherent tensions within and across the criteria applied (e.g. efficiency gains can come at the loss of some equity or sustainability). Nonetheless, our objective was not to find perfect or internally consistent models but rather to investigate in a methodologically transparent and comparative manner the kinds of criteria that make for successful alternatives to privatization in the PHC sector in Latin America. The fact that we ask as many questions as we answer is indicative of the ongoing tensions within the "alternatives" movement, as well as the friction these initiatives create with neoliberal capitalism.

FROM "COMPREHENSIVE PHC" TO "SELECTIVE PHC" IN LATIN AMERICA

The International Conference on Primary Health Care (ICPHC) in Alma-Ata, Kazakhstan, in 1978 resulted in an agreement signed by 134 nations committing themselves to incorporating PHC within the core planning of their country. The declaration is seen as a milestone in progressive PHC and established the following criteria for what is referred to as "comprehensive PHC" (WHO and UNICEF 1978):

- Health is a human right.
- There are enormous inequalities between and within developed and developing countries.
- There is a need for a New International Economic Order.
- Governments should assume responsibility for the health of their people.
- From the point of view of social justice, PHC should be the principal strategy for reaching "Health for All" in the year 2000.
- States should develop promotion and preventive health care models rather than just curative.
- PHC should be integrated within larger national health systems, leading to the increasing of coverage of comprehensive health care.
- Community participation in planning, organizing, running, and regulating PHC is critical.
- It is important to have cooperation amongst governments, workers, and communities.

The World Health Organization (WHO) and the United Nations Children's Fund (UNICEF) committed themselves to this declaration and gave advice on PHC to the countries involved (WHO and UNICEF 1978). Worldwide enthusiasm for the declaration was strong. With the help of international institutions and non-governmental organizations (NGOs), the strategy was adopted by nearly all countries in Latin America, with Cuba, Costa Rica and Brazil demonstrating exceptional community participation and government commitment (Werner et al, 2000, Giovanella et al, 2009). In Latin America today, there are many local comprehensive PHC teams, which continue to be inspired by this declaration and run integrated health systems that involve professional health care providers and the participation of communities. Two examples are the *Clínica Comunal* (Community Clinic) called *Ana Manganaro Guarjila* in El Salvador (Barten et al, 2009) and the community organization in a local health system in the *Región de Marqués de Comillas*, Chiapas, Mexico (Heredia 2007).

However, the Alma-Ata declaration contradicted the emerging neoliberal dictates of the 1980s in most of Latin America, particularly with the implantation of structural adjustment programmes created by the World Bank and the International Monetary Fund (IMF), which promoted privatization in the health care sector along with the reduction of state investment in health and education (World Bank 1993). Most Latin American countries acceded to these pressures, eroding their public health services, and allowing private operators and commercial principles to dominate. The only notable exception to this trend was Cuba (because of its socialist system), although Costa Rica and, to some extent, Brazil, showed considerable resistance to the implementation of neoliberal health policies.

According to the neoliberal orthodoxy of the day, the comprehensive version of PHC articulated in the Declaration of Alma-Ata was "too expensive and too unrealistic", with market-friendly policy makers suggesting it would be more efficient to redirect government spending towards low-cost, high-impact areas such as immunization. By 1983 UNICEF had also replaced the notion of comprehensive PHC with a group of specific interventions oriented to increasing child survival. This situation gave place to a much more limited policy known as GOBI—Growth Monitoring, Oral Re-Hydration Therapy, Breastfeeding, and Immunization (Wisner 1988). This new, more limited, version of service delivery has become known as "selective PHC" (Wisner 1988, Werner et al, 2000). As a result, the goal of Health for All was not reached, and was subsequently replaced by the Millennium Development Goals (MDGs).

Thus came about a succession of neoliberal health policy interventions, introduced mainly by the World Bank and the IMF, which gradually replaced the more progressive influence of the WHO and the Pan American Health Organization (PAHO). Amongst these interventions can be found the push for a "public-private mix" of service provision, which saw the development of national health policies headed by ministries/departments of health but in which the financing and ownership of services were both public and private (Eibenschutz 2007). After nearly 30 years of this neoliberal shift, the private sector has grown in every country in the region, yet equity in access to the services has not been achieved.

In Latin America, private expenditure on health—as a percentage of gross domestic product—rose from 3.2% in 1980 to 3.8% in 1990, due

Table 14.1 Health Care Expenditures in Selected Latin American Countries (as Percentage of GDP): 1995, 2000, and 2007

	General government expenditure on health			Prepaid and risk-pooling plans			Private households' out-of-pocket payment		
	1995	2000	2007	1995	2000	2007	1995	2000	2007
Argentina	5.0	5.0	4.6	0.9	1.3	2.7	2.3	2.5	2.1
Belize	2.8	2.4	2.8	NA	NA	NA	2.2	2.6	2.1
Brazil	2.9	2.9	4.9	1.2	1.5	1.2	2.6	2.7	2.4
Barbados	4.3	4.1	4.2	0.5	0.5	0.5	1.5	1.7	1.9
Chile	2.5	3.0	3.0	1.5	1.6	1.2	1.6	1.5	1.4
Colombia	4.3	6.2	6.4	0.5	0.6	0.6	2.6	0.9	0.4
Costa Rica	5.0	5.0	5.9	0.0	0.0	0.2	1.3	1.3	1.9
Cuba	5.2	6.1	9.9	0.0	0.0	0.0	0.5	0.6	0.6
Dominican Republic	1.2	2.2	1.9	0.8	0.8	0.6	3.2	3.0	2.1
Ecuador	2.3	1.3	2.4	0.3	0.1	0.2	1.3	2.4	2.7
Guatemala	1.3	2.2	2.0	0.1	0.1	0.2	2.2	3.0	4.1
Haiti	3.1	2.6	6.2	NA	NA	NA	3.5	3.2	2.3
Mexico	2.4	2.6	3.0	0.1	0.1	0.2	3.2	2.8	3.3
Nicaragua	4.8	3.7	4.9	0.0	0.2	0.1	1.3	3.1	5.0
Panama	4.8	5.3	5.7	0.4	0.5	0.4	1.9	2.0	1.7
Peru	2.2	2.5	2.6	0.2	0.4	0.4	2.0	1.8	1.5
Paraguay	2.4	3.7	2.6	0.4	0.6	0.5	3.9	4.9	4.0
El Salvador	2.5	3.6	3.6	0.0	0.2	0.3	3.9	4.1	2.0
Uruguay	4.6	3.5	3.5	2.6	5.2	3.2	2.0	1.8	1.4
Venezuela	2.3	3.2	2.7	0.1	0.1	0.1	2.0	2.5	2.4
Average	3.3	3.6	4.1	0.5	0.8	0.7	2.3	2.4	2.3

Source: Elaborated with data from WHO 2009.

mainly to increases in household out-of-pocket expenditures and growth in private health insurance and prepaid medical plans (PAHO 2007, 317). Since then there continues to be a general trend towards out-of-pocket expenditures and prepaid plans (see Table 14.1). Mexico, Venezuela, and Costa Rica are notable in this regard. In the Mexican case, it is more clearly a result of privatization.

On the other hand, Cuba stands out in terms of its relatively low out-of-pocket private expenditures (which refer principally to programmes for foreigners) and its high levels of government spending on health care (which have almost doubled since 2005 and are two-and a-half times the average of the countries listed in Table 14.1).

PHC IN TIMES OF CRISIS

There are, however, signs of change. Since abandoning the Alma-Ata principles, PAHO and the region's governments are now talking about revisiting comprehensive PHC. A growing number of academics, health workers, and non-governmental organizations have joined this initiative as well. Significantly, PAHO declared recently that "the principles that maintain a health system based on PHC require a process of renovation and include the responsibility and accountability of governments, as well as the capacity of the systems to meet, in a fair and sustainable way, the health needs of the people through participation, orientation towards quality and intersectoriality" (Macinko et al, 2007, 75).

Nevertheless, despite these enthusiastic efforts the social, economic, and political realities of long-term structural crisis in Latin America pose significant obstacles to meaningful change. By this we do not wish to dismiss the actions of governments in the region that appear committed to comprehensive PHC, but rather aim to point out obstacles that need to be overcome, including the ongoing push for privatization, the challenges of meeting citizen's rights, and the limited regulatory and delivery capacity of the region's states after three decades of liberalization. Of particular interest are questions of how we stimulate community participation in a context in which services depend on different public/private institutions of health and how we obtain participation among a polarized population (one that is increasingly divided into those who have private health insurance and those who do not).

THE SEARCH FOR ALTERNATIVES

In our search for public sector alternatives, we focused our attention on national-level programmes, which have explicitly attempted to prohibit (or at least minimize) private sector involvement in PHC. Cuba is exemplary in this regard, but Costa Rica is notable as well for its efforts to create health systems with the leadership of the public sector. We also look at the cases of Venezuela and Mexico City (the latter being a separate jurisdiction within the national Mexican state), both of which have experienced dramatic changes of government, with anti-neoliberal and anti-imperialist stances, creating opportunities for changes in health policy. Although more recent than Cuba and Costa Rica, these two cases provide valuable insights into an ongoing and dynamic state of change.

In all of these cases, we are exploring health provision by a formal state agency, working in part with local communities but largely as a single provider. Although there is some collaboration across different state agencies, we do not see the "public-public partnerships" that are increasingly common in other sectors in Latin America (notably in water) or the state-NGO collaborations found in the PHC sector in other parts of the world (see Chapters 8 and 11 on Asia and Africa, this volume). Nevertheless, the cases in this chapter demonstrate how the principles of Alma-Ata can be guaranteed through state-led national or subnational health systems because they can provide all three levels of care (clinic, general hospital, and specialty hospital) and can take advantage of economies of scale and reduce the disparities between geographic regions and social groups; none of which can be accomplished by disparate private providers or grassroots NGOs on their own. In addition, unlike non-commercialized initiatives in other sectors such as water, which lend themselves more easily to autonomous management options, PHC services require coordinated, multifaceted interventions by skilled professionals at a state level. In this regard, "alternatives to privatization" in PHC in Latin America are more limited and more narrowly defined than in some of the other sectors/regions discussed in this book but not necessarily less effective.

Information collection on the four cases was carried out primarily through the use of digital databases on the Internet (e.g. Academic Search Premier, Scielo, Medline), specialized health journals, data from ministries and departments of health in the selected countries, and relevant texts from the libraries of the Faculty of Medicine of the National Autonomous University of Mexico (UNAM), and the Autonomous Metropolitan University campus Xochimilco (UAM-X). We also consulted with the regional coordinators of the Latin American Association of Social Medicine (ALAMES, in its Spanish abbreviation), with detailed e-mail communication with representatives of Cuba and Costa Rica.

This information is very schematic, however, particularly the online material, making it difficult to find details on concrete processes and implementation of public health policy strategies and local-level experience. This difficulty demonstrates the absence of a systematization of documentation at both the local and national levels and highlights the challenge of conducting comparative research on this topic as well as the need for better coordination of information if progressive PHC policies and experiences are to be shared in the region. In this regard this research should be seen as a starting point for (re)constructing "alternative" experiences in Latin America and a step forward in the gathering, organization, and analysis of information, but there is much work that remains to be done on a more detailed case study basis.

THE CUBAN NATIONAL HEALTH SYSTEM

Following the triumph of the 1959 revolution, the organization and consolidation of the public health system in Cuba has passed through various stages. Before the revolution, health care was organized into three sectors: state, private, and mutual (or social security; Delgado 1996). During the post-revolutionary stage, there was a development of a universal and entirely public organization of the health system, guided by the principle of cost-free services as a way of ensuring universal access to health care. The first interventions were the nationalization of private clinics and drugstores, the reduction of prices of drugs and the creation of a Rural Medical Service with the objective of facilitating access to the remote communities (Delgado 1996).

In 1961 the Ministry of Public Health took on the leadership of all the country's health services, which led to the National Health System and the Cuban state eventually becoming the only provider of health care services in the country. In the 1970s, the services were reorganized, establishing "health areas" in the 14 provinces and 169 municipalities, which implanted a new model of community polyclinics (De Vos 2005). During that decade herbal medicine was also incorporated into formal health services.

The decade of the 1980s was the stage of the family physician model, known as "the family physician and nurse", giving PHC an added sense of priority within the Cuban National Health System (Rojas 2009). In the 1990s, with the loss of its main commercial partner and political ally due to the collapse of the Soviet Union, the "Special Period" saw a number of restrictive economic actions, including a lack of growth in the National Health System. Nevertheless, health programmes and education remained national priorities.

In the second half of the 1990s the economy began to grow again, which strengthened health services (De Vos 2005). In 2002 the Ministry of Public Health launched the "Revolution" project, which includes the following actions: maintenance on the facilities infrastructure; modernization of technology and services; training of staff at management level; updating the training of other staff; and extending to the polyclinics services that until then had only been available in hospitals (e.g. ultrasound, rehabilitation, endoscopy, and biliary drainage) or in certain clinics (e.g. optometry, dentistry, and traditional and natural medicine; Sansó 2005).

PHC is provided through the family medicine system and the family offices, secondary level care through the polyclinics, and tertiary level in hospitals and medical institutes. In Cuba PHC emerged, from 1984 onwards, through the family physician-and-nurse office model. In 1988 the "Family physician-and-nurse, polyclinic and Hospital Work Program" was established with the goal of "improving the population's health through comprehensive actions for individuals, families, the community and the environment, carried out in the context of close ties with the community itself" (MINSAP 1988, 3). The family physician and nurse's work was mainly aimed at promoting health, disease and damage prevention, and rehabilitation, contributing to the improvement of environmental sanitation, teaching, and research.

The physician and nurse work as a team and live within the community in which their office is located. In the mornings they do medical consultations at the office, and in the afternoons they make home visits. In terms of promotion and prevention, they carry out educational activities addressed at the reduction of health risk factors and early detection of disease. They also perform nutritional monitoring of family members and implement vaccination schemes. In addition to this, they carry out group activities for senior citizens, adolescents, children, and pregnant women, to encourage physical exercise, social integration and emotional well-being.

Regarding medical care, they guarantee regular and systematic attention for the community at the physician-and-nurse office, regular care for pregnant women, and child care consultations for newborns (MINSAP 1988). They have to provide medical care according to the community's needs, offer specialized consultations and emergency care at the family physician-and-nurse office or at home, and accompany the patient to the polyclinic or hospital if needed. They also do rehabilitation activities for new mothers, psychiatric patients, the mentally handicapped, or those with disabilities. The teaching tasks consist mainly of carrying out scientific activities with undergraduate medical students and with family physicians that have not yet begun their specialization.

Participation

After the revolution, social and community participation was very extensive and went through various stages according to the country's social, economic, and political organization. Social organizations such as Committees of Defence of the Revolution and the Cuban Woman's Federation contributed in very important ways to health education of the people and to the evaluation of services. Most recently, councils of health were organized starting in 2009. These actions have generated a set of activities to resolve problems of social concern, primarily deaths by transmissible and avoidable diseases (Sanabria 2001).

In the mid-1990s the National Council for Health Education and Promotion (NCHEP) was created, whose goal was to promote social participation and intersectoriality. The NCHEP is made up of Health Councils at different levels of government (national, provincial, municipal, and local; NCHEP 2009). Each of the three levels of government is involved not only in the planning but also in the delivery of the services (the National Health Council, the Provincial Assemblies of People's Power, and at municipal level the People's Council). These entities were created as part of the process of administrative decentralization and to promote community participation.

The system is not perfect, of course. In one study carried out in communities in Havana city and province, it was found that the weak aspects of social participation were a lack of adequate knowledge of the mechanisms of individual participation created in the community or by certain groups, a predominance of individual participation, and the limited influence of the community in the planning and implementation of the programmes (Sanabria 2001). It was found that there was a lack of training and information about specific participation mechanisms for both the health workers and the community. Equally, the practice of physicians and nurses focuses predominantly on curative actions at the expense of community health.

However, there have been successful experiences of social participation throughout the country. In one case study (Martínez 1998), in a neighbourhood attached to the People's Council *Balcón de Arimao* in the municipality of Lisa, it was found that health and socio-economic indicators improved as a result of the work with, and the close ties to, the Health Council, the People's Council, and the health team with the community.

In another case in a health area in the province of Havana, they turned to popular education as a means to increase community participation in the struggle against dengue fever. In this case they encouraged community participation in activities for learning about and investigating problems in order to find causes and to suggest and implement solutions. Over a two-year period (2002–2004), this process resulted in the reduction of vector density, and not one case of dengue was identified. In this case, "the leadership of health staff went from being paternalist to being shared with community leaders, as it took into account their opinions on action planning" (Sánchez et al, 2008, 71).

Equity

The Cuban government defines equity as equal opportunity to access resources, democratic distribution of power and knowledge within the health system, and a health policy that benefits all regardless of race, gender, nationality, disability, or any other form of individual or group trait (Gorry 2005). Due to the universal and integral character of the Cuban National Health System, this model covers virtually the entire population (99.4%), with 33,015 physicians in 14,074 offices (PAHO 2001; Presno and

González 2007). With regard to access, "no deaths occur without any form of medical care" (PAHO 2001, 19), and for the year 2004, 99.9% of births were attended by a professional health team (Gorry 2005).

With regard to access to drugs, although there is a shortage of supplies, there have been sustained efforts to ensure the population has access to them (*Granma* 2008). At present, the essential drug list consists of 866 drugs, of which 63% are produced domestically. In 2007, over 1 million dollars was invested in buying drugs that are not included in the list to treat certain patients, and the production of drugs grew by 26% compared to 2006, and 25 new drugs were introduced, of which 15 were created to replace imported ones.

The health services are funded directly by the national budget, with funding from general taxes, which means they are free for the public (WHO 2009). Statistics from the WHO indicate that for the year 2006 the total spending on health as a percentage of the GDP was 7.7%. External resources for health as a percentage of the total expenditure on health represent 0.2% of the GDP (WHO 2009).

Efficiency

From a macroeconomic perspective, Cuba has attained high levels of efficiency because it is the country with the best health indicators in Latin America, while its income level is relatively low (PAHO 2007). When the analysis is taken to the microeconomic level, we find a less even situation. In one evaluation of the efficiency of services in the province of Matanzas, it was estimated that between 60% and 80% of the polyclinics were deemed efficient (García et al, 2007). All of the polyclinics were classified efficient in seven of the 14 municipalities (Varadero, Jovellanos, Perico, Los Arabos, Calimete, Ciénaga, and Pedro Betancourt), while in two municipalities (Martí and Limonar), all the polyclinics were classified inefficient; while in the municipality of Jagüey, 66% of its units were found to be inefficient. It was concluded that amongst the causes of inefficiency were "weaknesses of management . . . inadequate monitoring of the most vulnerable groups of the population, poor preparation of human resources, and the lack of community participation in the health actions developed in the area" (García et al, 2007, 107).

The allocation of resources takes into account the assessment of the services and has been modified in relation to the efficiency of the care model. Between 1990 and 1994, expenditure on hospital care was reduced, while PHC expenditure was increased (Cárdenas and Cosme 2000). In 1998, as a consequence of home care, hospitalization was significantly reduced. The number of visits to hospital emergency departments was reduced, and visits to the emergency polyclinics increased.

Health indicators show that between 1994 and 2004, there was a fall in the infant mortality rate (from 9.9 to 5.8 per 1,000 live births), maternal mortality (from 57.0 to 38.5 per 100,000 live births), and the prevalence of newborns with low birth weight (from 8.9% to 5.5%) (Gorry 2005, PAHO 2001).

Quality

Evidence with respect to quality comes mainly from case studies. For example, between June 1998 and October 1999, the structure and process of medical care for workers in work places in the municipality of Santiago de Cuba was assessed (Sánchez et al, 2002). The availability of care materials and the number of physicians and nurses in the Family Physicians Offices were assessed as adequate, whereas the equipment (i.e. scales, stadiometers, multipurpose tables, autoclave sterilizers, examination lamps, sphygmomanometers, and stethoscopes) was considered inadequate. To assess the professional competence of the medical staff, there was an examination on relevant knowledge and procedures related to the specific health problems of the community. In this case, the results for 10 out of 11 indicators were inadequate.

In one polyclinic in the Playa municipality, the satisfaction of families, patients, and health staff concerning home care was studied (Márquez 2002). In this case 83.5% of patients and/or families said they were satisfied with the care, but 16.4% proved dissatisfied due to the lack of systemization of medical care. On the other hand, most of the physicians were satisfied with the home care as it allowed them to carry out closer monitoring of illness and improved physician-patient-family relationships; however, a significant number expressed dissatisfaction due to limited resources, overload of bureaucratic work, and lack of support by specialists.

In one polyclinic in the municipality of Yaguajay, it was reported that most of the patients were satisfied with the nurse care service (68.5%), while 98.4% said they trusted in the nurse, and 96.2% were satisfied with the level of interest the nurses showed in the patient (Pérez de Alejo y García 2005). Indicators of kindness and efficiency showed lower percentages of 70% and 63.1%, respectively, while 64% of those interviewed had known their nurse for over three years.

What these statistics indicate is a Cuban public health care system that is still in need of improvement but one with a remarkable record of success and a willingness to critically investigate and evaluate itself.

THE COSTA RICAN SOCIAL SECURITY SYSTEM

A number of institutions were created in Costa Rica in the 1940s, which together began to gradually integrate the Costa Rican health system. In 1941 the Costa Rican Social Security Fund (*Caja Costarricense de Seguridad Social*, CRSSF) was established, through the Law on Compulsory

Social Security, establishing universal health coverage (Gómez 2003). The subsequent Health Code (1949) stated that "the protection of health is a state duty" and charged the Ministry of Public Health with "the organization and supreme administration of the republic's hygiene and medical care, as well as of the centralization and coordination of all national, municipal and particular public health actions" (Villegas de Olazával 2005, 25).

In 1961 a law universalizing Compulsory Social Security was decreed, forcing the CRSSF to guarantee total coverage of social security benefits, as well as timely, comprehensive and equitable access to the health services (Gómez 2003). However, by the end of the 1960s health services were directed by various autonomous institutions (CRSSF, Social Welfare Boards, the Ministry of Health, and the National Insurance Institute), which rarely coordinated their efforts, with the result that actions were sometimes duplicated without improvement in outcomes.

In 1975 the CRSSF assumed responsibility of the administration of the non-contributive pensions scheme to protect low-income citizens. In the 1980s a process of integration between the CRSSF and the Ministry of Health began, and in 1993 the former took on full provision of health promotion, preventive, curative, and rehabilitation services.

At the end of the 1990s the Costa Rican health system underwent a reform, which included the strengthening of primary level health care, providing resources according to efficiency, and the deconcentration of CRSSF hospitals and clinics in order to grant it greater autonomy for budget management, administrative contracting, and human resource administration (Rodríguez 2006).

The CRSSF, built on the principles of universality, solidarity, and equity, is responsible for health promotion, prevention of disease and rehabilitation, as well as for disability, senior citizens, and death pension schemes. The health services are planned by hierarchical and administrative levels of the CRSSF and are made up of six central offices, seven health regions, and 94 health areas (PAHO et al, 2004).

Primary level health care is provided through the Basic Teams for Comprehensive Care (*Equipos Básicos de Atención Integral*, BTCC). Secondary level care is composed of 11 clinics, 14 peripheral hospitals, and seven regional hospitals. Tertiary level care takes place in three national general hospitals and five specialized hospitals. Primary level care is organized into 94 health areas and provides the services through the BTCC, made up of a physician, an auxiliary nurse, and one or more technical primary care assistants. In 2002 the CRSSF had 812 assigned BTCC; however, not all health areas have a complete team (PAHO et al, 2004, 29).

The objective of the BTCC is to ensure real access to health services, focusing on the health-illness process, emphasizing promotion, prevention, and community participation. The BTCC cover a geographic area with a population ranging from 2,500 to 6,000 inhabitants. This area is defined by demographic criteria, means of transport and communication and accessibility, allocation of resources according to necessity, use of lower cost-benefit infrastructures, and economies of scale (CRSSF 2009). The main activities and services of the BTCC are general medical consultations, educational talks, vaccination, home visits, and child, adolescent, women, adult, and senior citizen health care programmes.

Participation

The directive board of the CRSSF defines social participation as a process of interaction, negotiation and agreement between the people, the CRSSF, government, and non-governmental institutions (CRSSF 2004, 61). The health committees are the principal mechanisms responsible for organizing participation in health and are defined as an auxiliary body to the health services. The committees are made up of seven members (three representatives from insured people, two representatives from the pro-health organizations and associations, and two representatives from the employers sector) from the catchment area of that health area; they are elected by vote for a period of two years, with the possibility of being re-elected (CRSSF 2004). Despite these formal structures, in a study carried out by the Ministry of Health (MS 2004) on primary level care given by the BTCC, participation was the worst performing element, a situation that has not improved since then.

Equity

In 2002, through the PHC model, 812 BTCC covered 3,547,401 inhabitants (90% of the population). Costa Rica has one of the highest levels of coverage in Latin America at 81.8%. However, there is no universal coverage, and the excluded populations are generally the poorest, the indigenous, and immigrants (PAHO et al, 2004, 38).

It is important to point out that coverage is extended through other strategies but always under the direction of the CRSSF (Homedes and Ugalde 2002). One of these is the six cooperatives (NGOs) from whom the CRSSF buys services. Another strategy is "mixed-medicine", which means that the insured person pays for a consultation with a private physician registered with the CRSSF, and the CRSSF covers the laboratory tests and supplies the drugs. A third strategy is the "company physician" in which the corporate entity hires a physician who attends to its workers, and the CRSSF provides diagnostic services and medicine. Unlike the Cuban process, with predominance of the public sector, this situation in Costa Rica reflects a trend towards privatization.

In one case study carried out in Barrio Nuevo, in the region of San José, the coverage rates for different services were 100% for first time prenatal consultation, 82% for growth and development monitoring, 47.8% for preventive medicine, and 7% for family planning (Bonilla et al, 2006).

Concerning physical or geographical access to health services, 50% of Costa Ricans live 1 km away or less from medical care or primary care centres, but only 8% live this distance from a hospital (Rosero and Güell 1998). The average distance from a hospital is just over 5 km. The threshold of 4 km identifies 9% of the population with poor access to PHC and 13% with poor access to medical care. The reduction of the statistical difference in access is linked to the creation of the BTCC during the reforms of the 1990s. Thus, in the year 2000, inadequate access to health services was reduced from 30% to 22% in the areas where the reform was applied, while in the areas in which the reform had not been implemented, this proportion increased from 7% to 9% (Rosero and Güell 1998).

The CRSSF is funded by the contributions of salaried and non-salaried workers (35.3% of the total in 2004), employers (51.5%), pensioners (4.1%), and the government (8.9%; Rodríguez 2006). Part of the government contributions represents subsidies for salaried and non-salaried employees and pensioners.

Efficiency

Between 1990 and 2004, the number of consultations per inhabitant increased for general medical services (from 1.19 to 1.56) and dentistry (from 0.21 to 0.46). On the other hand, specialist consultations, decreased (from 0.72 to 0.64; Rodríguez 2006). These tendencies may be a reflection of improved problem-solving capacity at the primary level of care. However, the number of emergency consultations also rose (from 0.51 to 0.95), which is worrying, since as well as being more expensive, it could mean that other services do not resolve all cases or that people use the emergency services to avoid the administrative paperwork of PHC.

Taking a longer historical perspective, in 1941 the infant mortality rate was 123.5 per 1,000 live births (32.3 for neonatal mortality and 91.2 for postneonatal mortality), while in 2003 this had fallen to 10.10 (6.98 for neonatal and 3.13 for postneonatal; Villegas de Olazával 2005). According to the Ministry of Health, in 2008 the infant mortality rate decreased again to 8.9 per 1,000 infants (IPS 2009). Figures for maternal mortality are much less positive, however, with a significant rise of 85% between 2007 and 2008 (from 14 to 25 deaths per 100,000 live births). The causes of this rise are not yet known (IPS 2009).

Quality

In 2004 the Ministry of Health carried out a community study to assess the quality of health services provided by the BTCC (MS 2004). The classifications were as follows: less than 70% agreement was considered critical; from 70% to 79%, low; from 80% to 89%, acceptable; and from 90% to 100%, adequate. On a national level, the results obtained were 82% for physical structure, 78% for human resources, 93% for material resources, 82% for rules and procedures, 62% for programming and administration, 95% for supplies, and 84% for health education. Although people are generally satisfied with the public health services, users are dissatisfied with the long waiting lists for surgical interventions and specialized services, the ways in which services are disorganized, and wait times for services or pharmacies (Homedes and Ugalde 2002). A national opinion survey found that 70.3% of Costa Ricans agreed with the phrase "The CRSSF is irresponsible because it does not have enough drugs for the insured" and 70.8% agreed that "Hospital services have deteriorated" (Poltronieri 2006).

In general, the public acknowledges the important role of the CRSSF in the development of the country. In an opinion survey (Poltronieri 2006), 70.4% of the population disagreed with the phrase "Social security must be privatized", 72.3% interviewees believed that "The CRSSF is too important to be run by politicians", 40.3% disagreed with the phrase "It is a good thing that the CRSSF brings in private health services", and 40.2% agreed with the phrase "The physicians are destroying the CRSSF in order to set up their own clinics".

THE MINISTRY OF HEALTH IN THE FEDERAL DISTRICT OF MEXICO CITY (2000–2006)

Mexico is a federation formed by 31 states and a Federal District (or Mexico City), often with competing policy frameworks between states and the federal government. From the 1980s onwards, national governments have implemented neoliberal policies promoted by the World Bank and the IMF, including the privatization and commercialization of health care. In contrast, the local administration of the Federal District (during the period of 2000–2006) created policies aimed at restoring public institutions. Although this government was voted out in 2006, it is worth exploring the policies it implemented during that time.

To put these reforms in context, public health services have improved considerably since the 1940s but have never reached universal coverage, with services organized by people's work status: workers in the private and public sectors are covered by social security institutions, while the informal sector or non-salaried population and rural areas have services provided by local governments (called "states" in Mexico). According to the 2005 census, the coverage of both of these service groups is only 45.8% of total population (NISG 2005). The institution responsible for delivering these services is the *Secretaría de Salud,* which corresponds to a Health Ministry.

From the 1980s different measures have been implemented that have drastically affected these services, such as the decentralization of PHC services from the national level to the states, the reduction of the governmental budget for health from 3.4% of gross domestic product in 1980 to 2.6% in 2000 (Tamez and Valle 2005), the introduction of a package with 12 specific health measures (as opposed to "comprehensive" care) that included prenatal care, family planning, growth monitoring, immunization, home treatment of diarrhea and respiratory infections, and prevention and management of diabetes, hypertension, and injuries (Gomez-Dantes et al, 2004), and finally the promotion of health insurance (*Seguro Popular*) financed by the government but which can be used both in public and private services (Laurell 2007). These changes to the public sector have happened alongside the growth of private health services (Eibenschutz et al, 2007).

The assessment carried out to form the basis upon which to build the local government of Mexico City's health policy identified the following problems: poor and unequal quality of services due to chronic underfunding and deficient and/or deteriorated infrastructure of public institutions; high rates of corruption and embezzlement of resources; an institutional culture that views health services as a hand-out and not a right; and inequality in accessing the benefits of the Federal District health system, given that the uninsured population had to pay directly for the services and pharmaceutical drugs (HMFD 2002).

Consequently, the target group of the Health Ministry of the Federal District (HMFD) was the population without social security, which represented up to 3.9 million people (Laurell et al, 2004). In addition, the uninsured population is more prevalent in neighbourhoods with higher levels of marginalization (COPO-DF 2000, Laurell et al, 2004). Amongst the goals established by this administration were the reduction of inequality of health between social groups and geographic zones; the increase of timely access to required treatment; the decrease of inequality of access to sufficient and quality services; and the implementation of stable, sufficient, equitable, and supportive funding mechanisms (HMFD 2002). Consistent with the Mexico City government's social inclusion policy, the principle of public health policy is "the right to health as a civic right and, therefore, the government's responsibility to guarantee collective or common interest" (HMFD 2002, 21). Thus, the health programme for this period defined six strategies (HMFD 2002, Mussot 2007):

- The Free Medical Services and Drugs Programme (*Programa de Servicios Médicos y Medicamentos Gratuitos*, FMSDP) aimed at the uninsured population, which was free and included all services provided by the medical units of the Health Ministry of the Federal District and the pharmaceutical drugs listed in the institutional table of essential drugs. The HIV/AIDS programme and emergency services were also free, regardless of a person's insurance and place of residency.
- The Territorial Units Regionalization System was created to try to locate and identify highly marginalized groups to give them intensive care and thus to allocate resources according to demand.

- A new health care model, called the Expanded Health Care Model (*Modelo de Atención Ampliado a la Salud*) was implemented. This model consists of a series of integrated actions that cover four basic areas: sanitary and epidemiological vigilance, health promotion and education, building of a Unified Medical Emergency System (UMES), and extending citizen participation. The local government was committed to transparency in the use of public resources, and, therefore, the participation of citizens was promoted to supervise the application of programmes and definition of the health priorities in their neighbourhoods.
- Improvements to the buildings and maintenance or replacement of equipment; improvement of the technical quality of care and change in the institution's organizational culture; new organizational culture based on honesty, service vocation, and institutional loyalty values; good planning rather correcting bad actions; and promotion of the rationality and transparency criteria in the use of resources.
- To make the administrative process simpler and transparent and to optimize the medical supplies.
- Encouragement of citizen participation and social audits.

Participation

Through the territorial units, the participation mechanisms for health services users were formalized, with 1,325 territorial units created (HMFD 2005). Formally, social participation took place in the neighbourhood assembly, whose principal objective was to inform and make transparent both the administration of the budget and the correct application of the social programmes. Another level of participation took place within these assemblies, as they elected Local Committees by universal vote. The aim of these was to involve citizens in specific tasks such as the environment, health, and crime prevention, amongst others. With respect to health, the local committees were made up of two levels of health committees (local and regional) through which were promoted and put into action the citizens' initiatives and proposals to the assemblies.

Information about the programmes and accountability would pass initially through the local assemblies, which would also be responsible for publishing and distributing it door to door. Data from 2006 provides indications of the access to and availability of the information in quantitative terms: from 2001 up to the first quarter of 2006, approximately 11.4 million letters were delivered door to door. These gave information on the social programmes for each territorial unit, informed inhabitants about the budget allocated to each of the social programmes applied in the territorial units, the number of actions and beneficiaries, and the institutions responsible for administrating them (DGPC 2006). However, this quantitative data does not identify the beneficiaries' level of comprehension of the information received, nor does it tell us whether the population gave feedback to those in charge of the programmes.

Although social participation was a strategy of the health programme, no evidence of its successful implementation was found. The government employees in charge of the health policy have described the difficulties they faced in this field, acknowledging that the "historic absence of democratic and representative organizations has prevented the health commissions from being institutionalized" (Laurell 2008, 178). Likewise, there is no evidence of how the decisions, initiatives or observations of citizens during the participation activities were taken into account or not in the decision making or modification of programmes.

Equity

Within the health programme of this government, equity was defined as equal access to services for those with the same needs, which implies a commitment to guaranteeing the same level of services for all (HMFD 2002). One strategy that promoted equity of access was the convention signed by the public health institutions of Mexico City to create the Unified Medical Emergency Systems, which enabled emergency medical teams to see patients regardless of insurance and residency status. With the UMES there was a fall in the number of rejections and the time of journey to a hospital.

The government also initiated the universal pension scheme through a law that established the right to food pensions for seniors (*Gaceta Oficial* 2003), which consisted of monetary transfers to all citizens over 70 years of age residing in Mexico City, regardless of insurance or active job. In 2006, the coverage of this programme was 93.6% (IAAM-DF 2009).

Two speciality hospitals were created in the departments where highest demand was identified. One of these was located in a zone with a high density of people without social security insurance and a high level of marginalization (Iztapalapa County), and it also had adequate transport and communication access to other counties.

The FMSDP, in order to confront the economic barriers to accessing health services, simplified the procedure of affiliation, which could be realized even at the time of receiving a service (*Gaceta Oficial* 2006). Between 2002 and 2006, it is estimated that this programme represented a savings of around US$356 million for affiliated families (Laurell 2008). The programme's "no-cost" principle was achieved through the health expenditure that came from fiscal resources; therefore, financial sustainability was ensured. In 2001, the Federal District government distributed local tax funds to health and social programmes operated by the HMFD to a sum of US$27.3 million, which represented an increase of 171% with respect to the previous year (HMFD 2005).

Efficiency

By modifying the regulations, the HMFD achieved shorter delays for the purchase of medicine, the reduction of unused products, and savings in acquisition of materials (HMFD 2005). To ensure access to the services and to implement anti-discriminatory policies, the HIV/AIDS programme was assumed as priority, resulting in reduction of the AIDS mortality rate in 16% in four years and an improvement in detection and prevention (Laurell 2008).

Quality

In one assessment carried out on the FMSDP, it was observed that its beneficiaries—in comparison with those who were not insured—reported an equal waiting time (Laurell et al, 2004). In general, a high proportion of insured users rated the treatment received in public health services as good or very good (>85%). However, there was no difference between the beneficiaries of the programme and other services (i.e. social security services) in the quality of care.

Transparency

The HMFD administration páid special attention to correcting the prevailing culture of corruption. This culture was seen in practices such as *clientelismo* (i.e. obtaining work benefits in exchange for being a loyal supporter of a leader or political party), position inheritance (when an employee "bequeaths" their position to a family member), or payments for a particular job or bureaucratic position.

The strategies implemented to fight corruption included applying rank guidelines for newly hired staff; setting selection exams based on the job profile diagram; improving the time of the payments and benefits systems (by decentralizing the HMFD payroll, the delay for first payment of recently hired employees was reduced); improving the training and development programmes in all sectors of the institution; and ensuring that employees fulfil their obligations and remain in the service by applying work regulations and promoting a relationship with the union based on communication and respect (HMFD 2005). Finally, in order to comply with the Law of Transparency, in January 2004 the HMFD set up the Public Information Office (HMFD 2005), which supplied information of the services provided to different entities when requested.

VENEZUELA: "INSIDE THE NEIGHBOURHOOD MISSION"

In Venezuela, health care provision has historically come predominantly from the private sector. In 1997 this sector provided 73% of health services (Muntaner et al, 2006). The arrival of Hugo Chávez's government represented a turning point in this regard. In 1999 the New Constitution of the Bolivarian Republic of Venezuela established that health is "a fundamental social right which is an obligation of the State, who will guarantee it as part of the right to life" (Article 83), that "the State will create, govern and manage a public national health system . . . integrated with the social security system, ruled by principles of no-cost, universality, comprehensiveness, equity, social integration and solidarity", and that "public assets and services are the property of the State and cannot be privatized" (Article 85). In addition, Article 84 of the Constitution establishes the participation of organized community in the management of the health system.

The main health proposals implemented by the government of President Chávez since 1999 are, in chronological order: the application of the Comprehensive Health Care Model (1999) and the formulation of the Social Strategic Plan (2003; Alvarado et al, 2008). The Comprehensive Health Care Model was created to promote the PHC principles of the public establishments that existed at that moment and was replaced by the Inside the Neighbourhood Mission in 2003. The Social Strategic Plan was a policy instrument created to define the strategies to improve quality of life and health, which included the reorientation of public policies, the change of health care modelling, and the training of new public health leaders. This plan established the principles for the National Plan for Economic and Social Development 2001–2007 and the creation of new health norms and a national health system.

The Inside the Neighbourhood Mission programme originated from an act of solidarity by Cuban physicians when, in December 1999, they came to the help of communities affected by a flood in Vargas state. Following this experience, the Mayor's office of the Libertador municipality signed an agreement with the Cuban government to implement this project in low-income neighbourhoods of Caracas (MPPSP 2009). The project was subsequently extended to other states, and, in December 2003, President Chávez created a Presidential Commission—the *"Misión Barrio Adentro"* in Spanish—whose objective is the implementation and institutional coordination of the Comprehensive Programme for the provision of PHC. This special commission was made up of the Secretary of Health and Social Development (currently the Ministry of Popular Power for Health), the President of Venezuelan Oil (*Petróleos de Venezuela*), the President of Inside the Neighbourhood, the President of the Unified Social Fund, the mayors of the Municipalities of Libertador and Sucre, and representatives of the Francisco de Miranda Venezuelan Social Fighters Front (MPPSP 2009).

The Inside the Neighbourhood concept refers to the idea of penetrating into the heart of marginalized neighbourhoods and is characterized by the following (Alvarado et al, 2006, Armada et al, 2009, MPPSP 2009):

- Popular clinics are created for primary level care. These offer general medicine services, pediatrics, care for senior citizens, pre- and postnatal monitoring, and emergencies. Vaccination, dentistry, and smear testing are provided in some clinics. Catchment areas are defined in which each unit attends to between 250 and 400 families, representing around 1,250 people.

- It is a comprehensive care model as physicians and nurses give six hours of medical care in the popular clinic and then carry out home visits. Dentists and community promoters also participate.
- Health promotion activities are carried out at the health units and in schools and work places.
- Social participation is promoted through the health committees, which are formed by formal and informal leaders elected by the community and supported by the medical staff. The health committees formulate specific interventions for health promotion, which can be granted by the government.
- Each medical unit gives training for community health promoters and health technicians, at a professional and post-graduate level.
- It includes intersectoral action as it aims to improve living conditions through the coordination of health actions with other social interventions. The Inside the Neighbourhood Mission is articulated with other Missions, with foci on education (Simoncito, Ribas, and Sucre Missions), land and property (Zamora Mission), employment (*Vuelvan Caras* Mission), food security (Mercal Mission and Programme of Scholar Meals), housing (*Hábitat*), and sports and recreation (*Barrio Adentro Deportivo*).

The Inside the Neighbourhood Mission has nationwide coverage, with 13,000 physicians, 8,500 assistant nurses, and 4,600 dentists. It provides care at 8,500 consultation points and covers nearly 17 million people (MPPSP 2009). There are also approximately 200 community leaders of the Promotional Strategy of Equity as Life and Health, who deal with the needs of about 150 communities in the metropolitan area of Caracas. Each of these communities collects socio-demographic information and identifies high-risk sectors of the population. This information must be used as the basis for plans and projects in these communities.

These reforms have not been introduced without resistance, however. In 2002, the Venezuelan Medical Federation organized a strike of physicians because the government forbid medical fees in public establishments (Alvarado et al, 2006). In 2003, the Federation discouraged its members from working with Inside the Neighbourhood Mission, and since that time, the Federation has opposed the participation of Cuban physicians in these missions.

Notwithstanding these protests, the Venezuelan government has maintained its stance on free public health care and has attempted to deepen its regulation of the costs of private clinics and strengthen its supervision of private insurance companies. Until now little resistance has been put up by the private sector on these latter initiatives, possibly because the sector is composed primarily of small medical companies.

Participation

The health committees are the organ of social participation in health and are elected in neighbourhood assemblies. Their main tasks include identifying the community's health problems in order to prioritize them and then define the actions to be taken (Alvarado et al, 2006). They perform management tasks that support the work of the popular clinic and the comprehensive diagnostic centre. In 2006 there were 8,951 registered committees, and these had held 1,432,815 community health assemblies.

The activities carried out in the Libertador Municipality, a pioneer for Inside the Neighbourhood Mission, provide an illustration of social participation. In 2008, they held meetings with communities from different neighbourhoods within the municipality aimed at identifying and prioritizing local problems and constructing a strategy of political advocacy in the municipal government. The result was a citizen's agenda that was proposed to candidates running for elections that year. Community councils, residents from various neighbourhoods, an environmental group, a neighbourhood association, and a technical institution all participated in drawing up this agenda (Unión Vecinal 2009).

Conversely, in one case study carried out in a health unit in the municipality of Campo Elías in the Mérida state, it was observed that there was no culture of solidarity or participation in resolving its problems within the community (Romero and Zambrano 2007). However, signs of incipient awareness of their obligations and rights as citizens were also identified by some members of the community. The population also showed that they believed that health was a subject of "shared responsibility between the State and the community" (Romero and Zambrano 2007, 207). Medical staff studies provided further evidence of the need for greater communication with the communities they served.

Equity

The Inside the Neighbourhood Mission was created to provide care for the population of marginalized areas, which, generally speaking, have less access to health services; hence, equity is the core of the programme. Article 85 of the Constitution of Venezuela stipulates that "the funding of the public health system is the obligation of the State", while article 86 establishes that "every person has a right to social security as a non-lucrative public service. . . . Absence of contributory capacity will not be a motive for excluding people from its protection. . . . The contributions . . . may be administered for social purposes only by the governing body of the State".

In regard to access to prescription drugs, in 2003 drug modules were created, the task of which was to distribute 106 essential pharmaceuticals for free. A fortnightly distribution scheme delivers drugs to the popular clinics according to the demand made by the medical staff, based on the health needs of their area (Alvarado et al, 2006).

Sustainability

The programme's resources come from the Ministry of Health's regular budget, as well as from extraordinary resources from the sale of oil and a development fund (Alvarado et al, 2006). This is worrying as the latter two sources are not stable resources, bringing into question the long-term sustainability of the programme.

Efficiency

The number of medical visits has risen as a result of these reforms. While at the start of the Inside the Neighbourhood Mission less than 10,000,000 medical visits were registered, in 2004 there were 76,152,978 (Muntaner et al, 2006), and in 2007 approximately 236,458,980 (MPPSP 2009). Infant mortality dropped between 1998 and 2005 from 21.4 to 15.5 cases per 1,000 live births, while maternal mortality increased from 50.6 to 59.9 for each 1,000 live births (MPPSP 2009; with the latter figure possibly due to a higher rate of reporting that has accompanied the expansion of formal health care provision and not necessarily a rise in actual incidence of maternal mortality). Nevertheless, a long-term assessment of the Inside the Neighbourhood Mission is called for.

CONCLUSIONS

Given the social, political, and economic structures of the countries selected for this review, we have four very different experiences. Cuba is a socialist country that has based its social and health policy on collective well-being and a social distribution of resources that has given total predominance to public action for five decades. Venezuela is a country that, under the presidency of Chávez, has decided to try and implement socialism at a time with few international allies and internal corporate resistance. Costa Rica has social policies more advanced than other capitalist economies of the region but still experiences problems trying to contain the effects of neo-liberalism, while Mexico is a country marked by an almost blind adoption of the policies of the IMF and of the World Bank for more than 30 years but which nonetheless saw the election of a social democratic government in the Federal District based on the principles of civil participation and social justice. That is to say, national health systems, in general, and their primary health programmes, in particular, cannot be examined in isolation; nor can they be seen as a simple question in terms of addressing the health-sickness profiles of countries. Health care services are determined by socio-economic structures, the historic trajectories of a country, and power distribution within a society.

Cuba and Costa Rica are outstanding insofar as they have achieved high coverage levels through the provision of public services financed through contributions from employers and employees (in the case of the latter country) and general taxes. These two cases are evidence of how the principles of solidarity and equity can be achieved in peripheral countries, either through a social-democratic (Costa Rica) or socialist system (Cuba, and more recently Venezuela). The countries also suggest that it may only be possible to have equitable and/or universal health care systems when there exists a dominant public sector that guarantees access to medical care services and which is relegated sufficient resources.

The four cases discussed here have in common restricted financial resources, which limit the provision of public services in vital areas such as health. Thus, despite placing health at the centre of the governmental agenda, in each of the cases public service funding is still a constraint. Venezuela's ability to draw on oil revenues has allowed that country to increase its social spending rather dramatically, but it also raises serious questions about the long-term sustainability of that government's initiatives. On the other hand, the case of Costa Rica, and especially that of Cuba, demonstrates that even low-income peripheral countries can guarantee financial sustainability of national health services, ensuring long-term health access.

Regarding efficiency, we found that Cuba and Costa Rica, with the strongest public health systems, are amongst the countries with the best performance in health indicators. They also present the best epidemiological profiles, a product not only of health services, which have been developed over the past 40 years, but also due to the generally higher quality of living conditions in these countries as compared to other states in the region.

The use of "efficiency" to measure performance can be problematic, however, as it is one of the key principles used to promote neoliberal reforms in the health sector, whereby health services are evaluated using narrow cost-benefit principles and intervention-time ratios. From a social medicine perspective, efficacy takes priority (i.e. the improvement of health) over efficiency. What is more, it is possible to increase the efficiency of services by carrying out a large number of activities (e.g. health education talks), which have minimal impact on a population's health.

Although in all the cases discussed, there are formal structures of participation, the available data shows little evidence that the population exerts any determining control over the programming and provision of health services. Adequate social participation exists only in isolated cases (certain cities or municipalities), but the general assessment shows that participation has decreased. The absence of social participation could be the result of the conservative or non-democratic nature of Latin American states (Barba 2008). As a result, only certain segments of populations have achieved real social citizenship (i.e. their economic, social, and political rights are realized), while other ones are excluded. This conservative character could explain the absence of information on accountability and transparency as well.

Citizenship could be built by participating in organizations that are independent of the state such as organizations fighting for health on an individual and collective level and for the right to health in broad and collective terms. This growth of civic awareness is also a goal of PHC but is not always taken into account (Eibenschutz 2000). To summarize, incomplete citizenship is an obstacle and a challenge for PHC.

The role of the physician's guild must also be considered. For example, at the beginnings of the revolution in Cuba, and more recently in Venezuela, physicians have been reluctant to participate in PHC services since hospital work is generally valued over primary care work. In addition, in Venezuela private practice has been protected over the public one. In both countries part of the solution found for dealing with the bias of the physician against PHC has been the incorporation of research and teaching activities into PHC services.

It is a known fact that successful experiences of the so-called public-private mix in health care rest on the regulatory capacity of the state to ensure the complementarity of the private services and the quality of the public services, supported by a reasonable budget with which to run it. On the other hand, the experience of Latin American countries indicates that promotion of the private sector nearly always entails the progressive deterioration of public services, as part of the government's resources are allocated to the private sector.

In future debates the question of regulation—referred to by some authors as modulation—must also be covered (Londoño and Frenk 1997). In other words, although in most societies it might not be feasible to eliminate private sector participation in medical service provision, this participation must be complimentary to the governing role that the state plays in the funding, management and provision of health services. Therefore, in parallel to the opening up of the health systems into more open and diverse structures, regulations would have to be strengthened.

The regulation process must happen transparently and through public offices that act neutrally. Additionally, offices that participate in this activity must be predominantly public. The regulation must include policy building, strategic planning, establishing of priorities for the allocation of resources, intersectorial action, social mobilization for health—including community participation—and the development of criteria and standards to evaluate the performance of financial agencies, coordinating organizations, and individual and institutional benefits. The fact remains that some Latin American states do not have the governance capacity or competence to achieve this.

REFERENCES

Alvarado, C., Arismendi, C., Armada, F., Bergonzoli, G., Borroto, R., Castellanos, P.L., Castro, C., Feal, P., García J.M. Gusmao, R.A., Hernández, S., Martínez, M.E., Medina, E., Metzger, W., Muntaner, C., Muñoz, N., Nuñez, N., Pérez, J.C., and Vivas, S. 2006. *Barrio adentro: Derecho a la salud e inclusión social en Venezuela.* Caracas: Organización Panamericana de la Salud/Organización Mundial de la Salud para Venezuela.

Alvarado, C., Martínez, M., Vivas-Martínez, S., Gutiérrez, N. and Metzger, W. 2008. Cambio social y política de salud en Venezuela. *Revista Medicina Social* 3 (2): 113–129.

Armada, F., Muntaner, C., Chung, H., Williams-Brennan, L., and Benach, J. 2009. Barrio Adentro and the reduction of health inequalities in Venezuela: An appraisal of the first years. *International Journal of Health Services* 39 (1): 161–187.

Barba, C. 2008. Las reformas económica y social en América Latina: Regímenes de bienestar en transición. In Cordera, R. and Cabrera, C. (Eds), *Política social. Experiencias internacionales*, pp. 4182–4197. Mexico City: Universidad Nacional Autónoma de México.

Barten, F., Rovere, M. and Espinoza, E. 2009. *Salud para todos, una meta posible. Pueblos movilizados y gobiernos comprometidos en un nuevo contexto global.* Buenos Aires, Argentina: IIED-América Latina Publicaciones.

Bonilla, L., Díaz, A., Piedra, G., Guerrero, A., Mora, A. and Castillo, F. 2006. Caracterización de los determinantes de la salud del sector 9 de la localidad de José María Zeledón, Curridabat, perteneciente al Equipo Básico de Atención Integral de salud (EBAIS). *Enfermería Actual en Costa Rica* 5(9): 20.

Cárdenas, R.J. and Cosme, J. 2000. *Eficiencia en la atención primaria de salud. OPS-OMS.* Serie desarrollo de la representación OPS/OMS. Cuba, 22 Abril.

Constitución de la República Bolivariana de Venezuela. www.constitucion.ve/constitucion.pdf (accessed 1 May 2009).

COPO-DF (Consejo de Población del Distrito Federal). Breviario 2000. www.copo.df.gob.mx (accessed 20 February 2009).

CRSSF (Costa Rican Social Security Fund). 2004. Reglamento de las juntas de salud. *La Gaceta.* Diario Oficial. La Uruca, San José de Costa Rica. 30 January.

———. 2009. Perfil EBAIS. www.rree.go.cr/cooperacion/Ebais.php (accessed 28 March 2009).

Delgado, G. 1996. Etapas del desarrollo de la salud pública revolucionaria cubana. *Revista Cubana de Salud Pública* 22(1): 21–22.

De Vos, P. 2005. "No one left abandoned": Cuba's national health system since the 1959 revolution. *International Journal of Health Services* 35(1): 189–207.

DGPC (Dirección General de Protección Civil-DF). 2006. Distribución de Cartas PIT. www.dgpc.df.gob.mx/programas/actividades_intitucionales/acciones/distribucion_cartas_pit.pdf.

Eibenschutz, C. 2000. México: Gobierno autoritario, ciudadanía incompleta. In: Proceedings of Congreso Internacional LASA XXI. Miami, 16–18 Marzo, pp. 1–16.

———. 2007. Atención médica, neoliberalismo y reforma sanitaria en México. In Molina, R. (Ed), *La seguridad social: Retos de hoy*, pp. 23–48. Mexico City: Universidad Autónoma Metropolitana.

Eibenschutz, C., Tamez S., Ortiz-Hernández, L. and Camacho, I. 2007. *Justicia, desigualdad y exclusión en la salud de los mexicanos.* Mexico City: UNAM.

Gaceta Oficial del Distrito Federal. 2003. Ley que establece el derecho a la pensión alimentaria para los adultos mayores de setenta años, residentes en el Distrito Federal. 18 November.

————. 2006. Ley que establece el derecho al acceso gratuito a los Servicios médicos y medicamentos a las personas residentes en el Distrito Federal que carecen de seguridad social laboral. 22 May.

García, F.A., Sánchez, Z., Chaviano, M. and Muñiz, M. 2007. Niveles de eficiencia de las policlínicas de Matanzas, Cuba, según el método de análisis envolvente de datos. *Revista Panamericana de Salud Pública* 22(2): 100–109.

Giovanella, L., de Mendonça, M.H., de Almeida, P.F., Escorel, S., Senna, M. de C., Fausto, M.C., Delgado, M.M., de Andrade, C.L., da Cunha, M.S., Martins, M.I. and Teixeira, C.P. 2009. Family health: Limits and possibilities for an integral primary care approach to health care in Brazil. *Ciencia e Saude Coletiva* 14(3): 783–794.

Gómez, O. 2003. *Salud pública y políticas nacionales de salud en Costa Rica.* San José, Costa Rica: Editorial Universidad Estatal a Distancia.

Gomez-Dantes, O., Gómez-Jáuregui, J. and Inclán, C. 2004. La equidad y la imparcialidad en la reforma del sistema mexicano de salud. *Salud Pública de México* 46(5): 399–416.

Gorry, C. 2005. MDGs and health equity in Cuba. *MEDICC Review* 7(9): 2–4.

Granma. 2008. El Gobierno garantiza acceso a los medicamentos. 18 February.

Heredia, J. 2007. *Salud y desarrollo comunitario. Estudio de caso: Marqués de comillas, Chiapas. Tesis de Maestría en Desarrollo Rural.* Universidad Autónoma Metropolitana, Mexico.

Homedes, N. and Ugalde, A. 2002. Privatización de los servicios de salud: Las experiencias de Chile y Costa Rica. *Gaceta Sanitaria* 16(1): 54–62.

HMFD (Health Ministry of Federal District). 2002. *Programa de salud del gobierno del Distrito Federal al 2006.* Mexico Federal District: Secretaría de Salud del Gobierno del Distrito Federal.

————. 2005. *Informe de trabajo 2004.* Mexico Federal District: Secretaría de Salud del Gobierno del Distrito Federal.

IAAM-DF (Instituto para la Atención del Adulto Mayor del DF). 2009. *Pensión alimentaria.* www.adultomayor.df.gob.mx (accessed 1 February 2009).

IPS (Inter Press Service). 2009. SALUD-COSTA RICA: Sostenida caída de mortalidad infantil. www.ipsnoticias.net/ (accessed 27 March 2009).

Laurell, A.C. 2007. Health system reform in Mexico: A critical review. *International Journal of Health Services* 37(3): 515–535.

————. 2008. La reforma de salud en la Ciudad de México, 2000–2006. *Revista de Medicina Social* 3(2): 170–183.

Laurell, A.C., Mussot, M., Velteis, E. and Satines, G. 2004. *Reducción de la exclusión en salud, removiendo el obstáculo económico. La experiencia del gobierno del Distrito Federal.* Mexico City: Pan American Health Organization (PAHO).

Londoño, J.L. and Frenk, J. 1997. Structured pluralism: Towards an innovative model for health system reform in Latin America. *Health Policy* 41(1): 1–36.

Macinko, J., Montenegro, H., Nebot Adell, C., Etienne, C. and Grupo de Trabajo de Atención Primaria de Salud de la Organización Panamericana de la Salud. 2007. La renovación de la atención primaria de salud en las Américas. *Revista Panamericana de Salud Pública* 21(2–3): 73–84.

Márquez, N. 2002. Grado de satisfacción con el ingreso en el hogar. *Revista Cubana de Medicina General Integral* 18(5): 310–312.

Martínez, P.M. 1998. Sistematización de la experiencia en 2 años de trabajo. Consejo popular Arimao. *Revista Cubana de Enfermería* 14(2): 124–130.

MPPSP (Ministry of Popular Power for Health and Social Protection). 2009. Misión Barrio Adentro. www.mpps.gob.ve/ms (accessed 17 June, 2009).

MINSAP (Ministerio de Salud Pública). 1988. Programa de trabajo médico y enfermera de la familia, el policlínico y el hospital. PHC. sld.cu/bvs/materiales/programa/progra_tarbajo/programatrabajo.pdf (accessed 11 May 2009).

MS (Ministerio de Salud). 2004. *Evaluación de la atención integral del nivel I.* Sede EBAIS. Encuesta comunitaria 2004. Costa Rica: Ministerio de Salud de Costa Rica.

Muntaner. C., Guerra, S.R., Rueda, S. and Armada, F. 2006. Challenging the neoliberal trend. The Venezuelan health care reform alternative. *Canadian Journal of Public Health* 97(6): 19–24.

Mussot, L. 2007. Universalizar y territorializar las políticas en salud en el Distrito Federal. Premisa para garantizar la equidad e igualdad. In Proceedings of Congreso de Investigadores en Gobiernos Locales Mexicanos. Federal District, Mexico, 4–6 October.

NCHEP (National Council for Health Education and Promotion), Cuba. 2009. Infraestructura. www.cnpes.sld.cu/home.htm (accessed 25 March 2009).

NISG (National Institute of Statistics and Geography), Mexico. 2005. II Counting of population and housing 2005. Definitive results. www.inegi.org.mx (accessed 22 January 2010).

PAHO (Pan American Health Organization). 2001. Perfil del sistema de servicios de salud de Cuba. Washington, DC: PAHO.

———. 2007. *Health in the Americas.* Volume I. Regional Scientific and Technical Publication No. 622. Washington, DC: PAHO.

PAHO, Ministerio de Salud, Caja Costarricense de Seguro Social and OMS. 2004. *Perfil del sistema de servicios de salud de Costa Rica.* Serie Análisis de situación en salud No. 15. San José de Costa Rica: Ministerio de Salud.

Pérez de Alejo, B. and García, P. 2005. Grado de satisfacción de la población con los servicios de enfermería en un área de salud. *Revista Cubana de Enfermería* 21(2).

Poltronieri, J. 2006. Proyecto de investigación estructuras de la opinión pública. Encuesta 2006. Panorama global. www.ucr.ac.cr/documentos/Encuesta_Evolucion_de_las_estructuras_de_la_Opinion_Publica_2008.pdf.

Presno, C. and González, L. 2007. Medicina familiar en Cuba: Comienzo, presente y futuro. *Atención Primaria* 39(5): 265.

Rodríguez, A. 2006. *La reforma de salud en Costa Rica.* Serie Financiamiento del Desarrollo No.173. Santiago de Chile: CEPAL (Comisión Económica para América Latina).

Rojas, F. 2009. La salud pública revolucionaria Cubana en su aniversario 50. *Revista Cubana de Salud Pública* 35(1): 1–15.

Romero, Y. and Zambrano, D. 2007. Participación social en salud en la comunidad de Bella Vista Municipio Campo Elías Estado Mérida. *Revista Venezolana de Sociología y Antropología* 17(48): 181–209.

Rosero, L. and Güell, D. 1998. *Oferta y acceso a los servicios de salud en Costa Rica: Estudio basado en un sistema de información geográfica* (GIS). Costa Rica: INISA (Instituto de Investigaciones en Salud).

Sanabria, G. 2001. Participación social y comunitaria. Reflexiones. *Revista Cubana de Salud Pública* 27(2): 89–95.

Sánchez, I., Bonne, T., Pérez, C. and Botín, M. 2002. Evaluación de la calidad de la Atención Médica Integral a trabajadores del Municipio de Santiago de Cuba. *Revista Cubana de Salud Pública* 28(1): 38–45.

Sánchez, L., Pérez, D., Alfonso, L., Castro, M., Sánchez, L., Van der Stuyft, P. and Kouri, G. 2008. Estrategia de educación popular para promover la participación comunitaria en la prevención del dengue en Cuba. *Revista Panamericana de Salud Pública* 24(1): 61–69.

Sansó, F. 2005. Veinte años del modelo cubano de medicina familiar. *Revista Cubana de Salud Pública* 31(2).

Tamez, G. and Valle Arcos, R. 2005. Desigualdad social y reforma neoliberal en salud. *Revista Mexicana de Sociología* 67(2): 321–356.

Unión Vecinal. 2009. Agenda ciudadana del Municipio Libertador. www.unionveci-nalpc.blogspot.com/2008/12/agenda-ciudadana-del-municipio.html (accessed 2 June 2009).
Villegas de Olazával, H. 2005. Atención primaria de salud y salud para todos: Costa Rica y Centroamérica. Escenarios, participación, desafíos siglo XXI. In OPS, *Atención primaria de salud en Costa Rica 25 años después de Alma-Ata*, pp. 21–58. San José, Costa Rica: MS/CRSSF/PAHO/WHO.
Werner, D., Sanders, D., Weston, J., Babb, S. and Rodriguez, B. 2000. *Cuestionando la solución: Las políticas de atención primaria de salud y supervivencia infantil. Con una crítica detallada de la Terapia de Rehidratación Oral.* Palo Alto, CA: Health Wrights.
WHO (World Health Organization). 2009. National health accounts. Country information. www.who.int/nha/country/en/ (accessed 15 January 2010).
WHO and UNICEF (United Nations Children's Fund). 1978. Primary Health Care, Report of the International Conference on Primary Health Care. Alma-Ata, USSR, 6–12 September 1978. Geneva: WHO.
Wisner, B. 1988. GOBI versus PHC? Some dangers of selective primary health care. *Social Science and Medicine* 26(9): 963–969.
World Bank. 1993. *World Development Report 1993. Investing in health.* New York: World Bank and Oxford University Press.

15 Struggles for Water Justice in Latin America
Public and 'Social-Public' Alternatives

Susan Spronk, Carlos Crespo
and Marcela Olivera

Latin America was the first region to adopt neoliberalism as its hegemonic model, as well as the earliest to develop and implement explicit alternatives. In Latin America, struggles against water privatization have played an essential role in delegitimizing the neoliberal model, such as the infamous "Water War" in Cochabamba in 2000 and the constitutional referendum in Uruguay in 2004 (Kohl and Farthing 2006, Taks 2008). Thanks to these and other struggles that seek to defend water as a human right and common good, Latin America has changed from being a region in which the neoliberal model was dominant to a territory of hegemonic instability in which alternatives are being sought and contested (Sader 2009). For this reason, the world is looking to Latin America for alternative models of service delivery, which challenge the commercializing logic of neoliberal capitalism.

Due to these popular mobilizations, private water contracts in Argentina, Bolivia, and Uruguay have been cancelled, returning water delivery services to public and state control (Hall and Lobina 2006, Lobina and Hall 2007). It is no coincidence that these are also some of the countries in which the electorate has opted for left-of-centre governments that actively campaigned against neoliberalism, widely seen as an undemocratic form of development. As stated by the *Coordinadora de Defensa del Agua y de la Vida* (Coalition for the Defence of Water and Life—the Coordinadora), the organization that emerged to coordinate the protests during the Cochabamba water protests in 2000, the struggle for water is connected with the broader fight for popular control over natural resources: "[T]he fundamental problem is who decides about the present and future of the population, natural resources, work and living conditions. In relation to water, we want to decide for ourselves: this is what we call Democracy" (cited in Crespo Flores 2006b, 4; all Spanish translations by the authors).

This chapter provides an overview of a diversity of actually existing and proposed alternatives to privatization in the water sector and in urban and rural areas in Latin America. Whereas there is no "perfect" alternative, the region is replete with many examples of "successful" alternatives to privatization, including statist and communitarian solutions to the challenge of providing non-commercialized forms of water and sanitation for all.

HISTORICAL OVERVIEW

From a comparative perspective, it is not surprising that there has been a lot of social movement activity resisting privatization in the water sector during the neoliberal era (1970s to present). The Latin American and Caribbean region has a long history of revolution and social struggle (Wickham-Crowley 1992, John 2009). Indeed, the Mexican Revolution of 1910 was one of the first revolutions of the 20th century, followed by Bolivia in 1952, Cuba in 1959, and Nicaragua in 1979. Social movement organizations such as the Coalition for Water and Life in Bolivia and the Coalition for Water and Life in Uruguay have built on these traditions of revolution and struggle to defend the "commons" against the incursion of private capital, which made significant inroads in this region during the wave of international financial institution (IFI)-sponsored privatization in the 1990s.

In many ways, the Latin American region was a guinea pig for the World Bank and IMF policies of privatization of the 1990s. The reasons that privatization was such a popular policy choice at the height of neoliberalism in Latin America were twofold. First, 18 out of 21 countries in Latin America in the late 1970s were run by authoritarian governments that borrowed heavily from international banks, leaving a legacy of illegitimate debt (McMichael 2008, 126). By the time the Washington Consensus was implemented in the early 1980s, newly democratic governments were particularly vulnerable to the dictates of the international financial institutions, which made the extension of new structural adjustment loans conditional upon water privatization (Grusky and Fiil-Flynn 2004, Goldman 2007). Ideologically oriented towards neoliberalism, many governments followed suit, privatizing basic services, including water and sanitation.

Second, and perhaps most importantly, as a highly urbanized region with relatively wealthy populations, water utilities in Latin America were considered to be attractive, and the region attracted the bulk of private investment internationally in this sector (see Table 15.1). In many ways, the existence of numerous well-functioning municipal water utilities in the larger cities was a testament to success of the state-led development model of the previous era (Weisbrot et al, 2002). By the time governments opened up the water sector to private investment in the 1990s, the Latin American region was full of relatively well-functioning, government-owned utilities that were ripe for picking.

Although privatization made the furthest inroads in the Latin American region, it has been estimated that more than 90% of water still remains in public hands. A notable exception is Chile, where water privatization is well-advanced; it is the only other country in the world besides the UK to

Table 15.1   Total Private Investment Promised in Water and Sanitation in
Developing Countries, by Region, 1990–2002

Region	Private investment promised (US$ billion)	Percentage of investment in water and sanitation
East Asia and Pacific	17.0	39.0
Europe and Central Asia	3.5	8.0
Latin America and the Caribbean	21.3	48.9
Middle East and North Africa	1.3	3.0
South Asia	0.2	0.5
Sub-Saharan Africa	0.2	0.5
Total	43.6	100.0

Source: Hall and Lobina 2006, 41.

introduce fully private water markets and to privatize public water utilities by complete divestiture (Budds 2004). Mixed public-private companies
involving multinational water companies also continue to provide services
in several cities in Colombia, Brazil, Ecuador, and Peru. The shares of several of the renationalized water companies in Argentina were also sold to
local private companies (Lobina and Hall 2007). Nonetheless, most households in Latin America, which have access to an improved water source,
receive their water from a single individual public provider. And despite
the setback created by privatization, the Latin American region has higher
rates of access to improved water sources than Asia and Africa (Hall and
Lobina 2006). As of 2008, approximately 93% of the population of Latin
America and the Caribbean had access to potable water (80% in rural areas
and 97% in urban areas), while 79% had access to sanitation (55% in rural
areas and 86% in urban areas; WHO and UNICEF 2010, 38).

Given the relative success of former models of development, several
scholars have advocated for a resurrection of the "developmental state"
(Gwynne and Kay 2000). Between the 1940s and 1970s, central governments throughout the Latin American region centralized control over water
and sanitation services as part of an "import substitution industrialization"
(ISI) development strategy. In line with the Keynesian-developmentalist
thinking of the time, basic infrastructure and service provision were seen
as essential to maintain capital accumulation, to assist in the reproduction
of labour, and to help maintain social harmony.

By contrast, in this chapter we argue that although the state-led model
of development produced some undeniable benefits, such as the extension
of social benefits to large segments of the organized working class and
sustained rates of economic growth (Weisbrot et al, 2006, Sandbrook et al,
2007), it cannot be forgotten that the ISI model was highly exclusionary

(Nun 1969). Indeed, ISI was unable to overcome the deep-seated racial and class inequalities in the region (Thorp 1998, McMichael 2008) and served to further exacerbate uneven development between rural and urban areas (Lipton 1977). The social problems created by unplanned urbanization, such as large slum and shantytown populations that lack potable water and sanitation, tend to be particularly acute in one or two "primary" cities in each country (such as São Paulo and Rio de Janeiro in Brazil), where the ISI-sponsored commercial trade and secondary industries tended to be concentrated (Portes and Roberts 2005, 44), which are contrasted to "brown regions" that lie on the periphery of the capitalist world economy (such as the *favelas* of Rio or rural areas in Brazil's northeast region), which are similarly characterized by low levels of "stateness" and a deficit of public services (O'Donnell 1993). In the absence of the state, however, many local populations in these latter regions have come up with their own solutions to the problem of providing water and sanitation. Indeed, Latin America's water justice movement tends to look to these examples of "actually existing commons" in their search for ways to reinvent the social economy in the hopes of creating a more sustainable future.

SCOPE OF THE RESEARCH

The team conducting the research for this chapter was composed of academics and labour and social movement organizations in the region.[1] We began the project by conducting a survey of peer-reviewed articles and book chapters on "alternatives to privatization" in the water sector in Latin America. Not surprisingly, given the penetration of privatization in the sector, we found that the academic literature is much stronger on criticisms of privatization than on its alternatives; only 24 of the 200-odd documents address the issue of alternatives, and even these references are indirect (e.g. looking at anti-privatization campaigns or providing cursory overviews of municipal service reform). While this lacuna in the literature demonstrates the importance of the research, it also meant that we needed to rely on primary data more than initially expected. To collect primary data the research team conducted Web searches and interviews with social movement and union leaders throughout the region, largely those affiliated with the Red Vida and with Public Services International (PSI).

Conducting the research by working with Latin America's largest anti-privatization networks produced at least two limitations. First, we selected cases from countries that are part of the "left turn" in Latin America because they are of particular interest to scholars and activists seeking to learn more about the challenges involved with implementing alternatives in a post-neoliberal structural adjustment context. Second, we focused on cases that are fairly well-known in the activist community. We were able to collect more information on cases in which civil society organizations and trade unions have successfully defeated government campaigns for privatization. Previous research has demonstrated that given strong tendencies towards "cherry picking", public utilities threatened with privatization may be amongst the best-performing in the region. Nonetheless, there are case studies of "successful" public water utilities not included in the survey in countries where public utilities have never been threatened with privatization, such as Costa Rica. Given the fact that there is little public information about water operators in that country (since social movement organizations have other preoccupations), and our own resource limitations, we decided not to include Costa Rica in the survey. In addition, we included only one case study from Brazil (Porto Alegre), despite its importance in the sector. Given our team's Portuguese language limitations and the fact that Brazilian activists have already conducted their own survey on "successful" public water companies (da Costa et al, 2006, ASSAMAE 2007), we decided to focus our efforts on collecting data in countries with less capacity for progressive research. Finally, we decided to exclude Cuba—although it is evidently a relevant case for discussion of alternatives to neoliberal capitalism—given difficulties with access to information and the creeping commercialization taking place in the water sector there (see Cocq and McDonald 2010).

The case studies that are represented in the survey therefore reflect the regional strengths (and weaknesses) of the Red Vida network and come from countries where there has been a public debate on alternatives to privatization: Argentina, Brazil, Bolivia, Colombia, Costa Rica, Ecuador, Honduras, Peru, Uruguay, and Venezuela.[2] Despite the study's limitations, we believe that these cases are representative of a variety of service delivery experiences in different contexts, such as more "developed" states such as Brazil and Argentina and the poorest nations of the hemisphere such as Bolivia and Honduras. Furthermore, the exercise provides a map of actually existing alternatives and utopian visions of service delivery in the water sector in Latin America, representing examples of what social activists in the region consider to be best practices in the sector.

TYPES OF ALTERNATIVES FOUND

In total, our research team documented 26 successful alternatives in the water sector in Latin America (see Table 15.2) We documented nine cases of single public providers (municipal water utilities), 12 non-profit non-state providers (including community-run systems and cooperatives), three non-profit/non-profit partnerships, and two public/non-profit partnerships. In addition, we documented experiences of four national-level public-public partnerships (PuPs) and four examples of international PuPs (see Chapter 2, this volume, for a fuller discussion of research methodology and the typologies employed).

Table 15.2   Types of Alternatives in the Latin American Water Sector

Type of alternative	Name of entity	Location
SiP (single public sector)	Hidrocapital	Caracas, Venezuela
	Aguas Bonaerenses S.A./SOSBA	Province of Buenos Aires, Argentina
	EMAAP-Q	Quito, Ecuador
	ETAPA	Cuenca, Ecuador
	EAAB	Bogotá, Colombia
	Empresa Pública de Medellín	Medellín, Colombia
	EMCALI	Cali, Colombia
	OSE	Uruguay
	DMAE	Porto Alegre, Brazil
SiNP (single non-profit sector)	APAAS	Cochabamba (Sebastien Pagador), Bolivia
	Cooperativa de Servicio de Agua Potable 1 de mayo TUNTIRANCHO Ltda.	Cochabamba (Primer de Mayo), Bolivia
	SAGUAPAC	Santa Cruz de la Sierra, Bolivia
	COSMOL	Montero, Bolivia
	JAPOE	Rural Honduras
	COOPI	Villa Carlos Paz, Córdova, Argentina
	Aguas Santafesinas S.A.	Santa Fe, Argentina
	COOPLAN	Santa Cruz de la Sierra (Plan 3000), Bolivia

	Acueducto Comunal	Concepción de Naranjo, Costa Rica
	Servicio de Água	Vereda de la Palma, Colombia
	CENAGRAP	Rural Ecuador
	La Sirena	Cali, Colombia
NPNPP (non-profit-non-profit partnership)	ASICA-Sur	Cochabamba, Bolivia
	FEDECAAS	Santa Cruz, Bolivia
	Chilimarca	Tiquipaya, Department of Cochabamba, Bolivia
PuP (public–public partnership)		
National	AyA and ASADAS	Costa Rica
	SANAA	Honduras
	ASSAMAE	Brazil
	Aguasbonarenses S.A. and local water utilities	Argentina
International	OSE and ESSAP	Uruguay-Paraguay
	Sabesp and AyA	Brazil-Costa Rica
	Aguasbonarenses S.A. and SEDAM-Huancayo	Province of Buenos Aires, Argentina-Huancayo, Peru
	OSE and AAPOS	Uruguay-Potosí, Bolivia
PuNPP (public-non-profit partnership)	Cooperation between OSE and Maldonaldo Council (after 2005)	Uruguay
	ACUAVALLE S.A.	Valle de Cauca, Colombia

DEFENDING THE STATUS QUO

Given the legacy of the developmental state, the "status quo" in Latin America means supporting large, public utilities owned by the state and usually controlled by a board that is most often governed by some combination of elected politicians and representatives of civil society. When we asked Latin American water activists which public utilities were worthy of particular mention for excellence, two examples stood out: EAAB in Bogotá, Colombia, and EMAAP-Q in Quito, Ecuador. According to the "criteria for success" established for this research, however, these corporatized "public" companies are not necessarily non-commercialized "alternatives" since they operate much like private businesses, as corporatized entities.

Since 1955, the *Empresa de Acueducto y Alcantarillado de Bogotá* (EAAB) has been providing water and sanitation services to the capital Bogotá, Colombia, a city with over 7 million inhabitants. As of 2004, 96% of the population had potable water, and 88% had sanitary sewerage connections, which is a very high rate of coverage for a city in which almost one-third of the population lives under the poverty line—a service coverage that is comparable to wealthier cities such as Buenos Aires, Montevideo, Santiago, Porto Alegre, and São Paulo (Gilbert 2007, 1565). For many decades, the EAAB has employed a system of cross-subsidization in its tariff structure. The redistributive effect of this subsidization has diminished over time; however, the company has adopted more commercial practices in compliance with the neoliberal water sector reform law adopted in 1994 (Law 142). In 1995, the difference between the tariff paid by the rich and the poor was 7.4 times, and in 2004 it was 4.6 times (Gilbert 2007, 1566). Over the past decade or so, water tariffs have risen so much that consumption has dropped. The water company now has a production surplus, allowing it to sell water to the nine surrounding municipalities. Indeed, due to the drop in consumption, EAAB will not need to expand its water production until 2012 (Gilbert 2007, 1566).

The clearest indication that EAAB represents a commercial model of service delivery is the degree of private sector participation in the company. Since 1998, the French multinational water company Veolia has run the concession contract for a water purification plant, which serves 30% of the residents of Bogotá. In terms of "public ethos", the EAAB also scores rather low. The general manager of EAAB, Alberto Merlano, has even publicly endorsed the idea of privatization in the media (*BNAmericas* 2004), arguing the EAAB is an "exception" to the general trend of "inefficient" public services (see Spronk [2010] for a critical analysis of the erroneous way that the concept of "efficiency" is defined in contemporary debates about public services).

A similar trend towards corporatization was observed in the case of the *Empresa Metropolitana de Alcantarillado y Agua Potable* (EMAAP-Q), in Quito, another example of another well-performing public utility, which has adopted private sector business practices, including the granting of concession contracts. Originally founded in 1960, the company achieved major improvements in its coverage rates under the administration of progressive Mayor Paco Moncayo (2000 to present). The municipal council appointed General Manager Juan Neira Carrasco, who was recruited from the private sector to restructure the public utility and to inculcate a "corporate culture" (Belletini et al, 2006). The reforms have worked. Under new management, the public water company has made some impressive achievements. In August of 2000, the coverage was 72.28%; by March 2007, it was 96.87%. For sewerage, the coverage increased from 65.77% to 95.65% during the same period. This expansion is largely due to the utility's success in securing international loans from the Inter-American Development Bank (IDB), amongst other international financial institutions. The IDB has used its influence to pressure the management to privatize parts of its operations. In 2006 the mayor and the general manager proposed to grant a private concession in an area of new urban expansion near a new airport, which was defeated by a coalition of ecological and citizen groups who managed to convince the Mayor that privatization would not mean cost savings for the company (Buitrón 2008).

RECLAIMING PUBLIC SERVICES

Because social movement organizations have been so active in fighting the neoliberal water privatization agenda in Latin America, the region is home to many cancelled contracts. Most famous amongst these cases are the cancelled contracts following the 2000 "Water War" in Cochabamba, Bolivia, and the subsequent cancellation of a 40-year contract with Suez in the neighbouring cities of La Paz and El Alto, also in Bolivia. In Argentina, water companies were returned to state control following the economic crisis of 2001 in the cities of Buenos Aires and Santa Fe. A preliminary analysis suggests that none of these post-privatization cases present "successful" alternatives as of yet but are best described as works in progress.

Over the past eight years, the public water company in Cochabamba, SEMAPA, has lurched from one crisis to the next. After the population of Cochabamba successfully expelled Bechtel from Bolivia in 2000 (Olivera and Lewis 2004), a project to democratize the management of the utility— known as *"control social"* (social control)—was intended to resolve the problems with corruption that have historically plagued the public utility. While the former board of directors was staffed exclusively by professionals and politicians, since April 2002, three members elected from the macrodistricts (voting jurisdictions divided by population and territory) sat on the board. However, the many problems that have historically plagued public utilities have remained unresolved with a minimal degree of "social control" (Sánchez Gómez and Terhorst 2005, Crespo Flores 2006a, Driessen 2008).

Since the company was returned to public hands in 2000, two general managers have been dismissed for acts of corruption. General managers and the mayor, who sits on the board of directors, have used the company as a *botín político* (political booty), filling the company with their family members and friends. Due to these and other problems, the IDB cancelled payments on an $18-million loan, the first part of which was to be dedicated to the "modernization" of the company's management structure (Spronk 2007). The utility is once again scrambling for finances in order to maintain and expand the city's water and sanitation system. In May 2009 the Ministry of Water expressed in intent to intervene in the company and dismiss the board of directors due to mismanagement. Although there is public sentiment that the residents of Cochabamba "won the war" but "lost the water" (Caero 2009), residents in the poorest neighbourhoods have done as they always have and taken matters into their own hands, creating organizations of independent water committees.

In the case of La Paz-El Alto, social organizations also proposed a model for a "public-social company" with a very high level of popular participation, including a popular assembly with elected delegates from all regions of the city that would formulate the policy of the water company (Pérez 2005). Facing pressure from the mayors of La Paz and El Alto and international donor agencies—all of whom favour the formation of a public-private partnership (PPP)—the proposal has slowly transformed into a "light" version with a minimal level of public participation (Crespo Flores 2006c). In early 2009 all plans for introducing a participatory structure in the utility were scrapped, and the government Water Ministry commissioned a private consulting firm to propose a new model of management for the municipal utility.

In Argentina, the process of reversing some of the region's largest concessions has also been fraught with difficulty. Between 1991 and 1999, as part of one of the world's largest privatization programmes covering a range of sectors, water and sanitation concessions with the private sector were signed, covering 28% of the country's municipalities and 60% of the population (Galiani et al, 2005). In the years following the economic meltdown in December 2001, many of the concession contracts, which were already facing difficulty, were cancelled due to the devaluation of the peso, which made it nearly impossible to profit under the terms of the contracts. While the water company in the province of Buenos Aires was taken over by workers (see the case of ABSA, below), concession contracts in Buenos Aires and Santa Fe were cancelled and new water companies were formed. Whereas *Aguas y Saneamientos Argentinos* (AYSA) and *Aguas Santafesinas* (ASSA) have performed as well as could be expected under difficult conditions, having promised major investments (Lobina and Hall 2007), new managers have faced enormous challenges to repair the damage left by the previous concession owners. In the case of Buenos Aires, for example, the private concessionaire had failed to realize $900 million in projected investments (Lobina and Hall 2007).

In sum, returning water to public control has often been a frustrating process since public operators have had to clean up the mess left by the private sector, including large debts and underinvestment in infrastructure. It must also be noted, however, that local perceptions that public water utilities in Bolivia have "failed" need to be understood within the context of heightened public expectations following years of social movement mobilization, which has politicized the issue of service delivery. Although the public perception of the remunicipalized public utility in Cochabamba has not been satisfactory, SEMAPA may have performed better than the private company in terms of the concession contract on items such as the number of new water and sewer connections (Coordinadora 2005). To suggest that there might be a gap between perception and reality is not to deny, however, that progress at the local level has been frustrated by corruption, the lack of investment, and the slowness of reform at the national policy level.

There are a number of other examples in which public sector trade unions—as opposed to civil society organizations—have played a protagonist role in reclaiming public services by defending them against the threat of privatization. Workers in Cali and the Valley of Cauca, Colombia, and in the national water company of Uruguay have presented rescue plans to keep water under state control. In the Colombian cases, these efforts required sacrifices on the part of workers who have accepted revision of their collective agreement and a revision of the pension plan, the elimination of severance pay, certain bonuses, and benefits in order to keep the company in public hands. In the case of *Obras Sanitarias del Estado* (OSE) of Uruguay, the union was actively involved in investigating and trying cases of corruption within their own ranks, managing to save the enterprise from financial disaster (author interviews with Adriana Marquisio and Margarita López).

Originally founded in 1952, OSE provides water and sanitation services at the national level in Uruguay. According to the United Nations (UN), Uruguay is the only country in Latin America that has achieved nearly universal access to improved water sources and adequate sanitation (WHO and UNICEF 2010). Furthermore, around 70% of the wastewater collected is treated. The Federation of State Employees of OSE (*Federación de Funcionarios de Obras Sanitarias del Estado*, FFOSE) has played a key role in reversing privatization in the area of Maldonaldo, a wealthy suburb of Montevideo, which was granted a concession in 1993. When faced with the further threat of privatization in 2000, the trade union began to organize. Over the next two years, FFOSE held numerous assemblies to study the issue and to draft proposals for the company's restructuring. In 2002, the union organized a process to rid the company of corruption, sanctioning over 100 workers (author interview with Adriana Marquisio). Thanks to the participation of the trade union, the company was turned around in the space of a few years from a corrupt and inefficient institution to a public water company that runs a surplus budget and may now be considered a model public utility.

NEW FORMS OF PUBLIC SERVICE DELIVERY

Public-public partnerships

The initiative to promote PuPs has taken off quickly in the water sector in Latin America. Although there are many national-level PuPs in which national water regulators have supported the creation of partnerships between different utilities within countries, international PuPs are a newer phenomenon. Within the Red Vida, the initiative was first timidly approached in 2004 in Uruguay as part of conversations between OSE, FFOSE, and members of the Coordinadora in Bolivia. In August 2008, there was an event in Cochabamba specifically about this issue, and in May 2009, the principles were launched in Paso Severino, Uruguay (Red Vida 2009).

A cursory comparison of national and international PuPs suggests that while PuPs have both political and technical aims—to share experiences of "best practices" between two public, non-profit entities—the national PuPs place more emphasis on technical aspects, while the international PuPs have more political aims. International PuPs such as that between the workers operated water company in Buenos Aires, Argentina, and the public water company in Huancayo, Peru, are good examples of what social movement researchers Keck and Sikkink call the "boomerang effect", when groups in one country appeal to citizens of another through transnational alliances, and these citizens pressure their own government to pressure the offending regime (1998, 13).

There are several examples of national-level PuPs, including in Honduras, Colombia, Costa Rica, and Brazil, particularly in the rural areas where water systems are administered through community-based bodies and non-governmental organizations (NGOs; Phumpiu and Gustafsson 2009). The state water companies provide assistance to these PuPs by technicians employed by the national water corporations (SANAA, AyA, and ASSA-MAE). The Costa Rican case is particularly successful, where the national water institute has created a separate administrative body for this task, the ASADAS. In 2000, water supply coverage in Costa Rica was 98.5% at the urban level and 75.4% at rural level. Brazil also has a long history of internal collaboration between public water companies of larger and smaller size (da Costa et al, 2006, Hall et al, 2009, 8).

Interestingly, the most notable PuPs in the region have been trade union initiatives piloted by water workers' unions in Uruguay and Argentina. Two factors help to explain this. First, as social organizations, trade unions are in a privileged position to offer support to other social organizations since they have institutional sources of funding through trade union dues and employer support. Second, the Public Services International (PSI, an international public sector trade union umbrella group) and the Transnational Institute (TNI) have been active in the region promoting the formation of

PuPs. International travel has been financed by organizations such as TNI. In the Valley of Cauca, Colombia, and in the province of Buenos Aires, Argentina, trade union organizations affiliated with the PSI have been involved in providing technical support to the peri-urban and rural water committees. Building on these national experiences, the first international PuPs in the region were also initiatives of trade unions affiliated with the PSI, including the FFOSE in Uruguay and the *Sindicato Obras Sanitarias de la Provincia de Buenos Aires* (SOSBA), a trade union which runs the public water company in the province of Buenos Aires.

One of the best-known cases of international collaboration between two public-state water companies is the PuP signed between the worker-run cooperative water company ABSA (in the province of Buenos Aires), which is run by a trade union SOSBA, and SEDAM-Huancayo (Peru). The partnership aims to reform the municipal water company in Huancayo, which, along with all other public water companies in Peru, has been threatened by privatization. At the local level, the PuP has involved the cultivation of close relations between the local water workers' union (SUTAPAH), the Frente, the Federation of National Water Workers' Unions of Peru (FENTAP), and activists from TNI. Since 2002, social organizations in Huancayo, represented by the Defence Front for Water in the Junín Region (*Frente de Defensa del Agua de la Region Junín*, FREDEAJUN), have successfully staved off privatization through a series of public mobilizations, the largest of which brought thousands of people to the streets in March of 2005 (Terhorst 2008).

After signing the PuP in June 2007, SOSBA sent a team of engineers, which conducted a diagnostic of the public company. The report included suggestions for administrative reform of the company (that represent cost-savings of up to 35%) and advice on how to manage diminishing water supplies in the region with the melting of glaciers. As of 2008, the PuP hit a political impasse. Local authorities have resisted implementing the restructuring plan despite local and international civil society pressure. As one authority put it to Luis Isarra, a leader of FENTAP (the national federation of water workers' unions in Peru), during one of his visits to Huancayo, "where am I going to put the people who worked on my political campaign if I do not have control over the water company?" (author interview with Luis Isarra).

The experiences with PuPs have sponsored a debate within the Red Vida about how to evaluate the success of such initiatives. The initiative has provided political tools to local activists seeking to reform corrupt and politicized water companies, but the PuP model has had limited success in convincing local authorities to adopt measures to restructure utilities. Philipp Terhorst (author interview) reports that the administration of SEDAM-Huancayo is pursuing a PuP with the water company in Lima, which the central government has been trying to privatize for years. It is likely that the Peruvian government is implementing this alternative "PuP" as a political strategy to avoid restructuring and to prepare the ground for future privatization. If the government is successful in privatizing the company in Lima, there will be more pressure to do the same in Huancayo.

Civil society participation in large urban utilities

The water companies of Caracas, Venezuela, and Porto Alegre, Brazil, have improved services by democratizing decision making and therefore can be considered exemplary cases of successful alternatives to privatization in the water sector in Latin America. In these two cases, the institutionalization of popular participation in the processes of budgeting, planning, and even execution of water projects (particularly in the former case) has contributed to increased coverage rates and involved citizens in daily aspects of service delivery. These successful experiences of participatory decision making demonstrate that involving users in the planning and execution of water service delivery can make water utilities more "efficient" in social terms by making service provision more equitable.

Hidrocapital, which serves the capital city Caracas and the surrounding region, is amongst the most innovative public water companies in Latin America. Like many cities in the mountainous regions of South America, most of the urban population of Caracas has access to an improved water supply, but providing water to the poorer neighbourhoods that climb up the hillsides has been a challenge. Under the management of progressive mayor Aristóbulo Istúriz (1993–1996), the city established local forums to hear citizens' concerns about problems with water supply and sanitation. Whereas at first public participation was limited to protest, these forums were the forerunners of something more substantial. Following the national election of Hugo Chávez in 1999, a citywide communal water council was created in Caracas comprising representatives of the water company, local government, and civil society, and was later institutionalized as the technical water committees (*Mesas Técnicas de Agua*—MTAs). Indeed, the case of Caracas is a good example of how progressive mayors of major urban centres can sometimes influence national politics. In other words, municipal politics sometimes matter beyond the local scale.

The MTAs have been established as a way to involve the public in decision making. As Santiago Arconada Rodríguez describes it, the MTAs are a "way of co-ordinating all the knowledge the community [has] about their water network with the human, technical and financial resources that [belong] to them through their public water company. This was seen as necessary to harness the skills needed to solve the problems and the proposal suggested a huge change" (2005, 132). Through involvement in the *mesas técnicas*, communities are involved in the mapping, diagnosis, and planning for solutions to the water problem, as well as in project execution (e.g. digging the trenches for the pipes). Promoters of the project emphasize the importance of "co-responsibility" of the state and citizens in water services:

"Community that participates—Community that achieves results". The experience of the MTAs is remarkable because it scores highly in categories where many state companies are found lacking: participation, solidarity, public ethos, equity, sustainability, and even transferability of the model. According to one group of independent investigators, the participatory model also scores high in terms of gender equality (Allen et al, 2006, 348), which is a particularly weak point of most state utilities and many community systems (see Chapter 5, this volume, for an extended discussion of gender issues and "public" services).

Since the establishment of the MTAs, Caracas's coverage of drinking water service rose from 82% in 1998 to 89% in 2003, and sewerage from 64% to 72% (Simpson 2009, 8). In 2004, the national water regulator/holding company Hidroven announced that Venezuela had already achieved the Millennium Development Goal (MDG) water target of halving the proportion of people without access to safe water between 1990 and 2015. The Venezuelan government also predicted that they would reach the same MDG target for sanitation by 2010.

The municipal water company of Porto Alegre, the DMAE, is one of the better-known examples of participatory management in the Latin American region. It has been heralded by social movement organizations as a model of good public management. Technicians and activists from the DMAE have been involved in providing advice and solidarity to water warriors elsewhere, such as Bolivia (Souza and Kruse 2002). Under the participatory budgeting regime implemented by the left-of-centre Workers' Party (*Partido dos Trabalhadores*, PT; see, *inter alia*, Abers 1998, Baiocchi 2005), DMAE's coverage rates in poor areas of the city improved dramatically: potable water by 23% and sewerage by 40%, despite a high rate of urban growth (8%; Maltz 2005). As discussed in further detail below, however, the DMAE lost much of its social character after the PT was defeated in the elections in 2004, which raises questions about the sustainability of the model.

Cooperatives in urban areas

The cooperative model potentially presents an alternative form of collective ownership that defies the capitalist logic of private property. Compared to private businesses or state-owned utilities, which are controlled by shareholders or elected officials, cooperatives that provide basic services have certain organizational advantages that make them potentially more democratic (Ravina 1996). Nonetheless, as the following case studies of water cooperatives in Argentina and Bolivia suggest, cooperatives face the same market imperatives as private businesses and state-owned utilities, especially given increasing pressures of corporatization.

The experience of a worker-controlled water utility in the province of Buenos Aires, *Aguas Bonaerenses Sociedad Anónima* (ABSA), has been heralded by the UN as a model water company. The province of Buenos Aires has 10 million inhabitants distributed over 74 cities with 48 municipalities, which are served by ABSA. Azurix, a subsidiary of ENRON, was granted a concession in 1999, but it only lasted for three years, during which time the company failed to invest in the maintenance and expansion of services, leaving behind a severely debilitated company (Amorebieta 2005). In the wake of the financial crisis of 2001–2002 and the bankruptcy of ENRON, the union proposed to take over the company as its technical operator (replacing Azurix), forming a cooperative which is run by the workers called the *5 de Septiembre*. The provincial government agreed with the idea and bought Azurix's shares, leaving the union with the 10% of shares that they already had.

In its context, ABSA is a successful public water company, having achieved 70% of water coverage and 45% sewerage coverage over a vast and dispersedly populated geographical area. Under the administration of the workers' cooperative controlled by SOSBA, the company has improved the rate of payment among users from 30% to 80% (Amorebieta 2005). While the experience is a successful model of service delivery, the cooperative appears to measure its own success in commercial terms (e.g. number of workers per connection, rates of cost recovery from end users, etc). Public participation in the utility also appears to be low, although this is common amongst well-functioning public water companies that have enjoyed a high level of public investment.

Another example, SAGUAPAC, may be the largest urban cooperative in the world, serving the central part of the city of Santa Cruz de la Sierra, Bolivia. The cooperative was created in 1979 during the dictatorial period, during which time Santa Cruz was transformed from a colonial backwater into an economic powerhouse, largely due to the channelling of state funds to develop the agro-export sector and the discovery of oil and gas in the region (Eaton 2007). Today, SAGUAPAC provides water services to around 871,000 inhabitants (although the total urban population of Santa Cruz is around 1.5 million) and sewerage services to about 50% of the population (although it is unclear whether this refers to the total urban population or those with water connections with SAGUAPAC) (Yavarí 2005).

A study by researchers at the University of Birmingham (Nickson 1998) conducted in the late 1990s found that SAGUAPAC is one of the best-run water companies in Latin America, measured by criteria of efficiency, equity and effectiveness because it had:

- a low level of unaccounted-for water
- a low number of employees per 1,000 water connections
- efficient accounting: 100% of all connections are metered
- a 96% bill collection efficiency rate
- 80% water coverage, despite rapid population growth
- A 24-hour supply of clean water

While the cooperative has been heralded outside of Bolivia as a model (Constance 2005), Bolivian water activists see the cooperative less favourably. The major concerns pertain to public participation and coverage rates. Statements about the utility's supposedly high coverage rates ignore the fact that the utility's concession area is a restricted geographical area within the centre of the city. The peri-urban areas are served by nine small cooperatives, including Plan 3000 (discussed below). Indeed, SAGUAPAC's area of service does not extend beyond the "fourth ring", inside which live the wealthiest residents of the city. Furthermore, the claims of internal democracy need to be verified, since critics claim that SAGUAPAC, along with the telephone and electricity cooperatives, are run by secret societies similar to the Masons, referred to as *logías* (Ferreira 1994). In sum, there are serious questions about equity in service delivery given the failure of SAGUAPAC to extend its services beyond elite neighbourhoods at the centre of the city.

Testifying to the fact that SAGUAPAC is not the sole service provider in Santa Cruz de la Sierra is the existence of the Water Cooperative of Plan 3000 (*La Cooperativa de Aguas del Plan Tres Mil*, COOPLAN) in the poor suburb of Plan 3000. As Uruguay activist and political analyst Raúl Zibechi describes it,

> In the middle of a racist city of white elites, the nucleus of the agro-export oligarchy, Plan 3000 is an immense and poor suburb of almost 300,000 inhabitants mostly of Aymara, Quechua, and Guarani descent; a microcosm composed of 36 Bolivian ethnic groups. It is a city that—in the name of the struggle against inequality—the residents of Plan 3000 resist the machista, oppressive, and violent culture of the local elite. (2009a, 14)

COOPLAN was established in 1986 by the residents of Plan 3000 in order to address the problems created by reluctance of SAGUAPAC to expand services to peripheral neighbourhoods. Today it provides about 80% of households within its service area with potable water (121,000 of 151,000). In 2001, the national water regulator granted the cooperative a concession of 15 years as the sole service provider. The cooperative does not currently provide sewerage services, but it is planning to build a sanitary sewerage collection network thanks to a loan from the IDB and the European Union. Amongst other accomplishments, the amount of water unaccounted for was reduced from 63% to 29% between 2003 and 2008.

Community-run water systems in rural areas

In many ways, providing potable water to rural communities is a more challenging task than providing water to urban areas due to high rates of poverty and physically dispersed populations, which makes the provision of networked infrastructure more expensive and financing difficult.

According to WHO and UNICEF (2010), in 2008, 50 million people, or 9% of the population of Latin America and the Caribbean, did not have access to improved water supply, and 125 million, or 23%, did not have access to improved sanitation. As noted above, as a percentage of the unserved population, rural residents are over-represented, meaning that access to water and sanitation remains a problem in rural areas of Latin America.

Although there are a few countries, such as Costa Rica and Brazil, in which the national state has supported community initiatives in rural areas through the financing of water infrastructure, the story of service provision in rural areas of Latin America is generally one of state neglect. Nonetheless, in the absence of the state there are hundreds of examples of well-performing water systems that have been built by communities with additional support from local authorities and NGOs.

The Council of Potable Water in the Municipality of Jesús de Otoro (*La Junta de Agua Potable de la Municipalidad de Jesús de Otoro*, JAPOE) is considered to be the best example of a successful communal water system in Honduras (author interview with Erasto Reyes). Located in the Department of Intibucá, JAPOE is a communal water system that has been designed to protect the subwatershed of Rio Cumes. In 1993, the project received financial support from Catholic Relief Services in order to install a potable water system. In 2005, the system also received donations from AGUASAN of the Swiss Cooperation Agency (COSUDE) for institutional strengthening. In the beginning, JAPOE received financial help from the state through the Social Investment Fund of Honduras. The project has been executed directly by the water committees and represents a case of self-management financed by donor support. This committee is subdivided into 10 sectors, each of which has a board of directors that sends a representative to the assembly, which is the maximum authority of the project. Thanks to these projects, the coverage of potable water in the city rose from 50% of the population in 1993 to 91% of the population in 2005. At present, the system provides water to nearly 12,000 people with 1,500 connections. The water provided is not meant for domestic use, but it is suitable for human consumption because it is treated with chlorine. The project is also taking steps towards installing a treatment plant and micro- and macrometers in order to reduce the waste of water. Importantly, the JAPOE has promoted an integrated system of environmental management to take care of the watershed. It monitors a protected area of around 3,000 hectares, preventing deforestation and agricultural pollution, which affects the volume and quality of water.

The *acueducto comunal* of Costa Rica is another example of a communal water system that has been strengthened by state support (author interview with Marco Mellín). First created in 1961, the system today provides water and sewerage services to 1,600 inhabitants of the town of Concepción. It has been estimated that there are over 1,700 communal water systems in Costa Rica that provide water to about 26% of the population.

An association is responsible for capturing and distributing water to the community, constructing and maintaining the necessary infrastructure, charging for the services and managing the budget. The association has a quarterly newsletter that updates the members about activities, and once a year there is a general assembly at which members are informed about the status of the aqueduct. This example may be included as a "successful" model of communal service delivery that has also received state support.

Community-run[3] systems in peri-urban areas

Given the high rates of rural poverty, rural-urban migration has kept state water companies in Latin America scrambling to keep up with growing demand as cities have spread outwards. One of the major problems related to unplanned urban growth in many of these cities is that migrant populations have settled on increasingly precarious land, often establishing informal settlements climbing up the hillsides or next to rivers that are prone to flooding. In many of these areas, residents have come up with their own solutions to the urban water problem, establishing independent systems with little or no help from the state. There are at least two factors that appear to explain the emergence of communal water systems in peri-urban areas: a weak/absent state, and indigenous/campesino knowledge about water systems that is transferred from rural to urban areas. In both rural and peri-urban areas, these systems often serve a dual purpose, providing water for production (e.g. irrigation of crops, often for household consumption) and reproduction (e.g. drinking water for the household).

Peri-urban community water systems such as La Sirena in Cali, Colombia, and *Asociación de Producción y Administración de Agua y Saneamiento de Sebastián Pagador* (APAAS) in Cochabamba, Bolivia, provide high-quality services for relatively low cost (author interview with Fabian Condori). On a tour of the system's installations in May 2009, the president of the association in La Sirena, José Hoé Gareia Carreño, emphasized how the construction of their water tanks cost less than half what it would have cost the state water company to build, since the state water company must pay taxes and has higher staffing costs (author interview). La Sirena relies on local knowledge rather than hiring expensive consultants and engineers.

The other impressive aspect of these two systems is the democratic nature of management. The transparency of operations is facilitated by the small scale of operations, since these systems employ only two to three staff, including technical operators and administrators. In the case of Cali, bank account statements and information about the association's financial status are printed and posted on a bulletin board in the office where every user coming to pay their water bill can see it. In the case of APAAS in Cochabamba, the participatory structure of the water committee is mapped onto the neighbourhood councils that are institutionalized under the 1994 Law of Popular Participation. In both cases, the water systems are run by democratically elected, voluntary boards, which organize regular general assemblies to inform and consult users about the financial status and activities of the association.

The organizers and users of these independent systems express a strong sense of patrimony over the collective property that has been built and owned by local residents with little help from the state. In general, the system administrators tend to be highly suspicious of state attempts to regulate or absorb the system. These suspicions are linked to a fear that state involvement will mean higher water tariffs but also to the residents' general mistrust of the bureaucratic state for its inefficiency and corruption and a desire for self-governance.

UTOPIAN/PROPOSED MODELS

One of the difficulties associated with investigating proposed or "utopian" models of water delivery is that once the historical moment in which they were tried or discussed has passed, these dreams fade into memory unless there is written documentation about them. Thanks to the global attention paid to the Cochabamba Water War by both academics and activists, however, we know much more about the struggles there than have taken place elsewhere. For this reason, the Cochabamba struggles have served as key reference points within the global movement for water justice, including one of the most important aftermaths of the "War", the creation of the Association of Communal Potable Water Systems of the South (*Asociación de Sistemas Comunitarios de Agua Potable del Sur*, ASICA-Sur). While ASICA-Sur may appear to be an "actually existing" alternative, it is also a "utopian alternative" because it strives to attain and maintain community control over the day-to-day operations of the water system, while only depending on the state for the provision of bulk water at a fair price.

ASICA-Sur is an association of independent water communities in the poor, southern zone of Cochabamba. Its main objective is to strengthen local water committees, which deliver water and sanitation services in a poor, peri-urban area of the city. It negotiates with the government and the local municipal water company (SEMAPA) on behalf of its members and provides several technical, juridical, and political-organizational services.

The idea for ASICA-Sur emerged during the "Water War" of 2000. One of the main spokespersons, Abraham Grandydier, explained in an interview with one of the current authors in 2004 that they learned a lot from the example of FEDECOR (the Federation of Irrigators in the Department of Cochabamba), which played an active role in organizing the protests. In its early days, the *Centro Vicente Cañas* (the director of which was a Jesuit priest, Luis Sanchez) also facilitated the creation of ASICA-Sur (its first office was housed there) as well as the *Coordinadora de Defensa del Agua y la Vida* (Sánchez Gómez 2004, Sánchez Gómez and Olivera 2004, Sánchez Gómez and Terhorst 2005). More recently, ASICA-Sur has received financial support from NGOs such as the Foundation *France Libertés* and donor organizations such as the European Union. The central government is also channelling funds to ASICA-Sur through the programme *Bolivia cambia, Evo cumple*. These projects aim to build the infrastructure necessary to expand the amount of water available for distribution by the small water committees.

The experience of ASICA-Sur provides an interesting contrast with the technical water committees (*Mesas Técnicas de Agua*—MTAs) in Venezuela. Activists in both organizations promote an ideology of co-responsibility or co-management, but this concept in Venezuela has been introduced from top-down, while the notion of co-management in Bolivia is bottom-up. The water committees in Cochabamba have resisted the idea of surrendering control over management of their community water systems to any government entity since there is a general mistrust of the state (Zibechi 2009b). This mistrust is related to fears about losing control over water rates and a general notion that the systems are community, not state, patrimony. Given the long history of authoritarianism and racial exclusion, in poor communities in Bolivia, "the state" is not viewed as an entity which has collective interests at heart.

SUCCESSES AND FAILURES OF ALTERNATIVES

What, then, have been the overall successes and failures of "alternatives to privatization" in the water sector in Latin America? Judged in terms of service coverage, the most successful municipal water utilities are located in larger cities, such as Bogotá (Colombia), Quito (Ecuador), and Montevideo (Uruguay). These municipal water utilities represent the "old public" form of service delivery and management. That is, they are managed by highly professional staff, and the expansion of urban water and sanitation networks has been financed by large loans from international financial institutions such as the World Bank and IDB. But with the exception of the national utility in Uruguay, decision-making structures are very hierarchal, providing few spaces for participation by civil society and trade unions. By contrast, the bulk of alternatives that score highly for participation and equity are non-profit, non-state alternatives, which range from large cooperatives in urban areas of Bolivia and Argentina to community-run systems that provide low-cost, high-quality water services in rural areas of Costa Rica and Colombia. Alternatives that emphasize participatory forms of decision making tend to dominate in smaller cities and rural areas, although there are some noteworthy exceptions in urban metropolises of Venezuela and Brazil, such as Caracas and Porto Alegre, respectively.

Our research also reveals that some alternative forms of service delivery in large urban centres that have been heralded as successful—such as EAAB in Bogota and EMAAP-Q in Quito—are not all that positive when applying the evaluative criteria developed for this project. It should come as no surprise that corporatized utilities such EMAAP-Q of Quito, Ecuador, and EAAB of Bogota, Colombia, are weak on a number of important indicators, including public ethos, participation and quality of the workplace. Whereas these companies perform well in terms of economic efficiency and quality of service, workers have been expected to shoulder the burden of these efficiency gains. To illustrate, the EAAB pursued an aggressive policy of subcontracting as a way to reduce the costs of pensions, which at one point totalled approximately 20% of water tariffs (Gilbert 2007). Indeed, subcontracting is one of the pernicious trends in the large utilities throughout the region, both private and public.

Despite their supposed commitments to building "socialism of the twenty-first century", public utilities in Bolivia, Venezuela, and Ecuador are also not immune to these trends. In the case of renationalized enterprises such as Cantv, Venezuela's largest telecommunications provider, which was recuperated in 2007, local activists recognize that the government's promotion of cooperatives is a way to try to alleviate the worst situations of employer-employee abuse without raising the costs associated with absorbing the workers previously hired under subcontract by the privatized company. Instead of working for a private employer, workers in the renationalized companies in Venezuela have been encouraged to form cooperatives. Critical research on similar phenomena in the recuperated enterprises in Argentina and elsewhere, however, has suggested that workers must intensify their own self-exploitation in order to compete in the market (Kasmir 1996, Atzeni and Ghigliani 2007). In short, while cooperatives provide useful learning experiences for workers seeking to expand control over their working lives, they do not necessarily represent an alternative to capitalism because they fail to transform the meaning of the market, which is predicated on the alienation of labour and dependence of workers on the market for their own self-reproduction and subsistence (Marx [1993], McNally 1993).

Within the context of the battle against subcontracting, the public water company in Uruguay, OSE, represents one of the most successful public water companies in a large urban centre. Under the *Frente Amplio* government, the trade union is actively participating in a process to restructure the company, transforming a deficit into a surplus within a short period of time. The trade union has put forward proposals to reabsorb contract workers as full-time employees with benefits. While FFOSE leader Adriana Marquisio (author interview) acknowledges that "there is still a lot of work to be done", the OSE has maintained a high level of service coverage without sacrificing conditions of work.

The general acceptance by governments that promote "socialism of the 20th century" of the desirability of subcontracting suggests that there is the need for a public debate about the broader meaning of "efficiency". IFIs have waged a successful campaign in the region to encourage public managers to break strong unions and reduce the labour force. For example, the World Bank recommends that water and sanitation utilities employ two to three workers per thousand connections and uses this number politically to discipline managers into reducing the number of permanent staff. OSE (Uruguay) has four to five workers per connection, while ABSA under the management of SOSBA has two to three. While ASBA may be judged to be more efficient in this regard, contextual factors such as social and geographical considerations must also be considered. After all, it is much easier to achieve lower numbers of workers in a system in which there is one point of water capture and no sewerage treatment, because each physical installation requires staff to monitor.

Two other innovative public companies that may be considered amongst the most successful according to our research criteria are the public utilities of Caracas, Venezuela, and Porto Alegre, Brazil. In both cases state-owned and state-operated utilities have made dramatic improvements to service coverage by introducing institutional mechanisms to encourage the participation of citizens who lack services. Importantly, both of these experiments are unfolding in a context in which there is a strong state commitment to investment in infrastructure and long histories of democracy-building at both the local and national levels, which are two important factors in understanding their success. Indeed, in the absence of adequate public funds for infrastructure expansion and the democratization of larger power structures, including municipal and national governments, isolated participatory initiatives such as that in Cochabamba cannot be expected to succeed.

There are further questions to be asked, however, about the sustainability of these participatory initiatives. While one group of independent investigators in Venezuela notes that, "Despite being a government initiative, the [MTAs] are fairly autonomous" (Allen et al, 2006, 348), it is unclear if the initiative would continue if Hugo Chávez was to be replaced, particularly at the national level where the initiative was more recently launched.

There may be lessons in this regard from Brazil. According to many observers, the participatory budgeting process in Porto Alegre is not what it once was since the Workers' Party lost local elections in 2004 (Chávez 2006). Fernanda Levenzon (author interview) of the Centre on Housing Rights and Evictions (COHRE), an international NGO based in Porto Alegre, reports that her organization has received increased complaints from residents about the DMAE, which has allegedly adopted more commercial practices such as imposing a stricter policy on payment including higher water rates and more service cut-offs since the change in municipal administration.

Compared to water service delivery institutions in large urban areas, our survey suggests that with a couple of exceptions, smaller water systems run by committees and associations in rural and peri-urban areas score higher on the criteria of participation, transparency, and solidarity than public water providers in large urban settings. Indeed, the two main advantages of community-run systems such as JAPOE (Honduras), the *acueductos comunales* of Costa Rica and water committees in Cochabamba (Bolivia) and Cali (Colombia) are that they tend to be highly participatory, involving community members in decision making, and provide low-cost services to their members. In the absence of sophisticated monitoring systems and water-purification technology, however, service quality tends to vary and often depends on the quality of the crude water available in a given region.[4]

The main weaknesses of these small, community-run systems in rural and peri-urban areas relate to their environmental impact and the quality of services offered. First, sanitary sewerage is usually a lower priority in household budgets than potable water, so few of these communal systems provide sanitary sewerage. As a result, untreated waste water tends to be dumped directly into the ground and water supplies, creating potential health hazards for the community and those downstream. Second, the emergence of these fragmented and isolated systems makes it difficult to monitor and regulate water takings, which would ideally be part of an integrated watershed management scheme.

The question of service quality is an even larger ideological concern given the temptation of scholars and social movement actors alike to romanticize "indigenous" and "artisanal" forms of service delivery. In the context of deeply divided societies in which racial and class inequalities are expressed in the differential and unequal access to public services, improvements to social equity will require that a greater proportion of future investment be channelled to expansion and improvement of infrastructure in previously neglected areas, such as poor urban neighbourhoods and rural areas. Such public policy reform is even more badly needed in the aftermath of the decentralization mandated by neoliberal structural adjustment policies, by which governments transferred responsibility for service provision without transferring adequate resources to pay for these services. Given this recent historical legacy, the unwitting decision to endorse *different* solutions for urban and rural and economically advantaged and disadvantaged areas risks lending ideological legitimacy for the entrenchment of two-tiered service delivery systems that establish technologically sophisticated, formal water systems for the wealthy populations and piecemeal, informal solutions that provide inferior services to the poor (Crespo Flores 2001, Laurie and Crespo 2007, Spronk 2009a). Future research thus should specify ways to build on the experience of these artisanal systems without sacrificing environmental sustainability and service quality, especially for the poor.

WAYS FORWARD

In the debates about alternatives to privatization, particularly in the global North where public utilities have generally managed to extend public services to all urban citizens, "public" usually means "state" forms of ownership and control. And while this debate about "public versus private" is of fundamental importance, it tends to obscure the principal problem in countries in the South of systematic failure of water companies to connect the poorest of the poor, no matter who owns and operates them. As Swyngedouw argues in his book on the political economy of urban water infrastructure in Guayaquil, Ecuador, "[T]he water problem is not merely a question of management and technology, but rather, and perhaps in the first instance, a question of social power" (2004, 175). Indeed, the barriers that limit poor people's access to water—such as poverty and political powerlessness—are likely to persist whether the provider is publicly or privately owned and operated (Budds and McGranahan 2003).

Water activists in Latin America therefore recognize the limitations of public water authorities given the systematic failure of public utilities in the region to respond to the needs of the poor. These activists emphasize the need for "social" rather than simply public forms of management. While these activists who argue for social forms of management in order to "reclaim the commons" from corporate control agree that most forms of state ownership and control are preferable to private (profit-seeking) forms, they also share a common disdain for bureaucratic, centralized state control, which represents the "old public". The goal of initiatives such as the formation of PuPs that involve community organizations is therefore to democratize public forms of water delivery.

From a historical-sociological perspective, the emphasis on non-state solutions in Latin America is also coloured by the experience of the dictatorships that ruled 18 out of 21 nations from 1964 until the early 1990s. Amongst other effects, the history of corporatism has created a highly co-opted trade union movement, particularly in the larger industrialized countries such as Brazil, Argentina, and Mexico. Given the historical dominance of corporatist forms of relationships between workers and the state in the Latin American context, created under import substitution industrialization, workers in the most industrialized countries of the region have tended not to pursue "class conscious" trade unionism (Collier and Collier 1991). Municipal workers in these countries are even less likely to take on the state insofar as they depend on the state as their employers. Previous research on the topic suggests that with some exceptions, such as teachers and telephone and electrical workers in Mexico (Garza Toledo and Valdivia 1991), corporatist relations have dominated public sector trade unionism, even in countries in which the trade union is otherwise fiercely independent and even revolutionary (at least in the past), such as Bolivia (Spronk 2009b).

Since the 1990s, this situation has started to change. Neoliberal policies of privatization and austerity have reduced the amount of the "political goods", which are distributed through clientelist networks which formerly tied trade unions to the state. As a result, workers have increasingly found themselves in opposition to governments, defending their jobs against privatization. There are progressive trade unions in Peru, Uruguay, and Colombia that have placed themselves at the front of struggles for public services, building alliances with social movements, such as the environmental and indigenous movements, and NGOs. While these alliances are not without their tensions, the formation of coalitions has proven to be a successful strategy to fend off privatization and to build popular support for democratic reform of public utilities (Novelli 2004, Santos and Villarreal 2005, Spronk 2009b). As noted above, trade unions have also been the lead organizations in the formation of PuPs, which aim to improve the operations of public companies by sharing "best practices".

In the context of the emergence of self-defined "Left" governments—some of which have pledged their allegiance to an abstractly defined "socialism of the 20th century"—the relationship between labour, social movements, and the state is a theme being actively debated amongst academics, activists, and practitioners. As the Argentine, Bolivian, and Brazilian case studies demonstrate, there is a danger that when social movements ally themselves too closely to the state, left governments in power attempt to divide and co-opt them, which diminishes the social movement capacity for collective action and the possibility of putting forward proposals in their own interests. As Raquel Gutiérrez Aguilar has observed:

> These governments were born from Latin American societies' attempts to limit the brutality of neoliberalism. Yet they are governments which, nevertheless, lack direction and advance with an exasperating slowness, producing a frustration in their own societies that increases by the minute and that furthermore serve as the base on which the right wing reconstructs itself. (2008, 38)

As the *coup d'état* in Honduras in 2009 has demonstrated, even mildly reformist governments can be toppled by conservative reactionary forces when they are not supported by dense civil society networks.

The role of trade unions in public service delivery also deserves further exploration, as labour studies have largely fallen off the agenda in Latin America. As argued above, the subcontracting of public services remains a weakness of all formal water systems, whether they are owned and operated by the state or private capital, and whether or not the government in office embraces the value of the "New Left". As the Canadian Union of Public Employees (CUPE 1998) stated more than a decade ago, subcontracting is a form of "privatization by stealth" and presents the next barrier in the struggle against privatization and commercialization of public services. To date, there is very little information about the effects of subcontracting on workers and service quality in the water sector in Latin America, although trade union organizations such as the PSI have begun research on the question.[5]

Another research agenda that requires further attention relates to environmental questions—a pressing public issue in light of rapidly accelerating global climate change. Large urban centres in the Andes that are dependent on glacial melt-waters are particularly vulnerable. In cities such as Quito, Ecuador, and La Paz, Bolivia, it is predicted that urban populations will have to rely on new sources of water within the next 15 years. Public companies, just as private companies, have seldom prioritized the environment in their planning and development of water catchment systems. This lack of planning is evident in service indicators that allow companies to claim that they have met their goals in terms of "efficiency" and "sustainability" even though many of their practices will cost dearly in the long run, such as contaminating crude water sources with untreated waste, will cost dearly in the long run. The promotion of small, uncoordinated community water systems is not necessarily a solution, either, since these systems can just as easily contribute to environmental degradation in the absence of regulation or coordination at the level of the watershed.

Finally, it is necessary to critically investigate the strengths and weaknesses of our own "alternative" movements. Certain social movements and social movement organizations have manifested a tendency to *caudillismo* and centralization, which is expressed in the precariousness of democratic practices and the failure of leaders to be accountable to the rank and file, in trade unions and issue-or territorially based organizations. Such critical self-reflection will make for better social activism as well as better "alternatives to privatization".

NOTES

1. Our connections with Red Vida (the largest anti-privatization network in Latin America) were particularly important in this regard, while Ricardo Buitrón of Public Services International provided critical feedback on the project and facilitated contact with trade unions.
2. Although there is no Red Vida affiliate organization from Venezuela, we were able to make contact with Robin de la Motte, a PSI-affiliated researcher who has conducted extensive fieldwork on the water sector in Venezuela, and to conduct personal interviews with an activist and a government representative who were invited to a Red Vida workshop on public-public partnerships in Cochabamba, Bolivia, in August 2008.
3. The systems are termed "community systems" rather than cooperatives due to differences in their legal status. In Bolivia, for example, cooperatives and community systems are regulated by different laws and regulations.
4. There is a role for affordable appropriate technology that must be adapted to local conditions. See, for example, the study of solar purification technology in the Gualberto Villarroel province of Bolivia (Younger 2007).
5. For more information, see the website of PSI–Andean region, www.municipalesandinosisp.org/.

REFERENCES

Abers, R. 1998. From clientelism to cooperation: Local government, participatory policy, and civic organizing. *Politics and Society* 26(4): 511–538.

Allen, A., Dávila, J. and Hofmann, P. 2006. The peri-urban water poor: Citizens or consumers? *Environment and Urbanization* 18(2): 333–351.

Amorebieta, G. 2005. Argentina: Workers' co-operative takes over post-Enron. In Balanyá, B., Brennan, B., Hoedeman, O., Kishimoto, S. and Terhorst, P. (Eds), *Reclaiming public water: Achievements, struggles and visions from around the world*, pp. 149–157. Porto Alegre, Brazil: TNI (Transnational Institute) and CEO (Corporate Europe Observatory).

Arconada Rodríguez, S. (2005). The Venezuelan experience in the struggle for people-centred drinking water and sanitation services. In Balanyá, B., Brennan, B., Hoedeman, O., Kishimoto, S. and Terhorst, P. (Eds), *Reclaiming public water: Achievements, struggles and visions from around the world*, pp. 131–137. Porto Alegre, Brazil: TNI (Transnational Institute) and CEO (Corporate Europe Observatory).

ASSAMAE. 2007. Successful experiences in municipal public water and sanitation services from Brazil. In Warwick, H. and Cann, V. (Eds), *Going public: Southern solutions to the global water crisis*, pp. 40–51. London: World Development Movement. www.wdm.org.uk/going-public-southern-solutions-global-water-crisis.

Atzeni, M. and Ghigliani, P. 2007. Labour process and decision-making in factories under workers' self-management: Empirical evidence from Argentina. *Work Employment and Society* 21(4): 653–671.

Baiocchi, G. 2005. *Militants and citizens: The politics of participatory democracy in Porto Alegre*. Stanford: Stanford University Press.

Belletini, O., Carrillo, P., Brborich, W., Warner, M., Timme, L. and Coombs, E. 2006. Stay public or go private? A comparative analysis of water services between Quito and Guayaquil. Quito, Ecuador: Grupo FARO (Fundación para el Avance de las Reformas y las Oportunidades).

BNAmericas (Business News Americas). 2004. EAAB: Privatization cure for administrative ailments—Colombia. 11 March.

Budds, J. 2004. Power, nature and neoliberalism: The political ecology of water in Chile. *Singapore Journal of Tropical Geography* 25(3): 322–342.

Budds, J. and McGranahan, G. 2003. Are the debates on water privatization missing the point? Experiences from Africa, Asia and Latin America. *Environment and Urbanization* 15(2): 87–113.

Buitrón, R. 2008. *La concesión como estrategia de privatización*. Quito, Ecuador: Ediciones Abya-Yala.

Caero, G.A. 2009. *Cochabamba ganó la guerra y perdió el agua*. Cochabamba, Bolivia: Los Tiempos.

Chávez, D. 2006. Participation lite: The watering down of people power in Porto Alegre. *Red Pepper* 27. www.tni.org/detail_page.phtml?page=archives_chavez_participation.

Cocq, K. and McDonald, D. A. 2010. Minding the Undertow: Assessing Water "Privatization" in Cuba. *Antipode* 42(1): 6–45.

Collier, R.B. and Collier, D. 1991. *Shaping the political arena: Critical junctures, the labour movement, and regime dynamics in Latin America*. Princeton: Princeton University Press.

Constance, P. 2005. *Are cooperatives a better way to solve Latin America's water problems?* Inter-American Development Bank, 26 May. www.iadb.org/idbamerica/index.cfm?thisid=3497.

Coordinadora, T.S.T.O.T. 2005. Seminario Taller SEMAPA: El agua es nuestra: Construyendo una empresa social. Cochabamba, 7 April.

Crespo Flores, C. 2001. La concesión de la paz a los cinco años; elementos para una evaluación. 14 September. www.aguabolivia.org.

Crespo Flores, C. 2006a. La crisis sin fin de SEMAPA. *Observatorio de Conflictos Sociales* 3(5): 1–2.

———. 2006b. *Soberanía y autogestión en la terminación del contrato con AISA y el futuro del servicio*. Cochabamba: CESU-UMSS.

———. 2006c. Soberanía y autogestión en la terminación del contrato con AISA y el futuro del servicio. *Bolpress*, 1 December. www.bolpress.com/art.php?Cod=2006120123

CUPE (Canadian Union of Public Employees). 1998. *False savings, hidden costs: Calculating the costs of contracting out and privatization.* Ottawa, Canada: CUPE.

da Costa, S.S., Campos Borja, P., Heller, L., Santos Moraes, L.R. 2006. Successful municipal experiences in water supply and sanitation services in Brazil. Transnational Institute, 30 July. www.tni.org/archives/water-docs/dacosta.pdf.

Driessen, T. 2008. Collective management strategies and elite resistance in Cochabamba, Bolivia. *Development* 51: 89–95.

Eaton, K. 2007. Backlash in Bolivia: Regional autonomy as a reaction against indigenous mobilization. *Politics Society* 35(1): 71–102.

Ferreira, R. 1994. *Las logias en Santa Cruz.* Santa Cruz: Fondo de Ediciones Municipales.

Galiani, S., Gertler, P. and Schargrodsky, E. 2005. Water for life: The impact of the privatization of water services on child mortality. *The Journal of Political Economy* 113(1): 83–120.

Garza Toledo, E.d.l. and Valdivia, J.M. 1991. Sindicatos frente a la productividad: Telefonistas y electricistas. *El Cotidiano* 41.

Gilbert, A. 2007. Water for all: How to combine public management with commercial practice for the benefit of the poor? *Urban Studies* 44(8): 1559–1579.

Goldman, M. 2007. How "water for all!" policy became hegemonic: The power of the World Bank and its transnational policy networks. *Geoforum* 38(5): 786–800.

Grusky, S. and Fiil-Flynn, M. 2004. Will the World Bank back down? Water privatization in a climate of global protest. Washington, DC: Public Citizen Water for All Campaign.

Gutiérrez Aguilar, R. 2008. "We won but we lost". *Ukhampacha Bolivia.* 3 March. www.ubnoticias.org/en/article/we-won-but-we-lost.

Gwynne, R.N. and Kay, C. 2000. Views from the periphery: Futures of neoliberalism in Latin America. *Third World Quarterly* 21(1): 141–156.

Hall, D. and Lobina, E. 2006. *Pipe dreams: The failure of the private sector to invest in water services in developing countries.* London: PSIRU.

Hall, D., Lobina, E., Corral, V., Hoedeman, O., Terhorst, P., Pigeon, M. and Kishimoto, S. 2009. *Public-public partnerships (PUPs) in water.* Greenwich, UK: PSIRU.

John, S.S. 2009. *Bolivia's radical tradition: Permanent revolution in the Andes.* Tuscon, AZ: University of Arizona Press.

Kasmir, S. 1996. *The myth of Mondragón: Cooperatives, politics, and working-class life in a Basque town.* Albany: State University of New York Press.

Keck, M.E. and Sikkink, K. 1998. *Activists beyond borders: Advocacy networks in international politics.* Ithaca: Cornell University Press.

Kohl, B.H. and Farthing, L.C. 2006. *Impasse in Bolivia: Neoliberal hegemony and popular resistance.* London and New York: Zed Books.

Laurie, N. and Crespo, C. 2007. Deconstructing the best case scenario: Lessons from water politics in La Paz-El Alto, Bolivia. *Geoforum* 38(5): 841–854.

Lipton, M. 1977. *Why poor people stay poor: A study of urban bias in world development.* London: Temple Smith.

Lobina, E. and Hall, D. 2007. *Water privatization and restructuring in Latin America.* Greenwich, UK: PSIRU.

Maltz, H. 2005. Porto Alegre's water: Public and for all. In Balanyá, B., Brennan, B., Hoedeman, O., Kishimoto, S. and Terhorst, P. (Eds), *Reclaiming public water: Achievements, struggles and visions from around the world,* pp. 29–36. Porto Alegre: TNI.

Marx, K. 1993. *Grundrisse. Foundations of the critique of political economy.* London: Penguin Books and New Left Review.

McMichael, P. 2008. *Development and social change: A global perspective.* Los Angeles: Pine Forge Press.

McNally, D. 1993. *Against the market: Political economy, market socialism and the Marxist critique*. London: Verso.

Nickson, A. 1998. *A water co-operative for a large city: Does it work?* id21 Development Research. 6 February. www.id21.org.

Novelli, M. 2004. Globalisations, social movement unionism and new internationalisms: The role of strategic learning in the transformation of the municipal workers union of EMCALI. *Globalisation, Societies and Education* 2(2): 161–190.

Nun, J. 1969. Superpoblación relativa, ejército industrial de reserva y masa marginal. *Revista Latinoamericana de Sociología* 5(2): 178–235.

O'Donnell, G.A. 1993. On the state, democratization and some conceptual problems: A Latin American view with glances at some postcommunist countries. *World Development* 21(8): 1355–1369.

Olivera, O. and Lewis, T. 2004. *¡Cochabamba! Water War in Bolivia*. Cambridge, MA: South End Press.

Pérez, J. 2005. Social resistance in El Alto-Bolivia. In Balanyá, B., Brennan, B., Hoedeman, O., Kishimoto, S. and Terhorst, P. (Eds), *Reclaiming public water: achievements, struggles and visions from around the world*. Porto Alegre, Brazil: TNI and CEO. www.tni.org/books/waterelalto.pdf.

Phumpiu, P. and Gustafsson, J.E. 2009. When are partnerships a viable tool for development? Institutions and partnerships for water and sanitation service in Latin America. *Water Resources Management* 23(1): 19–38.

Portes, A. and Roberts, B.R. 2005. The free-market city: Latin American urbanization in the years of the neoliberal experiment. *Studies in Comparative International Development* 40(1): 43–82.

Ravina, A. O. 1996. Public services in the area of the social economy in Argentina. *Annals of Public and Cooperative Economics* 67(3): 451–462.

Red Vida. 2009. Acuerdo marco de compromiso. San Severino, Uruguay. Mimeo.

Sader, E. 2009. Postneoliberalism in Latin America. *Development Dialogue* 51: 171–179.

Sánchez Gómez, L. 2004. Directing SEMAPA: An interview with Luis Sánchez-Gómez. In Olivera, O. and Lewis, T. (Eds), *Cochabamba! Water War in Bolivia*, pp. 87–94. Cambridge, MA: Southend Press.

Sánchez Gómez, L. and Olivera, M. 2004. ¿Y después de la guerra del agua . . . qué? In Ceceña, A.E. (Ed), *La guerra por el agua y por la vida*, pp.160–166. Cochabamba: Coordinadora de Defensa del Agua y de la Vida.

Sánchez Gómez, L. and Terhorst, P. 2005. Cochabamba, Bolivia: Public-collective partnership after the Water War. In Balanyá, B., Brennan, B., Hoedeman, O., Kishimoto, S. and Terhorst, P. (Eds), *Reclaiming public water: Achievements, struggles and visions from around the world*, pp.121–130. Porto Alegre, Brazil: TNI and CEO.

Sandbrook, R., Edelman, M. Heller, P. and Teichman, J. 2007. *Social democracy in the global periphery: Origins, challenges, prospects*. Cambridge, UK: Cambridge University Press.

Santos, C. and Villarreal, A. 2005. Uruguay: Victorious social struggle for water. In Balanyá, B., Brennan, B., Hoedeman, O., Kishimoto, S. and Terhorst, P. (Eds), *Reclaiming public water: Achievements, struggles and visions from around the world*. Porto Alegre, Brazil: TNI and CEO.

Simpson, R. 2009. *Brazil and Venezuela: Civil society organisation involvement in urban water sector reform*. London, UK: WaterAid.

Souza, S. and Kruse, T. 2002. International solidarity strengthens the struggle. *Public Citizen*, 10 August. www.citizen.org/cmep/Water/cmep_Water/reports/bolivia/articles.cfm?ID=8913.

Spronk, S. 2007. Roots of resistance to urban water privatization in Bolivia: The "new working class", the crisis of neoliberalism, and public services. *International Labour and Working-Class History* 71: 8–28.

———. 2009a. Making the poor work for their services: Neo-liberalism and "pro-poor" privatization in El Alto, Bolivia. *Canadian Journal of Development Studies-Revue Canadienne D'Études du Développement* 28(3–4): 397–413.

———. 2009b. Water privatization and the prospects for trade union revitalization in the public sector: Case studies from Bolivia and Peru. *Just Labour: A Canadian Journal of Work and Society* 14: 164–176.

———. 2010. Water and sanitation utilities in the global South: Re-centering the debate on "efficiency". *Radical Review of Political Economics* 42(2): 156–174.

Swyngedouw, E. 2004. *Social power and the urbanization of water—Flows of power.* Oxford: Oxford University Press.

Taks, J. 2008. "El Agua es de todos/Water for all": Water resources and development in Uruguay. *Development* 51: 17–22.

Terhorst, P. 2008. Huancayo: From resistance to public-public partnership. In Balanyá, B., Brennan, B., Hoedeman, O., Kishimoto, S. and Terhorst, P. (Eds), *Reclaiming public water: Achievements, struggles and visions from around the world.* Porto Alegre, Brazil: TNI [Transnational Institute] and CEO [Corporate Europe Observatory]. [electronic document] http://www.tni.org/sites/www.tni.org/archives/books/waterhuancayo.pdf.

Thorp, R. 1998. *Progress, poverty and exclusion: An economic history of Latin America in the 20th century.* Washington, DC and Baltimore, MD: Inter-American Development Bank.

Weisbrot, M., Baker, D., Kraev, E. and Chen, J. 2002. The scorecard on globalization 1980–2000: Its consequences for economic and social well-being. *International Journal of Health Services* 32(2): 229–253.

———. 2006. The scorecard on development: 25 years of diminished progress. *International Journal of Health Services* 36(2): 211–234.

WHO (World Health Organization) and UNICEF. 2010. *Progress on sanitation and drinking water: 2010 update.* Geneva, Switzerland and New York: WHO and UNICEF.

Wickham-Crowley, T. 1992. *Guerrillas and revolution in Latin America: A comparative study of insurgents and regimes since 1956.* Princeton: Princeton University Press.

Yavarí, L.F. 2005. Management of basic drinking water and sanitation services by a co-operative in Bolivia. In Balanyá, B., Brennan, B., Hoedeman, O., Kishimoto, S. and Terhorst, P. (Eds), *Reclaiming public water: Achievements, struggles and visions from around the world.* Porto Alegre, Brazil: TNI and CEO.

Younger, P.L. 2007. Pro-poor water technologies working both ways: Lessons from a two-way, South-North interchange. *Geoforum* 38(5): 828–840.

Zibechi, R. 2009a. Bolivia: Plan 3000-Resistance and social change at the heart of racism. Upsidedownworld. 27 May. www.upsidedownworld.org/main/content/view/1849/68.

———. 2009b. Cochabamba: From war to water management. Center for International Policy (CIP), Americas Program, 2 June. www.alternet.org/water/140393/cochabamba:_from_war_to_water_management.

INTERVIEWS

Condori, Fabian. System Administrator, APAAS, Cochabamba, Bolivia, 19 May 2009 (conducted in person by Eva Carvajal).

Gareia Carreño and José Hoé. President of the Directorship of the Community Water System of La Sirena, Cali, Colombia, 22 May 2009 (conducted in person by Susan Spronk and Carlos Crespo).

Grandydier, Abraham. ASICA-Sur, Cochabamba, Bolivia, 14 September 2004, (conducted in person by Susan Spronk).

Isarra, Luis. Leader of FENTAP, Huancayo, Peru, 26 May 2008 (conducted in person by Susan Spronk).

Levenzon, Fernanda. Centre on Housing Rights and Evictions (COHRE, Porto Alegre, Brazil), Cali, Colombia, 19 May 2009 (conducted in person by Susan Spronk).

Margarita López. Secretary General, ACUAVALLE, Cali, Colombia, 21 May 2009 (personal interview by Susan Spronk and Carlos Crespo).

Marquisio, Adriana. FFOSE of Uruguay, Cali, Colombia, 30 May 2009 (conducted in person by Susan Spronk and Carlos Crespo).

Mellín, Marco. Board of Directors, Managing Association of the Communal Aqueduct of Naranjo, Costa Rica, 28 May 2009 (conducted by email by Eva Carvajal).

Reyes, Erasto. *Bloque Popular* of Honduras, Cali, Colombia, May 2009 (conducted in person by Susan Spronk).

Terhorst, Philipp. Researcher and activist with the Transnational Institute (TNI), Cali, Colombia, 20 May 2009 (conducted in person by Susan Spronk).

16 Alternatives in the Electricity Sector in Latin America

Daniel Chavez

On the night of October 10, 2009, while most Mexicans celebrated the qualification of their national football team to the World Cup 2010, police troops seized the premises of the state-owned electricity company *Luz y Fuerza del Centro* (LyFC, Central Region Light and Power), which served more than 6 million users in the capital city and adjacent municipalities. Such action followed a decree of liquidation signed by Mexican President Felipe Calderón that referred to the company's allegedly proven history of financial and operational inefficiency. A larger public enterprise, the *Comisión Federal de Electricidad* (CFE, Federal Electric Commission) took over the services until then provided by LyFC. The mighty *Sindicato Mexicano de Electricistas* (SME, Mexican Electrical Workers' Union) perceived the closure of the company as a virtual declaration of war against unionized labour, since approximately 45,000 employees would be fired. Thousands of SME members, backed by other workers, students, peasants, progressive intellectuals, and a wide range of social and political activists, marched in the streets to express their anger. The mobilization continued for several weeks, and included a huge demonstration on November 11, 2009 that virtually paralyzed traffic in downtown Mexico City. The government was forced to rule out privatization, but many social sectors believed that the closure of such a big company constituted a major step towards the full liberalization of the electricity sector, which most Mexicans see as a symbol of national pride worth defending.

Half a year later, on May 1, 2010, Bolivian President Evo Morales sent army troops to nationalize four electricity companies, including a subsidiary of the French transnational corporation GDF Suez, reaffirming the trend in that country towards greater state control over the economy. In previous years, Morales had also commemorated the International Workers' Day by nationalizing other companies controlled by foreign investors. "We are fulfilling the people's vociferous demand to recover and nationalize natural resources and basic services. We are here to nationalize all the hydroelectric plants that were previously owned by the state, in accordance with the new Bolivian Constitution. Basic services cannot be a private business. We are recovering the energy, the light, for all Bolivians", the President proclaimed in Cochabamba, announcing that the state had regained control of 80% of electricity generation and that his aim was to achieve in the near future the complete nationalization of the power sector (*Brecha* 2010, 23).

These two stories portray the core tensions and the social, economic, and political forces that have shaped the electricity sector in Latin America. During the past three decades, mainstream policy officials, business executives, consultants, and conservative researchers have been excessively optimistic about the potential impacts of market-oriented reforms in the sector. Many scholars considered privatization and deregulation to be the best and/or only means to increase efficiency of public services and promote economic and social development. But rather than regional convergence towards open markets, we see in Latin America a diverse mix of institutional arrangements, including the revival of state ownership and other emerging alternatives to marketization. Beginning in the 1980s, all Latin American countries implemented profound policy reforms in the electricity sector, which resulted in diverse models for market liberalization and institutional restructuring. The tide began to change in the late 1990s with the regional expansion of several left-of-centre governments, which meant strengthening state ownership and even the renationalization of power utilities (Barrett et al, 2008).

The purpose of this chapter is to contribute relevant information and analysis to ongoing national, regional, and global debates on reforms in the electricity sector in Latin America. We begin with an overview of the sector, followed by a summary of the types and trends of "alternatives to privatization" found in the region based on the same conceptual and methodological framework employed in the other studies presented in this book, including an analysis of their successes and failures. The concluding section summarizes the key findings and recommendations of the study.

This "mapping exercise" required surveying a wide range of organizational arrangements defined in the taxonomy originally outlined for the project (see Chapter 2, this volume, for more detail), which included different kinds of organizations with varying characteristics and service objectives. In practice, the most important type of alternative found in the region was the public enterprise (PE), which is sometimes also referred to as government controlled enterprise (GCE), state-owned enterprise, parastatals, public companies or public corporations. The electricity sector in Latin America includes various forms of PEs, with much heterogeneity in terms of inclusion in the broader ownership and managerial structures and diverse degrees of financial and administrative autonomy, as we shall see below.

The survey also covered non-profit and non-governmental service delivery arrangements, including both sizeable cooperatives and small-scale generation and distribution units such as microdams and wind turbines run by local communities and user cooperatives across the region. Although they comply with some of the criteria used to identify "alternatives", such small-scale private service providers are not very significant in Latin America. They might constitute an appropriate solution in remote and isolated areas, but they provide only a tiny fraction of the power consumed in the region. For the global South as a whole, between 10 and 50 million people were served by approximately 7,000 small-scale service providers, including both for- and non-profit (Kariuki and Schwartz 2005). The vast majority of those arrangements (85%) were located in Asia; less than 500 small-scale initiatives of this kind were found in Africa, the Middle East, and Latin America. Moreover, although larger cooperatives are strong players in the electricity market of some countries—in Costa Rica, for instance, the *cooperativas eléctricas* cover the needs of more than 12% of the population, and in Argentina a significant share of the distribution is also controlled by cooperatives (Zilocchi 1998)—in general they tend to operate as any other profit-seeking private company. From an idealistic perspective, user cooperatives might represent a valuable alternative to privatization, being a legitimate self-management or co-management option that guarantees coverage, participation, equity, and social control over the production and management of vital public services; however, the empirical evidence that supports such a view is weak.

The information and analysis presented in this paper derive from a combination of different sources and research methods, comprising (i) the author's own fieldwork in the region; (ii) a comprehensive desktop review of academic, technical and journalistic publications, and internal documents, including corporate Websites; and (iii) detailed surveys conducted by local researchers based in the Southern Cone, the Andean Region, and Central America.[1] The study relied on an extensive review of over 30 electricity companies in different national, regional, and municipal settings.

Despite the efforts undertaken to cover as wide a range of service providers as possible, and in as much depth as possible, the methodology faced clear limitations. Latin America is a vast and highly heterogeneous region. Drawing meaningful conclusions based on a comparative appraisal of the many and diverse experiences that evolved in the region is not an easy task. The institutional schemes, the managerial processes, and the social, economic and political actors engaged in the development of the electricity sector are many, and therefore it has been very difficult to document subtle features that often are key determinants of the categorization of an experience as an "alternative". But such is the nature of exploratory research of this type. It is hoped that future detailed case studies based on this initial mapping exercise will be able to provide more fine-grained insights.

ELECTRICITY SERVICES IN THE LATIN AMERICAN REGION

Energy, and electricity in particular, is a crucial component of social and economic development. As stated in a recent report published by the World Health Organization (WHO) and the United Nations Development Programme (UNDP):

lack of access to modern energy services dramatically affects health, limits opportunities and widens the gap between the haves and have-nots. The vulnerability of the poor is only worsened with recent challenges from climate change, a global financial crisis, and volatile energy prices. (Neira and Vandeweerd 2009, i)

Electricity, in particular, is and has been of critical importance to economic and social development across the global South. However, as acknowledged in a study published by the Economic Commission for Latin America and the Caribbean (ECLAC), UNDP, and the Club de Madrid, there has been little research "on the linkage between access to energy services and attainment of national goals for development, poverty reduction and environmental protection" (Bárcena et al, 2009, 5).

At present, the overall access to electricity in Latin America—where several countries have reached almost universal coverage—seems less problematic than in other parts of the world, as Figure 16.1 shows. Nevertheless, a closer look at the region reveals deeper problems:

[D]espite the high rates of urbanization in Latin America and the Caribbean, almost 30 million people still do not have electricity, of whom 21.4 million (73 percent) are poor. The lack of electrical services is directly related to poverty: it is estimated that, of the total poor in the region (200 million), about 10 percent have no electrical services and this figure rises to 30 percent in the case of the absolute poor. . . . Efficient and effective access to energy services is a vital requirement for attainment of the Millennium Development Goals, which in turn are intrinsically linked to the enhancement of human rights and of democracy. (Bárcena et al, 2009, 7)

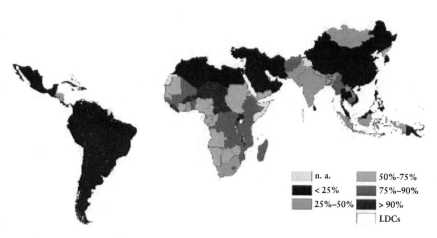

	n. a.		50%–75%
	< 25%		75%–90%
	25%–50%		> 90%
			LDCs

Figure 16.1   Share of population without access to electricity in the global South.

According to the most up-to-date official statistics by the Latin American Energy Organization (OLADE 2008), electricity accounted for 23% of the total energy consumed in the region in the year 2007, of which 56.7% was generated by hydroelectric power and 39.7% by thermoelectric facilities. Nuclear generation, being restricted to Argentina, Brazil, and Mexico, contributed 2.4% of the total supply, while the combined energy produced by geothermal, solar, and wind plants only reached 1.1%. However, while Brazil, Venezuela, and Peru are among the 10 countries in the world considered to have high levels of water resources, the installed hydroelectric capacity constitutes only 19.9% of the generating potential of the region, and the nine countries with higher consumption concentrate 95.6% of the hydroelectric generation across the region. The hydroelectric potential effectively used is only 5.2% in Peru and 40.1% in Venezuela. On the other hand, the rate of consumption of electricity in the region increases at around 4.0% per year, which means it doubles every 17 years (Goldemberg 2009). Table 16.1 presents a more detailed description of the electricity sector in 19 Latin American countries.

In institutional terms, the profile of the electricity sector has changed radically in Latin America in the past two decades. All countries in the region carried out profound reforms throughout the 1990s, adopting diverse institutional formats with a wide range of options as regards the degree of market openness and the promotion of private investment. The haste led in some cases to processes of privatization without having established a consistent regulatory framework prior to the sale of state-owned companies.

The pioneer of neoliberal reform in the region was Chile. The government launched a wave of privatization of public services in 1982, in the context of a brutal military dictatorship led by General Augusto Pinochet. Following the fundamentalist free-market principles advocated by a group of young economists trained in the US, the so-called *Chicago Boys* (Valdes 2008), Chile became the first country in the region to deregulate the power sector, soon followed by a group of neighbouring countries that between 1992 and 1996 implemented a similar model. Among them, the most radical case was Argentina, which privatized public services on a massive scale.

Brazil, Latin America's largest country, followed a different path. Around 1995, encouraged by the World Bank, the government "began efforts to try to impose a near exact copy of the 1990 British privatisation/liberalisation reforms to its electricity sector" (Thomas 2009b, 4), but a few years later the process concluded with the state still being the main actor, after the leftist *Partido dos Trabalhadores* (PT, Workers Party, led by Luis Inácio Lula da Silva) accessed national office in 2003. The current picture of the Brazilian power sector is one of a mixed public-private ownership system in which the state dominates electricity generation (being responsible for 85% of the total), while the private sector dominates distribution (80% of the national market), and transmission is relatively equally divided (17 of the 26 operating companies are private, but the public ones are larger). A recent

Table 16.1 Overview of the Electricity Sector in Latin American Countries, Year 2007

Country	Population (million)	Installed capacity			National annual consumption	Per capita residential consumption	Electricity coverage	Degree of privatization		
		Total	Hydro	Thermal				Generation	Transmission	Distribution
Argentina	39.0	28.1 GW	35%	61%	122.9 TWh	749.3 kWh	95.0%			
Bolivia	9.6	1.5 GW	32%	68%	5.3 TWh	177.5 kWh	69.0%			
Brazil	190.1	101.0 GW	76%	22%	486.0 TWh	472.5 kWh	97.9%			
Chile	16.4	15.9 GW	34%	66%	60.1 TWh	536.1 kWh	99.0%			
Colombia	46.8	13.7 GW	62%	34%	53.7 TWh	382.0 kWh	94.0%			
Costa Rica	4.4	2.1 GW	67%	21%	9.2 TWh	733.9 kWh	98.6%			
Cuba	11.4	5.4 GW	1%	99%	17.6 TWh	547.8 kWh	95.5%			
Dominican R.	9.8	5.5 GW	8%	92%	14.8 TWh	447.7 kWh	95.7%			
Ecuador	13.4	4.5 GW	46%	54%	18.2 TWh	301.7 kWh	90.2%			
El Salvador	7.0	1.4 GW	34%	51%	5.6 TWh	223.1 kWh	95.5%			
Guatemala	13.0	2.1 GW	36%	62%	8.6 TWh	174.8 kWh	84.7%			
Honduras	7.5	1.6 GW	32%	68%	6.3 TWh	287.5 kWh	67.0%			
México	107.5	49.9 GW	23%	72%	231.4 TWh	430.6 kWh	96.0%			
Nicaragua	5.6	0.8 GW	12%	77%	3.3 TWh	123.0 kWh	69.2%			
Panama	3.3	1.5 GW	58%	42%	6.4 TWh	478.3 kWh	83.0%			
Paraguay	6.4	8.1 GW	100%	0%	8.6 TWh	547.7 kWh	93.2%			
Peru	28.3	7.0 GW	46%	54%	29.9 TWh	229.3 kWh	78.1%			
Uruguay	3.5	2.2 GW	69%	31%	9.22 TWh	875.2 kWh	99.0%			
Venezuela	27.0	22.5 GW	65%	35%	110.1 TWh	741.4 kWh	97.0%			

References   ● Fully owned or managed by the state   ● Fully privatized

Source: Author's elaboration, based on data published by (OLADE 2008), national regulators, and electricity companies.

appraisal of the Brazilian power sector highlights the importance of public planning as a key component of the so-called "new model": [2]

> Power planners in Brazil have made a measured return from market to plan. Replacing a strategy of comprehensive deregulation where control and oversight are automated through the market, the New Model uses markets not in an integrated and interlinked manner, but in discretely delineated areas to achieve targets established by a coordinated planning exercise. It is the plan that links the various elements of the power sector together as opposed to the market, which was supposed to do so under the earlier policy. Its origin can be traced to Brazil's early successful experiments with state-led electric power development. (Tankha 2010, 193)

In terms of expansion of supply, Latin American countries attracted a significant amount of private investment until about 2000. One type of business that flourished in several places was small, independent producers with the ability to sell electricity to large customers, both public and private, mainly based on thermal generation. As the process of liberalization deepened, the number of major foreign investors in the region has been reduced to a handful of European and US corporations, predominantly Spanish firms, which have located in several countries in the region simultaneously (Hall 2007, Rozas Balbontín 2009, Thomas 2009a, Wilde-Ramsing and Steinweg 2010).

After more than two decades of market-driven reforms, previous promoters of the free market approach have already acknowledged that privatization has become out of favour or that previous reforms in this direction were too flawed (Andrés et al, 2007, 126). This is consistent with global trends: a comparative study published almost a decade ago had already stated that "while most technical assessments classify privatization as a success, it remains widely and increasingly unpopular, largely because of the perception that it is fundamentally unfair, both in conception and execution" (Birdsall and Nellis 2002, 1). By then, the interests of major transnational corporations in the power sector had already weakened, and several private investors had withdrawn from Latin America and other regions of the global South (Hall et al, 2009).

ALTERNATIVES TO MARKETIZATION IN THE ELECTRICITY SECTOR

Notwithstanding these concerns, and despite obvious limitations of the free-market paradigm in the wake of the global financial and economic crises since 2008, the hegemonic position amongst mainstream analysts of public services reform is still that public ownership and management of services constitutes the wrong approach for promoting economic and social development. They point to a number of reasons, including the failure of governments to infuse public enterprises with a strong developmental mission, equating the state with inefficiency, corruption, cronyism, clientelism, and other vices. As one of the most influential theorists in the field has put it, "The inherent limitations of state ownership render public enterprises ineffective" (Rondinelli 2008, 22).

Faced with such arguments, Latin American defenders of the public sector could retort today, reaffirming physicist Galileo Galilei's response to the orthodox church doctrine of his time about his theory that the earth revolves around the sun: *eppur si muove!* (and yet it moves). The empirical evidence portrayed in Table 16.1 shows that those countries in which electricity remained totally or mostly in the hands of the state have today equal or higher rates of coverage than those that opted for privatization. This does not mean to deny the many and profound problems of Latin American public enterprises, but we return to this later in the chapter.

Enthusiasm for market reforms and greater private participation in the electricity sector has receded across the region during the past decade, but there are several Latin American countries in which PEs were never privatized and/or the transfer of assets to private owners has been negligible, and others in which market-driven reforms have been reversed. The next section runs through the origin and evolution of the region's PEs, reviews the current governance arrangements of the public sector, and assesses the performance of the state in terms of service delivery.

ORIGIN AND EVOLUTION OF PUBLIC ENTERPRISES IN THE POWER SECTOR

Across Latin America, in the first half of the 20th century, electricity was mainly a for-profit endeavour. Prior to the 1930s, the private sector was the first, and in many places the only, entity responsible for generation, transmission, and distribution of electric power. Electricity generation had a fast and selective growth, to the point where, by the mid-1920s, Argentina, Chile, and Brazil were global leaders in penetration rates. Chile, in particular, had the second highest per capita power consumption in the world, behind France. Service provision, however, was concentrated in urban and affluent areas, since commercial operators were not interested in expanding the grids to rural and/or unprofitable localities (Millán 2006).

Between the 1930s and the 1960s, the failure of the market approach pushed Latin American governments towards the nationalization of private companies, in particular in those countries governed by charismatic nationalist leaders, such as Getulio Vargas in Brazil (1930–1945 and 1951–1954), Lázaro Cárdenas in Mexico (1934–1940), and Juan Domingo Perón in Argentina (1946–1955). In Brazil, the state challenged the predominantly foreign control, which was not meeting the electricity needs of the poorer, suburban, and rural sectors of the population. In 1934, the *Varguista* government passed legislation that required government authorization to run all hydropower plants and imposed tighter controls over the private sector, including a tariff freeze and the cancellation of new licenses to foreign-owned firms during World War II (Marques 1997, Baer and McDonald 1998). In Mexico, two foreign conglomerates controlled a substantial share of the electricity sector. In 1936, a major strike organized by the SME triggered government intervention, in line with Cárdenas' policy of cooperation between labour and the state, setting the political context for the creation, in 1937, of the Federal Electric Commission, which in the following years would become the country's second most powerful enterprise (Reséndiz Núñez 1994). In Argentina, between 1910 and 1930, three companies owned by foreign investors were accountable for 74% of national power generation capacity (Lanciotti 2008). The private sector continued to be the main actor until 1943, when the Argentine government created a regulatory agency and began to exert pressure towards nationalization. Such trends gathered speed and political support after 1946 under a *Peronista* government that promoted a more proactive role of the state in the electricity sector, within a much broader nationalist and welfarist agenda.

In the post-war period, most Latin American governments launched ambitious state-driven programmes aimed at expanding the electricity sector, as a way to promote economic growth and respond to the growing social needs of the population. In Brazil, the government promoted a national electrification plan and created new PEs for its implementation in the northeast and southeast regions. Regional (state level) authorities were also allowed to create their own electricity companies, with financial support from the National Economic and Social Development Bank (BNDES). As a result, the share of the private sector in generation dropped from 82% in 1952 to 34% in 1962.

South America's largest electricity company, the *Centrais Elétricas Brasileiras S.A.* (Eletrobras, Brazilian Electric Power Corporation) was founded in 1962, followed by the nationalization in 1964 and 1979 of the two biggest companies that had remained in private hands (Hamaguchi 2002). In Mexico, the government gained control in 1960 of the two large private corporations that were still active. The Mexican decree of nationalization was based on three premises: (i) the state's goal to secure harmonious national development, guaranteeing its benefits to all citizens; (ii) a coherent public response to the growing demand for electricity; and (iii) the state's responsibility for the provision of electric power "for the benefit of society, not for private interest" (Rodríguez 1994, 28).

Throughout the 1960s, the installed capacity grew substantially in most countries of the region, averaging 12% annually, which meant doubling in size every six years. Such growth was enthusiastically supported by international financial organizations such as the Inter-American Development Bank (IDB) and the World Bank, which financed large hydropower plants and new transmission lines that expanded the coverage and contributed to the higher economic efficiency of state-owned electricity companies (Millán 2006). Across the region, the state began to assume even bigger responsibilities. In Brazil, for instance, under the developmentalist administration of Juscelino Kubitschek, a quarter of all federal investments were directed towards the power sector, laying the foundation for a sustained cycle of growth during which the sector expanded at an annual rate of almost 10% over the following 10 years (Dias Leite 2007). Throughout the region, Latin American countries joined the global "Keynesian consensus", with governments taking a primordial role in the promotion of national economic growth, supporting industrial development and the expansion of social welfare programmes.

By the 1970s, the profile of the Latin American electricity sector was constituted by a diversity of institutional arrangements. In several countries the chosen public alternative had been the development of vertically integrated national enterprises, as exemplified by the *Instituto Costarricense de Electricidad* (ICE, Costa Rican Electricity Institute), the Uruguayan *Administración Nacional de Usinas y Trasmisiones Eléctricas* (UTE, National Electric Utilities Administration), and the Paraguayan *Administración Nacional de Electricidad* (ANDE, National Electricity Administration), among several other cases already mentioned. In Brazil, diverse public bodies became shareholders of Eletrobras, which developed as a massive federal holding company with large generation and transmission enterprises as subsidiaries: *Companhia Hidro Elétrica de São Francisco* (Chesf), *Furnas Centrais Elétricas* (Furnas), *Centrais Elétricas do Norte do Brasil* (Eletronorte), and *Empresa Transmissora de Energia Elétrica do Sul do Brasil* (Eletrosul). Moreover, Eletrobras was made accountable for many responsibilities usually assigned in other countries to the Ministry of Energy, such as strategic planning and research in the field of electric power, energy efficiency programmes, and financial support to other PEs.

In some countries, powerful regional and municipal power utilities had also emerged as important players. Three subnational PEs in particular are often referred to as good examples of the capacities of the subnational state as an efficient entrepreneur in the electricity sector: in Brazil, the *Companhia Paranaense de Energia* (COPEL, Energy Company of Parana) and the *Companhia Energetica de Minas Gerais* (CEMIG, Energy Company of Minas Gerais), both owned by regional authorities; and in Colombia, the *Empresas Públicas de Medellín* (EPM, Public Enterprises Conglomerate of Medellín), owned by a municipal authority. Brazil has a strong tradition of subnational PEs in the electricity sector as well. The majority of the distribution companies, with the exception of the enterprises that served the cities of Rio de Janeiro, Espírito Santo, and Brasilia, were owned by regional authorities. Besides COPEL of Parana, the largest state companies—in São Paulo, Minas Gerais, Rio Grande do Sul, and Rio de Janeiro—were in full or in part also vertically integrated.

In Colombia, by the turn of the century, when other countries had already completed the cycle of privatization, the state was still in control of over 60% of generation, 100% of transmission, and 60% of distribution. Two municipal companies, the already-mentioned EPM and the *Empresa de Energía Eléctrica de Bogotá* (EEEB, Electric Public Enterprise of Bogotá) have been generating and distributing around 40% of the country's electric power for several decades. The public system also included regional companies, owned by the national state, including the *Instituto Colombiano de Energía Eléctrica* (ICEL), the *Corporación Eléctrica de la Costa Atlántica* (CORELCA), the *Corporación Regional del Valle del Cauca* (CVC), and *Interconexión Eléctrica S.A.* (ISA, Electric Interconnections Ltd.). The latter, a national enterprise jointly owned by the municipal and regional companies mentioned above, evolved as the owner of the interconnecting grid and generated a big portion of the power consumed in Colombia.

Besides national, regional and municipal PEs, the public power sector in Latin America is also composed of three binational entities that were established to operate very large hydroelectric projects in neighbouring rivers: Itaipú (jointly built by Brazil and Paraguay with a generating capacity of 12,500 MW was for many years the world's largest hydropower project), Yaciretá (Argentina–Paraguay), and Salto Grande (Argentina–Uruguay). These initiatives evolved in the 1970s in the context of agreements between repressive military regimes. The construction of Salto Grande and Yaciretá relied on strong financial support from multilateral development banks. Despite its tainted origin, Salto Grande is generally perceived as a successful project that delivered its anticipated developmental objectives. In the other two cases, the evaluation is much more negative, since the projects were constructed with many delays and with heavy additional and unaccounted costs. The case of Itaipú is often also mentioned in political debates as an example of Brazil's "sub-imperialist" identity, based on the abusive share of revenues that overwhelmingly benefit the Brazilian interests to the detriment of Paraguay, the weaker partner.

CURRENT OWNERSHIP AND MANAGERIAL PROFILES

In terms of ownership, three scenarios coexist in the region:

- *Exclusive state ownership.* As noted above, this was the situation in most countries of the region before market-driven reforms. At present, only two countries—Paraguay and Venezuela—are included in this category. Bolivia is expected to join this group in the future, after the government announced in May 2010 the forthcoming full renationalization of the electricity sector.
- *Mixed property.* Private investors can be shareholders of companies partially owned by the state. It also refers to diverse forms of private-public

partnerships and the existence of independent power producers that sell electricity to the state or to large industrial consumers.

- *Private property.* This category refers to those countries in which the electricity system is predominantly privately owned. In this case, two options are possible: the first refers to vertical segmentation, with mandatory separation of generation, transmission, and distribution (unbundling), while the second allows the possibility of vertical integration.

In terms of electricity sector management, there are four distinct situations:

- *Monopolistic control.* Before liberalization, most countries of the region based the delivery of electricity services on a single state-owned company. The power sector was considered a "natural monopoly", as the functioning of one entity as owner and operator of services in one area made economic sense, whether property was public or private. At present, there are only two Latin American countries in which private companies are *not* part of the system.
- *Single buyer.* This is a situation that applies to many countries in the region where the state remains the main player, which has allowed the incorporation of private actors through a limited opening. It has occurred predominantly·in generation.
- *Integration.* This situation implies a distinct division of roles between the state and private companies. The latter plan and implement their activities according to their own rationality. The state plays mainly the role of regulator, taking the main decisions concerning investments, tariffs, and the overall development of the sector. Competition in each subsector is open to both public and private companies. This situation, therefore, does not imply vertical or horizontal disintegration. Competition in each subsector is open to public, private or mixed-property companies. However, in practice, competition is very often limited by concession contracts and by the strict demarcation of market shares by geographic areas or types of customers.
- *Open market.* The idea of a natural monopoly remains in place only for transmission and distribution of electricity, where open competition seems unfeasible or inappropriate. In systems large enough to allow and ensure full competition, several players are allowed to compete in the segments of generation and marketing.

Table 16.2 presents the diversity of ownership and managerial schemes in the region in 2007, after Venezuela nationalized its power sector.

The current institutional framework of the power sector is constantly challenged by social discontent in many Latin American countries. Many plans for further privatization had to be cancelled due to violent riots, as happened in Peru in 2000, while annual surveys show that public support for privatization has remained low, falling from 48% to 22% between 1998

Table 16.2 Latin American and Caribbean Electricity System Structures, 2007

Ownership options			a. Monopolistic control	b. Single buyer	c. Integration	d. Open market
Private property	Vertical segmentation					Argentina Bolivia Guatemala Panama
	Vertical integration allowed					Chile El Salvador Peru Dominican Republic
	Mixed property			Brazil Ecuador Honduras Jamaica Mexico Trinidad and Tobago	Costa Rica Grenada Guyana Uruguay Cuba	Colombia Nicaragua
Exclusive state property			Venezuela	Suriname	Paraguay Venezuela	
					Managerial options	

Source: Author's elaboration, adapted from Poveda 2004

and 2003, reaching 33% in 2009 (Corporación Latinobarómetro 2009). Based on the analysis of the same data, Checchi et al argue that "less dogmatism and more realism is needed" in the region; "after all, in the EU as in the US, public ownership in water and energy industries and progressive tariff cross-subsidies are widespread" (2009, 348).

APPRAISAL OF ALTERNATIVES TO PRIVATIZATION

As national economies around the world strive to respond to the global crisis, states are back on the political agenda, and "it is widely accepted that they have no option but to rescue the market from itself" (Ramesh and Araral 2010, 1). It might be argued that this is exactly what states do in capitalist economies all the time, in a cyclical way. In several Latin American countries, however, the trend towards stronger and/or more dynamic states is not just a momentary phenomenon. Thus, this is a very timely moment to assess the alternative potential of PEs. This section provides a general appraisal of Latin American PEs in the power sector, based on some of the indicators of "success" used for this research. As already noted, the lack of detailed or disaggregated data pertaining to certain variables has prevented an in-depth analysis of all the criteria suggested by the research project's conceptual framework, but the summary below offers indications of general trends and will hopefully provoke further case study investigations.

Equity

Compared with Africa and Asia, the situation with electricity provision in Latin America is less dire, as many countries—particularly those that retained public ownership and management of utilities—have reached almost universal coverage. Moreover, those systems that were marketized had the advantage of "inheriting" well-developed public electrical systems, with accessibility levels well above 70% to begin with. As a result, electricity costs have been relatively low, with one study concluding that "only" about 20% of the region's households would have to pay more than 5% of household income for water or electricity if tariffs were set at cost recovery levels (Foster and Yepes 2006)—not ideal, but much better than Asia and Africa. However, the same report warned that reaching full cost recovery would generate, in the poorer countries, a real affordability problem for around half of the population.

By definition, privatization requires making the private sector profitable, so in some countries that implemented market-friendly reforms, tariffs increased based on the justification that they were below the cost of service provision. Public enterprises were not compelled to seek profits, but price inequality for residential and industrial consumption is a reality in several Latin American countries, with (low-income) citizens subsidizing big business. In 2009, several months before the closure of LyFC, the Mexican Electrical Workers' Union had presented a proposal to the federal government calling for the elimination of the so-called "high domestic consumption" rate and the creation of a "social rate", as well as an increase in the industrial tariff. In the words of a union leader interviewed by the author in November 2009:

> The President has forgotten that CFE and LyFC were established as public enterprises and therefore should not be run as private companies. They should never have profit as their top institutional priority. The Mexican people should not have to choose whether to eat or to pay the electricity bill. For us, it was unacceptable that tariffs averaged 99 cents per kWh for industrial consumers while the average for household consumers was 2.5 pesos per kWh [two-and-a-half times as high]. Last January [2009], the government approved a 20% reduction in the industrial rate, arguing that it was needed to support the national production in times of crisis. When he ordered the liquidation of LyFC, 70% of the company's revenues came from the industrial sector, and they were approximately 40,000 consumers. But LyFC had more than six million domestic users. We proposed a social tariff and the elimination of the high consumption domestic rate, because we knew that the industrial consumers could effortlessly pay twice or more what they were paying.

As a whole, Latin America has a long and ample tradition of social tariffs (Foster and Yepes 2006) that continues to evolve today. As this chapter was being written, several PEs were developing new schemes to subsidize power consumption by the poor. The Uruguayan company UTE, for instance, announced in July 2010 the introduction of a new tariff category expected to benefit low-consuming residential users. In a country of little more than 3 million inhabitants, around 150,000 users could benefit from the new social tariff. According to the Chair of the Board of Directors of the Uruguayan company:

> UTE is willing to participate in the social policies implemented by the Ministry of Social Development (Mides). Historically, UTE has contributed in terms of developing the power sector and securing access to electricity to every citizen, reaching in particular those in greater need. In fact, tariffs have been designed as a form of redistribution of wealth. The previous government had launched a special tariff that targeted households with low consumption, which had great results, and now we are fulfilling that objective and therefore they pay very little for electricity. Our technical team is working on new social programmes. That is something we have always done, but now we put greater emphasis on the social. (Matos 2010, 3)

Efficiency

Efficiency, or rather its absence, has been one of the main excuses used by advocates of the market to legitimize their offensive against PEs. In truth, many public electricity utilities had real troubles with poor collection of revenues, financial and technical losses, obsolete and decaying networks, and high costs of operation. The real or assumed governmental inefficiency during the fiscal crises of the 1970s and 1980s became the ideal argument used by the promoters of privatization against public ownership across the region. In this respect, Colombia constitutes an interesting case: on the one hand, the state-owned system succeeded in expanding national access to electrical services, but by 1990 it was responsible for 30% of the country's foreign debt. However, not every Colombian PE performed the same way: the municipal utility EPM managed to expand its services, while keeping healthy financial balances; it did not request constant cash transfers from the national government and is even today highlighted as one of the best examples of efficient public management (Millán 2006).

Based on the availability of published academic and journalistic litera-ture, it would seem that efficient Latin American PEs nowadays constitute a very small group. Efficiency was an issue that the Mexican government pointed at in 2009 to justify its liquidation of LyFC, the case highlighted at the beginning of this chapter. A press clip from that period summarizes the main allegations:

> The company was obsolete and ineffective, largely because it was almost totally controlled by a very strong workers' union, which had steadily gained power, prerogatives and absurd privileges, which meant that until its bankruptcy the company had lived out of governmental subsidies. The inhabitants of Mexico City, a metropolitan area of more than 20 million people, suffered from a bad electrical service: constant blackouts triggered by almost any cause, frequent voltage irregularities which hurt appliances, improper charges for energy consumption, old transmission posts at a high risk of falling, poles and repair materials abandoned in the streets and medians, slow repairs and consideration of complaints, bureaucracy, mistreatment and abuse of clients and awful customer service. (Bastidas Colinas 2009, 20)

There are multiple indicators that show that management and service pro-vision were indeed decaying long before LyFC was liquidated, in a way that resembled the reality of many Latin American utilities in previous decades. Nonetheless, from the perspective of the unionized workers and other critics (e.g. Sheinbaum Pardo 2009), the arguments given by the con-servative government are flawed. Because the national electricity system is interconnected and LyFC had been denied enough resources to build new generating plants, it was forced to buy power from CFE; as a result, LyFC generated less than 10% of the energy it transmitted and distributed. But despite being a public company, the energy received from CFE was bought at the same rate that the Federal Electricity Commission applied to any other buyer, public or private, even with some penalties. Moreover, the delayed introduction of automation systems would explain much of LyFC's inefficiency and bad service provision. Funding was very much required for the modernization and expansion of facilities, and the same applies today to the larger Mexican company CFE.

Beyond the recent debate about the performance record of Mexican power utilities, a broader regional and historical perspective shows that the ideological assumption about the alleged "inherent limitations" of state ownership has been invalidated by plenty of data from across Latin America. Historical analysis of the evolution of the power sector in Brazil, for instance, shows that PEs were able to evolve as highly successful companies, as a classic study on entrepreneurship in the public sector illustrates (Tendler 1968). State-owned electric companies, particularly in the area of generation, were able for many years to maintain a high degree of technical excellence. In a similar vein, more recent studies (Dubrovsky and Ruchansky 2010, Tankha 2010) maintain that PEs continue to be well-managed under state ownership. The success of state-driven power development in Brazil and other countries can be explained by a combination of technical and political factors. More than in other areas of public service provision, the electricity sector demands enormous investments that imply substantial coordination not only among the three subsectors (generation, transmission, and distribution) but also among diverse political, social, and economic actors, and therefore the matter of long-term technical planning becomes essential.

Previous studies have also highlighted the importance of decentralization and even competition among PEs (Tendler 1968). In Brazil there was a combination of centralized planning and decentralized operation, with several nationally and regionally owned PEs competing to build power generation plants across the country. "Rival" public utilities would compete eagerly to push their own projects in search of federal financing. Tankha has observed that this rivalry somehow replicated the dynamics of the private sector (competition *for* the market) in a healthy way. It stimulated higher efficiency of the public sector, even though there was no competition *in* the market. Some PEs performed poorly, but in general the power sector managed to overcome many of the shortcomings that neoliberal critics attribute to state ownership and management, such as irresponsible financial administration, "because the existence of multiple companies owned by the states as well as the federal government meant that as they competed, the stronger companies distinguished themselves and the federal and state governments eventually subsumed the weaker companies into them"

(Tankha 2010, 184). Such "competitive spirit", which at its extreme can become a clear sign of "corporatization" and can dangerously undermine the public ethos, can in certain contexts become a force towards a progressive reform of the public sector.

Quality

A real problem in the power sector of many Latin American countries has been the quality of supply. Market reform was supposed to be the solution, but the evidence from within and outside the region, with dramatic blackouts in quite different places around the world, demonstrates that in many cases privatization was not the best response (Chavez 2002, Bouille and Wamunkoya 2003). Meanwhile, in countries where the state remained as the only or main provider of electrical services, such as Costa Rica or Uruguay, blackouts are currently unheard of or limited to extreme situations caused by adverse weather conditions.

Nevertheless, quality of supply is today also a very present concern in other countries that have resisted or even reversed privatization. Cuba is one of those countries that had succeeded in previous decades in reaching practically universal coverage of electricity services, but its power sector almost collapsed between 2005 and 2006. The breakdown of utilities managed by the national state company *Unión Eléctrica* caused a series of blackouts lasting up to 18 hours a day. In response, the government launched, at the beginning of 2006, the so-called "energy revolution", a programme that combined energy efficiency projects, tariff increases, and the deployment of small power generator units throughout the country. At present, Cuba has overcome the worst of the power crisis, but the electricity sector is still characterized by an obsolete infrastructure, inadequate levels of energy efficiency, losses of about 30% in transmission and distribution, and a heavy reliance on fossil fuels for power generation, including a strong dependence on Venezuelan oil contributions (Belt 2009).

During the past three years, a number of other Latin American countries experienced similar disruptions in the provision of electric power. Venezuela, where the electricity sector was fully nationalized in 2007, has been the most problematic case. Throughout 2009 and 2010, the country suffered a deep power crisis, with continuous blackouts across the national grid. The main cause of the crisis has been the over-dependence on hydro capacity—despite being one of the world's largest oil exporters—which left the country almost paralyzed when a prolonged drought associated with a *La Niña* oscillation (a periodic disturbance of climate patterns that occurs across the tropical Pacific Ocean on average every five years) left the country's main dam dangerously close to the critical point where water cannot feed its turbines. Electricity supply in Venezuela relies on the Guri hydro plant, which, with an installed capacity of more than 10 GW, supplies more than half of the country's production. Some local experts interviewed by the author in

March 2010 criticized the poor governmental response and lack of long-term planning. According to one of them: "The drought is real, but the true problem has been the government not being ready for it. Over the past decade or so, there has not been enough investment in the national power system. The dam levels will sooner or later return to normal, but the infrastructure of transmission and the distribution networks are already overloaded".

From another perspective, it may be argued that the response to the Venezuelan crisis would have been much worse if the power sector had been privatized, considering the performance of private utilities when they had to face equivalent meteorological disruptions in other countries of the region. From the perspective of the *Corporación Eléctrica Nacional* (CORPOELEC, National Electric Corporation, the holding company that currently integrates all Venezuelan power utilities since the conclusion of the process of nationalization in 2007), the government is doing all it can to ensure that Venezuela does not suffer a similar crisis in the future. According to company officials interviewed for this research, public investments in the power system will reach US$18.5 billion over the next eight years.

Citizens' participation

Latin America is awash with academic studies about "participation", based on the diversity, strength, and originality of its citizens' engagement in policy planning and implementation, particularly at the local level. Some of the most creative and radical innovations in citizen participation that originated in the region are now being replicated around the world, with *orçamento participativo* (participatory budgeting) being perhaps the most celebrated (Goldfrank 2007). Yet, participation in the electricity sector is practically non-existent, with the only exception being Venezuela.

Participation can have very different meanings, of course. According to Goetz and Gaventa (2001), the concept refers to three different modalities: consultation, representation, and influence, with varying degrees of engagement allowed to citizens. Consultation implies opening channels for the transfer of information and dialogue; representation involves institutionalizing regular engagement of certain sectors of the population in decision making; influence means enabling citizens to have a substantial impact on policy design and/or the implementation of service delivery. Across the Latin American power sector, the most citizens can expect is consultation; regulatory frameworks in several countries stipulate that all or some decisions taken by the regulatory body or by public or private utilities should be made public and consulted with representatives of the users (or "consumers") of the service.

The case of Venezuela is different, rooted in the notion of *poder popular* (people's power), a key component of the Bolivarian Revolution launched by President Hugo Chávez in 1999. Several years before Chávez came to power, a series of community-driven initiatives aimed at expanding social control over the provision of urban services were already developing in the country. One experience of citizen organization that had emerged before the "official" launch of the revolution was the *Mesas Técnicas de Agua* (MTAs, Grassroots Technical Water Committees), currently being expanded from water to the telecommunications and electricity sectors. The MTAs are in charge of elaborating a diagnosis of their own neighbourhood's problems in terms of access to water and other public services, as well as being co-responsible for developing viable solutions, in partnership with local or national government. The Caracas water utility *Hidrocapital* was the first to institutionalize such a citizen-centred approach, but since 2007, other PEs have promoted their own versions of participatory democracy; Cantv launched the *Mesas Técnicas de Telecomunicaciones*, and the Ministry of Energy launched the *Mesas Técnicas de Energía*, currently promoted by CORPOELEC and with specific responsibilities focused on the planning and development of electric power projects at the grassroots level.

Nevertheless, despite having access to substantial financial resources and real political influence, the future of the *mesas técnicas* should not be taken for granted. In an article, which is both supportive and critical of this process, López Maya argues the following:

> To expand and deepen experiences such as this one [in the water sector], which provides management skills and power to poor communities, has been a challenge to both authorities and neighbours committed to develop these innovations. The difficult socioeconomic conditions that affect poor people constitute a serious obstacle to the right and duty of participation. Many people, especially women, cannot participate because they face a double shift at work: in the workplace and at home. Sometimes people cannot or do not want to participate in community work because it is unpaid. Crime and violence are also a limiting factor, because the most convenient time for meetings is the evening, too dangerous. . . . Another big problem is the constant uncertainty of Chávez's policies, where the removal of the official in charge usually means a stop in the transfer of resources or a full change of plans. . . . Finally, this type of innovation, if it is not developed within a more comprehensive programme aimed at improving the unplanned urban spaces where today nearly half of the families in Venezuela live, runs the risk of being useless. . . . But nevertheless, the MTA is an innovation in the right direction. When its members are interviewed, most women respond that this experience changed their lives. . . . They have learned a set of skills and assumed a set of responsibilities that have allowed them to grow both as persons and as citizens. (2009, 119)

Workers' engagement

Workers' direct engagement in the development of the electricity sector in Latin America goes a long way back. One of the region's most interesting and radical experiences developed in Argentina, where for almost three years, until the military coup of March 1976, a local section of the *Sindicato de Luz y Fuerza* (Light and Power Workers' Union) exerted worker control over the *Servicios Eléctricos del Gran Buenos Aires* (SEGBA, Greater Buenos Aires Power Company), a large public corporation that provided energy services to the capital city and the surrounding metropolitan area. The union's management and administration of SEGBA "represented the apogee of influence for the light and power workers in Argentina" and "also symbolized the emergence of electric power workers generally as key players in Latin American post-war industrial economies" (Brennan 1995, 39).

Another country in which the unions historically had significant political weight is Mexico. Electrification developed earlier, faster, and deeper in this country than in the rest of the region, giving its electricity workers a great influence, despite their relatively small size. Mexican electricity workers had an active role in labour politics during the revolution (between 1910 and 1920) and were responsible for organizing in 1916 the country's first general strike.

At the wider regional level, however, labour's participation in the management and administration of the electricity sector has been a recurrent and mostly unfulfilled demand of unions for many decades. Nevertheless, the strategic importance of electricity gave the power sector workers greater leverage in collective bargaining than other trade unions. After nationalization, when wages began to be negotiated in the framework of the national public budgets, electricity workers were less prone than other segments of the working class to strike over wages. Throughout the second half of the last century, the employees of public utilities became some of the best-paid workers in the region. In Mexico, for instance, due to the institutionalized nature of collective bargaining in the sector and the favourable treatment awarded by the state, relations between the CFE and its labour force remained relatively peaceful. Furthermore, despite its privileged status, the Mexican electricity workers' unions remained relatively free of corruption and nepotism. In Mexico and in other Latin American countries, much of the mobilization of workers was focused on questions of labour-state relations, as Brennan notes:

> Disputes over models of economic development and how to resolve the specific problems of the electric power industry were subsumed into political categories for the labour activists who led the reform movements. From the perspective of Mexican light and power workers, deepening nationalization and resolving the industry's problems first required consolidating their unions into a single industrial union and democratizing the Mexican labour movement. (1995, 59)

More recently, events in the Mexican electricity sector constitute a window into contemporary debates about the role and influence of unions within PEs across the region. The liquidated company LyFC was constantly criticized by conservative analysts for being less efficient than its bigger sister, CFE, due to the excessive power of the former's union, which allegedly derived from inflated salaries that prevented the company from using the budget it received for investments. The union retorted that only 35%–37% of LyFC's annual revenues were used to cover labour costs, including salary, benefits, and pensions. One SME leader interviewed for this study in November 2009 argued:

> LyFC was not performing well, but it was a profitable enterprise, and any accusation that the company's problems were caused by the collective labour agreement or the result of workers' actions is a fallacy. The company began to malfunction when it was denied the budget that was needed for physical investment, meaning the modernization, maintenance or replacement of equipment, transmission and distribution lines, circuit breakers and transformers. The deterioration of the physical investment was the federal government's fault, not a problem caused by us, the workers.

The Mexican union also contends that under the framework of the LyFC labour agreement the workers had pushed to reform work processes at all levels and areas of LyFC's operations, seeking to provide better service to the population, but the workers' perspectives were not considered in the official plans to modernize and restructure the sector. Vested interests, corporatism, and corruption have been identified by other studies as real problems of the Mexican labour movement (De la Garza Toledo 2003), but they are not even remotely the main causes of the financial and operation problems of state-owned public utilities, at least in this case.

In some countries, the traditional amicable relationship between the state and the power sector workers has been radically affected by the corporatization of PEs. One of the clearest examples of such trend is Colombia, where an investigation into the impacts of commercialization of public services found that:

> [In the 1990s] the specific articulation between the trade unions and the managerial units of public enterprises broke down when *mercantilización* [marketization] became the new axis of public policy in the sector. The relationship moved from a situation of relative cooperation, or at least of pragmatic agreements between the managers and the unions, to a situation of open confrontation. The workers' unions radicalized their political positions, expelling the centrist tendencies from the leadership and waving new oppositional flags against the process of commercialization of public services. (Varela Barrios 2008, 76)

Sustainability

In terms of environmental sustainability, the track record of PEs is not necessarily better than that of private companies. Most Latin American governments have declared their commitment to the development of renewable energy, often in the context of rural electrification programmes implemented with financial support from the IDB, the World Bank, and other multilateral financial institutions. In practice, however, the real process of supporting decentralized power generation is evolving in a piecemeal fashion, without a long-term strategy or integral vision. Several PEs have plans to develop their own projects in wind, solar, geothermal, and other areas of renewable energy, but in general the "greening" of the power sector is becoming a new golden opportunity for private capital, with the rapid expansion of public-private partnerships (PPPs), which we have excluded from our definition of "alternatives to privatization". The national state-owned energy corporation *Energía Argentina Sociedad Anónima* (ENARSA), for instance, announced in May 2009 the launch of a tender for 500 MW of new wind capacity, and new plans for the construction of private wind farms were publicized by Spanish investors in June 2010 (while they put pressure on the government to increase power tariffs in order to guarantee a return on their investment).

If the expansion of renewable energy is to be taken seriously by the governments of the region, the issue of financing its development will have to be discussed and properly planned. Solar projects, for instance, can be cleaner than other forms of generation, but they are still too costly to be deployed on a mass scale. The technology is not fully advanced and is being developed outside the region, and for at least some years the electricity generated from solar plants will predictably be much more expensive. A positive sign is the proactive role that some municipal governments have begun to play; for instance, in São Paulo (Brazil), it is now compulsory for every official building in the city to mount solar panels. The Brazilian government, for its part, is also contributing to the expansion of the solar alternative by mandating the installation of solar power collectors in new federal housing programmes.

Other renewable options, such as microhydro projects, are much less likely to develop in the near future on a large scale. Microhydro initiatives generally require additional and expensive transmission lines and substations, which often make projects infeasible from a financial point of view. It is not clear how to promote the expansion of microhydro generation in Latin America without seeking funding from the very questionable "clean development mechanism" scheme, a market-driven component of the Kyoto Protocol based on the trading of carbon emission rights (see Gilbertson and Reyes 2009) or other dubious funders.

Across the region, there is growing awareness that wind and solar projects are far more environmentally friendly than coal, oil, natural gas, or nuclear plants (GTZ 2007). Wind and photovoltaic generation do not require water, have very low emissions, and do not create long-term waste. Nevertheless, attempts to develop green energy projects are rapidly becoming the target of widespread opposition. On the Chilean side of the Patagonia, for example, the indigenous Mapuche nation has strongly resisted

Trayenko (a subsidiary of Norway's SN Power), and Endesa Chile's plans to develop hydro and geothermal projects on its ancestral land, with support from local environmental organizations. Similarly, the Mexican unit of *ACCIONA Energía* (a Spanish firm) plans to build three wind farms in the southern state of Oaxaca, but local farmers and indigenous communities are very reluctant to lease their land. Local communities are not opposed to renewable energy, per se; they are afraid of the negative externalities of such projects, including possible displacement. If renewable energy is to become a real priority for Latin American PEs—quite a remote prospect at present—most likely it will not be a smooth ride, and they might encounter the same hostility that many private companies across the region are already facing today, unless proper consultation and/or inclusion of local communities in planning and implementation take place.

And although hydropower is generally seen as "renewable", an ominous environmental and social threat on the horizon is a possible return to the era of massive hydro, with a series of projects in various stages of development once again being enthusiastically supported by governments and public electric utilities. These sorts of mega projects are strongly resisted by a wide range of civic organizations such as the Movement of People Affected by Dams (MAB), the Brazilian Network for Environmental Justice (REBRIP), and the Sustainable Southern Cone Programme, which have extensively documented the destruction of environmental systems, the loss of cultural heritage, and the displacement and impoverishment of communities (Larraín and Haedo 2008). In Brazil, the government has approved the construction of the mammoth 11.3 GW Belo Monte hydro plant, to be built on the Xingu River, in the Amazonian state of Para. Eletrobras will hold a 15% stake in the consortium that will construct and operate the dam, which consists of 18 Brazilian and foreign partners, public and private. In Colombia, the public corporation ISAGEN has already begun the construction of the 820 MW Sogamoso dam, which is expected to become operational by December 2013, while the municipally owned utility EPM recently signed an agreement with the agency for local development promotion of the department of Antioquia (IDEA) to build the 2.4 GW HidroItuango project, set to be online in 2018.

Another factor that might diminish the sustainability dimension of PEs is the recent revival of the nuclear option. Brazil, for instance, has announced that it will resume its atomic programme, after years of discontinuity, with plans (discussed in the media but unconfirmed by the government) to build up to eight nuclear plants in the coming two decades. Argentina has announced that it is analyzing the possible expansion of its existing capacity, and Chile, Panama, Uruguay, and Venezuela are apparently mulling the possibilities. The region's growing fascination with nukes could even mean opening another door to the private sector, as privately managed small-scale nuclear plants able to supply electric power in remote regions are also being considered. So far, all nuclear generators in the region are owned and managed by the state, but because of environmental, public safety, and social concerns they are *not* presented here as an "alternative".

Finally, a positive trend in a sustainable direction is the expansion of a series of governmental initiatives focused on a more rational and sustainable use of electric power, under the broad umbrella of energy efficiency programmes (CEPAL et al, 2009). The Ecuadorian government, for instance, is launching the *Plan de Acción de Energía Sostenible para Ecuador* (PAES, Sustainable Energy Action Plan), initially conceived as a way to offset a prolonged drought, consisting of several new measures to promote efficiency and increase supply, including renewed support for wind generation.

Public ethos

In an article focused on public-public partnerships (PuPs) in the water sector, Boag and McDonald (2010) discuss the meaning of the concept of "public" and present a series of concerns that are also very relevant for the analysis of current trends in the Latin American electricity sector. In particular, the article warns about the uncritical celebration of state (or "community") ownership without deeper discussion of how "public" entities are configured, the incentives and constraints that frame their operations, and the way they relate to larger public service objectives. In short, the authors refer to three concrete risks arising from corporatization:

- the deterioration and replacement of traditional principles of the public sector, including the prioritization of efficiency objectives ahead of equity and affordability
- the introduction of market mechanisms and practices imported from the private sector, such as competitive bidding, cost-benefit analysis, tariff indexation, performance-targeted salaries, and demand-driven investments and the matching abandonment of principles of integrated planning, (cross)subsidization, and supply-driven decision making
- the change of managerial ethos, focusing on narrow and short-term financial gains and losses

Looking at the current regional scenario, it is clear that corporatization is indeed a fact that undermines the value of many of the public utilities mentioned in this chapter as "alternatives". The hegemonic rhetoric of the region's reformers since the mid-1990s, inspired by the experience of New Zealand and other countries that reformed their public services according to "new public management" (NPM) principles, has been that the more public companies are exposed to market governance, the less confusion and overlap there is between political and managerial responsibilities and tasks, hence, more efficiency and efficacy and less corruption and clientelism. In practice, however, corporatization has often undermined control and accountability, because redefined public companies have looser institutional affiliations with the government, the parliament, and society at large. This affects even those PEs that have managed to place themselves on top in terms of efficiency and equity, such as UTE in Uruguay. In a recent newspaper interview, Eleuterio Fernández Huidobro, a leading figure of the Uruguayan Left, a former guerrilla commander and a current national senator, declared the following:

> There are some companies that we believed were public enterprises, but which in fact had been privatized. We discovered that when we won the national government [in 2004]. For instance, UTE, the electric power company, is not being managed to serve the interests of the country; it is a public enterprise only in name, owned by its managers. (López San Miguel 2009, 7)

On the one hand, these declarations address a very valid and worrisome trend widespread throughout the region (i.e. the excessive "professionalization" of public management, which leads to situations in which elected government officials and legislators exert little or no control over the managers of PEs). On the other hand, these concerns can be unfair and ungrounded, because (i) UTE's directors are indeed accountable to both the state and society and operate following the course of action established by the national government; and (ii) the Uruguayan people have mobilized on many occasions, via plebiscites and referendums, to defend the public nature of UTE and other PEs, expressing a strong identification and satisfaction with the country's state-owned companies (Oria Giordan 2006).

In the end, the characteristics and scope of corporatization in the region depend on the specific history and political culture of each country. While some states with stronger political systems and democratic traditions—Uruguay and Costa Rica being the two clearest cases—have developed a certain style of public management that perceives public enterprises as important instruments for economic and social development, serving well-defined political goals, there are other countries in which the links between public companies and the broader institutional system are much weaker and the objectives of public utilities and other state-owned enterprises are less clear. With the rise of progressive national governments in Latin America, more countries are moving towards the first category, with the potential for previously decayed or corporatized public companies becoming real alternatives to market-driven provision of services, as components of a broader project towards national liberation and development.

A crucial question therefore in the current period of transition—and in some cases a transition to socialism (Raby 2006)—is whether the values and procedures associated with the old-style management of public companies match the objectives and values of the new left governments. In Venezuela, for instance, the unions have strongly criticized the current administration of CORPOELEC (electricity), Cantv (telecommunications), and other PEs for keeping the old bureaucratic structures and cultures of the previous era, including a large number of managerial cadres "inherited" from the private companies that were in control before the socialist government of Hugo Chávez nationalized them. Although some of these criticisms are sustained by empirical evidence, the most radical critics tend to forget that "Rome wasn't built in a day", and that it would be unthinkable to dismantle a whole corporate structure in a period of a few months (the process of nationalization of the two mentioned Venezuelan companies was only completed in mid-2007, and internal changes are ongoing).

Some of the worst examples of corporatization can be observed in Colombia. The national electric enterprise, ISA, followed by municipal utilities, promoted the so-called *proceso de democratización accionaria* (shareholder democratization process), which enable private individuals to own part of the public company as any other business opportunity. Although the state remains the majority owner, the presidency of the Board of Directors is granted to minority owners. Advocates of corporatization (Millán 2006) point to the fact that ISA has on several occasions been praised by Transparency International as an example of a transparent and honest corporation. They also celebrate that ISA has become one of the region's most prosperous enterprises in financial terms, including the expansion of its portfolio to Bolivia, Ecuador, and Peru, and its participation in SIEPAC, a business investment in Central America heavily criticized by civil society organizations.

Moreover, presenting PEs as a viable alternative to marketization does not mean assuming that they are always corruption-free. Even the best examples of efficient public management can be tainted; a political crisis erupted in Costa Rica in October 2004 when a former Director of ICE appeared in the national press admitting that high officials of the company, as well as a former president of the country, had received a hefty bribe from the French transnational corporation Alcatel in 2001 (Artavia Araya 2008).

Nevertheless, the resilience of the *estado empresario* (entrepreneur state) is notable. In Mexico, notwithstanding several attempts aimed at liberalizing the electricity sector, CFE and LyFC (until 2009) were icons of the "big state", inherited from the Mexican Revolution, acting as bulwarks against neoliberal legislation. In Uruguay, building upon the strong ideological legacy of the welfare state built by President José Batlle y Ordóñez in the early 20th century, direct democracy mechanisms have been used to reject privatization of practically every PE. In Costa Rica, the institutions at the core of the public electricity system have proven remarkably resistant to change, to a great extent due to resistance from multiple sectors of society.

International cooperation and solidarity

Unlike the water sector in Latin America, where some promising PuPs have emerged in the region (see Chapter 15, this volume), there are many PuPs in the Latin American power sector where profit, not solidarity, seems to be the main motivation. Regional integration is today a big challenge, particularly in the Mercosur region (the trade bloc set up by Argentina, Brazil, Uruguay, and Paraguay as founding members, and Bolivia, Chile, Colombia, Ecuador, and Peru as associate members, with the long-delayed full incorporation of Venezuela to be ratified by the Paraguayan parliament). Binational intergovernmental agreements have already established strong links between several electricity PEs, but larger and deeper integration is increasingly seen as a way to prevent the frequent power shortages that affect most of the region. In this sense, two scenarios are foreseeable: (i) that private transnational power companies take the lead of this process, linking the different countries where they are currently doing business; and (ii) that the largest state-owned electricity companies expand to neighbouring countries and/or launch new forms of association with other PEs.

Eletrobras is actively looking for business opportunities in the region. It has announced a number of projects outside Brazil, particularly in Peru and Venezuela, and the Brazilian national development bank BNDES (one of its main shareholders) is already financing new power projects in other countries. The giant public company plans to follow the strategy previously implemented by Portuguese and Spanish corporations. President Lula has declared several times that he aspired to see Eletrobras become the Petrobras (the Brazilian state-owned energy entity, one of the world's 10 largest oil companies) of the electricity sector. The analogy openly challenges the "alternative" potential of Eletrobras, because Petrobras has been charged with behaving internationally like any other private transnational corporation, with profits being its main concern and little regard for social or environmental sustainability (León 2008).

Another clear example of the for-profit expansion of some state-owned companies across national borders is the participation of the strong Mexican (CFE), Colombian (ISA), and Costa Rican (ICE) PEs in the very controversial *Sistema de Interconexión Eléctrica de los Países de América Central* (SIEPAC, Central American Electrical Interconnection System). This is a business endeavour led by the Spanish transnational corporation Endesa in association with several public utilities, consisting of an electricity transmission network that will interconnect Guatemala, Honduras, El Salvador, Nicaragua, Costa Rica, and Panama (Martin 2010). The programme has been criticized by non-governmental organizations, which point the finger at the social, environmental, and political implications of a very costly initiative being pushed forward without real public consultation or debate.

Transferability

Previous studies about the evolution of the public sector in Latin America and elsewhere have tried to explain why some PEs are more efficient than others and have questioned the replicability of the most successful ones.

The factors that contribute to higher success might be mainly related to peculiar features of concrete localities, as argued by the "new comparative economics" approach. A study published some years ago (Djankov et al, 2003) focused on the impact of different institutional arrangements for social control of managerial practices, drew attention to the importance of local legal systems, institutional patterns and cultural characteristics, condensed into what the authors call—without proposing any tangible definition—"civic capital" and "institutional possibility frontier". The authors argue that "efficient institutional design depends on specific characteristics of countries and sectors, which can only be ascertained empirically" (2003, 604).

Following such an approach, it has been argued that those societies with more plentiful "civic capital" will be prone to stronger and more efficient PEs. In the context of the electricity sector, that would explain how the Antioquian society, in Colombia, favoured the development of EPM, while Costa Rica and Uruguay—two countries often referred to as Latin America's most democratic and institutionally robust—favoured the development of ICE and UTE, respectively. Without accepting the full and rather simplistic argumentation offered by the proponents of the "civic capital" idea,[3] our own research supports the proposition that the specific social, economic, and political context surrounding each experience has been a strong enabling factor in the development of robust and efficient PEs in the three concrete cases mentioned above. The experience of EPM, in particular, shows a combination of positive results produced by the synergy of the rent generated by hydropower resources and the human resources that have allowed it to be properly exploited and developed, as well as the strong citizens' control over the company's governance, which would prevent the opportunistic takeover of management by the political class. Similar favourable conditions can be also observed in at least two other successful experiences: the national public corporation ICE in Costa Rica and the regional company COPEL in the state of Parana, Brazil.

Another factor that should not be dismissed when the transferability of positive developments in the state-owned electricity sector is discussed, is the profound national pride associated with some PEs. In Costa Rica, popular discontent blew up in the year 2000, including road blockades and large demonstrations throughout the country, in reaction to a legislative proposal that would have eventually privatized ICE (Hoffmann 2007, Frajman 2009). Similarly, Uruguay's relatively small size, the existence of a long and strong statist tradition, and the extended use of direct democracy mechanisms (referendums and plebiscites) to resolve conflicts on issues of fundamental importance for the country, help explain the characteristics and rhythms of the unusually stubborn defence of UTE and other PEs (Bergara et al, 2006, Dubrovsky and Ruchansky 2010).

CONCLUSION

Although the most relevant alternative to market-driven provision of electricity in Latin America is the PE, none of them are "chemically pure" in terms of being acceptable alternatives to privatization. Nonetheless, the region has a long and rich tradition of successful PEs, and despite pressures from neoliberal advocates to get rid of them, few countries have dismantled them completely, creating in many cases a grey area between companies still under tight public control and wholly privatized ones. Across Latin America, the crucial question is how governments and civil society can wield political control over public companies that are going through a process of corporatization, transforming them into an effective tool for economic and social development in sustainable and equitable ways.

To try and answer this question it is necessary to note that a state apparatus is an intrinsically contradictory system, where different units seek not merely to maximize a simple set of goals but are also required to compromise between conflicting objectives, interests, and values. This means that the managers of state-owned companies are permanently confronted by tensions and dilemmas to which there is no simple solution. Many public companies responsible for the provision of electricity services across the region are now highly corporatized, having adopted the core principles of new public management and other market-oriented ideas that make them hard to distinguish from private firms. Nevertheless, for as long as public entities remain under state ownership they are accountable to the government and society—at least in theory—and there are possibilities to reclaim them. There is an intrinsic connection between public ownership and the purpose of essential public services such as electricity, water, education, and health, which is broken when they are privatized.

As we have observed, many public companies have been operating under the continuous threat of privatization and/or subject to the neglect of governments, political parties, and even trade unions, which have caused the deterioration or stagnation of service delivery. Faced with this situation, there is a clear need to concentrate on strengthening existing public entities, even those currently corporatized, by using whatever means available at practical and policy levels. This might involve further critical research, advocacy, and intellectual support to campaigns already initiated by labour and other social organizations. At the same time, it is necessary to work on creating awareness and changing the mindset of public managers, user organizations, trade unions, and other relevant stakeholders, seeking to make them more open to change their old approaches and think anew, beginning with the revival of the public service ethos and an increased role for workers in the day-to-day administration and long-term planning of the power sector.

Another kind of public service is in the making in Latin America. Unfortunately, change in the electricity sector is still not as obvious as in the water sector, but there are positive precedents and good prospects for future development. A new type of convergence between new left governments, and the interests and proposals of social movements, community groups, and committed researchers has revealed that reclaiming the state is a very viable option in the region. Moreover, experiences such as participatory budgeting in Brazil, Uruguay, and other Latin American countries (Chavez 2004, Chavez and Goldfrank 2004, Goldfrank and Schrank 2009), the *mesas técnicas* of water, energy, and telecommunications in Venezuela, and several other innovations in public management based on citizens' participation, have demonstrated that "people's knowledge" rooted in experience can be as important and needed as that of the "experts" in order to rebuild public services in the region. There is a critical mass of new and good ideas already available for public sector policy makers and administrators seeking for democratic approaches to public management specific to the challenges of power provision, and which confronts the by now not-so-new NPM ideas.

If the processes of reconstruction and development in countries run by "new left" or "progressive" forces evolve in a positive direction, the reorganization of public companies in these and other countries of the region might also respond to external pressure, as has happened before. During the past two decades many Latin American countries embraced international norms and beliefs about how a public company should be organized and run, simply because these had become the hegemonic doctrine. Nowadays, another isomorphic trend is evolving in the region, and the expansion of progressive new models for public service management in countries governed by the new left may lead to the extension of a counter-hegemonic ideological climate and create pressure towards similar reforms and deeper structural change across the region.

Not everything in the current situation of Latin American PEs is positive, progressive, or constitutes a real alternative to marketization. There is plenty of room for improvement and change, but the available options cannot mean swinging back the pendulum of history to the "golden age" of development of state-owned public utilities because the objective and subjective conditions that existed between the 1940s and 1970s no longer exist. Nevertheless, the experiences of several national and subnational companies from across the region demonstrate that PEs can certainly be a real and viable alternative to the privatization of the power sector. Good or bad performance in provision of electrical services is very much related to the commitment of managers and workers and the resources that they can access to perform their tasks. Performance is not determined solely by the nature of ownership and management in terms of private versus public, as the neoliberals have argued for over three decades.

NOTES

1. The author benefited from the valuable assistance of four researchers working on public services reform in Latin America: Pablo Bertinat (Taller Ecologista, Argentina), who focused on the Southern Cone; Claudia Torelli (REDES, Uruguay, currently based at Tufts University in the US), who conducted research on Central America; Sara Forch (TNI, based in Barcelona), and Tatiana Roa (CENSAT Agua Viva, Colombia), who researched the Andean Region.

2. The so-called "New Model" was designed by a working group created by the PT during the presidential campaign of 1992 to respond to the huge electricity crisis inherited from previous governments and to come up with innovative ideas. The group consisted of experts from the public electric utilities and academics based at public universities. The model proposes a new public-private mix. "If public sector utilities are significantly less efficient than private sector ones, they will not be able to match private sector offers without incurring losses. If the private sector bids too high, the public sector will be able to undercut them" (Tankha 2010, 192).

3. The notion of "civic capital" derives from the much-used and abused concept of "social capital". For a comprehensive discussion of the ideological profile and shortcomings of the "social capital" approach, see Fine 2010.

REFERENCES

Andrés, L.A, Diop, M., and Guasch, J.L. 2007. Un balance de las privatizaciones en el sector infraestructura. *Nueva Sociedad* 207: 113–129.

Artavia Araya, F. 2008. Decisiones públicas, beneficios privados. Consideraciones teóricas en torno a la corrupción. *Revista de Ciencias Sociales* 119: 13–26.

Baer, W. and McDonald, C. 1998. A return to the past? Brazil's privatization of public utilities: The case of the electric power sector. *Quarterly Review of Economics and Finances* 38(3): 503–523.

Bárcena, A, Grynspan, R. and Lagos Escobar, R. 2009. Foreword. In *Contribution of energy services to the Millennium Development Goals and to poverty alleviation in Latin America and the Caribbean*. Santiago: Economic Commission for Latin America and the Caribbean (ECLAC), United Nations Development Programme (UNDP) and Club de Madrid.

Barrett, P., Chavez, D. and Rodriguez-Garavito, C (Eds). 2008. *The new Latin American left: Utopia reborn*. London: Pluto Press.

Bastidas Colinas, S. 2009 !Se fue la luz!. *El País*, Madrid, 12 October.

Belt, J. 2009. *The Electric Power Sector in Cuba: Potential ways to increase efficiency and sustainability*. Washington, DC: United States Agency for International Development (USAID).

Bergara, M., Pereyra, A., Tansini, R., Garce, A., Chasquetti, D., Buquet, D. and Moraes, J.A. 2006. *Political institutions, policymaking processes, and policy outcomes: The case of Uruguay*. Washington, DC: Inter-American Development Bank.

Birdsall, N. and Nellis, J. 2002. *Winners and losers: Assessing the distributional impact of privatization*. Washington, DC: Center for Global Development.

Boag, G. and McDonald, D. 2010. A critical review of public-public partnerships in water services. *Water Alternatives* 3(1): 1–25.

Bouille, D. and Wamunkoya, N. 2003. Power sector reform in Latin America: A retrospective analysis. In Wamunkoya, N. (Ed), *Electricity reforms: Social and environmental challenges*, pp. 99–115. Roskilde: United Nations Environmental Programme (UNEP).

Brecha. 2010. Evo nacionaliza y se enfrenta a sindicatos. 7 May.

Brennan, J.P. 1995. Industrial sectors and union politics in Latin American labour movements. Light and power workers in Argentina and Mexico. *Latin American Research Review* 30: 39–68.

CEPAL, OLADE and GTZ. 2009. Situación y perspectivas de la eficiencia energética en América Latina y El Caribe. Santiago: Comisión Económica para América Latina y el Caribe (CEPAL), Organización Latinoamericana de Energía (OLADE), and Deutsche Gesellschaft für Technische Zusammenarbeit (GTZ).

Chavez, D. 2002. *Lights off! Debunking the myths of power liberalisation.* Amsterdam: Transnational Institute (TNI).

———. 2004. *Polis and demos. The left in municipal governance in Montevideo and Porto Alegre.* Utrecht: Institute of Social Studies (ISS) and Shaker Publishers.

Chavez, D. and Goldfrank, B. (Eds). 2004. *The left in the city: Progressive and participatory local governments in Latin America.* London: Latin America Bureau.

Checchi, D., Florio, M. and Carrera, J. 2009. Privatisation discontent and utility reform in Latin America. *Journal of Development Studies* 45(3): 333–350.

Corporación Latinobarómetro. 2009. *Informe 2009.* Santiago: Corporación Latinobarómetro.

De la Garza Toledo, E. 2003. Mexican trade unionism in the face of political transition. In Keister, L.A. (Ed.), *Labour revitalization: Global perspectives and new initiatives.* Bingley: Emerald Group Publishing.

Dias Leite, A. 2007. *A energia do Brasil.* Rio de Janeiro: Elsevier.

Djankov, S., Glaeser, E., LaPorta, R., Lopez de Silanes, F. and Shleifer, A. 2003. The new comparative economics. *Journal of Comparative Economics* 31: 595–619.

Dubrovsky, H. and Ruchansky, B. 2010. *El desarrollo y la provisión de servicios de infraestructura: La experiencia de la energía eléctrica en Uruguay en el período 1990–2009.* Santiago: Comisión Econonómica para América Latina y el Caribe (CEPAL).

Fine, B. 2010. *Theories of social capital: Researchers behaving badly.* Pluto Press.

Foster, V. and Yepes, T. 2006. *Is cost recovery a feasible objective for water and electricity? The Latin American experience.* Washington, DC: The World Bank.

Frajman, E. 2009. Information and values in popular protests: Costa Rica in 2000. *Bulletin of Latin American Research* 28(1): 44–62.

Gilbertson, T. and Reyes, O. 2009. *Carbon trading. How it works and why it fails.* Uppsala: Dag Hammarskjöld Foundation.

Goetz, A.M. and Gaventa, J. 2001. *Bringing citizen voice and client focus into service delivery.* Brighton: Institute of Development Studies (IDS), University of Sussex.

Goldemberg, J. 2009. Renewable energy in Latin America and the Caribbean. *Enerlac. Latin American and the Caribbean Energy Magazine* 1(1): 16–18.

Goldfrank, B. 2007. Lessons from Latin America's experience with participatory budgeting. In Shah, A. (Ed), *Participatory budgeting*, pp. 91–126. Washington, DC: World Bank Institute.

Goldfrank, B. and Schrank, A. 2009. Municipal neoliberalism and municipal socialism: Urban political economy in contemporary Latin America. *International Journal of Urban and Regional Research* 33(2): 443–462.

GTZ (Gesellschaft für Technische Zusammenarbeit). 2007. *Energy-policy framework conditions for electricity markets and renewable energies. 23 country analyses.* Eschborn: Deutsche GTZ, Division Environment and Infrastructure.

Hall, D. 2007. *Electricity companies in Latin America 2007.* London: Public Services International Research Unit (PSIRU), University of Greenwich.

486 *Daniel Chavez*

Hall, D., Thomas, S. and Corral, V. 2009. *Global experience with electricity liberalisation*. London: Public Services International Research Unit (PSIRU), University of Greenwich.

Hamaguchi, N. 2002. Will the market keep Brazil lit up? Ownership and market structural changes in the electric power sector. *The Developing Economies* 40(4): 522–552.

Hoffmann, B. 2007. *Why reform fails: The "politics of policies" in Costa Rican telecommunications liberalization*. Working Paper. Hamburg: German Institute of Global and Area Studies/Leibniz-Institut für Globale und Regionale Studien (GIGA).

Kariuki, M. and Schwartz, J. 2005. *Small-scale private service providers of water supply and electricity. A review of incidence, structure, pricing and operating characteristics*. Washington, DC: World Bank.

Lanciotti, N.S. 2008. Foreign investments in electric utilities: A comparative analysis of Belgian and American companies in Argentina, 1890–1960. *Business History Review* 82(3): 503–528.

Larraín, S. and Haedo, M.P. (Eds). 2008. *Política energética en América Latina: presente y futuro. Críticas y propuestas de los pueblos*. Santiago: Programa Chile Sustentable.

León, A. 2008. *Petrobras en Centroamérica: El caso de los agrocombustibles*. Guatemala City: Centro de Estudios Políticos Alternativos (CEPA).

López Maya, M. 2009. Innovaciones participativas y poder popular en Venezuela. *Umbrales de América del Sur* (6): 115–126.

López San Miguel, S. 2009. Eliminamos pobreza pero aún falta (interview with Eleuterio Fernández Huidobro). *Página 12*, Buenos Aires, 11 October.

Marques, G.L. 1997. *Restructuring the Brazilian electrical sector*. Washington, DC: Instituto Cultural Minerva, Institute of Brazilian Issues, The George Washington University.

Martin, J. 2010. *Central America electric integration and the SIEPAC project: From a fragmented market toward a new reality*. Miami: Center for Hemispheric Policy, University of Miami.

Matos, V. 2010. Plan Quinquenal. La UTE entre el carbon y el gas natural. *La Diaria* (*Energia* 32), 29 June, p. 3.

Millán, J. 2006. *Entre el mercado y el Estado. Tres décadas de reformas en el sector eléctrico de América Latina*. Washington, DC: Banco Interamericano de Desarrollo.

Neira, M. and Vandeweerd, V. 2009. Foreword. In UNDP and WHO *The energy access situation in developing countries: A review focusing on the least developed countries and Sub-Saharan Africa*, p. i. New York: United Nations Development Programme (UNDP) and World Health Organization (WHO).

OLADE. 2008. *Informe de estadísticas energéticas 2007*. Quito: Organización Latinoamericana de Energía (OLADE).

Oria Giordan, S.E. 2006. Referéndum y proceso de privatización de empresas públicas en Uruguay. Paper presented at the XI Congreso Internacional del CLAD sobre la Reforma del Estado y de la Administración Pública, Guatemala City, Guatemala, 7–10 November.

Poveda, M. 2004. *Competencia en mercados energéticos. Una evaluación de la restructuración de los mercados energéticos en América Latina y el Caribe*. Quito: Latin American Energy Organization (OLADE), Canadian International Development Agency (CIDA) and University of Calgary.

Raby, D.L. 2006. *Democracy and revolution: Latin America and socialism today*. London: Pluto Press.

Ramesh, M. and Araral, E. 2010. Introduction: Reasserting the role of the state in public services. In Ramesh, M., Araral, E. and Wu, X. (Eds), *Reasserting the public in public services: New public management reforms*, pp. 1–16. London: Routledge.

Reséndiz Núñez, D. (Ed). 1994. *El sector eléctrico en México*. Mexico, DF: Fondo de Cultura Económica.

Rodríguez, G.R. 1994. Evolución de la industria eléctrica en México. In Reséndiz Núñez, D. (Ed), *El sector eléctrico en México*, pp. 15–42. Mexico, DF: CFE and FCE.

Rondinelli, D.A. 2008. Can public enterprises contribute to development? A critical assessment and alternatives for management improvement. In UNDESA, *Public enterprises: Unresolved challenges and new opportunities. Publication based on the Expert Group Meeting on Re-inventing Public Enterprise and their Management. 27–28 October 2005*, pp. 21–42. New York: United Nations, Division for Public Administration and Development Management, Department of Economic and Social Affairs.

Rozas Balbontín, P. 2009. *Crisis económica y enérgetica en América Latina: Su impacto en las operadoras españolas*. Santiago de Chile: Comisión Econonómica para América Latina y el Caribe (CEPAL).

Sheinbaum Pardo, C. 2009. Ilegalidades y mentiras de la extinción de LFC. *La Jornada*, 16 October.

Tankha, S. 2010. Lessons from three generations of Brazilian electricity reforms. In Ramesh, M., Araral, E. and Wu, X. (Eds), *Reasserting the public in public services: New public management reforms*, pp. 178–196. London: Routledge.

Tendler, J. 1968. *Electric power in Brazil: Entrepreneurship in the public sector*. Cambridge: Harvard University Press.

Thomas, S. 2009a. *Corporate policies in the EU energy sector*. London: Public Services International Research Unit (PSIRU), University of Greenwich.

———. 2009b. *Energy Planning in Brazil*. London: PSIRU, University of Greenwich.

Valdes, J.G. 2008. *Pinochet's economists: The Chicago School of Economics in Chile*. Cambridge: Cambridge University Press.

Varela Barrios, E. 2008. El impacto de la mercantilización de los servicios públicos sobre las empresas estatales del sector. *Semestre Económico* 11(22), 91–109.

Wilde-Ramsing, J. and Steinweg, T. 2010. *Down to the wire. The impact of transnational corporations on sustainable electricity provision in developing countries: Case studies in Argentina and Peru*. Amsterdam: SOMO, Centre for Research on Multinational Corporations.

Zilocchi, G. 1998. Autogestión social de obras y servicios públicos locales. Lo "público no estatal" a partir de un estudio de caso en la ciudad de Córdoba, Argentina. In Bresser Pereira, L.C. and Cunill Grau, N. (Eds), *Lo público no-estatal en la reforma del estado*. Buenos Aires: Centro Latinoamericano de Administración para el Desarrollo (CLAD) and Editorial Paidós.

INTERVIEW

Martín Esparza, Secretary General of the Mexican Electrical Workers' Union (SME).

Part III

Looking Ahead

17 Conclusion
Ways Forward for Alternatives in Health, Water and Electricity

David A. McDonald and Greg Ruiters

The number of people in the global South without access to (adequate) basic services is staggering. Globally, more than 1.1 billion people are not able to obtain safe water supplies, 2.4 billion people do not have access to any type of improved sanitation facility, and 1.4 billion do not have electricity services; the vast majority of these people live in Asia, Africa, and Latin America (IEA 2010, WHO 2011a). These numbers would be much higher if one were to include other criteria such as affordability, quality of supply, and ease of access. Figures for health care are more difficult to estimate given the wide range of health services one needs to consider, but access to maternal health services, anti-retroviral drugs and a suite of other primary care facilities and support is depressingly low in many parts of the South, despite some gains made on the Millennium Development Goals health objectives (WHO 2011b).

The interconnectivity of these service deficits makes matters even worse, with diarrheal diseases alone killing about 2 million people a year, most of whom are children less than five years of age (WHO 2011a). A lack of clean water, inadequate sanitation (including in health centres), an absence of electricity for the refrigeration of foods and health supplies, and a shortage of medical personnel all combine to create a vortex of weak health systems that wreak havoc on people's lives.

Service gaps are most pronounced in Sub-Saharan Africa, and rural areas are generally worse off than urban areas in quantitative terms (only 14.3% of rural Sub-Saharan Africans have access to electricity, for example, as compared to 98.8% of urban Latin Americans [IEA 2010]). However, urban areas suffer their own form of qualitative service deficiencies and inequities, and they are growing rapidly, with the majority of new service needs expected to be in large cities in the South in the future. China alone is expecting to add 350 million new urban residents by 2030 (Deutsche Bank 2008).

The capital and operating costs of these service gaps are going to be enormous, with an estimated US$41 billion a year needed on energy infrastructure in Africa alone if universal access to electricity is going to be attained by 2030 on that continent (Foster and Briceño-Garmendia 2010). Universal access to improved water and sanitation services is less costly, but still estimated at US$22.6 billion per year globally (WHO 2011b). Once again, health investments are harder to quantify because of the complex nature of this service sector, but the Global Health Workforce Alliance (2010) estimates that between 2.6 and 3.5 million additional health workers will be needed in the 49 highest burden countries alone by 2015.

The sources of finance to build these new/improved service facilities, and the methods of paying for their ongoing operation and maintenance, will be crucial to determining their "public" versus "private" character. Combined with debates about the future of already existing services, it is obvious that the struggles over privatization and its "alternatives" are going to feature prominently in research, policy discussions, and grassroots activism for many years to come.

The push for more "publicness" in this rush to expand service delivery will not be an easy one. Public alternatives require different classes to share a common space and fate, yet the trend is precisely towards the opposite: global apartheid in (urban) life (Davis 1990, Harvey 1996). Uneven flows of capital over the globe create, sustain and destroy built environments, making for a scale and quality of difference that renders equitable, sustainable, and democratic public service delivery difficult to imagine.

Against these stark realities, this book has considered the roles of key actors (states, trade unions, social movements, women in services) and normative principles that could inform progressive alternatives to privatization and commercialization. But rather than fixating on one particular response to the experience of uneven development or on particular localistic solutions, we have suggested a different procedure that starts with faint outlines of a vision of a better world. Despite the decidedly undemocratic pronouncement by neoliberals that "there is no alternative" to its free market utopia, the authors in this book have argued that the necessity of alternatives has been thrust onto our agenda by capital's chaos and the failures of privatization. Indeed, the original ambitious rhetoric and goals of neoliberalism have proved largely unrealizable as the state is being "brought back in" to mop up capital's disarray.

In thinking about alternatives, it became clear that a systematic study of concrete practices needed to be grounded in principles—objective realities of uneven developments and varying political circumstances in diverse parts of the world—not just a random collection of case studies. Visions and principles require more than a mere summary of what activists and progressive policy makers have to say. They require an historical and multiscalar view of links between public services and democratic governance. And while activists can share stories of oppression and repression, and distill principles of justice and visions for alternatives from their own experiences, this needs to be complemented by analysis and synthesis informed by understandings of market crises.

The arguments and evidence presented in this book make it clear that "another world"—and perhaps several, "conjoined" ones—"is possible".

There are a multitude of interesting and progressive alternatives to marketization and privatization. From nationalized electricity providers in Latin America, to community-led health initiatives in Africa, to water services by non-governmental organizations (NGOs) in Asia, public services in the global South are breaking new ground (and sometimes ploughing old) in the search for socially effective, progressive, and sustainable non-commercialized services. In many respects the alternatives we have brought forward in this book entail refashioning and redesigning existing public institutions and/or radicalizing what exists, rather than leaping into the dark.

The research thus raises as many questions as it answers. Is there a convergence around democratic public values and practices that can inform alternatives? What are we to make of the highly differentiated trends across regions and sectors? How do we weigh trade-offs between criteria such as affordability and quality, transparency and efficiency, participation and urgency, and centralized and decentralized alternatives? And, most problematically, how do we evaluate the robustness of "public" services in a "private" world dominated by finance capital that remains hostile to public values, where millions of households can no longer afford quality services, and where capital can move to sites of low taxation and high corporate subsidies, pitting equity-oriented service providers against market-oriented ones keen to attract business at any cost? The answers to these questions will not be easy.

Conceptually, there is much to be learned still about defining and refining the scale and boundaries of notions of "public" in understanding the relationship of public services to (non)capitalist systems of production and consumption, and in situating "alternatives to privatization" within larger theoretical frameworks of social and economic analysis. If neoliberalism fails to provide us with adequate conceptual tools for conceiving and constructing acceptable systems of public service provision, then what school(s) of thought do we turn to? The chapters in this book tend towards a historical materialist account, but this is not uniform, and the highly context-specific nature of the services discussed here makes any singular theoretical framework difficult. Marxian insights into the uneven and crisis-prone nature of capitalism and its alternation between bourgeois nationalization and privatization are invaluable to understanding why privatization occurs, why it fails, why renationalization or bailouts take place, and why certain market-friendly reforms are bound to fail, but these critiques are limited in their ability to anticipate concrete alternative forms of services and different cultural interpretations of resources. The fact that faith-based health services can be progressive and non-marketized in one place but chauvinistic and class/caste-oriented in another is one indication of the need for more sophisticated ways of thinking about the political economy of public services.

Additional theoretical and empirical work is required to move this conceptual debate forward. The material in this book is a step in this direction, but finer-grained evidence is required, and lots of it. Getting there is going to require an iterative theoretical and methodological approach, one which should include "universal norms" (of the sort outlined in Chapter 2, this volume) but which allows for contextualized difference so as not to blot out the possibility of progressive outcomes from very different social and economic formations. Nor do simplistic counterpositions (reformism versus revolution, local versus global issues, particularist versus universal claims) advance the debate.

It must also be remembered that no service delivery system is going to be perfect. There will be trade-offs in every case. The challenge—practically and conceptually—is how to measure and weigh these imperfections and how to evaluate their overall "success", without which we are left with little more than interesting case studies. Is it acceptable, for example, to give up efficiency for better transparency, and if so, how much? Is equity for women and girls a more important objective than health and safety for workers? Can we accept some market-oriented management principles in exchange for more immediate capital injections into desperately needed service infrastructures? These are desirable, necessary or unalterable trade-offs, but they do represent the sort of real-world imperfections that activists, policy makers, and other frontline stakeholders must grapple with, and which researchers must help conceptualize.

Our approach to further research is to combine empirical, evidence-based research with conceptual questions and frameworks. Rather than simply identifying a series of interesting experiments—and thereby amplifying the "apples and oranges" syndrome that has plagued research on alternatives to privatization to date (see Chapter 1, this volume)—we think it better to explore important thematic areas of interest, some of which have emerged from the "mapping exercise" research in this book, such as the remunicipalization of water services, debates over new scales of governance, and the role of technology in shaping policy choices. The themes we have chosen are not the only ones that could be explored, but it is a starting point based on what we consider to be the most promising and/or the most vexing findings from the research to date. The following sections briefly describe these thematic areas.

FUTURE RESEARCH THEMES

Reclaiming public services

Despite the hype about privatization, many local, regional, and national level authorities have been taking back ownership and/or management of services from the private sector. As private contracts run out, or as popular opposition to private contracts has arisen, governments (sometimes in collaboration with non-state, non-profit entities) have begun to remunicipalize or renationalize services in the name of being "public". From municipal water provision in Dar es Salaam, Tanzania, to national electricity services in Bolivia, there has been a significant rise in this trend—most notable in water, and largely at the local level. It is important to understand the conditions that have given rise to this trend in each place, the balance of forces that have allowed it to come to fruition, and the successes and failures of the newly "public" entities that have assumed control. Comparative studies will allow for consistent research methodologies to be applied and "universal" lessons to be drawn, while still permitting highly differentiated explanations and outcomes.

Legislative and rights-based approaches

Since the 1970s, from the micro level of municipal bylaws to the global level of trade agreements, the world has become increasingly corporate-friendly, giving freer movement to capital while sheltering it from prosecution (Harvey 2005). The trend continues, but important cracks have begun to emerge in the form of a revolt against the globalization of capital. Capital has become especially vulnerable in areas of critical service provision, with communities, unions and progressive policy makers and politicians pushing back free-trade agreements and corporate-friendly legislation. Water and universal access to health care are at the forefront: Uruguay has a constitutional amendment that makes it illegal to "privatize" water; South Africa has announced a National Health Insurance plan, and its constitution guarantees all citizens the right to a supply of "free basic water"; and on July 28, 2010, the UN General Assembly passed a resolution "calling on States and international organizations to provide financial resources, build capacity, and transfer technology, particularly to developing countries, in scaling up efforts to provide safe, clean, accessible, and affordable drinking water and sanitation for all".[1]

Though problematic, concessions such as the right to water cannot be dismissed as insignificant victories. Fraser (2009), in a major review of feminist struggles over the last 40 years, suggests that some feminists shot themselves in the foot by rejecting the welfare state and citizenship rights, playing into the agenda and discourse of neoliberals. The UN agreement on water as a basic human right is a victory and wins progressive space to press for better public solutions and for jobs and food and other essential goods and services to be declared basic human rights as well. Ideally, citizens should be able to action these social rights of citizenship through the courts and through popular pressure.

But as Bakker warns, rights-based discourse also may feed into the push for privatization, pointing to the "limitations of the human right to water as a conceptual counterpoint to privatization, and as an activist strategy" (2007, 442) (if water is a human right, argues the private sector, then who better to satisfy this right than the private companies with the resources and skills to deliver them!). In contrast, she argues that "alter-globalization strategies—centred on concepts of the commons—are more conceptually coherent, and also more successful as activist strategies" (2007, 442). In principle, we agree but fear that a rigid political stance may miss the dialectic of "reform and revolution". They are not a panacea, but rights discourse and popular notions of justice can be elemental in creating meaningful change and in mobilizing people (Harvey 1996, Fraser 2009). No citizen in a decent society should be left to die on the pavement; homeless, thirsty, hungry, or sick. It is far better to have rights (even bourgeois ones) than not in the fight against injustice. Small gains do not overcome capitalism, to be sure, but they can improve the ability of the working class and others to defend themselves and advance their interests. More needs to be known about the potential and limitations of such rights in the struggle to create meaningful alternatives to privatization, particularly as it applies to legal and constitutional efforts to make "public" services a national right.

Information campaigns

One of the reasons that commercialization and privatization have spread so rapidly over the past few decades is the enormous amount of resources put into "promoting" the benefits of market-oriented service delivery. This disinformation campaign against the state and the public sector has often been direct: donor-sponsored conferences on the advantages of commercialization for government officials, full-page advertisements by private multinational service providers, "research" sponsored by pro-market think tanks, and consultancies for academics linked to the World Bank. But it is also indirect, with the "common sense" acceptance of neoliberalism, crass consumerism, and individualism peddled by television hosts, journalists, bureaucrats, educators, NGOs, and others perpetuating a dogma of anti-state principles. Even some post-modernist and new social movements were swept into this anti-welfarist tide. This is hegemony in action—a non-coercive acceptance of a dominant ideology that may or may not actually benefit one's own personal material standing. It is a powerful force, and one that takes years, if not decades, to change (Strinati 2004).

Against this tide of opinion it can be difficult to imagine how messages of pro-public, solidaristic service delivery can be effective. And yet it is happening the world over. Some of this "counter-propaganda" is very effective, making inroads at union conferences, social movement events, in churches, in academic papers, and, increasingly, with politicians and bureaucrats who have seen the failures of privatization first-hand and who are actively trying to resist or reverse the trend. Even buried inside the neoconservative view is a yearning for lost sociality. All over the world, there are increasing questions about whether we can ever trust the market mechanism. The merits of privatization have been fundamentally challenged (most notably with water), as the lived realities of millions, if not billions, of people have given way to growing resentment of commercialized service delivery and outright resistance.

This counter-information about alternatives and collectivized forms of service delivery has not been as ideologically consistent, as voluminous, or as sophisticated as that of the pro-privatizers. This is due to the relative lack of resources, as well as to the fragmented interpretations of what is wrong with privatization and what kinds of alternatives might be better. The latter is part of the "poverty of practice and thinking around alternatives" discussed in Chapter 1, but it is also a reflection of the non-linear and highly variegated realities of alternatives on the ground and the kinds of communities that build them. In other words, there is unlikely anything approaching the monolithic neoliberal messaging of privatization in the world of "alternatives to privatization", and this is a good thing.

All of this makes research into the content and effectiveness of pro-public service messaging important and difficult. What kinds of information campaigns have worked in locations where public services have thrived or made a comeback? What messages are being used, how are they being delivered and by whom, how is it being financed and how reproducible are the messages elsewhere? Slick information campaigns are no substitute for good ideas and real practice, but the best public systems in the world need good messaging to support them, at least while they continue to swim in shark-infested waters. Systematic and comparative studies of such initiatives should help.

Corporatized entities

Considerable debate remains as to the merits of state-owned and state-managed services that are run on (some) private sector principles—i.e. corporatization. Evidence of the degree of "publicness" in these service organizations is mixed—including the cases in this book—and there is a need for finer-grained analyses of success factors for a more consistent comparison across regions and sectors. Are there positive lessons to be learned from Uruguay's corporatized water entity, *Obras Sanitarias del Estado* (OSE), that could be applied elsewhere, and if so, under what conditions? Can the negative experiences of South Africa's parastatal electricity provider, Eskom, be avoided in other countries? Are there inherent structural tensions within the corporatization model that cut across experiences with new public management and can these be resolved? The debate needs more and better, empirical data and more transparent and comparable research methods if we are to advance our understanding of what is arguably the single most important trend in "public" service delivery today.

Financing alternatives

Virtually every development organization in the world recognizes the need to pour resources into services and infrastructure in the global South. As noted above, tens of billions of dollars a year are needed to provide the most basic levels of services to the hundreds of millions without adequate access.

But we must also be careful with these estimates, in part because the costs of services and the package of services built into the assumptions, are based on the private sector model. The national health insurance debate in South Africa, for example, was almost derailed by private insurance companies exaggerating the costs of such a programme. Although there is clearly a need for massive amounts of capital we should not accept the international financial institutions' estimates at face value. The key financial debates must also revolve around how we can better use existing resources and how to manage the operating costs through greater participation of users.

There are, for example, massive expenditures on military and infrastructure projects that do little to assist low-income households. Public monies spent to build showcase infrastructure that benefit a wealthy, global elite at the cost of marginalized urban and rural poor remains a major problem, as the billions of dollars spent on the FIFA World Cup and the Delhi Commonwealth games in 2010 amply demonstrate (Desai and Vahed 2009, Uppal 2009). Country-specific and sector-specific accounting of public capital expenditures are needed to further expose spending biases and to reveal the true potential of public coffers.

Nor are these public coffers static entities, shaped as they are by tax regimes that typically favour elites and transnational capital, requiring a deconstruction of the structural nature of fiscal deficits and an extrapolation of spending potentials in the global South. Such accounts are unlikely to have much effect on neoliberal policy makers and footloose capitalists steeped in an ideology of "competitive governance", but as advocates of the Tobin Tax on global financial transactions have demonstrated, even relatively small changes can create substantial sums of capital for reinvestment in public services and infrastructure (Palley 2001). A fuller accounting of the impacts of more progressive forms of general taxation in different countries/regions/sectors would be a useful counterweight to "the cupboard is bare" and "we can't raise taxes" rhetoric of those in favour of private sector investment.

The other major financial challenge is how to manage operating costs. Even if public monies are spent on infrastructure and equipment, the day-to-day operating costs of services are increasingly paid for out of cost-reflexive pricing policies that often make it difficult for low-income families to consume enough of what they need. South Africa's water and electricity providers offer a particularly sobering example, with billions of dollars spent by the post-apartheid state since the mid-1990s to build trunk infrastructure and connect people to the grid, but cost-reflexive pricing on consumption having resulted in millions of these new "consumers" being cut off for varying lengths of time due to an inability to pay (too often portrayed as a "culture of non-payment"; Fjeldstad 2004). Are there better ways to envision "lifeline" supplies of cheap or free services? Is a "universal" approach to service pricing better than "targeted" approaches to indigence? How do these different financing strategies relate to the "publicness" of a service?

Operating and capital spending need to be seen in multiscalar terms as well. The push to decentralize service delivery over the past 20 years has not always been accompanied by a concomitant shift in financial resources, leaving local authorities with unfunded mandates and little opportunity to raise the funds locally, either because they are constrained by national-level policy making that restricts levels of taxation and deficit financing, and/or because they feel trapped by the increasing competition between municipalities to keep taxes low and infrastructural support for business high so as to attract and retain private capital.

At the other end of the spectrum, a shift to supranational infrastructure projects, notably in electricity, has meant an even greater loss of financial accountability and measurability, as regional bodies such as the Southern African Development Community spend billions of public dollars to develop regional-level infrastructural projects that have little if any public input and benefit big capital at the expense of low-income households (McDonald 2009). Connecting the dots of this financial architecture between various levels of governance, public resources, and private capital is critical.

There are also massive public sector pension funds, which are often overlooked in spending debates, partly because they remain sheltered from public scrutiny (Clark 2000). A better accounting of what is available in countries in the South, and how this money is being used, would shed further light on the scale of public resources that are available for productive investment. So too would a closer accounting of public sector pensions in the North be useful, partly given their size and partly given that some are actually investing in privatized services in the South. The Ontario Teachers' Pension Plan in Canada, for example, with some $96 billion in assets in 2009,[2] owns 50% of Chile's water and sanitation systems (though there have been calls from some union members to disinvest [*Canadian Press* 2010]). Could these monies be used for public-sector services instead?

Sovereign wealth funds may be another source of "public" money. With about US$3.8 trillion available internationally—and an additional $6.5 trillion held in other sovereign investment vehicles such as pension reserve funds, development funds, and state-owned corporations' funds, and $6.1 trillion in other official foreign exchange reserves—these are arguably the largest sources of public funds available in the world. Some sovereign funds are immense, including those of the government of China (combined total of US$925 billion), the Abu Dhabi Investment Authority (US$627 billion), the government pension fund of Norway (US$445 billion), the Kuwait Investment Authority (US$250 billion), and the government of Singapore (US$330 billion; see www.swfinstitute.org). Could these funds be tapped into to support public services?

And finally, there is publicly financed donor funding, much of which is in favour of commercially oriented service delivery, either through direct funding of pro-privatization think tanks and government agencies (e.g. DFID's support for the Adam Smith Foundation), support for loan conditionalities, or indirect pressure on states to adopt the "common sense" of commercialization. There is also the increasingly influential role of private donor agencies. The latter may not represent "public" money in the way that official multilateral and bilateral agencies do, but the lines are increasingly blurred as private donors such as the Gates Foundation team up with public donor agencies to deliver aid and often take the lead in developing new aid priorities, even though these programmes tend to be stand-alone, verticalized interventions, which often obstruct systemic change (Equinet 2007).

There are some bright lights, however, such as the creation of the Global Water Operators' Partnerships Alliance (GWOPA) by UN-Habitat to explore "public-public partnerships" and the recognition by the European Parliament that "financing and technical support available from a variety of donors for PPPs" needs to be balanced by "dedicated funds made available for PuPs [public-public partnerships]" (Tucker et al, 2010). But as noted in Chapter 1, the first example is compromised by the presence of multinational corporations, and the latter is a drop in the proverbial funding bucket. Nevertheless, they are indicators of a growing awareness from mainstream actors of the need to put public financial resources into an exploration of alternatives to privatization, and it is a trend that itself needs attentive research.

Non-state actors

With the inclusion of non-state actors in many definitions of "public" and the mushrooming numbers of services provided by these groups, it is important to develop better insights into how these organizations have emerged, what their objectives are, whether they are sustainable, and so on. But rather than exploring unconnected case studies, we hope to conduct research that compares and contrasts the strengths and weaknesses of different social actors (unions, social movements, NGOs, faith-based organizations, community groups) across regions/sectors and their potential/limitations for working together.

We also see scope for participatory research on the part of these groups, be they frontline workers, community activists or NGO leaders. For it is through their perspectives that we gain the richest range of insights into the complex dynamics of non-traditional service delivery mechanisms, and it is here that we have the best potential for developing a more permanent mechanism of critical inquiry into the nature of public service provision through ongoing monitoring and evaluation by those who remain part of the system.

Technology

One of the key findings of this book was the potential for technology to shape political and economic outcomes of a service delivery system. Large-scale and capital-intensive services can be prone to unaccountability and a lack of transparency, while small-scale, low-tech systems may lend themselves to more democratic participation and environmental sustainability. But there is nothing automatic or deterministic about technology (or scale), and there is a need to explore more closely the relationships between technological choice and the "publicness" of a service. Renewable energy sources may, for example, open up new opportunities for locally controlled electricity services, weakening the grip of big capital on energy, but it is equally true that the push for solar and wind power over the past decade has seen a rush of small- and large-scale capital into greenfield developments, a sort of privatization by stealth under the guise of "alternative" energy systems (Hepbasli and Ozgener 2004, Mitchell and Connor 2004, van Niekerk 2010).

Gender

As discussed in Chapter 5, gender considerations must be factored into all research on alternatives to privatization; for example, by asking questions of the gendered nature of equity, participation, and affordability of a particular public service. The same applies to questions of race, class, caste, and a host of other demographic and socio-economic factors, but gender is particularly important, not least because it has received so little attention in the research on alternatives to privatization to date. Gender-specific studies are therefore necessary to provide deeper insights into the gendered dynamics of alternative service delivery systems. Detailed ethnographic accounts of women's and girls' experiences with services, combined with conceptual frameworks of place-based knowledge and practice, will help to develop better context-specific understandings and generate a pool of comparative thematic studies.

Historical research

Finally, we hope to explore a range of historical models of non-commercialized service delivery. From Soviet health care to the municipal socialisms of the 19th century to post-colonial experiences with state services since the 1950s there is a wealth of non-privatized service delivery models that have been un(der)explored and which lack a consistent methodological and conceptual framework for comparative purposes. There may be little that binds the Tanzania of the 1960s with the England of a century earlier, but in both cases there were explicit efforts to exclude the private sector from the delivery of basic municipal services. Why this happened, how these "public goods" were interpreted, and who benefited from them may provide useful insights into contemporary debates over the same questions.

CONCLUSION

In the 1930s Ernst Bloch coined the phrase "the utopian intention", which he described as "the real motor force of history" (cited in Panitch and Gindin 1999, 2). In his book *Spaces of Hope*, Harvey (2000) similarly invoked the idea of "social imaginary". In this spirit, we hope to have generated some new ideas about "public" service delivery, drawing on innovative and exciting developments on the ground, with the aim of moving beyond the defensive, rearguard actions that too often characterize the response to privatization. There can be real value in incremental change and thinking, but it is also necessary to push aside the (apparent) barriers to transformation and to think and act in more sweeping terms. Decisions about what to produce, how to produce, how to consume, and how to distribute are in the end not technical decisions to be left to professionals and bureaucrats, but political ones to be made by active citizens operating within a meaningful public realm.

Rigorous, critical, and innovative research must be part of this agenda. Existing conceptual and methodological frameworks can help us see through the seemingly mysterious and enigmatic nature of the commodification process, but it is not clear that we yet have the appropriate analytical tools to move beyond this commodified world, to be more creative in our thinking about alternative utopias, or to adequately understand the imaginative realities of those who are pushing for new systems of production and consumption. The analyses in this book have hopefully opened new doors in this respect, but the process has also shown just how far we have to go.

Equally important is the need to better connect critical research with frontline action. Abstract theory must be meaningful in some way to those with the lived experience of change, and communication needs to be multidirectional, contributing to a more synergetic relationship than has traditionally been the case in academic work. For if we cannot democratize our own sphere of research, how are we to contribute to a more meaningful world of alternatives to privatization? Water services, health care, and electricity may only be one part of this larger picture, but they are critical to the livelihoods of billions of people and a potential "motor force" for bigger things to come.

NOTES

1. See www.un.org/News/Press/docs/2010/ga10967.doc.htm (accessed 12 August 2010).
2. See Ontario Teachers' Pension Fund. Fast facts. www.otpp.com/wps/wcm/connect/otpp_en/Home/Investments/Fast+Facts/.

REFERENCES

Bakker, K. 2007. The "commons" versus the "commodity": Alter-globalization, anti-privatization and the human right to water in the Global South. *Antipode* 39(3): 430–455.

Canadian Press. 2010. Water activists to put pension petition before teachers, 21 August 2010. www.toronto.ctv.ca/servlet/an/local/CTVNews/20100831/water-teachers-pension-100831/20100831/Dancing%20with%20the%20Stars (accessed 23 October 2010).

Clark, G.L. 2000. *Pension Fund Capitalism*. Oxford: Oxford University Press.

Davis, M. 1990. *City of quartz: Excavating the future in Los Angeles*. London: Verso.

Desai, A. and Vahed, G. 2009. World Cup 2010: Africa's turn or the turn on Africa? *Soccer and Society* 11(1): 154–167.

Deutsche Bank. 2008. By 2030 China's cities have to be equipped for at least 350 million new inhabitants. Talking point: Deutsche Bank research, 29 August. www.dbresearch.com/PROD/DBR_INTERNET_EN-PROD/PROD0000000000230655.pdf (accessed 25 September 2010).

Equinet. 2007. *Reclaiming the resources for health: A regional analysis of equity in health in east and southern Africa*. Uganda: Fountain Publishers.

Fjeldstad, O.H. 2004. What's trust got to do with it? Non-payment of service charges in local authorities in South Africa. *Journal of Modern African Studies* 42(4): 539–562.

Foster, V. and Briceño-Garmendia, C. (Eds). 2010. *Africa's infrastructure: A time for transformation*. Washington, DC: World Bank.

Fraser, N. 2009. Feminism, capitalism and the cunning of history. *New Left Review* 56: 97–117.

Global Health Workforce Alliance. 2010. No health workforce. No health MDGs. Is that acceptable? Summary of discussions at the Side Event on Human Resources for Health at the UN MDG Summit, Geneva, 21 September. www.who.int/workforcealliance/media/news/2010/mdgcommitstatement/en/ (accessed 18 April 2011).

Harvey, D. 1996. *Justice, nature and the geography of difference*. Oxford: Basil Blackwell.

———. 2000. *Spaces of hope*. Berkeley: University of California Press.

———. 2005. *A brief history of neoliberalism*. Oxford: Oxford University Press.

Hepbasli, A. and Ozgener, O. 2004. A review on the development of wind energy in Turkey. *Renewable and Sustainable Energy Reviews* 8(3): 257–276.

IEA (International Energy Agency). 2010. World Energy Outlook 2010: The electricity access database. www.worldenergyoutlook.org/electricity.asp (accessed online on 15 April 2011).

McDonald, D.A. (Ed). 2009. *Electric capitalism: Recolonizing Africa on the power grid*. London: Earthscan.

Mitchell, C. and Connor, P. 2004. Renewable energy policy in the UK 1990–2003. *Energy Policy* 32: 1935–1947.

Palley, T. 2001. Destabilizing speculation and the case for an International Currency Transactions Tax. *Challenge* 44(3): 70–89.

Panitch, L. and Gindin, S. 1999. Transcending pessimism. In Panitch, L. and Leys, C. (Eds), *Socialist register 2000, necessary and unnecessary utopias*, pp. 1–29. Suffolk: Merlin Press.

Strinati, D. 2004. *An introduction to theories of popular culture*. New York: Routledge.

Tucker, J., Calow, R., Nickel, D. and Thaler, T. 2010. A comparative evaluation of public-private partnerships for urban water services in ACP countries. European Parliament, Director-General for External Policies of the Union, Directorate B, Policy Department, May. www.europarl.europa.eu/activities/committees/studies.do?language=EN (accessed 10 September 2010).

Uppal, V. 2009. *The impact of the Commonwealth Games 2010 on urban development of Delhi*. Theoretical and Empirical Researchers in Urban Management, No 1(10). New Delhi: Centre for Civil Society.

van Niekerk, S. 2010. *Desertec: What are the implications for Africa?* Public Services International Research Unit, Policy Paper, October. London: PSIRU.

WHO (World Health Organization). 2011a. Water Sanitation and Health (WSH) Section. www.who.int/water_sanitation_health/hygiene/en/ (accessed 15 April 2011).

———. 2011b. *World health statistics 2011.* Geneva: WHO.

Contributors

Al-Hassan Adam is Coordinator at Africa Water Network, Accra, Ghana.

Cheryl Batistel works at the Institute for Social Research and Development Studies, Visayas State University, Baybay, Leyte, Philippines.

Kate Bayliss is Researcher Coordinator in the Privatization Working Group and Department of Development Studies, School of Oriental and African Studies, University of London, UK.

Daniel Chavez is Coordinator in the New Politics Programme at the Transnational Institute (TNI) and a lecturer at the Institute of Social Studies in Den Hague, Netherlands.

Jenina Joy Chavez is Philippines Programme Coordinator and Research Associate in Focus on the Global South, Quezon City, Philippines.

Carlos Crespo is Coordinator at *Centro de Estudios Superiores Universitarios* (CESU), University Mayor San Simón, Cochabamba, Bolivia.

Iliana Camacho Cuapio is Research Assistant in the Department of Health Care, Metropolitan Autonomous University Xochimilco Campus, Mexico City, Mexico.

Yoswa Mbulalina Dambisya is senior professor, Pharmacology in the School of Health Sciences at University of Limpopo, Sovenga, South Africa.

Buenaventura Dragantes is Professor of Socio-ecology and Coordinator, Programme on Integrated Water Resources Management (IWRM) Research, Development and Extension, Visayas State University, Baybay, Leyte, Philippines.

Ben Fine is Professor in the Department of Economics, School of Oriental and African Studies, University of London, UK.

Silvia Tamez González is Professor-researcher in the Department of Health Care, Metropolitan Autonomous University Xochimilco Campus, Mexico City, Mexico.

David Hall is Director of the Public Services International Research Unit (PSIRU), University of Greenwich, London, UK.

Catalina Eibenschutz Hartman is Professor-researcher in the Department of Health Care, Metropolitan Autonomous University Xochimilco Campus, Mexico City, Mexico.

Terri Hathaway is former Africa Programme Director at International Rivers, Yaoundé, Cameroon, and founder of Energy for Africa's Kitchens, Farms and Jobs.

Luis Ortiz Hernández is a professor-researcher in the Department of Health Care, Metropolitan Autonomous University Xochimilco Campus, Mexico City, Mexico.

Hyacinth Eme Ichoku works in the Department of Economics, University of Nigeria, Nsukka, Nigeria.

Nepomuceno Malaluan is Trustee at Action for Economic Reforms, Quezon City, Philippines.

Mary Ann Manahan is Research Associate in Focus on the Global South, Quezon City, Philippines.

David A. McDonald is Professor in Global Development Studies and Department of Geography, Queen's University, Kingston, Canada, and Codirector of the Municipal Services Project.

Sarah Miraglia is a doctoral candidate in Sociology, Syracuse University, New York, US.

Marcela Olivera is Latin American Coordinator, Water for All Campaign, Food and Water Watch, Washington DC and Cochabamba, Bolivia.

Chandra Talpade Mohanty is Professor and chair, Department of Women's and Gender Studies, Syracuse University, New York, US.

Greg Ruiters is Professor of Governance and Public Policy, School of Government, University of Western Cape, South Africa, and Codirector of the Municipal Services Project.

Amit Sengupta is Associate Coordinator of People's Health Movement and General Secretary of All India Peoples Science Network, Delhi, India.

Susan Spronk is Assistant Professor, School of International Development and Global Studies, University of Ottawa, Canada.

Phillip Terhorst is Coordinator of the Platform for Public-Community Partnerships of the Americas.

Hilary Wainwright is Research Director in the New Politics Programme, Transnational Institute, Amsterdam, Netherlands, and editor of *Red Pepper Magazine*.

Index